U.S. Private-Sector Privacy

Law and Practice for Information Privacy Professionals, Fourth Edition

Peter Swire, CIPP/US

DeBrae Kennedy-Mayo, CIPP/US

An IAPP Publication

Copy editor: Libby Sweeney
Indexer: Hyde Park Publishing Services

ISBN: 978-1-948771-75-7

Library of Congress Control Number: 2023946048

Contents

About the IAPP

The International Association of Privacy Professionals (IAPP) is the largest and most comprehensive global information privacy community and resource, helping practitioners develop and advance their careers and organizations manage and protect their data.

The IAPP is a not-for-profit association founded in 2000 with a mission to define, support and improve the privacy profession globally. In 2023, the IAPP expanded our work with the launch of the AI Governance Center which provides professionals tasked with AI governance, risk and compliance with the content, resources, networking, training, and certification needed to respond to the complex risks in the AI field. We are committed to providing a forum for privacy and AI governance professionals to share best practices, track trends, advance privacy, and AI management issues, standardize the designations for professionals and provide education and guidance on opportunities in the fields of information privacy and AI governance.

The IAPP is responsible for developing and launching the only globally recognized credentialing programs in information privacy and AI governance: the Certified Information Privacy Professional (CIPP®), the Certified Information Privacy Manager (CIPM®), the Certified Information Privacy Technologist (CIPT®), and the AI Governance Professional Certification (AIGP). The CIPP, CIPM and CIPT are the leading privacy certifications for thousands of professionals around the world who serve the data protection, information auditing, information security, legal compliance and/or risk management needs of their organizations. The AIGP is the first designation of its kind. AIGP certification demonstrates that an individual can ensure safety and trust in the development and deployment of ethical AI and ongoing management of AI systems.

In addition, the IAPP offers a full suite of educational and professional development services and holds annual conferences that are recognized internationally as the leading forums for the discussion and debate of issues related to privacy policy and practice as well as AI governance.

About the IAPP

Preface

I write this preface in July 2023, a little over three years after the preface for the previous edition of this textbook. As with previous editions, I offer some reflections on what has happened since.

The first comprehensive state privacy law, the California Consumer Privacy Act, went into effect in 2020. By the end of 2022, five states had such laws, and that number has already doubled in 2023. Although Congress has acted more slowly than it ought, organizations across the United States are ramping up to respond to these new laws.

Also in 2020, the Court of Justice of the European Union (CJEU) issued its Schrems II decision, calling into question the enormous volume of data flows across the Atlantic. Now, the EU and U.S. have created the Trans-Atlantic Data Privacy Framework, including new redress provisions that were the subject of much of my research with the Cross-Border Data Forum. More generally, data has become so important that countries around the world are considering new laws to regulate or prohibit cross-border data flows. Privacy professionals today often list cross-border flows as the most challenging part of their job.

Privacy professionals must cope with constant technological change. Recently, large learning models such as ChatGPT have exploded onto the scene. One result is that the governance and ethics expertise of privacy professionals is being tapped in many organizations to address new AI challenges.

The first edition of this book, published in 2007, focused on the privacy issues for a limited number of sectors, such as health care and financial services, as well the online technology companies whose existence is defined by the processing and transfer of information. By contrast, the importance of privacy professionals has spread into companies and sectors that were historically based in the physical world, as data collection and connectivity spread throughout human activity. For instance, automobiles for decades were physical objects fixed by wrenches and similar tools. Then, software became important to diagnose and repair cars. Today the average new car is approaching 20 antennas, while the average American spends over six percent of their waking time in a car. Imagine the volume, variety, and velocity of data that privacy professionals will need to consider in the future of the auto sector. Across the economy, privacy and cybersecurity governance have become essential components of organizational success.

You are holding the fifth version of this textbook. When Sol Bermann and I wrote the first iteration of the book, published in 2007, it was the first official International Association of Privacy Professionals textbook and was created to prepare for the first Certified Information Privacy Professional examination. Kenesa Ahmad and I revamped the text for the next version (and first edition with this name), published in 2012. DeBrae Kennedy-Mayo has been the co-author for the 2018, 2020, and 2023 editions, and her knowledge and insights are apparent in every part of the book. DeBrae's twice-yearly teaching of the Privacy for Professionals course at Georgia Tech means that our updates are informed by literally hundreds of students who use this text. Thanks as well to all the others that DeBrae lists by name in her preface. All of us have worked hard to create a book that gives you, a new person in the field, a readable introduction to our profession.

In the IAPP, thanks to Nicole Russell as our lead contact for this edition. Under the direction of Trevor Hughes, the IAPP, which was founded in 2000, has grown into a vibrant, global organization with more than 80,000 members.

On a personal level, my special thanks to my wife, Annie Antón, for her wisdom and partnership in privacy and more importantly in life.

I believe that we, as privacy professionals, have a profound ethical responsibility to handle personal information in responsible ways. I hope this book fosters the knowledge and awareness to help make that a reality.

Peter Swire, CIPP/US
Atlanta, Georgia, USA
July 2023

This edition of the book has numerous updates, likely more than any previous edition. The need for such updates was triggered both by the amazing speed at which the technological innovations that shape the contours of privacy are happening and by the efforts of regulators to respond to these changes.

As authors, we also realize that by the time this book has been published, another round of edits will already be on the horizon. With this realization in mind, we made the decision to remove Chapter 15 – Emerging Issues because in a published book, that chapter cannot keep pace with the changes occurring in the regulation of privacy. We have added relevant discussions of emerging technologies into the chapters on medical privacy, financial privacy, and education privacy.

Each chapter in the book has been refreshed (at a minimum) and several have been entirely rewritten. Chapter 1 – Introduction to Privacy has been updated to include the recent work by the OECD and APEC to enhance cross-border data flows. In Chapter 2 – U.S. Legal Framework, the book now has a discussion of the United States Supreme Court case of Dobbs v. Jackson Women's Health Organization, which overturned Roe v. Wade. Chapter 3 – Introduction to Technological Aspects of Privacy is an entirely new chapter that replaces the chapter previously known as Online Privacy. Chapter 4 – Information Management and Privacy Risk Management has been overhauled in its treatment of information management and now also explores privacy risk management. Chapter 5 – Federal and State Regulators has been edited to remove certain historical information, refreshed to focus on new cases, and expanded in its treatment of state-level developments.

Chapter 6 – State Comprehensive Privacy Laws is an entirely new chapter that replaces the 2020 chapter known as the California Consumer Privacy Act. Realizing that additional state comprehensive privacy laws would almost inevitably be passed (and the number of enacted state laws has doubled since the chapter was written in January 2023), this chapter focuses on trends and outliers among these older state laws as well as providing the reader with an approach for examining any such state laws which may be enacted in the future. Chapter 7 – State Data Breach Notification Laws has been edited to remove details of the specific state laws and to instead focus on the trends and outliers among these laws. The chapters focused on sectoral privacy laws, Chapter 8 – Medical Privacy, Chapter 9 – Financial Privacy, Chapter 10 – Education Privacy, Chapter 11 – Telecommunications and Marketing, and Chapter 12 – Workplace Privacy, have been updated to incorporate the long-term effects of the pandemic, the implications of the Dobbs case, and the efforts to regulate emerging technologies. In Chapter 13 – Civil Litigation and Government Investigations, the implications of the Dobbs case are addressed. In addition, this chapter examines the Second Additional Protocol to the Budapest Convention. The updates to Chapter 14 – The GDPR and International Privacy Issues explore data transfers from Europe to the United States as well as developments in global data flows.

Also, we have reordered two chapters in the book. In the 2020 edition, Chapter 3 focused on federal and state regulators while Chapter 5 explored the various aspects of the topic dubbed online privacy. In this edition, we have swapped that order. For this edition, the first three chapters of the book are introductory material important to the study of privacy and its regulation. These three chapters are then followed by chapters that focus on different aspects of the regulation of privacy.

In several chapter updates, we have intentionally linked the updates to the material found in the relevant books associated with additional certifications offered by the IAPP—CIPT, CIPM, and CIPP/E, respectively. Chapter 3 provides an introduction to technical issues relevant to privacy, which are discussed in more detail in the IAPP's book entitled *An Introduction to Privacy for Technology Professionals*. Chapter 4 provides an introduction to information management and privacy risk management, topics discussed in more detail in the IAPP's book *Privacy Program Management*. Chapter 14 provides an overview of the EU data protection framework and the legal basis for data flows to the United States. The IAPP's book entitled *European Data Protection: Law and Practice* explores these topics in detail.

On a personal note, I want to express my appreciation to Peter Swire for the positive working relationship that resulted in our co-authorship of this latest edition of this book.

In the IAPP, Nicole Russell was our lead contact for this edition of the book. Her work in getting this edition to the publisher was invaluable.

A list of thank yous is inevitably incomplete, but the effort is still worthwhile. Thank you to Theodore Christakis, Ken Propp, and Dan Felz at the Cross-Border Data Forum for their insights into data flows across national borders. Thank you to Nathan Lemay for his insight concerning the technical aspects of privacy, his focus on deidentification, and his efforts to further democratization of education in the field of privacy. Thank you to Jan Hankins for her insights into Fourth Amendment protections and her perspective related to criminal defense. Thank you to Tino Chikate, Gemma Davies, Jake Gord, Dwight Hakim, Will Hankins, Justin Hemmings, James Jones, Ben Jury, Emily Le, Tamara Lev, Muhammad Nauman, Hal Overman, Emily Powell, and Sepehr Saberian for providing ideas for chapter update, reviewing drafts of chapters, and working on footnotes.

To my students at Georgia Tech, thank you for all the insights you have provided to me and, more importantly, for all those that you have imparted to the communities where you live. To everyone who reads this book, thank you for the time you take to increase your knowledge and understanding of the complex concept referred to as privacy and for how you implement these ideas, both in your professional and private lives.

Finally, thank you to my remarkable husband Garrett for his insights, his unwavering support, and his willingness to watch our dog, Luke, and our cat, Miss Kitty, on those days when I am working long hours researching the intersection of privacy and technology.

DeBrae Kennedy-Mayo, CIPP/US
Savannah, Georgia, USA
July 2023

Acknowledgments

The IAPP is pleased to present *U.S. Private-Sector Privacy: Law and Practice for Information Privacy Professionals, Fourth Edition in* support of the Certified Information Privacy Professional/United States (CIPP/US®) program.

We are grateful for the many privacy professionals who provide their time and expertise to support our training programs. This list starts with our Training Advisory Board, a group of highly-respected professionals representing a broad range of jurisdictions and industries. Current members include:

Olufunke Babatunde, CIPP/E, CIPM, FIP
Shay Babb, CIPP/C, CIPM
Robin Anise Benns, CIPP/US
James Boyle, CIPP/E
Dave Brown, CIPP/US, CIPM, FIP
Erin Butler, CIPM
Jonathan Cantor, CIPP/G, CIPP/US
Smriti Chandrashekar, CIPP/A, CIPP/US, CIPM, FIP
Ben Daley-Gage, CIPP/E, CIPM, CIPT
Nitin Dhavate, CIPP/E, CIPM, FIP
Preeti Dhawan, CIPP/C
Kathryn Fox, CIPM
Roberto Girardi, CIPP/E
Francesco Gualtieri, CIPP/E, CIPM, CIPT, FIP
Leyla Gurbanova, CIPP/E
Adebola Hamed, CIPP/US, CIPM, FIP
Adam Higgins, CIPP/E, CIPM, CIPT, FIP
Stacey Keegan, CIPP/C, CIPP/US, CIPM
Milla Keller, CIPP/E
Kok Kwang Lui, CIPP/E, CIPM, CIPT, FIP
Maria-Cristina Macocinschi, CIPP/E, CIPM
Fiona Makaka, CIPP/E
Nicholas Merker, CIPT
Esteban Morin, CIPP/C, CIPP/E, CIPP/US, CIPM, FIP, PLS

Michael O'Rourke, CIPP/G
Ross Parker, CIPM
Jason Peterson, CIPP/A, CIPP/C, CIPP/E, CIPP/US, CIPM, CIPT, FIP
Natasha Petterson, CIPP/E, CIPM
Petruta Pirvan, CIPP/E, CIPP/US, CIPM, FIP
Tiina Suomela, CIPP/E, CIPM, CIPT, FIP
Kalpana Sundaram, CIPP/US
Roja Tanamala, CIPM
Liisa Thomas
Mary Kay Thurlkill, CIPP/US, CIPM, FIP
Paul Törnblom, CIPP/E
Victoria van Roosmalen, CIPP/C, CIPP/E, CIPP/US, CIPM, CIPT, FIP
Sok Woo Yoon, CIPP/US

I am enormously grateful to Peter Swire and DeBrae Kennedy-Mayo for their time and dedication to this project. Thank you, Peter and DeBrae for sharing your expertise in government and privacy law to clearly and comprehensively explain the changes in and complexity of the U.S. privacy landscape within these pages.

We are appreciative of Libby Sweeney's attention to detail in her copy edit of the textbook and for Hyde Park Publishing Services who created the book index.

As with previous editions, I hope you find this textbook to be a valuable resource in preparing for your CIPP/US certification and a practical reference in your daily professional lives.

Marla Berry, CIPT
Training Director
International Association of Privacy Professionals

Introduction

It has become cliché in the world of data privacy to remark on the pace of change within our field. We speak of a landslide of U.S. state consumer privacy laws. We drink from the fire hose of international compliance obligations. We swim endlessly in the vast and turbulent waters of regulatory scrutiny.

But through it all, privacy professionals can return always to the strong core at the base of our practice. Like a martial artist descending comfortably into a fighting stance, privacy's principles-based foundation provides us with the flexibility we need to adapt to new realities without compromising the lived experience of those we serve. Whether we conceive of new risks in corporate terms or by reference to the privacy rights of individuals, we find ourselves armed with the tools we need to adapt and maintain consistent outcomes. It is books like the one you hold in your hands that make the flexible strength of our profession possible.

As this edition goes to print, the newest wave of technologies—often described imprecisely and unsatisfyingly as "artificial intelligence"—are challenging many of the fundamental concepts in data privacy. What is "personal data" when new inference engines can spin powerful and accurate guesses about consumers' lives from mundane inputs? What is "sensitive data" when the movements of our bodies or even the electrical emanations of our thoughts can be used to infer our health conditions, our emotions, our very identities? How can we rely on individualized controls to respond to the collective privacy risks raised by opaque algorithms deployed at scale?

Yet even as AI questions our assumptions, the field of privacy is reaching a maturity level that could only have been dreamed of a few decades ago. The policy innovations to which privacy pros respond largely require the same time-tested tools of practice that began to be developed in the 1970s.

This book helps us to understand and use those tools, whether we do so in service of the Privacy Act of 1974, the Connecticut Data Privacy Act of 2022, or our own values and principles.

We could not ask for a better guide. Peter Swire continues to inspire with the depth and rigor of his privacy credentials. Swire wears many hats. In addition to his work handcrafting each subsequent edition of this textbook, he is a Senior Counsel at Alston & Bird, LLP and serves as Professor of Law and

Ethics in the Georgia Technology Scheller College of Business, while holding the J.Z. Liang Chair in the Georgia Technology School of Cybersecurity and Privacy. Professor Swire has served important roles in government, including groundbreaking privacy management and oversight roles in Clinton's Office of Management and Budget and the Obama White House. He is a Senior Fellow with the Future of Privacy Forum and has been a member of the National Academies' Forum on Cyber-Resiliency. He has received awards for his scholarship and leadership in the privacy community from the IAPP and FPF. More importantly, Swire has left his mark on a wide range of long-lasting privacy developments that feature in this book, from the Health Insurance Portability and Accountability Act Privacy Rule to the EU-U.S. Privacy Shield agreement.

The impact of DeBrae Kennedy-Mayo to the effectiveness of this resource can also not be understated. As Kennedy-Mayo makes clear in her preface, this textbook is forged in the fires of real-world education. The focus on robust pedagogy is apparent throughout its pages, refreshed in this edition with new angles and examples, always with an eye toward bringing data privacy alive for the student and practitioner alike.

Since the time my own privacy career was but a twinkle, this book has served as the definitive resource for privacy law and regulation in the United States. The fourth edition of *U.S. Private-Sector Privacy: Law and Practice for Information Privacy Professionals* continues to benefit from its authors' careful stewardship. Because of its comprehensive treatment of the principles, practice, and evolving compliance obligations of data privacy, it will continue to serve as an indispensable resource for every privacy professional—even in the swiftly moving digital world we now occupy.

As you peruse the pages of this rich resources, whether for the first time or on a repeat journey, I hope you will take to heart the lesson that data privacy remains a powerful tool for centering the lives of individuals within organizational practice, not because of new compliance obligations, but because of the timeless principles it embraces.

Laws change, technology changes, but the ideal of data privacy remains the same, challenging us always to continue to improve.

Cobun Zweifel-Keegan, CIPP/US, CIPM
Managing Director, Washington, D.C.
International Association of Privacy Professionals

CHAPTER 1

Introduction to Privacy

This chapter provides an introduction to the subject of protection of information about individuals. In the United States and other countries, laws in this area are known as **privacy law**, or sometimes **data privacy** or **information privacy law**. In the European Union and other countries, laws in this area are known as **data protection law**. The discussion introduces the relevant vocabulary and describes the common principles and approaches used throughout the world for information privacy and data protection. This chapter continues by providing an understanding of the legal and policy structures for privacy and data protection around the world. It then outlines key models of privacy protection: the comprehensive, sectoral, self-regulatory or co-regulatory, and technology models.

1.1 Defining Privacy

In 1890, Samuel Warren and Louis Brandeis published "The Right to Privacy" in the *Harvard Law Review*, setting forth the essential definition of privacy as "the right to be let alone."[1] Both fundamental and concise, this definition underscored the personal and social dimensions of the concept that would linger long after publication of this landmark essay. Similar to this U.S. experience, most other countries have historical reasons that individuals, organizations, and government bodies have proposed their own privacy definitions. International organizations have also addressed the issue of privacy.

Privacy has been defined as the desire of people to freely choose the circumstances and the degree to which individuals will expose their attitudes and behavior to others.[2] It has been connected to the human personality and used as a means to protect an individual's independence, dignity, and integrity.[3] Establishing an understanding of how privacy is defined and categorized—as well as how it has emerged as a social concern—is critical to understanding data protection and privacy laws as they have been established today in the United States, Europe and elsewhere around the world.

1.2 Classes of Privacy

As previously discussed, privacy can be defined in many ways. When examining data protection and privacy laws and practices, it can be helpful to focus on four categories or classes of privacy.[4]

1. **Information privacy** is concerned with establishing rules that govern the collection and handling of personal information. Examples include financial information, medical information, government records, and records of a person's activities on the internet.
2. **Bodily privacy** is focused on a person's physical being and any invasion thereof. Such an invasion can take the form of genetic testing, drug testing, or body cavity searches. It also encompasses issues such as birth control, abortion, and adoption.
3. **Territorial privacy** is concerned with placing limits on the ability to intrude into another individual's environment. "Environment" is not limited to the home; it may be defined as the workplace or public space. Invasion into an individual's territorial privacy typically takes the form of monitoring such as video surveillance, identification checks, and use of similar technology and procedures.
4. **Communications privacy** encompasses protection of the means of correspondence, including postal mail, telephone conversations, email, and other forms of communicative behavior and apparatus.

While some of these categories may interrelate, this book will focus primarily on the legal, technological and practical components of information privacy.

1.3 The Historical and Social Origins of Privacy

Information privacy as a social concept is rooted in some of the oldest texts and cultures.[5] Privacy is referenced numerous times in the laws of classical Greece and in the Bible. The concept of the freedom from being watched has historically been recognized by Jewish law.[6] Privacy is similarly recognized in the Qur'an and in the sayings of Mohammed, where there is discussion of the privacy of prayer as well as in the avoidance of spying or talking ill of someone behind their back.[7]

The legal protection of privacy rights has a similarly far-reaching history. In England, the Justices of the Peace Act, enacted in 1361, included provisions calling for the arrest of "peeping Toms" and eavesdroppers.[8]

In 1765, British Lord Camden protected the privacy of the home, striking down a warrant to enter the home and seize papers from it. He wrote, "We can safely say there is no law in this country to justify the defendants in what they have done; if there was, it would destroy all the comforts of society; for papers are often the dearest property any man can have."[9] Parliamentarian William Pitt shared this view, declaring that "the poorest man may in his cottage bid defiance to all the force of the Crown. It may be frail: its roof may shake; the wind may blow through it; the storms may enter; the rain may enter—but the King of England cannot enter; all his forces dare not cross the threshold of the ruined tenement."[10]

This British tradition of privacy protection was built into the U.S. Constitution, ratified in 1789. Although the word "privacy" does not appear in the Constitution, a number of provisions relate to privacy, including the Third Amendment, banning quartering of soldiers in a person's home; the Fourth Amendment, generally requiring a search warrant before the police can enter a home or business; the Fifth Amendment, prohibiting persons from being compelled to testify against themselves; and, later, the Fourteenth Amendment, with its requirement of due process under the law, including for intrusions into a person's bodily autonomy.

By contrast, the California Constitution contains an explicit guarantee of the right to privacy, which the people of California added to the California Constitution by a ballot measure in November 1974. Article 1, Section 1 of the California Constitution states:

> *All people are by nature free and independent and have inalienable rights. Among these are enjoying and defending life and liberty, acquiring, possessing, and protecting property, and pursuing and obtaining safety, happiness, and privacy.*[11]

In many parts of the world, modern privacy has arisen within the context of human rights. In December 1948, the General Assembly of the United Nations adopted and proclaimed the Universal Declaration of Human Rights.[12] This declaration formally announced that "no one shall be subjected to arbitrary interference with his privacy, family, home or correspondence."[13] In 1950, the Council of Europe set forth the European Convention for the Protection of Human Rights and Fundamental Freedoms.[14] Article 8 of that Convention, which has been the subject of extensive litigation, provides that "everyone has the right to respect for his private and family life, his home and his correspondence," with this right conditioned where necessary to protect national security and other goals, as necessary to preserve a democratic society.[15]

1.4 Fair Information Practices

Since the 1970s, fair information practices (FIPs), sometimes called fair information privacy practices or principles (FIPPs), have been a significant means for organizing the multiple individual rights and organizational responsibilities that exist with respect to personal information. The precise definitions of FIPs have varied over time and by geographic location; nonetheless, strong similarities exist for the major themes. In practice, there are various exceptions to the clear statements provided here and the degree to which the FIPs are legally binding.

Important codifications of FIPs include:

- The 1973 U.S. Department of Health, Education and Welfare Fair Information Practice Principles
- The 1980 Organisation for Economic Co-operation and Development (OECD) Guidelines on the Protection of Privacy and Transborder Flows of Personal Data ("OECD Guidelines")
- The 1981 Council of Europe Convention for the Protection of Individuals with Regard to Automatic Processing of Personal Data ("Convention 108")
- The Asia-Pacific Economic Cooperation (APEC), which in 2004 agreed to a Privacy Framework
- The 2009 Madrid Resolution—International Standards on the Protection of Personal Data and Privacy

1.4.1 Overview of Fair Information Practices

FIPs are guidelines for handling, storing, and managing data with privacy, security, and fairness in an information society that is rapidly evolving.[16] These principles can be conceived in four categories: rights of individuals, controls on the information, information life cycle, and management.

1.4.1.1 Rights of Individuals

With regard to the rights of individuals, organizations should address notice, choice, and consent, as well as data subject access.

- **Notice.** Organizations should provide notice about their privacy policies and procedures and should identify the purpose for which personal information is collected, used, retained, and disclosed.
- **Choice and consent.** Organizations should describe the choices available to individuals and should get implicit or explicit consent with respect to the collection, use, retention, and disclosure of personal information. Consent is often considered especially important for disclosures of personal information to other data controllers.
- **Data subject access.** Organizations should provide individuals with access to their personal information for review and updates.

1.4.1.2 Controls on the Information

Regarding controls on the information, organizations should focus on information security and information quality.

- **Information security.** Organizations should use reasonable administrative, technical, and physical safeguards to protect personal information against unauthorized access, use, disclosure, modification, and destruction.
- **Information quality.** Organizations should maintain accurate, complete, and relevant personal information for the purposes identified in the notice.

1.4.1.3 Information Life Cycle

Organizations should address the life cycle of information, including collection, use and retention, and disclosure.

- **Collection.** Organizations should collect personal information only for the purposes identified in the notice.
- **Use and retention.** Organizations should limit the use of personal information to the purposes identified in the notice and for which the individual has provided implicit or explicit consent. Organizations should also retain personal information for only as long as necessary to fulfill the stated purpose.

- **Disclosure.** Organizations should disclose personal information to third parties only for the purposes identified in the notice and with the implicit or explicit consent of the individual.

1.4.1.4 Management

Regarding management, organizations should ensure that they address both management and administration as well as monitoring and enforcement.

- **Management and administration.** Organizations should define, document, communicate, and assign accountability for their privacy policies and procedures.
- **Monitoring and enforcement.** Organizations should monitor compliance with their privacy policies and procedures and have procedures to address privacy-related complaints and disputes.

1.4.2 U.S. Health, Education and Welfare FIPs (1973)

The FIPs used widely today date back to a 1973 report by the U.S. Department of Health, Education and Welfare Advisory Committee on Automated Systems.[17]

The original Code of Fair Information Practices provided:

- There must be no personal data recordkeeping systems whose very existence is secret
- There must be a way for a person to find out what information about the person is in a record and how it is used
- There must be a way for a person to prevent information about the person that was obtained for one purpose from being used or made available for other purposes without the individual's consent
- There must be a way for a person to correct or amend a record of identifiable information about the person
- Any organization creating, maintaining, using or disseminating records of identifiable personal data must assure the reliability of the data for its intended use and must take precautions to prevent misuse of the data

1.4.3 Organisation for Economic Co-operation and Development Guidelines (1980)

In 1980, the OECD, an international organization that originally included the United States and European countries but has since expanded, published a set of privacy principles entitled "Guidelines on the Protection of Privacy and Transborder Flows of Personal Data."[18] Updated in 2013, the OECD Guidelines are perhaps the most widely recognized framework for FIPs and have been endorsed by the U.S. Federal Trade Commission (FTC) and many other government organizations.[19]

The guidelines provide the following privacy framework:

> ***Collection Limitation Principle.*** *There should be limits to the collection of personal data and any such data should be obtained by lawful and fair means and, where appropriate, with the knowledge or consent of the data subject.*
>
> ***Data Quality Principle.*** *Personal data should be relevant to the purposes for which they are to be used, and, to the extent necessary for those purposes, should be accurate, complete and kept up to date.*
>
> ***Purpose Specification Principle.*** *The purposes for which personal data are collected should be specified not later than at the time of data collection and the subsequent use limited to the fulfillment of those purposes or such others as are not incompatible with those purposes and as are specified on each occasion of change of purpose.*
>
> ***Use Limitation Principle.*** *Personal data should not be disclosed, made available or otherwise used for purposes other than those specified in accordance with [the Purpose Specification Principle] except: (a) with the consent of the data subject or (b) by the authority of law.*
>
> ***Security Safeguards Principle.*** *Personal data should be protected by reasonable security safeguards against such risks as loss or unauthorized access, destruction, use, modification or disclosure of data.*
>
> ***Openness Principle.*** *There should be a general policy of openness about developments, practices and policies with respect to personal data. Means should be readily available of establishing the existence and nature of personal data, and the main purposes of their use, as well as the identity and usual residence of the data controller.*
>
> ***Individual Participation Principle.*** *An individual should have the right: (a) to obtain from a data controller, or otherwise, confirmation of*

whether or not the data controller has data relating to him; (b) to have communicated to him, data relating to him, within a reasonable time, at a charge, if any, that is not excessive, in a reasonable manner, and in a form that is readily intelligible to him; (c) to be given reasons if a request made under subparagraphs (a) and (b) is denied, and to be able to challenge such denial; and (d) to challenge data relating to him and, if the challenge is successful to have the data erased, rectified, completed or amended.

Accountability Principle. *A data controller should be accountable for complying with measures which give effect to the principles stated above.*[20]

In 2022, the OECD adopted a declaration on common principles for government access, both for law enforcement and national security purposes, to personal data held by private companies.[21]

1.4.4 Council of Europe Convention (1981)

In 1981, the Council of Europe passed the Convention for the Protection of Individuals with Regard to Automatic Processing of Personal Data ("Convention 108"). This convention required member states of the Council of Europe that signed the treaty to incorporate certain data protection provisions into their domestic law.[22]

Convention 108 provided for the following:

- **Quality of data.** Data of a personal nature that is automatically processed should be obtained and stored only for specified and legitimate purposes. Data should be stored in a form that permits identification of the data subject no longer than needed for the required purpose.
- **Special categories of data.** Unless domestic law provides appropriate safeguards, personal data revealing the following categories cannot be automatically processed: racial origin, political opinions, religious beliefs, health, sex life, or criminal convictions.
- **Data security.** Appropriate security measures should be taken for files containing personal data. These measures must be adapted for the particular function of the file as well as for risks involved.
- **Transborder data flows.** When transferring data from one party of the Convention to another party, privacy concerns shall not prohibit

> the transborder flow of data. Exceptions to this provision include special regulations concerning certain categories of personal data.[23]

The Convention was broadly similar to the OECD Guidelines, and its principles were important contributors to national data protection laws in Europe in the 1980s and 1990s.[24]

In 2018, the Council of Europe adopted an update to the convention, referred to as Convention 108+.[25] The changes brought the Convention in line with the EU's General Data Protection Regulation (GDPR). In particular, the updates focus on necessary and proportionate requirements for data processing; obligations on controllers to provide notice when a data breach occurs; and requirements for transborder data flows.[26] As of the writing of this book, the United States is not expected to ratify Convention 108 or Convention 108+.[27]

1.4.5 APEC Privacy Framework (2004)

APEC is a multinational organization with 21 Pacific Coast members in Asia and the Americas. Unlike the European Union, the APEC organization operates under nonbinding agreement. It was established in 1989 to enhance economic growth for the region.

In 2003, the APEC Privacy Subgroup was established under the auspices of the Electronic Commerce Steering Group in order to develop a framework for privacy practices. This framework was designed to provide support to APEC-member economic legislation that would both protect individual interests and ensure the continued economic development of all APEC member economies. The APEC Privacy Framework was approved by the APEC ministers in 2004 and updated in 2015.[28]

It contains nine information privacy principles that generally mirror the OECD Guidelines, but in some areas are more explicit about exceptions. The APEC privacy principles spelled out in the framework are:

1. ***Preventing Harm.*** *Recognizing the interests of the individual to legitimate expectations of privacy, personal information protection should be designed to prevent the misuse of such information. Further, acknowledging the risk that harm may result from such misuse of personal information, specific obligations should take account of such risk and remedial measures should be proportionate to the likelihood and severity of the harm threatened by the collection, use and transfer of personal information.*

2. ***Notice.*** *Personal information controllers should provide clear and easily accessible statements about their practices and policies with respect to personal information that should include:*
    a. *the fact that personal information is being collected;*
    b. *the purposes for which personal information is collected;*
    c. *the types of persons or organizations to whom personal information might be disclosed;*
    d. *the identity and location of the personal information controller, including information on how to contact it about its practices and handling of personal information;*
    e. *the choices and means the personal information controller offers individuals for limiting the use and disclosure of personal information, and for accessing and correcting it.*

    All reasonably practicable steps shall be taken to ensure that such information is provided either before or at the time of collection of personal information. Otherwise, such information should be provided as soon after as is practicable. It may not be appropriate for personal information controllers to provide notice regarding the collection and use of publicly available information.

3. **Collection Limitation.** *The collection of personal information should be limited to information that is relevant to the purposes of collection and any such information should be obtained by lawful and fair means, and, where appropriate, with notice to, or consent of, the individual concerned.*

4. ***Uses of Personal Information.*** *Personal information collected should be used only to fulfill the purposes of collection and other compatible purposes except:*
    a. *with the consent of the individual whose personal information is collected;*
    b. *when necessary to provide a service or product requested by the individual; or,*
    c. *by the authority of law and other legal instruments, proclamations and pronouncements of legal effect.*

5. **Choice.** *Where appropriate, individuals should be provided with clear, prominent, easily understandable, accessible and affordable mechanisms to exercise choice in relation to the collection, use and disclosure of their personal information. It may not be appropriate for personal information controllers to provide these mechanisms when collecting publicly available information.*

6. ***Integrity of Personal Information.*** *Personal information should be accurate, complete and kept up-to-date to the extent necessary for the purposes of use.*

7. ***Security Safeguards.*** *Personal information controllers should protect personal information that they hold with appropriate safeguards against risks, such as loss or unauthorized access to personal information, or unauthorized destruction, use, modification or disclosure of information or other misuses. Such safeguards should be proportional to the likelihood and severity of the harm threatened, the sensitivity of the information and the context in which it is held, and should be subject to periodic review and reassessment.*

8. ***Access and Correction.*** *Individuals should be able to:*
    a. *obtain from the personal information controller confirmation of whether or not the personal information controller holds personal information about them*
    b. *have communicated to them, after having provided sufficient proof of their identity, personal information about them*
        i. *within a reasonable time;*
        ii. *at a charge, if any, that is not excessive;*
        iii. *in a reasonable manner;*
        iv. *in a form that is generally understandable; and,*
    c. *challenge the accuracy of information relating to them and, if possible and as appropriate, have the information rectified, completed, amended or deleted.*
    d. *such access and opportunity for correction should be provided except where:*

> i. *the burden or expense of doing so would be unreasonable or disproportionate to the risks to the individual's privacy in the case in question;*
>
> ii. *the information should not be disclosed due to legal or security reasons or to protect confidential commercial information; or*
>
> iii. *the information privacy of persons other than the individual would be violated*
>
> *If a request under (a) or (b) or a challenge under (c) is denied, the individual should be provided with reasons why and be able to challenge such denial.*

9. ***Accountability.*** *A personal information controller should be accountable for complying with measures that give effect to the principles stated above. When personal information is to be transferred to another person or organization, whether domestically or internationally, the personal information controller should obtain the consent of the individual or exercise due diligence and take reasonable steps to ensure that the recipient person or organization will protect the information consistently with these principles.*[29]

In 2022, Canada, Japan, the Republic of Korea, the Philippines, Singapore, Chinese Taipei, and the United States announced that they will establish an international certification system based on the existing APEC Cross-Border Privacy Rules and Privacy Recognition for Processors (PRP) Systems. The new approach, known as the Global Cross-Border Privacy Rules Forum (Global CBPR Forum), will technically be independent of the existing APEC framework, allowing non-APEC members to participate.[30]

1.4.6 Madrid Resolution (2009)

In 2009, the Madrid Resolution was approved by the independent data protection and privacy commissioners (not the governments themselves) at the annual International Conference of Data Protection and Privacy Commissioners held in Madrid, Spain.[31] There were dual purposes for the Madrid Resolution: to define a set of principles and rights guaranteeing (1) the effective and internationally uniform protection of privacy with regard to the processing of personal data and (2) the facilitation of the international flows of personal data needed in a globalized world.

The resolution has several basic principles:

- **Principle of lawfulness and fairness.** Personal data must be fairly processed, respecting the applicable national legislation as well as the rights and freedoms of individuals. Any processing that gives rise to unlawful or arbitrary discrimination against the data subject shall be deemed unfair.
- **Purpose specification principle.** Processing of personal data should be limited to the fulfillment of the specific, explicit, and legitimate purposes of the responsible person; processing that is noncompatible with the purposes for which personal data was collected requires the unambiguous consent of the data subject.
- **Proportionality principle.** Processing of personal data should be limited to such processing as is adequate, relevant, and not excessive in relation to the purposes. Reasonable efforts should be made to limit processing to the minimum necessary.
- **Data quality.** The responsible person should at all times ensure that personal data is accurate, sufficient, and up to date in such a way as to fulfill the purposes for which it is processed. The period of retention of the personal data shall be limited to the minimum necessary. Personal data no longer necessary to fulfill the purposes that legitimized its processing must be deleted or rendered anonymous.
- **Openness principle.** The responsible person shall provide to the data subjects, as a minimum, information about the responsible person's identity, the intended purpose of processing, the recipients to whom their personal data will be disclosed, and how data subjects may exercise their rights. When data is collected directly from the data subject, this information must be provided at the time of collection unless it has already been provided. When data is not collected directly from the data subject, the responsible person must inform them about the source of personal data. This information must be provided in an intelligible form, using clear and plain language, in particular for any processing addressed specifically to minors.
- **Accountability.** The responsible person shall take all the necessary measures to observe the principles and obligations set out in the resolution and in the applicable national legislation and have the necessary internal mechanisms in place for demonstrating such observance both to data subjects and to the supervisory authorities exercising their powers.

1.5 Information Privacy, Data Protection, and the Advent of Information Technology

Modern ideas about privacy have been decisively shaped by the rapid development of information technology (IT). Mainframe computers emerged by the 1960s to handle the data processing and storage needs of business, government, educational, and other institutions. As hardware and software evolved, there were clear and large benefits to individuals and society, ranging from increased economic growth to easier communications for individuals. The unprecedented accumulation of personal data, and the resulting potential for increased surveillance, also triggered an acute interest in privacy practices and the privacy rights of individuals. A vivid image of the risk came from George Orwell's 1949 book *1984*, in which the government kept citizens under surveillance at all times, warning them with the slogan "Big Brother is watching you."[32] To prevent the creation of "Big Brother," by the late 1960s, nearly two decades after Orwell wrote his masterpiece, there were increasing demands for formal rules to govern the collection and handling of personal information.

In response to this sort of concern, in 1970 the German state of Hesse enacted the first known modern data protection law. This German law was motivated in part by the growing potential of IT systems as well as a desire to prevent a reoccurrence of the personal information abuses that took place under Hitler's Third Reich before and during World War II. Such concerns were not confined to Germany, and over the next decade, several European countries enacted national privacy laws of differing objectives and scope. In 1970, the United States passed its first national privacy law, the Fair Credit Reporting Act (FCRA), which focused solely on information about consumer credit.

1.6 Personal and Nonpersonal Information

Because information privacy is concerned with establishing rules that govern the collection and handling of personal information, an understanding of what constitutes personal information is key. A central issue to determine is the extent to which information can be linked to a particular person. This can be contrasted with aggregate or statistical information, which generally does not raise privacy compliance issues.

1.6.1 Personal Information

In the United States, the terms "personal information" and "personally identifiable information" (PII) are generally used to define the information that is covered by privacy laws. These definitions include information that makes it possible to identify an individual. Examples include names, Social Security numbers, or passport numbers. The terms also include information about an "identified" or "identifiable" individual. For instance, street address, telephone number, and email address are generally considered sufficiently related to a particular person to count as identifiable information within the scope of privacy protections. The definitions generally apply to both electronic and paper records.

Sensitive personal information is an important subset of personal information. The definition of what is considered sensitive varies depending on jurisdiction and particular regulations. In the United States, Social Security numbers and financial information are commonly treated as sensitive information, as are driver's license numbers and health information. In general, sensitive information requires additional privacy and security limitations to safeguard its collection, use and disclosure.

1.6.2 Nonpersonal Information

If the data elements used to identify the individual are removed, the remaining data becomes nonpersonal information, and privacy and data protection laws generally do not apply.[33] Similar terms used include "deidentified" or "anonymized" information. This type of information is frequently used for research, statistical, or aggregate purposes. Pseudonymized data exists where information about individuals is retained under pseudonyms, such as a unique numerical code for each person, that renders data temporarily nonpersonal. Pseudonymized data can be reversed, reidentifying the individuals. This reversibility can be important in certain situations, such as a drug trial where the medicine is discovered to have adverse side effects.[34]

1.6.3 The Line between Personal and Nonpersonal Information

The difference between personal and nonpersonal information depends on what is identifiable. The line between these two categories is not always clear, and regulators and courts in different jurisdictions may disagree on what counts as personal information.

Other Information Assets of an Organization

As part of their normal activities, organizations also may collect and generate information that, by its nature, would not be considered personal information but is nevertheless a key part of the information assets of the organization. Examples of such information include:

- *Financial data*
- *Operational data*
- *Intellectual property*
- *Information about the organization's products and services*

Though not personal information, such information needs to be protected and secured to ensure its confidentiality.

As an example of how different regimes have defined the line between personal and nonpersonal information, consider the internet protocol (IP) address: the numbers that identify the location of computers in communications over the internet. The European Union generally considers IP addresses personal data" taking the view that IP addresses are identifiable.[35] In the United States, federal agencies operating under the Privacy Act do not consider IP addresses to be covered by the statute.[36] However, the Federal Trade Commission, an independent agency in the United States, has stated that in connection with breaches of health care information, IP addresses are personal information.[37] For the privacy professional, it is important to check the line between personal and nonpersonal information for the appropriate regulatory regime.

Assessing an Organization's Personal Information Responsibilities

The line between personal and nonpersonal information illustrates a critical first step in assessing an organization's personal information responsibilities—determining whether the organization is covered by a law or other obligation.

With globalization, information privacy professionals may need to determine when the laws of a particular jurisdiction apply. In addition, some laws apply only to particular sectors or types of information. The Health Insurance Portability and Accountability Act (HIPAA) in the United States, for instance, applies only to certain organizations ("covered entities") and certain information ("protected health information").

Changes in technology can also shift the line between personal and nonpersonal information. For instance, historically, IP addresses were usually dynamic—individuals would generally get a new IP address assigned by their internet service provider each time they logged on to the internet. Over time, more individuals have had static IP addresses, which stay the same for each computer device, linking the device more closely to an identifiable person.[38] The increasingly used version of the internet protocol (IPv6) employs a new numbering scheme that, by default, uses information about the computer to generate an IPv6 address, making it even easier to link devices (including smartphones) and their users.

1.7 Sources of Personal Information

Sometimes the same information about an individual is treated differently based on the source of the information. To illustrate this point, consider three sources of personal information: public records, publicly available information, and nonpublic information.

1. **Public records** consist of information collected and maintained by a government entity and available to the public. These government entities include the national, state, provincial, and local governments. Public records laws vary considerably across jurisdictions.[39]

2. **Publicly available information** is information that is generally available to a wide range of persons. Some traditional examples are names and addresses in telephone books and information published in newspapers or other public media. Today, search engines are a major source of publicly available information.

3. **Nonpublic information** is not generally available or easily accessed due to law or custom. Examples of this type of data are medical records, financial information, and adoption records. A company's customer or employee database usually contains nonpublic information.

Organizations should be alert to the possibility that the same information may be public record, publicly available, and nonpublic. For example, a name and address may be a matter of public record on a real estate deed, publicly available in the telephone book, and included in nonpublic databases, such as in a health care patient file. To understand how to handle the name and address, one must understand the source that provided it—restrictions may apply to use of the name and address in the patient file, but not to public records or publicly available information.

1.8 Processing Personal Information

As previously introduced, almost anything that someone may do with personal information might constitute processing under privacy and data protection laws. The term "processing" refers to the collection, recording, organization, storage, updating or modification, retrieval, consultation, and use of personal information. It also includes the disclosure by transmission, dissemination or making available in any other form, linking, alignment or combination, blocking, erasure, or destruction of personal information. The following common terms, first widely used in the European Union, apply to data processing:

- **Data subject** is the individual about whom information is being processed, such as the patient at a medical facility, the employee of a company, or the customer of a retail store.
- **Data controller** is an organization that has the authority to decide how and why personal information is to be processed. This entity is the focus of most obligations under privacy and data protection laws—it controls the use of personal information by determining the purposes for its use and the manner in which the information will be processed.[40] The data controller may be an individual or an organization that is legally treated as an individual, such as a corporation or partnership.
- **Data processor** is an individual or organization, often a third-party outsourcing service, that processes data on behalf of the data controller. Under the HIPAA Privacy Rule, these data processors are called "business associates." A data controller might not have the employees or expertise in-house to do some types of activities, or might find it more efficient to get assistance from other organizations. For instance, a data controller may hire another organization to do accounting and back-office operations. The first data processor, in turn, might hire other organizations to act as data processors on its behalf, for example, if a company providing back-office operations hired a subcontractor to manage its website. Each organization in the chain—from data controller, to data processor, to any subsequent data processor acting on behalf of the first data processor—is expected to act in a trusted way, doing operations that are consistent with the direction of the data controller. The data processors are not authorized to do additional data processing outside of the scope of what is permitted for the data controller itself.

1.9 Sources of Privacy Protection

There is no single approach to protecting privacy and security. Rather, privacy protection is derived from several sources: market forces, technology, legal controls, and self-regulation.

- **Markets.** The market can be a useful way of approaching privacy protection. When consumers raise concerns about their privacy, companies respond. Businesses that are brand-sensitive are especially likely to adopt strict privacy practices to build up their reputations as trustworthy organizations. In turn, this can create market competition, spurring other companies to also implement privacy practices into their operations.
- **Technology**. Technology also can provide robust privacy protection. The rapid advancement of technology such as encryption provides people with new and advanced means of protecting themselves. Even if privacy protection from law or market forces is weak, information privacy and security best practices can remain strong.
- **Law.** Law is the traditional approach to privacy regulation. However, simply enacting more laws does not necessarily result in better privacy and security. Laws may not be well drafted and may be poorly enforced. Laws should be understood as one very important source of privacy protection, but in practice, actual protection also depends on markets, technology and self-regulation.
- **Self-regulation and co-regulation**. Self-regulation (and the closely related concept of co-regulation) is a complement to law that comes from the government. The term "self-regulation" can refer to any or all of three components: legislation, enforcement, and adjudication. Legislation refers to the question of who defines privacy rules. For self-regulation, this typically occurs through the privacy policy of a company or similar entity, or by an industry association. Enforcement refers to the question of who should initiate enforcement action. Actions may be brought by data protection authorities (DPAs), other government agencies, industry code enforcement, or, in some cases, the affected individuals. Finally, adjudication refers to the question of who should decide whether an organization has violated a privacy rule. The decision-maker can be an industry association, a government agency, or a judicial officer. Thus, the term "self-regulation" covers a broad range of institutional arrangements. For a clear understanding

of data privacy responsibilities, privacy professionals should consider who defines the requirements, which organization brings enforcement action, and who makes the judicial decisions.

1.10 World Models of Data Protection

As of the writing of this book, more than 160 countries have privacy or data protection regimes, and more than half of them first enacted such laws after the year 2000.[41] In varying degrees, the different data protection models around the world all draw upon law, markets, technology and self-regulation as sources for privacy protection.[42] Comprehensive data protection laws are those in which the government has defined requirements throughout the economy. On the other hand, sectoral laws, such as those in the United States, exist in selected market segments, often in response to a particular need or problem. The scope of data protection laws, as described above, varies depending on how much the specific country relies on government laws versus industry codes and standards. The various data protection models used globally also differ in enforcement and adjudication. However, each regime falls along a continuum, with clearly defined legislative, enforcement and adjudication mechanisms established by the government at one end and no stated, defined baseline at the other. In practice, no regime is so comprehensive that all laws are written, enforced and adjudicated by the government. Even in the United States, however, which is often used as an example of a less regulatory-oriented regime, the government has written numerous privacy laws.

Some of the most common data protection models in use today are comprehensive and sectoral frameworks, co-regulatory or self-regulatory models, and the technology-based model. Following are the basic approaches, along with major arguments for and against each approach.

1.10.1 Comprehensive Model

Comprehensive data protection laws govern the collection, use and dissemination of personal information in the public and private sectors.[43] Generally speaking, a country that has enacted such laws hosts an official or agency responsible for overseeing enforcement.[44] This official or agency, often referred to as a DPA in Europe, ensures compliance with the law and investigates alleged breaches of the law's provisions. In many countries, the official also bears responsibility for educating the public on data protection matters and acts as an international liaison for data protection issues. Enforcement and funding are two critical issues in a comprehensive data protection scheme. Data protection officials are granted varying degrees of enforcement power from country to country. Further, countries choose to allocate varying levels of resources to the enforcement of data protection laws, leaving some countries inadequately funded to meet the laws' stated goals.

Over time, countries have adopted comprehensive privacy and data protection laws for a combination of at least three reasons:[45]

- **Remedy past injustices.** A number of countries, particularly those previously subject to authoritarian regimes, have enacted comprehensive laws as a means to remedy past privacy violations. For instance, Germany is widely regarded as having one of the strictest privacy regimes. At least part of the reason is likely a reaction to its history during the Nazi regime and under the heavy surveillance by the Stasi (Ministry of State Security) in East Germany before the two parts of Germany were reunified in 1990.
- **Ensure consistency with European privacy laws.** As discussed later in the book, the GDPR in the European Union limits transfer of personal data to countries that lack "adequate" privacy protections.[46] Some countries passed privacy laws as part of the process of joining the European Union. Other countries have enacted privacy laws at least in part to prevent any disruption in trade with EU countries.
- **Promote electronic commerce.** Countries have developed privacy laws to provide assurance to potentially uneasy consumers engaged in electronic commerce.

Critics of the comprehensive approach express concern that the costs of the regulations can outweigh the benefits. One-size-fits-all rules may not address risk well. If the rules are strict enough to ensure protection for especially sensitive data, such as medical data or information that can lead to identity theft, that same level of strictness may not be justified for less sensitive data. Along with the strictness of controls, comprehensive approaches can involve costly paperwork, documentation, audits and similar requirements even for settings where the risks are low.

A different critique of comprehensive regimes is that they may provide insufficient opportunity for innovation in data processing. With the continued evolution of IT, individuals have access today to many products and services that were unimaginable a decade or two ago, from smartphones to social networks and the full range of services that have developed since the internet emerged in the 1990s. To the extent that comprehensive laws may discourage the emergence of new services involving personal information or require prior approval from regulators, the pace and diversity of technological innovation may slow.

1.10.2 Sectoral Model (United States)

This framework protects personal information by enacting laws that address a particular industry sector.[47] For example, in the United States, different laws delineate conduct and specify the requisite level of data protection for video rental records, consumer financial transactions, credit records, law enforcement, and medical records. Even in a comprehensive model, laws addressing specific market segments may be enacted to provide more specific protection for data particular to that segment, such as the health care sector.

Supporters of the sectoral approach emphasize that different parts of the economy face different privacy and security challenges; it is appropriate, for instance, to have stricter regulation for medical records than for ordinary commerce. Supporters also underscore the cost savings and lack of regulatory burden for organizations outside of the regulated sectors.

Critics of the sectoral approach express concern about the lack of a single DPA to oversee personal information issues. They also point out the problems of gaps and overlaps in coverage. Gaps can occur when legislation lags technological change, and unregulated segments may suddenly face privacy threats with no legislative guidance. Whereas laws under the comprehensive approach apply to new technologies, there are no similar governmental rules under the sectoral approach until the legislature or other responsible body acts. As a recent example, drones are becoming more common in the United States, but there have not been any national privacy rules governing surveillance by drones. Moreover, there can be political obstacles to creating new legislation if industry or other stakeholders oppose such laws. An example of a gap being filled is the Health Information Technology for Economic and Clinical Health (HITECH) Act of 2009, which introduced a breach notification requirement for vendors of personal health records. These were not covered entities under HIPAA. The new law addressed a gap, where entities not traditionally involved in health care offered services involving the collection and use of large volumes of health care information.

Similarly, overlaps can exist in a sectoral approach. For instance, HIPAA-covered entities such as medical health care providers are subject to enforcement either by the U.S. Department of Health and Human Services (HHS) under HIPAA or by the FTC under its general authority to take action against unfair and deceptive practices. As the boundaries between industries change over time, previously separate industries can converge, potentially leading to different legal treatment of functionally similar activities.

1.10.3 The Co-Regulatory and Self-Regulatory Models

Co-regulation and self-regulation are quite similar, with co-regulation generally referring to laws such as those in Australia, which are closer to the comprehensive model, and self-regulation generally referring to approaches such as those in the United States, where there are no general laws applying to personal information.[48] Under both approaches, a mix of government and nongovernment institutions protects personal information.

The **co-regulatory model** emphasizes industry development of enforceable codes or standards for privacy and data protection against the backdrop of legal requirements by the government. Co-regulation can exist under both comprehensive and sectoral models. One example is the Children's Online Privacy Protection Act (COPPA) in the United States, which allows compliance with codes to be sufficient for compliance with the statute once the codes have been approved by the FTC.

The **self-regulatory model** emphasizes creation of codes of practice for the protection of personal information by a company, industry or independent body. In contrast to the co-regulatory model, there may be no generally applicable data protection law that creates a legal framework for the self-regulatory code.[49] A prominent example that affects the wide range of businesses that process credit card data is the global Payment Card Industry Data Security Standard (PCI DSS), which enhances cardholder data security and facilitates the broad adoption of consistent data security measures globally.

Seal programs are another form of self-regulation. A seal program requires its participants to abide by codes of information practices and submit to some variation of monitoring to ensure compliance.[50] Companies that abide by the terms of the seal program are then allowed to display the program's privacy seal on their website. Seal programs recognized by the FTC for adhering to the COPPA are Children's Advertising Review Unit (CARU), Entertainment Software Rating Board (ESRB), iKeepSafe, kidSAFE, PRIVO, and TrustArc (formerly TRUSTe).[51]

Supporters of a self-regulatory approach tend to emphasize the expertise of the industry to inform its own personal information practices, and thus use the most efficient ways to ensure privacy and security.[52] Self-regulatory codes may also be more flexible and quicker to adjust to new technology without the need for prior governmental approval.

Critics of the self-regulatory approach often express concerns about adequacy and enforcement. Industry-developed codes can provide limited data protection and may not adequately incorporate the perspectives and interests of consumers and other stakeholders who are not part of the industry. The strength of enforcement can also vary. In some cases, where an organization has signed up for a code, any violation is treated just like a violation of a statute. In others, however, penalties can be weak, and there may be no effective enforcement authority.

An alternative to the protections that arise from an organization's administrative compliance with laws or self-regulatory codes that is worth considering is a technology-based model. Individuals and organizations in some settings can use technical measures that reduce the relative importance of administrative measures for overall privacy protection. For example, global web email providers such as Google and Microsoft have increased their use of encryption between the sender and recipient. Chapters 3 and 4 further discuss the interrelated roles of technical, administrative, and physical safeguards for personal information.

1.11 Conclusion

This chapter introduced key terminology about privacy and data protection laws and policies. It traced the history of these topics and the continued growth of legal requirements to accompany the evolution of IT since the 1960s. As legal requirements have increased, the number of data protection and privacy professionals has grown rapidly, and the role has expanded in many organizations. Similar but not identical forms of FIPS have been the basis of privacy and data protection laws in numerous countries around the globe. This chapter introduces the reader to the legal and policy structures for privacy and data protection around the world. The key models of privacy protection have been examined: the comprehensive, sectoral, self-regulatory or co-regulatory, and technology models.

Endnotes

1 Samuel Warren and Louis Brandeis, "The Right to Privacy," *Harvard Law Review* 4, no. 5 (December 15, 1890): 193, http://groups.csail.mit.edu/mac/classes/6.805/articles/privacy/Privacy_brand_warr2.html. There are numerous sources of legal privacy, including tort privacy (Warren and Brandeis's original conception), Fourth Amendment privacy, First Amendment privacy, fundamental-decision privacy and state constitutional privacy. Ken Gormley, "One Hundred Years of Privacy," *Wisconsin Law Review* 1335 (1992), https://cyber.law.harvard.edu/privacy/Gormley--100 Years of Privacy--EXCERPTS.htm.

2 Alan F. Westin, *Privacy and Freedom* (New York: Atheneum, 1967).

3 Edward J. Bloustein, "Privacy as an Aspect of Human Dignity: An Answer to Dean Prosser," *New York University Law Review* 39 (December 1964): 962–971.

4 David Banisar and Simon Davies, "Global Trends in Privacy Protection: An International Survey of Privacy, Data Protection, and Surveillance Laws and Developments," *John Marshall Journal of Computer & Information Law* 18 (Fall 1999), http://papers.ssrn.com/sol3/papers.cfm?abstract_id=2138799.

5 Gary M. Schober et al., "Colloquium on Privacy & Security," *Buffalo Law Review* 50, no. 2 (April 2002): 703–726; Electronic Privacy Information Center & Privacy International, *Privacy and Human Rights: An International Survey of Privacy Laws and Developments,* 2002.

6 *Privacy and Human Rights,* 5; *see EPIC-Privacy and Human Rights Report,* 2006, www.worldlii.org/int/journals/EPICPrivHR/2006/PHR2006-The.html.

7 Qur'an, an-Noor 24:27–28 (Yusufali); al-Hujraat 49:11–12 (Yusufali).

8 "Justices of the Peace Act 1361, CHAPTER 1 34 Edw 3," Legislation.gov.uk, accessed January 2020, www.legislation.gov.uk/aep/Edw3/34/1.

9 Entick v. Carrington [1765] EWHC KB J98, www.bailii.org/ew/cases/EWHC/KB/1765/J98.html.

10 William Pitt, Speech on the Excise Bill, House of Commons (March 1763).

11 Cal. Const. art. I, § 1. *See* Lothar Determann, *California Privacy Law: Practical Guide and Commentary,* (Portsmouth, NH: IAPP, 2016), Chapter 2-2.

12 Universal Declaration of Human Rights, United Nations, accessed January 2020, www.un.org/en/universal-declaration-human-rights/.

13 Universal Declaration of Human Rights at Article 8.

14 Convention for the Protection of Human Rights and Fundamental Freedoms, Council of Europe, April 11, 1950, www.coe.int/en/web/conventions/full-list/-/conventions/treaty/005.

15 Convention for the Protection of Human Rights and Fundamental Freedoms at Article 8.

16 Pam Dixon, "A Brief Introduction to Fair Information Practices," World Privacy Forum, updated December 19, 2007, https://www.worldprivacyforum.org/2008/01/report-a-brief-introduction-to-fair-information-practices/. To view the code itself, *see* "The Code for Fair Information Practices," Electronic Privacy Information Center, accessed January 2020, https://www.epic.org/privacy/consumer/code_fair_info.html.

17 U.S. Department of Health, Education and Welfare, Pub. No. (OS) 73-94, "Records, Computers, and the Rights of Citizens," July 1973, https://www.justice.gov/opcl/docs/rec-com-rights.pdf. For a historical overview of this report, view Chris Hoofnagle, "The Origin of Fair Information Practices," Archive of Meetings of the Secretary's Advisory Committee on Automated Personal Data Systems, Berkeley Center for Law and Technology, July 15, 2014, https://papers.ssrn.com/sol3/papers.cfm?abstract_id=2466418.

18 Organisation for Economic Co-operation and Development, *Guidelines on the Protection of Privacy and Transborder Flows of Personal Data,* September 23, 1980. An important distinction between the Organisation for Economic Co-operation and Development and the Council of Europe is the involvement and support of the U.S. government. For more information, *see* https://www.oecd.org/digital/privacy/ (accessed May 2023).

19 The Organisation for Economic Co-operation and Development Privacy Framework, accessed March 2023, https://www.oecd.org/digital/privacy/; Jordan M. Blanke, "'Safe Harbor' and the European Union's Directive on Data Protection," *Albany Law Journal of Science & Technology* (2000).

20 Recommendation of the Council concerning Guidelines Governing the Protection of Privacy and Transborder Flows of Personal Data, OECD, adopted September 22, 1980 and amended July 10, 2013, https://legalinstruments.oecd.org/en/instruments/OECD-LEGAL-0188.

21 This recent OECD effort is discussed in more detail in Chapter 14. Declaration on Government Access to Personal Data Held by the Private Sector, OECD, December 13, 2022, https://legalinstruments.oecd.org/en/instruments/OECD-LEGAL-0487; see Natasha Lomas, "OECD Adopts Declaration on Trusted Government Access to Private Sector Data," TechCrunch, December 14, 2022, https://techcrunch.com/2022/12/14/oecd-declaration-trusted-government-access/.

22 Convention for the Protection of Individuals with Regard to the Automatic Processing of Personal Data (Convention 108), January 8, 1981, Council of Europe, https://www.coe.int/en/web/conventions/full-list/-/conventions/treaty/108; see Council of Europe Privacy Convention, Electronic Privacy Information Center, https://epic.org/privacy/intl/coeconvention/ (accessed January 2020); see also 46 Member States, accessed May 2023, https://www.coe.int/en/web/portal/46-members-states.

23 See *Explanatory Report to the Convention for the Protection of Individuals with Regard to Automatic Processing of Personal Data,* Council of Europe, European Treaty Series No. 108, January 28, 1981, https://rm.coe.int/16800ca434.

24 Banisar and Davies, "Global Trends," 11. See also Jeffrey B. Ritter, Benjamin S. Hayes and Henry L. Judy, "Emerging Trends in International Privacy Law," *Emory International Law Review* (Spring 2001).

25 Later that year, Convention 108+ was opened for signatures for the members of the Council of Europe. Convention 108+: Convention for the Protection of Individuals with Regard to Automatic Processing of Personal Data, opened for signature January 28, 1981, Council of Europe, https://rm.coe.int/convention-108-convention-for-the-protection-of-individuals-with-regar/16808b36f1.

26 Jennifer Baker, "What Does the Newly Signed Convention 108+ Mean for UK Adequacy?" IAPP Privacy Advisor, October 30, 2018, https://iapp.org/news/a/what-does-the-newly-signed-convention-108-mean-for-u-k-adequacy/; Amelia Williams, "International Origins of Data Protection Day and the Convention 108." DataGuidance, January 2022, https://www.dataguidance.com/opinion/international-origins-data-protection-day-convention.

27 The U.S. is an observer to the Convention. "Chart of Signatures and Ratifications of Treaty 108," Council of Europe, https://www.coe.int/en/web/conventions/full-list?module=signatures-by-treaty&treatynum=108.

28 The framework provides guidance on both domestic and international implementation. *APEC Privacy Framework,* Asia-Pacific Economic Cooperation, August 2017, https://www.apec.org/Publications/2017/08/APEC-Privacy-Framework-(2015).

29 *APEC Privacy Framework,* Asia-Pacific Economic Cooperation.

30 U.S. Department of Commerce, "Global Cross Border Privacy Rules (CBPR) System." Commerce.gov, July 22 2020, https://www.commerce.gov/global-cross-border-privacy-rules-declaration; see Mark Scott & Vincent Manancourt, "Washington Goes on the

Global Privacy Offensive," *Politico*, May 6, 2022, https://www.politico.eu/article/washington-data-privacy-global-rules-restrictions/; APEC Cross-Border Privacy Rules Go Global," *The National Law Review*, April 21, 2022, https://www.natlawreview.com/article/apec-cross-border-privacy-rules-go-global.

31 *International Standards on the Protection of Personal Data and Privacy: The Madrid Resolution*, from the International Conference of Data Protection and Privacy Commissioners, November 5, 2009; see Calli Schroeder, "When the World's DPAs Get Together: Resolutions of the ICDPPC, IAPP Privacy Advisor, November 28, 2017, https://iapp.org/news/a/when-the-worlds-dpas-get-together-resolutions-of-the-icdppc/.

32 Image of "Big Brother is Watching You" book cover, accessed June 2023, https://images-na.ssl-images-amazon.com/images/I/51AZNmwwgxL._SY550_.jpg.

33 At the writing of this book, some countries, including the EU and India, are considering regulation of nonpersonal data. Although these protections may fulfill various government objectives, the motivations are not necessarily primarily related to privacy and instead may address concerns such as foreign theft of intellectual property or trade secrets. See Ken Propp, "Cultivating Europe's Digital Garden," Lawfare, March 4, 2022, (discussing proposed regulation of nonpersonal data in the EU Data Act and Digital Markets Act), https://www.lawfareblog.com/cultivating-europes-data-garden; Sourabh Lele, "Governance Policy Will Ensure Fair Access to Non-Personal Data," Business Standard, June 17, 2022 (discussing India's National Data Governance Framework), https://www.business-standard.com/article/economy-policy/governance-policy-will-ensure-fair-access-to-non-personal-data-meity-122061600954_1.html.

34 See Phil Lee, "Anonymisation is Great, but Don't Undervalue Pseudonymisation," *Data and Privacy* (blog), Fieldfisher, April 26, 2014, https://www.fieldfisher.com/en/services/privacy-security-and-information/privacy-security-and-information-law-blog/anonymisation-is-great-but-dont-undervalue-pseudonymisation.

35 See Daniel Felz, "ECJ Declares IP Addresses Are Personal Data," *Privacy & Cybersecurity* (blog), Alston & Bird, October 19, 2016, https://www.alstonprivacy.com/ecj-declares-ip-addresses-personal-data/.

36 Office of Management and Budget Memorandum 07-16, "Safeguarding Against and Responding to the Breach of Personally Identifiable Information," May 22, 2007, https://obamawhitehouse.archives.gov/sites/default/files/omb/memoranda/fy2007/m07-16.pdf.

37 Federal Trade Commission, 16 CFR Part 318, "Health Breach Notification Rule," *Federal Register* 74, no. 163 (August 25, 2009), https://www.ftc.gov/sites/default/files/documents/federal_register_notices/health-breach-notification-rule-16-cfr-part-318/090825healthbreachrule.pdf.

38 At least one Federal Trade Commission official has noted that static IP addresses generally meet the definition of personally identifiable data. Jessica Rich, director of the Federal Trade Commission Bureau of Consumer Protection, "Keeping Up with the Online Advertising Industry," *FTC Business Blog*, April 21, 2016, https://www.ftc.gov/news-events/news/public-statements/keeping-online-advertising-industry.

39 The categorization of government records as "public records" can sometimes be less than straightforward. For instance, real estate records in some jurisdictions contain detailed information about ownership, assessed value, amount paid for the parcel, taxes imposed on the parcel, and improvements. Making this information public has certain advantages, such as enabling a person who owns real estate to determine if the taxes assessed are fair

relative to other parcels in the area. Other jurisdictions, by contrast, do not release such information, considering it to be private.

40 General Data Protection Regulation, Article 4, accessed March 2020, https://gdprm.eu/article-4-definitions/; see Detlev Gabel and Tim Hickman, "Chapter 10: Obligations of Controllers – Unlocking the EU General Data Protection Regulation," White & Case, April 5, 2019, https://www.whitecase.com/publications/article/chapter-10-obligations-controllers-unlocking-eu-general-data-protection.

41 Graham Greenleaf, "*Global Data Privacy Laws: 2023: 162 National Laws and 20 Bills,* 181 Privacy Laws and Business International Report 1, 2-4, https://papers.ssrn.com/sol3/papers.cfm?abstract_id=4426146. For a searchable database, see "Data Protection Laws of the World," DLA Piper, accessed October 2023, https://www.dlapiperdataprotection.com/#handbook/world-map-section/c1_RU.

42 See Digital Economic Report 2021 - Cross-Border Data Flows and Development: For Whom the Data Flows, United Nations Conference on Trade and Development, 2021, https://unctad.org/system/files/official-document/der2021_en.pdf

43 Banisar and Davies, "Global Trends," 18.

44 Banisar and Davies, "Global Trends," 14.

45 Banisar and Davies, "Global Trends," 11.

46 GDPR is discussed in detail in Chapter 14.

47 Banisar and Davies, "Global Trends," 14.

48 Office of the Australian Information Commissioner, "Australian Privacy Principles," accessed January 2020, https://www.oaic.gov.au/privacy-law/privacy-act/australian-privacy-principles; see "Australia," Data Protection Laws of the World, DLA Piper, last modified December 31, 2022, https://www.dlapiperdataprotection.com/index.html?t=law&c=AU; Sven Burchartz, Karla Brown and Brighid Virtue Kalus Kenny Intelex, "The Privacy, Data Protection and Cybersecurity Law Review: Australia," The Law Reviews, October 27, 2022, https://thelawreviews.co.uk/title/the-privacy-data-protection-and-cybersecurity-law-review/australia. As of the writing of this book, Australia is considering a significant overhaul of its privacy laws. Jake Evans, "Government to Overhaul Privacy Laws, Including Right to Opt Out of Advertising, a Right to Be Forgotten, and New Rules for Small Businesses," ABC News, September 28, 2023, https://www.abc.net.au/news/2023-09-28/government-agrees-to-sweeping-privacy-reforms/102912458; "Overhaul of Australian Privacy Laws Imminent," Ashurst, February 16, 2023, https://www.ashurst.com/en/insights/overhaul-of-australian-privacy-laws-imminent/.

49 Banisar and Davies, "Global Trends," 13–14.

50 "COPPA Safe Harbor Program," Federal Trade Commission, accessed January 2020, https://www.ftc.gov/safe-harbor-program.

51 "COPPA Safe Harbor Program," Federal Trade Commission.

52 For a discussion of the pros and cons of self-regulation, see Peter Swire, "Markets, Self-Regulation, and Government Enforcement in the Protection of Personal Information," in *Privacy and Self-Regulation in the Information Age,* U.S. Department of Commerce, last revised June 10, 2017, http://papers.ssrn.com/sol3/papers.cfm?abstract_id=11472.

CHAPTER 2

U.S. Legal Framework

This chapter introduces basic concepts and terms used by privacy professionals in the United States. Much of the material in this chapter will be familiar to lawyers. Privacy compliance in most organizations today, however, involves substantial participation by nonlawyers, including people whose primary background ranges from marketing, information technology (IT) and human resources to public relations and other areas. For all readers, the goal of this chapter is to provide a helpful introduction to the terminology used by privacy professionals.

2.1 Branches of the U.S. Government

The U.S. Constitution establishes the framework of the legal system, creating three branches of government. The three branches—legislative, executive, and judicial—are designed to provide a separation of powers with a system of checks and balances among the branches. These three branches are also generally found at the state (and often the local) levels.[1] The legislative branch is made up of elected representatives who write and pass laws. The executive branch's duties are to enforce and administer the law. The judicial branch interprets the meaning of a law and how it is applied, and may examine such issues as a law's constitutionality and the intent behind its creation.

Table 2-1: Three Branches of U.S. Government

	Legislative Branch	Executive Branch	Judicial Branch
Purpose	Makes laws	Enforces laws	Interprets laws
Who	Congress (House and Senate)	President, vice president, cabinet, federal agencies (such as FTC)	Federal courts
Checks and Balances	Congress confirms presidential appointees, can override vetoes	President appoints federal judges, can veto laws passed by Congress	Determines whether the laws are constitutional

The U.S. Congress, consisting of the Senate and the House of Representatives, is the legislative branch. Aside from passing laws, Congress can override presidential vetoes; the Senate confirms presidential appointees. When enacting legislation, Congress may also delegate the power to promulgate regulations to federal agencies. For example, Congress has enacted several laws that give the U.S. Federal Trade Commission (FTC) the authority to issue regulations to implement the laws.

The executive branch consists of the president, the vice president, the president's cabinet, and federal agencies that report to the president. The agencies implement the laws through rulemaking and enforce the laws through civil and criminal procedures. In addition, the president has veto power over laws passed by Congress and the power to appoint federal judges.

The judicial branch encompasses the federal court system. The lowest courts in the federal system are the district courts, which serve as federal trial courts. Cases decided by a district court can be appealed to a federal appellate court, also referred to as a circuit court. The federal circuit courts are not trial courts but serve as the appeals courts for federal cases. The appeals courts are divided into 12 regional circuits, and each district court is assigned to a circuit; appeals from a district court are considered by the appeals court for that circuit. In addition, there are special courts such as the U.S. Court of Federal Claims and the U.S. Tax Court.

At the top of the federal court system is the U.S. Supreme Court, which hears appeals from the circuit courts and decides questions of federal law, including interpreting the U.S. Constitution. In certain circumstances, the Supreme Court may also hear appeals from the highest state courts. In rare instances, the Supreme Court also has the ability to function as a trial court.

As mentioned above, when given the authority by Congress, federal agencies may promulgate and enforce rules pursuant to law. In this sense, agencies may wield power that is characteristic of all three branches of government. This means that agencies may operate under statutes that give them legislative power to issue rules, executive power to investigate and enforce violations of rules and statutes, and the judicial power to settle particular disputes.

2.2 Sources of Law in the United States

The numerous sources of law in the United States include federal and state constitutions, legislation, case law, contract law, tort law, regulations issued by agencies, and consent decrees.

2.2.1 Constitutions

The supreme law in the United States is the U.S. Constitution, drafted originally by the Constitutional Convention in 1787. The Constitution does not contain the word "privacy." Some parts of the Constitution directly affect privacy, such as the limits on government searches in the Fourth Amendment. The Supreme Court has also recognized an individual's right to privacy over certain personal decisions, by discussing a "penumbra" of unenumerated constitutional rights arising from numerous constitutional provisions as well as the more general protections of due process of law.[2]

In the 2022 case Dobbs v. Jackson Women's Health Organization, the U.S. Supreme Court overturned Roe v. Wade, which had provided constitutional restraints on the ability of state governments to outlaw abortion. The 2022 decision overturning Roe v. Wade explicitly stated that the decision was limited to the topic of abortion.[3] Constitutional scholars and privacy advocates, however, have expressed concern that the 2022 Dobbs decision could affect previous decisions of the Supreme Court that founded a constitutional right to privacy to protect an individual's use of contraception, to marry a person of a different race, and to marry a person of the same sex. These other right-to-privacy decisions were based on the "penumbra" of privacy rights relied upon in Roe v. Wade.[4] This is an area for privacy professionals to watch for developments.

State constitutions are also sources of law and may create stronger rights than the U.S. Constitution provides. For example, the California Constitution states, "All people are by nature free and independent and have inalienable rights. Among these are enjoying and defending life and liberty, acquiring, possessing, and protecting property, and pursuing and obtaining safety, happiness, and privacy."[5] As of the writing of this book, 11 state constitutions—including California—expressly recognize a right to privacy.[6]

2.2.2 Legislation

Both the federal Congress and the state legislatures have enacted a variety of privacy and security laws. These regulate many different matters, including certain applications of information (such as use of information for marketing or preemployment screening), certain industries (such as financial institutions or health care providers), certain data elements (such as Social Security numbers or driver's license information) or specific harms (such as identity theft or children's online privacy).

In the United States, law-making power is shared between the national and state governments. The U.S. Constitution states that the Constitution and laws passed pursuant to it is "the supreme law of the land." Where federal law does not prevent it, the states have power to make law. Under the Tenth Amendment to the Constitution, "the powers not delegated to the United States by the Constitution, nor prohibited by it to the States, are reserved to the States respectively, or to the people." In understanding the effect of federal and state laws, it is important to consider whether a federal law preempts—or overrides—any state laws on the subject. In many instances, such as for the Health Insurance Portability and Accountability Act (HIPAA) Privacy Rule, states may pass privacy or other laws with stricter requirements than federal law. In other instances, such as the limits on commercial emails in the Controlling the Assault of Non-Solicited Pornography and Marketing (CAN-SPAM) Act, federal law preempts state law, and the states are not permitted to pass stricter provisions.[7]

Aside from this governmental ability to make and enforce laws and regulations, the U.S. legal system relies on legal precedent based on court decisions, the doctrines implicit in those decisions, and their customs and uses. Two key areas of the common law are contracts and torts, discussed in Sections 2.2.4 and 2.2.5.

2.2.3 Case Law

Case law refers to the final decisions made by judges in court cases. When similar issues arise in the future, judges look to past decisions as precedents and decide the new case in a manner that is consistent with past decisions. The following of precedent is known as *stare decisis* (a Latin term meaning "to let the decision stand"). As time passes, precedents often change to reflect technological and societal changes in values and laws.

Common law refers to legal principles that have developed over time in judicial decisions (case law), often drawing on social customs and expectations. Common law contrasts with law created by statute. For privacy, the common law has long upheld special privilege rules such as doctor-patient or attorney-client confidentiality, even in the absence of statutes protecting that confidentiality.

2.2.4 Contract Law

A contract is a legally binding agreement enforceable in a court of law. The contract may include provisions on issues such as data usage, data security, breach notification, jurisdiction, and damages. For example, a company often has a contract with its service providers requiring the latter to implement privacy and security protections when processing personal data provided by the first company.

However, not every agreement is a legally binding contract. There are certain fundamental requirements for forming a binding contract:[8]

- An **offer** is the proposed language to enter into a bargain. An offer must be communicated to another person, and it remains open until it is accepted, rejected, retracted, or has expired. Some terms of an offer, such as price, quantity and description, must be specific and definite. Note that a counteroffer ends the original offer.
- **Acceptance** is the assent or agreement by the person to whom the offer was made that the offer is accepted. This acceptance must comply with the terms of the offer and must be communicated to the person who proposed the deal.
- **Consideration** is the bargained-for exchange. It is the legal benefit received by one person and the legal detriment imposed on the other person. Consideration usually takes the form of money, property, or services. Note that an agreement without consideration is not a contract.

A breach of contract occurs when one party fails to meet its obligations under the contract. The injured party can file a lawsuit asking a court to award monetary damages for the injured party's losses or to enforce the terms of the contract.[9]

It is important to understand contracts that would otherwise be valid may be unenforceable due to reasons such as misrepresentation or conflict with public policy.[10]

A privacy notice may be a contract if a consumer provides data to a company based on the company's promise to use the data in accordance with the terms of the notice.

2.2.5 Tort Law

Torts are civil wrongs recognized by law as the grounds for lawsuits. These wrongs result in an injury or harm that constitutes the basis for a claim by the injured party. Primary goals of tort law are to provide relief for damages incurred and deter others from committing the same wrongs.

There are three general tort categories:

1. **Intentional torts.** These are wrongs that the defendant knew or should have known would occur through their actions or inactions; for example, intentionally hitting a person or stealing personal information.

2. **Negligent torts.** These occur when the defendant's actions were unreasonably unsafe; for example, causing a car accident by not obeying traffic rules or not having appropriate security controls.
3. **Strict liability torts.** These are wrongs that do not depend on the degree of carelessness by the defendant but are established when a particular action causes damage.[11] Product liability torts fall into this category since they concern potential liability for making and selling defective products, without the need for the plaintiff to show negligence by the defendant.

Historically, the concept of a personal privacy tort has been a part of U.S. jurisprudence since the late 1890s.[12] Privacy torts continue today for actions such as intruding on seclusion, public revelation of private facts, interfering with a person's right to publicity, and casting a person in a false light. These traditional privacy torts, however, are often subject to the defense that the speaker is exercising free speech rights under the First Amendment. In addition, courts in recent years have considered a range of other privacy-related torts, such as allegations that a company was negligent for failing to provide adequate safeguards for personal information and thus caused harm due to disclosure of the data. The lack of adequate safeguards thus may expose a company to damages under tort law. Privacy torts remain an unsettled area of law, and courts across the United States have not taken a uniform approach in applying tort principles to privacy-related cases.

2.2.6 Regulations and Rules

As described further in Section 2.4, some federal laws require regulatory agencies such as the FTC or the U.S. Federal Communications Commission (FCC) to issue regulations and rules. These place specific compliance expectations on the marketplace. For example, U.S. Congress passed the CAN-SPAM Act in 2003, which requires the senders of commercial email messages to offer an "opt-out" option to recipients of these messages. CAN-SPAM provides the FTC and the FCC with the authority to issue regulations that set forth exactly how the opt-out mechanism must be offered and managed.

Aside from promulgating rules and enforcing them, agencies provide guidance in the form of formal opinions. Agency opinions do not necessarily carry the weight of law but do give specific guidance to interested parties trying to interpret agency rules and regulations.[13] Agencies often provide even more informal guidance through published reports, content on their websites, congressional testimony, and speeches at conferences or industry gatherings. These channels are not so much explicit requirements as they are valuable insight into the agency's mindset, view of the law, and priorities in enforcement.

2.2.7 Consent Decrees

A consent decree is a judgment entered by consent of the parties whereby the defendant agrees to stop alleged illegal activity, typically without admitting guilt or wrongdoing.[14] This legal document is approved by a judge and formalizes an agreement reached between a federal (or state) agency and an adverse party. The consent decree describes the actions the defendant will take, and the decree itself may be subject to a public comment period. Once approved, the consent decree has the effect of a court decision.

In the privacy enforcement sphere, the FTC has entered into numerous consent decrees with companies as a result of alleged violations of privacy laws, such as the Children's Online Privacy Protection Act (COPPA).[15] These consent decrees generally require violators to pay money to the government and agree not to violate the relevant law in the future.

2.3 Key Definitions for Understanding the U.S. Privacy Law Framework

Here are a few legal terms and definitions that are important for understanding the framework of U.S. privacy law:

- **Person.** Any entity with legal rights, including an individual (a "natural person") or a corporation (a "legal person").
- **Jurisdiction.** The authority of a court to hear a particular case. A court must have jurisdiction over both the type of dispute ("subject matter jurisdiction") and the parties ("personal jurisdiction"). Government agencies have jurisdictional limits also.
- **General versus specific authority.** A governmental body can have two types of authority. "General authority" is blanket authority to regulate a field of activity. "Specific authority" is targeted at singular activities that are outlined by legislation. Many agencies have both types of authority. For example, the FTC has general authority over "unfair and deceptive trade practices" and specific authority to enforce COPPA.

- **Preemption.** A superior government's ability to have its laws supersede those of an inferior government.[16] For example, the U.S. federal government has mandated that state governments cannot regulate email marketing. The federal CAN-SPAM Act preempts state laws that might impose greater obligations on senders of commercial electronic messages.
- **Private right of action.** The ability of an individual harmed by a violation of a law to file a lawsuit against the violator.

It is also useful to review the concepts of notice, choice and access in the context of U.S. privacy law.

2.3.1 Notice

Notice is a description of an organization's information management practices. Notices have two purposes: (1) consumer education and (2) corporate accountability. The typical notice tells the individual what information is collected, how the information is used and disclosed, how to exercise any choices about uses or disclosures, and whether the individual can access or update the information. However, it is important to note that many U.S. privacy laws have additional notice requirements. With the states enacting breach notification laws that have varying requirements for notice, the federal government is now considering a preemptive law to standardize breach-related notification. In addition, for most industries, the promises made in a company's privacy notice are legally enforceable by the FTC and the states.

Privacy notices may also be called privacy statements or even privacy policies, although the term "privacy policy" is often used to refer to the internal standards used within the organization, whereas "privacy notice" refers to an external communication issued to consumers, customers, or users. Additionally, protocols, standards, and instructions are used by companies to direct their employees to comply with data privacy laws.[17]

2.3.2 Choice

Choice is the ability to specify whether personal information will be collected and/or how it will be used or disclosed. Choice can be express or implied.

The term "opt-in" means an affirmative indication of choice based on an express act of the person giving the consent. For example, a person opts in if they say yes when asked, "May we share your information?" Failure to answer would result in the information not being shared.

The term "opt-out" means a choice can be implied by the failure of the person to object to the use or disclosure. For example, if a company states, "unless you tell us not to, we may share your information," the person has the ability to opt out of the sharing by saying no. Failure to answer would result in the information being shared.

Choice is not always appropriate, but if it is offered, it should be meaningful—that is, it should be based on a real understanding of the implication of the decision.

2.3.3 Access

Access is the ability to view personal information held by an organization. This may be supplemented by allowing updates or corrections to the information. U.S. laws often provide for access and correction when the information is used for substantive decision-making, such as for credit reports.

2.4 Regulatory Authorities Focused on Privacy Issues in the Private Sector

At the federal level, a number of agencies engage in regulatory activities concerning privacy in the private sector. The FTC has general authority to enforce against unfair and deceptive trade practices, notably including the power to bring "deception" enforcement actions where a company has broken a privacy promise.[18] In certain areas, such as marketing communications and children's privacy, the FTC has specific regulatory authority.

Other federal agencies have regulatory authority over particular sectors. These include the federal banking regulatory agencies (such as the Consumer Financial Protection Bureau, Federal Reserve, and Office of the Comptroller of the Currency), the FCC, the U.S. Department of Transportation (DOT), and the U.S. Department of Health and Human Services (HHS) through its Office of Civil Rights. The U.S. Department of Commerce (DOC) does not have regulatory authority for privacy, but often plays a leading role in privacy policy for the executive branch.

At the state level, state attorneys general have traditionally brought a variety of privacy-related enforcement actions, often pursuant to state laws prohibiting unfair and deceptive practices.[19] Each state attorney general serves as the chief legal advisor to the state government and as the state's chief law enforcement officer.[20] Many states have successfully pursued such actions, including Washington and Minnesota.[21] California, under the California Privacy Rights Act (CPRA), is the first state in the nation to stand up an independent agency dedicated to enforcing its state comprehensive law, similar to the data protection authorities (DPAs) found in Europe to enforce the General Data Protection Regulation (GDPR).[22]

2.5 Self-Regulation

As discussed in Chapter 5, self-regulatory regimes play a significant role in governing privacy practices in various industries. Examples include the Network Advertising Initiative (NAI), the Association of National Advertisers (formerly the Direct Marketing Association) and the Children's Advertising Review Unit (CARU).[23] Some trade associations also issue rules or codes of conduct for members. In some regulatory settings, government-created rules expect companies to sign up for self-regulatory oversight.

2.6 Keys to Understanding Laws

To understand any law, statute or regulation, it is important to ask six key questions:

1. Who is covered by this law?
2. What types of information (and what uses of information) are covered?
3. What exactly is required or prohibited?
4. Who enforces the law?
5. What happens if I don't comply?
6. Why does this law exist?

The first two questions relate to the scope of the law. Even if an organization or person is not subject to the law, it may still be useful to understand it. For example, the law may suggest good practices that an organization or individual would want to emulate. It may provide an indication of legal trends. It may also provide a proven way to achieve a particular result, such as protecting individuals in a given situation.

Assuming one is subject to the law, question three explains how to comply with it. Questions four and five help the individual or corporation assess the risks associated with noncompliance or less than perfect compliance. In most cases, companies do what it takes to be materially compliant with applicable laws. There may, however, be a situation where the costs of compliance outweigh the risks of noncompliance for a particular period of time. For example, if a system that is not appropriately compliant with a new law going to be replaced in a few months, a company may decide that the noncompliance outweigh the costs and risks of trying to accelerate the system transition.

The final question helps foster understanding of the motivation behind the law. Most companies try to comply with both the letter and the spirit of the law. Knowing why the law was written helps them understand the spirit of the legislation and can also help improve other processes and thus achieve desired results. It may also help companies anticipate regulatory trends.

As an example, consider the security breach notification law in California (California SB 1386), which was the first such law enacted and covers the largest population.[24]

- **Who is covered?** This law regulates entities that do business in California and that own or license computerized data, including personal information. It applies to natural persons, legal persons and government agencies.

  Those that do business only in Montana or New York are not subject to this law (although they may wish to be careful about what counts as "doing business"). Even if they conduct business in California, they are not subject to this law if they don't have computerized data.

- **What is covered?** This law regulates the computerized personal information of California residents. "Personal information" is an individual's name in combination with any one or more of the following: (1) Social Security number; (2) California identification card number; (3) driver's license number; or (4) financial account, credit, or debit card number in combination with security code, access code, or password information required to permit access to an individual's financial account, when either the name or the data elements are not encrypted.

  Databases that contain only names and addresses or only encrypted information are not subject to this law.[25]

- **What is required or prohibited?** This law requires all persons to disclose any breach of system security to any resident of California whose unencrypted personal information was or is reasonably believed to have been acquired by an unauthorized person. A breach of the security of the system means unauthorized acquisition of computerized data that compromises the security, confidentiality, or integrity of personal information maintained by the person. The disclosure must be made in as expedient a manner as possible.

There is an exception for the good faith acquisition of personal information by an employee or agent of the business, provided the personal information is not used or subject to further unauthorized disclosure. One may also delay providing notice, if law enforcement requests such a delay.

- **Who enforces the law?** The California attorney general enforces the law, and there is a private right of action.
- **What is the consequence for noncompliance?** The California attorney general or any citizen can file a civil lawsuit against a noncompliant party seeking damages and forcing compliance.
- **Why does this law exist?** SB 1386 was enacted because security breaches of computerized databases are feared to cause identity theft—and individuals should be notified about these breaches so they can take steps to protect themselves. Anyone with a security breach that puts people at real risk of identity theft should consider notifying them even if they are not subject to this law.

2.7 Conclusion

This chapter has introduced legal concepts and terminology about basic topics, including the structure of the U.S. government and legal system. Privacy compliance requires knowing the applicable legal rules as well as fulfilling each organization's policies and goals. Chapter 5 examines the structure of enforcement actions for alleged privacy violations in the United States.

Endnotes

1 "The U.S. Constitution mandates that all states uphold a 'republican form' of government, although the three-branch structure is not required." The White House: President Barack Obama, State & Local Government; see U.S. Constitution of the United States: A Transcription, Article 4, Section 4, National Archives, accessed June 2023, https://www.archives.gov/founding-docs/constitution-transcript.

2 Many of the cases relevant to this discussion have their foundation in protecting private sexual conduct. The term "penumbra" was introduced in the case of Griswold v. Connecticut (1965), voiding a state statute preventing the use of contraceptives. The legal theory introduced in Griswold was followed in multiple U.S. Supreme Court cases, including Roe v. Wade (1973), overturning state law that barred abortion; and Lawrence

v. Texas (2003), striking down antisodomy laws. See "The Right to Privacy," Section 3.4, Criminal Law, Open Textbooks at University of Minnesota Libraries, accessed June 2023, http://open.lib.umn.edu/criminallaw/chapter/3-4-the-right-to-privacy/.

3 Dobbs v. Jackson Women's Health Organization, Oyez, June 24, 2022, https://www.oyez.org/cases/2021/19-1392. For the full opinion, read Dobbs v. Jackson Women's Health Organization, Slip Opinion, Supreme Court of the United States, June 24, 2022, https://www.supremecourt.gov/opinions/21pdf/19-1392_6j37.pdf.

4 "Roe v. Wade Overturned," *The New York Times*, June 24, 2022, https://www.nytimes.com/2022/06/24/us/roe-wade-overturned-supreme-court.html; Jedidiah Bracy, "Leaked Roe v. Wade Opinion Sparks Right-to-Privacy Concerns," *Privacy Advisor*, IAPP, May 3, 2022, https://iapp.org/news/a/leaked-roe-v-wade-opinion-sparks-right-to-privacy-concerns/.

5 California State Constitution, Article I, Section 1, accessed July 2022, https://leginfo.legislature.ca.gov/faces/codes_displaySection.xhtml?lawCode=CONS§ionNum=SECTION%201.&article=I.

6 Privacy Protections in State Constitutions, National Conference of State Legislatures, accessed July 2022, https://www.ncsl.org/research/telecommunications-and-information-technology/privacy-protections-in-state-constitutions.aspx.

7 For additional discussion of preemption in federal privacy laws, view the Future of Privacy Forum (FPF) series on this topic. See Stacey Gray, "Preemption in U.S. Federal Privacy Laws," Future of Privacy Forum, June 14, 2021, https://fpf.org/blog/preemption-in-us-federal-privacy-laws/.

8 Richard Stim, "What is a Contract?" Nolo, accessed June 2023, www.nolo.com/legal-encyclopedia/contracts-basics-33367.html.

9 "Breach of Contract," Legal Information Institute, Cornell University Law School Cornell Law School, updated June 2022, https://www.law.cornell.edu/wex/breach_of_contract. Study.com provides a video lesson on numerous aspects of breach of contract. "What is a Breach of Contract," Study.com, accessed July 2022, https://study.com/academy/lesson/types-of-contract-breach-partial-material-total.html.

10 See "What Makes a Contract Valid," *Forbes*, November 20, 2006, https://www.forbes.com/2006/11/20/smallbusiness-statelaw-gifts-ent-law-cx_nl_1120contracts.html; "Unenforceable Contracts: What to Watch Out For," Nolo, accessed January 2020, https://www.nolo.com/legal-encyclopedia/unenforceable-contracts-tips-33079.html.

11 "Tort," Legal Information Institute, Cornell University Law School, accessed January 2020, https://www.law.cornell.edu/wex/Tort.

12 "The Privacy Torts," Privacy and Business, Privacilla, accessed September 2023, https://techliberation.com/wp-content/uploads/2007/10/privacytorts.html.

13 "Legal Library: Advisory Opinions," Federal Trade Commission, accessed January 2020, https://www.ftc.gov/policy/advisory-opinions.

14 The Law Dictionary, featuring Black's Law Dictionary, 2nd ed. (2023), s.v. "consent decree." http://thelawdictionary.org/consent-decree/.

15 United Stated v. The Ohio Art Company, "Reasons for Settlement," April 22 2002, https://www.ftc.gov/enforcement/cases-proceedings/022-3028/ohio-art-company; "FTC Protecting Children's Privacy Online," Federal trade Commission, April 22, 2002, https://www.ftc.gov/news-events/press-releases/2002/04/ftc-protecting-childrens-privacy-online.

16 For a list of resources on preemption, view Future of Privacy Forum's Recommended Reading List. "Understanding Federal Preemption," Future of Privacy Forum, December 19, 2019, https://fpf.org/fpf-event/understanding-federal-preemption/. For a discussion of the complexity of preemption when the U.S. Congress is considering enacting a federal comprehensive privacy law, view "U.S. Federal Privacy Preemption - Part 1: History of Federal Preemption of Stricter State Laws" and "Part 2: Federal Preemption of State Privacy Laws and the Issues That May Arise." Peter Swire, "U.S. Federal Privacy Preemption - Part 1: History of Federal Preemption of Stricter State Laws," Daily Dashboard, IAPP, January 19, 2019, https://iapp.org/news/a/us-federal-privacy-preemption-part-1-history-of-federal-preemption-of-stricter-state-laws/; Peter Swire, "Part 2: Federal Preemption of State Privacy Laws and the Issues That May Arise," Daily Dashboard, IAPP, January 10, 2019, https://iapp.org/news/a/swire-part-2-federal-preemption-of-state-privacy-laws-and-the-issues-that-may-arise/.

17 For more guidance on the function and drafting considerations regarding privacy notices, policies, protocols and other documentation, *see* Lothar Determann, *Determann's Field Guide to Data Privacy Law: International Corporate Compliance*, 2nd ed., (Cheltenham, UK: Edward Elgar, 2015), Chapter 3.

18 FTC ACT, 15 U.S.C. § 45 (2011), "unfair or deceptive acts or practices in or affecting commerce, are hereby declared unlawful. . . The [Federal Trade Commission] is hereby empowered and directed to prevent persons, partnerships, or corporations, except [certain institutions] . . . from using unfair methods of competition in or affecting commerce and unfair or deceptive acts or practices in or affecting commerce." For a listing of recent enforcement actions, *see* "Legal Library: Cases and Proceedings," accessed June 2023, https://www.ftc.gov/enforcement/cases-proceedings.

19 For general information on actions by state attorneys general, *see* Danielle Keats Citron, "The Privacy Policymaking of State Attorneys General," *Notre Dame Law Review* 92, no. 2 (2016): 747–816, http://ndlawreview.org/wp-content/uploads/2017/02/NDL205.pdf.

20 National Association of Attorneys General. "What Attorneys General Do," National Association of Attorneys General, accessed June 2023, https://www.naag.org/attorneys-general/what-attorneys-general-do/.

21 "Washington e-Commerce Company May Owe You Money," Office of the Attorney General, Washington State, March 30, 2011, http://atg.wa.gov/news/news-releases/washington-e-commerce-company-may-owe-you-money; "Minnesota Settles Consumer Fraud Suit with MemberWorks," *ConsumerAffairs, April 19, 2000,* https://www.consumeraffairs.com/news/index/2000/04/. For an in-depth discussion of state actions, see Citron, "The Privacy Policymaking of State Attorney Generals."

22 The agency is known as the California Privacy Protection Agency (CPPA). California Privacy Protection Agency, "Home Page." cppa.ca.gov, https://cppa.ca.gov/#:~:text=The%20CPRA%20added%20new%20privacy,by%20a%20five%2Dmember%20Board.

23 "The NAI Code and Enforcement Program: An Overview," Network Advertising Initiative, accessed January 2020, https://www.networkadvertising.org/code-enforcement; "Welcome from the theDMA.org." Association of National Advertisers, accessed June 2023, https://www.ana.net/content/show?id=thedmaorg-redirect; "Children's Advertising Review Unit, BBB National Programs," accessed June 2023, https://bbbprograms.org/programs/all-programs/children's-advertising-review-unit.

24 California Legislative Information, CIV Sect. 1798.82, accessed November 2017, https://leginfo.legislature.ca.gov/faces/codes_displaySection.xhtml?lawCode=CIV§ionNum=1798.82. For a summary of the current statute, see M. Scott Koller, "California Amends its Breach Notification Statute," *Data Counsel*, BakerHostetler, October 12, 2015, https://www.bakerdatacounsel.com/data-breach-notification-laws/california-amends-its-breach-notification-statute/.

25 As of January 1, 2016, the definition of personal information has been expanded to include data collected from automated license plate recognition systems. https://leginfo.legislature.ca.gov/faces/billNavClient.xhtml?bill_id=201520160SB34.

CHAPTER 3

Introduction to Technological Aspects of Privacy

3.1 Overview

This chapter introduces the technological aspects of privacy protection.[1] An organization's overall privacy program is often shaped initially by legal requirements and the policy decisions of the organization about what personal data to collect and use. Multiple chapters in this book discuss such laws and policies, including for specific sectors such as health care or financial services. To implement the relevant laws and policies, organizations need to manage the processing of personal data. Chapter 4 introduces the relevant management concepts. In addition, organizations need to build and operate a technical infrastructure so that the laws, policies, and management objectives of the organization are implemented in practice.

In addressing the technological aspects of privacy, this chapter seeks to be understandable to the nontechnical reader, while also providing insights and links that will be helpful for both technical and nontechnical readers. This chapter draws extensively on the IAPP textbook *An Introduction to Privacy for Technology Professionals*.[2] We recommend that book (or any following update) for those wishing to dig deeper into the technological aspects of privacy. We have drawn from its text, sometimes closely, in writing this chapter.

This chapter discusses the basics of the internet, including definitions of numerous terms relevant to privacy protection. It next addresses computing architectures, such as client/server and cloud systems. The chapter provides a bit more detail on types of digital surveillance and tracking, such as web tracking like cookies. Along with online tracking, other technologies like smartphones and home assistants deploy sensors that can track individuals, including location, audio, and video tracking capabilities.

Because technology creates the possibility of so much tracking, we next turn to the realm of privacy-enhancing technologies (PETs), including encryption and the deidentification of data. The chapter concludes with some key components of cybersecurity—even the best privacy policy will not protect data if it is easy for malicious attackers to grab the data.

3.2 Basics of the Internet

The internet is a network of networks. The precursor of the internet we know today is the Advanced Research Projects Agency Network, known as the ARPANET, a computer network developed in the 1960s by the U.S. military, which expanded to scientific research in the 1970s.[3] Commercial activity did not become substantial on the internet until the early 1990s.[4] Distant in time and size from its origins, the internet today has the same basic architecture as when it was first designed. The open and dynamic nature of the internet enables its speed, functionality, and continued growth. However, as will be described later in this chapter, this also exposes it to information privacy vulnerabilities.

Transmission control protocol (TCP) is the internet protocol suite the internet uses to enable communication among networks and devices. TCP enables two devices to establish a reliable data connection. Before it transmits data, TCP establishes a connection between a source and its destination, which it ensures remains live until communication begins. It then breaks large amounts of data into smaller packets, while ensuring data integrity is in place throughout the process.[5]

The **internet protocol (IP)** specifies the format of data packets that travel over the internet and also provides the appropriate addressing protocol. An IP address is a unique number assigned to each connected device—it is similar to a phone number because the IP address shows where data should be sent, such as when a website transmits text, videos, and other information to a user's IP address. The most recent version of the protocol is IPv6, which is in the process of replacing the earlier IPv4 version.[6]

To move information from the source to the destination, TCP/IP relies on packet switching.[7] Data in the header of each packet directs the packet to its destination. The payload of the packet—such as text or video—is extracted upon arrival. To arrive at the destination, different packets in the same communication, such as parts of a video, may travel on a different route, or nodes, on the internet. Upon arrival, the receiving device re-assembles the packets in the correct order, essentially putting all the pieces of a video back together correctly. Any packets that do not arrive are retransmitted.

3.2.1 Web Infrastructure

Although the terms are often used interchangeably, the "internet" has a broader meaning than the "web" or "World Wide Web." The internet carries a wide range of information types, including both web traffic and non-web traffic such as electronic mail, IP telephony, file sharing, and many communications for the Internet of Things (IoT).

The most familiar way of accessing the internet, however, is through the web. Historically, the web functioned based on two key technologies, both of which have received updates:

- **Hypertext transfer protocol (HTTP)** is an application protocol that manages data communications over the internet and defines how messages are formatted and transmitted over a TCP/IP network for websites. It also defines what actions web servers and web browsers take in response to various commands.
- **Hypertext markup language (HTML)** is a content-authoring language used to create web pages. Today, HTML is used together with other computer languages including JavaScript, CSS, and JSON, the details of which we do not discuss in this chapter. A key task for these languages is to enable the web browser to determine how the content on the page should be rendered. Document tags can be used to format and lay out a web page's content and to hyperlink—to jump to other web content. Forms, links, pictures, and text may all be added with minimal commands. Headings are also embedded into the text and are used by web servers to process commands and return data with each request.[8]

Sir Tim Berners-Lee, a British computer scientist, invented HTTP and HTML in the early 1990s while working at the European Organization for Nuclear Research (CERN). Berners-Lee recognized the inherent limitations of the early internet and advanced the HTML language as a means for research scientists such as himself to dynamically tie documents and files together—a capability he referred to as **hyperlinking**.

Numerous advancements have occurred since the web's creation. The development of **hypertext transfer protocol secure (HTTPS)** allows the transfer of data from a browser to a website over an encrypted connection.[9] By 2016, the total amount of HTTPS traffic sent over the internet was greater than HTTP traffic.[10]

HTML has continually evolved since it was first developed in the 1990s. Today, many browsers support features of HTML5, the fifth and most recent version of the HTML standard.[11] HTML5 has new capabilities and features, such as the ability to run video, audio, and animation directly from websites without the need for a plug-in (a piece of software that runs in the browser and renders media such as audio or video). Another feature of HTML5 is an increased ability to store information offline, in web applications that can run when not connected to the internet.[12]

Extensible markup language (XML) is another language that facilitates the transport, creation, retrieval, and storage of documents. Like HTML, XML uses tags to describe the contents of a web page or file. HTML describes the content of a web page in terms of how it should be displayed. Unlike HTML, XML describes the content of a web page in terms of the data that is being produced, enabling automatic processing of data in large volumes and consequently requiring additional attention to privacy issues.[13]

The web browser software is considered a web client application in that it is used by the computer or other device (the "client") to navigate the web and retrieve web content from web servers for viewing. Some web server firewalls also function as a web client.[14] To protect the inner system, the firewall will interact with the inner web proxy as a client and then relay the same request out to the web server.

Two of the more common web-browser-level functions are uniform resource locators (URLs) and hyperlinks.

A **uniform resource locator (URL)** is the address of documents and other content that are located on a web server. An example of a URL is https://www.iapp.org. This URL contains (1) an HTTPS prefix to indicate its use of the protocol; (2) often, "www" to signify a location on the World Wide Web, (3) a domain name (e.g., "iapp") and (4) an indicator of the top-level domain (".org"). Today there are over 1,500 top-level domains.[15] Some of the most familiar include "com" for a commercial organization, "org" for an organization, "gov" for government, "edu" for an educational institution, or a two-letter country code, such as "uk" for United Kingdom or "jp" for Japan.[16] A URL can also include a "deep link" to a specific page within the domain, such as "news" in https://iapp.org/news, or even to a specific paragraph within a page.

URLs are a subset of a larger class of identifiers called **uniform resource identifier (URI)**, which are formatted as URLs but may not include information to locate the resource on a network. Another term also used is a **uniform resource name (URN)**. The distinctions are confusing and not relevant in most usages, but privacy professionals should be aware of them as they may appear interchangeably in some documents.

A **hyperlink** is used to connect an end user to other websites, parts of websites, and/or web-enabled services. The URL of another site may be embedded in the HTML code of a site so that when a user clicks on the link in the web browser, the end user is transported to the destination page.

3.2.2 Key Web Infrastructure Definitions

The web is built from a conglomeration of hardware and software technologies that include server computers, client applications (such as browsers), and various networking protocols.

A **web server** is a computer that is connected to the internet, hosts web content, and is configured to share that content. Documents that are viewed on the web are actually located on individual web servers and accessed by a browser.

A **proxy server** is an intermediary server that provides a gateway to the web. Employee access to the web often goes through an organization's proxy server. A proxy server may mask what is happening behind the organization's firewall, so that an outside website may see only the IP address and other characteristics of the proxy server and not detailed information about which part of an organization is communicating with the outside website. A proxy server generally logs each user interaction, filters out malicious software downloads, and improves performance by caching popular, regularly fetched content.

Virtual private networks (VPNs) are similar to proxy servers, widely used in the United States for employee web access but not used as widely by consumers. VPNs can encrypt the information from the user to the organization's proxy server, potentially masking both the content and the final destination from the internet service provider (ISP).

An **internet service provider (ISP)** connects users and their devices to the internet. Common examples of ISPs are cable or wireless providers. ISPs can dedicate a specific IP address to a specific user or business. This is called a **static IP address**. ISPs can also assign IP addresses dynamically as needed. This can happen on a session-by-session basis, but other ISPs sometimes assign the same **dynamic IP address** to a particular customer for months or even longer. When an IP address does not change, a website can use the IP address as a way to recognize a device that returns to the site.[17] This persistent link to a device is a basis for the European Union and some other regulators considering an IP address as personal information, due to the greater likelihood that data can be linked to a specific user.[18]

Caching occurs when a server saves a copy of content, reducing the need to download the same content again from the web server.

A **web server log** is sometimes automatically created when a visitor requests a web page. Examples of the information automatically logged include the IP address of the visitor, the date and time of the web page request, the URL of the requested file, the URL visited immediately prior to the web page request, and the visitor's web browser type and computer operating system. Depending on how the web server is configured, it is possible for personal information such as a username and password to appear in web server logs. IP addresses themselves, and thus web server logs containing them, are considered personal information by some regulators but not by others. While passwords should not be logged, they have been on many occasions, causing privacy and security problems.

Transport layer security (TLS) is a protocol that ensures privacy between a user and a web server. When a server and client communicate, TLS secures the connection to ensure that no third party can eavesdrop on or corrupt the message. TLS is a successor to secure sockets layer (SSL).[19]

3.3 Computing Architectures

In order to perform tasks such as a privacy impact assessment (PIA) and ensure privacy by design, privacy professionals often need to understand the key elements of IT architecture. This section explains client-server architecture, cloud computing, and edge computing. It also explains the basics of how emails and text messages work.

3.3.1 Client-Server Architecture

Figure 3-1: Common elements of the client-server architecture.

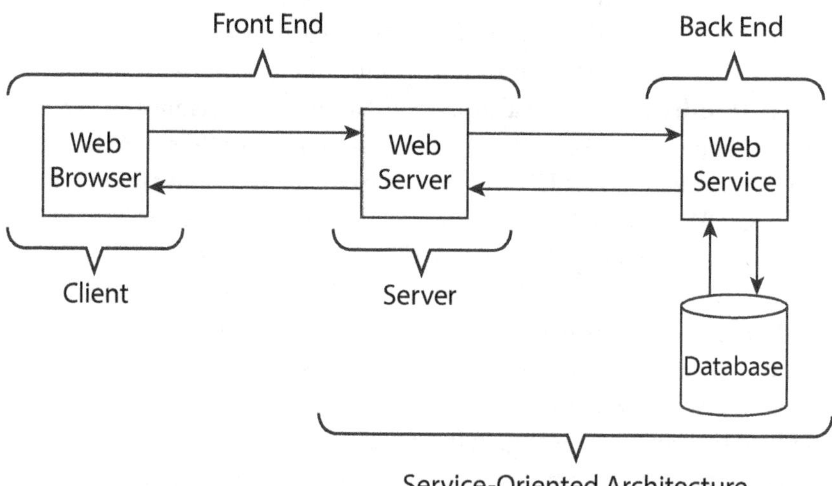

Individual consumers are most familiar with the perspective of the client, a piece of computer hardware or software that accesses a service made available by a server in the client-server model of computer architecture. Familiar clients include a desktop, laptop, or mobile phone. The term also applies generally to a computer or program that relies on sending a request to a server in order to access a service. A thick client is capable of performing many data processing actions itself, such as a computer or mobile phone that can run many programs even when not connected to the internet. A thin client relies predominantly on processing performed remotely, such as a cloud-based application that the user can only operate when connected to that application. An example of running as a thin client is a computer that only runs a web browser and uses web-based editing tools such as Google Suite or Microsoft's web-based Office 365.

The client often uses a web browser to interact with the server. In addition to a browser, the client may interact using a different protocol, such as the Simple Mail Transfer Protocol (SMTP) used in sending and receiving email.

The client communicates with the **server**, which is the computer process that responds to client requests. For instance, the server on a news website will make a news story available, and the server on an e-commerce site will enable the customer to place an order. These interactions of the client and the server are called the front end of the organization's computer system. At present, front end is generally used to describe a web-based interface coded in HTML, CSS, and JavaScript.

The organization often chooses to have other devices and software operate significantly separate from the web server. These other devices and software are the **back end**, including databases and other computing activity not essential for operating the server. Separation of the front end and back end can help protect privacy and security. Suppose that a hacker is able to put malicious code on the front end of the server. If the front end and back end interact only in limited ways, the organization may be able to carefully monitor those interactions, preventing the malicious code from infecting the back end. A database in the back end thus becomes better protected, reducing the likelihood of a data breach of sensitive personal information.

3.3.2 Cloud Computing

Organizations have been shifting a growing fraction of their data processing to **cloud computing**, defined as on-demand availability of computing resources. Multiple reasons have driven the shift away from computing on resources owned and managed by the organization itself, sometimes called on-premises computing. These reasons include cost savings, the ability to scale without costly capital investment, and the increase in demand for remote access at any time.[20]

For many organizations, there are cybersecurity and privacy reasons to select cloud computing.[21] Cloud architectures tend to be homogeneous and easier to manage, in contrast to legacy on-premises systems. For smaller organizations, it can be challenging to hire top IT talent in-house, while cloud providers can have dedicated in-house staff for security and privacy. Each organization must analyze its particular situation, but the scale of a cloud provider can often assist in meeting the complexity of security and privacy compliance.

Although vendors and experts differ on precisely what is covered by each category, there are three commonly used categories of cloud computing.[22]

- **Software as a service (SaaS)** uses the internet to deliver applications, which are managed by a third-party vendor, to its users. Many SaaS applications run directly through a web browser, which means they do not require any downloads or installations on the client side.
- **Platform as a service (PaaS)** provides cloud components to certain software while mainly being used for applications. PaaS delivers a framework for developers to build upon and use to create customized applications.
- **Infrastructure as a service (IaaS)** is self-service for the user, for accessing and monitoring computers, networking, storage, and other services. Although the infrastructure is provided by the third party, such as physical control over data storage, the company buying the service retains complete control over what is done with the infrastructure, including the management of databases of personal information.

3.3.3 Edge Computing

Edge computing is a distributed IT architecture where data is processed at the periphery of the network, often as close to the originating source as possible.[23] One driver for edge computing is the IoT (further discussed in Section 3.4). The IoT means that the number of Internet-connected sensors is growing exponentially, raising the costs of having all data processed through a centralized data center. Processing data close to the origin reduces the cost of connecting to a centralized data center. By keeping data closer to the edge, it also reduces the delay in communicating over a network, known as latency.

3.3.4 How Emails and Texts Work

Privacy professionals should be aware of key technologies used for emails and texts. Here we highlight the various protocols used to implement these communications.

For sending emails, the most common protocol is SMTP.[24] For receiving emails, Internet Message Access Protocol (IMAP) has become more common over time, with Post Office Protocol (POP, or POP3 referring to the latest version) becoming less used. IMAP typically leaves messages on the server, enabling synchronization of multiple devices, while POP typically deletes the mail on the server.[25] The key difference is that IMAP allows management of multiple mailboxes and executing search commands on the server. Commercial email services such as Gmail and Microsoft Outlook support all of these protocols, but with different degrees of fidelity. Privacy professionals should be aware of the CAN-SPAM Act, discussed in Chapter 11, which requires commercial email marketing to honor customer opt-outs.

Text messages became pervasive using SMS, the message service that uses the Short Message Peer to Peer Protocol.[26] SMS is "short" because the maximum size of text messages is 160 characters—longer messages need to be split into multiple short messages. SMS can operate through cell service, without the need for an internet connection.[27] More recently, many text messages have shifted to what are called over-the-top (OTT) services, which are services that stream content using the internet.[28] (The service is delivered "over the top" of another service, such as cell or cable service). Many users now use OTT messaging services, such as Apple's iMessage, Signal, Telegram, or WhatsApp. These OTT services do not have the limitations of SMS and can provide end-to-end encryption. Privacy professionals should be aware of laws such as the Telephone Consumer Protection Act, discussed in Chapter 11, which regulates how businesses can use text messages for marketing purposes.

3.4 Digital Surveillance and Tracking

The smartphone in your pocket likely has greater processing power than the world's largest mainframe computers in the 1970s. In computer science, the rapid progress in computing is often symbolized by Moore's Law, the statement in the 1980s by computer scientist Gordon Moore that the capacity of a digital transistor doubles roughly every two years.[29] It is roughly correct to say that the power and speed of computers has doubled every two years going back multiple decades.

As computers improve, they can handle far larger databases of personal information, process the data more quickly in unprecedented ways, and thus pose new threats to personal privacy. With faster and cheaper computers, it becomes economical to place new internet-connected sensors into more and more devices, creating and adding to the IoT. Smartphones now take incredibly detailed pictures measured in mega-pixels, while many homes and businesses increasingly create and store video footage in a quantity and quality that would have been impossible or unaffordable in the recent past.

These advances in computing technology thus create the possibility—and often the reality—of new types of digital surveillance and tracking. The discussion here first explains key aspects of tracking over the internet, including for online advertising purposes. It then turns to the variety of sensors that increasingly collect personal information. The discussion here relies in many places on the "Tracking and Surveillance" chapter from the IAPP text, *An Introduction to Privacy for Technology Professionals.*[30]

3.4.1 Internet Monitoring

The internet provides many opportunities for tracking and surveillance. These include protective measures like detecting malicious software, or criminal measures to steal passwords and account information. This section describes deep-packet inspection; Wi-Fi and other wireless eavesdropping; internet monitoring by those in control of systems, such as employers; and spyware and other phishing attacks. Each section explains the techniques for monitoring as well as measures that can address privacy concerns.

3.4.1.1 Deep Packet Inspection

As discussed in Section 3.2, communications from sender to receiver on the internet are split into packets. Only the header of the packet is needed to route the packet to the correct IP address. Those administering a node on the internet, however, can also examine some or all of the packet for a variety of purposes. When a node looks at this additional data, it is called deep packet inspection.

Deep packet inspection can serve useful purposes. For instance, examining packets before they enter a company network can help determine whether the packets contain known viruses or other malicious content. Similarly, examining packets before they leave a network can help detect and prevent data leaks of sensitive information.

On the other hand, deep packet inspection can also be used for purposes that raise serious privacy issues. A company might use this inspection to track all user's online behavior, such as to target ads. A government might use it to censor or track citizens' online behaviors, as has occurred in China as part of the "Great Firewall."[31]

In the early years of the internet, deep packet inspection was technically possible for most communications. When communications are effectively encrypted, however, deep packet inspection can no longer see the contents of the communication. Major email providers shifted to encrypted emails after the U.S. intelligence disclosures by Edward Snowden in 2013. The email content is protected from deep packet inspection as it moves over the network, but it can still be reviewed by the email provider on the mail server, which is used to allow for spam filtering. For web browsing, recent years have seen rapid growth in the use of HTTPS, the encrypted version of the HTTP protocol. Going forward, deep packet inspection will only operate on the diminished fraction of internet traffic that fails to use encryption, or where encryption is broken such as by use of stolen keys.

3.4.1.2 Wireless Eavesdropping

In the absence of effective encryption, it is possible to eavesdrop on data sent through a wireless network, including Wi-Fi networks: packet-sniffing systems can capture packets sent over such networks. This risk is often present in Wi-Fi hotspots in public places, such as hotels or coffee shops, where many users share a network that is either unprotected or protected with a password known to a large group of users.

Several defenses can address this risk. Using any password to access a modern encrypted Wi-Fi network forces the network to negotiate a per-user encryption key, which makes it nearly impossible for an eavesdropper to gain access to the contents of wireless communications. The communications can still be monitored by the wireless router, however. VPNs encrypt communications from a user's device to the VPN server, such as when an employer deploys a VPN for its employees, providing a much higher degree of protection against not just the wireless access point, but also the local ISP. This is especially important when traveling internationally. In addition, regardless of the security of the network itself, encrypting web requests using HTTPS can prevent eavesdroppers from intercepting passwords and other sensitive information, although a system can be misconfigured so that sensitive information leaks out even when HTTPS is being used.

3.4.1.3 Internet Monitoring by Employers, Schools, and Parents

Some systems enable people in positions of authority to monitor local networks, which also raises potential privacy issues. Such monitoring may be used to protect security and control behavior on the network, perhaps by blocking access to websites (sometimes called blacklisting) and other internet activity considered inappropriate.

As discussed in more detail in Chapter 12, employers in the United States are generally allowed to monitor their employees' internet usage on the organization's network or company-owned devices. Reasons given for such monitoring include maintaining security within the corporate network and ensuring appropriate behavior among employees. In addition to monitoring internet browsing, many companies scan emails, with one reason being to detect possible phishing attacks.

The U.S. Children's Internet Protection Act (CIPA) requires public schools and libraries to install filters to prevent children from viewing inappropriate content online.[32] Many schools also track students' internet usage to prevent inappropriate and illegal behavior. Civil liberties organizations have long voiced concern about this practice on free speech and other grounds, but CIPA remains in place.

Parents as well can monitor their children's internet usage. Tools allow parents to limit the types of sites their children can visit, often by lists of restricted sites or keyword filters. Such tools enable parents to supervise their child's online activities.

Privacy concerns can arise from any of the monitoring and control performed by persons in authority, such as employers, schools, or parents. What some may consider appropriate blocking of sites, others may see as a form of censorship. What some may consider standard security practice, such as monitoring emails, others may see as an intrusion on privacy. In addition, the context of monitoring can matter greatly—software considered appropriate to track a young child's internet usage may be considered objectionable, and even criminal stalking. Considering such privacy concerns, the mere technical ability to monitor internet usage should not automatically lead to the conclusion that such monitoring is legal or ethical.

3.4.1.4 Spyware and Phishing

Beyond monitoring the network connection, malicious software may surveil data before it even leaves the user's own device. Spyware is malicious software that is covertly installed on a user's computer, often by tricking the user to click on a link that results in downloading of the spyware. Once spyware is installed, it can monitor the user's activities and send sensitive personal information to the attacker. One type of spyware is keylogging, which is malware that tracks all keystrokes performed by the user. Data about the keystrokes can then be sent back to the attacker. Other spyware can take control of the device's camera or microphone, capturing audio or video streams without the user's knowledge.

Spyware may be installed on a user's device via a phishing attack. Phishing is a form of social engineering that uses a routine, trusted communication channel to fool the user into providing unauthorized access to the user's device or to sensitive personal information.[33] Phishing occurs commonly in email messages that appear to be authentic and encourage the user to click on a link or respond to the message by disclosing personal information, such as passwords or financial account numbers. For example, when a person clicks a link in an email sent to a work email account, the employee may be led to a website that collects information, or the link may result in installing spyware or other malicious software onto the user's device.[34]

Fraudsters have developed variations on phishing attacks:

- **Spear phishing** is a phishing attack that is tailored to the individual user, for example, when an email appears to be from the user's boss instructing the user to provide information.
- **Whaling** is a specialized type of spear phishing that is targeted at C-suite executives, celebrities, and politicians. The aim is the same as spear phishing—to download malicious software or use an email or website to obtain personal and/or sensitive information from the victim.
- **Smishing** is phishing by use of SMS. Instead of the attack coming via email, the fraudulent link or request for information arrives via text message.
- **Vishing** is the use of a fraudulent voice message or phone call to trick an individual to provide sensitive personal information or take some other action.

To protect against spyware downloads, technical measures may be able to limit an employee's ability to download **executable code** (code that can run a computer program). For phishing, smishing, or similar attacks, a first line of defense can be software that filters incoming communications and then blocks or flags suspected phishing communications. For phishing messages that make it through such filters, the principal defense is training for employees and other individuals. Individuals should learn to be cautious about clicking on links or opening attachments except from clearly trusted sources.

Although the discussions of phishing and spyware are often intertwined, it is important to understand that the preliminary step of defining software as spyware is dependent in large part on the intent and knowledge of the user, and whether it is reasonable to believe the user wished to have the information transmitted back to the remote location. There is no simple distinction between illegal or inappropriate spyware and legitimate software that performs as intended. Spyware cannot be defined simply by the technical act of sending personal information from the user's computer to a remote computer. For instance, a user might wish to have software that allows someone at a remote location to read what is on the screen. A common example is when a computer user receives technical help from a technician who can see the user's screen or each keystroke. By contrast, the same ability to read the screen, without the knowledge or consent of the user, would in many contexts be considered spyware, and is used in technical support scams.[35]

3.4.2. Tracking Used in Advertising

3.4.2.1 HTTP Cookies

Cookies are widely used on the internet to enable someone other than the user to link a computing device to previous web actions by the same device. The HTTP and HTTPS protocols are stateless, which means the protocols are not designed to remember past interactions with a particular user. For instance, a website should be able to remember if a user is logged in—it would be a bad user experience if the user were required to log in to a website each time they clicked on a link or navigated to a new page.

The basic function of an HTTP cookie is to maintain continuity for the user and website. Cookies can be set for a particular visit to a website or for extended periods of time. **Session cookies** are stored only until the web browser is closed, and thus contain only limited information about that session. Session cookies can be used, for instance, to keep a user logged-in during a session or to allow the user to fill a shopping cart on a particular visit to an e-commerce site. **Persistent cookies**, by contrast, can be saved indefinitely—the website that sets the cookie determines how long the persistent cookie stays in place. Persistent cookies, for instance, can recognize a user who logged in on previous days, or keep a shopping cart filled until the purchase is completed on a later date.

Web domains, such as an e-commerce site or advertising network, can only read and write cookies that they themselves have set—a cookie set by one company cannot be read by others. However, multiple cookies can result from a user's visit to a webpage. For instance, an online news site might load cookies from its own internet domain. These cookies from the primary page that the user is visiting are known as **first-party cookies.** However, a user visiting that site often receives cookies from other entities, such as online advertising networks or a social network when the user is logged in. Cookies set from any company other than the first-party website are known as **third-party cookies**. The second party is understood to be the user who is surfing the web.

3.4.2.2 First-party data collection

Cookies are one important way that first parties collect information about a user's web activities. In a growing number of jurisdictions, including California and the European Union, first parties provide notice before setting cookies on the user's browser.

The IAPP website, for example, has the following cookie notice:

> *When you visit our website, the site asks your browser to store a small piece of data (text file) called a cookie on your device in order to remember information about you, such as your language preference or login information. Those cookies are set by us and called first-party cookies. We also use third-party cookies, which are cookies from a domain different than the domain of the website you are visiting, for our advertising and marketing efforts. More specifically, we use cookies and other tracking technologies for the following purposes: strictly necessary cookies, performance cookies, marketing cookies, and third-party website cookies.*[36]

As with the IAPP website, the user typically has a choice whether to accept all cookies (which may include cookies from third parties) or to refuse all cookies that are not necessary for the site's functioning. The latter may include, for instance, the ability to place items in a shopping cart during that user session. We briefly note some prominent forms of first-party data collection related to web activity.

Cookies can enable personalization, such as where the site suggests music, books, or online shopping based on the user's previous interactions with the site. In general, advertisers will pay a higher price per advertisement when detailed information exists about the user's interests and likely economic activity.

Personalization can be especially strong for search engines, where the user selects searches that may reveal the user's current intentions. For instance, advertisers may pay a search engine especially high prices for advertisements when the search suggests the user may make major purchases, such as a search for "mortgage rates this week" or "auto sales this week."

Social networks and other websites often collect and retain user-generated content (UGC), which is text, photos, or videos the user posts to the website. UGC can provide particularly granular information about a user's interests and activities, including details about the user's offline activities, such as attendance at a restaurant or concert. Social networks often do not sell the data to a third party; instead, the advertiser may pay, for instance, for 1,000 advertisements to individuals that the social network knows have interest in a particular product. In such an advertising campaign, the advertiser may learn the identity only of those individuals who subsequently come to the advertiser's website to purchase the product.

The first party may learn greater details if the user is logged in. The consent to cookies, as discussed in the example with IAPP's website, is consent only to set the cookies. By contrast, a user who creates an account with a social media or other website typically agrees to a longer website policy, called its terms of use, terms of service, or terms and conditions. Such terms often state that the service provider will have additional rights to collect and process data as a condition of the user joining the service. Such rights may include common uses, such as to develop, test, and improve the product or service. They may also include privacy-relevant provisions, such as the right to track a user's location or sell the user's information to third parties.

First parties may also purchase or otherwise gain access to user data from other sources. First parties may append data from third parties in order to fill in gaps, correct and update existing data, and gain other insights.[37] This third-party data may come from data brokers, which are businesses that obtain information from one or more sources, process it to cleanse it or otherwise increase its usefulness, and then license the data for use by the first party.[38] The U.S. Federal Trade Commission (FTC) and other privacy regulators have often scrutinized data brokers due to privacy concerns.[39] Although definitions of what constitutes a data broker can vary, studies put the annual data brokerage market at above $250 billion.[40]

3.4.2.3 Third-Party Data Collection

Prior to the last few years, a large portion of online advertising was previously facilitated by third-party cookies. For instance, advertising networks would often set cookies on a user's device when the user went to a first party, such as a news or e-commerce site. The advertising networks could then observe a user's activity across multiple sites and serve targeted ads to that user based on the interests revealed by the user's web browsing.

A variety of market and regulatory changes, however, are reducing the prevalence of third-party cookies. In the European Union, there have been multiple challenges to the legality of third-party cookies for advertising purposes.[41] The California Privacy Rights Act (CPRA), which entered into effect January 2023, requires notice and an opt-out right for third-party cookies. As discussed in Chapter 11, major browsers have taken steps to block or make it more difficult for third-party cookies to operate. Edge, Firefox, and Safari had third-party cookies blocked by default by the end of 2022, with Chrome announcing it was in the process of blocking such cookies by default.[42]

In light of these major changes concerning third-party cookies, there is now considerable uncertainty about what types of third-party data collection will continue at anything close to the previous scale. Advertisers have the incentive to create new technologies and market models for third-party data collection, but regulators likely will seek to block approaches that they believe threaten privacy. Privacy professionals involved in advertising should be alert to the possibility of new technological, market, and regulatory developments.

3.4.2.4 Tracking Email Recipients

Techniques used to track what websites are visited from a particular computer can also indicate whether an email has been opened or when a particular link in the email has been clicked on.[43] Many email programs can display emails containing HTML code and enabling functionality similar to web page tracking. One technique for tracking is to load a small image when a user opens an email. The image has a link or file name unique to the user, known and accessible to the sender of the email. To prevent such tracking, the user can disable HTML, and read the email in plain text.

3.4.2.5 Cross-Device Tracking

Companies use both deterministic and probabilistic techniques to enable cross-device tracking, which is the ability to link a user to multiple devices, such as smartphones, tablets, and laptops.[44] Deterministic tracking is usually based on the user logging in, so that a company can observe the same login for the multiple devices. Probabilistic tracking relies on inferences that the same user may be using multiple devices.[45] The inferences can arise from sources including IP addresses, cookies, location data, and other behavioral data. Cross-device tracking can raise privacy issues, especially where users are not aware that their activities on different devices can be linked. It can assist users, such as when the user can access emails or content from different devices. Companies have an incentive to use cross-device tracking in order to increase their ability to target advertisements or other content, but regulators have expressed increasing concern about the practice of cross-device tracking.[46]

3.4.3. Location Tracking

The technical ability to track location has become pervasive for the first time in human history. In a 2000 survey, only 28 percent of U.S. respondents reported having a cellphone.[47] By 2021, 85 percent of Americans had a smartphone, and 97 percent owned a cellphone of some kind.[48] Cellphones necessarily reveal the person's location, if only because the service provider needs to know where to send the signal to make the phone ring. In addition to cellphones, an increasing number of other technical means exist to track a person's location, including the cars we drive and the cameras that can recognize our faces when we are in public.

Location information has important privacy implications.[49] The details of an individual's location reveal potentially sensitive information about numerous aspects of a person's life, such as our friends and associates, the medical services we receive, and where we spend the night. Although location information can be useful in solving crimes, such as identifying all of those at the scene of a robbery, it can also be used by an authoritarian government to keep tabs on the political opposition and stifle dissent.

The discussion here first addresses location-tracking technologies, and then turns to location-based services.

3.4.3.1 Location-Tracking Technologies

Although others exist, we describe three location tracking technologies: cell tower and Wi-Fi triangulation; global positioning satellites (GPS); and metadata.

Cellphones communicate with cell towers that receive their signal and connect phones to a global network. Service providers can gain information about the phone's location through the time it takes a message from a particular tower to arrive at a phone, the strength of the signal from that tower, and the towers with which a phone can communicate. After determining the phone's position relative to a handful of towers whose location are known by the cellular provider, the position of the phone can be determined geometrically through triangulation.[50]

GPS satellites can enable the phone to determine location, specifically the device's longitude, latitude, and altitude. As with triangulation, the GPS receiver can determine its location based on the differences in time it takes for messages from each satellite to reach the receiver. Devices do not automatically reveal their information when they receive information to determine their location. However, smartphones and other devices often subsequently, and automatically, share the GPS information with an app or the phone provider.[51]

Location information can also be automatically stored in the metadata of content, such as photos. For photos taken with cellphones or other GPS-enabled devices, location is often automatically stored in the camera metadata, sometimes without the user's awareness. A user who accesses the photo can then often access the location (and often the time) when the photo was taken.

3.4.3.2 Location-Based Services

Location-based services draw upon the data provided by location-tracking technologies. Modern smartphones and automobiles pervasively offer map-related functions, such as directions for walking, driving, or taking public transport. Apps often personalize an experience based on user location, such as weather reports or nearby restaurants or gas stations. Location also plays a role in many social media apps, such as finding one's friends. Advertisers value location information, such as the ability to offer a coupon when an individual is near a store or restaurant. The location of individuals can be integrated with other databases, such as geographic information systems used widely for business purposes.

Along with clearly positive uses, such as correctly arriving at a destination, location services also can enable tracking and intrusive surveillance. Parents can use location services to know where their children are (or at least where their phones are). Employers can use location services to keep track of their employees and assets, such as the location of a company truck. In the United States, law enforcement investigates a crime or attempt to prevent a terrorist attack, they can request location information from companies holding the data. The U.S. Supreme Court held in Carpenter v. United States that police need to get a warrant when doing long-term tracking of an individual's movements. For shorter periods, the holders of location information may be able to respond voluntarily to police requests. In other countries, such as China, governments have established extensive systems for tracking individuals, without the need for prior judicial approval.

3.4.3.3 Preventing and Controlling Location Tracking

The United States has historically had relatively few legal restrictions on businesses that collect and use location information. In recent years, as discussed in Chapter 6, the states that enacted comprehensive privacy laws have often included location information in their definitions of sensitive data.[52] The Children's Online Privacy Protection Act (COPPA), discussed in Chapter 5, also specifically includes location data in its definition of personal data.[53] Both users and controllers of personal information, however, can take action to moderate the use of location information and address the privacy risks.

On the user side, smartphones reveal location information to the cellular providers, and many streams of location data on smartphones are enabled by default. With that said, smartphone operating systems have provided more detailed user controls over time. Individuals today can often specify which apps may collect location information, how granular the collection will be, and whether the location information goes to the app continuously or only when the app is being used.[54] Users often have the ability to turn on and off the automatic metadata in photos taken by a smartphone or other smart camera. More generally, designers of consumer-facing technology face increasing pressure to enable user controls over location data, as good practice in the United States and under legal requirements in the European Union and other countries.

On the side of the data controller, location services often benefit from a privacy impact assessment to understand both the benefits of collecting and using such data and to become aware of privacy risks. Privacy risks can often be mitigated by limiting the retention period of location data, deidentifying the data, and limiting who has access to location data and for what purposes. Organizations should be aware that location data can also be combined with other databases, enabling more detailed profiling than would be possible with company's location data alone. Although location data can enable maps and many other useful services, developers can benefit from the "friends and family test"—how would I feel about the use of location data if it applied to my family or friends? If there are scenarios the developer does not want for family members, then quite possibly greater privacy safeguards are worth considering.

3.4.4 Surveillance by Audio, Video, and Other Sensors

In addition to tracking a device's location, smartphones and other modern devices come equipped with audio (microphone), video (camera), and other sensors. We examine some scenarios where such sensors can raise privacy risks, and then discuss steps to mitigate such risks.

Smartphones, laptops, and desktop computers are all typically connected to the internet and potentially can have their microphones and cameras activated remotely without the knowledge of the user. Malware can be loaded onto these devices, such as when the user unsuspectingly clicks on a link that downloads the malware. These types of malware are often known as remote access trojans (RATs). Malware, for instance, may turn on the webcam of a desktop or laptop, and even turn off the light that indicates the webcam is in use. Malware may also infect microphones, such as on a smartphone, a smart television, or the remote control used with a smart television or other device. In addition to malware, employers or others with lawful access to the device may activate the microphone or camera. Employers often have the technical ability to activate microphones or other sensors on work-issued devices, and police may get a warrant under wiretap laws to listen to a criminal suspect.

The decreasing cost of cameras, microphones, and other sensors also enables surveillance of individuals in public from sources other than a user's devices. There have been policy debates about the extent and use of closed-circuit television (CCTV), police body cameras, and other video surveillance, especially when paired with facial recognition technology.[55] Use of such video surveillance systems by the government is generally legal in the United States, although not where the individual has a "reasonable expectation of privacy" (such as in a bathroom), and not in some cities that have set limits on police and municipal agencies from using facial recognition.[56] Drones, called unmanned aerial vehicles by government agencies, are often equipped with video cameras, and may also include infrared cameras, radar, or other sensors.[57] By contrast with the general legality of video surveillance, U.S. wiretap laws set limits on wiretapping and other secret audio surveillance.

Audio, video, and other sensors increasingly exist in a user's home or automobile. The term "smart home" can apply to the increasing number of home devices that are internet-connected, including thermostats and home security systems. The term "connected cars" focuses on the trend toward an increasing number of these sensors in new cars, many of which send data to the cloud.

The discussion of managing the privacy risks of location tracking applies as well to audio, video, and other sensors. On the user side, designers of consumer-facing technology can enable greater user control over data collection. For example, designers of smart toys for children (and even general smart home devices) can set privacy by default so data does not go outside of the home or provide usable choice interfaces concerning data about children. For many kinds of video and remote sensing, however, there is no effective notice or choice for users, such as for data collected by drones or security cameras.[58]

Data controllers should consider the full life cycle of personal data when deploying audio, video, and other sensors. Under the principle of data minimization, there may be ways to achieve an organization's goals with more limited collection, processing, and dissemination of personal data.

3.5 Privacy-Enhancing Technologies

Just as new technology can enable greater privacy invasions, it can also enable new types of privacy protection. Privacy by design has become more important over time, and that approach is now legally required in California and the European Union, among others. Privacy by design means to embed privacy principles in architectures, products, and service from the onset.[59] In recent years, privacy engineering has emerged as an increasingly important role related to engineering requirements for privacy into systems. Privacy engineers have a growing number of mathematically sophisticated tools that seek to preserve privacy while maintaining utility of the analyzed information.[60]

The discussion here provides an explanation of issues relating to deidentification and reidentification of data. To the extent that data can indeed be deidentified, then privacy is preserved. We next turn to two important general tools for protecting privacy—encryption and hashing, and conclude with some broader observations.

3.5.1 Altering Data: Data Deidentification

The word "anonymous" derives from the Greek *anonymos,* meaning "without a name."[61] Privacy laws and governance apply to "personally identifiable information" or "personal data." When the data is no longer able to be traced back to a person, then privacy laws no longer apply. One important category of privacy-preserving technology, therefore, is any technique that can alter the data so that it is no longer identifiable.

Although U.S. law provides few clear definitions, privacy professionals should be aware of the difference between data that is either "anonymous" or "pseudonymous."[62] Useful definitions come from the UK Information Commissioner's Office, which states that anonymous data is "in a form that does not identify individuals and where identification through its combination with other data is not likely to take place."[63] By contrast, pseudonymization is "the process of distinguishing individuals in a dataset by using a unique identifier which does not reveal their 'real world' identity."[64]

To understand pseudonymization, consider the medical records of an individual patient, where the patient is described as Patient 13579. Some organizations, such as the hospital that treated the patient, assigned that patient the number. That hospital may be able to link the patient number to the actual identity easily. On the other hand, medical researchers elsewhere only see Patient 13579, and the identity of the patient is thus masked when the records are used in a research study. (As later discussed, it may be possible for recipients of the records to reidentify the data, but the pseudonyms rather than the names are provided to the outside medical researchers.) Note that EU law treats pseudonymized information as personal data covered by the GDPR, in contrast to anonymized data, which falls outside of the GDPR.[65]

3.5.1.1 Strong Versus Weak Identifiers and Linkability

It is far from simple, however, to determine when data is truly **deidentified**. Some information is considered clearly identifying, such as a Social Security or passport number. These are called **strong identifiers**. Names can be strong identifiers, although common names may not be uniquely identifying. Identifiers that must be used in combination with other information to determine identity are **weak identifiers**. A related concept is **quasi-identifiers**, or data that can be combined with external knowledge to link data to an individual.[66]

Date of birth is an example of a quasi-identifier that can often assist in identification—there are 366 possible birthdays in a year (including leap year), and the population is spread out over more than 80 years, so that each unique date of birth is one of over 25,000 cells (366 times 80) in a spreadsheet. Even in a large population, only a small portion (perhaps 1 in 25,000) share the exact same birthdate. If a data set provides an individual's date of birth, and someone knows the individual's date of birth, then it becomes relatively easy to learn the other information in the data set about that individual.

A related topic is linked data (or identified data) versus linkable data (or identifiable data). An example of linked data is having both a bank account number and the person's name. If someone other than the bank only has the bank account number, however, is that truly identifying? Having the bank account number alone is an example of linkable or identifiable data—the bank account number gives us a strong clue to a unique account owner, but we may not have a method to learn the name of the account owner. In a 2016 speech, FTC Chair Edith Ramirez addressed the definition of "personally identifiable." FTC Chair Ramirez stated, "We now regard data as personally identifiable when it can be reasonably linked to a particular person, computer, or device. In many cases, persistent identifiers, such as device identifiers, MAC addresses, static IP addresses, and retail loyalty card numbers meet this test."[67] Online search engines often enable linkability, such as when a quasi-identifier can be linked to an individual using publicly available information.

3.5.1.2 Approaches to Deidentification

Many approaches to deidentification rely on one or more of three techniques to hide identity.[68] The simplest approach is **suppression**, which is the process of removing identifying values from a record. One example is when part of the organization is doing machine-learning or statistical analysis of a customer data set. Those performing the calculations are looking for statistical patterns and generally have no need to see the customer names or other strongly identifying information such as phone numbers.

Some types of data are amenable to **generalization**, where a detailed data element is replaced by a more general data element. For example, using year of birth rather than date of birth greatly reduces identifiability—the population then has roughly 80 categories (if persons over 80 years of age are placed together), rather than the 25,000 categories for date of birth. A common example of generalization is to provide less granularity for location data, such as by revealing only the municipality rather than a precise GPS coordinate.

A third approach is **noise addition**. In this approach, actual data values are replaced with similar, but different, values. Often, the noise addition seeks to preserve statistical properties of the data, such as the average value, while disrupting the ability of outsiders to spot the data associated with a specific individual. For instance, suppose there is a report that contains detailed information about each participant, including their precise annual salary. An employer might know the annual salary from payroll records, and then seek other information from the survey about the individual. With noise addition, that precise annual salary information no longer appears in the report, blocking such efforts.

3.5.1.3 The Risk of Reidentification and Differential Privacy

Computer scientists have had surprising success at reidentifying data that appeared to be deidentified.[69] In an early study by Latanya Sweeney, she was able to uniquely identify the governor of Massachusetts from public voter files that contained only gender, zip code, and date of birth. (The study illustrates the extent to which precise date of birth is highly identifying.)[70] Since then, an entire academic field has developed on techniques for reidentifying supposedly anonymized information.[71] New privacy professionals should thus be alert to the possibility, for a data set that is supposedly deidentified, that there may in fact be technical means to reidentify at least some of the data.

Partly in response to these reidentification attacks, researchers have developed **differential privacy**, which is a mathematical definition of privacy in the context of statistical and machine-learning analysis.[72] Here is the definition of the mathematical guarantee from differential privacy: "Anyone seeing the result of a differentially private analysis will essentially make the same inference about any individual's private information, whether or not that individual's private information is included in the input to the analysis."[73] Differential privacy defines the necessary amount of statistical noise that must be added to a data set to meet the desired level of privacy for a specific set of queries.

Researchers continue to explore the set of circumstances where differential privacy can apply. The U.S. Census used differential privacy for certain data sets as part of the 2020 Census.[74] For more complex data sets, however, the Census decided in 2022 that application of differential privacy would not yield sufficiently useful data to be worthwhile.[75] Overall, there will likely be an increasing range of applications for differential privacy in the coming years.

3.5.1.4 Conclusion on Deidentification

Privacy professionals will continue to face issues of deidentification and reidentification. The entire effort to protect privacy depends on defining what is in scope—covered by privacy rules—rather than deidentified/anonymized and thus out of scope. Most global privacy regulations are not applicable to data that cannot reasonably be traced back to an individual. Internationally, the terms used to describe the boundaries of personal data rights vary as well as the approaches to risk assessment, and which threats for reidentification need to be considered. Definitions and interpretations of the relevant legal terms vary tremendously in different jurisdictions.

The longest-standing deidentification rules in the United States are under the Health Insurance Portability and Accountability Act (HIPAA), concerning protected health information. There are two methods for deidentification under HIPAA. Under the safe harbor, covered entities must eliminate 18 specific types of potentially identifying information. For instance, postal codes can be no more specific than the first three digits of a five-digit ZIP code. Alternatively, deidentification can be achieved via the "expert determination" method, under which an expert determines and documents that "the risk is very small that the information could be used, alone or in combination with other reasonably available information, by an anticipated recipient to identify an individual."[76] Many new reidentification attacks have developed, however, since the promulgation of the HIPAA rule over twenty years ago.

Outside of the HIPAA context, privacy professionals often look to non-binding guidance from the FTC, which has stated that data is not "reasonably linkable" to the extent that a company: "(1) takes reasonable measures to ensure that the data is deidentified; (2) publicly commits not to try to reidentify the data; and (3) contractually prohibits downstream recipients from trying to reidentify the data."[77]

In conclusion, privacy professionals should be alert to the possibility that others in an organization may wish to use data without privacy protections while asserting incorrectly that the data is actually anonymized. Such data use creates risk for the organization. In 2022, a senior FTC official stated about location, health, and other sensitive information that "claims that data is 'anonymous' or 'has been anonymized' are often deceptive." The official concluded that "companies that make false claims about anonymization can expect to hear from the FTC."[78]

3.5.2 Shielding of Data

Anonymization and other altering of the original data leaves data available for processing but does so in a way that makes the data anonymous or less identifiable. By contrast, encryption shields data to prevent unauthorized persons from accessing it but enables the data to be read in its original form if an authorized person uses a key.

Shielding of data can occur at different stages. Encryption in transit is encrypted between the sender and the recipient. For the use of this chapter, we shall refer to the sender as "Alice" and the recipient as "Bob." Encryption in transit is commonly used on the internet, to prevent "man in the middle" attacks by a malicious actor intercepting the communication as it moves from Alice to Bob. Encryption at rest means that data is stored in a system when it is not being used. For instance, a well-encrypted hard drive means that the data remains secure even if a malicious actor steals the hard drive. Under most data breach laws, such encryption creates an exception from the requirement to report the breach. Chip manufacturers have sought to develop trusted execution environments, also called secure enclaves, within the processors themselves to provide stronger privacy guarantees.[79] In some instances, there is also encryption in use, although many types of processing need to see the actual data—the plaintext—in order to do the processing.

Research continues on expanding various techniques for operating with encrypted data. These topics include secure multiparty computation and fully homomorphic encryption, which would enable processing of data while the data remains in encrypted form.[80] Details on these topics and important tools such as zero-knowledge proofs are beyond the scope of this chapter.[81]

3.5.2.1 Encryption

Encryption has become a pervasive privacy-enhancing technology.[82] The use of encryption has grown enormously since the spread of the internet and society's reliance on software and computing for so many tasks of everyday life and commerce. The discussion here can only provide a brief introduction to the topic.

Encryption is a reversible process that converts original data from plaintext into data that is scrambled and cannot be read, called cyphertext. Decryption converts the ciphertext back to the original plaintext. A cryptographic algorithm takes the original plaintext and performs mathematical operations on it to create the ciphertext.

To achieve decryption, a user must have (or guess) a key. The key is a string of characters (the longer and more complex the key, the stronger the security). When the cryptographic algorithm applies the key to the ciphertext, the plaintext becomes available.

Symmetric key cryptography (also called private-key cryptography) uses the same key both to encrypt and decrypt data. Symmetric keys are relatively short, and they are often faster and less resource-intensive than other approaches. The disadvantage, however, is that Alice has to share the symmetric key with Bob in order to enable Bob to read the message. That means Alice must trust Bob with the key and find a secure way to provide the key to Bob, even if he is far away.

With the rise of the internet, asymmetric cryptography (also called public-key cryptography) has become widespread. In this approach, a pair of keys is generated for each user. One of the keys is public—the whole world sees it, like a telephone number in a traditional phone book. The other key is private—

only the user knows it, and the user never needs to share the private key with others. When Alice wants to send a message to Bob, she encrypts it using his public key; Bob then uses his private key to convert back to plaintext. Public-key cryptography is scalable—Alice's computer can look up and use the public key of recipients all over the world, such as to send an encrypted message or log into a website.

Asymmetric encryption also enables digital certificates, widely used in the authentication process. Alice can encrypt a message using her private key. Then, only Alice's public key can reveal the underlying plaintext. When the plaintext becomes readable, Bob can verify that the communication came from Alice's private key.

A certificate authority (CA) is a trusted third party that validates a person's identity and either generates a public/private key pair on Alice's behalf or associates an existing public key provided by Alice to that person.[83] Once a CA validates someone's identity, they issue a digital certificate that is digitally signed by the CA. The digital certificate can then be used to verify a person associated with a public key. Public key infrastructure (PKI) refers to the policies, standards, people, and systems that support the distribution of public keys and the identity validation of individuals or entities with digital certificates and a certificate authority.

3.5.2.2 Hashing

Hashing is a cryptographic function that transforms an input into a new output of alphanumeric characters. The goal is to have a one-way function—the hash will work the same way each time the algorithm operates on the original file or other input; however, seeing the output should not reveal anything about the original input. To get the idea, consider how a potato can be converted into hashed brown potatoes. That is a one-way process, however—you can't convert the hash back into a potato.

Hashing, similar to encryption, transforms data into an unintelligible format. Hashing in some instances is used to protect privacy, notably by creating a pseudonym. For instance, hashing might be applied to a patient's name and date of birth, and all the records associated with that patient would be accessed by using the hash, with no visibility for the name and birth date. More simply, some organizations have used a hash on a relatively short string such as a person's Social Security number.

This approach to deidentification, however, may not work in practice. For instance, an attacker might create a table that shows the hashed outcome for each possible Social Security number.[84] Then, the attacker may be able to look up the Social Security number matched with each hash. There are ways to make this look-up strategy more difficult. Notably, the organization performing the hash can add "salt" to the hash, which approximates the use of a key for encryption. Privacy professionals should be aware both possibilities of using hashing to shield data and the risk that attackers may be able to circumvent that shield.

Hashes are often used to show the integrity of the communication—that the content of the communication has remained the same between Alice and Bob, because the hashed value is the same before and after communication.

For a digital signature, Alice uses her private key to create a string of characters. Bob then applies Alice's public key to the communication. If the public key works—if it creates a readable plaintext—then Bob learns that the message received is the same as the message sent.

3.5.2.3 Hardware and Other Shielding of Data

In addition to the use of encryption and hashing, there are other technologies that can shield data. Some technologies are simple and physical, such as a physical cover over a webcam or a privacy screen that makes it difficult for a stranger to observe your laptop. Other technologies prevent data from being accessed except under specified conditions. For instance, a biometric reader on a laptop or other device blocks access except by the authorized user. More generally, the device may only operate when certain hardware or software conditions are met, such as anti-interdiction mechanisms that detect tampering and prevent operation of the device when tampering is detected.[85]

3.5.3 Conclusion on privacy-enhancing technologies

The discussion here on some key categories of PETs focused on ways of altering data (e.g., deidentification) and ways for shielding data (e.g., encryption, hashing). Privacy professionals should be alert to the development of a variety of other PETs in the future, as researchers and regulators seek to expand technical measures to protect privacy.[86] Reduction of privacy risk also can come from effective systems and processes for data activities, many of which are discussed in Chapter 4.

The privacy professional should keep in mind that weak organizational measures can undermine the quality of technical measures. In practice, most encryption is cracked due to a mistake in implementation rather than a flaw in the encryption algorithm itself.[87] Overall reduction of privacy risk comes from a combination of technical measures, such as encryption and hashing, as well as organizational measures, such as limiting which employees gain access to data.

3.6 Cybersecurity

Security is an essential component of providing privacy protection—the best privacy policy will not protect data if it is easy for malicious attackers to grab the data. That is why all versions of the Fair Information Practices in Chapter 1 include a security principle providing that organizations should use reasonable administrative, technical, and physical safeguards to protect personal information against unauthorized access, use, disclosure, modification, and destruction.

In practice, privacy professionals often coordinate closely with security professionals in their organization. This part of the chapter cannot possibly teach all aspects of cybersecurity; instead, the goal is to familiarize the reader with some key concepts, enabling more effective communication with cybersecurity professionals when appropriate.

3.6.1 Confidentiality, Integrity, and Availability

In considering privacy and security together, a useful first approximation is that privacy means deciding which uses of personal data are authorized, while security means preventing unauthorized access to data.[88] More broadly, computer security traditionally addresses CIA: confidentiality, integrity, and availability. In this setting, confidentiality means protecting information from unauthorized access. Integrity means data is trustworthy, complete, and has not been accidentally altered or modified by an unauthorized user. Availability means data is accessible when it is needed.[89] Computer security, often called cybersecurity or information security, thus adds protection of integrity and availability to the privacy protections against unauthorized access.

3.6.2 The NIST Cybersecurity Framework

Since its first publication in 2014, one of the most important cybersecurity documents has been the U.S. National Institute of Standards and Technology (NIST) Cybersecurity Framework (CSF).[90] Although the CSF is guidance rather than a set of legal requirements, it provides "a set of industry standards and best practices to help organizations manage cybersecurity risks."[91]

The CSF popularized five Framework Core Functions designed to assist organizations in addressing ever-changing cybersecurity risks. NIST emphasizes that all five functions should operate "concurrently and continuously to form an operational culture that addresses the dynamic cybersecurity risk."

- **Identify.** Organizations should develop the understanding to manage cybersecurity risk to systems, assets, data, and capabilities. Organizations need to manage assets, understand their business environment, and assess risks.
- **Protect.** Organizations should develop and implement the appropriate safeguards to ensure confidentiality, integrity, and availability.
- **Detect.** Organizations should develop and implement appropriate activities to identify the occurrence of a cybersecurity event. For instance, organizations should identify anomalous activities, and follow up on anomalies in order to determine whether they indicate a compromise.
- **Respond.** Organizations should develop and implement appropriate activities to take action regarding a detected cybersecurity event. These activities are often called incident responses, where organizations may be required to provide notice to government agencies and affected individuals.
- **Recover.** Organizations should develop and implement the appropriate activities to maintain plans for resilience and to restore any capabilities or services that were impaired due to a cybersecurity event.

In short, the CSF provides a systematic, widely known, and relatively concise source of information for privacy professionals seeking to learn more about cybersecurity or about how to integrate the privacy and cybersecurity activities in an organization.

3.6.3 The Adversarial Mindset

An organizing principle in learning cybersecurity is to adopt the adversarial mindset.[92] Many of us go through our daily lives without feeling like we are constantly under direct attack by malicious actors. In cybersecurity, however, we all live in a "bad neighborhood"—the attackers, from all over the globe and at any second, can unleash a potentially devastating attack on our system.[93]

To address this unceasing risk of attack, organizations must perform threat modeling to identify the most salient risks for the organization.[94] Along with the widely used MITRE ATT&CK Framework, a helpful mnemonic is the STRIDE framework for modeling computer security threats.[95] STRIDE stands for:

- **Spoofing:** an attempt to undermine authentication.
- **Tampering:** changes to the desired hardware and software specifications.
- **Repudiation:** an application or system does not adopt controls to accurately track users' action.[96]
- **Information disclosure:** the loss of private information.
- **Denial of service:** a website or service becomes inoperable due to a bombardment of attempts to log on to the site, in what is called a distributed denial of service attack.
- **Elevation of privilege:** an attacker gets inside an organization's firewall and tries to gain additional privileges to manipulate the computer system. If the attacker gains the greatest authority of any user of the system, that is often called root access to the system.

The process of cybersecurity threat modeling can differ in practice from other aspects of compliance. Many compliance programs have a checklist of required actions or do a gap analysis of where the current state differs from the organization's goals. Such compliance lists and gap analyses also occur in cybersecurity.

With that said, the adversarial mindset highlights the possibility that a single failure can lead to catastrophic consequences—the attacker gaining control of the entire computer system. Over time, given the possible consequences of a single failure, cybersecurity defense has placed more emphasis on the concept of resilience—the ability of an organization to bounce back from an intrusion or other malicious action.[97]

In 2022, the U.S. government announced the goal of adopting the "zero-trust" approach: "The foundational tenet of the Zero Trust Model is that no actor, system, network, or service operating outside or within the security perimeter is trusted. Instead, we must verify anything and everything attempting to establish access."[98] The goal is that "all traffic must be encrypted and authenticated as soon as practicable," including internal traffic. With the zero-trust approach, the idea is that a single intrusion will be able to cause only limited damage—even if the adversary is in the system, there will be a limited scope of harm.

The adversarial mindset also is consistent with other foundational aspects of cybersecurity. Because defenders must be on the lookout for serious attacks, each user should only receive "least privilege"—the most limited scope of action on the system that can get the user's job done. To implement the least privilege principle, organizations strive to build role-based access controls—a doctor or nurse might need the detailed medical record, while the cafeteria only needs to know about a patient's low-salt diet. Legal requirements related to privacy, such as the HIPAA Security Rule (discussed in Chapter 8), often require these role-based access controls.[99]

In addition, because attackers may get past the first line of defense, organizations try to build "defense in depth," so that an initial intrusion still faces multiple obstacles before harm occurs. Because attackers may try to gain advantage when new hardware and software is installed, it is important to have security by default, such as strong passwords even upon initial use.

3.6.4 Conclusion on Cybersecurity

Some aspects of cybersecurity closely parallel important privacy principles. The idea of security by default is similar to privacy by default. For new systems, there should be thorough consideration of risks, through both the security development life cycle and the privacy development life cycle. Implementing role-based access controls is a standard part of both security and privacy programs.

One difference is the nature of the threat. In cybersecurity, the most common perspective is that of the system owner—keep the adversary out of the system. In privacy, however, it is far more common to adopt the perspective of the data subject—the individual user. The company, agency, or other organization may itself be seen as a source of risk, such as if a company acts unfairly or deceptively toward the individual. As previously discussed, the simplest distinction may be that security means preventing unauthorized access to data, while privacy often means deciding which uses of personal data should be authorized.

3.7 Conclusion

This chapter seeks to introduce the reader to key terms and concepts related to technology and privacy. For the nontechnical reader, learning this terminology can serve multiple uses, not least of which is easing the fear of sitting in a meeting when others are talking about things that you do not understand. When you have at least the basic vocabulary for these technical issues, it becomes far easier to follow up and learn more when that is necessary.

A growing number of privacy professionals will need to dig quite a bit deeper into technical issues as part of their job. The role of the privacy engineer has become far more prominent in recent years, in order to provide stronger technical protections than privacy policies alone can deliver. Computing technology will keep changing, so both the technical and the nontechnical reader should expect to engage in continuous learning to keep up with best practices involving technology and privacy.

Endnotes

1 For helpful comments on a draft of this chapter, the authors thank Simson Garfinkel, Katherina Koerner, and Nathan Lemay. Any errors remain those of the authors.

2 Travis Breaux, *An Introduction to Privacy for Technology Professionals*, (Portsmouth: IAPP, 2020).

3 Jack L. Brock Jr. and Keith A. Rhodes, "Information Security: Computer Hacker Information Available on the Internet, Testimony Before the Permanent Subcommittee on Investigations, Committee on Governmental Affairs, U.S. Senate," U.S. General Accounting Office, June 5, 1996, https://www.gao.gov/assets/t-aimd-96-108.pdf.

4 "A brief history of NSF and the Internet," National Science Foundation, August 13, 2003, https://www.nsf.gov/news/news_summ.jsp?cntn_id=103050.

5 "What is Transmission Control Protocol TCP/IP?, Transmission Control Protocol (TCP)," Fortinet, Inc., accessed July 2023, https://www.fortinet.com/resources/cyberglossary/tcp-ip.

6 "What is IPv6?" Geeks for Geeks, accessed July 2023, https://www.geeksforgeeks.org/what-is-ipv6/.

7 Kinza Yasar and Andrew Zola, "Definition: Network Packet," TechTarget, accessed July 2023, https://www.techtarget.com/searchnetworking/definition/packet.

8 "Web Accessibility Best Practices from NASA Webmaster Community," National Aeronautics and Space Administration, accessed November 2017, https://www.hq.nasa.gov/webmaster/accessibility/AccessibilityBestPractice.htm.

9 "Introduction to HTTPS," The HTTPS-Only Standard, accessed February 2023, https://https.cio.gov/faq/.

10 Peter Swire, Justin Hemmings and Alana Kirkland, "Online Privacy and ISPs: ISP Access to Consumer Data is Limited and Often Less than Access by Others," Working Paper, Institute for Information Security & Privacy, Georgia Tech, February 29, 2016, www.iisp.gatech.edu/sites/default/files/images/online_privacy_and_isps.pdf.

11 Brenda Barron, "HTML vs HTML5: Learn the Crucial Differences Between Them," Kinsta, November 24, 2022, https://kinsta.com/blog/html-vs-html5/; "HTML: Living Standard," WhatWG, updated July 13, 2022, https://html.spec.whatwg.org/multipage/; Adam Wood, "HTML5 Basics for Everyone Tired of Reading About Deprecated Code," HTML.com, accessed July 2023, https://html.com/html5/.

12 Jaime Morrison, HTML 5.1 Expected for Release in September 2016," WhatPixel, accessed February 2023, http://whatpixel.com/html51-expected-release-rc-2016/; "HTML: Living Standard," WhatWG.

13 Paul Madsen and Carlisle Adams, "Privacy and XML, Part I," XML.com, April 17, 2002, www.xml.com/pub/a/2002/04/17/privacy.html.

14 "Technology Assessment: Cybersecurity for Critical Infrastructure Protection," U.S. General Accounting Office, May 2004, 151, https://www.gao.gov/assets/gao-04-321.pdf.

15 Farsight Security, "Farsight Security Reveals Most Popular Top-Level Domains Over 10-Year Period," Yahoo! Finance, May 4, 2021, https://finance.yahoo.com/news/farsight-security-reveals-most-popular-110000789.html; see Brett McKay, "How Many TLDs Are There? What Are The Types? We Answer Your Common TLD Questions!" Dynadot Inc., June 26, 2020, https://dynadot.com/community/blog/how-many-TLDs-are-there-and-what-are-the-types.html.

16 There are currently more than 1,000 top-level domains available, "List of Top-Level Domains," Internet Corporation for Assigned Names and Numbers, accessed January 2020, https://www.icann.org/resources/pages/tlds-2012-02-25-en. The International Corporation for Assigned Names and Numbers (ICANN) controls the creation of top-level domains. (The application can be viewed at ICANN's website, www.icann.org.) As of October 2016, Public Technical Identifiers is responsible for the operation of IANA (Internet Assigned Numbers Authority) functions, namely domain names. "Public Technical Identifiers," accessed July 2023, https://pti.icann.org/.

17 "What Is the Difference between a Static and Dynamic IP Address?" Brand Media, Inc., modified November 18, 2018, https://www.iplocation.net/static-vs-dynamic-ip-address.

18 See Lindsey Tonsager, "FTC's Jessica Rich Argues IP Addresses and Other Persistent Identifiers Are 'Personally Identifiable,'" Inside Privacy, Covington, April 29, 2016, https://www.insideprivacy.com/united-states/ftcs-jessica-rich-argues-ip-addresses-and-other-persistent-identifiers-are-personally-identifiable/.

19 John Gates, "Which TLS Version is Obsolete," CalCom, July 25, 2022, https://www.calcomsoftware.com/which-tls-version-is-obsolete/.

20 "7 Reasons why Cloud is the Future," eHosting Datafort, February 5, 2014, https://www.ehdf.com/blog/7-reasons-why-cloud-is-the-future/.

21 See Johnnie Konstantas, "7 Reasons Why the Cloud is More Secure," *Oracle Cloud Security* (blog), September 16, 2019 https://blogs.oracle.com/cloudsecurity/post/7-reasons-why-the-cloud-is-more-secure.

22 See Stephen Watts and Muhammad Raza, "SaaS vs PaaS vs IaaS: What's the Difference & How to Choose." *BMC Blogs*, June 15, 2019, https://www.bmc.com/blogs/saas-vs-paas-vs-iaas-whats-the-difference-and-how-to-choose.

23 See Stephen J. Bigelow, "What is edge Computing? Everything you need to know," Techtarget, accessed July 2023, https://techtarget.com/searchdatacenter/definition/edge-computing

24 See Bettina Specht, "Everything you need to know about SMPTP (Simple Mail Transfer Protocol)," ActiveCampaign, updated September 13, 2022, https://postmarkapp.com/guides/everything-you-need-to-know-about-smtp.

25 "IMAP vs POP3 vs SMTP – The Ultimate Comparison," Courier, accessed July 2023, https://www.courier.com/guides/imap-vs-pop3-vs-smtp/.

26 Risa Takenaka, "What is SMS? How Short Message Service Works," Telnyx, January 4, 2021, https://telnyx.com/resources/what-is-sms.

27 SMS-Magic Documentation, "SMS 101 – Basics of SMS Technology", Screen-Magic Mobile Media Pvt. Ltd., accessed February 2023, https://www.sms-magic.com/docs/messaging-guides/knowledge-base/sms-101-basics-of-sms-technology/.

28 Henry Cazalet, "What Are OTT Messaging Platforms?" The SMS Works, accessed July 2023, https://thesmsworks.co.uk/blog/ott-messaging-apps/; Cemal Dikman and David Anstiss, "Applying Lawful Intelligence to OTT Messaging Platform Communications," January 28, 2022, https://www.ss8.com/applying-lawful-intelligence-to-ott-messaging-platform-communications/.

29 Gordon E. Moore, "Cramming More Components onto Integrated Circuits," Electronics, April 19, 1965, 114-117, https://www.hte.hu/documents/10180/1032032/Moore_reprint.pdf. Carla Tradi, "What is Moore's Law and Is it Still True?" Investopedia, July 17, 2022, https://www.investopedia.com/terms/m/mooreslaw.asp#:~:text=Moore's%20Law%20states%20that%20the,will%20pay%20less%20for%20them.

30 Breaux, *An Introduction to Privacy for Technology Professionals*, Chapter 6: Tracking and Surveillance by Lorrie Faith Cranor, Blase Ur, and Manya Sleeper.

31 Richard Clayton, Steven Murdoch, Robert Watson, "Ignoring the Great Firewall of China," *A Journal of Law and Policy* 3, no. 2 (2007): 273-298, https://www.cl.cam.ac.uk/~rnc1/ignoring.pdf.

32 "Children's Internet Protection Act (CIPA)," U.S. Federal Communications Commission, updated December 19, 2019, https://www.fcc.gov/consumers/guides/childrens-internet-protection-act; "Children's Interent Protection Act (CIPA, 2000), Chegg, accessed July 2023, https://www.chegg.com/learn/business/business-law/childrens-internet-protection-act-cipa-2000.

33 Noah Campbell, "Employee-Targeted Social Engineering Continues to Infiltrate Corporate Systems: ZTNA Can Help," Blackberry, September 19, 2022, https://blogs.blackberry.com/en/2022/09/employee-targeted-social-engineering-continues-to-infiltrate-corporate-systems-ztna-can-help. See Pijus Jaunikskis, "10 Famous Phishing Attacks that Targeted People and Corporations," Surfshark, March 7, 2022, https://surfshark.com/blog/biggest-phishing-attacks.

34 Phishing is often used as an approach for a bad actor to carry out a ransomware attack, where malware is installed on the victim's system to prevent the victim from accessing their own data and the bad actor demands money, or "ransom," to restore the victim's access. Many experts warn against victims paying these ransoms. Also, paying the ransom is not a guarantee that the bad actor will restore the victim's access to the data. Danny Palmer, "Ransomware: Attacks that Start with Phishing Emails are Suddenly Back in Fashion Again," ZDNet, June 29, 2020, https://www.zdnet.com/article/ransomware-attacks-that-start-with-phishing-emails-are-suddenly-back-in-fashion-again/; see "2021 Trends Show Increased Globalized Threat of Ransomware," Cybersecurity & Infrastructure Security Agency, February 10, 2022, https://www.cisa.gov/news-events/cybersecurity-advisories/aa22-040a; see also Ransomware, Federal Bureau of Investigation, accessed March 2023, https://www.fbi.gov/how-we-can-help-you/safety-resources/scams-and-safety/common-scams-and-crimes/ransomware.

35 Clare Stouffer, "Spyware: What is Spyware + How to Protect Yourself," Norton, December 13, 2021, https://us.norton.com/blog/malware/spyware; see Amanda Gillies, "Research Finds Most Companies Have Installed Spyware on Work Equipment," NewsHub, June 6, 2022, https://www.newshub.co.nz/home/technology/2022/06/research-finds-most-companies-have-installed-spyware-on-work-equipment.html; see also Bobby Allyn, "Your Boss is Watching You: Work-From-Home Boom Leads to More Surveillance," NPR, May 13, 2020, https://www.npr.org/2020/05/13/854014403/your-boss-is-watching-you-work-from-home-boom-leads-to-more-surveillance.

36 "Cookie Notice," IAPP, updated March 2023, https://iapp.org/about/cookie-notice/.

37 See Heather Mateus, "What is a Data Append?" LiftEngine, last modified June 27, 2022, https://www.liftengine.com/articles/what-is-a-data-append/.

38 "Data Broker," Information Technology Gartner Glossary, Gartner, accessed February 2023, https://www.gartner.com/en/information-technology/glossary/data-broker.

39 "Data Brokers: A Call for Transparency and Accountability," Federal Trade Commission, May 2014, https://www.ftc.gov/system/files/documents/reports/data-brokers-call-transparency-accountability-report-federal-trade-commission-may-2014/140527databrokerreport.pdf.

40 "Data Broker Market: Global Industry Forecast (2023-2029)," Maximize Market Research, accessed July 2023, https://www.maximizemarketresearch.com/market-report/global-data-broker-market/55670/.

41 Natasha Lomas, "Hold-Outs Targeted in Fresh Batch of NOYB GDPR Cookie Consent Complaints," TechCrunch, August 9, 2022, https://techcrunch.com/2022/08/08/noyb-gdpr-cookie-consent-complaints/; Commission Nationale de l'Informatique et des Libertés, "Cookies and other tracking devices: the Council of State issues its decision on the CNIL guidelines", June 29, 2020, https://www.cnil.fr/en/cookies-and-other-tracking-devices-council-state-issues-its-decision-cnil-guidelines; "ICO's Guidance On Cookie Consent And The PECR", Seers, accessed February 2023, https://seersco.com/articles/ico-guidance-and-the-pecr-cookie-consent/.

42 Nick Statt, "Apple Updates Safari's Anti-Tracking Tech With Full Third-Party Cookie Blocking," The Verge, March 24, 2020, https://www.theverge.com/2020/3/24/21192830/apple-safari-intelligent-tracking-privacy-full-third-party-cookie-blocking; see "Apple Block on Third Party Cookies will Change Digital Media Forever," GlobalData Thematic Intelligence, June 23, 2021, https://www.verdict.co.uk/apple-halts-third-party-cookies/; Christine Parizo, "Will Google Kill Third-Party Cookies," TechTarget, March 22, 2022, https://www.techtarget.com/searchcustomerexperience/tip/Will-Google-kill-third-party-cookies.

43 Breaux, *An Introduction to Privacy for Technology Professionals*, page 257.

44 Swire, Hemmings and Kirkland, "Online Privacy and ISPS," Chapter 9, 116.

45 Aloni Cohen, "CCPA, Cross-Device Tracking, and Probabilistic Identifiers," Tech Policy Press, accessed February 2023, https://www.protegopress.com/ccp-and-probabilistic-identifiers/.

46 For a detailed discussion on cross-device tracking, view Swire, Hemmings and Kirkland, "Online Privacy and ISPS."

47 Peter Tuckel and Harry O'Neill, "Ownership and Usage Patterns of Cell Phones: 2000-2005," AAPOR – ASA Section on Survey Research Methods, American Statistical Association, 2005, http://www.asasrms.org/Proceedings/y2005/files/JSM2005-000345.pdf.

48 "Mobile Fact Sheet," Pew Research Center, April 7, 2021, https://www.pewresearch.org/internet/fact-sheet/mobile/.

49 Andrew J. Blumberg and Peter Eckersley, "On Locational Privacy, and How to Avoid Losing it Forever," Electronic Frontier Foundation, August 2009, https://www.eff.org/wp/locational-privacy.

50 Breaux, *An Introduction to Privacy for Technology Professionals*, 273.

51 Breaux, *An Introduction to Privacy for Technology Professionals*, 273.

52 Alan Friedman, Robin Wilcox, Austin Manes, "Comparing the 5 Comprehensive Laws Passed by the US," Kramer Levin, June 10, 2022, https://www.kramerlevin.com/en/perspectives-search/comparing-the-5-comprehensive-privacy-laws-passed-by-us-states.html.

53 COPPA defines a child's location as personal data. Stacey Gray, "Policy Brief: Location Data Under Existing Privacy Laws," December 2020, https://fpf.org/wp-content/uploads/2020/12/FPF_Guide_Location_Data_v2.2.pdf. See *Protecting Consumer Privacy in an Era of Rapid Change: Recommendations for Business and Policymakers*, FTC Report, Federal Trade Commission, March 2012, https://www.ftc.gov/sites/default/files/documents/reports/federal-trade-commission-report-protecting-consumer-privacy-era-rapid-change-recommendations/120326privacyreport.pdf.

54 "App Store Review Guidelines," Apple Developer, accessed July 2023, https://developer.apple.com/app-store/review/guidelines/; "Developer Policy Center," Google Play, accessed July 2023, https://play.google.com/about/developer-content-policy/.

55 Dave Davies, "Surveillance and Local Police: How Technology is Evolving Faster Than Regulation," NPR, January 27, 2021, https://www.npr.org/2021/01/27/961103187/surveillance-and-local-police-how-technology-is-evolving-faster-than-regulation; "What's Wrong with Video Surveillance," ACLU, February 25, 2002, https://www.aclu.org/other/whats-wrong-public-video-surveillance.

56 Katz v. United States, 389 U.S. 347 (1967), accessed July 2023, https://supreme.justia.com/cases/federal/us/389/347/case.html; see United States v. Jones, 565 U.S. 400 (2012), accessed July 2023, https://supreme.justia.com/cases/federal/us/565/400/; see also Carpenter v. United States, 585 U.S. __ (2018), accessed July 2023, https://supreme.justia.com/cases/federal/us/585/16-402/; Louis Casiano, "New Orleans Reverses Facial Recognition Ban to Help Police Fight Crime; Privacy Experts are Wary," Fox News, December 1, 2022, https://www.foxnews.com/us/new-orleans-reverses-facial-recognition-ban-help-police-fight-crime-privacy-experts-are-wary; see Eli Brand, "New Orleans Mayor Signs Ordinance to Allow NOPD to Use Facial Recognition, WDSU News, July 28, 2022, https://www.wdsu.com/article/new-orleans-facial-recognition/40743163; see "Real-Time Crime Center," NOLA.gov, accessed July 2023, https://nola.gov/homeland-security/real-time-crime-center/.

57 Breaux, *An Introduction to Privacy for Technology Professionals*, 283.

58 "Figure 2: Different Views of Surveillance Video and Remote Sensing Sensors When Capturing the Same Scene," Research Gate, accessed July 2023, https://www.researchgate.net/figure/Different-views-of-surveillance-video-and-remote-sensing-sensors-when-capturing-the-same_fig1_343076694.

59 Anne Cavoukian, "Privacy by Design: The 7 Foundation Principles," Information and Privacy Commissioner of Ontario, revised January 2011, https://www.ipc.on.ca/wp-content/uploads/resources/7foundationalprinciples.pdf.

60 Katharina Koerner and Brandon Lalonde, "Cheering Emerging PETs: Global Privacy Tec Support on the Rise," January 24, 2023, *Privacy Advisor*, IAPP, https://iapp.org/news/a/cheering-emerging-pets-global-privacy-tech-support-on-the-rise/.

61 "Anonymity," Online Etymology Dictionary, accessed July 2023, https://www.etymonline.com/word/anonymity.

62 Three of the state comprehensive privacy laws—California, Colorado, and Virginia—provide definitions of deidentified data. Peter Karalis, "Analysis: Nothing Personal—States Are Eyeing De-Identified Data," February 7, 2022, https://news.bloomberglaw.

com/bloomberg-law-analysis/analysis-nothing-personal-states-are-eyeing-de-identified-data. Colorado, for example, defines deidentified as "data that cannot reasonably be used to infer information about, or otherwise be linked to, an identified or identifiable individual, or a device linked to such individual." Nanc Perkins, Jason Raylesberg, Sunneta Hazra, Ronald Lee and Jami Vibbert, "Colorado Enacts Broad Data Privacy Law, Following Lead of California and Virginia," Arnold & Porter, July 8, 2021, https://www.arnoldporter.com/en/perspectives/advisories/2021/07/colorado-enacts-broad-data-privacy-law.

63 "Anonymization: Managing Data Protection Risk Code of Practice," UK Information Commissioners Office, November 2012, https://ico.org.uk/media/1061/anonymisation-code.pdf.

64 "Anonymization: Managing Data Protection Risk Code of Practice," UK Information Commissioners Office.

65 "Anonymisation and Pseudonymisation," University College London, accessed July 2023, https://www.ucl.ac.uk/data-protection/guidance-staff-students-and-researchers/practical-data-protection-guidance-notices/anonymisation-and.

66 Breaux, An Introduction to Privacy for Technology Professionals, 162.

67 Edith Ramirez, "Protecting Consumer Privacy in the Digital Age: Reaffirming the Role of Consumer Control," Keynote Address of FTC Chairwoman Edith Ramirez at Technology Policy Institute Aspen Forum, August 22, 2016, https://www.ftc.gov/system/files/documents/public_statements/980623/ramirez_-_protecting_consumer_privacy_in_digital_age_aspen_8-22-16.pdf.

68 Breaux, An Introduction to Privacy for Technology Professionals, 163.

69 Paul Ohm, "Broken Promises of Privacy: Responding to the Surprising Failure of Anonymization," UCLA Law Review, August 13, 2009, https://papers.ssrn.com/sol3/papers.cfm?abstract_id=1450006.

70 See "Keeping Secrets: Anonymous Data Isn't Always Anonymous," Berkley School of Information, March 15, 2014, https://ischoolonline.berkeley.edu/blog/anonymous-data/; see Caroline Perry, "You're Not So Anonymous," The Harvard Gazette, October 18, 2011, https://news.harvard.edu/gazette/story/2011/10/youre-not-so-anonymous/

71 Gregory E. Simon, MD, MPH, Susan M. Shortreed, R. Yates Coley, PhD, Robert B. Penfold, Rebecca C. Rossom, Beth E. Waitzfelder, Katherine Sanchez, and Frances L. Lynch, "Assessing and Minimizing Re-identification Risk in Research Data Derived from Health Care Records," National Library of Medicine, March 29,2019, https://www.ncbi.nlm.nih.gov/pmc/articles/PMC6450246/.

72 Kobbi Nissim, Thomas Steinke, Alexandra Wood, Micah Altman, Aaron Bembenek, Mark Bun, Marco Gaboardi, David R. O'Brien, and Salil Vadhan, "Differential Privacy: A Primer for a Non-technical Audience," February 14, 2018, https://privacytools.seas.harvard.edu/files/privacytools/files/pedagogical-document-dp_new.pdf.

73 Nissim, Steinke, Wood, Altman, Bembenek, Bun, Gaboardi, O'Brien, and Vadhan, "Differential Privacy."

74 Hansi Lo Wang, "For the U.S. Census, Keeping Your Data Anonymous and Useful is a Tricky Balance," NPR, August 2, 2021, https://www.npr.org/2021/05/19/993247101/for-the-u-s-census-keeping-your-data-anonymous-and-useful-is-a-tricky-balance; see "Differential Privacy and the 2020 Census," U.S. Census Bureau, July 22, 2021, https://www.census.gov/library/fact-sheets/2021/differential-privacy-and-the-2020-census.html.

75 Simson Garfinkel, "Differential Privacy vs. the American Community Survey," Database Nation, December 22, 2022, https://www.linkedin.com/comm/pulse/differential-privacy-vs-american-community-survey-simson-garfinkel.

76 "Guidance Regarding Methods for De-Identification of Protected Health Information in Accordance with the Health Insurance Portability and Accountability Act (HIPAA) Privacy Rule," U.S. Department of Health and Human Services, October 25, 2022, https://www.hhs.gov/hipaa/for-professionals/privacy/special-topics/de-identification/index.html.

77 Protecting Consumer Privacy in an Era of Rapid Change, FTC Report, Federal Trade Commission.

78 Kristin Cohen, "Location, Health, and Other Sensitive Information: FTC Committed to Fully Enforcing the Law Against Illegal Use and Sharing of Highly Sensitive Data," Federal Trade Commission, July 11, 2022, https://www.ftc.gov/business-guidance/blog/2022/07/location-health-and-other-sensitive-information-ftc-committed-fully-enforcing-law-against-illegal.

79 Offensive Con, Blue Frost Security, accessed July 2023, https://www.offensivecon.org/trainings/2022/teepwn-breaking-trusted-execution-environments-extended-edition.html.

80 David Evans, Vladimir Kolesnikov, Mike Rosulek, "A Pragmatic Introduction to Secure Multi-Party Computation," NOW Publishers, April 15, 2020, https://www.cs.virginia.edu/~evans/pragmaticmpc/pragmaticmpc.pdf; Katharina Koerner, "Legal Perspectives on PETs: Homomorphic Encryption," July 20, 2021, https://medium.com/golden-data/legal-perspectives-on-pets-homomorphic-encryption-9ccfb9a334f; Lars Larson, "But What if We Just Use Encryption?—Practical GDPR for CTOs," *Elastisys Tech Blog,* June 30, 2021, https://elastisys.com/but-what-if-we-just-use-encryption-practical-gdpr-for-ctos/; Marcelo Corrales Compagnucci, Marck Fenwick, Mateo Aboy, Timo Minssen, "Supplementary Measures and Appropriate Safeguards for International Transfers of Personal Data after Schrems II," SSRN, February 23, 2022, https://papers.ssrn.com/sol3/papers.cfm?abstract_id=4042000.

81 Zero Knowledge Proofs, accessed July 2023, https://zk-learning.org.

82 The encryption discussion here follows Kaitlin Asrow, "Privacy Enhancing Technologies: Categories, Use Cases, and Considerations," Federal Reserve Bank of San Francisco, June 1, 2021, https://www.frbsf.org/banking/wp-content/uploads/sites/5/Privacy-Enhancing-Technologies_FINAL_V2_TOC-Update.pdf. For a more detailed discussion, see Cryptography and the Intelligence Community: Future of Encryption, National Academies Sciences Engineering Medicine (2022), https://www.nationalacademies.org/our-work/future-of-encryption; Breaux, An Introduction to Privacy for Technology Professionals, Chapter 3.

83 "Understanding Digital Signatures, Cybersecurity & Infrastructure Security Agency, February 01, 2021, https://www.cisa.gov/tips/st04-018.

84 See Latanya Sweeney, "Risk Assessments of Personal Identification Technologies for Domestic Violence Homeless Shelters," Carnegie Mellon University Technical Report, November 2005, https://dataprivacylab.org/projects/homeless/index.html; see generally Michael Platzer, "AI-Based Re-Identification Attacks – and How to Protect Against Them," Mostly AI, April 22, 2022, https://mostly.ai/blog/synthetic-data-protects-from-ai-based-re-identification-attacks.

85 Kaitlin Asrow, "Privacy Enhancing Technologies."

86 Data Protection Engineering, ENISA Report, European Union Agency for Cybersecurity, January 2022, https://www.enisa.europa.eu/publications/data-protection-engineering.

87 Proton Team, "Privacy Decrypted #3: Can encryption be broken?" Proton Blog, updated November 8, 2022, https://proton.me/blog/can-encryption-be-broken.

88 Peter Swire and DeBrae Kennedy-Mayo, "The Effects of Data Localization on Cybersecurity – Organizational Effects," SSRN, February 18, 2022 (revised June 16, 2023), https://papers.ssrn.com/sol3/papers.cfm?abstract_id=4030905.

89 "Confidentiality, Integrity, and Availability: The CIA Triad," Washington University in St. Louis, accessed July 2023, https://informationsecurity.wustl.edu/items/confidentiality-integrity-and-availability-the-cia-triad/.

90 Cybersecurity Framework, NIST, accessed July 2023, https://www.nist.gov/cyberframework.

91 Cybersecurity Framework, NIST, at 1.

92 Jerry Perullo, "Adversarial Risk Management," November 2021, https://www.fsisac.com/insights/adversarial-risk-management.

93 Shawn Robinson, "Successful Security in the High Crime Neighborhood of the Internet," October 31, 2019, https://www.linkedin.com/pulse/security-high-crime-neighborhood-internet-d-shawn-robinson.

94 Adam Shostack, Threat Modeling: Designing for Security (Indianapolis: Wiley, 2014), https://shostack.org/books/threat-modeling-book.

95 ATT&CK, MITRE, accessed July 2023, https://attack.mitre.org; Loren Kohnfelder and Praerit Garg, "The Threats to Our Products," Microsoft Interface, April 1, 1999, https://shostack.org/files/microsoft/The-Threats-To-Our-Products.docx.

96 "Repudiation Attack, OWASP, accessed July 2023, https://owasp.org/www-community/attacks/Repudiation_Attack.

97 "Forum on Cyber Resilience," National Academies Sciences Engineering, Medicine, accessed July 2023, https://www.nationalacademies.org/our-work/forum-on-cyber-resilience.

98 Shalanda D. Young, "Moving the U.S. Government Toward Zero Trust Cybersecurity Principles," Executive Office of the President, January 26,2022, https://www.whitehouse.gov/wp-content/uploads/2022/01/M-22-09.pdf.

99 Matthew Scholl, Kevin Stine, Joan Hash, Pauline Bowen, Arnold Johnson, Carla Dancy Smith, and Daniel I. Steinberg, "An Introductory Resource Guide for Implementing the Health Insurance Portability and Accountability Act (HIPAA) Security Rule, National Institute of Standards and Technology, October 2008, https://www.hhs.gov/sites/default/files/ocr/privacy/hipaa/administrative/securityrule/nist80066.pdf.

CHAPTER 4

Information Management and Privacy Risk Management

The first three chapters in this book have introduced key material in the study of privacy. Chapter 1 explored fundamental concepts for modern protection of privacy. Chapter 2 explained essential aspects of the U.S. legal system. Chapter 3 introduced the technological aspects of privacy. This chapter focuses on principles that businesses must address as they handle data: information management and privacy risk management.[1]

Almost every business, regardless of industry, faces a plethora of decisions in how to handle personal data. These decisions grow more complicated as consumers and regulators demand more from businesses related to the privacy and security of this personal data. Businesses that handle so-called sensitive data, which often includes medical, financial, or children's data, are expected to meet an even higher bar as they make decisions about how to collect, use, and possibly disseminate this data. Businesses that operate on a global scale, which is far more common with the internet than it once was, face cross-border data issues that include multiple sets of regulation related to privacy and security.

Businesses face significant costs to come into compliance with federal and state privacy requirements as well as legal requirements in other countries. When the EU General Data Protection Regulation (GDPR) was enacted in 2018, a joint survey by the IAPP and EY found that companies reported spending more than $1 million per year on GDPR compliance.[2] In the absence of a federal comprehensive privacy law in the United States, the Information Technology and Innovation Foundation (ITIF) estimated in 2022 that the yearly out-of-state cost for compliance in a scenario where all 50 states enact privacy laws would be approximately $100 billion per year.[3]

It is worth pointing out that the cost of mishandling personal data can be significant for a business, both for the short-term impact to the business' profits and also potentially for its long-term viability as a business.[4] For example, in 2022 IBM found that the global average cost of a data breach is more than $4 million, with costs even higher in health care and financial industries.[5] In the longer term, as it relates to the treatment of personal data, numerous studies have indicated that consumer trust (or lack thereof), can have a positive (or negative) impact on a consumer's decision to engage with a particular business.[6] According to Edelman's Trust Barometer, trust of a company is linked to purchase decisions, and ethics are more important in creating consumers' trust of a company than competence.[7] Cisco's 2022 survey reported that elements of trust are key to consumers' decisions to associate with a business. According to the research, consumers expect businesses to be both truthful and transparent about the handling of personal data, and also expect businesses to handle their personal data responsibly. More than 80 percent of participants in the survey reported that the way a business treats personal data is indicative of the degree to which the business respects its customers. Approximately 75 percent of those surveyed stated they would not buy from a business that they did not trust with their data.[8]

When examined through the lens of trust, privacy can be viewed as a core business priority that has the potential to increase consumer loyalty, improve brand perception, drive business outcomes, and lead to higher earnings.[9] This chapter begins by discussing best practices for developing an information management program that addresses privacy and other information management concerns, including security. The chapter then turns to an examination of privacy risk management, focusing on privacy impact assessments (PIAs), vendor/third-party risk assessments, and data breach readiness assessments. The chapter concludes with an overview of key global issues related to data traveling to or from the United States.

This material should be read in the context of more detailed discussions of legal rules in the other chapters of this book. Numerous chapters in the book look at the legal regulation of privacy, including Chapter 5 (State and Federal Regulators of Privacy), Chapter 8 (Medical Privacy), Chapter 9 (Financial Privacy), Chapter 10 (Education Privacy), Chapter 11 (Telecommunications and Marketing), and Chapter 12 (Workplace Privacy). Two chapters focus on state regulation of privacy – Chapter 6 (State Comprehensive Laws) and Chapter 7 (State Data Breach Notification Laws). Chapter 14 (The GDPR and International Privacy Issues) provides additional insight into the global landscape – with particular emphasis of the EU's GDPR. This chapter provides a management perspective on how to meet any and all such legal requirements.

This chapter draws heavily on the IAPP book *Privacy Program Management: Tools for Managing Privacy Within Your Organization.*[10] We recommend that book (or any update) for those wishing to gain a deeper understanding of these concepts.

loyalty, where businesses would be required to act in the best interests of those whose personal data is processed.[22]

Although established techniques exist for information security, such as installing firewalls or using industry-standard encryption for communications,[23] there is less consensus about good practice for many privacy issues. Laws vary across jurisdictions and industry sectors, and views about good practice often differ, both within an organization and as defined by external norms.[24]

The role of the privacy professional may include: researching laws, guidelines, common practices and tools; educating and communicating to the organization; designing and recommending policies; and monitoring and managing organizational risk. Privacy professionals engage in numerous tasks, such as alerting their organizations to these often-divergent perspectives. Privacy professionals also help their organizations manage a range of risks that can arise from processing personal information and do so in a manner consistent with meeting the organization's growth, profitability and other goals. Privacy professionals can assist the organization in identifying areas where compliance is difficult in practice, and in designing policies to close gaps between stated policies and actual operations.

Setting up the privacy team includes several important tasks. One early task for the privacy team is establishing responsibilities and a reporting structure that is appropriate to the size of the organization. It is important to note that the reporting structure can vary considerably from organization to organization.[25] The privacy team should designate a point of contact for privacy issues. Also, the privacy team should determine how to evaluate the work of the team. Another critical task that the privacy team can undertake is to operationalize privacy across the organization.[26] This involves: ensuring that an ethical code of conduct is in place for the organization, with privacy as a core value; developing practical approaches for addressing privacy challenges and designing to engender trust; and using privacy best practices throughout the privacy program's life cycle.[27]

Depending on the size of the organization, numerous individuals with various job titles may be part of the privacy team. The team may include the following roles:

- The **chief privacy officer (CPO)** is charged with developing and implementing policies related to the data processing and properly handling of personal information. The CPO is typically in a leadership position at the organization.[28]

- The **data protection officer (DPO)**, a term more widely used in Europe than the United States, is tasked with ensuring that the organization's processing and handling of personal information is in compliance with legal privacy requirements. The DPO cannot be directly involved with decision-making regarding data processing activities and cannot have other responsibilities within the organization that are in conflict with the DPO role.[29]

- The **chief legal officer** is responsible for the legal affairs of the entire organization. Privacy would be one area of concern among many. This function can also be performed by an attorney within the legal department; in a large organization, such an attorney might be dedicated to privacy matters.

- The **privacy engineer** works to ensure that compliance with legal requirements has occurred through the technical processes of the organization. Although concerned generally with compliance, the focus of a privacy engineer is also to ensure that the strategic direction of the organization better supports customers and those affected by the practices of the organization.[30] For many organizations, this job title can be relatively new, but typically is given a significant amount of responsibility.

- The **privacy manager** is responsible for development, maintenance and enforcement of privacy policies and procedures within an organization.[31] A privacy manager is typically a mid-level manager within the organization and may work within a particular business unit.

- The **privacy analyst** manages legal and operational risks related to personal information held by the organization. The privacy analyst assesses business unit operations. In addition, the privacy analyst develops policies, procedures, and trainings. The position of privacy analyst can be an entry-level position in many organizations.[32]

Within an organization, there can also be individuals who play more informal parts related to privacy: privacy champions and first responders. Privacy champions can be in an area of the organization. These are individuals within the organization who are passionate about privacy and/or who focus on the details of the legal requirements related to privacy. These individuals do their best to understand and implement privacy requirements. First responders are those individuals within an organization who are "on the front lines" so they respond when the organization deals with a specific difficulty.[33]

4.1.2 Data Sharing and Transfers

For a company seeking to develop a privacy program, it is critical to identify the types, sources, and uses of PI within an organization. For a company that already has a privacy program, it is important to remember that this is a process that requires constant updates as business practices evolve and technology changes. In addition, the regulatory landscape is not static.

Before examining the practices and controls related to data sharing and transfers, it is likely helpful to remember that data should be managed through its life cycle, and that approaches which are privacy-protecting in one stage may not be as appropriate to accomplish these goals in another stage. The stages of the **data life cycle** are:

- Data creation
- Data storage
- Data sharing and usage
- Data archival
- Data deletion[34]

It is also worth noting that legal requirements may arise at different stages of the life cycle. For example, numerous states have data destruction laws (discussed in Chapter 7) that mandate requirements in the last stage of the data life cycle.[35]

This section examines practices and controls for managing personal information in the often-complex flows among U.S. business enterprises, both within the United States and across geographic boundaries: data inventory, data classification, data flow mapping, and data accountability.

4.1.2.1 Data Inventory

It is important for an organization to undertake an inventory of the PI it collects, stores, uses, or discloses—whether within the organization or to outside entities. This inventory should include both customer and employee data records. It should document data location and flow as well as evaluate how, when, and with whom the organization shares such information—and the means for data transfer used.

One benefit of the inventory can be that it identifies risks that could affect reputation or legal compliance. If a problem subsequently occurs, current enforcement practices indicate penalties are likely to be less severe if the company has an established system of recording and organizing this inventory. The organization's inventory should be reviewed and updated on a regular basis. This sort of inventory is legally required for some institutions, such as those covered by the Gramm-Leach-Bliley Act (GLBA) Safeguards Rule discussed in Chapter 9.

4.1.2.2 Data Classification

After completing an inventory, the next step is to classify data according to its level of sensitivity. The data classification level defines the clearance of individuals who can access or handle that data, as well as the baseline level of protection appropriate for that data.

Most organizations handle different types of PI, such as personnel and customer records, as well as other information the organizations treats as sensitive, such as trade secrets and business plans. Data that is more sensitive generally requires greater protection than other information held by the organization. It may be segregated from less sensitive data, for instance, through access controls that enable only authorized individuals to retrieve the data, or even kept in an entirely separate system. If all data is held in the same system, temporary or lower-level employees might gain access to sensitive data. Holding all data in one system can increase the consequences of a single breach.

In the United States, classification is often important for compliance purposes because of sector-specific privacy and security laws. As discussed throughout this book, different rules apply to financial services information, medical information, and numerous other categories. An effective data classification system helps organizations address compliance audits for a particular type of data, respond to legal discovery requests without producing more information than necessary, and use storage resources in a cost-effective manner.

4.1.2.3 Data Flow Mapping

Once data has been inventoried and classified, data flows should be examined and documented. Questions to be answered in data mapping include: What data does the organization process? Where does the organization process data? Why does the organization process data? An organization chart can be useful to help map and document the systems, applications, and processes for handling data. Documenting data flows helps identify areas for compliance attention.[36]

There can be different approaches to data mapping. Two common examples are top-down and bottom-up. When undertaken primarily for regulatory purposes, the top-down approach is typically employed. This top-down approach often starts with the record of processing activities (RoPA) which is required under the GDPR. The RoPA process involves documenting the purpose for processing the PI; the parties to whom any PI was disclosed; the retention period for PI; and details about the safeguards in place for PI. Because this process can be difficult to validate and keep up to date, many organizations have chosen to automate the RoPA process by utilizing technological solutions.[37]

For privacy professionals, the bottom-up approach can be insightful and can also incorporate RoPA in one of the steps. This approach includes the following steps: understanding the data assets; data inventory and classification; delineating data processes; and documenting data lineage. With data assets, there are several important questions to ask: Is the environment for hosting data on-premises or cloud-based? Is the data in a structured or unstructured system? Does the organization utilize mainframes or legacy systems? Next, inventory and classification (discussed earlier in this subsection) help to ensure that the data carries with it both identities and risk values. The third step of delineating data processes can be accomplished using RoPA. Finally, data lineage adds context to the data; metadata is added to the mapping process. Data lineage can be used to identify "the original source of the data [;] the most critical data within the inventory"; and "how data sets are subsequently built and aggregated."[38]

4.1.2.4 Data Accountability

Privacy professionals often have significant responsibility within an organization for ensuring compliance with privacy laws and policies. Here are some helpful questions for privacy professionals when doing due diligence and for organizations to consider as they address privacy risks:

- **Where, how, and for what length of time is the data stored?** Data breach laws have focused increasing attention on where and how an organization stores PI.[39] The organization needs policies to address potential risks of data lost from laptops as well as centralized computer centers. An organization should also have retention policies that limit the time PI is stored. A limited retention period reduces the risk from data breach—no breach will occur once the data is removed from the system. Some laws require data to be deleted after a certain period or after the reason for collection has ceased to be relevant.[40]

- **How sensitive is the information?** As discussed, data should be classified according to its level of sensitivity. The data management cycle includes many participants—from the data owner to the privacy professional, the information security professional, the vendor (if applicable), the auditor (if applicable) and the end user. Ultimately, however, the data owner is responsible for assigning the appropriate sensitivity level or classification to the information based on company policy. Common categories include confidential, proprietary (i.e., property of the organization), sensitive, restricted (i.e., available to select few) and public (i.e., generally available).

- **Should the information be encrypted?** Under many breach notification laws, no notice is required if the lost PI is sufficiently encrypted or protected by some other effective technical protection. Such laws have encouraged greater use of encryption for stored data, and good security practices have included a wider use of encryption over time.[41] Encryption in transit has become far more widespread, including for emails and communications over the web that use HTTPS (the secure version of the widely used HTTP web protocol). On the other hand, encryption can be difficult to implement correctly and may reduce function in some applications. IT professionals should be consulted about how to take advantage of encryption while achieving other organizational goals.[42]
- **Will the information be transferred to or from other countries, and if so, how will it be transferred?** Because different countries have significantly different privacy laws, an organization should familiarize itself with the privacy requirements of both origination and destination countries for transborder data flows.
- **Who determines the rules that apply to the information?** U.S. privacy professionals have increasingly used some terms that are included in the GDPR—for example, a "controller" is an entity that "determines the purposes and means of the processing of personal data" and a "processor" is an entity that "processes personal data on behalf of the controller."[43] Similar terms for processor in the United States include "business associate" under the Health Insurance Portability and Accountability Act (HIPAA) or "service provider" under the GLBA. Privacy professionals should assess which organization determines the rules that apply to the processing of data. If an organization stores data on behalf of another, the organization should expect to be required to meet the privacy policy guarantees of the other entity (the controller) in the use and storage of such data. Most likely, a storing company (or processor) will be required to sign a contract to this effect.

- **How is the information to be processed, and how will these processes be maintained?** The procedures through which personal information is processed also must be defined. Steps should be taken to train staff members involved in the processes. Computers on which the information will be processed should be secured appropriately to minimize the risk of data leak or breach. Physical transfer of the data also should be secured.
- **Is the use of such data dependent upon other systems?** If the use of personal data depends on the working condition of other systems, such as a cloud provider or a specialized computer program, the condition of those systems must also be evaluated and updated if necessary. A system that is outdated may call for developing a new method or program for using the relevant data.

4.1.3 Privacy Program

A privacy program is critical for most organizations to establish accountability and legal compliance with how personal data is handled. At a minimum, the goals of a privacy program are to: demonstrate an effective and auditable framework to enable compliance with applicable privacy laws and regulations; promote trust and confidence in the organization's handling of personal data; respond effectively to requests by consumers; address privacy and security breaches; and continually monitor and improve the maturity of the privacy program.

In designing and administering a privacy program, an organization should consider and balance four types of business risks: legal risks, reputational risks, operational risks, and strategic risks.

- **Legal risks.** The organization must comply with applicable state, federal, and international laws regarding its use of information or potentially face litigation or regulatory sanctions such as consent decrees, which may last for many years.[44] The company must also comply with its contractual commitments, privacy promises, and commitments to follow industry standards, such as the Payment Card Institute Data Security Standard (PCI DSS).[45]
- **Reputational risks.** The organization can face reputational harm if it announces privacy policies but does not carry them out.[46] It may also face enforcement actions—particularly from the U.S. Federal Trade Commission (FTC).[47] An organization should seek to protect its reputation as a trusted institution with respected brands.

- **Operational risks.** The organization must ensure that its privacy program is administratively efficient. If a privacy program is too heavy-handed, it may interfere with relationships and inhibit lawful uses of PI that benefit the organization and its customers, such as for personalization or risk management.[48]
- **Strategic risks.** The organization must be able to receive an appropriate return on its investments in information, information technology, and information-processing programs in light of evolving privacy regulations, enforcement, and expectations.[49]

This section focuses on two main topics: the privacy program framework and the privacy operational life cycle.

4.1.3.1 Privacy Program Framework

With a privacy program framework, the organization designs a manageable approach to operationalizing the controls needed to handle and protect personal information. The term framework can refer to numerous processes, templates, tools, and standards that may assist with privacy program management. Using an appropriate privacy framework to build an effective privacy program can: (1) help achieve compliance with the various privacy laws and regulations relevant to the organization; (2) support business commitments and objectives relating to stakeholders, customers, and vendors; and (3) serve as a competitive advantage by reflecting the value that the organization places on the protection of personal data, thereby encouraging trust.

Steps in the privacy program framework include: developing the privacy program framework; implementing the privacy program framework; and ensuring appropriate metrics for the privacy program framework. Before undertaking the development of a privacy program, the organization should lay the groundwork for the program by developing the privacy mission statement, and/or the privacy vision. The privacy mission statement can be incorporated into the organization's overall mission statement or can be a standalone statement; however, the privacy mission statement should align with the organization's overall purposes or objectives. Typically, the privacy mission statement is a concise statement describing the core function of privacy within the organization. For example, Stanford University's privacy mission statement is to "enable Stanford to navigate a dynamic future in privacy through transparent, ethical, and innovative uses of personal data."[50] As is mentioned in the Stanford approach, ethics can be one of the guiding principles when designing the organization's approach to privacy. When ethical considerations are baked into the privacy vision for the organization, the approach to privacy can be motivated by building trustworthy relationships with individuals and be less focused on the desire to avoid fines imposed by multiple regulatory schemes.[51]

Developing the privacy program framework involves (1) creating organizational privacy policies, procedures, standards, and guidelines (see Section 4.1.4); and (2) defining privacy program activities. Privacy program activities can cover a variety of topics including: data inventories, data flows, and data classifications designed to identify what personal information the organization processes; risk assessment (such as PIAs); education and awareness; monitoring and responding to the regulatory environment; monitoring internal privacy policy compliance; incident response; remediation oversight; audits; and handling of complaints by customers and regulators.

Implementing the privacy program framework involves numerous components. The organization must communicate the framework to internal and external stakeholders. The organization must understand applicable laws and regulations, and seek to align with regulatory changes. Ensuring continuous alignment with applicable laws and regulations can be challenging, and is also a multifaceted requirement. The organization needs to understand territorial laws and regulations; sectoral and industry laws and regulations; penalties for noncompliance with these laws and regulations; and the scope of authority of oversight agencies. The organization must review data sharing agreements, including international data sharing agreements, vendor agreements, and affiliate/subsidiary agreements.

Ensuring appropriate metrics for the privacy program framework is also critical. The four main steps for ensuring these metrics are (1) identifying intended audience for metrics; (2) defining reporting sources; (3) defining privacy metrics for oversight and governance; and (4) identifying systems/application collection points. Notably, although defining privacy metrics can vary by organizations, there are numerous topics to consider. Compliance metrics can include: responses to data subject requests, disclosures to third parties, incidents (such as breaches), employees trained, PIA metrics, and privacy risk indicators. Additional privacy metrics beyond those specifically focused on compliance include privacy program return on investment (ROI), business resilience metrics, privacy program maturity level, trend analysis, and resource utilization.

4.1.3.2 Privacy Operational Life Cycle

The privacy operational life cycle should consider measurements, improvements, and the ability to support the program. This approach focuses on refining and improving the privacy processes, with the goal of continuously monitoring and upgrading the program. The privacy operational life cycle has four stages: assess, protect, sustain, and respond.

Assessing or measuring an organization's privacy regime includes: document the baseline of the privacy program; evaluate processors and third parties; identify operational risks; and document the assessment.

Protecting information assets, through the implementation of industry-leading privacy and security control and technology, includes: reviewing access controls and technical controls; reviewing incident response plan; and integrating privacy requirements into functional areas of the organization (such as Human Resources).

Sustaining or evaluating the privacy program through communication, training, and management actions involves several steps. These include: monitoring compliance with privacy policies; monitoring regulatory changes; auditing compliance with privacy policies and standards; and holding employee, management, and contractor trainings.

Responding has numerous possible topics ranging from supporting consumer rights to addressing privacy incidents. Organizations are expected to respond to consumer requests for information as well as ensure privacy rights are respected. Request from consumers can relate to numerous topics, including access, redress, and correction. Consumers may also make requests concerning rights, such as the right to erasure or the right to be informed. Organizations must also address consumer complaints as well as any appeal processes. With regard to privacy incidents, organizations are expected to have measures in place related to legal compliance, incident response planning, incident detection, incident handling, incident reduction techniques, and incident metrics.

4.1.4 Privacy Policy and Privacy Notice

This section focuses on two interrelated topics: the privacy policy and the privacy notice. In this chapter, the term privacy policy is used to refer to the internal document in an organization that is used to implement privacy goals and strategic vision. The privacy policy informs relevant employees and contractors about how PI must be handled. A privacy notice is an external statement that provides transparency concerning the organization's privacy practices and is directed at customers (and potential customers), users, and employees, in certain instances. Both the privacy policy and the privacy notice describe how personal information will be collected, used, shared, and stored. If a U.S. organization violates a promise made in a privacy policy that is also communicated in the privacy notice, then the FTC or state attorney general may bring an enforcement action for a deceptive practice.[52]

4.1.4.1 Privacy Policy

The **privacy policy** is a high-level document that helps an organization meet policy goals contained within an organization's privacy vision or mission statement. One of the main focuses of the privacy policy is to explain how personal information is handled by the organization. This means privacy policies are central to privacy programs. As discussed in the numerous chapters in this book, privacy policies also are important as legal documents. It should be noted that privacy policies are distinct from the standards, guidelines, and handbooks that focus on methodologies for meeting policy goals.[53]

Typically, the privacy policy will have the following components: purpose, scope, applicability, roles and responsibilities, compliance, and sanctions for noncompliance.

- **Purpose.** The purpose explains why the policy exists and explains the goals of the organization's privacy program.
- **Scope.** The scope defines the resources (such as information) that the privacy policy protects.
- **Applicability.** Applicability explains whether the privacy policy applies to customers, employees, contractors, third parties, etc.
- **Roles and responsibilities.** The privacy policy assigns responsibilities for privacy to roles throughout the organization. The privacy policy delineates responsibilities of leaders, managers, and employees as well as contractors and vendors.
- **Compliance.** Compliance is typically one of the main topics in the privacy policy, and generally entails monitoring activities and enforcement through disciplinary actions. Organizations should keep records of actions taken for noncompliance with the privacy policy.
- **Penalties and sanctions for noncompliance.** Noncompliance with laws and regulations can subject the organization to significant penalties and sanctions. Privacy practitioners should keep abreast of the changing legal and regulatory requirements to which the organization is subject.

An organization must determine whether to have one privacy policy that applies globally to all its activities or multiple policies. One policy will work if an organization has a consistent set of values and practices for all its operations. Multiple policies may make sense for a company that has well-defined divisions or lines of business, especially if each division uses customer data in very different ways, does not typically share PI with other divisions, and is perceived in the marketplace as a different business.

Sometimes separate corporations decide to use a common privacy policy. For financial holding companies, the same corporate name may be used by multiple subsidiaries and affiliates, and a single privacy policy can avoid complications in handling PI. For example, mutual funds and their advisors are separate corporations, but may decide to adopt a joint privacy policy and a joint form of notice.[54] All the mutual funds in a corporate "family" may use joint notices.

Conversely, using multiple policies can create complications. One division's privacy policy may be more stringent in a particular way than another division's, and prevent sharing of customer information between two parts of the same company. Where multiple policies are used, it makes sense to align policies as closely as possible so as not to hinder cooperation between divisions.

With all these considerations, an organization should not finalize a privacy policy without legal consultation followed by executive approval. If a policy is too strict, then open-ended statements or overly ambitious security promises can result in legal penalties or reputational problems if the organization cannot satisfy its promises. If the policy is not strict enough, then consumers, regulators, and the press may criticize the company for its failure to protect privacy.

If a privacy policy is revised, the organization should announce the change first to employees, then to both current and former customers through its privacy notice. According to the FTC, companies should obtain express affirmative consent (opt-in) before making material retroactive changes to privacy representations, noting that a "material" change "at a minimum includes sharing consumer information with third parties after committing at the time of collection not to share the data."[55]

Additionally, an organization's privacy policy will need to be updated as its information collection, use and transfer needs evolve. To ensure this update occurs on a timely basis, an organization should ensure it reviews the privacy policy periodically. With the rapid changes in technology and business practices, this evaluation should be scheduled to take place at least once a year. As such changes occur, a new version of the privacy policy must be drafted to replace the older version. Replacement of the policy must occur systematically across all areas of posting (physical and electronic) to reduce the risk that representations made under different versions of the policy will be implemented. Privacy policies should reflect the policy revision date along with a version number, if used.

For compliance purposes, it is useful to save and store older versions of the privacy policy and its associated notice. These earlier versions may be useful internally, for example, to show what representations have been made in connection with which customer transactions. The earlier versions may also be useful in the event of an enforcement action, to reduce the risk that the company will be held to an incorrect set of representations. Data should only be used in compliance with the policy notice in effect at the time the data was collected, unless the data subject later agrees to the terms of a revised notice.

4.1.4.2 Privacy Notice

A privacy notice is an external statement that provides transparency concerning the organization's privacy practices—how it collects, uses, shares, retains, and discloses personal information based on the organization's privacy policy. In certain instances, a privacy notice must be provided to consumers when an organization collects information from individuals. Importantly, a privacy notice should be considered a promise that organization makes to consumers.[56]

Both the privacy notice and the privacy policy describe how personal information will be collected, used, shared, and stored. While the privacy policy is typically an internal document directed at employees and contractors, the privacy notice is directed at customers (and potential customers), users, and employees, in certain instances. The goal of the privacy notice should be to assist the recipient in making informed decisions concerning privacy and to facilitate the reader in exercising rights.

The content of privacy notices is based on laws as well as fair information practices such as the Organisation for Economic Co-operation and Development (OECD) Guidelines and Asia-Pacific Economic Cooperation (APEC) Principles. Some laws, such as HIPAA (see Chapter 8), specify the content of privacy notices.

The easiest method to communicate an organization's privacy notice, as well as to review the privacy notices of competitors or business partners, is to review the relevant organizations' websites. Organizations may use multiple methods to communicate privacy notices to consumers and other external stakeholders.

- **Make the notice accessible online.** The websites of most organizations, even those primarily involved in offline commerce, today contain the privacy notice. It is standard to have a link from the company's front page.
- **Make the notice accessible in places of business.** Clearly post the organization's privacy notice at the location of business in areas of high customer traffic and in legible form. Organization staff also should have ready access to copies of the up-to-date company privacy policy in case a customer wishes to obtain a copy for review.
- **Provide updates and revisions.** For financial institutions, GLBA requires that customers receive the privacy notice annually, with clear notice of the customer's right with respect to opt-outs.[57] Institutions without this sort of required updating will need to provide good notice when the privacy policy is revised, with express customer consent for material changes and a clear opportunity to opt out for smaller changes.
- **Ensure that the appropriate personnel are knowledgeable about the policy.** Organization staff who interact with PI should receive training in the organization's privacy policy. HIPAA creates specific training requirements for all employees of covered entities.[58] Especially for employees working with sensitive data, organizations should provide regular training and keep records of which employees have been trained.

As one type of appropriate training, customer service representatives (CSRs), such as in customer call centers, should receive a summary statement or script that describes the privacy notice and can be used to answer customer questions. CSRs should have a full copy of the privacy notice in their standard reference material and should retain the ability to send or direct customers to a copy of the privacy notice that they can review in detail. They should know how to escalate privacy issues or incidents once observed.

As data practices has evolved and become more complex, many privacy notices have become quite lengthy. Companies over time have increasingly used a layered privacy notice approach. The basic idea is to offer "layers" that provide the key points on top in a short notice but give users the option to read a detailed notice or click through to greater detail on particular parts of the notice. Users typically click a link or scroll to read more about a particular topic.[59]

- **The short notice** is the top layer. Often using a standard format, it summarizes the notice's scope as well as basic points about the organization's practices for personal information collection, choice, use, and disclosure. Details for contacting the organization on information privacy matters are also included along with links to the full notice.
- **The full notice** is the bottom layer. Often referenced from the short notice via a hyperlink, it is a comprehensive information disclosure that articulates the organization's privacy notice in its entirety. The full notice is thus available for end users who are interested. The full notice also guides an organization's employees on permitted data practices and can be used for accountability by enforcement agencies or the general public.

Another way that organizations help facilitate meaningful choice is by using a "just-in-time" notice, which follows the principle of notice "at or before the point of information collection" or before a user accepts a service or product. Many websites choose to provide a link on every page to cover passive information collection. The best choice is an easy-to-find location, in a font that is no less prominent than other links on the page.

Finally, an organization can provide transparent privacy notices as well as user control through the use of a privacy dashboard. A dashboard offers a summary of privacy-related information in a format that is intended to be easy to access and navigate.

When designing a privacy notice, it is important for the organization to consider intended audience and how the user will view the privacy policy (on a computer screen or on a mobile device).

Numerous privacy challenges arise in the mobile environment because of the vast amount of personalized information available on mobile devices. Privacy issues concerning geolocation data were previously discussed. Other categories of data are created more often on mobile devices than on traditional computers, including text messages, metadata from telephone calls, medical monitoring, and other information generated by the numerous apps that users download.

The small screens available on most mobile devices make notices an especially challenging issue. Small screens make it difficult to convey the amount of information previously provided in privacy notices to laptops and desktops.[60] Because of the complexity of the issues regarding privacy in the mobile environment, the FTC has recommended best practices for platforms, advertising networks, app developers, and app developer networks.[61] Overarching principles to address privacy and security in the mobile environment include privacy by design (or even privacy by default), transparency, and simplification of consumer choices.[62] Privacy practitioners should be aware that privacy notices have been criticized in numerous ways including being written in "legalese"—dense prose, written by lawyers to reduce the risk of enforcement actions, and difficult to understand. When privacy notices are written in this way, research suggests that users rarely read these privacy notices.[63]

4.1.5 Managing User Preferences and User Requests

In following their privacy policies, organizations can face management challenges on topics including how to manage user preferences and respond to user requests related to consumer rights. Legal rules may set basic requirements for what must be done, but privacy professionals must often choose options within those requirements and ensure that implementation occurs correctly.

Choice of the individual is a key concept related to processing of personal information by a company. In this context, there are two central concepts of choice. The individual can consent to processing by opting in or the individual can withhold (or revoke) consent by opting out. Prior to discussing the concepts of opting in and opting out, it is important to discuss choice. Individuals who do not have a choice about the processing of their personal information should not be led to believe that they do. Individuals who have a choice should be given the ability to exercise that choice. If consent is required by a law or regulation, the organization must ensure that it properly obtains this consent. For example, U.S. state privacy laws increasingly prohibit so-called "dark patterns" as a legitimate form of consent. Dark patterns are generally defined as any interface designed to substantially subvert an end user's autonomy.[64]

The discussion here illustrates major areas where user preferences are handled through opt-in, opt-out, or no option, and then examines management issues for handling user preferences and customer access and redress requests.

4.1.5.1 Opt-in, Opt-out, and No Option

Privacy professionals should become aware of situations that call for different approaches to consumer preferences: notably, opt-in, opt-out, or no option.

Opt-in is sometimes called affirmative or express consent. Some U.S. federal privacy laws require **affirmative consumer consent**, or **opt-in**, before data is used or collected. As discussed in Chapter 5, the Children's Online Privacy Protection Act (COPPA) requires express consent from a parent before a child's PI is collected.[65] The HIPAA requires opt-in consent before protected health information (PHI) is disclosed to third parties, subject to important exceptions discussed in Chapter 8.[66]As detailed in Chapter 9, the Fair Credit Reporting Act (FCRA) requires opt-in before a consumer's credit report may be provided to an employer, lender, or other authorized recipient.[67] The FTC believes that opt-in consent should occur before PI collected under one privacy notice is processed under a materially changed privacy notice.[68]

Some industry segments commonly employ opt-in, such as email marketers that send a confirmation email requiring a response from the subscriber before the subscriber receives actual marketing emails. This email approach is sometimes called "double opt-in" or "confirmed opt-in," because a consumer first indicates interest in the mailing list and then confirms that interest in response to the follow-up email. In addition, the European Union takes a general position that opt-in consent is the appropriate way for marketing to occur, and this position is underscored in the General Data Protection Regulation (GDPR), as discussed in Chapter 14. Opt-in is often the preferred consent mechanism when collecting sensitive information such as a customer's geolocation data.

In many instances in the United States, it is common practice for companies to offer an **opt-out**, sometimes referred to as **consumer choice**, before customer information is sold or shared with third parties. Although a less stringent approach to using or collecting consumers' data than the opt-in approach, this privacy approach nonetheless creates an enforceable promise. If an individual sells the information of individuals who have opted out, the FTC or state enforcers may bring suit under the unfair and deceptive trade practices laws.

Some U.S. statutes require that companies provide consumers with the opportunity to opt-out. As discussed in Chapter 9, the GLBA requires that an individual have the opportunity to opt out before a financial institution transfers the customer's PI to an unaffiliated third party for the latter's own use. As discussed in Chapter 11, the Video Privacy Protection Act (VPPA) requires providing an opportunity for a consumer to opt out before covered movie and other rental data is provided to a third party. Also detailed in Chapter 11, the Controlling the Assault of Non-Solicited Pornography and Marketing Act (CAN-SPAM Act) requires email marketers to provide consumers with a means to opt out of unwanted communications. The Do Not Call rules provide the opportunity to opt out of telemarketing phone calls, both in general or on a company-by-company basis.

Opt-outs are required for companies that subscribe to any number of self-regulatory systems. For instance, the Data & Marketing Association has long operated an opt-out system for consumers who do not wish to receive commercial mail sent to their homes.[69] The Network Advertising Initiative (NAI), TrustArc, and the Digital Advertising Alliance (DAA) operate opt-out systems in connection with online advertising.[70]

In certain circumstances, the consumer is provided **no option when an organization** uses or collects the consumer's data because that organization has been given implied authority to share PI. The 2010 preliminary FTC staff report, "Protecting Consumer Privacy in an Era of Rapid Change," called these situations "commonly accepted practices." For example, a consumer who orders a product online expects her PI to be shared with the shipping company, the credit card processor and others who are engaged in fulfilling the transactions. The consumer does not expect to have to sign an opt-in or be offered an opt-out option for the shipping company to learn the address.

In addition to product fulfillment, other examples provided by the FTC include "internal operations such as improving services offered, fraud prevention, legal compliance and first-party marketing" by the seller to the customer.[71] The FTC received public comments that the term "commonly accepted practices" would not work well for companies providing innovative services. The final report, in 2012, addressed the same issue by saying: "Companies do not need to provide choice before collecting and using consumers' data for practices that are consistent with the context of the transaction, consistent with the company's relationship with the consumer, or as required or specifically authorized by law."[72]

4.1.5.2 Managing User Preferences

Effective management of user preferences can become quite challenging, especially for organizations that interact with their customers with multiple channels and for multiple products. The following are some of these challenges:

- The **scope** of an opt-out or another user preference can vary. As mentioned above, financial institutions must provide an opt-out by law prior to sharing personal information with third parties, but sharing with affiliates can be done without offering such an opt-out. An organization must decide how broadly an opt-out or another user preference will apply. Some opt-out rules are by channel, such as specific limits on phone calls or commercial emails.

- The **mechanism** for providing an opt-out or another user preference can also vary. A good rule of thumb is that the channel for marketing should be the channel for exercising a user preference. This rule is written into law for the CAN-SPAM Act, where an email solicitation must be exercisable by the consumer through an online mechanism; it is not acceptable under the law to require customers to mail or call in their opt-out.[73] Similarly, if communication with a customer is done via a website, good practice is to enable user preferences to be expressed through a web channel, and not to insist on mailing or a phone call.
- **Linking** a user's interactions through multiple channels, including in person, by phone, by email or by web, can be a management challenge when customers interact with an organization. Good practice is for the organization to implement the opt-out or other user preference across channels and platforms. Under GLBA, a bank receiving an opt-out request from a customer must comply across all communications regardless of the media used to communicate the request.[74]
- The **time period** for implementing user preferences is sometimes provided by law. For instance, the CAN-SPAM Act and Telemarketing Sales Rules mandate specific time periods for processing customer preferences.[75]
- **Third-party vendors** often process PI on behalf of the company that has the customer relationship. In such instances, the user preferences expressed to the first organization should be honored by the vendor.[76]

It is important to note that choice and control should be offered to individuals even after the opt-in stage. In other words, when individuals can freely give consent, they must be able to freely revoke that consent. In certain circumstances, laws and regulations may require an organization to provide individuals with access to their personal information, as well as information about the processing performed on it and to allow individuals to correct this information.

4.1.5.3 Responding to User Requests Related to Consumer Rights

Many federal and state laws provide individuals with rights of control related to their personal information. Although these rights are not encompassed in one federal law in the United States, numerous federal laws across sectors include these rights. Also, state laws grant individuals these types of rights. These rights include: the right to access; the right to correction (or rectification); the right to delete; the right to portability; the right against automated decision-making; and the right to nondiscrimination.

Individuals typically exercise these rights by making a request to a business or government agency. Typically, the business or government agency has a defined period to provide a timely response. If the individual's request is denied, the individual may have the right to request that the business or government agency reconsider, often referred to as a right to appeal. If the individual is dissatisfied, the person may complain to a regulator.

Some U.S. laws provide consumers with clear rights to access the PI held about them. For instance, individuals have the right to access their credit reports under FCRA and rectify incorrect data.[77] Patients can access their medical records under HIPAA, with records that the patient believes are incorrect noted as such in the patient files.[78] Under the Judicial Redress Act of 2015, the United States expressly extended the right to a civil action against a U.S. government agency for qualifying non-U.S. individuals to obtain access to covered records, as well as rectification of incorrect records.[79] In the European Union, access and the opportunity to correct mistakes are required by the GDPR.[80] Where customer access is not required under a specific statute, access is included in statements of fair information practices such as the OECD Guidelines and the APEC Principles.[81]

4.2 Privacy Risk Management

Privacy risk management is an important topic for organizations as they deal with privacy concerns. Privacy risk management is a process that identifies and assesses the risks to an organization's information assets and then implements appropriate mitigation strategies to reduce or eliminate these risks.[82]

According to the National Institute of Standards and Technology (NIST), privacy risk management is intended to "help enterprises weigh the benefits of data processing against the risk of doing so and determine which risk response measure should be adopted."[83] According to resources from the Information Systems Audit and Control Association (ISACA), privacy risk management is intended to build consumer trust by safeguarding personal data throughout the data life cycle.[84] Having an organizational code of ethics in place may help in assessing the benefits and risk of processing personal data. A code of ethics focuses on topics such as: how to respect the individuals whose personal data is held by the organization; what are the downstream uses of the personal data; what are the consequences of utilizing analytical tools; whether to collect data that the organization does not need; and how should the organization design practices to ensure transparency, accountability, and auditability.[85]

Privacy risk is defined as "the likelihood that individuals will experience problems resulting from data processing, and the impact of these problems should they occur."[86] Privacy risks focus on data processing throughout the data life cycle such as collection, storage, adaptation (or alteration), transmission, and dissemination. Example of privacy risks include: lack of appropriate safeguards; third party access; lack of encryption; mobile malware; social media attacks; social engineering; and outdated security software.[87]

As discussed below, privacy risk management activities often include conducting PIAs, vendor/third-party risk assessments, and data breach readiness assessments.

4.2.1 Privacy Impact Assessments

From a practical standpoint, privacy risk management includes: privacy risk assessment (assess privacy risk); privacy risk treatment (select security and privacy controls); and privacy controls implementation (implement security and privacy controls). PIAs, similar to data protection impact assessments (DPIAs), typically combine privacy risk assessment and privacy risk treatment. In some instances (and under some regulatory schemes), the PIA can be restricted to only privacy risk assessment while other PIAs may include privacy risk assessment, privacy risk treatment, and privacy controls implementation.[88] According to NIST, PIAs provide an analysis of how personal information is handled to: (1) ensure handling conforms to applicable legal, regulatory, and policy requirements regarding privacy; (2) determine the risks and effects of collecting, maintaining, and disseminating personal information in identifiable form; and (3) examine and evaluate protections and alternative processes for handling information to mitigate potential privacy risks.[89]

The core of the PIA process is privacy risk assessment, which focuses on determining the level of privacy risk by looking at two variables. The first is the privacy impact, which focuses on the privacy harm to individuals and businesses. The second variable is the likelihood of privacy harm given the controls. For this assessment (or calculation), the term "privacy harms" is key. It can include loss of self-determination (such as loss of autonomy, exclusion, loss of liberty, and physical harm), discrimination, loss of trust, and economic loss.[90]

4.2.2 Vendor/Third-Party Risk Assessments

Many U.S. organizations elect to outsource information processing to an outside vendor or plan to sell the collected information to a third party. Specific precautions must be taken if a company plans to share personal data with a third-party data processor.[91]

Companies are responsible for the actions of vendors they contract to collect, analyze, catalog, or otherwise provide data management services on the company's behalf.[92] The claims in a privacy policy also apply to third parties when they are working with an organization's data. To ensure the responsibility and security of data once it is in the hands of a contractor or vendor, precautions to consider incorporating in written contracts include:

- **Confidentiality provision.** Contractors and vendors involved in personal information collection for an organization—or with whom an organization shares data—should be required to sign a contract containing a confidentiality provision before engaging in business that uses the information.
- **No further use of shared information.** The contract with the vendor managing personal information on the organization's behalf should specify that the data be used only for the purposes contracted.
- **Use of subcontractors.** If the vendor intends to use subcontractors in the collection, use, or processing of personal information, the contractor organization should require all subcontractors to follow the privacy and security protection terms in the vendor's contract (which, in turn, should be consistent with the organization's own privacy protection terms). Vendor contracts should also address whether the data can flow across borders to ensure that the organization's policy on this issue is not violated.
- **Requirement to notify and to disclose breach.** An organization should require prompt notification in the event of a data breach or breach of contract. Details of the breach should be disclosed promptly and in detail.

- **Information security provisions.** Contracts may include provisions concerning specific security controls; encryption of data in transit, on media and on portable devices; network security; access controls; segregation of data; employee background checks; audit rights and so on.
- **End of relationship.** The contract with the vendor should contemplate the termination of the relationship and how the data will be handled at that time. In particular, the contract should include a provision concerning the return of the data at the conclusion of the relationship or the deletion of the data after a certain timeframe. In addition, the contract may include provisions to address either the return or the deletion of the data while the relationship is ongoing—particularly if the organization suspects or is investigating potential misuse of specific data by the vendor.[93]

Vendor due diligence focuses on a procuring organization having specific standards and processes in place for vendor selection. A prospective vendor should be evaluated against these standards. Standards for selecting vendors may include:

- **Reputation.** A vendor's reputation with other companies can be a valuable gauge of the vendor's appropriate collection and use of personal data. Requesting and contacting references can help determine a vendor's reputation.
- **Financial condition and insurance.** The vendor's finances should be reviewed to ensure the vendor has sufficient resources in the case of a security breach and subsequent litigation. A current and sufficient insurance policy can also protect the procuring organization in the event of a breach.
- **Information security controls.** A service provider should have sufficient security controls in place to ensure the data is not lost or stolen. Service providers often provide evidence of their controls, such as a certification by an auditor that an organization is compliant with the SOC 2 controls defined by the American Institute of Certified Public Accountants.[94]
- **Point of transfer.** The point of transfer between the procuring organization and the vendor is a potential security vulnerability. Secure transfer mechanisms should be developed and maintained.

- **Disposal of information.** Appropriate destruction of data in any format or media is a key component of information management—for both the contracting organization and its vendors. As discussed in Chapter 9, the Disposal Rule under the Fair and Accurate Credit Transactions Act of 2003 (FACTA) sets forth required disposal protections for financial institutions. The Disposal Rule requirements provide a good baseline for disposal of PI more generally.
- **Employee training and user awareness.** The vendor should have an established system for training its employees about its responsibilities in managing personal or sensitive information.
- **Vendor incident response.** Because of the potentially significant costs associated with a data breach, the vendor should clearly explain in advance its provisions for responding to any such breach, with required cooperation to meet the organization's business and legal needs.
- **Audit rights.** Organizations should be able to monitor the vendor's activities to ensure it is complying with contractual obligations. Audit needs can sometimes be satisfied through periodic assessments or reports by independent trusted parties regarding the vendor's practices.[95]

The high-profile breach of SolarWinds resulted in important lessons for vendor management. SolarWinds was a company that provided software to more than 18,000 organizations. In 2020, SolarWinds' software system was compromised by hackers. Subsequently, SolarWinds inadvertently sent out software updates to its customers that included this malicious code. Hackers used the malicious code to create backdoors that ultimately permitted them to spy on the customers of SolarWinds, including Fortune 500 businesses and multiple agencies in the U.S. government. The example of SolarWinds highlights the risks associated with vendors and demonstrates the devastating consequences that can result.[96]

According to a recent IAPP survey, the most common type of risk assessment performed by organizations is the vendor/third-party risk assessment. Note that the more an organization relies on vendors and third parties, the more complex the assessment can be. When conducting a vendor/third-party risk assessment, and organization should consider doing the following:

- Review data sources, data types, data location, local regulatory requirements, data retention period, minimum safeguards, and additional processing purposes (such as subcontracts)

- Determine whether a PIA or DPIA has been conducted for the data processing operations performed by the third party
- Review potential data uses that may impact the level of risks for individuals, such as artificial intelligence (AI) and cloud computing
- Review whether the third party has certifications such as SOC 2 or the PCI DSS
- Disclose to customers any use of subcontractors to process personally identifiable information
- Inform customers of any intended changes concerning the addition or replacement of subcontractors[97]

4.2.3 Risks Related to Information Security

As discussed in detail in Chapter 3, information security is the protection of information for the purpose of preventing loss, unauthorized access, or misuse.[98] Information security requires an ongoing assessment of threats and risks to information as well as the procedures and controls to preserve the information, consistent with three key attributes:

- **Confidentiality.** Access to data is limited to authorized parties
- **Integrity.** Assurance that the data is authentic and complete
- **Availability.** Knowledge that the data is accessible, as needed, by those who are authorized to use it[99]

Security controls are mechanisms put in place to prevent, detect, or correct a security incident. The three types of security controls are:

- **Physical controls**, such as locks, security cameras, and fences
- **Administrative controls**, such as incident response procedures and training
- **Technical controls**, such as firewalls, antivirus software, and access logs[100]

Information security is different from information privacy. Generally, information security is the protection of information, whether it is personal or other types of information, from unauthorized access, use, and disclosure. Information privacy notably includes deciding what sorts of use and disclosure of personal information should be authorized. Despite this distinction, the two concepts are similar and overlap in certain respects. Information security is a necessary component of privacy protection—if security is breached, then privacy controls will not be effective. Information privacy and information security both include the use, and confidentiality of as well as access to personal information. Information privacy, however, also involves the individual's (often called the data subject in European usage) right to control the data, such as rights to notice and choice.

The NIST Cybersecurity Framework is a voluntary tool for organizations to better manage and reduce cybersecurity risks. The framework can be used as a strategic planning tool to assess risks. Core elements of the NIST Cybersecurity Framework include:

- **Identify**, which looks at people, systems, data, and capabilities to understand what a potential risk could be.
- **Protect**, which focuses on safeguards for risks that an organization wants to mitigate.
- **Detect** is defined as activities that identify a cybersecurity incident such as anomalies in the network.
- **Respond** refers to what activities an organization takes when there is an incident.
- **Recover** is defined as plans to restore business operations from a cybersecurity incident.[101]

4.2.4 Data Breach Readiness Assessments

A data breach readiness assessment examines the level of risk of a data breach coupled with the likelihood and severity of a personal data breach. In a data breach readiness assessment, the following factors are examined in determining the likelihood and severity of a personal data breach:

- Type and nature of personal data involved, particularly sensitive personal information
- Whether appropriate technical safeguards have been applied (e.g., encryption, pseudonymization)
- Whether the data subject will be directly or indirectly affected
- Possibility that personal data can be maliciously used
- Possibility of substantial damage on a physical level[102]

4.3 Global Perspective

Governments around the world vary in their approach to privacy law, policy, and regulation—as was discussed in Chapter 1. As of this writing, more than 160 nations globally have enacted significant privacy laws that apply to companies doing business within their borders and with their citizens.[103] As of the writing of this book, the greatest attention has focused on the legal responsibility of companies, including those based in the United States, to comply with the comprehensive EU privacy requirements of the GDPR, as discussed in greater detail in Chapter 14.[104] Much of this concern has been prompted by fines for violations of the GDPR that are based on a company's worldwide revenues, making sanctions significant enough to garner the attention of even top management in businesses.

When companies are designing compliance programs for the GDPR, top management should be cognizant of that fact that numerous countries around the world have adopted laws that are similar to Europe's regulation,[105] at least in part to benefit from a preferential trading status that allows free flow of data with Europe.[106] Companies should keep in mind that the requirements of the GDPR and those of the countries that are deemed by Europe to be legally similar are not identical, meaning that it is critical for companies to comply with the particular legal regimes in each country where they do business.

Most basically, privacy professionals should advise management that countries are re-evaluating legal protections—which often have privacy at their core—in an effort to address concerns raised by technological advances. Noteworthy countries that have enacted significant privacy protections during this timeframe include China,[107] India,[108] Brazil,[109] Japan,[110] and South Korea.[111] Companies with cross-border data flows should be particularly astute to follow updates concerning regulation of transfers of data from one country to another as well as to stay abreast of the increasing trend towards requirements related to data localization.[112]

When examining the regulation of cross-border data flows, it can be helpful to examine the multiple mechanisms that exist to help enable trust with these data flows:

- **Domestic approaches (or unilateral mechanisms).** According to a recent report by the OECD, more than half of countries with safeguards for cross-border data flows employ pre-authorization safeguards. This means these countries use government adequacy determinations and/or standard contractual clauses.

- **Multilateral arrangements.** Multilateral arrangements include: OECD Privacy Guidelines; APEC Cross-Border Privacy Rules; and Council of Europe Convention 108 and 108+.
- **Trade agreements.** Trade agreements increasingly include provisions concerning data flows. Note that these provisions are not identical. Some include binding language concerning data flows. Even those with binding language generally have exceptions that allow parties to restrict data flows to meet "legitimate public policy objectives."
- **Standards and technology-driven initiatives.** Standards and technology-driven initiatives, such as ISO standards and privacy-enhancing technologies (PETs), are increasingly being used to protect and control data access in the context of cross-border data flows.[113]

4.4 Conclusion

The often-quoted adage is that the law lags behind technological developments.[114] For privacy practice within an organization, this can be an opportunity to put in place a privacy program built on best practices and to assess the privacy and security risks related to the personal data held by the business. In such a program, the decisions related to handling data are made based on the business' overall mission statement as well as the privacy vision for the company, and not merely in response to concerns for fines from privacy regulators. The business approach can balance profit and return on investment with ethical practices related to the treatment of customers, including their personal data. In this scenario, businesses will have a mature privacy program in place when new laws and regulations are enacted by federal or state enforcers of privacy.

When considering information management and privacy risk assessment, it is important to remember that protection of privacy requires far more than the writing of policies that comply with applicable law; actual implementation must occur within the fast-paced and demanding setting of modern business. By designing and implementing a good information management program and a detailed approach to privacy risk management, privacy professionals can play a vital role in helping their companies achieve both business success and good privacy practices. For companies doing business outside the United States, an increasingly important aspect of information management is ensuring compliance with the laws in other countries, and specifically with rules governing international data flows.

Endnotes

1 See Abhinav Palia, Carlton Mathis, Daneil Nieters and Rebecca Gonzales, "Privacy: An Organization's Responsibility for Building Trustworthy Systems, IAPP, August 23, 2022, https://iapp.org/news/a/privacy-an-organizations-responsibility-for-building-trustworthy-systems/.

2 *IAPP-EY Annual Privacy Governance Report 2018*, IAPP and EY, 2018, https://assets.ey.com/content/dam/ey-sites/ey-com/en_gl/topics/financial-services/ey-iapp-ey-annual-privacy-gov-report-2018.pdf; see Jennifer Huddleston, "The Price of Privacy: The Impact of Strict Data Regulations on Innovation and More," American Action Forum, June 3, 2021, https://www.americanactionforum.org/insight/the-price-of-privacy-the-impact-of-strict-data-regulations-on-innovation-and-more/.

3 Daniel Castro, Luke Dascoli and Gillian Diebold, "The Loomin Cost of a Patchwork of State Privacy Laws," Information Technology & Innovation Foundation, January 24, 2022, https://itif.org/publications/2022/01/24/looming-cost-patchwork-state-privacy-laws/; see "Report: Projected $1T Compliance Costs for State Privacy Law Patchwork," IAPP, January 28, 2022, https://iapp.org/news/a/report-projected-1t-compliance-costs-for-state-privacy-law-patchwork-2/.

4 See Michael Hall, "The 12 Biggest Data Breach Fines, Penalties, and Settlements So Far," CSO, September 12, 2022, https://www.csoonline.com/article/3410278/the-biggest-data-breach-fines-penalties-and-settlements-so-far.html;
"Cooley Privacy Talks: Overview of Privacy Enforcement Actions in the US and EU," Cooley, February 17, 2022, https://cdp.cooley.com/cooley-privacy-talks-overview-of-privacy-enforcement-actions-in-the-us-and-eu/.

5 IBM's study examined costs for data breaches in a variety of industries, including healthcare, financial, technology, education, entertainment, and hospitality. The average cost for a data breach in the healthcare industry was approximately $10 million. In the financial industry, the average cost of a breach was nearly $6 million. The study also reports on the total average cost of a data breach by country. According to the report, the United States has the highest average cost for the 12th year in a row, at nearly $10 million. *Cost of a Data Breach Report 2022*, IBM Security, https://www.ibm.com/downloads/cas/3R8N1DZJ. The 2023 report can be found here, https://www.ibm.com/reports/data-breach.

6 See Palia, Mathis, Nieters and Gonzales, "Privacy: An Organization's Responsibility for Building Trustworthy Systems, IAPP; see also Eszter Harittai and Alice Marwick, "What Can I Really Do? Explaining h Privacy Paradox with Online Apathy," *International Journal of Communication* 10 (2016), https://ijoc.org/index.php/ijoc/article/view/4655.

7 "2022 Edelman Trust Barometer," Edelman, accessed July 2023, https://www.edelman.com/trust/2022-trust-barometer; see Catherine Cote, "5 Principles of Data Ethics for Business," Harvard Business School Online, March 16, 2021, https://online.hbs.edu/blog/post/data-ethics.

8 "Data Transparency's Essential Role in Building Consumer Trust," CISCO 2022 Consumer Privacy Survey, CISCO Secure, https://www.cisco.com/c/dam/en_us/about/doing_business/trust-center/docs/cisco-consumer-privacy-survey-2022.pdf.

9 See Palia, Mathis, Nieters and Gonzales, "Privacy: An Organization's Responsibility for Building Trustworthy Systems; Scott Ikeda, " 'Mission Critical': Report Documents Increasing Primacy of Digital Privacy, Consumer Distrust of AI," https://www.cpomagazine.com/data-privacy/mission-critical-report-documents-increasing-primacy-

of-digital-privacy-consumer-distrust-of-ai/; Huddleston, "The Price of Privacy: The Impact of Strict Data Regulations on Innovation and More; Deepa Seshadri, "Data Privacy: From Compliance to Trust," ISACA, April 4, 2022, https://www.isaca.org/resources/news-and-trends/industry-news/2022/data-privacy-from-compliance-to-trust; see "Develop Stronger Privacy Practices," ISACA, accessed July 2023, https://www.isaca.org/resources/privacy.

10 Russell Densmore, *Privacy Program Management: Tools for Managing Privacy Within Your Organization, Third Edition* (Portsmouth: IAPP, 2022), https://iapp.org/resources/article/privacy-program-management/.

11 See "Privacy Management Framework," AICPA, accessed July 2023, https://us.aicpa.org/interestareas/informationtechnology/privacy-management-framework; "Understanding ISO 27701: Privacy Information Management System (PIMS)," ISMS.online, accessed July 2023, https://www.isms.online/privacy-information-management-system-pims/; Becky Simon, "Information Management Strategies: From Punch Cards to Data Warehouses, and Looking to the Future with Big Data and AI, October 24, 2017, https://www.smartsheet.com/information-management; see also William Stallings, "Information Privacy Engineering and Privacy by Design," (Pearson Education: 2020), https://dl.acm.org/doi/book/10.5555/3384141.

12 Ponnurangam Kumaraguru and Lorrie Faith Cranor, *Privacy Indexes: A Survey of Westin's Studies,* Carnegie Mellon University, Institute for Software Research International, (December 2005), www.casos.cs.cmu.edu/publications/papers/CMU-ISRI-05-138.pdf

13 "Treasury Announces Steps to Increase Privacy Protections," U.S. Treasury Department, August 31, 2000, https://www.treasury.gov/press-center/press-releases/Pages/ls859.aspx.

14 According to Statista.com, the global social network penetration was 31 percent in 2016. In the U.S., the rate was 78 percent. S. Dixon, "Social Media – Statistics & Facts," July 11, 2023, https://www.statista.com/topics/1164/social-networks/.

15 Lee Rainie, "The State of Privacy in Post-Snowden America," Pew Research Center, September 21, 2016, www.pewresearch.org/fact-tank/2016/09/21/the-state-of-privacy-in-america/.

16 Americans have an initially strong reaction to data breaches but hold onto these negative feelings for less time than British consumers. "Consumer Attitudes Towards Security Breaches are Changing Significantly," Help Net Security, February 27, 2019, https://www.helpnetsecurity.com/2019/02/27/consumer-attitudes-towards-security-breaches/.

17 Josh Fruhlinger, "Equifax Data Breach FAQ: What Happened, Who Was Affected, What Was the Impact?" CSO, October 14, 2019, https://www.csoonline.com/article/3444488/equifax-data-breach-faq-what-happened-who-was-affected-what-was-the-impact.html; Phil Hudson, "Which Atlanta Company is the 'Most Hated' in the United States," Atlanta Business Chronicle, February 6, 2018, https://www.bizjournals.com/atlanta/news/2018/02/06/which-atlanta-company-is-the-most-hated-in-the.html.

18 Eric Mandel, "Report: Public Opinion in Equifax is Nearly Back to Normal," Atlanta Business Chronicle, November 12, 2018, https://www.bizjournals.com/atlanta/news/2018/11/12/report-public-opinion-in-equifax-is-nearly-back-to.html.

19 Alvin Chang, "The Facebook and Cambridge Analytica Scandal, Explained with a Simple Diagram," Vox, May2, 2018, https://www.vox.com/policy-and-politics/2018/3/23/17151916/facebook-cambridge-analytica-trump-diagram; Issie Lapowsky, "How Cambridge Analytica Sparked the Great Privacy Awakening," Wired

(March 17, 2019), https://www.wired.com/story/cambridge-analytica-facebook-privacy-awakening/; see Casey Newton, "The Tech Backlash is Real, and It's Accelerating," The Verge, September 17, 2019, https://www.theverge.com/interface/2019/9/17/20869495/tech-backlash-nyt-rob-walker-antitrust-privacy.

20 Joanna Kavenna, "Shoshana Zuboff: 'Sureveillance Capitalism is an Assault on Human Autonomy," October 4, 2019, https://www.theguardian.com/books/2019/oct/04/shoshana-zuboff-surveillance-capitalism-assault-human-automomy-digital-privacy; John Laidler, "In New book, Business School Professor emerita Says Surveillance Capitalism Undermines Autonomy – and Democracy," The Harvard Gazette, March 4, 2019, https://news.harvard.edu/gazette/story/2019/03/harvard-professor-says-surveillance-capitalism-is-undermining-democracy/.

21 "Justice Department Sues Google for Monopolizing Digital Advertising Technologies," Office of Public Affairs, U.S. Department of Justice, January 24, 2023, https://www.justice.gov/opa/pr/justice-department-sues-google-monopolizing-digital-advertising-technologies; Josh Sisco, "Antitrust Agency Takes Aim at the the Metaverse by Suing Facebook," *Politico*, July 27, 2022, https://www.politico.com/news/2022/07/27/ftc-sues-facebook-vr-acquisition-metaverse-strategy-00048248; Muge Fazlioglu, "Distilling the Essence of the American Data Privacy and Protection Act Discussion Draft," IAPP, June 6, 2022, https://iapp.org/news/a/distilling-the-essence-of-the-american-data-privacy-and-protection-act-discussion-draft/; see Daisuke Wakabayashi, Katie Benner, Steve Lohr, "Justice Department Opens Antitrust Review of Big Tech Companies," *The New York Time*, July 23, 2019, https://www.nytimes.com/2019/07/23/technology/justice-department-tech-antitrust.html; John McKinnon and Brent Kendall, "States to Move Forward with Antitrust Probe of Big Tech Firms," *The Wall Street Journal*, August 19, 2019, https://www.wsj.com/articles/attorneys-general-to-move-forward-with-antitrust-probe-of-big-tech-11566247753; see Foo Yun Chee, "EU May Need to Regulate Tech Giants' Data Use: EU Antitrust Chief," *Reuters*, September 13, 2019, https://www.reuters.com/article/us-eu-antitrust-data/eu-may-need-to-regulate-tech-giants-data-use-eu-antitrust-chief-idUSKCN1VY1GU.

22 See Woodrow Hartzog and Neil Richard, "We're So Close to Getting Data Loyalty Right," IAPP, June 14, 2022, https://iapp.org/news/a/were-so-close-to-getting-data-loyalty-right/.

23 The National Institute of Standards and Technology's (NIST) Cybersecurity Framework is a guide for best practices. Cybersecurity Framework, NIST, https://www.nist.gov/cyberframework.

24 The NIST Cybersecurity Framework is an example of a voluntary standard developed in partnership between the U.S. federal government and the private sector. Cybersecurity Framework, NIST. An example of mandatory requirements can be found in the EU, where recently approved rules impose security and reporting obligations on companies, which are implemented through national legislation. "The Directive on Measures for a High Common Level of Cybersecurity Across the Union (NIS2 Directive), European Commission, accessed July 2023, https://digital-strategy.ec.europa.eu/en/policies/nis2-directive.

25 *The Reporting Structure of Legal, Compliance, Risk, and Privacy Leadership*, Barker Gilmore, April 2022, https://www.barkergilmore.com/research-report/the-reporting-structure-of-legal-compliance-risk-and-privacy-leadership/; Lucy Saddleton, "The Reporting Structure of Legal, Company, Risk, and Privacy Leadership," Canadian Lawyer, April 20,

2022, https://www.canadianlawyermag.com/news/general/the-reporting-structure-of-legal-compliance-risk-and-privacy-leadership/365905.

26 Certain companies may add a data ethicist to their privacy team. See "What Skills Do You Need for Working in Data Ethics?" *U.K. Data in Government Blog*, September 7, 2021, https://dataingovernment.blog.gov.uk/2021/09/07/what-skills-do-you-need-for-working-in-data-ethics/; Stephanie Walden, "What is a Data Ethicist and Should Your Company Hire One?" Dell Technologies, May 8, 2019, https://www.dell.com/en-us/perspectives/what-is-a-data-ethicist-and-should-your-company-hire-one/.

27 See Palia, Mathis, Nieters and Gonzales, "Privacy: An Organization's Responsibility for Building Trustworthy Systems; see Stallings, "Information Privacy Engineering and Privacy by Design."

28 Nicholai Pfeiffer, "Data Protection Office or Chief Privacy Officer?" White Label Consultancy, January 4, 2022, https://whitelabelconsultancy.com/2022/01/chief-privacy-officer-or-data-protection-officer/#:~:text=The%20primary%20difference%20between%20the,processing%20needs%20of%20the%20organisation.

29 Pfeiffer, "Data Protection Office or Chief Privacy Officer?"

30 Lea Kissner and Lorrie Cranor, "Privacy Engineering Superheroes," Communications of the ACM 64, no. 11 (November 2021): 23-25, https://cacm.acm.org/magazines/2021/11/256380-privacy-engineering-superheroes/fulltext; Benjamin Brook, "The Discipline of Modern Data Privacy Engineering," September 9, 2022, https://iapp.org/news/a/the-disciplines-of-modern-data-privacy-engineering/; see Stallings, "Information Privacy Engineering and Privacy by Design"; Courtney Bowman. Aro Gesher, John Grant, Daniel Slate an Elissa Lerner, "The Architecture of Privacy," (Boston: O'Reilly Media, 2015) https://www.oreilly.com/library/view/the-architecture-of/9781491904503/.

31 "Working as a Privacy Manager," Infosec, accessed July 2023, https://www.infosecinstitute.com/podcast/working-as-a-privacy-manager-cybersecurity-career-series/#:~:text=A%20Privacy%20Manager%20is%20responsible,privacy%2Drelated%20laws%20and%20regulations.

32 Chris Stevens and Stephen Holland, "Privacy Analysts Should Be More than Compliance Officers," IAPP, May 7, 2014, "https://iapp.org/news/a/privacy-analysts-should-be-more-than-compliance-officers-2/.

33 "Privacy Champions – Building a Culture of Privacy," The Privacy Guru, October 11, 2021, https://www.theprivacyguru.com/post/privacy-champions-building-a-culture-of-privacy.

34 "What is Data Lifecycle Management?" IBM, accessed July 2023, https://www.ibm.com/topics/data-lifecycle-management; Prateek Panda, "Best Practices for Data Lifecycle Management," Intertrust, February 1, 2022, https://www.intertrust.com/blog/data-lifecycle-management/; "Integrity in the Data Lifecycle," Dataworks, accessed July 2023, https://www.dataworks.ie/5-stages-in-the-data-management-lifecycle-process/.

35 See Manny Rivelo, "Why Data Security Lifecycle is Essential for Reducing Costs and Risk," May 1, 2023, https://www.forbes.com/sites/forbestechcouncil/2023/05/01/why-the-data-security-lifecycle-is-essential-for-reducing-cost-and-risk/?sh=271ec743cf52; Hossein Rahnama an Alex Pentland, "The New Rules of Data Privacy," February 25, 2022, https://hbr.org/2022/02/the-new-rules-of-data-privacy; David Deming, "Balancing Privacy with Data Sharing for Public Good," *The New York Times*, February 19, 2021, https://www.nytimes.com/2021/02/19/business/privacy-open-data-public.html.

36 Caitlin Fennessy, "Microsoft Launces Open-Source Privacy Mapping Tool," February 21, 2020, https://iapp.org/news/a/microsoft-launches-open-source-privacy-mapping-tool/; "Best Practices for Effective Data Mapping" DataGrail, July 15, 2022, https://www.datagrail.io/blog/data-privacy/best-practices-for-effective-data-mapping/.

37 Although data flow mapping is similar to the term known as RoPA under the EU's GDPR, it is not the same. "GDPR Data Mapping an RoPA: What's the Difference?" Soveren, June 9, 2021, https://soveren.io/blog/data-map-ropa-difference and Heather Federman, "Redefining Data Mapping," IAPP, May 29, 2022, https://iapp.org/news/a/redefining-data-mapping/.

38 Federman, "Redefining Data Mapping; see Pratik Dwivedi, "What is Data Mapping? : A Comprehensive Guide 101," Hevo, December 3, 2021, https://hevodata.com/learn/data-mapping/; Olga Annenko, "Data Mapping Best Practices | A Guide to Types, Approaches, Tools," November 2, 2022, https://www.elastic.io/integration-best-practices/data-mapping-best-practices/.

39 The requirements of state data breach notification laws in the U.S. vary considerably. A listing can be found at the website maintained by the National Conference of State Legislatures (NCSL). Security Breach Notification Laws, NCSL, accessed February 2023, www.ncsl.org/research/telecommunications-and-information-technology/security-breach-notification-laws.aspx. For a detailed discussion of the topic, see Chapter 7 (State Data Breach Notification Laws).

40 For example, the FCRA requires delinquent debts to be removed from credit reports after seven years and bankruptcies to be removed from credit reports after ten years. "Consumer Reports: What Information Furnishers Need to Know," FTC, accessed November 2017, https://www.ftc.gov/tips-advice/business-center/guidance/consumer-reports-what-information-furnishers-need-know.

41 Peter Swire, *From Real-Time Intercepts to Stored Records: Why Encryption Drives the Government to Seek Access to the Cloud,* The Ohio State University Mortiz College of Law (2012), http://ssrn.com/abstract=2038871.

42 "Protecting Personal Information: A Guide for Business," Federal Trade Commission, October 2016, https://www.ftc.gov/business-guidance/resources/protecting-personal-information-guide-business; see Palia, Mathis, Nieters and Gonzales, "Privacy: An Organization's Responsibility for Building Trustworthy Systems"; see also Peter Swire, "Encryption and Globalization," *Columbia an Technology Law Review* 23, no. 157 (2012), https://papers.ssrn.com/sol3/papers.cfm?abstract_id=1960602; " Cryptography and the Intelligence Community: The Future of Encryption," National Academies of Sciences, Engineering, an Medicine, 2002, https://nap.nationalacademies.org/catalog/26168/cryptography-and-the-intelligence-community-the-future-of-encryption.

43 Directive 95/46/EC of the European Parliament and of the Council of 24 October 1995 on the protection of individuals with regard to the processing of personal data and on the free movement of such data (EU Data Protection Directive 95/46/EC), Article 2, accessed November 2017, http://eur-lex.europa.eu/legal-content/en/ALL/?uri=CELEX:31995L0046. The General Data Protection Regulation addresses these issues and replaces Directive 95/46/EC. Regulation (EU) 2016/679 of the European Parliament and of the Council of 27 April 2016 on the protection of natural persons with regard to the processing of personal data and on the free movement of such data, and repealing Directive 95/46/EC (General Data Protection Regulation), Article 4, accessed November 2017, http://eur-lex.europa.eu/legal-content/EN/TXT/?uri=uriserv:OJ.L_.2016.119.01.0001.01.ENG&toc=OJ:L:2016:119:TOC.

44 The consent orders entered into between the FTC and various companies have placed compliance and reporting requirements on the companies for 20 years. See In the Matter of Facebook, accessed November 2017, https://www.ftc.gov/sites/default/files/documents/cases/2011/11/111129facebookagree.pdf; *United States of America v. InMobi Pte Ltd.*, accessed November 2017, https://www.ftc.gov/system/files/documents/cases/160622inmobistip.pdf.

45 PCI Security, accessed November 2017, https://www.pcisecuritystandards.org/pci_security/.

46 Cara McGoogan, "WhatsApp Met with Backlash After Giving Users' Data to Facebook," *The Telegraph,* August 26, 2016, www.telegraph.co.uk/technology/2016/08/26/whatsapp-met-with-backlash-after-giving-users-data-to-facebook/.

47 A detailed analysis of enforcement actions can be found in Chapter 5 (Federal and State Regulators and Enforcement of Privacy Laws).

48 "Privacy and Personal Information," New Zealand Government, accessed July 2023, https://www.digital.govt.nz/standards-and-guidance/governance/managing-online-channels/security-and-privacy-for-websites/foundations/privacy-and-personal-information/; see Troy Segal, "Operational Risk Overview, Importance, and Examples," January 16, 2023, https://www.investopedia.com/terms/o/operational_risk.asp.

49 Will Kenton, "What is Business Risk? Definition, Factors, and Examples," updated March 25, 2022, https://www.investopedia.com/terms/b/businessrisk.asp#:~:text=Business%20risk%20usually%20occurs%20in,operational%20risk%2C%20and%20reputational%20risk.

50 "About the University Privacy Office," Standford University, accessed July 2023, https://privacy.stanford.edu/about-upo.

51 See Alex Edquist, Liz Grennan, Sian Griffiths and Kayvaun Rowshankish, "Data Ethics: What is Means and What it Takes," McKinsey Digital, September 23, 2022, https://www.mckinsey.com/capabilities/mckinsey-digital/our-insights/data-ethics-what-it-means-and-what-it-takes; Palia, Mathis, Nieters and Gonzales, "Privacy: An Organization's Responsibility for Building Trustworthy Systems"; see "An Introduction to Data Ethics: What is the Ethical Use of Data?" DataCamp, February 2023, https://www.datacamp.com/blog/introduction-to-data-ethics; see also Deepa Seshadri, "Data Privacy: From Compliance to Trust," April 4, 2022, https://www.isaca.org/resources/news-and-trends/industry-news/2022/data-privacy-from-compliance-to-trust.

52 "Privacy Policy," Resource Center, IAPP, accessed July 2023," https://iapp.org/resources/article/privacy-policy/; "Privacy Notice," IAPP, accessed July 2023, https://iapp.org/resources/article/privacy-notice/; see "Benjamin Brook, "The Discipline of Modern Data Privacy Engineering," IAPP, September 9, 2020, https://iapp.org/news/a/the-disciplines-of-modern-data-privacy-engineering/; see Stallings, "Information Privacy Engineering and Privacy by Design."

53 "Privacy Policy," Resource Center, IAPP; see Brook, "The Discipline of Modern Data Privacy Engineering"; see Stallings, "Information Privacy Engineering and Privacy by Design."

54 Robert G. Bagnall, *Investment Company Regulation and Compliance Conference: Privacy,* SJ095 ALI-ABA 209 (2004).

55 *Protecting Consumer Privacy in an Era of Rapid Change: Recommendations for Businesses and Policy Makers,* Federal Trade Commission (March 2012), https://www.ftc.gov/sites/

default/files/documents/reports/federal-trade-commission-report-protecting-consumer-privacy-era-rapid-change-recommendations/120326privacyreport.pdf.

56 "Privacy Notice," IAPP; see Brook, "The Discipline of Modern Data Privacy Engineering"; Stallings, "Information Privacy Engineering and Privacy by Design."

57 Public Law 106-102, Gramm-Leach Bliley Act, November 12, 1999, https://www.gpo.gov/fdsys/pkg/PLAW-106publ102/pdf/PLAW-106publ102.pdf.

58 45 C.F.R. § 164.530(b)(1), accessed November 2017, https://www.law.cornell.edu/cfr/text/45/164.530.

59 Mehmet Munur, Sarah Branam and Matt Mkrobrad, "Best Practices in Drafting Plain-Language and Layered Privacy Policies," IAPP, September 13, 2012, https://iapp.org/news/a/2012-09-13-best-practices-in-drafting-plain-language-and-layered-privacy/. For an independent ranking of several major companies' privacy notices based on their collection, handling, and transparency practices, visit "Directory," Privacy Spy, accessed November 2019, https://privacyspy.org/directory/.

60 Mark Brennan, "Mobile App Privacy Considerations," *Lexis Practice Advisor Journal*, November 9, 2016, https://www.lexisnexis.com/lexis-practice-advisor/the-journal/b/lpa/archive/2016/11/08/mobile-app-privacy-considerations.aspx.

61 "Mobile Privacy Disclosures: Building Trust Though Transparency," Federal Trade Commission, February 2013, https://www.ftc.gov/sites/default/files/documents/reports/mobile-privacy-disclosures-building-trust-through-transparency-federal-trade-commission-staff-report/130201mobileprivacyreport.pdf.

62 "Mobile Privacy Disclosures," Federal Trade Commission. For a more detailed discussion on how design could be important, view Mark Wilson, "Most People Don't Understand Privacy, and That's a Huge Opportunity for Design," *Fast Company*, October 9, 2019, https://www.fastcompany.com/90414691/most-people-dont-understand-privacy-and-thats-a-huge-opportunity-for-design.

63 Woodrow Hartzog, "User Agreements are Betraying You," Medium, June 5, 2018, https://onezero.medium.com/user-agreements-are-betraying-you-19db7135441f; Dan Solove, "The Myth of the Privacy Paradox," *George Washington Law Review* 89, no. 1 (January 29, 2021), https://papers.ssrn.com/sol3/papers.cfm?abstract_id=3536265 (citing Bruce Schneier, "It's Not Just Facebook. Thousands of Companies Are Spying on You," CNN, March 26, 2018, https://www.cnn.com/2018/03/26/opinions/data-company-spying-opinion-schneier/index.html); Alexis Madrigal, "Reading the Privacy Policies You Encounter in a Year Would Take 76 Work Days," *Atlantic*, March 1, 2012, https://www.theatlantic.com/technology/archive/2012/03/reading-the-privacy-policies-you-encounter-in-a-year-would-take-76-work-days/253851/.

64 See Colorado Revised Statutes § 6-1-1303, accessed July 2023, https://casetext.com/statute/colorado-revised-statutes/title-6-consumer-and-commercial-affairs/fair-trade-and-restraint-of-trade/article-1-colorado-consumer-protection-act/part-13-effective-712023-colorado-privacy-act/section-6-1-1303-effective-712023-definitions.

65 Children's Online Privacy Protection Act, accessed November July 2023, http://www.columbia.edu/~mr2651/ecommerce3/2nd/statutes/ChildrenOnlinePrivacyProtectionAct.pdf.

66 Health Insurance Portability and Accountability Act of 1996, accessed November 2017, https://www.gpo.gov/fdsys/pkg/PLAW-104publ191/pdf/PLAW-104publ191.pdf.

67 Fair Credit Reporting Act, Federal Trade Commission, accessed July 2023, https://www.ftc.gov/legal-library/browse/statutes/fair-credit-reporting-act

68 State laws may also have opt-in requirements. For a discussion in the California Consumer Privacy Act (CCPA), see Chapter 6 (State Comprehensive Privacy Laws).

69 Take Control, accessed July 2023, DMAchoice.org.

70 "Opt Out of Interest-Based Adverting," Network Advertising Initiative, accessed February 2023, https://optout.networkadvertising.org/?c=1; Your Advertising Choices, TrustArc, accessed November 2017, https://preferences-mgr.truste.com/; DAA Webchoices Browsers Check, Digital Advertising Alliance, accessed July 2023, https://optout.aboutads.info/.

71 *Protecting Consumer Privacy in an Era of Rapid Change, A Proposed Framework for Businesses and Policymakers,* Federal Trade Commission, Preliminary Staff Report, December 2010, https://www.ftc.gov/reports/preliminary-ftc-staff-report-protecting-consumer-privacy-era-rapid-change-proposed-framework.

72 *Protecting Consumer Privacy in an Era of Rapid Change, A Proposed Framework for Businesses and Policymakers,* Federal Trade Commission.

73 CAN-SPAM Act, accessed November 2017, https://www.ftc.gov/sites/default/files/documents/cases/2007/11/canspam.pdf.

74 "How to Comply with the Privacy Consumer Financial Information Rule of the Gramm-Leach-Bliley Act," Federal Trade Commission, July 2002, https://www.ftc.gov/business-guidance/resources/how-comply-privacy-consumer-financial-information-rule-gramm-leach-bliley-act.

75 "CAN-SPAM Act: A Compliance Guide for Business," Federal Trade Commission, September 2009, https://www.ftc.gov/tips-advice/business-center/guidance/can-spam-act-compliance-guide-business.

76 D. Reed Freeman Jr. and Maury Riggan, "A Primer on FTC Expectations for Your Partner and Vendor Relationships: Enforcement Shows You Are Your Brother's Keeper," *Bloomberg BNA* 14, May 5, 2015, https://www.jdsupra.com/legalnews/a-primer-on-ftc-expectations-for-your-pa-23784/.

77 Fair Credit Reporting Act, Federal Trade Commission.

78 "Your Medical Records," U.S. Department of Health and Human Services, reviewed November 2, 2020, https://www.hhs.gov/hipaa/for-individuals/medical-records/index.html?language=es.

79 Judicial Redress Act of 2015, codified at 5 U.S.C. § 552a, accessed November 2017, https://www.congress.gov/114/plaws/publ126/PLAW-114publ126.pdf.

80 General Data Protection Regulation (GDPR), accessed February 2023, https://eur-lex.europa.eu/EN/legal-content/summary/general-data-protection-regulation-gdpr.html. For a discussion of the regime in the EU, see "Data Protection," European Commission, accessed February 2023, https://commission.europa.eu/law/law-topic/data-protection_en.

81 "Recommendation of the Council concerning Guidelines Governing the Protection of Privacy and Transborder Flows of Personal Data," OECD Legal Instruments, accessed February 2023, https://legalinstruments.oecd.org/en/instruments/OECD-LEGAL-0188; APEC Privacy Framework (2015), https://www.apec.org/Publications/2017/08/APEC-Privacy-Framework-(2015).

82 "Data Risk Management Framework," Infolock, accessed July 2023, https://www.infolock.com/wp-content/uploads/2018/10/infolock-drmf.pdf; "What is Data Risk Management" Why Should you Care?" The ECM Consultant, September 11,

2022, https://theecmconsultant.com/data-risk-management/; "7 Steps in Privacy Risk Management," in Blog, Data Privacy Manager, November 5, 2020, https://dataprivacymanager.net/7-steps-and-elements-of-privacy-risk-management/; "Privacy Management Framework," AICPA.

83 The NIST Privacy Framework is a voluntary tool intended to help organizations identify and manage privacy risks. "NIST Privacy Framework," NIST, accessed July 2023, https://www.nist.gov/privacy-framework.

84 Andrea Tang, "Privacy Risk Management," *ISACA Journal* 4 (June 30, 2020), https://www.isaca.org/resources/isaca-journal/issues/2020/volume-4/privacy-risk-management#:~:text=It%20is%20about%20managing%20consumer,build%20trust%20and%20protect%20data.; see https://www.isaca.org/resources/news-and-trends/industry-news/2022/performing-an-information-security-and-privacy-risk-assessment.

85 "Ethics in Privacy and Security," *OneTrust* (blog), November 9, 2020, https://www.onetrust.com/blog/ethics-in-privacy-and-security/; see Palia, Mathis, Nieters and Gonzales, "Privacy: An Organization's Responsibility for Building Trustworthy Systems"; Adam Hayes, "Code of Ethics: Understanding its Types, Uses Through Examples," Investopedia, June 29, 2022, https://www.investopedia.com/terms/c/code-of-ethics.asp#:~:text=What%20Is%20a%20Code%20of%20Ethics%20in%20Business%3F,promote%20a%20benefit%20to%20society; see Michele Loi, et al., "Toward an Ethical Code for Data-Based Businesses," 6th Swiss Conference on Data Science, 2019, https://digitalcollection.zhaw.ch/bitstream/11475/18333/2/2019_Heitz_Towards%20an%20ethical%20code%20for%20data-based%20business_IEEE.pdf.

86 Tang, "Privacy Risk Management."

87 Tang, "Privacy Risk Management"; see Andre Pitkowski and Daniel Bispo de Jesus, "Performing an Information Security and Privacy Risk Assessment," ISACA, May 18, 2022, https://www.isaca.org/resources/news-and-trends/industry-news/2022/performing-an-information-security-and-privacy-risk-assessment; see also Stallings, "Information Privacy Engineering and Privacy by Design."

88 "The Analyst's Inbox: DPIA vs PIA - What Are the Differences?" OneTrust DataGuidance (blog), April 28, 2022, https://www.dataguidance.com/resource/analysts-inbox-dpia-vs-pia-what-are-differences; Verrion Wright, "PIA vs. DPIA: The Art of Privacy Risk Assessments," February 9, 2021, https://bigid.com/blog/pia-vs-dpia/.

89 "NIST Privacy Framework," NIST.

90 Tang, "Privacy Risk Management"; see Emily Leach and Rosemary Kim, Assessing Risk: Determining the Appropriate Risk Flags for Your Privacy Risk Assessments," *Privacy Advisor*, IAPP, April 26, 2022, https://iapp.org/news/a/assessing-risk-determining-the-appropriate-risk-flags-for-your-privacy-risk-assessments/; see also Stallings, "Information Privacy Engineering and Privacy by Design."

91 Peter Swire, "Vendor Management by Banks: How Law Firms are Affected," ABA Antitrust Meeting, Spring 2016, https://peterswire.net/wp-content/uploads/CLE-ABA-law-firm-and-vendors.040716.pptx.

92 For a detailed discussion for requirements of "processors" of data under the GDPR, see Chapter 14.

93 "Vendor Management," Resource Center, IAPP, accessed July 2023, https://iapp.org/resources/article/vendor-assessment/; see "The Ultimate Guide to Privacy Management," *OneTrust* (blog), May 21, 2021, https://www.onetrust.com/blog/privacy-management/.

94 "SOC 2 Compliance," Imperva, accessed July 2023, https://www.imperva.com/learn/data-security/soc-2-compliance/.

95 Tang, "Privacy Risk Management"; see "Top 14 Cyber Security Vendor Due Diligence Questions," CyberSecOp, November 30, 2020, https://cybersecop.com/news/2020/11/30/top-14-cybersecurity-vendor-due-diligence-questionnaire; Sarah Harvey, "What is a Due Diligence (Vetting) Process?" KirkpatrickPrice, January 24, 2020, https://kirkpatrickprice.com/blog/vendor-due-diligence-checklist/.

96 Sandra Gittlen, "5 Cybersecurity Lessons from the SolarWinds Breach," TechTarget, accessed July 2023, https://www.techtarget.com/searchsecurity/feature/5-cybersecurity-lessons-from-the-SolarWinds-breach; Isabella Jibilian and Katie Canales, "The U.S. is Readying Sanctions Against Russia Over the SolarWinds Cyber Attack. Here is a Simple Explanation of How the Massive Hack Happened and Why It's Such a Big Deal," Business Insider, April 15, 2021, https://www.businessinsider.com/solarwinds-hack-explained-government-agencies-cyber-security-2020-12.

97 Tang, "Privacy Risk Management"; see Cameron Kerry, "Protecting Privacy in an AI-Driven World," Brookings, February 10, 2020, https://www.brookings.edu/research/protecting-privacy-in-an-ai-driven-world/.

98 For an overview of major cybersecurity events during the last decade, view Catalin Cimpanu, "A Decade of Hacking: The Most Notable Cybersecurity Events of the 2010s," *ZDNet*, December 11, 2019, https://www.zdnet.com/article/a-decade-of-hacking-the-most-notable-cyber-security-events-of-the-2010s/.

99 Harry Lau, "What is the CIA Triad: Confidentiality, Integrity, & Availability," *Allot* (blog), October 7, 2019, https://www.allot.com/blog/cia-triad/; see Michael Nieles, Kelley Dempsey, and Victoria Yan Pillitteri, "An Introduction to Information Security," NIST Special Publication 800-12 Revision 1, National Institute of Standards and Technology , June 2017, https://nvlpubs.nist.gov/nistpubs/SpecialPublications/NIST.SP.800-12r1.pdf; see also Stallings, "Information Privacy Engineering and Privacy by Design."

100 Debbie Walkowski, "What Are Security Controls?" F5 Labs, August 22, 2019, https://www.f5.com/labs/articles/education/what-are-security-controls.

101 Elisha Girken, "Incident Response Steps and Frameworks for SANS and NIST, AT&T Business, January 3, 2020, https://cybersecurity.att.com/blogs/security-essentials/incident-response-steps-comparison-guide.

102 Tang, "Privacy Risk Management."

103 Graham Greenleaf, "*Global Data Privacy Laws: 2023: 162 National Laws and 20 Bills,* 181 Privacy Laws and Business International Report 1, 2-4, https://papers.ssrn.com/sol3/papers.cfm?abstract_id=4426146. For a searchable database, *see* "Data Protection Laws of the World," DLA Piper, accessed October 2023, https://www.dlapiperdataprotection.com/#handbook/world-map-section/c1_RU.

104 GDPR became effective in May 2018. See "EU Data Protection Rules," European Commission, accessed November 2019, https://ec.europa.eu/commission/priorities/justice-and-fundamental-rights/data-protection/2018-reform-eu-data-protection-rules/eu-data-protection-rules_en.

105 See "Comparing Privacy Laws: GDPR v. LGPD, OneTrust DataGuidance, August 9, 2022, https://www.dataguidance.com/resource/comparing-privacy-laws-gdpr-v-lgpd-0; Alex Wall, "GDPR Matchup: South Korea's Personal Information Protection

Act, *Privacy Tracker*, IAPP, January 8, 2018, https://iapp.org/news/a/gdpr-matchup-south-koreas-personal-information-protection-act/; Kensaku Takase, "GDPR Matchup: Japan's Act on the Protection of Personal Information," Privacy Tracker, IAPP, August 29, 2017, https://iapp.org/news/a/gdpr-matchup-japans-act-on-the-protection-of-personal-information/.

106 Under the GDPR, the European Commission determines whether a country outside of the EU has "adequate" data protections for the free flow of data between the EU and the third country. See "Adequacy Decisions," European Commission, accessed February 2023, https://commission.europa.eu/law/law-topic/data-protection/international-dimension-data-protection/adequacy-decisions_en. For example, South Korea's privacy protection regime was deemed 'adequate' in 2021. "EU Adopts Adequacy Decision with South Korea," *Daily Dashboard*, IAPP, December 20, 2021, https://iapp.org/news/a/eu-adopts-adequacy-decision-with-south-korea/; see "Decision on the Adequate Protection of Personal Data by the Republic of Korea with Annexes, December 17, 2021, "https://commission.europa.eu/document/e9453177-f192-4416-a147-3c57adc468c4_en.

107 Jedidiah Bracy, "China Adopts National Privacy Law, Privacy Advisor, IAPP, August 20, 2021, https://iapp.org/news/a/china-adopts-national-privacy-law/; see "Topic Page: China," IAPP, accessed July2023, https://iapp.org/resources/topics/china-3/.

108 Ravin Nandle, "India's Digital Personal Data Protection Bill 2022: Does it Overhaul the Former PDPB? IAPP, *Privacy Tracker*, IAPP, November 22, 2022, https://iapp.org/news/a/indias-digital-personal-data-protection-bill-2022-does-it-overhaul-the-former-pdpb/; Rishi Wadwa and Grace Bains, "The Evolution of India's Data Privacy Regime in 2021, Privacy Tracker, IAPP, March 17, 2022, https://iapp.org/news/a/the-evolution-of-indias-data-privacy-regime-in-2021/; Julie McCarthy, "Indian Supreme Court Declares Privacy a Fundamental Right," NPR, August 24, 2017, https://www.npr.org/sections/thetwo-way/2017/08/24/545963181/indian-supreme-court-declares-privacy-a-fundamental-right; see "Topic Page: India," IAPP, accessed July 2023, https://iapp.org/resources/topics/india-2/.

109 Sarah Rippy, "An Overview of Brazil's LGPD, *Privacy Tracker*, IAPP, September 18, 2020, https://iapp.org/news/a/an-overview-of-brazils-lgpd/; see Comparing Privacy Laws: GDPR v. LGPD, OneTrust DataGuidance; Scott Ikeda, "New IAPP Report: Brazil's Newly Activated LGPD Will Likely Create a Need for At Least 50,000 DPOs, October 20, 2020, https://www.cpomagazine.com/data-protection/new-iapp-report-brazils-newly-activated-lgpd-will-likely-create-a-need-for-at-least-50000-dpos/; see also LGPD, Brazilian General Data Protection Law, IAPP, updated October 2020, https://iapp.org/resources/article/brazilian-data-protection-law-lgpd-english-translation/.

110 Hiroyuki Tanaka and Noato Shimamura, "Practical Notes for Japan's Important Updates of the APPI Guidelines and Q&As, IAPP, January 10, 2022, https://iapp.org/news/a/practical-notes-for-japans-important-updates-of-the-appi-guidelines-and-qas/; Hiroyuki Tanaka and Noboru Kitayama, "Japan Enacts Amendments to the Act on te Protection of Personal Information," IAPP, June 9, 2020, https://iapp.org/news/a/japan-enacts-the-act-on-the-protection-of-personal-information/; Kensaku Takase, "GDPR Matchup: Japan's Act on the Protection of Personal Information," *Privacy Tracker*, IAPP, August 29, 2017, https://iapp.org/news/a/gdpr-matchup-japans-act-on-the-protection-of-personal-information/.

111 "EU Adopts Adequacy Decision with South Korea, *Daily Dashboard*, IAPP, December 20, 2021, https://iapp.org/news/a/eu-adopts-adequacy-decision-with-south-korea/; Wall, GDPR Matchup: South Korea's Personal Information Protection Act"; see "South Korea Privacy Law – Personal Information Protection Act," Resoruce Center, IAPP, accessed July 2023, https://iapp.org/resources/article/south-korea-privacy-law-personal-information-protection-act/.

112 "Garner Identifies Top Five Trends in Privacy Through 2024," Gartner, May 31, 2022, https://www.gartner.com/en/newsroom/press-releases/2022-05-31-gartner-identifies-top-five-trends-in-privacy-through-2024#:~:text=%E2%80%9CBy%20year%2Dend%202024%2C,Henein%2C%20VP%20Analyst%20at%20Gartner; see Jana Subramanian, "Challenges in Cross Border Data Flows and Data Localizaion Amidst New Regulations," SAP, January 19, 2022, https://blogs.sap.com/2022/01/19/challenges-in-cross-border-data-flows-and-data-localization-amidst-new-regulations/; see also Peter Swire and DeBrae Kennedy-Mayo, "The Effects of Data Localization on Cybersecurity – Organizational Effects, Georgia Tech Scheller College of Business Research Paper No. 4030905, June 15, 2023, https://papers.ssrn.com/sol3/papers.cfm?abstract_id=4030905.

113 "Dashboard: Trade Rules on Data Transfers," Global Data Alliance, accessed July 2023, https://globaldataalliance.org/wp-content/uploads/2021/07/gdadashboard.pdf; see "2023 National Trade Estimate Report on Foreign Trade Barriers," United Staes Trade Representative, 2023, https://ustr.gov/sites/default/files/2023-03/2023%20NTE%20Report.pdf; see Joseph Whitlock, "Global Alliance: 3 Years of Leading on Digital Trust Across Borders," BSA, January 23, 2023, https://techpost.bsa.org/2023/01/23/global-data-alliance-3-years-of-leading-on-digital-trust-across-borders/; "White Paper: Data Localization an Barriers to Cross-Border Data Flows Towards a Multitrack Approach," World Economic Forum, January 2018, https://www3.weforum.org/docs/White_Paper_Data_Localization_Barriers_Cross-Border_Data_Flows_report_2018.pdf.

114 Daniel Malan, "The Law Can't Keep Up with New Tech. Here's How to Close the Gap," World Economic Forum, June 21, 2018, https://www.weforum.org/agenda/2018/06/law-too-slow-for-new-tech-how-keep-up/; "Law & Technology: Risks and Opportunities from the Tectonic Forces at Work," White & Case, June 18, 2018, https://www.whitecase.com/insight-our-thinking/law-technology-risks-and-opportunities-tectonic-forces-work; Julia Griffith, "A Losing Game: he Law is Struggling To Keep Up With Technology," *Journal of High Technology Law*, Suffolk University, April 12, 2019, https://sites.suffolk.edu/jhtl/2019/04/12/a-losing-game-the-law-is-struggling-to-keep-up-with-technology/#:~:text=It%20has%20been%20estimated%20that,an%20attempt%20to%20keep%20up.

CHAPTER 5

Federal and State Regulators and Enforcement of Privacy Law

In the United States, privacy is regulated at both the federal and state level. At the federal level, the United States has numerous regulators whose jurisdictions can overlap—with these regulators primarily dedicated to specific sectors such as medical, financial, and education. The U.S. Federal Trade Commission (FTC) is often considered to be the lead privacy enforcer as this agency can address a variety of privacy violations that relate to consumer protection. At the state level, all 50 states have in place Unfair and Deceptive Acts and Practices statutes that, although there are variations among these state laws, provide similar consumer-protection safeguards to those found in the FTC Act. As of the writing of this book, the United States has not enacted a federal comprehensive privacy law. In the absence of such a federal law, state privacy enforcement takes on additional importance, particularly as states have begun enacting their own comprehensive privacy laws.

This chapter introduces the interplay of federal and state regulators of privacy, including many concepts that will be developed in later chapters of the book. The chapter begins with an overview of the many agencies that play a part in regulating privacy at the federal level. Much of the chapter then focuses on the FTC and Section 5 of the FTC Act. We examine the prominent role that the FTC has played among federal agencies in the development of U.S. privacy standards as well as in the enforcement of privacy protections at the federal level. The chapter then gives an overview of state laws that provide privacy protections and examines the role of state attorneys general in enforcing these laws. The chapter concludes with a discussion of self-regulation.

This chapter begins our examination of this interplay between federal and state enforcement of privacy. Chapter 6 examines recently enacted state comprehensive privacy laws. Chapter 7 examines state data breach notification laws, state data security laws, and state data security laws. Chapters 8, 9, 10, 11, and 12 return to a focus on federal privacy protections, looking in turn at medical privacy, financial privacy, education privacy, privacy in telecommunications and marketing, and workplace privacy.

5.1 Types of Litigation and Enforcement

For nonlawyers, it is useful to define the main categories of legal actions: civil litigation, criminal prosecution and administrative enforcement actions. As a reminder, these topics are discussed in additional detail in Chapter 2.

Civil litigation occurs in the courts, when one person (the plaintiff) sues another person (the defendant) to redress a wrong. The plaintiff often seeks a monetary judgment from the defendant. The plaintiff may also seek an injunction, which is a court order mandating the defendant to stop engaging in certain behaviors. Important categories of civil litigation include contracts and torts. For instance, a plaintiff might sue for a breach of a contract that promised confidential treatment of personal information. In a tort action, a plaintiff might sue for an invasion of privacy—for example, where the defendant surreptitiously took pictures in a changing room and broadcast the pictures to the public. Some privacy laws create private rights of action, enabling an individual plaintiff to sue based on violations of the statute. The Fair Credit Reporting Act of 1970 (FCRA), for instance, has a private right of action, allowing individuals to sue a company if their consumer reports have been used inappropriately.

Criminal prosecution involves actions brought by the government for violations of criminal laws. This contrasts with civil litigation, which generally involves an effort by a private party to correct specific harms. Criminal prosecution can lead to imprisonment and criminal fines. In the federal government, criminal laws are prosecuted by the U.S. Department of Justice (DOJ). States typically place criminal prosecutorial power in the hands of the state attorneys general and local officials such as district attorneys.

Administrative enforcement actions are carried out pursuant to the statutes that create and empower an agency, such as the FTC. In the federal government, the basic rules for agency enforcement actions occur under the Administrative Procedure Act (APA).[1] The APA sets forth rules for adjudication within an agency, where court-like hearings may take place before an administrative law judge (ALJ). Federal agency adjudications can generally be appealed to federal court. In addition, a federal agency may sue a party in federal court, with the agency as the plaintiff in a civil action. How the FTC typically conduct privacy enforcement actions, notably by the use of consent decrees, is discussed in more detail in Section 5.3.2.

5.2 Federal Privacy Enforcement and Policy Outside the FTC

Much of this chapter examines the FTC and its focus on unfair and deceptive trade practices as well as children's privacy. Before concentrating on the FTC, it is important to highlight federal agencies other than the FTC that may be responsible for privacy enforcement, depending on the statutes or regulations violated. In certain instances, the FTC may have overlapping responsibilities with these agencies to enforce privacy protections.[2] For example, the following agencies are discussed in chapters of this book:

- **Medical privacy (Chapter 8)**. The Office of Civil Rights (OCR) in the U.S. Department of Health and Human Services (HHS) enforces the Health Insurance Portability and Accountability Act (HIPAA).
- **Financial privacy (Chapter 9)**. The Consumer Financial Protection Bureau (CFPB) is responsible generally for financial consumer protection issues. Federal financial regulators such as the Federal Reserve and the Office of Comptroller of the Currency (OCC) have privacy enforcement responsibilities for institutions under their jurisdiction under the Gramm-Leach-Bliley Act (GLBA).
- **Education privacy (Chapter 10)**. The U.S. Department of Education enforces the Family Educational Rights and Privacy Act (FERPA).
- **Telecommunications and marketing privacy (Chapter 11)**. The Federal Communications Commission (FCC) has responsibilities under the Telephone Consumer Protection Act (TCPA) and other statutes.
- **Workplace privacy (Chapter 12).** Agencies, including the Equal Employment Opportunity Commission (EEOC), are responsible for enforcing the protections in the Americans with Disabilities Act (ADA) and other antidiscrimination statutes.

As new technologies emerge, federal agencies seek to address negative impacts—often by using the regulatory frameworks that are already in place.[3] For example, as of the writing of this book, the United States lacks a federal law that specifically regulates the privacy concerns raised by artificial intelligence (AI). The OCR is expected to address improper collection of protected health information (PHI) by companies employing AI.[4] The EEOC is expected to address complaints of discrimination when companies utilize algorithms to make decisions in the hiring process.[5]

In addition, other federal agencies are involved in privacy oversight, enforcement, and policy. Privacy professionals should thus be alert to the possibility that federal agencies other than the FTC will be relevant to their organizations' activities.[6]

- The **U.S. Department of State (DOS)** has been increasingly active over time on privacy, especially by negotiating internationally on privacy issues with other countries and in multinational groups such as the United Nations (UN) or the Organisation for Economic Co-operation and Development (OECD).
- The **U.S. Department of Commerce (DOC)** plays a leading role in federal privacy policy development and has traditionally administered the agreement on privacy protections for data flows between the United States and the European Union.[7] The DOC negotiates internationally on privacy issues with other countries and in multinational groups, such as the UN and the OECD.
- The **U.S. Department of Transportation (DOT)** is the agency responsible for transportation companies under its jurisdiction and has traditionally enforced violations of the agreement on privacy protections for data flows between the United States and the European Union for some transportation companies. Within the DOT, the Federal Aviation Administration (FAA) has recently played an increasing role for drones. The National Highway Traffic Safety Administration (NHTSA), also within the DOT, addresses privacy and security issues for connected cars.
- The President's **Office of Management and Budget (OMB)** is the lead agency for interpreting the Privacy Act of 1974, which applies to federal agencies and private-sector contractors to those agencies. OMB also issues guidance to agencies and contractors on privacy and information security issues, such as data breach disclosure and privacy impact assessments.
- The **Internal Revenue Service (IRS)** is subject to privacy rules concerning tax records, including disclosures of such records in the private sector. Other parts of the U.S. Department of Treasury are also involved with financial records issues, including compliance with money-laundering rules at the Financial Crimes Enforcement Network (FinCEN).

- The **U.S. Department of Homeland Security (DHS)** faces numerous privacy issues, such as: the E-Verify program for new employees; rules for air traveler records, under the Transportation Security Administration (TSA); and immigration and other border issues, under Immigration and Customs Enforcement (ICE).
- As new technologies emerge, additional agencies become involved in privacy. For instance, the development of the Smart Grid has made privacy an important issue for the electric utility system, thus involving the **Department of Energy (DOE)**. The increased use and surveillance implications of unmanned aerial vehicles (UAVs), also known as drones, have raised privacy issues for the **Federal Aviation Administration (FAA)**. In short, almost every agency in the federal government is or may soon become involved with privacy in some manner within that agency's jurisdiction.
- The **U.S. Department of Justice (DOJ)** is the sole federal agency to bring criminal enforcement actions, which can result in imprisonment or criminal fines. Some statutes, such as HIPAA, provide for both civil and criminal enforcement. In such cases, procedures exist for the roles of both HHS and the DOJ.[8]

5.3 The FTC and the FTC Act

The FTC is typically considered the lead privacy enforcer in the United States. The FTC is an independent agency governed by the decision of its chair and four other commissioners, instead of falling under the direct control of the president as the head of the executive branch.[9] The FTC was founded in 1914 to enforce antitrust laws, and its general consumer protection mission was established by a statutory change in 1938.[10] The FTC navigates both roles today, and privacy and information security issues have become an important part of its work.[11] This section details: (1) FTC Jurisdiction; (2) FTC Enforcement Process and Consent Decrees; (3) Deceptive Trade Practices; and (4) Unfair Trade Practices.

5.3.1 FTC Jurisdiction

The FTC enforces consumer protections for nearly all areas of commerce.[12] Before proceeding with a discussion of the details related to Section 5 of the FTC Act, it is important to mention those entities that are not covered due to limitations found in the act itself. Because Section 5 of the FTC Act refers to unfair and deceptive practices "in commerce," this means that nonprofit organizations are not covered.[13] Also, under the FTC Act, the commission's powers do not extend to certain industries, including banks and other federally regulated financial institutions, as well as common carriers, such as the transportation and communications industries.[14]

This subsection examines: the FTC's authority under the FTC Act and its application to privacy and information security; the FTC's enforcement tools under the FTC Act; the FTC's rulemaking authority under Magnuson-Moss; and the FTC's joint enforcement with states.

5.3.1.1 FTC Authority under the FTC Act and its Application to Privacy and Information Security

Section 5 of the FTC Act is perhaps the single most important piece of U.S. privacy law. Section 5 notably says that "unfair or deceptive acts or practices in or affecting commerce, are hereby declared unlawful."[15] To date, the FTC has pursued notable enforcement actions related to privacy and cybersecurity against social media companies, data brokers, mobile app developers, and others.[16]

Despite the fact that Section 5 of the FTC Act does not mention privacy or information security, the application of Section 5 to privacy and information security is clearly established today.[17] The FTC has enforced privacy violations for decades, beginning with credit reporting and debt collection practices under FCRA.[18] During the 1990s, the FTC began bringing privacy enforcement cases under its jurisdiction to address unfair and deceptive practices.

Several recent court cases about privacy and information security have confirmed and clarified the FTC's authority related to the application of Section 5 to privacy and information security—namely, the 2015 case in FTC v. Wyndham Worldwide Corporation and the 2018 case of FTC v. LabMD.

FTC v. Wyndham. The FTC's unfairness authority related to cybersecurity was upheld in the federal courts in litigation against Wyndham Worldwide Corporation. The facts of this enforcement action relate to three hacks suffered by Wyndham, a hotel company, from 2008 to 2009. Based on these breaches, the FTC investigated Wyndham for unfair and deceptive trade practices. When the FTC sought to sanction Wyndham, the company initially chose not to settle the case. In 2012, the FTC filed suit against the company in U.S. District Court. Wyndham challenged the FTC's authority to require the company to meet more than the minimum standards set forth in Section 5 of the FTC Act. The federal district court ruled for the FTC. In a 2015 decision, the Third Circuit Court of Appeals (a federal appellate court) confirmed that the FTC's longstanding authority to regulate "unfair methods of competition in or affecting commerce" under Section 5 of the FTC Act extended to regulation of cybersecurity practices that are harmful to consumers.[19]

FTC v. LabMD. In this case, the federal courts recognized the FTC's authority to regulate privacy and information security while announcing constraints on the ability of the FTC to require companies to institute comprehensive cybersecurity programs.[20] The underlying facts of the case focus on LabMD being significantly hacked on two separate occasions in 2009 and 2012.[21] In 2013, the FTC brought an enforcement action against LabMD under Section 5 of the FTC Act. Rather than enter into a consent order with the FTC, LabMD chose to proceed with an administrative hearing before an ALJ. The ALJ dismissed the action against LabMD, citing the FTC's failure to establish harm to the consumers.[22] The FTC reversed the decision by the ALJ, and issued a Final Order requiring the company to implement a comprehensive security program. LabMD appealed the FTC's Final Order to the Eleventh Circuit Court of Appeals (another federal appellate court).[23] In 2018, that court vacated the FTC's order—meaning the FTC order was unenforceable. According to the Eleventh Circuit, the FTC order "does not enjoin a specific act or practice. Instead, it mandates a complete overhaul of LabMD's data-security program and says precious little about how this is to be accomplished."[24]

5.3.1.2 FTC Enforcement Tools under the FTC Act

The FTC has traditionally relied on a variety of enforcement tools in the FTC Act—including Section 5(l) for administrative enforcement and Section 13(b) and Section 19 for judicial enforcement.[25] Under Section 5(l), the FTC issues a complaint and then determines via an administrative proceeding whether a violation has occurred. If a violation is found, the FTC issues a cease-and-desist order; the FTC can pursue civil penalties if the company subsequently violates the order.[26] Section 13(b) has been used by the FTC to seek "equitable money relief" such as restitution and disgorgement without first issuing a final cease-and-desist order. Restitution refers to recouping money losses of consumers while disgorgement means requiring companies to repay profits from wrongful conduct.[27] Section 19 allows courts to grant necessary relief if the FTC first issued a final cease-and-desist order to the company.[28]

In the 2021 case of AMG Capital Management v. FTC, the Supreme Court of the United States determined that the FTC was not authorized to obtain monetary relief, or damages, pursuant to Section 13(b) of the FTC Act.[29]

5.3.1.3 FTC Joint Enforcement with States

The FTC shares its consumer protection responsibility with the states. All 50 states have enacted statutes to protect consumers, commonly known as Unfair and Deceptive Acts and Practices (UDAP) statutes, as discussed in Section 5.6.[30] In 2022, FTC Chair Lina Khan spoke to a gathering of state attorneys general where she stated that, while there was already an incentive for federal/state partnerships in privacy enforcement, "[t]he AMG decision underscored how state partnerships help maximize relief for Americans subject to unlawful behavior."[31]

5.3.1.4 FTC Rulemaking Authority Under Magnuson-Moss

The FTC has general authority in theory to issue regulations for implementing protections against unfair and deceptive acts and practices.[32] Such regulations, however, are not promulgated under the usual rulemaking procedures of the APA, where the agency publishes a notice of proposed rule, the public then comments, and the agency finalizes the rule. Instead, any such regulation must comply with the complex and lengthy procedures under Section 18 of the FTC Act, also known as the Magnuson-Moss Warranty Federal Trade Commission Improvements Act of 1975 ("Magnuson-Moss").[33] According to Magnuson-Moss, the FTC can promulgate a trade rule regulation, which defines an act or a practice as unfair or deceptive "only where it has reason to believe that the unfair or deceptive acts or practices which are the subject of the proposed rulemaking are prevalent."[34] For rulemaking pursuant to Magnuson-Moss, the FTC must establish the following (among other requirements): the prevalence of the acts or practices; how the acts and practices are unfair or deceptive; and the economic effect of the rule, including on consumers and small businesses.[35]

In 2022, the FTC announced its intent to consider rules on surveillance practices and data security. As of this writing, possible topics for inclusion in the rules include: data minimization and targeted advertisements; consent framework; algorithmic discrimination; dark patterns; misuse of apps; and harm to minors.[36] Also, in 2022, the FTC responded to the AMG decision by proposing rules that would allow the FTC to recover funds for harm suffered by consumers.[37]

It is worth noting that the 2022 U.S. Supreme Court case of West Virginia v. EPA could narrow the breadth of rules that the FTC can enact in the future. Although the details of the legal rationale are beyond the scope of this book, this case evinced a shift from courts deferring to rules that agencies believe are appropriate to an expectation that courts would review agency rules to determine compliance based on the "major questions doctrine"—which restricts the authority of federal agencies to issue substantial regulations without precise directions from Congress. As of the writing of this book, commentators have speculated that this case could curtail the FTC's traditionally broad approach to defining unfair and deceptive trade practices.[38]

5.3.2 FTC Enforcement Process and Consent Decrees

The FTC enforcement process has numerous steps, beginning with the FTC alleging a claim against a company. When discussing enforcement by the FTC, it is important to recognize that the majority of enforcement actions end in consent decree.[39]

5.3.2.1 Enforcement Process

The typical FTC enforcement action pursuant to Section 5 of the FTC Act begins with a claim that a company has committed an unfair or deceptive practice or has violated a specific consumer protection law. The need for an enforcement action can be brought to the FTC's attention in numerous ways, such as press reports covering questionable practices or complaints from consumer groups or competitors. If the violation is minor, the FTC may work with the company to resolve the problem without launching a formal investigation. If the violation is more significant or there is a pattern of noncompliance, the FTC may proceed to full enforcement.

The FTC has broad investigatory authority, including the authority to subpoena witnesses, demand civil investigation, and require businesses to submit written reports under oath.[40] Following an investigation, the commission may initiate an enforcement action if it has reason to believe a law is being or has been violated.[41] The commission issues a complaint, and an administrative trial can proceed before an ALJ. If a violation is found, the ALJ can enjoin the company from continuing the practices that caused the violation. The decision of the ALJ can be appealed to the five commissioners. That decision, in turn, can be appealed to federal court.[42]

Although the FTC lacks the authority to assess civil penalties, if an FTC ruling is ignored the FTC can seek civil penalties in federal court of up to $50,120 per violation—as of the writing of this book—and can seek compensation for those harmed by the unfair or deceptive practices.[43]

5.3.2.2 Consent Decrees

In practice, FTC privacy enforcement actions have usually been settled through consent decrees and accompanying consent orders. In a consent decree, the respondent does not admit fault but promises to change its practices and avoids further litigation on the issue. Consent decrees are posted publicly on the FTC's website, and the details of these decrees provide guidance about what practices the FTC considers inappropriate. Once an individual or company has agreed to a consent decree, any violation of that decree can lead, following an FTC investigation, to enforcement in federal court, including civil penalties. The federal court can also grant injunctions and other forms of relief. The FTC's Enforcement Division, within the Bureau of Consumer Protection (BCP), monitors and litigates violations of consent decrees in cooperation with the DOJ.

Consent decree terms vary depending on the violation. Usually, the consent decree states what affirmative actions the respondent needs to take and which practices the respondent must refrain from engaging in. Consent decrees often require the respondent to maintain proof of compliance with the decree and to inform all related individuals of the consent decree obligations. The respondent is also usually required to provide the FTC with confirmation of its compliance with the decree and must inform the FTC if company changes will affect the respondent's ability to adhere to its terms. Respondents may also face civil penalties. Increasingly, in privacy cases, companies are subject to periodic outside audits or reviews of their practices, or they may be required to adopt and implement a comprehensive privacy program. Over time, consent decrees have become more specific in nature.

Both the company and the FTC have incentives to negotiate a consent decree rather than proceed with a full adjudication process. The company avoids a prolonged trial as well as negative ongoing publicity. It also avoids having the details of its business practices exposed to the public. The FTC: (1) achieves a consent decree that incorporates good privacy and security practices, (2) avoids the expense and delay of a trial, and (3) gains an enforcement advantage because monetary fines are much easier to assess in federal court if a company violates a consent decree than if no decree is in place.

5.3.3 Deceptive Trade Practices

Today, the application of "deceptive trade practices" in Section 5 of the FTC Act to privacy and information security is well established. As the FTC is tasked with addressing concerns raised by emerging technology, this interpretation evolved during the commercialization of the internet.

In the 1990s, organizations began to post privacy notices on their websites. These privacy notices helped inform consumers about how their personal information was being collected and used. During this period, the FTC, along with the DOC, began convening public workshops and conducting other activities to highlight the importance of privacy protection on websites.[44]

By 2000, privacy notices had become a standard feature of legitimate commercial websites.[45] If a company promised a certain level of privacy or security on its website or elsewhere and did not fulfill its promise, then the FTC considered that breach of promise a "deceptive" practice under Section 5 of the FTC Act.[46]

In addition, the absence of a privacy notice is easily visible—any consumer advocate or regulator visiting the site can tell whether a notice is posted. In practice, today most commercial websites are expected to post a privacy notice. Although there is no omnibus federal law requiring companies to have public privacy notices, certain federal sector-specific statutes such as HIPAA, GLBA, and the Children's Online Privacy Protection Act (COPPA), do impose notice requirements. Also, as discussed in Chapters 6 and 7, state laws often require companies and organizations doing in-state business to post privacy notices on their websites.

The early focus on privacy notices by the FTC has evolved into numerous privacy and security "deceptive" practices cases in a typical year. For a practice to be deceptive, it must involve a material statement or omission that is likely to mislead consumers who are acting reasonably under the circumstances.[47] Deceptive practices include false promises, misrepresentations, and failures to comply with representations made to consumers, such as statements in privacy notices or certifications of compliance with an industry or government set of standards.[48] Two recent cases highlight enforcement practices of the FTC related to deceptive trade practices—In the Matter of Facebook and In the Matter of Everalbum.

5.3.3.1 In the Matter of Facebook

In 2019, Facebook agreed to pay a $5 billion fine to settle allegations that the company deceived users about their ability to control the privacy of personal data.[49] At the time of the consent order, this fine was the largest penalty the FTC had ever imposed on a company for alleged violations of consumer privacy.[50]

In 2012, Facebook agreed to a consent order that prohibited the company from misrepresenting the extent to which users could control the privacy of their information and the extent to which the company made the information available to third parties.

According to the allegations by the FTC that resulted in the 2019 fine, Facebook violated this 2012 consent order. The FTC alleged that Facebook failed to restrict third-party developers from accessing and collecting the data of users' friends.[51]

As part of the 2019 settlement agreement, Facebook agreed to restructure its corporate approach to privacy and to create increased accountability at the level of the board of directors.[52]

5.3.3.2 In the Matter of Everalbum

In a 2021 settlement, the photo app Everalbum agreed to a novel remedy. The company agreed to delete the facial recognition algorithms developed using consumer data inappropriately obtained—a remedy referred to as algorithmic disgorgement.[53] Much as the FTC has historically sought to have companies disgorge profits from unlawful practices, it may also seek disgorgement of the algorithmic fruits of unlawful behavior.

With regard to the facts of the enforcement action, Everalbum told users that the company would not apply facial recognition technology to users' content, such as photos and videos, unless they affirmatively chose (opted in) to facial recognition. Everalbum also informed users that, when users deactivated accounts, their content would be deleted. At the time of the FTC complaint, Everalbum had 12 million users globally.

According to the allegations by the FTC, Everalbum misled users by automatically activating the facial recognition feature—noting that the facial recognition could not be turned off by most users. In addition, Everalbum failed to keep its promise to users to delete their account when users deactivated accounts. Instead, Everalbum kept the users' photos and videos indefinitely.[54]

After the U.S. Supreme Court case of AMG Capital Management v. FTC, that precluded the FTC from seeking "equitable monetary remedies" (damages) pursuant to Section 13(b), the FTC can likely still seek non-monetary remedies such as algorithmic disgorgement—which is seen as an important new remedy for the FTC.

As of the writing of this book, the FTC lacks specific regulation related to AI, which is software reliant on algorithms. To address unfair or deceptive AI practices, algorithmic disgorgement may become a more prominent enforcement tool. Experts suggest that the FTC is likely to continue to use this new remedy in consent orders unless and until courts rule that the remedy exceeds the commission's authority.

5.3.4 Unfair Trade Practices

Section 5 of the FTC Act applies to "unfair" as well as "deceptive" trade practices. The FTC began to enforce "unfair" practices by 2004.

The scope of the term "unfairness" has been clarified by the FTC numerous times over the years. Unfair practices are those that: cause or are likely to cause substantial injury to consumers (which are not merely speculative); which is not reasonably avoidable by consumers themselves; and not outweighed by countervailing benefits to consumers or competition.

Claims of unfair trade practices can exist even where the company has not made any deceptive statements if the injury is substantial, lacks offsetting benefits, and cannot be easily avoided by consumers.[55] Each step involves a detailed, fact-specific analysis that must undergo careful consideration by the commission.[56]

The FTC has sanctioned companies for unfair practices when they failed to implement adequate protection measures for sensitive personal information or when they provided inadequate disclosures to consumers.[57]

Two recent cases highlight enforcement practices of the FTC related to unfair trade practices—In the Matter of Equifax and In the Matter of Uber.

5.3.4.1 In the Matter of Equifax

The 2019 Equifax settlement showed the significant consequences faced by a company for a massive data breach. Equifax suffered a breach in 2017 that affected approximately 150 million consumers. The breach exposed Social Security numbers and home addresses of these individuals.

According to the allegations in the case, the consumer reporting agency's failure to engage in reasonable security measures to protect its network led to the 2017 data breach.[58]

In the 2019 settlement with the FTC, the CFPB, and 50 states and territories, Equifax agreed to pay $300 million to set up a fund for affected customers to receive credit monitoring: $175 million to 48 states, the District of Columbia, and Puerto Rico; and $100 million in civil penalties to the CFPB.[59] In addition, Equifax agreed to implement a comprehensive security program for 20 years.[60]

5.3.4.2 In the Matter of Uber

In 2018, Uber entered into a consent order with the FTC related to two data breaches—the first in 2014 and the second in 2016. The Uber case is significant because it marks the first time that a company executive has faced criminal prosecution related to the handling (or mishandling) of a data breach.

In the 2014 data breach, an intruder gained access to personal information of approximately 100,000 drivers. A second, larger breach occurred in 2016 where hackers accessed the personal information of approximately 60 million

Uber drivers and riders. According to the allegations in the FTC enforcement action, Uber failed to monitor employees' access to consumers' personal information; reasonably secure sensitive consumer data in the cloud; and timely disclose the second breach.[61]

The criminal prosecution focused on events in 2016. At that time, Uber was under investigation by the FTC related to the 2014 breach. Uber's chief of security (and his team) learned of the second breach when hackers demanded a $100,000 ransom from Uber. The team did not report the 2016 breach to Uber's general counsel, as required by internal policies of the company. Instead, they paid the ransom and had the hackers sign a nondisclosure agreement. The chief of security (and his team) failed to notify the FTC of the breach. In 2017, Uber hired a new CEO. After the CEO took office, Uber publicly disclosed the 2016 breach and notified the FTC of the event. In 2022, Uber's former chief of security was found guilty by a jury of the following crimes: obstructing an FTC investigation and concealing a felony from authorities.[62]

5.4 Additional FTC Authority to Protect Consumer Privacy and Security

The FTC has specific authority over privacy and security issues beyond Section 5 of the FTC Act, including COPPA, the Health Information Technology for Economic and Clinical Heath (HITECH), FCRA, and the Controlling the Assault of Non-Solicited Pornography and Marketing (CAN-SPAM) Act.

5.4.1 COPPA

The FTC is the rulemaking and enforcement agency for COPPA. This 1998 law was passed specifically to protect children's use of the internet—particularly websites and services targeted toward children, who are defined as under the age of 13.[63] COPPA requires website operators to provide clear and conspicuous notice of the data collection methods employed by the website, including functioning hyperlinks to the website privacy policy on every web page where personal information is collected. It also requires consent by parents prior to collection of personal information for children under the age of 13. This means COPPA requires express consent from a parent before a child's personal information is collected. Although COPPA does not mandate a precise method that website operators must employ to obtain consent from parents, operators are required to utilize a method that is reasonably designed, in light of the technology available, to make sure that the consent is provided by the parent of the child.[64]

As states begin to enact comprehensive privacy laws, these state laws generally contain protections for children and often refer to COPPA—particularly in relation to the requirements for obtaining consent from parents. These state laws are discussed in Chapter 6.

5.4.2 HITECH

The FTC shares rulemaking and enforcement authority with HHS for data breaches related to medical records under HITECH, which applies to personal health record providers. The notice of breach requirements under HITECH are similar to those under HIPAA (see Chapter 8). These requirements apply even if the provider does not seek electronic reimbursement from the U.S. government. This rule is enforced by the FTC.

5.4.3 FCRA

The FCRA regulates the consumer reporting industry and provides privacy rights in consumer reports. Until the creation of the CFPB, the FTC issued rules and guidance for the FCRA, as amended by the Fair and Accurate Credit Transactions Act (FACTA) of 2003. The CFPB now has authority to issue rules for those areas. The CFPB shares enforcement authority with the FTC for financial institutions that are not covered by a separate financial regulator. Also, state attorneys general are required to give notice to the FTC prior to filing suit, and the FTC retains the authority to intervene in the cases brought by the state attorneys general (see Chapter 9).

5.4.4 CAN-SPAM

CAN-SPAM restricts unsolicited commercial electronic mail. Both the FTC and the FCC have the authority to issue regulations implementing CAN-SPAM. The FCC has issued rules regarding mobile service commercial messages (MSCMs), including many commercial text messages. CAN-SPAM grants enforcement authority to the FTC and the FCC as well as state attorneys general (see Chapter 11).

5.5 Future of Federal Enforcement by the FTC

The focus of the FTC's regulatory efforts evolves with changing technology and practice. The FTC's mandate includes a focus on the cutting edge of emerging technology and practices.[65] In 2023, the FTC created an Office of Technology to further this part of its mandate.[66] This focus on emerging technology and practices by the FTC means that it is important for privacy practitioners to examine recent publications of the FTC to learn where future enforcement actions are likely to be directed.

Important guidance from the FTC on the future of privacy and security enforcement has recently come from proposed rules, workshops, reports, and advice, including: 2022 Proposed Rules concerning Commercial Surveillance, 2020 Workshop on Data Portability, 2022 Advice for Health App Developers, 2022 Staff Report on Dark Patterns, and 2022 Vision on Section 5 Authority to Address Unfair Methods of Competition.

5.5.1 FTC's Proposed Rules concerning Commercial Surveillance

In 2021, President Joe Biden issued Executive Order 14036 where he urged the FTC to exercise its rulemaking authority to address "unfair data collection and surveillance practices."[67] In 2022, the FTC announced its intent to consider rules on surveillance practices and data security. The proposed rule focus on surveillance practices defined as "the collection, aggregation, analysis, retention, transfer, or monetization of commercial data and the direct derivatives of that information." As of this writing, the FTC has started this rulemaking process under Magnuson-Moss, but it is unclear whether these rules will be enacted. Even if the rules are adopted, they would be further developed after this writing.[68]

5.5.2 FTC Workshop on Data Portability

In 2020, the FTC held a workshop concerning the benefits and challenges posed by data portability, which refers to the ability of individuals to obtain and reuse their personal data for their own purposes across different services. Attendees of the workshop included regulators, industry representatives, consumer advocates, and academics. Specific topics discussed at the FTC workshop included: (1) how data portability can empower consumers and promote competition without compromising data security; and (2) the tension between opening data flows—promote competition and to allow for user control—and closing data flows—which would protect consumer privacy and prevent unauthorized access.[69]

5.5.3 FTC Advice for Health App Developers

In 2022, the FTC issued advice tailored to health app developers regarding data security, including data minimization, limiting access and permissions, focusing on authentication, considering the mobile ecosystem, and implementing security by design. The FTC suggested that health app developers consider the following questions, which are questions that may provide insights for companies in other sectors as they grapple with how to address security concerns:

- Do you need to collect and retain people's information?
- Can you keep the data in a deidentified form?
- What permissions does your app really need?
- How does your app generate credentials?
- Are you relying on a mobile platform to protect sensitive data?
- Do you incorporate data security at every stage of your app's life cycle—design, development, launch, and post-market?
- Do you use strong encryption at rest and in transit?
- Are you taking advantage of what experts have already learned about security?[70]

These inquiries may help many companies, particularly those that deal with sensitive data, as they grapple with how to address security concerns.

5.5.4 FTC Staff Report on Dark Patterns

Following an FTC workshop on the topic in 2021, the FTC issued its 2022 Staff Report on Dark Patterns, which are sophisticated design practices that can trick or manipulate consumers into buying services/products or into giving up personal information. The report focuses on four common dark pattern practices: disguising ads and misleading consumers about content; making it difficult to cancel charges or subscriptions; hiding or obscuring key terms and sham fees; and tricking consumers into sharing data.[71]

5.5.5 FTC Vision on Section 5 Authority to Address Unfair Methods of Competition

In 2022, the FTC issued a policy statement announcing its intent to broaden its vision of Section 5 FTC enforcement. Section 5 analysis focuses on "stopping unfair methods of competition in their incipiency based on their tendency to harm competitive conditions," which is not focused only on whether the conduct caused actual harm. The FTC notes that the focus is on whether the company's conduct has a tendency to create negative consequences, such as: raise prices; limit choices; lower quality; reduce innovation; impair other market participants; or reduce likelihood of competition. The 2022 statement by the FTC emphasized that Section 5 "does not require a separate showing of market power or market definition" when the evidence indicates a tendency of anticompetitive effects. Such a showing is required for virtually all other antitrust statutes.[72]

5.6 State Enforcement

There is a complex interplay of federal and state privacy protections. We dedicate two chapters of the book to examining state comprehensive privacy laws and state data breach notification laws.

In this section, we provide an overview of the state-level framework for enforcing privacy protections. This section begins by examining the role of the state attorneys general, the primary enforcer of these protections in most states. Next, we discuss the tradition of UDAP statutes in all 50 states. We then introduce the state comprehensive privacy laws recently enacted in a handful of states, and how these laws acknowledge protections provided at the federal level (and further examined in Chapter 6). We will next introduce state data breach notifications, which have been passed in all 50 states (which are further discussed in Chapter 7). This section concludes by providing an overview of additional privacy protections at the state level.

5.6.1 State Attorneys General

In all 50 states, state attorneys general (state AGs) are constitutional officers, whose office is established under the applicable state constitutions. State AGs are popularly elected in nearly all states. State AGs are typically viewed as one of the most powerful officials in their respective states.[73]

State AGs have traditionally enforced privacy protections at the state level. Although the state AGs often have sole enforcement authority related to state-level privacy protections, sometimes there is a private right of action, or the AGs share enforcement authority with another entity within the state. In addition, certain federal statutes allow state AGs to bring enforcement actions along with the relevant federal agency. These federal laws include HIPAA (Chapter 8), GLBA (Chapter 9), and CAN-SPAM (Chapter 10).[74]

5.6.2 State UDAP Statutes

The states have had a lengthy legal tradition of providing consumer protections, especially since the 1960s. As previously mentioned, each of the 50 states have UDAP statutes which are roughly similar to Section 5 of the FTC Act. The FTC Act does not preempt state laws on unfair and deceptive trade practices so long as they do not conflict with the requirements of the federal law. Some statutes also allow enforcement against "unconscionable" practices, a contract law term for a range of harsh seller practices.[75] Several states allow private rights of action under their state UDAP laws so individuals can bring suit against violators.[76] UDAP laws are enforced by state attorneys general.[77]

5.6.3 State Comprehensive Privacy Laws

With the lack of a federal comprehensive privacy law, a number of states have recently enacted comprehensive privacy laws, and many other states are considering this type of legislation. Chapter 6 details the five state laws that were enacted as of the conclusion of 2022: California, Colorado, Connecticut, Utah, and Virginia. The definition of personal information found in these state comprehensive privacy laws, which is broader than the definition of personal information found in state data breach notification laws, typically applies to any data that can be associated or linked with a particular individual.

These state comprehensive privacy laws acknowledge the various federal privacy laws by incorporating numerous references to these laws. This section examines the interaction with federal protections for children's data as well as federal sectoral privacy laws.

5.6.3.1 Interaction with Federal Protection for Children's Data

Each of the state comprehensive privacy laws has special rules governing how companies address the data of children, although variation exists in the specific approach taken. Most of these state laws reference COPPA for procedures on how to obtain consent from parents for children's data.

5.6.3.2 Interaction with Federal Sectoral Privacy Laws

The state comprehensive privacy laws provide two types of exemptions in their laws related to the interplay with federal sectoral privacy laws. Some states exempt from compliance those entities that are subject to a specific federal law, referred to as entity-level exemptions. Other states exempt only that data that is protected by the federal law. This is known as data-based exemptions.

The Health Insurance and Portability Act (HIPAA) focuses on protected health information (PHI) held by covered entities, such as health care providers seeking electronic reimbursement. Out of the five state comprehensive privacy laws passed by 2023, Connecticut, Utah, and Virginia's privacy laws exempt HIPAA entities. California, Colorado, Connecticut, Utah, and Virginia generally exempt data that is regulated under HIPAA.

The Gramm-Leach-Bliley (GLBA) applies to the use of nonpublic personal information of financial institutions, a broad term including banks and securities firms (see Chapter 9). Out of the five state comprehensive privacy laws passed by 2023, Colorado, Connecticut, Utah, and Virginia's laws all exempt GLBA entities. California, Colorado, Connecticut, Utah, and Virginia generally exempt data that is regulated under GLBA.

The Fair Credit Reporting Act (FCRA) regulates consumer reporting agencies (CRAs) that furnish consumer reports (see Chapter 9). All five states with passed comprehensive privacy laws by 2023 exempt entities covered by the FCRA. These states generally exempt data that is regulated under this law.

The Driver's Privacy Protection Act (DPPA) of 1994 prohibits state departments of motor vehicles (DMVs) from releasing personal information of drivers without their express permission, except in situations where a permissible use exists.[78] The DPPA defines personal information to include the information used by the state department in connection with obtaining the driver's license such as: name, address, telephone number, and driver identification number.[79] The DPPA further limits the permissible uses of highly restricted personal information, including Social Security numbers, photographs of individuals, and medical or disability information.[80] The DPPA has recently received attention because it is discussed in numerous state comprehensive privacy laws. All five states provide an exemption for personal data that is "collected, processed, sold, or disclosed" pursuant to DPPA.[81]

5.6.4 State Data Breach Notification Laws

State enforcement of information security lapses has been especially prominent, driven by data breach notifications. Since California enacted the first breach notification law in 2002, every state has passed a breach notification law (see Chapter 7).[82]

The definition of personal information found in state data breach notification laws is tailored to protecting individuals from identify theft and fraud. This means, in the majority of state data breach notification laws, the focus is on categories such as an individual's first name or first initial and last name in combination with one, or more, of the following: (1) Social Security number; (2) driver's license number or state identification card number; or (3) financial account number or credit or debit card number. Note that many of these laws require organizations to furnish state AGs with reports about breaches when they occur. These laws also often confer enforcement authority on state AGs if the breach notification reveals the implementation of inadequate security controls.

Data breaches often involve the theft of identifiers unique to an individual, such as Social Security numbers, that can lead to identify theft. This subsection thus turns to state protections for Social Security numbers as well as state identity theft laws.

5.6.4.1 State Protections for Social Security Numbers

In the United States, a Social Security number is a nine-digit number issued to U.S. citizens, permanent residents, and certain other residents. The number is associated with retirement benefits under the federal law known as the Social Security Act of 1935. Under this act, states are permitted to require individuals to furnish this number to establish eligibility for unemployment compensation and various welfare programs.[83] The federal government places a variety of limits on disclosure of Social Security numbers, including a prohibition on having the numbers visible through the window of Treasury-disbursed check envelopes.[84] The DPPA curtailed the widespread use of Social Security numbers by state departments of motor vehicles (DMVs).[85]

Over time, Social Security numbers became a de facto identifier requested—and often required—in government and business transactions.[86] Once this evolution in the use of Social Security numbers occurred, these numbers became key in successful identity theft schemes. Largely in response to concerns related to identity theft, state have enacted a variety of legal protections for Social Security numbers—these protections can be found in state comprehensive privacy laws, state data breach notification laws, and specific state laws limiting businesses' right to use Social Security numbers.[87] California law, for example, prohibits businesses as well as state and local agencies from using Social Security numbers for a variety of purposes including public posting, printing on mailings (unless mandated by federal law), and printing on ID or membership cards.[88] Additionally, this law prohibits businesses from requiring that customers transmit their Social Security numbers over an unencrypted internet connection.

5.6.4.2 State Identity Theft Laws

In 2003, Congress made substantial amendments to FCRA when it passed the Fair and Accurate Credit Transactions Act (FACTA), discussed in Chapter 9.[89] Although FACTA preempted many state laws related to consumer credit reports, states retained the power to enact laws addressing identity theft.[90] As of the writing of this book, all 50 states have enacted identity theft laws. More than half of the states permit restitution for victims of identity theft.[91]

5.6.5 Additional Privacy Protections at the State Level

States provide a variety of privacy protections in addition to the laws already detailed in this subsection. As discussed in Chapter 2, numerous state constitutions expressly recognize a right to privacy. State common law is an additional source of privacy enforcement. Plaintiffs can sue under the privacy torts, which traditionally have been categorized as intrusion upon seclusion, appropriation of name or likeness, publicity given to private life, and publicity placing a person in false light.[92] Plaintiffs may also sue under a contract theory in certain situations, such when a physician, financial institution, or other entity holding sensitive information breaches a promise of confidentiality and causes harm.

States also have many other specialized statutes protecting privacy. These state laws exist for the medical, financial, workplace, and other sectors.[93] As with federal law, new issues arise with changing technology. States, for instance, are examining the appropriate rules for personal information collected in connection with smart cities.[94]

Examples of two state laws provide insight into the national implications that can result when a state addresses specific privacy concerns, particularly in the absence of federal legislation on the topic.

In 2008, Illinois enacted the **Biometric Information Privacy Act (BIPA)** which requires companies, including employers, to notify individuals of their biometric practices and to obtain informed consent prior to using individuals' biometric data as part of these practices. In 2015, the private right of action in BIPA gained national attention with the filing of a series of class-action lawsuits. Businesses continue to struggle with how to address the requirements of BIPA in their nationwide approaches to the use of biometric information.[95]

In 2022, California enacted the **Age-Appropriate Design Code Act**, modeled on the UK's act, which places legal obligations on businesses that provide online services or products that are likely to be accessed by children under the age of 18. As the name implies, the law requires covered businesses to make design choices with their services and products that protect children, such as configuring default privacy settings to provide a high level of privacy for children. The law also mandates restrictions on the use of children's data by covered businesses and extends these requirements to situations that would negatively impact the child's physical or mental well-being.[96] California's actions in this area are particularly important and influential because of the size of the state's economy and of California's jurisdiction over the country's largest technology companies and platform providers.

5.7 Self-Regulation and Enforcement

The term "self-regulation" refers to a variety of approaches to privacy protection. Self-regulation, similar to government regulation, can occur through the three separation-of-powers components: legislation, enforcement, and adjudication.[97] Legislation refers to the question of who should define appropriate rules for protecting privacy. Enforcement refers to the question of who should initiate enforcement actions. Adjudication refers to the question of who should decide whether a company has violated the privacy rules, and with what penalties.

For enforcement under Section 5 of the FTC Act or state UDAP laws, self-regulation only occurs at the quasi-legislative stage (i.e., voluntary industry rulemaking). A company writes its own privacy policy, or an industry group drafts a code of conduct that companies agree to follow. Under Section 5, the FTC can then decide whether to bring an enforcement action, and adjudication can occur in front of an ALJ, with appeal to federal court. Referring to this approach as self-regulation is somewhat confusing because a government agency is involved at the enforcement and adjudication stage.

Other self-regulatory systems engage in all three roles without the involvement of a government agency. For example, the Payment Credit Card Industry Data Security Standard (PCI DSS) provides an enforceable security standard for payment card data. The rules were drafted by the PCI DSS Council, which built on previous rules written by the various credit card companies.[98] Except for small companies, compliance with the standard requires hiring a third party to conduct security assessments and detect violations. Failure to comply can lead to enforcement, decision-making, and penalties as set forth in the standard. Consequences can include cutting off the violator from being able to receive payments from Visa, MasterCard or payment card systems, as well as penalties of $5,000 to $100,000 per month.[99]

Third-party privacy seal and certification programs play an important role in providing assurances that companies are complying with self-regulatory programs. Services offered by the Better Business Bureau, companies like TrustArc, and others provide methods for third parties to oversee compliance.[100] Companies may demonstrate compliance and thus improve consumer confidence by displaying a trust mark in the form of a seal, logo or certification showing that the company is part of a certification program. It can serve as a way to comply with legal requirements.

One prominent self-regulatory effort involves the Digital Advertising Alliance (DAA), a coalition of media and advertising organizations. The DAA helped develop an icon program intended to inform consumers about how they can exercise choice with respect to online behavioral advertising. The AdChoices system allows users to click on an icon near an ad or to visit the AdChoices website and choose to what extent the user will view behavioral ads from participating advertisers.[101]

It is important to note that self-regulation is controversial. Privacy advocates and supporters of the European approach to data protection often express concern that industries are not strict enough when creating, adhering to, and enforcing privacy rules or codes of conduct. European regulators, for instance, say that privacy is a fundamental human right, and data protection authorities (DPAs) should be involved in defining and protecting that right.[102] Supporters of self-regulation tend to emphasize the fact that industry has greater expertise about how its systems operate and therefore should lead the creation, establishment, and enforcement of those rules.[103]

5.8 Conclusion

In this chapter, we have examined the complex legal framework for providing privacy protections in the United States, including the interplay between federal and state enforcement of privacy. In the absence of a federal law that provides comprehensive privacy protections, privacy practitioners need to understand how the different parts of this framework interact.

At the federal level, the FTC is generally considered to have the main role for enforcing consumer protection law. This enforcement has evolved over time from focusing on deceptive practices to a more comprehensive approach—moving beyond the mere punishment of violators to consent decrees that require the implementation of best practices in privacy and security. The FTC is also the enforcer of COPPA, the primary federal law addressing children's privacy. When examining the privacy framework in the

United States, the large number of federal agencies and other actors involved in U.S. privacy enforcement are important to consider. This chapter provides an overview of these players, noting that many of these topics will be discussed in more detail later in this book.

State laws should not be overlooked when examining the privacy framework in the United States. The state UDAP laws have been in place for decades, in large part following the lead of the federal government in enacting the consumer protections found in the FTC Act. In recent years, the states have taken the lead in enacting comprehensive privacy protections for their citizens. This chapter serves as a preview for the two chapters in the book that focus on state laws: Chapter 6 (State Comprehensive Privacy Laws) and Chapter 7 (State Data Breach Notification Laws).

In Chapter 14 (The GDPR and International Privacy Issues), we layer on the additional complexity that companies must face related to privacy protections when we explore cross-border enforcement.

Endnotes

1 "Administrative Procedure Act (5 U.S.C. Subchapter II)," Federal Register, National Archives, accessed January 2020, https://www.archives.gov/federal-register/laws/administrative-procedure/.

2 "Consumer Financial Protection Circular 2022-04: Insufficient Data Protection or Security for Sensitive Consumer Information," CFPB, August 11, 2022, https://www.consumerfinance.gov/compliance/circulars/circular-2022-04-insufficient-data-protection-or-security-for-sensitive-consumer-information/; "Data Protection Law: An Overview," Congressional Research Service, March 25, 2019, https://crsreports.congress.gov/product/pdf/R/R45631; see Maneesha Mithal, et al., "Privacy and Security of Health Information: A Primer for Digital Health Companies," Wilson Sonsini, June 1, 2022, https://www.wsgr.com/en/insights/privacy-and-security-of-health-information-a-primer-for-digital-health-companies.html.

3 See Eli MacKinnon and Jennifer King, "Regulating AI Through Data Privacy," Stanford University Human-Centered Artificial Intelligence, January 11, 2022, https://hai.stanford.edu/news/regulating-ai-through-data-privacy; Cameron Kerry, "Protecting Privacy in an AI-Driven World," Brookings, February 10, 2020, https://www.brookings.edu/research/protecting-privacy-in-an-ai-driven-world/.

4 Kristi Kung, Dan Kagan, an Andrew Serwin, "OCR Releases Important Guidance Regarding HIPAA and the Use of Tracking Technologies," December 15, 2022, https://www.dlapiper.com/en-us/insights/publications/2022/12/ocr-releases-important-guidance-regarding-hipaa-and-the-use-of-tracking-technologies.

5 Sharon Perley Masling, "EEOC Releases Guidance on Algorithms, AI, and Disability Discrimination in Hiring," May 20, 2022, https://www.morganlewis.com/pubs/2022/05/eeoc-releases-guidance-on-algorithms-ai-and-disability-discrimination-in-hiring; see Deven Desai, Swati Gupta, and Jad Salem, "Using Algorithms to Tame Discrimination: A Path to Algorithmic Diversity, Equity, and Inclusion," UC Davis

Law Review (October 10, 2022), https://papers.ssrn.com/sol3/papers.cfm?abstract_id=4244925. Privacy concerns also exist related to government use of AI, such as biometric surveillance and social media monitoring. In the absence of a specific federal law regulating the use of AI by government actors in the United States, commentators also expect that the existing legal frameworks to restrain government actions will be applied to AI. These protections are described in detail in Chapter 13 (Civil Litigation and Government Investigations). See Steven Feldstein, Eduardo Ferreyra, and Danilo Krivokapic, *The Global Struggle Over AI Surveillance: Emerging Trends and Democratic Responses*, National Endowment for Democracy and International Forum for Democratic Studies, Working Paper June 2022, https://www.ned.org/global-struggle-over-ai-surveillance-emerging-trends-democratic-responses/; Karl Manheim and Lyric Kaplan, "Artificial Intelligence: Risks to Privacy and Democracy," *Yale Journal of Law & Technology* 21 (2019), https://yjolt.org/sites/default/files/21_yale_j.l._tech._106_0.pdf.

6 See Cobun Zweifel-Keegan, "US Institutions Privacy Stakeholder Map," Resource Center, IAPP, Marc 2023, https://iapp.org/resources/article/us-institutions-privacy-stakeholder-map/.

7 This topic is discussed in Chapter 14. "EU-U.S. Privacy Shield," U.S. Department of Commerce, accessed August 2023, https://www.commerce.gov/tags/eu-us-privacy-shield.

8 Federal Trade Commission Act, 42 U.S.C. § 1320d–6(a), Legal Information Institute, Cornell Law School, accessed January 2020, https://www.law.cornell.edu/uscode/text/42/1320d-6.

9 Zweifel-Keegan, "U.S. Institutions Privacy Stakeholder Map"; see Chris Jay Hoofnagle, *Federal Trade Commission Privacy Law and Policy,* (Cambridge, UK: Cambridge University Press, 2016); see also Andrew Serwin, "The Federal Trade Commission and Privacy: Defining Enforcement and Encouraging Adoption of Best Practices," San Diego Law Review 48, (2011), https://digital.sandiego.edu/sdlr/vol48/iss3/4/.

10 J. Howard Beales III, "The FTC's Use of Unfairness Authority: Its Rise, Fall, and Resurrection," Federal Trade Commission, May 30, 2003, https://www.ftc.gov/public-statements/2003/05/ftcs-use-unfairness-authority-its-rise-fall-and-resurrection.

11 "Federal Trade Commission," Resource Center, IAPP, accessed August 2023, https://iapp.org/resources/article/federal-trade-commission-2/; see Cobun Zweifel-Keegan, "IAPP Enforcement Guide to FTC Privacy Enforcement," IAPP White Paper, May 2017, https://iapp.org/resources/article/iapp-guide-to-ftc-privacy-enforcement/.

12 "What the FTC Does," Federal Trade Commission, accessed August 2023, https://www.ftc.gov/news-events/media-resources/what-ftc-does.

13 Nonprofit working with companies for profit.

14 15 U.S.C. § 45, Legal Information Institute, Cornell Law School, accessed January 2020, https://www.law.cornell.edu/uscode/text/15/45; K.C. Halm, Christin McMeley, John Seiver, an Bryan Thompson, "Ninth Circuit Rules All Common Carriers Beyond Reach of FTC's Consumer Protection Authority," September 1, 2016, https://www.dwt.com/insights/2016/09/ninth-circuit-rules-all-common-carriers-beyond-rea; FCC-FTC Consumer Protection Memorandum of Understand, Federal Trade Commission, accessed August 2023, https://www.ftc.gov/system/files/documents/cooperation_agreements/151116ftcfcc-mou.pdf.

15 15 U.S.C. § 45, Legal Information Institute, Cornell Law School.

16 "The FTC's Use of Its Authorities to Protect Consumer Privacy and Security," Federal Trade Commission, 2020, https://www.ftc.gov/system/files/documents/reports/reports-response-senate-appropriations-committee-report-116-111-ftcs-use-its-authorities-resources/p065404reportprivacydatasecurity.pdf.

17 15 U.S.C. § 45(a)(1), Legal Information Institute, Cornell Law School, accessed January 2020, https://www.law.cornell.edu/uscode/text/15/45.

18 "The FTC is nimble and can adapt to new technologies without an act of Congress. ... Many privacy issues are thought to be new. But the Federal Trade Commission has decades of experience handling privacy problems, particularly in credit reporting and debt collection." Chris Jay Hoofnagle, Woody Hartzog, and Daniel Solove, "The FTC Can Rise to the Challenge, but Not Without Help from Congress," *TechTank* (blog), Brookings, August 8, 2019, https://www.brookings.edu/blog/techtank/2019/08/08/the-ftc-can-rise-to-the-privacy-challenge-but-not-without-help-from-congress/; see "The FTC's Use of Its Authorities to Protect Consumer Privacy and Security," Federal Trade Commission.

19 "FTC Held to Have Authority to Regulate Cybersecurity Practices under Section 5 Of The FTC Act," Norton Rose Fulbright, December 28, 2015, https://www.nortonrosefulbright.com/en/knowledge/publications/4872772b/ftc-held-to-have-authority-to-regulate-cybersecurity-practices-under-section-5-of-the-ftc-act; see Lesley Fair, "Third Circuit Rules in FTC v. Wyndham Case," *Business Blog*, Federal Trade Commission, August 25, 2015, https://www.ftc.gov/business-guidance/blog/2015/08/third-circuit-rules-ftc-v-wyndham-case; see also "FTC v. Wyndham Worldwide Corp.," *Harvard Law Review* 129, no. 4, February 10, 2016, https://harvardlawreview.org/2016/02/ftc-v-wyndham-worldwide-corp/.

20 See Jim Harvey, Larry Sommerfeld, and Kate Hanniford, "LabMD: The End of the FTC in Cyber, or Just a New Path?" Privacy & Data Security Advisory, Alston & Bird, July 9, 2018, https://www.alston.com/-/media/files/insights/publications/2018/07/183465-labmd-client-alert.pdf; Lydia Parnes and Eddie Holman, "Eleventh Circuit LabMD Decision Significantly Restrains FTC's Remedial Powers in Data Security and Privacy Actions," Wilson Sonsini, June 18, 2018, https://www.wsgr.com/en/insights/eleventh-circuit-labmd-decision-significantly-restrains-ftc-s-remedial-powers-in-data-security-and-privacy-actions.html; Kirk Nahra, "Takeaways from the 11th Circuit FTC v. LabMD Decision," *Privacy Tracker*, IAPP, June 7, 2018, https://iapp.org/news/a/takeaways-from-the-11th-circuit-ftc-vs-labmd-decision/.

21 According to the FTC's complaint, sensitive patient information for thousands of LabMD customers was taken in the 2009 hack and placed on a peer-to-peer file-sharing network. The types of information included names, Social Security numbers, birth dates, health insurance provider information, and standardized medical treatment codes. The second hack, in 2012, resulted in at least 500 customer names and Social Security numbers being found in the possession of identity thieves. Initial decision of administrative law judge in the case of In the Matter of LabMD, November 13, 2019, https://www.ftc.gov/system/files/documents/cases/151113labmd_decision.pdf.

22 As to the 2009 incident, the ALJ decided that the FTC failed to establish that there was actual harm to the customers, as required under the legal test for unfairness. Notably, the ALJ stated that consumer's "embarrassment or other emotional harm" from exposure of sensitive information on a peer-to-peer network was not sufficient to be a basis to sanction LabMD. With regard to the 2012 incident, the ALJ determined that the FTC failed to introduce evidence that LabMD was the source of the information found with the identity

thieves. See Section 5(n) defines an "unfair" practice as one that "causes or is likely to cause substantial injury to consumers," 15 U.S. Code § 45, Legal Information Institute, Cornell Law School, accessed January 2020, https://www.law.cornell.edu/uscode/text/15/45.

23 LabMD also requested a stay of the Final Order, meaning that it asked not to have to implement the security program while the appeal was pending. The Court granted the request for a stay. *See* Rita Heimes, "US Appeals Court Narrows FTC's 'Unfair' Standard in LabMD Case," Privacy Bar Section, IAPP, November 14, 2016, https://iapp.org/news/a/us-appeals-court-narrows-ftcs-unfair-standard-in-labmd-case/; see Angelique Carson, "LabMD Argues 'Matter of Principle' in FTC Data Security Appeal," *Privacy Advisor*, IAPP, June 26, 2017, https://iapp.org/news/a/11th-circuit-hears-arguments-in-labmd-v-ftc-appeal/.

24 Kirk Nahra, "Takeaways from the 11th Circuit FTC v. LabMD Decision," *Privacy Tracker*, IAPP, June 7, 2018, https://iapp.org/news/a/takeaways-from-the-11th-circuit-ftc-vs-labmd-decision/; see Lydia Parnes and Eddie Holman, "Eleventh Circuit LabMD Decision Significantly Restrains FTC's Remedial Powers in Data Security and Privacy Actions," Wilson Sonsini, June 18, 2018, https://www.wsgr.com/en/insights/eleventh-circuit-labmd-decision-significantly-restrains-ftc-s-remedial-powers-in-data-security-and-privacy-actions.html. It is worth noting that LabMD ceased operations in 2014 and blamed the Federal Trade Commission enforcement action. See Dune Lawrence, "A Leak Wounded This Company. Fighting the Feds Finished It Off," *Bloomberg*, April 25, 2016, https://www.bloomberg.com/features/2016-labmd-ftc-tiversa/; Cheryl Conner, "When the Government Closes Your Business," *Forbes*, February 1, 2014, https://www.forbes.com/sites/cherylsnappconner/2014/02/01/when-the-government-closes-your-business/#48e190041435.

25 "The FTC's Enforcement Power: How AMG Reshapes the Landscape," Proskauer, April 23, 2021, https://www.proskauer.com/alert/the-ftcs-enforcement-power-how-amg-reshapes-the-landscape; see "A Brief Overview of the Federal Trade Commission's Investigative, Law Enforcement, and Rulemaking Authority," Federal Trade Commission, revised May 2021, https://www.ftc.gov/about-ftc/mission/enforcement-authority.

26 15 U.S. Code § 45, Legal Information Institute, Cornell Law School.

27 15 U.S. Code § 53, Legal Information Institute, Cornell Law School, https://www.law.cornell.edu/uscode/text/15/53.

28 15 U.S. Code § 57b, Legal Information Institute, Cornell Law School, https://www.law.cornell.edu/uscode/text/15/57b.

29 "Section 13(b) does not authorize the Commission to seek, or a court to award, equitable monetary relief such as restitution or disgorgement. … Congress granted the Commission authority to enforce the Act's prohibitions on 'unfair or deceptive acts or practices,' … by commencing administrative proceedings pursuant to §5 of the Act. Section 5(l) of the Act authorizes the Commission, following completion of the administrative process and the issuance of a final cease and desist order, to seek civil penalties, and permits district courts to 'grant mandatory injunctions and such other and further equitable relief as they deem appropriate in the enforcement of such final orders of the Commission' … Section 19 of the Act further authorizes district courts (subject to various conditions and limitations) to grant 'such relief as the court finds necessary to redress injury to consumers,' … in cases where someone has engaged in unfair or deceptive conduct with respect to which the Commission has issued a final

cease and desist order applicable to that person." Syllabus, AMG Capital Management v. FTC, the United States Supreme Court (2021), https://www.supremecourt.gov/opinions/20pdf/19-508_l6gn.pdf; see AMG Capital Management, LLC v. Federal Trade Commission, Oyez, April 2, 2021, https://www.oyez.org/cases/2020/19-508; see also So Jung Kim, "Post-FTC v. AMG: Consumer Redress Through Other Means," *The University of Chicago Law Review Online* (September 20, 2022), https://lawreviewblog.uchicago.edu/2022/09/20/kim-ftc-amg/; AMG v. FTC: US Surpreme Court Severely Limits FTC's Ability to Seek Monetary Relief," Cooley, April 29, 2021, https://www.cooley.com/news/insight/2021/2021-04-29-amg-v-ftc; Leonard L. Gordon, Alexandra Megaris, and Michael A. Munoz, "Rolling with the Punches: The FTC Goes with Civil Penalties after AMG Capital Management Takes Away Section 13(b) Authority," Venable LLP, June 29, 2021, https://www.allaboutadvertisinglaw.com/2021/06/rolling-with-the-punches-the-ftc-goes-with-civil-penalties-after-amg-capital-management-takes-away-section-13b-authority.html.

30 "Defining Unfair or Deceptive Practices," Comment of Federal Trade Commissioner Rohit Chopra, 2019, https://www.ftc.gov/system/files/documents/public_statements/1576174/chopra_-_comment_to_department_of_transportation_no_dot-ost-2019-0182.pdf; see "Interjurisdictional Collaboration," National Association of Attorney's General, accessed August 2023, https://www.naag.org/issues/consumer-protection/interjurisdictional-collaboration/.

31 Paul Singer, Abigail Stempson, and Beth Chun, "Statements to the State AGs: CFPB and FTC Priorities for 2023, December 9, 2022, https://www.adlawaccess.com/2022/12/articles/statements-to-the-state-ags-cfpb-and-ftc-priorities-for-2023/.

32 15 U.S.C. § 57A, Legal Information Institute, Cornell Law School, accessed January 2023, https://www.law.cornell.edu/uscode/text/15/57a.

33 15 U.S. Code § 45, Legal Information Institute, Cornell Law School.

34 15 U.S.C. § 57A, Legal Information Institute, Cornell Law School; see Ian Davis, "Resurrecting Magnuson-Moss Rulemaking: The FTC at a Data Security Crossroads," *Emory Law Journal* 69, (February 20, 2019), https://papers.ssrn.com/sol3/papers.cfm?abstract_id=3363925.

35 15 U.S.C. § 57A, Legal Information Institute, Cornell Law School.

36 Lesley Fair, "FTC Undertakes Inquiry into Commercial Surveillance Practices and Wants Your Insights," Business Blog, Federal Trade Commission, August 16, 2022, https://www.ftc.gov/business-guidance/blog/2022/08/ftc-undertakes-inquiry-commercial-surveillance-practices-and-wants-your-insights; "FTC Launches Commercial Surveillance an Data Security Rulemaking, Holds a Public Forum, and Seeks Public Input," Gibson Dunn, September 27, 2022, https://www.gibsondunn.com/ftc-launches-commercial-surveillance-and-data-security-rulemaking-holds-a-public-forum-and-seeks-public-input/.

37 "FTC's Rulemaking Authority: Update Following Recent Developments," Concurrences Law & Economics Webinar, October 24, 2022, https://peterswire.net/wp-content/uploads/Concurrences-synthesis-FTC-Rulemaking-Authority-2022.pdf; see "FTC to Explore Rulemaking to Combat Fake Reviews and Other Deceptive Endorsements," Federal Trade Commission, October 20, 2022, https://www.ftc.gov/news-events/news/press-releases/2022/10/ftc-explore-rulemaking-combat-fake-reviews-other-deceptive-endorsements; "FTC Proposes New Rule to Combat Government and Business Impersonation Scams," Federal Trade Commission, September 15, 2022, https://www.

ftc.gov/news-events/news/press-releases/2022/09/ftc-proposes-new-rule-combat-government-business-impersonation-scams.

38 David DiMolfetta and Sarah Barry James, "Supreme Court Decision to Complicate FCC, FTC Rulemaking Process, Experts Say," S&P Global, June 30, 2022, https://www.spglobal.com/marketintelligence/en/news-insights/latest-news-headlines/supreme-court-decision-to-complicate-fcc-ftc-rulemaking-processes-experts-say-70952924; Eirk Weibust and Stuart Gerson, "The FTC Seemingly Thumbs Its Nose at the Supreme Court," *The National Law Review*, July 21, 2022, https://www.natlawreview.com/article/ftc-seemingly-thumbs-its-nose-supreme-court; "Cases Granted Review: West Virginia v. EPA, 20-1530; North American Coal Corp. v. EPA, 20-1531; Westmoreland Mining Holdings, LLC v. EPA, 20-1778; North Dakota v. EPA, 20-1780," National Association of Attorney's General, November 9, 2021, https://www.naag.org/attorney-general-journal/supreme-court-report-west-virginia-v-epa-20-1530-north-american-coal-corp-v-epa-20-1531-westmoreland-mining-holdings-llc-v-epa-20-1778-north-dakota-v-epa-20-1780-2/; Omer Tene, "The FTC's Privacy Rulemaking: Risks and Opportunities," IAPP, August 17, 2022, https://iapp.org/news/a/the-ftcs-privacy-rulemaking-risks-and-opportunities/.

39 See Ian Davis, "Resurrecting Magnuson-Moss Rulemaking: The FTC at a Data Security Crossroads," *Emory Law Journal* (2020), https://scholarlycommons.law.emory.edu/elj/vol69/iss4/4/; J. William Binkley, "Fair Notice of Unfair Practices: Due Process in FTC Data Security Enforcement After Wyndham," *Berkeley Technology Law Journal* (2016), https://btlj.org/data/articles2016/vol31/31_ar/1079_1108_Binkley_WEB.pdf.

40 15 U.S.C. § 46, 49, 57b-1, Legal Information Institute, Cornell Law School, accessed January 2020, https://www.law.cornell.edu/uscode/text/15/46, https://www.law.cornell.edu/uscode/text/15/49; and https://www.law.cornell.edu/uscode/text/15/57b-1.

41 "A Brief Overview of the Federal Trade Commission's Investigative, Law Enforcement, and Rulemaking Authority," Federal Trade Commission.

42 "A Brief Overview of the Federal Trade Commission's Investigative, Law Enforcement, and Rulemaking Authority," Federal Trade Commission.

43 The precise amount of the civil penalty is adjusted for inflation each year. 16 C.F.R. § 1.98, Legal Information Institute, Cornell Law School, accessed January 2023, https://www.law.cornell.edu/cfr/text/16/1.98; 15 U.S.C. § 45, Legal Information Institute, Cornell Law School.

44 Peter P. Swire, "Trustwrap: The Importance of Legal Rules to Electronic Commerce and Internet Privacy," *Hastings Law Journal* 54 (August 6, 2003): 847, https://papers.ssrn.com/sol3/papers.cfm?abstract_id=424167.

45 *Privacy Online: Fair Information Practices in the Electronic Marketplace: A Federal Trade Commission Report to Congress*, Federal Trade Commission, May 2000, https://www.ftc.gov/reports/privacy-online-fair-information-practices-electronic-marketplace-federal-trade-commission.

46 "Gateway Learning Settles FTC Privacy Charges," Federal Trade Commission, July 7, 2004, https://www.ftc.gov/news-events/press-releases/2004/07/gateway-learning-settles-ftc-privacy-charges.

47 "FTC Policy Statement on Deception," Federal Trade Commission, October 14, 1983, https://www.ftc.gov/public-statements/1983/10/ftc-policy-statement-deception; see *Big Data: A Tool for Inclusion or Exclusion? Understanding the Issues*, Federal Trade Commission, January 2016, https://www.ftc.gov/reports/big-data-tool-inclusion-or-exclusion-understanding-issues-ftc-report.

48 Sidley Austin, *Essentially Equivalent: A Comparison of the Legal Orders for Privacy and Data Protection in the European Union and United States*, January 2016, www.sidley.com/~/media/publications/essentially-equivalent---final.pdf.

49 "FTC Imposes $5 Billion Penalty and Sweeping New Privacy Restrictions on Facebook," Federal Trade Commission, July 24, 2019, https://www.ftc.gov/news-events/press-releases/2019/07/ftc-imposes-5-billion-penalty-sweeping-new-privacy-restrictions; see Ryan Chiavetta, "U.S. Lawmakers Respond to Facebook's $5B FTC Settlement," *Privacy Tracker*, IAPP, July 15, 2019, https://iapp.org/news/a/us-lawmakers-respond-to-facebooks-5b-ftc-settlement/.

50 "FTC Imposes $5 Billion Penalty and Sweeping New Privacy Restrictions on Facebook," Federal Trade Commission , July 24, 2019, https://www.ftc.gov/news-events/press-releases/2019/07/ftc-imposes-5-billion-penalty-sweeping-new-privacy-restrictions; see Mike Snider and Edward Baig, "Facebook Fined $5 Billion by FTC, Must Update and Adopt New Privacy, Security Measures," *USA Today*, July 24, 2019, https://www.usatoday.com/story/tech/news/2019/07/24/facebook-pay-record-5-billion-fine-u-s-privacy-violations/1812499001/.

51 United States v. Facebook, Complaint against Facebook, Federal Trade Commission (2019), https://www.ftc.gov/system/files/documents/cases/182_3109_facebook_complaint_filed_7-24-19.pdf.

52 "FTC Imposes $5 Billion Penalty and Sweeping New Privacy Restrictions on Facebook," Federal Trade Commission.

53 Avi Gesser, Paul Rubin, and Anna Gressel, "Model Destruction – FTC's Powerful New AI and Privacy Enforcement Tool," *Data Blog*, Debevoise & Plimpton, March 22, 2022, https://www.debevoisedatablog.com/2022/03/22/model-destruction-the-ftcs-powerful-new-ai-enforcement-tool/; see In the Matter of Everalbum, Inc., Complaint against Everalbum, Federal Trade Commission (2019), https://www.ftc.gov/system/files/documents/cases/everalbum_complaint.pdf. Rebecca Slaughter, Former Acting Chair of the FTC, explained the concept of algorithmic disgorgement in relation to disgorgement of ill-gotten monetary gains, a remedy that the FTC has routinely used when consumers pay for a product that is marketed deceptively. According to Former Acting Chair Slaughter, "Everalbum shows how we can apply this principle to privacy cases where companies collect and use consumers' data in unlawful ways. We should require violators to disgorge not only ill-gotten data, but also to the benefits – the algorithms – generated from that data." Kate Kaye, "The FTC's New Enforcement Weapon Spells Death for Algorithms," Protocol, March 14, 2022, https://www.protocol.com/policy/ftc-algorithm-destroy-data-privacy.

54 See In the Matter of Everalbum, Inc., Complaint against Everalbum, Federal Trade Commission.

55 15 U.S.C. § 45(n), Legal Information Institute, Cornell Law School, accessed January 2020, https://www.law.cornell.edu/uscode/text/15/45; "FTC Policy on Unfairness," Federal Trade Commission, December 17, 1980, https://www.ftc.gov/public-statements/1980/12/ftc-policy-statement-unfairness; See *Big Data: A Tool for Inclusion or Exclusion?*, Federal Trade Commission.

56 J. Howard Beales III, "The FTC's Use of Unfairness Authority."

57 Austin, *Essentially Equivalent*.

58 Federal Trade Commission v. Equifax, Complaint for Permanent Injunction and Other Relief, accessed January 2020, https://www.ftc.gov/system/files/documents/cases/172_3203_equifax_complaint_7-22-19.pdf.

59 In addition, Equifax could be required to pay up to $125 million to compensate consumers for their losses. See Federal Trade Commission v. Equifax, Stipulated Order for Permanent Injunction and Monetary Judgment, 2019, https://www.ftc.gov/system/files/documents/cases/172_3203_equifax_proposed_order_7-22-19.pdf; Alfred Ng and Sean Keane, "Equifax to Pay at Least $575 Million As Part of FTC Settlement," *CNet,* July 22, 2019, https://www.cnet.com/news/equifax-to-pay-at-least-575m-as-part-of-ftc-settlement/.

60 Federal Trade Commission v. Equifax, Stipulated Order for Permanent Injunction and Monetary Judgment.

61 "Federal Trade Commission Gives Final Approval Settlement with Uber," Federal Trade Commission, October 26, 2018, https://www.ftc.gov/news-events/news/press-releases/2018/10/federal-trade-commission-gives-final-approval-settlement-uber and In the Matter of Uber Technologies, Inc., Complaint against Uber Technologies, inc., Federal Trade Commission, accessed August 2023, https://www.ftc.gov/system/files/documents/cases/152_3054_c-4662_uber_technologies_revised_complaint.pdf.

62 "Former Uber Security Chief Found Guilty in Criminal Trial for Failure to Disclose Breach to FTC," *Privacy & Information Security Law Blog,* Hunton Andrews Kurth, October 2022, https://www.huntonprivacyblog.com/2022/10/06/former-uber-security-chief-found-guilty-in-criminal-trial-for-failure-to-disclose-breach-to-ftc/; see Colin Jennings, Ericka Johnson, and Dylan Yepez, "Executive responsibilities and Consequences: A Case Study of Uber's Data Breaches," Corporate Compliance Insights, September 1, 2020, https://www.corporatecomplianceinsights.com/responsibilities-consequences-uber-data-breaches/.

63 Recognizing that teenagers between the ages of 13 and 18 are not protected under COPPA, states have made efforts to address privacy issues for this age group. As early as the 2000s, state attorneys general focused their attention on the privacy rights of middle school and high school students. Danielle Keats Citron, "The Privacy Policymaking of State Attorneys General," *Notre Dame Law Review* 92, no. 2 (2016): 775-76, http://ndlawreview.org/wp-content/uploads/2017/02/NDL205.pdf.

64 Children's Online Privacy Protection Act, accessed November 2017, http://www.columbia.edu/~mr2651/ecommerce3/2nd/statutes/ChildrenOnlinePrivacyProtectionAct.pdf; "Complying with COPPA: Frequently Asked Questions," Federal Trade Commission, July 2020, https://www.ftc.gov/business-guidance/resources/complying-coppa-frequently-asked-questions; "Verifiable Parental Consent and the Children's Online Privacy Rule," Federal Trade Commission, accessed August 2023, https://www.ftc.gov/business-guidance/privacy-security/verifiable-parental-consent-childrens-online-privacy-rule.

65 "FTC Launches New Office of Technology to Bolster Agency's Work," FTC, February 17, 2023, https://www.ftc.gov/news-events/news/press-releases/2023/02/ftc-launches-new-office-technology-bolster-agencys-work; "Combatting Online Harms Through Innovation," FTC, June 2022, https://www.ftc.gov/reports/combatting-online-harms-through-innovation; see Rob Verger, "FTC is Trying to Get More Tech-Savvy," Popular Science, February 25, 2023, https://www.popsci.com/technology/ftc-office-of-technology/; see also Davide Castelvecchi, "Are Quantum Computers About to Break Online Privacy," Nature, January 6, 2023, https://www.nature.com/articles/d41586-023-00017-0; Nita Farahany, "The Battle for Your Brain: Defending the Right to Think Freely in the Age of Neurotechnology," St. Martin's Press, 2023, https://philosophy.duke.edu/books/battle-your-brain-defending-right-think-freely-age-neurotechnology;

Katharina Koerner, "Privacy and Responsible AI," *Privacy Advisor,* IAPP, January 11, 2022, https://iapp.org/news/a/privacy-and-responsible-ai/.

66 Stephanie Nguyen, "A Century of Technological Evolution at the Federal Trade Commission," Federal Trade Commission, February 17, 2023, https://www.ftc.gov/policy/advocacy-research/tech-at-ftc/2023/02/century-technological-evolution-federal-trade-commission.

67 "Executive Order on Promoting Competition in the American Economy," The White House, July 9, 2021, https://www.whitehouse.gov/briefing-room/presidential-actions/2021/07/09/executive-order-on-promoting-competition-in-the-american-economy/.

68 Fair, "FTC Undertakes Inquiry into Commercial Surveillance Practices and Wants Your Insights"; see "Commercial Surveillance and Data Security Rulemaking," Federal Trade Commission, August 11, 2022, https://www.ftc.gov/legal-library/browse/federal-register-notices/commercial-surveillance-data-security-rulemaking.

69 Peter Swire, one of the authors of this book, presented on the topic of "Using the Portability and Other Required Transfers Assessment (PORT-IA) in Antitrust Law." Guilherme Roschke and Andrea Zach, "Data on the Go: The FTC's Workshop on Data Portability," CPI Antitrust Chronicle, November 2020, https://www.ftc.gov/system/files/documents/public_events/1568699/data-portability-workshop-summary.pdf.

70 "New FTC Guidance for Mobile Health Apps," Sidley, February 7, 2023, https://www.sidley.com/en/insights/newsupdates/2023/02/new-ftc-guidance-for-mobile-health-apps; see "Mobile Health App Developers: FTC Best Practices," Federal Trade Commission, December 2022, https://www.ftc.gov/business-guidance/resources/mobile-health-app-developers-ftc-best-practices; see also Jennifer Wagner, "The Federal Trade Commission and Consumer Protections for Mobile Health Apps," Journal of Law, Medicine and Ethics, 2020, https://www.ncbi.nlm.nih.gov/pmc/articles/PMC8329941/.

71 Lesley Fair, "Shedding Light on Dark Patterns: Protecting Consumers from Digital Deception," National Association of Attorney's General, accessed August 2023, https://www.naag.org/attorney-general-journal/shedding-light-on-dark-patterns-protecting-consumers-from-digital-deception/; "Bringing Dark Patterns to Light," Federal Trade Commission, September 2022, https://www.ftc.gov/reports/bringing-dark-patterns-light; FTC Report Shows Rise in Sophisticated Dark Patterns Designed to Trick and Trap Consumers," Federal Trade Commission, September 15, 2022, https://www.ftc.gov/news-events/news/press-releases/2022/09/ftc-report-shows-rise-sophisticated-dark-patterns-designed-trick-trap-consumers; Lesley Fair, "FTC Issues Illuminating Report on Digital Dark Patterns, September 9, 2022, https://www.ftc.gov/business-guidance/blog/2022/09/ftc-issues-illuminating-report-digital-dark-patterns.

72 "FTC Announces Broader Vision of Its Section 5 Authority to Address Unfair Methods of Competition," Gibson Dunn, November 14, 2022, https://www.gibsondunn.com/ftc-announces-broader-vision-of-its-section-5-authority-to-address-unfair-methods-of-competition/; see "Policy Statement Regarding the Scope of Unfair Methods of Competition Under Section 5 of the Federal Trade Commission Act," Commission File No. P221202, Federal Trade Commission, November 10, 2022, https://www.ftc.gov/system/files/ftc_gov/pdf/P221202Section5PolicyStatement.pdf; see also "FTC Report to Congress on Privacy and Security," Federal Trade Commission, September 13, 2021, https://www.ftc.gov/system/files/documents/reports/ftc-report-congress-privacy-security/report_to_congress_on_privacy_and_data_security_2021.pdf.

73 Attorneys General, National Association of Attorneys General (NAAG), accessed August 2023, https://www.naag.org/attorneys-general/; see Michael Signer, "Constitutional Crisis in the Commonwealth: Resolving the Conflict Between Governors and Attorneys General," *University of Richmond Law Review 41, no.1* (2006), https://scholarship.richmond.edu/lawreview/vol41/iss1/.

74 See Singer, Stempson, and Chun, "Statements to the State AGs"; see also Dee Pridgen, "The Dynamic Duo of Consumer Protection: State and Private Enforcement of Unfair and Deceptive Trade Practices Laws," University of Wyoming College of Law Faculty Scholarship, February 16, 2018, https://scholarship.law.uwyo.edu/cgi/viewcontent.cgi?article=1012&context=faculty_articles; Bilyana Petkova, "The Safeguards of Privacy Federalism," *Lewis & Clark Law Review* 20, no. 2 (2016), https://papers.ssrn.com/sol3/papers.cfm?abstract_id=2637933.

75 In the 1960s and the 1970s, states enacted consumer protections statutes. Many states enacted "little FTC Acts" that prohibited "unfair or deceptive acts or practices" (mirroring the language of the federal act) and instruct that "due consideration ... shall be given" to the FTC's and federal courts' interpretations of federal law. Even with these references to federal law, many of these state "mirror" statutes no longer closely resemble the federal approach. More than half the states did not follow the precise "little FTC Acts" approach, opting instead for varying approaches that could include regulation of deceptive trade practices, unfair trade practices, unconscionable acts, and/or consumer fraud. Pridgen, "The Dynamic Duo of Consumer Protection"; Henry N. Butler and Joshua D. Wright, "Are State Consumer Protection Acts Really Little-FTC Acts?," *Florida Law Review*, 2011, https://scholarship.law.ufl.edu/flr/vol63/iss1/5/.

76 California Business and Professions Code § 17200-17210, California Legislative Information, accessed November 2017, http://leginfo.legislature.ca.gov/faces/codes_displayText.xhtml?lawCode=BPC&division=7.&title=&part=2.&chapter=5.&article=.

77 Carolyn Carter, "Consumer Protection in the States: A 50-State Evaluation of Unfair and Deceptive Practices Law, National Consumer Law Center," March 2018, https://www.nclc.org/resources/how-well-do-states-protect-consumers/; see Charles Byrd, "A 50-State Survey of Consumer Protection Acts and Their Connections to the Federal Trade Commission Act," Pro Te Solutio, March 13, 2019, https://protesolutio.com/2019/03/13/a-50-state-survey-of-consumer-protection-acts-and-their-connections-to-the-federal-trade-commission-act/; see also Eric Posner, "Contract Law in the Welfare State: A Defense of the Unconscionability Doctrine, Usury Laws, and Related Limitations on the Freedom to Contract," The Journal of Legal Studies, 1995, https://www.journals.uchicago.edu/doi/abs/10.1086/467961. Hawaii provides one example of a UDAP statute. HI § 480-2, accessed February 2023, https://www.capitol.hawaii.gov/hrscurrent/vol11_ch0476-0490/hrs0480/hrs_0480-0002.htm. A detailed definition of "unconscionable" is contained in Ohio's law. 13 Ohio Revised Code § 1345.03, accessed February 2023, http://codes.ohio.gov/orc/1345.

78 Permissible uses include legitimate government functions; use by employer in verifying commercial driver's license; and use by insurers for claims investigations, anti-fraud, and underwriting. See "Preparing for 2023, State Privacy Law Compliance," Squire Patton Boggs, August 2022, https://www.squirepattonboggs.com/-/media/files/insights/publications/2022/05/preparing-for-2023-state-privacy-law-compliance/preparingfor2023stateprivacylawcompliance.pdf;

79 The five-digit zip code not considered protected information. "The Drivers Privacy Protection Act (DPPA) and the Privacy of Your State Motor Vehicle Record," Electronic Privacy Information Center, accessed August 2023, https://epic.org/dppa/.

80 See 18 U.S. Code § 2721, Legal Information Institute, Cornell Law School, accessed August 2023, https://www.law.cornell.edu/uscode/text/18/2721; see Corinne Bernstein, "Definition: Driver's Privacy Protection Act (DPPA), TechTarget, updated October 2017, https://www.techtarget.com/whatis/definition/Drivers-Privacy-Protection-Act-DPPA; Mike Slipsky, "The Drivers Privacy Protection Act," Poyner Spruill LLP, August 4, 2016, https://www.poynerspruill.com/thought-leadership/the-drivers-privacy-protection-act/; "The Social Security Number: Legal Developments Affecting Its Collection, Disclosure, and Confidentiality," Every CRSReport.com, January 21, 20225, https://www.everycrsreport.com/reports/RL30318.html.

81 In 1994, Congress passed the Driver's Privacy Protection Act of 1994 to protect the personal identifiable information of licensed drivers from improper use or disclosure by state governments. The DPPA was enacted in response to complaints that states were raising revenue by selling driver's information to direct marketers and auto insurance companies. In addition, several high-profile stalking cases, including the death of actress Rebecca Schaeffer, illustrated the possibility for tragic outcomes resulting from the lack of restrictions on accessing the data held by state departments of motor vehicles. 18 U.S. Code § 2721, Legal Information Institute, Cornell Law School; see also Angela Karras, "The Constitutionality of the Driver's Privacy Protection Act: A Fork in the Information Access Road," *Federal Communications Law Journal* 52, no. 1 (1999), https://www.repository.law.indiana.edu/cgi/viewcontent.cgi?article=1219&context=fclj;

82 Chapter 7 also discussed state data security laws and state data destruction laws.

83 "Program Operations Manual System (POMS)," Social Security, May 29, 2018, https://secure.ssa.gov/apps10/poms.nsf/lnx/0203325005#b1; "The Social Security Number: Legal Developments Affecting Its Collection, Disclosure, and Confidentiality," EveryCRSReport.com, January 21, 2005-February 14, 2014, https://www.everycrsreport.com/reports/RL30318.html.

84 "GN 03325.002 Disclosure and Verification of Social Security Numbers (SSN) Without Consent," Social Security, July 9, 2008, https://secure.ssa.gov/apps10/poms.nsf/lnx/0203325002; Social Security Number Confidentiality Act of 2000, https://www.congress.gov/106/plaws/publ433/PLAW-106publ433.pdf.

85 "The Social Security Number," EveryCRSReport.com.

86 "GN 03325.002 Disclosure and Verification of Social Security Numbers (SSN) Without Consent," Social Security.

87 A list of states with laws regulating the use of Social Security numbers can be found at National Council of State Legislatures. See "Social Security Number 2010 Legislation," National Council of State Legislatures, June 21, 2010, http://www.ncsl.org/research/financial-services-and-commerce/social-security-number-2010-legislation.aspx.

88 Cal. Civ. Code § 1798.85, California Legislative Information, accessed November 2019, http://leginfo.legislature.ca.gov/faces/codes_displaySection.xhtml?lawCode=CIV§ionNum=1798.85. For a summary of the California statute on the confidentiality of Social Security numbers, see the California attorney general's website. Social Security Number Confidentiality, California Law—General Privacy Laws, Privacy Laws, Office of the Attorney General, State of California Department of Justice, accessed November 2019, https://oag.ca.gov/privacy/privacy-laws.

89 16 C.F.R. Part 682, Legal Information Institute, Cornell Law School, accessed November 2017, https://www.law.cornell.edu/cfr/text/16/part-682; see "The Fair Credit Reporting Act (FCRA) and the Privacy of Your Credit Report," Electronic Privacy Information Center, accessed November 2017, https://epic.org/privacy/fcra/.

90 "CFPB Affirms Ability of States to Police Credit Reporting Markets," Consumer Financial Protection Bureau, June 28, 2022, https://www.consumerfinance.gov/about-us/newsroom/cfpb-affirms-ability-for-states-to-police-credit-reporting-markets/. In addition, FACTA specifically identified certain state laws that would remain in effect. With regard to credit scores, state laws in California and Colorado, as well as state insurance laws regulating the use by insurers of credit-based insurance scores, remain in effect. Pertaining to frequency of free credit reports, the federal law permitted state laws in Colorado, Georgia, Maine, Maryland, Massachusetts, New Jersey, and Vermont to remain in effect. 2003 Changes to the Fair Credit Reporting Act, Consumers Union, accessed February 2020, https://consumerfed.org/pdfs/credit_reporting_summary_of_final_law.pdf."

91 "Federal and State Identity Theft Laws," Debt.com, modified January 9, 2023, https://www.debt.com/identity-theft/federal-state-laws/.

92 Restatement (Second) of Torts, § 652A-E, accessed November 2017, www.tomwbell.com/NetLaw/Ch05/R2ndTorts.html.

93 Robert Ellis Smith, *Compilation of State and Federal Privacy Laws* (Providence: Privacy Journal, 2012).

94 Ashley Johnson, "Balancing Privacy and Innovation in Smart Cities and Communities," Information Technology & Innovation Foundation, March 6, 2023, https://itif.org/publications/2023/03/06/balancing-privacy-and-innovation-in-smart-cities-and-communities/; see Hannah Hess, "Smart Grids Need Smart Privacy Laws: Reconciling the California Consumer Privacy Act with Decentralized Electricity Models," Ecology Law Quarterly, August 18, 2020, https://www.ecologylawquarterly.org/currents/smart-grids-need-smart-privacy-laws-reconciling-the-california-consumer-privacy-act-with-decentralized-electricity-models/; Phil Goldstein, "The Power of Smart Street Lighting in Smart Cities," State Tech, January 31, 2020, https://statetechmagazine.com/article/2020/01/power-smart-street-lighting-smart-cities-perfcon; see also Elvira Ismagilova, "Security, Privacy, and Risks Within Smart Cities: Literature and Development of a Smart City Interaction Framework," Information Systems Frontier, 2020, https://www.ncbi.nlm.nih.gov/pmc/articles/PMC7373213/; Liesbet van Zoonen, "Privacy Concerns in Smart Cities," Government Information Quarterly, July 2016, https://www.sciencedirect.com/science/article/pii/S0740624X16300818.

95 "Illinois Biometric Information Privacy Act FAQs," Jackson Lewis, accessed February 2023, https://www.jacksonlewis.com/sites/default/files/docs/IllinoisBIPAFAQs.pdf; see "The $17 Billion Slider? Illinois Supreme Court Decides White Castle BIPA Case," *The National Law Review, February 17, 2023,* https://www.natlawreview.com/article/17-billion-slider-illinois-supreme-court-decides-white-castle-bipa-case#:~:text=The%20landscape%20of%20biometric%20privacy,Information%20Privacy%20Act%20(BIPA). ; "Here's a Look at Settlements Stemming From Illinois' Biometric Privacy Act," NBC Chicago, August 24, 2022, https://www.nbcchicago.com/news/local/heres-a-look-at-all-the-settlements-stemming-from-illinois-biometric-privacy-act/2922736/; "Recent Surge in Class Actions Involving "Biometric" Data: What Employers Need to Know an Do Now," Epstein Becker Green, January 3, 2018, https://www.ebglaw.com/insights/recent-surge-in-class-actions-involving-biometric-data-what-employers-need-to-know-and-do-now/.

96 "California Enacts the California Age-Appropriate Design Code Act," *Privacy & Information Security Law Blog*, Hunton Andrew Kurth, September 15, 2022, https://www.huntonprivacyblog.com/2022/09/15/california-enacts-the-california-age-appropriate-design-code-act/; see Alvaro Maranon, "2023 US Privacy Landscape: Trifectas and the Age of Age-Appropriate Design Code," Disruptive Competition Project, December 12, 2022, https://www.project-disco.org/privacy/061222hed-2023-us-privacy-landscape-trifectas-and-the-age-of-age-appropriate-design-code/.

97 Peter P. Swire, "Markets, Self-Regulation, and Government Enforcement in the Protection of Personal Information, in Privacy and Self-Regulation in the Information Age by the U.S. Department of Commerce," U.S. Department of Commerce, revised June 10, 2017, http://ssrn.com/abstract=11472.

98 In 2025, the requirements of PCI DSS 4.0 will be fully effective. Prior to that time, there will be a phase in period for the new requirements. Lauren Holloway, "Countdown to PCI DSS v4.0," PCI Security Standards Council, accessed August 2023, https://blog.pcisecuritystandards.org/countdown-to-pci-dss-v4.0; see Ian Terry, "Changes to Expect with the Transition to PCI 4.0," IS Partners, February 22, 2023, https://www.ispartnersllc.com/blog/pci-dss-version-4-0-launching-2020/#:~:text=is%20currently%20moving.-,PCI%204.0%20Compliance%20Date%3A%20March%2031%2C%202025,March%202025%20is%20already%20underway.

99 Mike Mariano, "PCI Non-Compliance Fines & Consequences," IS Partners, August 11, 2022, https://www.ispartnersllc.com/blog/pci-non-compliance-fines-consequences/; see Josh Fruhlinger, "PCI DSS Explained: Requirements, Fines, and Steps to Compliance," CSO, May 16, 2022, https://www.csoonline.com/article/3566072/pci-dss-explained-requirements-fines-and-steps-to-compliance.html.

100 "Enterprise Privacy Certification, TrustArc, accessed February 2023, https://trustarc.com/truste-certifications/enterprise-privacy-certification/; Digital Advertising Accountability Program, BBB National Programs, accessed February 2023, https://bbbprograms.org/programs/all-programs/daap.

101 Your AdChoices Gives You Control, YourAdChoices, accessed February 2023, https://youradchoices.com/; see "White House, DOC, and FCC Recommend DAA's Self-Regulatory Program to Protect Consumer Online Privacy," Digital Advertising Alliance, February 23, 2012, https://digitaladvertisingalliance.org/press-release/white-house-doc-and-ftc-commend-daa%E2%80%99s-self-regulatory-program-protect-consumer-online.

102 See Ana Isabel Segovia Domingo and Nathalie Desmet Villar, "Self-Regulation in Data Protection," BBVA Research, October 2018, https://www.bbvaresearch.com/wp-content/uploads/2018/10/Watch_Self-regulation-and-data-protection-1.pdf.

103 See Council of Better Business Bureaus' Letter to National Telecommunications and Information Administration, Comment on Consumer Privacy and Self-Regulation, November 9, 2018, https://www.ntia.doc.gov/files/ntia/publications/cbbb_comment_to_ntia_on_consumer_privacy_-_11.09.18.pdf.

CHAPTER 6

State Comprehensive Privacy Laws

An increasing number of states have adopted comprehensive privacy laws and numerous other states have considered legislation with comprehensive privacy requirements. The path to U.S. states adopting comprehensive privacy laws, which provide similar protections for data to those provided in the European Union and other parts of the world, is a long and complex one. As discussed in Chapter 1, the majority of countries in the world have adopted a comprehensive approach to privacy. Many of the laws around the world are modeled on the EU's General Data Protection Regulation (GDPR) and its comprehensive approach to privacy—or data protection, as it is termed in many parts of the world.

As of this writing, the United States lacks a federal law that addresses privacy for all types of personal data. Much of the material presented in other chapters of this book will focus on the federal regulation of privacy in certain sectors, such as HIPAA (see Chapter 8), the GLBA (see Chapter 9), and COPPA (see Chapter 5). Over the years, there have been numerous attempts at the federal level to enact a comprehensive approach to privacy in the United States. In recent years, pressure has mounted in the United States to adopt such legislation both to better protect individual's personal information and to require companies to comply with privacy rules in the United States that are similar to those they comply with in other parts of the world.

As the federal government in the United States has been unable to respond to these calls for regulation by enacting a comprehensive privacy law, states examined these issues. California was the first state in the U.S. to pass a state comprehensive privacy law. The history of the California privacy framework, as it stands at the writing of this book, is worth mentioning. The California Consumer Privacy Act (CCPA) was enacted in 2018, with an effective date of January 1, 2020. The CCPA provides a number of consumer privacy rights, such as those found in data protection laws outside the United States—most prominently the GDPR.[1] Almost immediately after passage of the CCPA in 2018, efforts began to amend the law. The ballot initiative known as the California Privacy Rights Act (CPRA) passed in late 2020. The CPRA amended and extended the CCPA, in some respects to be even more similar to the protections provided under the EU's GDPR.[2] The CPRA became effective January 1, 2023.

California's enactment of comprehensive privacy requirements is seen as impactful for numerous reasons. The saying "as California goes, so goes the nation" is one such reason. Looking at trends in the privacy space, California was the first state to enact a state data breach notification law in 2003. All 50 states have now enacted state data breach notification laws. In 2004, California was also the first state to enact a state data security law; as of the writing of this book, approximately two-thirds of states in the U.S. have adopted data security laws.[3] Many believe that a similar trend could emerge over time with comprehensive state privacy laws.

The size and influence of the California economy also mean that the state's comprehensive privacy requirements affect a substantial number of consumers and businesses. California's gross domestic product (GDP) ranks it as the fifth largest economy in the world—behind the United States, China, Japan, and Germany, respectively. Predictions are that California will soon take Germany's spot as the fourth largest economy in the world.[4] Notably, California's population is approximately 40 million people.[5] In addition, California is home to many of the world's largest technology companies as well as to Silicon Valley.

After California enacted its comprehensive privacy requirements, numerous other states either considered or enacted state comprehensive privacy laws. At the writing of this book, more than half the states in the U.S. have considered legislation with comprehensive privacy requirements and an increasing number of states have passed laws with comprehensive privacy requirements. This chapter will focus on California and the four other laws that were in effect in 2023, rather than the laws that have since passed. These laws are the Colorado Privacy Act (CPA), the Connecticut Data Privacy Act (CTDPA), the Utah Consumer Privacy Act (UCPA), and the Virginia Consumer Data Protection Act (VCDPA).

Before continuing, it is important to point out that this chapter will use the name of the state, such as California, when discussing the state's comprehensive privacy framework in an effort to avoid confusion. The reason for this naming convention can be illustrated by focusing on what would be the acronyms for these laws—many are similar to one another.

This chapter begins with a discussion of the lack of a federal comprehensive privacy law in the United States. The chapter then moves to a focus on the state comprehensive privacy laws. The first topic from these laws is key terms, such as "business" and "consumer." Next, the discussion moves to consumer rights, such as the right to access and the right to correction. Another topic is business obligations, such as notice/transparency and risk assessments. The discussion of these laws concludes with the topic of enforcement.

Realizing that additional states are expected to adopt state comprehensive privacy laws and that states can readily amend these laws and tweak their meaning through rules and regulations, this chapter focuses on trends and outliers among these state laws. Instead of detailing the requirements of each law enacted at the time of writing, the intent of this chapter is to provide the reader with an approach for examining the laws that have been enacted as well as any which may be enacted in the future. Privacy practitioners should be aware that this is a complex area of law where a lawyer would likely need to be engaged if a particular company was seeking to ensure compliance with the specific legal requirements in force.

6.1 Lack of Federal Comprehensive Privacy Law

For decades, privacy advocates have encouraged Congress to implement a federal law that would generally address privacy protections for personal data.[6] Although the details of such proposals have evolved over time as technology has changed, the basic idea would be for the United States to adopt a comprehensive approach to privacy instead of a sector-based approach. As of the writing of this book, no federal comprehensive privacy law exists. Among numerous recent bills, one novel approach to privacy protection being considered would place fiduciary duties on those companies that handle data, based in the idea that these companies should act in good faith on behalf of consumers.[7]

The passage of numerous state comprehensive privacy laws has increased interest at the federal level for enacting a general U.S. privacy law.[8] This interest is in part because of the belief that, without federal intervention, the number of state laws will continue to increase and include inconsistent requirements.[9] For companies, compliance costs continue to increase, particularly as these state requirements multiply.[10]

In debates about a possible national U.S. privacy statute, one of the most politically charged and complicated issues has been whether and to what extent the new statute would preempt state privacy protections.[11] Preemption occurs when a federal statute overrides an inconsistent state statute, such as the prohibition in the federal Controlling the Assault of Non-Solicited Pornography And Marketing Act (CAN-SPAM) law on state laws that expressly regulate the use of electronic mail to send commercial messages. The preemption debate takes place principally between industry, which generally favors broad preemption, and "privacy advocates"—meaning those public interest groups, academics, and others who generally support stricter privacy law. The latter have historically either opposed preemption or sought to narrow whatever preemption exists.[12] With the passage of state comprehensive privacy laws (discussed in Section 6.2), state officials—such as governors and state attorneys general—have publicly opposed broad preemption in a federal approach to comprehensive privacy protections.[13]

For any general U.S. privacy legislation, a complex set of questions concerning preemption would have to be answered. These include:

- Whether state attorneys general would retain the ability to use state consumer protection law to bring civil suits to protect individuals' privacy
- Whether state tort, contract, and property laws would be preempted
- Whether state medical privacy laws, state financial privacy laws, and state cybersecurity laws would be preempted
- Whether provisions in the federal wiretap law and many other federal privacy laws that permit stricter state laws would be maintained[14]

A second issue has been whether a federal law would include a private right of action, allowing individuals to file suit if a violation occurred instead of simply allowing a government official to fine a company for a violation. As with preemption, the debate concerning a private right of action typically finds industry opposed to such a right for individuals and privacy advocates supporting a private right of action.[15]

6.2 Overview of State Comprehensive Privacy Laws

Among the state comprehensive privacy laws that have passed as of the writing of this book, there is notable variation even though the similarities can sometimes be striking. When reviewing these laws, there is a natural tendency to want to label one as the strictest and another as the weakest. This approach would oversimplify a complex web of requirements under these state laws. For privacy practitioners, a more helpful approach is to review the historical context of the implementation of these laws coupled with an examination of the types of requirements found in these laws.[16]

As to historical context, it is important to remember that the EU's GDPR became effective in 2018, which is the same year that California's CCPA was enacted. Even though the CCPA was amended and extended in 2020 with the enactment of the CPRA, it should not come as a surprise that the individual protections and business requirements in California's framework mirror those in the GDPR in many ways—though perhaps sometimes in spirit more than in the letter of the law. Even California's implementation of the California Privacy Protection Agency (CPPA), a newly created agency dedicated to the regulation of privacy protections, was viewed by many as an effort to match California's approach to the practice in the European Union of utilizing a data protection authority (DPA) to investigate complaints and enforce rights.[17]

In both 2021 and 2022, there was a flurry of state activity that resulted in the enactment of four additional state comprehensive privacy laws. Virginia was the second state to enact such a law, and initially Virginia's law was touted as the pro-business approach to regulation, in contrast to the California approach—viewed as the most privacy-protecting as well as the most similar to the GDPR. Once additional states enacted their laws, this distinction—if it ever existed at all—became muddied.

Before looking at the distinctions in these laws, which are important to understand when practicing in this area, it is worth noting that the overall frameworks in these five states have a great deal of similarity and overlap; so much so that some commentators speak of interoperability among these state laws. Each of the laws includes core concepts that allow them to be defined as comprehensive approaches to privacy, including detailed consumer rights and business obligations.[18] That said, the numerous distinctions among these laws provide insight into understanding the intricacies of the comprehensive privacy requirements at the state level.

- **California** defines several terms using a broad brushstroke, which is indeed similar to the EU approach. When determining which entities are subject to regulation, California automatically regulates companies that do business in its state that meet a threshold for annual gross revenues, in addition to including approaches that are similar to those taken by other states. California is alone among the states in including employees in its definition of a consumer. California is also the only state to take an expansive view of regulated behavior of businesses by including both selling and sharing personal information. California provides consumer rights and imposes business obligations that are structured in a similar manner to the GDPR. Importantly, the substance of the rights and obligations in

California are echoed in the four other states. Notably, however, California lacks certain rights found in Colorado, Connecticut, and Virginia, including the explicit right of appealing to the business to reconsider its decision of denying a request (Utah also lacks this right of appeal).

- **Colorado, Connecticut,** and **Virginia** have numerous similarities in their regulatory frameworks. These states have similar key terms, consumer rights, and business obligations. Although distinctions exist among these three states on the term "business," the overall approach is similar with the differences found in the threshold numbers to qualify as a regulated entity. Each of these three states also provides rights not explicitly provided by California, including the right to opt in to the sale of sensitive personal information and the right to appeal.
- Although **Utah** has a regulatory framework that is akin to Colorado, Connecticut, and Virginia, its definition of business is narrower, and it provides fewer rights to consumers and puts fewer obligations on businesses.

In this section, the following topics related to state comprehensive privacy laws will be discussed: key terms, consumer rights, business obligations, and enforcement. As a reminder, the approach taken in this chapter is to provide a framework to assist the reader in understanding the state laws in place at the time of the writing of this book as well as any future state laws that are enacted.[19]

6.2.1 Key Terms

The state comprehensive privacy laws have many commonalities, such as the inclusion of similar key terms. For practitioners, it is important to note that these state laws also have subtle, and sometimes significant, differences. Critical to understanding the scope of each law is knowing which entities must comply with a particular law, which individuals are protected by the law, the type of data of "consumers" that is covered by the law, and the type of activities of "businesses" that are regulated by the law. This section reviews the following key terms: business, consumer, personal information (including sensitive personal information), and sale.[20]

These state laws generally have two main types of exemptions: entity-level exemptions and data-based exemptions. Entity-level exemptions refer to a type of entity that is exempt from the laws. Nonprofits, institutions of higher education, and local governments typically fall into this type of exemption under these state laws. The second type of exemption, data-based exemptions, focus on a class of data is exempt. An example would be an exemption for data that is covered by a federal law, such as the Driver's Privacy Protection Act (DPPA) discussed in Chapter 5.

It is worth noting that these state laws often acknowledge that certain data is protected by federal laws, such as HIPAA and the GLBA. The approach taken in these instances varies, with some states exempting the entity from compliance with the state law (entity-level exemptions) and other states exempting only that data which is protected by the federal law (data-based exemptions). Privacy practitioners should be aware that the result of this regulatory approach involving data-based exemptions is that a business may have some data that is exempt from the state law yet hold other data, such as human resources records, that is subject to the state law.

6.2.1.1 Business

The term "business" provides insight into one aspect of the breadth of state comprehensive privacy laws. California is viewed as having the broadest definition of the term, meaning the greatest number of companies subject to the requirements of its law. Of the five states with laws in effect in 2023, Utah's definition of business has the narrowest scope among those states with comprehensive privacy laws.[21]

The term business delineates which entities that conduct business in the state are subject to the requirements of the law.[22] For companies doing business in a state, the following requirements apply:

- In California, the size of the company alone can subject a company to regulation, as California has an annual revenue threshold that subjects an entity to the law's requirements, regardless of the type of company. A company doing business in California with a total annual gross revenue of $25 million is subject to regulation.
- California, Colorado, Connecticut, and Virginia each have a separate requirement that subjects companies to regulation if they meet the threshold requirement related to the number of customers in that state whose data is processed. In these states, a company is subject to regulation if it processes the data of at least 100,000 consumers. Notably, Connecticut excludes payment transactions from its calculation.

- In California, Colorado, Connecticut, and Virginia, companies are subject to regulation if they meet a threshold that includes gross revenues from selling or sharing data.
    - California's threshold is met when a company derives at least 50 percent of their gross revenues from selling or sharing data.
    - In Colorado, Connecticut, and Virginia, the requirement related to gross revenues focuses only on selling data. These three states couple a threshold for processing consumer data with a threshold for gross revenues.
        - In Colorado, a company is subject to regulation when it processes the data of at least 25,000 consumers and derives any revenue or receives any discount on goods or services from selling personal data.[23]
        - In Connecticut, a company is subject to regulation when it processes data of at least 25,000 consumers and derives at least 25 percent of its gross revenues from selling data.[24]
        - In Virginia, a company is subject to regulation when it processes data of at least 25,000 consumers and derives at least 50 percent of its gross revenues from selling data.
- As the outlier, Utah takes a multiple threshold approach that combines a minimum annual gross revenue with other threshold requirements. In Utah, a company is subject to regulation if it has at least $25 million in annual gross revenue and meets one of the following: (1) processes the data of at least 100,000 Utah consumers; or (2) processes data of at least 25,000 Utah consumers and derives at least 50 percent of its gross revenues from selling data.[25]

These states exclude numerous types of organizations from the definition of business. All five states typically exempt governments and nonprofits. Connecticut, Utah, and Virginia exempt institutions of higher education. Colorado and Connecticut exempt registered national securities associations. In addition, the interaction with federal law plays into which entities are covered by these state laws. Connecticut, Utah, and Virginia exempt HIPAA entities. Colorado, Connecticut, Utah, and Virginia exempt GLBA entities. All five states exempt entities covered by the FCRA.[26]

6.2.1.2 Consumer

The definition of consumer in these state laws explains which individuals are covered. Note that privacy rights under these state comprehensive privacy laws are *not* limited to consumers commonly understood as individuals who purchase products and services for their own purposes. All five states define their own residents to be protected by their respective laws.

California includes employees in its definition of consumer. Colorado, Connecticut, Utah, and Virginia exclude individuals "acting in a commercial or employment context."[27]

6.2.1.3 Personal Information

With the definition of personal information (and any accompanying definition of sensitive personal information), these state comprehensive privacy laws move beyond the definition of personal information found in state data breach notification laws (Chapter 7) to protect individuals from identify theft and fraud.

In all five states, the definition of personal information focuses on any data that can be associated or linked with a particular individual. California extends the definition to include the information of the consumer and the consumer's household. Note that California is the only state to include employment data in its definition of personal information.[28]

California provides examples of the type of data that would generally fall within the definition of personal information in these laws:

- Real name, postal address, email address, Social Security number, driver's license number, passport number
- Internet protocol (IP) address
- Characteristics of protected classifications under California or federal law (such as race, religion, disability, sexual orientation, and national origin)
- "Commercial information, including records of personal property, products or services purchased, obtained, or considered, or other purchasing or consuming histories or tendencies"
- Biometric information
- Internet and network activity, including "browsing history, search history, and information regarding a consumer's interaction with an internet website, application, or advertisement"
- Geolocation information

- "Audio, electronic, visual, thermal, olfactory, or similar information"
- Professional or employment information and certain education information[29]

These state laws have numerous exclusions from the definition of personal information. Although the specific definitions of these terms vary by state, the types of exclusions include:

- **Deidentified data.** The term "deidentified data" focuses on data that cannot reasonably fall within the definition of personal information—meaning it cannot reasonably be associated or linked with a particular individual.[30] All five states exclude data that qualifies as deidentified.[31]
- **Data that is publicly available.** The term "publicly available" refers to information that is lawfully made available by federal, state, or local governments.[32] All five states exclude from regulation data that is publicly available.[33]
- **Aggregate data.** The term "aggregate data" means information relating to a group of consumers where the identities of individual consumers have been removed, meaning that the information is not reasonably linkable to a consumer. California, Utah, and Virginia explicitly exclude aggregate data from the definition of personal information.[34]
- **Employee data.** The term "employee data" refers to records kept by businesses related to applicants, employees, and contractors. Connecticut, Utah, and Virginia exclude employment data from regulation. Colorado has this exemption but limits it to employment records.
- **Data that is subject to specific federal privacy requirements.** These states generally exempt data that is federally regulated, including data subject to HIPAA, the GLBA, FCRA, and the DPPA. All five states generally exempt data that is regulated under these federal laws.[35]

In all five states, the definition of **sensitive personal information** includes citizenship; genetic and/or biometric information; physical or mental health conditions, race or ethnicity; religion; and sexual orientation. Some states include additional categories to their definition of sensitive personal information. Colorado, Connecticut, and Virginia define children's data as sensitive data. California, Connecticut, Utah, and Virginia include geolocation as sensitive data. Notably, California includes additional categories, such as union membership, philosophical beliefs, and the content of consumer's mail, email, and text messages.[36]

6.2.1.4 Sale

In examining the type of business activities that are regulated, each state focuses on the sale of personal data. California also regulates the sharing of personal information.

The definition of the term sale varies by state. Utah and Virginia restrict their regulation of a sale to those transactions involving monetary compensation. The definition of sale in California, Colorado, and Connecticut includes both transactions involving monetary compensation and situations that involve bartering for the data—meaning any exchange for value.

Often these laws identify those activities that are not considered to be a sale. These exclusions to the definition of sale often include:

- Disclosures of personal data to a processor for the purpose of processing the data for the business
- Disclosures of personal data to a third party for purposes of providing services or products that are requested by the consumer
- Disclosures of personal data where the consumer directs the business to disclose the personal data or intentionally uses the business to interact with a third party
- Disclosures or transfers of personal data, considered to be an asset, for purposes of a merger, acquisition or bankruptcy, where the third party assumes control of the business's stake in the asset[37]

Notably, California also regulates the sharing of personal information. In California, the term "sharing" is defined as "sharing, renting, leasing, disclosing, disseminating, making available, transferring, or otherwise communicating … a consumer's personal information by the business to a third party for cross-context behavioral advertising, whether or not for monetary or other valuable consideration."[38] Colorado, Connecticut, Utah, and Virginia do not explicitly regulate the sharing of personal information.

6.2.2 Consumer Rights

The state comprehensive privacy laws in California, Colorado, Connecticut, Utah, and Virginia provide a variety of rights to consumers who are covered by these laws. These rights are similar to those found in the GDPR, described in Chapter 14.[39]

Under these state comprehensive privacy laws, consumer rights include: right to access; right to correction; right to delete; right to data portability; right to opt out of sales; right to opt out of targeting/cross-contextual behavioral advertising; right against automated decision-making; right concerning sensitive personal information; and right to nondiscrimination.[40] In most instances, all five states provide these rights, with Utah as the outlier in its treatment of certain rights.

It is worth noting that a consumer exercises these rights by making a request of a business, such as a request to delete personal information or a request to opt out of sales. Each state provides a defined period of time for a timely response by businesses. Colorado, Connecticut, Utah, and Virginia allow businesses 45 days to respond, and permit an additional 45 days for response "when reasonably necessary." Although California takes this approach with certain types of requests from consumers, the state alters the approach for opt-out requests. In California, when a consumer asks to opt out, the business is given 15 days to comply.[41] In addition, certain states provide consumers with the ability to ask for a reconsideration from the business for denied requests, known as the right to appeal. Colorado, Connecticut, and Virginia provide consumers with this right to appeal. Consumers in California and Utah are not explicitly afforded this opportunity.[42]

This subsection provides details on these consumer rights and discusses which states provide each right, as of the writing of this book. Importantly, an individual state may provide additional consumer rights not detailed here.

6.2.2.1 Right to Access

Under this right, consumers generally have the ability to access specific pieces of personal information collected or held by businesses. The details of this right vary by state, with consumers having access to the personal information or categories or personal information collected by the business; access to the personal information or categories of personal information shared with third parties; and/or access to the third parties or categories of third parties with which the personal information was shared. As part of this right, the consumer is typically able to confirm whether the business is processing the consumer's personal data. All five states provide consumers with the right to access.[43]

6.2.2.2 Right to Correction

The right to collection means that consumers have the ability to correct inaccuracies in the personal information collected or held by businesses. Consumers in California, Colorado, Connecticut, and Virginia have the right to correction. Consumers in Utah lack this right.[44]

6.2.2.3 Right to Delete

Consumers have the right to delete the personal information held by a business, unless an exception applies.[45] The exceptions generally override the right when the personal information at issue is needed to for a specific permitted purpose. Examples of these exceptions include completing a transaction requested by a consumer, detecting or protecting against security incidents, and complying with legal obligations.[46] In all five states, consumers have the right to delete. In Colorado, Connecticut, and Virginia, this right applies to all personal information held by the business. California and Utah limit this right to personal information collected from the consumer by the business.[47] California adds a requirement that the business must notify service providers, contractors, and third parties (if possible) to delete a consumer's personal information.[48]

6.2.2.4 Right to Data Portability

The right to data portability means that data, which is in "a readily useable format," should be made available to the consumer to facilitate the consumer's ability to provide the information to another entity. This provision reflects a policy aimed to support consumers' ability to transfer their personal information from the initial business to a different destination.[49] All five states provide consumers with the right to data portability.[50]

6.2.2.5 Right to Opt Out of Sales

The right to opt out of sales means that the consumer can choose to opt out of the sale of personal information held by businesses. It is important to recall that "sale" is a defined term under these laws. In all five states, the definition of a sale refers to monetary transactions. In California, Colorado, and Connecticut, the term sale is also defined to include any other exchange for value.

In all five states, consumers have the right to opt out of sales.[51] California extends this right to provide consumers with the right to opt out of sharing of personal information.

6.2.2.6 Right to Opt Out of Targeting/Cross-Context Behavioral Advertising

The right to opt out of targeting/cross-context behavioral advertising means that the consumer can choose to opt out of advertising selected based on personal information collected about the consumer over time from a variety of online sources.

In Colorado, Connecticut, Utah, and Virginia, consumers have the right to opt out of targeting/cross-context behavioral advertising. California likely provides this protection through the right to opt out of the selling or sharing personal information.[52]

6.2.2.7 Right Against Automated Decision-Making

The right against automated decision-making means that the consumer can choose to opt out of automated processing of personal information that results in decisions about the consumer and/or profiling of the consumer. California, Colorado, Connecticut, and Virginia provide consumers the right against automated decision-making. Utah does not provide this right.[53]

6.2.2.8 Right Concerning Sensitive Personal Information

The right concerning personal information means that the consumer has a right related to how their sensitive personal information is handled by businesses. In Colorado, Connecticut, and Virginia, a business needs consent to process this data, meaning that the consumer needs to opt-in. It is worth noting that these three states define children's data as sensitive personal information. In Utah, businesses must provide notice, and the opportunity for consumers to opt out. California's approach is more complex, with businesses either able to, in essence, self-restrict to certain uses of sensitive personal information or to provide consumers notice and an opportunity to opt out.[54]

6.2.2.9 Right to Nondiscrimination

The right to nondiscrimination means that businesses cannot discriminate against consumers for exercising their rights under these laws. Although the specifics for each state vary, examples of prohibited activity may include: (1) businesses may not deny goods or services; (2) businesses may not charge different prices; and (3) businesses may not degrade (or provide different) quality in goods or services. All 5 state prohibit businesses from discriminating against consumers who exercise any of the rights in the respective laws.[55]

6.2.3 Business Obligations

The state comprehensive privacy laws in California, Colorado, Connecticut, Utah, and Virginia impose a variety of obligations on businesses that are covered by these laws. These obligations are similar to the key principles found in the GDPR.

Although specific requirements vary by state, the core business obligations in these state laws are quite similar: notice/transparency requirements; opt-in default for children's data; purpose/processing limitations; risk assessments;

and security requirements.[56] In most instances, all five states impose these business obligations, with Utah as the outlier in its treatment of certain obligations.

6.2.3.1 Notice/Transparency Requirements

The notice/transparency obligation means that a business is required to provide consumers with notice of certain data practices, privacy programs, and/or privacy operations.

- **Privacy notice.** All five states mandate that a business provide consumers with a privacy notice. The core requirements for the privacy notice are similar in all five states. These core requirements include explaining: categories of data; purpose for processing each category of data; any sale and how to opt out; categories of data shared with third parties; and how to exercise consumer rights. California adds additional elements that must be included in the privacy notice, such as duration of retention of each category of personal data as well as categories of sensitive personal data.[57]
- **Notice of right to opt out.** All five states require that businesses provide consumers with notice of the right to opt out and a conspicuous method to allow consumers to exercise these rights.[58] In California, businesses that sell or share personal information must provide a link on the business's web pages that says "Do Not Sell or Share My Personal Information." For those businesses that use or disclose sensitive personal information, California requires the businesses to have a "Limit the Use of My Personal Information" link on their websites.[59]
- **Notice at point of collection.** Notice at point of collection is required by one state. California requires that consumers be informed "at or before the point of collection" about the categories of personal data collected and the purposes of their use. Colorado, Connecticut, Utah, and Virginia do not require this notification.[60]

6.2.3.2 Opt-in Default for Children's Data

Opt-in default can be viewed as a type of age requirement where a business is obligated to obtain consent from a consumer under a certain age before handling their data in specific ways. The detailed implementation of these laws can be quite complicated, as parental consent is likely required for children under the age of 13.[61] California requires that businesses obtain opt-in consent to sell or share personal information of consumers under the age of 16. Connecticut requires that businesses obtain opt-in consent from consumers under the age of 16 (but at least 13 years old) to sell their personal information or to process their personal information for targeted advertising. As a reminder, Connecticut as well as Colorado and Virginia treat the personal information of consumers under the age of 13 as sensitive personal information—requiring opt-in consent from these consumers to process their data.[62] Utah requires opt-in consent for the processing of personal information of consumers under the age of 13.

6.2.3.3 Purpose/Processing Limitations

Purpose/processing limitations mean that a business is prohibited from collecting and/or processing personal information except for a specific purpose. In California, Colorado, Connecticut, and Virginia, businesses are obligated to enact purpose and/or processing limitations. Typically, the terms "necessary" and "proportionate" are used in describing the restrictions related to the purpose and/or processing by the business, which is similar to the approach in the GDPR. Utah does not impose this obligation on businesses.[63]

6.2.3.4 Risk Assessments

Risk assessments mean that a business is obligated to conduct a formal risk assessment related to privacy and/or cybersecurity. In states requiring risk assessments, businesses are required to conduct risk assessments for processing that presents a "heightened risk of harm to a consumer." The processing activities that can trigger the need for a risk assessment include:

- Processing personal information for the purpose of targeting advertisement
- Selling personal data
- Processing sensitive data
- Processing personal data for profiling under certain circumstances

California, Colorado, Connecticut, and Virginia require businesses to undertake risk assessments. Utah lacks this requirement.[64]

6.2.3.5 Security Requirements

Security requirements mean that a business is obligated to ensure security measures are in place related to data, including "reasonable administrative, technical, and physical data security practices" that are designed to protect the confidentiality and the integrity of the data. All five states require businesses to ensure security measures are in place related to data.[65]

6.2.4 Enforcement

Variations exist among the states for the enforcement of these state comprehensive privacy laws. This subsection examines the penalties for noncompliance; who enforces the law; and whether there is a period for a business to cure a violation. This discussion concludes by examining the absence of a private right of action in most of these state laws and briefly mentions the limited private right of action in California, noting that this right is primarily directed toward breaches.[66]

6.2.4.1 Penalties

Although all five states can impose penalties for noncompliance, the amount per violation varies. In California, civil penalties can be up to $2,500 for typical violations and up to $7,500 for intentional violations.[67] In Utah and Virginia, civil penalties can reach $7,500 per violation. In Colorado, violations are treated as "deceptive trade practices" under Colorado's Consumer Protection Act, where fines can be up to $20,000 per violation. In Connecticut, violations are treated as "unfair trade practices" under Connecticut's Unfair Protection Act, where fines can be up to $5,000 per willful violation. [68]

6.2.4.2 Enforcer

With regard to who enforces the state comprehensive privacy law, the state attorney general has either sole or joint enforcement power in each of these states.[69] In Virginia and Utah, the state attorney general is solely responsible for enforcement. In Connecticut, the state attorney general works in conjunction with the Division of Consumer Protection to enforce the law. In Colorado, both the state attorney general and local district attorneys have the power to enforce the law. Although the details of California's enforcement approach are beyond the scope of this book, both the state attorney general and the CPPA have the power to enforce the requirements in California.[70]

6.2.4.3 Cure Period

In certain states, a business is given a specified number of days to address a violation without being subject to sanction. This is known as a cure period, where the enforcer must notify the business of the violation and permit the business a set number of days to rectify the violation. The states split on the topic of a cure period. California initially had a cure period, but it expired prior to the writing of this book. Colorado and Connecticut currently have a cure period, which is set to sunset, or expire, on December 31, 2024. Utah and Virginia have a cure period of 30 days, with no statutory date when the cure period ends.[71]

6.2.4.4 Private Right of Action

It is worth noting, particularly in light of the contention at the federal level over a private right of action in proposed comprehensive privacy legislation, that none of the five state comprehensive privacy laws discussed in this section have a traditional private right of action. Colorado, Connecticut, Utah, and Virginia do not provide consumers with a private right of action as part of their laws. California does not include an expansive private right of action related to the consumer rights discussed in this chapter. Instead, California provides a limited private right of action related to security breaches that compromise personal information—as defined in California's data breach notification law (see Chapter 7)—as well as usernames and passwords that permit access to accounts.[72]

6.3 Conclusion

In the absence of a comprehensive privacy law at the federal level in the United States, more than half the states have considered legislation with comprehensive privacy protections. An increasing number of states have enacted laws. Five of the laws were in effect in 2023. Although these state laws vary in their detail, each of the five reviewed in this chapter addresses consumer rights and business obligations that are similar to those found in the GDPR. As more of these state laws are likely to pass, commentators suggest pressure will continue to mount to enact a federal law in the United States that addresses comprehensive privacy protections.

Endnotes

1 The EU's General Data Protection Regulation became effective on May 25, 2018, approximately one month before the passage of The California Consumer Privacy Act. It will be discussed in detail in Chapter 14—GDPR and International Privacy Issues. For a comparison of California Consumer Privacy Act requirements and General Data Protection Regulation requirements, see CCPA and GDPR Comparison Chart, Thomson Reuters, accessed February 2023, https://www.bakerlaw.com/webfiles/Privacy/2018/Articles/CCPA-GDPR-Chart.pdf; See "Comparing Privacy Laws: GDPR vs. CCPA," DataGuidance and Future of Privacy Forum, accessed February 2023, https://fpf.org/wp-content/uploads/2018/11/GDPR_CCPA_Comparison-Guide.pdf.

2 "Comparing GDPR, CCPA, and CPRA," OneTrust DataGuidance and Newmeyer & Dillion LLP, January 2022, https://www.dataguidance.com/sites/default/files/gdpr_v_ccpa_and_cpra_v6.pdf.

3 State data breach notification laws and state data security laws are discussed in detail in Chapter 7.

4 Andrew Sheeler, "California Soon to Become the World's Fourth Largest Economy," Governing, October 25, 2022, https://www.governing.com/finance/california-soon-to-become-the-worlds-fourth-largest-economy.

5 State of California Department of Finance, "Estimates E-1: Population and Housing Estimates for Cities, Counties, and the State—January 1, 2002 and 2023," January, may 2023, https://dof.ca.gov/forecasting/demographics/estimates-e1/.

6 "Reforming the U.S. Approach to Data Protection and Privacy," Council on Foreign Relations, January 30, 2018, https://www.cfr.org/report/reforming-us-approach-data-protection.

7 Müge Fazioglu, "Distilling the Essence of the American Data Privacy and Protection Act Discussion Draft," *Privacy Tracker*, IAPP, June 6, 2022, https://iapp.org/news/a/distilling-the-essence-of-the-american-data-privacy-and-protection-act-discussion-draft/; Neil Richards and Woodrow Hartzog, "Professors Hartzog and Richards Advocate for Data Loyalty in Privacy Legislation," *Technology, Academics, Policy* (blog) July 25, 2022, https://www.techpolicy.com/blog-posts/professors-hartzog-and-richards-advocate-data-loyalty-privacy-legislation.

8 Robert Gellman, "The Long and Difficult Road to a U.S. Privacy Law: Part 2," *Privacy Perspectives*, IAPP, August 8, 2018, https://iapp.org/news/a/the-long-and-difficult-road-to-a-u-s-privacy-law-part-2/.

9 Travis Brennan, Raj Shukla, and Scott Schneider, "California Sets De Facto National Data Privacy Standard," *Corporate Counsel Business Journal*, July 6, 2019, https://ccbjournal.com/articles/california-sets-de-facto-national-data-privacy-standard; *see* Ian Adams and Pasha Moore, "Only the Right Kind of State 'Techlash' Will Lead to Meaningful Privacy Protection," *InsideSources*, July 15, 2019, https://www.insidesources.com/only-the-right-kind-of-state-techlash-will-lead-to-meaningful-privacy-protection/. Chapter 7 discusses state-specific privacy, security, and data breach notification laws in detail.

10 Sintia Radu, "50-State Patchwork of Privacy Laws Could Cost $1 Trillion More than a Single Federal Law, New ITIF Report Finds," Information Technology & Innovation Foundation, January 24, 2022, https://itif.org/publications/2022/01/24/50-state-patchwork-privacy-laws-could-cost-1-trillion-more-single-federal.

11 Peter Swire and Pollyanna Sanderson, "A Proposal to Help Resolve Federal Privacy Preemption," *Privacy Tracker*, IAPP, January 13, 2020, https://iapp.org/news/a/a-proposal-to-help-resolve-federal-privacy-preemption/; *see* Peter Swire, "U.S. Federal Privacy Preemption Part 1: History of Federal Preemption of Stricter State Laws," IAPP January 9, 2019, https://iapp.org/news/a/us-federal-privacy-preemption-part-1-history-of-federal-preemption-of-stricter-state-laws/.

12 Robert Gellman, "The Long and Difficult Road to a U.S. Privacy Law: Part 3," Privacy Perspectives, IAPP, August 15, 2018; Swire, "U.S. Federal Privacy Preemption Part 1"; see Gellman, "The Long and Difficult Road to a U.S. Privacy Law: Part 2."

13 Cameron F. Kerry and Caitlin Chin, "Will California Be the Death of National Privacy Legislation?" *TechTank* (blog), Brookings, November 18, 2022, https://www.brookings.edu/blog/techtank/2022/11/18/will-california-be-the-death-of-national-privacy-legislation/; Meghan Stoppel, "AGs Unite to Ensure Federal Privacy Legislation Sets Floor, Not Ceiling, for States," Reuters, August 22, 2022, https://www.reuters.com/legal/litigation/ags-unite-ensure-federal-privacy-legislation-sets-floor-not-ceiling-states-2022-08-22/.

14 For a more detailed analysis of the preemption issues related to a general U.S. privacy law, read the complete article by Peter Swire, "U.S. Federal Privacy Preemption Part 2: Examining Preemption Proposals," *Privacy Tracker*, IAPP, January 10, 2019; see Swire, "U.S. Federal Privacy Preemption Part 1."

15 Cameron F. Kerry and Caitlin Chin, "Will California Be the Death of National Privacy Legislation?" *TechTank* (blog), Brookings Institution, November 18, 2022, https://www.brookings.edu/blog/techtank/2022/11/18/will-california-be-the-death-of-national-privacy-legislation/.

16 See Myriah Jaworski and Paul Schmeltzer, "An Enterprise-Wide Data Solution to the State Privacy Law Problem," SHRM, November 2, 2022, https://www.shrm.org/resourcesandtools/legal-and-compliance/state-and-local-updates/pages/state-data-privacy-laws.aspx.

17 DPAs are independent public authorities that are dedicated to handling data protection, or privacy, requirements. "What Are Data Protection Authorities (DPAs)?," European Commission, accessed April 12, 2023, https://commission.europa.eu/law/law-topic/data-protection/reform/what-are-data-protection-authorities-dpas_en. When examining the enforcement framework in the 4 states without an agency dedicated to privacy protections, it should be noted that State Attorneys General are independent officers, who are typically viewed as one of the most power officials in their respective states. State Attorneys General are put into office and removed only by popular election in nearly all states. In all 50 states, State Attorneys General are constitutional officers, meaning their office is required under their respective state constitutions. Attorneys General, National Association of Attorneys General (NAAG), https://www.naag.org/attorneys-general/; see Michael Signer, "Constitutional Crisis in the Commonwealth: Resolving the Conflict Between Governors and Attorneys General," *University of Richmond Law Review*, November 1, 2006, https://scholarship.richmond.edu/lawreview/vol41/iss1/5/.

18 Anokhy Desai, "U.S. State Comprehensive Privacy Laws Report," Resource Center, IAPP, March 2023, https://iapp.org/resources/article/us-state-privacy-laws-overview/; see David Stauss, "State Data Privacy Legislation: Takeaways from 2022 and What to Expect in 2023," *Privacy Advisor*, IAPP, August 23, 2022, https://iapp.org/news/a/state-data-privacy-legislation-takeaways-from-2022-and-what-to-expect-in-2023/; see also Joseph Duball, "State Privacy Prospects Bring New Paradigm in 2023," *Privacy Advisor*, IAPP, February 28, 2023, https://iapp.org/news/a/2023-state-privacy-prospects-bring-new-paradigm.

19 Note the classification of consumer rights and business obligations can vary by state.

20 Cathy Cosgrove and Sarah Ropy, "Comparison Chart: Comprehensive Data Privacy Laws - Virginia, California, Colorado," Resource Center, IAPP , July 2021, https://iapp.org/media/pdf/resource_center/comparison_chart_comprehensive_data_privacy_laws_virginia_california_colorado.pdf; Sheila A. Millar and Tracey P. Marshall, "A State-by-State U.S. Privacy Law Comparison," *The National Law Review*, May 24, 2022, https://www.natlawreview.com/article/state-us-state-privacy-laws-comparison; Alan R. Friedman, Robin Wilcox and Austin Manes, "Comparing the 5 Comprehensive Privacy Laws Passed by U.S. States," Kramer Levin, June 10, 2022, https://www.kramerlevin.com/en/perspectives-search/comparing-the-5-comprehensive-privacy-laws-passed-by-us-states.html.

21 Taylor Kay Lively, "Utah Becomes Fourth U.S. State to Enact Comprehensive Consumer Privacy Legislation," *Privacy Advisor*, IAPP, March 25, 2022, https://iapp.org/news/a/

utah-becomes-fourth-state-to-enact-comprehensive-consumer-privacy-legislation/; Alan R. Friedman, Robin Wilcox and Austin Manes, "Comparing the 5 Comprehensive Privacy Laws Passed by U.S. States," Kramer Levin, June 10, 2022, https://www.kramerlevin.com/en/perspectives-search/comparing-the-5-comprehensive-privacy-laws-passed-by-us-states.html.

22 It is worth noting that California uses the term business, while the other four states use the term controller to refer to those entities covered by the law. The term "business" is used in this chapter for ease of reading. See Anokhy Desai, "U.S. State Comprehensive Privacy Laws Report—Overview," Resource Center, IAPP, March 2023, https://iapp.org/resources/article/us-state-privacy-laws-overview/.

23 Friedman, Wilcox and Manes, "Comparing the 5 Comprehensive Privacy Laws Passed by U.S. States"; Taylor Kay Lively "Connecticut Enacts Comprehensive Consumer Data Privacy Law," *Privacy Advisor*, IAPP, May 11, 2022, https://iapp.org/news/a/connecticut-enacts-comprehensive-consumer-data-privacy-law/.

24 Office of the Connecticut Attorney General, "The Connecticut Data Privacy Act," State of Connecticut, last modified May 10, 2022, https://portal.ct.gov/AG/Sections/Privacy/The-Connecticut-Data-Privacy-Act.

25 The annual-revenue requirement is absent in Connecticut, Colorado, and Virginia. Friedman, Wilcox and Manes, "Comparing the 5 Comprehensive Privacy Laws Passed by U.S. States."

26 Friedman, Wilcox and Manes, "Comparing the 5 Comprehensive Privacy Laws Passed by U.S. States."

27 Lively, "Connecticut Enacts Comprehensive Consumer Data Privacy Law"; "Preparing for 2023 State Privacy Law Compliance," Squire Patton Boggs, August 2022, https://www.squirepattonboggs.com/-/media/files/insights/publications/2022/05/preparing-for-2023-state-privacy-law-compliance/preparingfor2023stateprivacylawcompliance.pdf.

28 "Preparing for 2023 State Privacy Law Compliance," Squire Patton Boggs.

29 Cal. Civ. Code § 1798.140(o), "1798.140 Definitions," California Consumer Privacy Act (CCPA), https://ccpa-info.com/home/1798-140-definitions/; see Hans Skillrud, "Guide to Collecting Personal Information under CCPA," Termageddon, May 6, 2022, https://termageddon.com/guide-to-collecting-personal-information-under-the-ccpa.

30 Peter Karalis, "Analysis: Nothing Personal: States Are Eyeing De-Identified Data," Bloomberg Law, February 7, 2022, https://news.bloomberglaw.com/bloomberg-law-analysis/analysis-nothing-personal-states-are-eyeing-de-identified-data.

31 Friedman, Wilcox and Manes, "Comparing the 5 Comprehensive Privacy Laws Passed by U.S. States"; Lively "Connecticut Enacts Comprehensive Consumer Data Privacy Law."

32 "Preparing for 2023 State Privacy Law Compliance," Squire Patton Boggs.

33 Friedman, Wilcox and Manes, "Comparing the 5 Comprehensive Privacy Laws Passed by U.S. States"; Lively "Connecticut Enacts Comprehensive Consumer Data Privacy Law"; see David Stauss and Stacey Weber, "How Do CPRA, CPA, & VCDPA Treat Publicly Available Information?" Husch Blackwell, January 27, 2022, https://www.bytebacklaw.com/2022/01/how-do-the-cpra-cpa-vcdpa-treat-publicly-available-information/.

34 "Preparing for 2023 State Privacy Law Compliance," Squire Patton Boggs.

35 "Preparing for 2023 State Privacy Law Compliance," Squire Patton Boggs; Desai, "U.S. State Comprehensive Privacy Laws Report—Overview."

36 Millar and Marshall, "A State-by-State U.S. Privacy Law Comparison"; Friedman, Wilcox and Manes, "Comparing the 5 Comprehensive Privacy Laws Passed by U.S. States"; Robb Hiscock, "The Ultimate Guide to U.S. Privacy," *OneTrust Blog*, https://www.onetrust.com/blog/the-ultimate-guide-to-us-privacy/.

37 Friedman, Wilcox and Manes, "Comparing the 5 Comprehensive Privacy Laws Passed by U.S. States"; Lively "Connecticut Enacts Comprehensive Consumer Data Privacy Law"; see California and Colorado.

38 Cal. Civ. Code § 1798.140(ah).

39 "United States - Comprehensive State Privacy Laws," Government of Canada, accessed June 2023, https://www.tradecommissioner.gc.ca/guides/state_privacy_laws_lois_confidentialite.aspx?lang=eng; see Fredric Bellamy, "U.S. Data Privacy Laws to Enter New Era in 2023," Reuters, January 12, 2023, https://www.reuters.com/legal/legalindustry/us-data-privacy-laws-enter-new-era-2023-2023-01-12.

40 "U.S. State Privacy Legislation Tracker: 2023," IAPP; Friedman, Wilcox and Manes, "Comparing the 5 Comprehensive Privacy Laws Passed by U.S. States."

41 Friedman, Wilcox and Manes, "Comparing the 5 Comprehensive Privacy Laws Passed by U.S. States."

42 "10 Key Differences Between the 2023 California, Virginia, and Colorado Privacy Laws," Engage, Hogan Lovells, June 30, 2021, https://www.engage.hoganlovells.com/knowledgeservices/news/10-key-differences-between-the-2023-california-virginia-and-colorado-privacy-laws; Friedman, Wilcox and Manes, "Comparing the 5 Comprehensive Privacy Laws Passed by U.S. States"; Office of the Connecticut Attorney General, "The Connecticut Data Privacy Act."

43 "Preparing for 2023 State Privacy Law Compliance," Squire Patton Boggs; "U.S. State Privacy Legislation Tracker: 2023," IAPP.

44 "Preparing for 2023 State Privacy Law Compliance," Squire Patton Boggs; "U.S. State Privacy Legislation Tracker: 2023," IAPP; see Utah State Legislature, "Utah Consumer Privacy Act," Utah Code Annotated Title 13 Chapter 61, last modified May 4, 2022, https://le.utah.gov/xcode/Title13/Chapter61/C13-61_2022050420231231.pdf.

45 The right to deletion can also be referred to as the right to erasure or the right to be forgotten. The approach in state comprehensive privacy laws has some distinctions from the requirements under the EU's GDPR. See "The Reason Why Europe's 'Right to be Forgotten' Hasn't Made it to the United States," Modern Diplomacy, March 10, 2023 (discussing the right to be forgotten in relation to the First Amendment to the U.S. Constitution), https://moderndiplomacy.eu/2023/03/10/the-reason-why-europes-right-to-be-forgotten-hasnt-made-it-to-the-united-states/; see also Laura Jehl and Alan Friel, "CCPA and GDPR Comparison Chart," Practical Law, Baker Hostetler, updated, (comparing California's approach to the EU's approach under the GDPR), https://www.bakerlaw.com/webfiles/Privacy/2018/Articles/CCPA-GDPR-Chart.pdf

46 Glenn A. Brown, "Consumers' 'Right to Delete' Under U.S. State Privacy Laws," *Privacy World* (blog), Squire Patton Boggs, March 3, 2021, https://www.privacyworld.blog/2021/03/consumers-right-to-delete-under-us-state-privacy-laws/; Kate Berry, Nancy Libin, and John D. Seiver, "Utah Consumer Privacy Act Signed into Law," Privacy & Security Law Blog, Davis Wright Tremaine LLP, updated March 31, 2022, https://www.dwt.com/blogs/privacy--security-law-blog/2022/03/utah-consumer-privacy-act; see Natasha G. Kohne, Michelle A. Reed, Lauren E. York, Rachel Claire Kurzweil, "Virginia's New Amendments to the VCDPA," Akin, April 19, 2022, https://www.

akingump.com/en/insights/blogs/ag-data-dive/virginias-new-amendments-to-the-vcdpa.

47 "Preparing for 2023 State Privacy Law Compliance," Squire Patton Boggs.

48 Cal. Civ. Code § 1798.105(d).

49 The data portability right is arguably one of the few provisions of these state comprehensive privacy laws that do not reflect a clear privacy or security purpose; instead, this right is apparently designed to serve a pro-competition interest. See Daniel Castro, "Improving Consumer Welfare with Data Portability," Center for Data Innovation, November 29, 2021, https://www2.datainnovation.org/2021-data-portability.pdf; "10 Key Differences Between the 2023 California, Virginia, and Colorado Privacy Laws," Engage, Hogan Lovells; see also Peter Swire, "The Portability and Other Required Transfers Impact Assessment (PORT-IA): Assessing Competition, Privacy, Cybersecurity, and Other Requirements," *Georgetown Law Technology Review*, February 2022, https://georgetownlawtechreview.org/the-portability-and-other-required-transfers-impact-assessment-port-ia-assessing-competition-privacy-cybersecurity-and-other-considerations/GLTR-02-2022/.

50 "Preparing for 2023 State Privacy Law Compliance," Squire Patton Boggs; "U.S. State Privacy Legislation Tracker: 2023," IAPP.

51 Friedman, Wilcox and Manes, "Comparing the 5 Comprehensive Privacy Laws Passed by U.S. States"; "Preparing for 2023 State Privacy Law Compliance," Squire Patton Boggs; "The Ultimate Guide to California Privacy Laws," OneTrust DataGuidance, https://www.dataguidance.com/resource/ultimate-guide-california-privacy-laws#CCPA v CPRA.

52 "Preparing for 2023 State Privacy Law Compliance," Squire Patton Boggs; "Connecticut Data Privacy Act—What Businesses Need to Know," Akin, May 26, 2022, https://www.akingump.com/en/news-insights/connecticut-data-privacy-act-what-businesses-need-to-know.html; David A. Zetoony, "Under the Colorado Privacy Act, Will Companies Be Required to Offer Consumers the Ability to Opt Out of Behavioral Advertising if They have Already Received Opt-in Consent?," *The National Law Review*, November 4, 2021, https://www.natlawreview.com/article/under-colorado-privacy-act-will-companies-be-required-to-offer-consumers-ability-to; Glenn Brown, "Virginia: Consumers' opt-out Rights Under CDPA," OneTrust DataGuidance, July 2021, https://www.dataguidance.com/opinion/virginia-consumers-opt-out-rights-under-cdpa.

53 Brown, "Virginia: Consumers' opt-out Rights Under CDPA"; W. Reece Hirsch, Gregory T. Parks, Carla B. Oakley, Ezra D. Church, and Kristin Hadgis, "California Consumer Privacy Act: Employee and B2B Exemptions Expire January 1, 2023," Morgan Lewis, October 14, 2022, https://www.morganlewis.com/pubs/2022/10/california-consumer-privacy-act-employee-and-b2b-exemptions-expire-january-1-2023; see Kyle Fath, Shea Leitch, and Gicel Tomimbang, "Profiling and Automated Decision-Making: How to Prepare in the Absence of Draft CPRA Regulations," Privacy World (blog), Squire Patton Boggs, October 14, 2022, https://www.privacyworld.blog/2022/10/profiling-and-automated-decision-making-how-to-prepare-in-the-absence-of-draft-cpra-regulations/#:~:text=CTPA%20provides%20the%20right%20to,distinct%20from%20VCDPA%20and%20CPA.

54 "Preparing for 2023: State Privacy Law Compliance," Squire Patton Boggs, August 2022, https://www.squirepattonboggs.com/-/media/files/insights/publications/2022/05/preparing-for-2023-state-privacy-law-compliance/

preparingfor2023stateprivacylawcompliance.pdf; "U.S. State Privacy Legislation Tracker: 2023," IAPP.

55 "Preparing for 2023: State Privacy Law Compliance," Squire Patton Boggs; "U.S. State Privacy Legislation Tracker: 2023," IAPP

56 It should be noted that a state may have additional requirements for businesses. See "U.S. State Privacy Legislation Tracker: 2023," IAPP; Friedman, Wilcox and Manes, "Comparing the 5 Comprehensive Privacy Laws Passed by U.S. States"; Millar and Marshall, "A State-by-State U.S. Privacy Law Comparison."

57 "U.S. State Privacy Legislation Tracker: 2023," IAPP; Friedman, Wilcox, and Manes, "Comparing the 5 Comprehensive Privacy Laws Passed by U.S. States"; Millar and Marshall, "A State-by-State U.S. Privacy Law Comparison."

58 David A. Zetoony, "Where Exactly Does an Opt-Out of Targeted Advertising Link Need to Be Placed?," Data Privacy Dish, GreenbergTraurig, May 24, 2022, https://www.gtlaw-dataprivacydish.com/2022/05/where-exactly-does-an-opt-out-of-targeted-advertising-link-need-to-be-placed/; see Robb Hiscock, "The Ultimate Guide to U.S. Privacy," OneTrust Blog, December 9, 2022, https://www.onetrust.com/blog/the-ultimate-guide-to-us-privacy/; see also, Steven G. Stransky and Thora Knight, "2023 U.S. State Data Protection Laws Compliance Chart," Thompson Hine LLP, https://iapp.org/media/pdf/resource_center/thompson_hine_2023_us_state_data_protection_laws_compliance_chart.pdf; Liisa M. Thomas and Julia Kadish, "Comparing and Contrasting the Opt-Out Preference Signal Across States," The National Law Review, October 24, 2022, https://www.natlawreview.com/article/comparing-and-contrasting-opt-out-preference-signal-across-states.

59 Cal. Civ. Code § 1798.135(a), California Legislative Information, "California Consumer Privacy Act," California Civil Code § 1798.100 et seq. (2022), https://leginfo.legislature.ca.gov/faces/codes_displayText.xhtml?division=3.&part=4.&lawCode=CIV&title=1.81.5.

60 "Preparing for 2023 State Privacy Law Compliance," Squire Patton Boggs.

61 The rules for processing children's data under the Children's Online Privacy Protection Act (COPPA) are discussed in many of these state laws. COPPA is discussed in Chapter 5. See Jessica B. Lee and Nerissa Coyle McGinn, "Changes in Children's Privacy Protection in Response to the Pandemic," Loeb & Loeb LLP, July 2022, https://www.loeb.com/en/insights/publications/2022/07/changes-in-childrens-privacy-protection-in-response-to-the-pandemic.

62 U.S. State Privacy Legislation Tracker: 2023," IAPP; Millar and Marshall, "A State-by-State U.S. Privacy Law Comparison"; Shelby Dolen and Mike Summers, "How Do the CPRA, VCDPA, and the CPA Treat Children's Data?," Byte Back, Husch Blackwell, March 29, 2022, https://www.bytebacklaw.com/2022/03/how-do-the-cpra-vcdpa-and-the-cpa-treat-childrens-data/.

63 "U.S. State Privacy Legislation Tracker: 2023," IAPP; "Preparing for 2023 State Privacy Law Compliance," Squire Patton Boggs.

64 "U.S. State Privacy Legislation Tracker: 2023," IAPP; see Theodore P. Augustinos, "Emerging Requirements for Data Protection Impact Assessments," Locke Lord, Spring 2022, https://www.lockelord.com/newsandevents/publications/2022/05/emerging-requirements; David Strauss and Shelby Dolen, "How Do the CPRA, CPA, and VCDPA Approach Data Protection Assessments?," Byte Back, Husch Blackwell, February 9, 2022, https://www.bytebacklaw.com/2022/02/how-do-the-cpra-cpa-and-vcdpa-approach-

data-protection-assessments/; see also Wayne Matus and Rich Vestuto, "You're Not Ready for CPRA if Your Vendors Aren't," ANA, September 7, 2022, https://www.ana.net/miccontent/show/id/ii-2022-09-CPRA-breakdown.

65 Taylor Kay Lively, "Utah Becomes Fourth State to Enact Comprehensive Consumer Privacy Legislation"; Natasha G. Kohne, Michelle A. Reed, Jo-Ellyn Sakowitz Klein, Rachel Claire Kurzweil, Lauren E. York, Tina M. Jeffcoat, "Utah Consumer Privacy Act: What Businesses Need to Know," Akin, April 8, 2022, https://www.akingump.com/en/news-insights/utah-consumer-privacy-act-what-businesses-need-to-know.html.

66 "United States – Comprehensive State Privacy Laws," Government of Canada, last modified June 6, 2022, https://www.tradecommissioner.gc.ca/guides/state_privacy_laws_lois_confidentialite.aspx?lang=eng; Friedman, Wilcox and Manes, "Comparing the 5 Comprehensive Privacy Laws Passed by U.S. States."

67 "Any person who engages, has engaged, or proposes to engage in unfair competition shall be liable for a civil penalty not to exceed two thousand five hundred dollars ($2,500) for each violation." Section 17206(a) of the California Business and Professional Code, accessed November 2019, http://leginfo.legislature.ca.gov/faces/codes_displaySection.xhtml?lawCode=BPC§ionNum=17206; see Nicholas Schmidt, "Top 5 Operational Impacts of CCPA: Part 5—Penalties and Enforcement Mechanisms," *Privacy Advisor*, IAPP, August 21, 2018, https://iapp.org/news/a/top-5-operational-impacts-of-cacpa-part-5-penalties-and-enforcement-mechanisms/.

68 Friedman, Wilcox and Manes, "Comparing the 5 Comprehensive Privacy Laws Passed by U.S. States"; Lively "Connecticut Enacts Comprehensive Consumer Data Privacy Law."

69 Sam Pfeifle, "The Expert's Guide to California Data Privacy Law," Osano, August 2, 2022, https://www.osano.com/articles/california-privacy-laws-ccpa-cpra; Millar and Marshall, "A State-by-State U.S. Privacy Law Comparison."

70 Millar and Marshall, "A State-by-State U.S. Privacy Law Comparison." "The CCPA vests the California Attorney General with enforcement authority. Although the CPRA grants the California Privacy Protection Agency 'full administrative power, authority, and jurisdiction to implement and enforce' the CCPA, the Attorney General still retains enforcement powers. Cal. Civ. Code § 1798.199.90 provides that the California Privacy Protection Agency 'may not limit the authority of the Attorney General to enforce this title.'" "California Consumer Privacy Laws," Bloomberg Law, accessed June 2023, https://pro.bloomberglaw.com/brief/the-far-reaching-implications-of-the-california-consumer-privacy-act-ccpa/.

71 Millar and Marshall, "A State-by-State U.S. Privacy Law Comparison"; Friedman, Wilcox and Manes, "Comparing the 5 Comprehensive Privacy Laws Passed by U.S. States."

72 "U.S. State Privacy Legislation Tracker: 2023," IAPP; Millar and Marshall, "A State-by-State U.S. Privacy Law Comparison"; see "CPRA Expanded Private Right of Action," *Securiti* (blog), December 16, 2022, https://securiti.ai/blog/cpra-privacy-right-of-action/.

CHAPTER 7

State Data Breach Notification Laws, State Data Security Laws, and State Data Destruction Laws

- *Security,* September 8, 2022: "A data breach of student loan servicer Nelnet Servicing (Nelnet) has affected over 2.5 million student loan borrowers throughout the United States. The breach … compromised the names, addresses, email addresses, phone numbers and Social Security numbers of borrowers. … Nelnet reported … that they had discovered a vulnerability believed to be the source of the breach."[1]
- *HIPAA Journal,* September 1, 2022: "The number of individuals affected by the ransomware attack on the Hartland, WI-based mailing and printing vendor [for various healthcare companies], OneTouchPoint, has now increased to 2,651,396 individuals. … Customers have reported the breach as involving names, subscriber ID numbers, diagnoses, medications, addresses, dates of birth, sexes, physician demographics information, family histories, social histories, allergies, vitals, immunizations, and other information."[2]
- *Business Insider,* April 3, 2021: "The exposed data includes the personal information of over 533 million Facebook users from 106 countries, including over 32 million records on users in the U.S., 11 million on users in the UK, and 6 million on users in India. It includes their phone numbers, Facebook IDs, full names, locations, birthdates, bios, and, in some cases, email addresses. … A Facebook spokesperson told Insider that the data had been scraped because of a vulnerability that the company patched in 2019."[3]
- *Reuters,* February 14, 2021: "A hacking campaign, … likely orchestrated by Russia, breached software made by SolarWinds Corp., giving hackers access to thousands of companies and government offices that used its products. … The breach could have compromised up to 18,000 SolarWinds customers that used the company's Orion network monitoring software."[4]

As these examples show, companies across a variety of industries collect and process large amounts of personal data. When companies store large amounts of data, this data can become a target for bad actors—creating significant cybersecurity challenges. Of particular importance in this book about privacy regulation, problems with cybersecurity can lead to data being accessed and (mis)used in ways not intended or agreed to by the user. When unauthorized persons do gain access to this data, data breach notification laws are triggered.

The spread of state data breach notification laws to all 50 states over the last two decades has had a major impact on private-sector information security practices. When breaches occur, top management often focuses intensively on information management practices, discussed in Chapter 4. In many instances, the budget and visibility increase for information security activities in the wake of a breach. Similarly, concerns about the possibility of data breaches, with the resulting negative publicity, financial penalties, and other effects provide an important incentive for companies to develop strong information security practices. While significant differences remain among the state laws, the end result today is that entities processing personal data in the United States are compelled to disclose data breaches in an expeditious manner.[5]

This chapter begins with a discussion of the state data breach notification laws. An overview of the material provisions of the laws in all 50 states is provided. Because California has been an innovator in this area, enacting the first state data breach law in 2003 and recently becoming the first state to provide consumers with the ability to recover a set amount of money when their data is compromised in a data breach, pertinent details of California's legal framework are also highlighted.[6]

Recognizing that regulators may review whether entities used reasonable data security measures and data destruction policies in the wake of a data breach, the chapter also reviews state data security laws that are designed to help prevent data breaches as well as state data destruction laws that are enacted to prevent breaches at the end of the data life cycle.

It is worth noting that, although both state comprehensive privacy laws and state data breach notification laws define "personal information," the definitions in these laws may differ significantly.[7] This is primarily due to the fact that the laws are focused on different protections. State comprehensive privacy laws intend to limit what authorized entities are properly able to do with an individual's data. State data breach notification laws put protections in place in an effort to avoid instances where an unauthorized user can misuse an individual's data—such as for purposes of fraud or identity theft.[8] For privacy practitioners, the landscape at the state level can be complex, with multiple types of state laws and accompanying requirements in place.

7.1 State Data Breach Notification Laws

With all 50 states having implemented data breach notification laws and California having enacted a provision that permits consumers to recover a set amount of money for the unauthorized release of certain personal information, these state laws can result in significant enforcement actions by state attorneys general as well as notable class action settlements in states that permit a private right of action.[9] Privacy practitioners should be prepared to assist companies in developing policies to comply with the various requirements of these laws as well as to help coordinate responses in the event of breaches.

With massive, high-profile data breaches making the front pages, calls for a uniform federal data breach law have been ongoing for decades.[10] These discussions began at the national level in 2003, when Senator Dianne Feinstein of California introduced the first federal breach notification bill. Over the years, numerous comprehensive federal data breach notification laws have been considered by Congress. As of the writing of this book, no comprehensive federal law with data breach notification requirements has been enacted.[11] Reaching consensus on such a law is difficult; privacy advocates have generally supported approaches that would match federal law to the strictest state laws, while businesses have generally supported a federal law with fewer regulatory requirements as well as preemption of stricter state laws.

In the absence of a federal law, states have taken the lead in setting requirements related to data breaches. These laws create important incentives for companies to develop good information security practices. Companies who operate nationally are faced with compliance with all 50 state data breach laws.[12]

When examining these state laws, it is important to realize that state data breach notification laws generally contain the same basic topics:

- **Key terms** such as the definition of personal information (meaning the specific data elements that trigger reporting requirements), the definition of what entities are covered, and the definition of a security breach (including whether an analysis of risk of harm is permitted)

- **Notification requirements** including whom to notify, when to notify affected parties, what to include in the notification letter to affected parties, how to notify affected parties, when to notify state attorneys general or state agencies, when notice is required to consumer reporting agencies, whether exceptions may exist to the obligation to notify, and when notification may be delayed
- **Enforcement** such as penalties and private rights of action[13]

Each of the following subsections highlights trends common among the majority of states and details states with outlying requirements. Because California's recently enacted comprehensive privacy framework (discussed in Chapter 6) includes a provision that permits consumers to recover a set amount of money for certain data breaches, pertinent parts of California's legal framework are detailed here.

7.1.1 Key Terms

For data breach notification laws, it is important to focus on definitions of key terms when assessing the applicability of these state laws. Three key terms discussed below are "personal information," "covered entities," and "security breach."

7.1.1.1 Personal Information

The definition of personal information found in the majority of state data breach notification laws includes an individual's first name or first initial and last name in combination with any one, or more, of the following data: (1) Social Security number; (2) driver's license number or state identification card number; or (3) financial account number or credit or debit card number, often in combination with any required security code, access code, or password that would permit access to an individual's financial account.[14]

Approximately two-thirds contain additional elements as meeting the definition of personal information.[15] These include medical and health care information, any federal or state identification number, unique biometric data, tax information, and mother's maiden name.[16] Almost all states exclude publicly available information from the definition of personal information.[17]

7.1.1.2 Covered Entities

In most states, covered entities that are subject to these state laws include those: (1) that conduct business in the state; and (2) that, in the ordinary course of such person's business, maintain computerized data that includes personal information. Some states limit the definition of covered entities to those that conduct business in that state.[18] Georgia's definition is significantly more limited, with covered entities defined as "information brokers."[19]

7.1.1.3 Security Breach

The definition of a "security breach" in these state laws often includes the following elements: unauthorized access to or acquisition of electronic files or computerized data containing personal information, which compromises confidentiality, security, or integrity of information; when access to the personal information has not been secured by encryption or by any other method; or technology that renders the personal information unreadable or unusable.

Nearly all states apply a risk-of-harm analysis in determining whether an incident involving personal data constitutes a regulated breach.[20] Although the exact requirements vary by state, an incident is commonly excluded where it is not reasonably likely that either harm or substantial harm will result to the affected party. The harm envisioned by these laws typically includes identity theft, fraud, and other financial loss. It is worth noting that the language related to this risk analysis can be found either in the state law's definition of a security breach or in the requirements for notification to affected parties.[21]

7.1.2 Notification Requirements

With notification requirements, it is important for companies to understand who they are required to notify—affected parties, state attorneys general, and national consumer reporting agencies (CRAs). In addition, companies must understand when they are required to make these notifications and what they must include in these notifications. Because each state has its own set of requirements, this subsection focuses primarily on the trends that are common among states, with some mention of those states with requirements that are atypical. The subsection concludes by reviewing exceptions to the notification requirements as well as permitted delays when law enforcement is investigating the breach.

7.1.2.1 Whom to Notify

Data breach notification laws commonly require notifications to affected parties, state attorneys general or other state agencies, and nationwide CRAs.

- The primary recipients of a breach notification are those state residents who are at risk because their personal information has (potentially) been exposed based on the level of unauthorized access or harm. All 50 states require notification to those affected.

- Approximately two-thirds of the states require covered entities that have detected a data breach to notify the state attorney general and/or other state agencies.
- About two-thirds of states require that these entities notify CRAs of a data breach.[22]

7.1.2.2 When to Notify Affected Parties

These state laws use similar language to describe the required timing of notifications to affected individuals. The most common phrase used in conjunction with timing is "as expeditiously as possible and without unreasonable delay"—which allows the affected entity to conduct a reasonable investigation to determine the scope of the breach and restore the reasonable integrity of the data system. Numerous states specify a limit to the time allowed when this common phrase is utilized, with 45 days after the discovery of the breach being the most common timeframe permitted by these states.[23] For companies operating nationally, it is important to note that the industry best practice is to report within 30 days after the discovery of the breach, meaning that a delay of 45 days could be considered unreasonable (without a valid explanation) in certain states.

7.1.2.3 What to Include in the Notification Letter to Affected Parties

Approximately half of these state laws mandate specific content be included in the notification to the affected parties. Privacy professionals dealing with the required notifications in those states that do not mandate specific information in the notice to affected parties can use the requirements in states with mandates (detailed in this subsection) as guidance.

Although the particular requirements for the content of the notification to affected parties vary, many of these state laws require:

- A description of the incident in general terms
- An approximate date of the incident
- A description of the type of personal information that was subject to the unauthorized access and acquisition
- A description of the general acts of the business to protect the personal information from further unauthorized access
- A telephone number for the business that the person may call for further information and assistance

- A conspicuous notice on the company's website indicating how the person may contact the company for further information and assistance
- A list of steps that the person may take to protect against identity theft
- The toll-free numbers and addresses for the major consumer reporting agencies
- The toll-free numbers, addresses, and websites for the FTC and relevant offices of attorneys general, along with a statement that the individual can obtain information from these sources about preventing identity theft[24]

For companies that operate nationally, the notification to affected parties should be developed with caution as the sometimes diverging requirements in the 50 states can lead to problematic results. For example, while almost all state laws require the notification to include a general description of the incident, Massachusetts law prohibits including a description of the nature of the breach in the notification or the number of residents affected by the breach.[25]

With regard to content of the notice, it is worth noting that when Social Security numbers are compromised, the Federal Trade Commission (FTC) suggests companies offer affected parties at least a year of free credit monitoring or other identity theft protection in the notification letter.[26] As of the writing of this book, three states require companies to provide certain affected parties with free credit monitoring for at least 12 months. The requirement comes into play when Social Security numbers or other similar data have been exposed, increasing the likelihood of the victims suffering identity theft or fraud. California became the first state to enact this requirement in 2015.[27] Since then, Delaware[28] and Massachusetts[29] have also added a credit-monitoring requirement.[30]

7.1.2.4 How to Notify the Affected Parties

State laws generally focus on providing written notification to affected parties using postal mail. These laws typically permit notice by email or telephone as acceptable alternatives, but usually only if the affected party previously and explicitly chose one of these as the preferred communication method.[31]

The notification requirements for nearly all states recognize that data breach notifications involving thousands or even millions of affected parties could place an undue financial burden on the organization if it was required to individually notify each affected party.[32] Under certain circumstances, these laws permit substitute notice by methods such as conspicuous posting on websites or notification to major state-wide media, including newspapers, radio, and television.[33]

7.1.2.5 When Notice is Required to State Attorney General or State Agency

Approximately two-thirds of states require entities who detected a data breach to notify the state attorney general and/or other state agencies. Nearly half of the state laws have a threshold for the number of people affected before notification to the state attorney general or state agency is required; some of these states focus on the number of state residents impacted, while other states are concerned with the number of individuals affected. In state laws with this triggering requirement, the number of people affected typically varies from a low of 250 to a high of 1,000.[34]

States vary regarding the timing of the notice to the attorney general or state agency.

- The most commonly used approach focuses on the notice being made as soon as possible. Numerous states specify a limit to the time allowed when this common phrase is utilized, and the timeframe often mirrors the requirement for notification to affected parties.
- Several states have a requirement that the notification to the state attorney general or state agency must be no later than the time of notification to the affected parties or must be simultaneous to that notice.
- At the writing of this book, the shortest enumerated time frame is found in Vermont's law which provides the required notification must be made within 14 business days of discovery of the breach or when notifying affected individuals, whichever is sooner.[35]
- Maryland, New Hampshire, and New Jersey require this notification to the state entity *prior* to sending notices to affected parties.
- It is worth noting that a minority of state laws contain no provisions regarding the timing of the notice to the state attorney general or state agency.[36]

Most states require notification to the state attorney general or state agency only if the entity determines, after an investigation into the breach, that the breach has harmed the consumers or is reasonable likely to do so.[37]

Notification to attorneys general and regulators may be sent via letter or email. Some states have specific online forms that must be used for this reporting.

7.1.2.6 When Notice is Required to Consumer Reporting Agencies

Similar to the reporting requirements for state attorneys general and/or state agencies, approximately two-thirds of states require that entities notify nationwide CRAs of a data breach.

Nearly half of the state laws have a threshold for the number of people affected before notification to nationwide CRAs is required. In state laws with this triggering requirement, the number of people affected typically varies from a low of 250 to a high of 1,000. In some of these states, the number of state residents affected is critical, but in other states the number of individuals impacted is key.[38]

The timing required for notification to national CRAs varies.

- The most commonly used approach focuses on the notice being provided without unreasonable delay.
- The second most common approach is to defer to the timing requirements in federal statutes.
- As of the writing of this book, the shortest timeframe for reporting to national CRAs that is found in Minnesota's state law. Minnesota requires reporting within 48 hours.[39]
- It is worth pointing out that a minority of state laws contain no provisions regarding the timing of the notice to the CRAs.[40]

The CRAs have established email addresses to receive breach notification reports.

7.1.2.7 Exceptions to Notification

There are three basic exceptions for providing data breach notification:

- Entities subject to another more stringent data breach notification law
- Entities subject to their own notification policy
- Data that is subject to the safe harbor provision within the state data breach notification law.

The first and most common exception allowed by states is for entities that are subject to other, more stringent data breach notification laws. This includes entities covered by the Health Insurance Portability and Accountability Act

(HIPAA), discussed in Chapter 8, and financial institutions subject to and in compliance with the Gramm-Leach-Bliley Act (GLBA) Safeguards Rule, discussed in Chapter 9.

Second, most states allow exceptions for entities that already follow breach notification procedures as part of their own information security policies as long as these are compatible with the requirements of the state law.[41]

The third exception involves data that falls within the safe harbor provision of a state data breach notification law. All state data breach notification laws include a safe harbor for data that was encrypted, redacted, unreadable, or unusable.[42] The specific requirements related to the safe harbor vary by state and are subject to change. Some states exclude encrypted data from the definition of a data breach. In other states, the notification requirement is avoided if the data is encrypted based on the idea that there has not been a compromise (or, more pointedly, there is no risk of harm).[43] Importantly, these laws help motivate many organizations to use encryption to protect data, and thus avoid the burden of providing notice of breaches, as well as the embarrassment and potential brand damage of a public data breach. It is important to note that this encryption exception typically applies only when the key remains secure: most state breach notification laws, such as the Illinois law, make this requirement explicit by stating that the exception does not apply when the decryption key is breached along with the encrypted data.[44]

7.1.2.8 When Notification May Be Delayed

When a data breach is suspected to be the result of criminal activity, all states allow delays of required notifications for a reasonable period of time if law enforcement determines that the notification will impede a criminal investigation.[45] The covered entity is, however, expected to issue the notification as soon as possible after such an investigation is complete or the law enforcement agency decides that notification will not compromise the criminal investigation.

7.1.3 Enforcement

All 50 states provide for enforcement of state data breach notification laws when covered entities fail to properly provide notice under these laws. Most typically this enforcement involves penalties assessed against the company by the state attorney general. Additionally, in many states, affected parties can file a lawsuit pursuant to the state law's private right of action. In 2020, California became the first state in the nation to permit consumers to recover a set amount of money after a breach.

7.1.3.1 Penalties

In each of the 50 states, covered entities are subject to civil penalties if they violate the state data breach notification law. In approximately one-third of these states, the state attorney general (or other appropriate state agency) can impose fines. Under many of these laws there is a maximum cap per breach, with $750,000 being the highest amount at the time of writing this book.[46] A minority of laws impose a fine per day for failure to comply with certain notification requirements.[47] Notably, a few of these state laws include criminal penalties that can be imposed under egregious circumstances, such as when notice of a breach is provided with the intent to defraud.[48]

7.1.3.2 Right of Action

Nearly 15 states grant a private right of action to individuals harmed by disclosure of their personal information. The recovery in these suits is often capped at the amount of money lost by the party as a result of the breach, called actual damages, along with attorneys' fees and costs of the lawsuit.[49] Suits are also common by businesses directly harmed by a breach, such as banks that undergo costs to replace stolen credit card numbers.[50]

7.1.3.3 Statutory Damages

As of 2020, California became the first U.S. state to allow consumers to recover a certain amount of money set by statute, known as statutory damages, as a result of data breaches.[51] Realizing that actual damages can be difficult to prove in a data breach, California took the approach of providing an avenue for consumers to recover statutory damages—dispensing with the need for a consumer to prove an actual amount of loss suffered as a result of a breach.[52]

Under California's private right of action, consumers may be entitled to statutory damages between $100 and $750 per incident, actual damages, or other remedies the court deems appropriate.[53] To be entitled to these remedies, the breach of the consumer's personal information must result from the business's failure to "implement and maintain reasonable security procedures and practices."[54] A consumer who is seeking statutory damages must give the business the ability to cure the alleged violation, meaning that if the business successfully cures the violation within 30 days then the consumer cannot pursue statutory damages.[55]

The provision for statutory damages was passed as part of the private right of action in the California Consumer Privacy Act (CCPA) and then updated in the California Privacy Rights Act (CPRA) (see Chapter 6). This California framework provides consumers the opportunity to receive statutory damages when a company's poor cybersecurity practices result in a data breach involving the consumers' personal information as defined under California's data breach notification law.[56]

7.2 State Data Security Laws

Since each state has enacted a data breach notification law, many practitioners are aware that such requirements exist and that care must be taken to abide by these laws. Less well known is the fact that many states have enacted data security laws. While some of these laws call for reasonable security and others mandate specific security requirements, all these state laws are intended to ensure that companies develop and maintain appropriate data security practices.

7.2.1 Federal Requirements for Data Security

Although no federal legislation directly imposes information security standards across all industries, the health care and financial sectors have federally imposed information security provisions.[57] In addition, the FTC uses its Section 5 power (under the FTC Act) to bring actions against companies misrepresenting their information security practices (as a deceptive trade practice) or failing to provide "reasonable procedures" to protect personal information (as an unfair trade practice).[58]

7.2.2 Details of State Laws on Data Security Measures

In the absence of comprehensive federal requirements, approximately two-thirds of the states have laws requiring companies to take data security measures to protect citizens' personal information.[59]

Approximately 20 states have enacted laws that impose a reasonableness standard for security but do not provide specific cybersecurity requirements. California is an example of this "reasonable security" approach. One year after enacting the first state security breach notification law in 2003, California put in place Assembly Bill 1950 (AB 1950, added to California Civil Code as section 1798.81.5)—the country's first state security law—to "encourage businesses that own or license personal information about Californians to provide reasonable security."[60] Specifically, the law requires a business "that owns or licenses personal information about a California resident" to "implement and maintain reasonable security procedures and practices appropriate to the nature of the information, to protect the personal

information from unauthorized access, destruction, use, r
disclosure."[61]

About 10 state security laws take the approach of imposi
cybersecurity requirements. For example, the Massachusett
law—generally considered one of the most prescriptive in th
establishes detailed minimum standards to "safeguard . . . per
information contained in both paper and electronic records."[62] ...m a technical perspective, the Massachusetts law mandates user authentication, access controls, encryption, monitoring, firewall protection, updates, and training.[63]

In a more recent development, four states—Connecticut, Iowa, Ohio, and Utah—have "safe harbor" laws in place for cybersecurity instead of enacting security obligations. In these states, a company has the possibility of defeating a lawsuit resulting from a data breach if the company had put in place the appropriate safeguards, detailed in the relevant law, prior to the breach.[64]

Privacy practitioners should be alert that certain states have additional laws imposing security mandates on specific sectors, such as financial services or insurance, with New York having the most prominent of such laws.[65]

7.3 State Data Destruction Laws

While state data breach notification laws and, to a lesser degree, state security laws receive media attention, state data destruction laws have received relatively little attention. These state laws are put in place to make sure that data is handled appropriately at the end of the data life cycle. These laws require companies to implement the data minimization principle that data should only be kept so long as necessary to fulfill its purpose. Securely destroying unnecessary data also reduces the amount of data that a company holds in case of a breach.

7.3.1 Federal Requirements for Data Destruction

Although no federal legislation directly imposes data destruction standards across all industries, privacy practitioners should be alert that data destruction requirements, sometimes called data disposal mandates, may be found as part of federal privacy laws for certain sectors. For example, the FTC enforces the disposal rule for consumer reports and information derived from consumer reports.[66]

Details of State Laws on Data Destruction

In the absence of comprehensive federal requirements, approximately two-thirds of states have enacted data destruction laws.[67] Typically, these states require that the companies destroy or dispose of personal information in such a way that it is no longer readable or decipherable. The term personal information is often defined in these laws similarly to how it is defined in data breach notification laws. Most of these laws have common elements describing to whom the law applies (government and/or private businesses), the required notice, exemptions (e.g., GLBA, HIPAA, FCRA), the covered media (electronic and/or paper), and the penalties.[68]

7.4 Conclusion

State data breach laws, combined with state data security laws and state data destruction laws, have become an important component in protection of personal data in the United States. The lack of comprehensive private-sector data breach notification, data security, and data destruction requirements in the United States leads some observers to suggest the nation is less stringent about protection of personal data than other jurisdictions, such as Europe. In practice to date, the intensive attention to data breaches in the United States has quite often led to more rigorous information security programs than present in other jurisdictions outside the United States.[69]

Endnotes

1 Madeline Lauver, "Data Breach Exposed Records of 2.5 Million Student Loan Borrowers," Security, September 8, 2022, https://www.securitymagazine.com/articles/98306-data-breach-exposes-records-of-25-million-student-loan-borrowers; see Olivia Powell, "The Biggest Data Breaches and Leaks of 2022," Cyber Security Hub, December 9, 2022, https://www.cshub.com/attacks/articles/the-biggest-data-breaches-and-leaks-of-2022.

2 Steve Adler, "OneTouchPoint Ransomware Victim Count Increases to 2.65 Million," *HIPAA Journal*, September 1, 2022, https://www.hipaajournal.com/onetouchpoint-ransomware-victim-count-increases-to-2-65-million/; see Jessica Davis, "Most of the 10 Largest Healthcare Data Breaches in 2022 are Tied to Vendors," SC Media, December 12, 2022, https://www.scmagazine.com/feature/breach/most-of-the-10-largest-healthcare-data-breaches-in-2022-are-tied-to-vendors.

3 Aaron Holmes, "533 Million Facebook Users' Phone Numbers and Personal Data May Have Been Leaked Online," Insider, April 3, 2021, https://www.businessinsider.com/stolen-data-of-533-million-facebook-users-leaked-online-2021-4?r=US&IR=T.

4 Reuters Staff, "SolarWinds Hack was 'Largest and Most Sophisticated Attack' Ever: Microsoft President," Reuters, February 14, 2021, https://www.reuters.com/article/us-

cyber-solarwinds-microsoft/solarwinds-hack-was-largest-and-most-sophisticated-attack-ever-microsoft-president-idUSKBN2AF03R.

5 Data breach requirements under the EU's GDPR are discussed in Chapter 14.

6 Tom Kemp, "Drilling Down on the California Data Breach Notification Law," *Tom Kemp* (blog), May 16, 2020, https://tomkemp.blog/2020/05/16/drilling-down-on-the-california-breach-notification-law/; Jonathan Schenker, Michael Buchanan, and Alejandro Cruz, "A Closer Look at the CCPA's Private Right of Action and Statutory Damages," *Data Security Law Blog*, Patterson Belknap, August 22, 2019, https://www.pbwt.com/data-security-law-blog/a-closer-look-at-the-ccpas-private-right-of-action-and-statutory-damages.

7 The focus of Chapter 6 is state comprehensive privacy laws.

8 See W. Reece Hirsch, "California Consumer Privacy Act Could Spell a Sea Change in U.S. Privacy Law," Morgan Lewis, June 6, 2018, https://www.morganlewis.com/pubs/2018/06/california-consumer-privacy-act-could-spell-a-sea-change-in-us-privacy-law. For a discussion of a proposed approach to updating laws to secure data, view Daniel Solove and Woodrow Hartzog, "Breached! Why Data Security Fails and How to Improve It (Chapter 1)," SSRN, March 1, 2022, https://papers.ssrn.com/sol3/papers.cfm?abstract_id=4043111.

9 See Frederic Bellamy, "Data Breach Class Action Litigation and the Changing Legal Landscape," June 27, 2022, Reuters, https://www.reuters.com/legal/legalindustry/data-breach-class-action-litigation-changing-legal-landscape-2022-06-27/; "The Rise of Privacy Litigation in California," Baker Botts, June 6, 2022, https://www.bakerbotts.com/thought-leadership/publications/2022/june/the-rise-of-privacy-litigation-in-california; "50 State Attorneys General Secure $600 Million from Equifax in Largest Data Breach Settlement in History," Oregon Department of Justice, July 22, 2019, https://www.doj.state.or.us/media-home/news-media-releases/50-state-attorneys-general-secure-600-million-from-equifax-in-largest-data-breach-settlement-in-history/.

10 For a timeline of major data breaches, view "World's Biggest Data Breaches & Hacks," Information is Beautiful, updated September 2022, http://www.informationisbeautiful.net/visualizations/worlds-biggest-data-breaches-hacks/.

11 Chapter 8 [Medical Privacy] discusses relevant data breach notification requirements relevant to the medical field.

12 For a detailed chart of requirements found in state data breach notification laws, view Cheryl Saniuk-Heinig, "State Data Breach Notification Chart," Resource Center, IAPP, March 2021, https://iapp.org/resources/article/state-data-breach-notification-chart/.

13 "Security Breach Notification Laws," National Conference of State Legislatures, January 17, 2022, https://www.ncsl.org/research/telecommunications-and-information-technology/security-breach-notification-laws.aspx.

14 Note that numerous states treat the last four digits of the Social Security number with less protection than the entire nine-digit number. "State Data Breach Notification Laws," Mintz, April 1, 2019, https://www.mintz.com/sites/default/files/media/documents/2019-03-27/APRIL19_-_State_Data_Breach_Matrix.pdf; "State Data Breach Notification Laws," Mintz, April 1, 2019, https://www.mintz.com/sites/default/files/media/documents/2019-03-27/APRIL19_-_State_Data_Breach_Matrix.pdf.

15 Key Issues Filter – "Personal Information" is Broader Than the General Definition, "Breach Notification Law Interactive Map," BakerHostetler, 2022, https://www.bakerlaw.com/BreachNotificationLawMap.

16 "State Data Breach Notification Laws," Foley & Lardner, December 6, 2022, https://www.foley.com/-/media/files/firm/state-data-breach-notification-laws.pdf?la=en. For detailed charts that include additional elements in particular states, view Michael Buckabee, "Data Breach Definition by State," Data Security (blog), Varonis, June 6, 2017, https://www.varonis.com/blog/data-breach-definition-by-state.

17 "State Data Breach Notification Laws," Mintz.

18 "Security Breach Notification Chart," Perkins Coie, September 2021, https://www.perkinscoie.com/images/content/2/4/246420/Security-Breach-Notification-Law-Chart-Sept-2021.pdf.

19 As of the writing of this book, Georgia's definition of covered entities is "persons or commercial entities who engage in whole or in part in the business of collecting, evaluating, transmitting, or otherwise communicating information concerning individuals for the primary purpose of furnishing personal information to nonaffilated third parties." O.C.G.A. § 10-1-911, https://law.justia.com/codes/georgia/2010/title-10/chapter-1/article-34/10-1-911; see "Georgia – Quick Facts," Davis Wright Tremaine LLP, February 15, 2022, https://www.dwt.com/gcp/states/georgia.

20 At the time of the writing of this book, California, Georgia, Illinois, Minnesota, North Dakota, and Texas do not include a risk-of-harm analysis. "State Data Breach Notification Laws," Foley & Lardner; see Key Issues Filter – Risk of Harm Analysis is Permitted, "Breach Notification Law Interactive Map," BakerHostetler, 2022, https://www.bakerlaw.com/BreachNotificationLawMap; see also "Seeking Solutions: Aligning Data Breach Notification Laws Across Borders," U.S. Chamber of Commerce and Hunton Andrews Kurth, 2019, https://www.huntonak.com/images/content/5/6/v2/56941/Data-Breach-Notification-paper.pdf.

21 Kelly Burg, "Risk of Harm Standards in Breach Notification," Risk Management, June 15, 2021, https://www.rmmagazine.com/articles/article/2021/06/15/risk-of-harm-standards-in-breach-notification.

22 Saniuk-Heinig, "State Data Breach Notification Chart."

23 For example, Colorado and Florida provide for a 30-day time frame. New Mexico, Ohio, Oregon, Rhode Island, Tennessee, Vermont, and Wisconsin mandate a 45-day time frame. Louisiana stipulates a 60-day requirement. Saniuk-Heinig, "State Data Breach Notification Chart"; see Key Issues Filter – Specific Time Frame Requirement for Notice, "Breach Notification Law Interactive Map," BakerHostetler, 2022, https://www.bakerlaw.com/BreachNotificationLawMap; see also "Seeking Solutions: Aligning Data Breach Notification Laws Across Borders," U.S. Chamber of Commerce and Hunton Andrews Kurth.

24 "Data Breach Notification in the United States 2022 Report," PrivacyRights.org, January 27, 2023, https://privacyrights.org/resources/data-breach-notification-2022. For a sample letter to send to affected parties, view "Data Breach Response: A Guide for Business," Federal Trade Commission, February 2021, https://www.ftc.gov/business-guidance/resources/data-breach-response-guide-business.

25 Massachusetts' prohibition complicates the idea of treating all breach victims the same if the breach crosses state lines. See Requirements for Data Breach Notifications, Mass.gov, accessed November 2022, https://www.mass.gov/info-details/requirements-for-data-breach-notifications#notification-letter-to-ma-consumers-.

26 "Data Breach Response: A Guide for Business," Federal Trade Commission.

27 Pursuant to California's AB 1710, "the data breach notification must inform the affected persons that the [credit monitoring] services will be provided for at least 12 months and at no cost." Joseph Lazzaroti, "California Takes the Lead Again in Data Breach Laws," JacksonLewis, October 1, 2014, https://www.jacksonlewis.com/resources-publication/california-becomes-first-state-require-credit-monitoring-services-information-following-data-breach.

28 Delaware's law requires "an entity to provide credit monitoring services for at least one year to any individuals whose Social Security numbers were compromised, or reasonably believed to have been compromised, as the result of a data breach. The notification to these individuals must include all information necessary to enroll in these services and place a credit freeze." Caleb Skeath, "Delaware Amends Law to Require Credit Monitoring, Attorney General Notification," Covington, August 28, 2017, https://www.insideprivacy.com/data-security/data-breaches/delaware-amends-data-breach-notification-law-to-require-credit-monitoring-attorney-general-notification/.

29 Massachusetts HB 4806 mandates that companies contract with third parties to provide "free credit monitoring services to impacted Massachusetts residents following breaches involving Social Security numbers" for at least 18 months. Caleb Skeath, "Massachusetts Amends Data Breach Notification Law to Require Free Credit Monitoring," Covington, January 21, 2019, https://www.insideprivacy.com/data-security/data-breaches/massachusetts-amends-data-breach-notification-law-to-require-free-credit-monitoring/.

30 "Data Breach Notification Laws by State: How to Notify, Who to Notify and When," Spirion, October 13, 2021, https://www.spirion.com/blog/data-breach-notification-laws-state/; see "State Data Breach Notification Laws," Foley & Lardner.

31 "The Definitive Guide to U.S. State Data Breach Laws," DigitalGuardian, accessed June 2023, https://info.digitalguardian.com/rs/768-OQW-145/images/the-definitive-guide-to-us-state-data-breach-laws.pdf.

32 "Seeking Solutions: Aligning Data Breach Notification Laws Across Borders," U.S. Chamber of Commerce and Hunton Andrews Kurth.

33 "Data Breach Notification Laws by State," IT Governance, July 2018, https://www.itgovernanceusa.com/data-breach-notification-laws. For additional information on substitute notice, view "Substitute Notice," Resource Center, IAPP, accessed November 2022, https://iapp.org/resources/article/substitute-notice/; "Substitute Notice – Definition," IRMI, accessed November 2022, https://www.irmi.com/term/insurance-definitions/substitute-notice#:~:text=Substitute%20notice%20is%20a%20type,their%20personal%20information%20being%20exposed.

34 "State Data Breach Notification Chart," IAPP.

35 "Security Breach Notification Chart - Vermont," Perkins Coie, accessed November 2022, https://www.perkinscoie.com/en/news-insights/security-breach-notification-chart-vermont.html#:~:text=Attorney%20General%2FAgency%20Notification.,to%20consumers%2C%20whichever%20is%20sooner.

36 "State Data Breach Notification Chart," IAPP; see State Data Breach Notification Laws: Overview of Requirements for Responding to a Data Breach," Keller and Heckman, June 2021, https://www.khlaw.com/sites/default/files/2021-6/State_Data_Breach_Notification_Laws_Chart_June%202021.pdf.

37 For a summary of different states' approaches to harm analysis, view "States That Require a Risk of Harm Analysis in Determining When Notification is Triggered,"

BakerHostetler, July 2018, https://www.bakerlaw.com/files/uploads/documents/data%20breach%20documents/data_breach_charts.pdf.

38 "State Data Breach Notification Chart," IAPP.

39 "Security Breach Notification Chart - Minnesota," Perkins Coie, accessed November 2022, https://www.perkinscoie.com/en/news-insights/security-breach-notification-chart-minnesota.html.

40 "State Data Breach Notification Chart," IAPP.

41 "Security Breach Notification Chart," Perkins Coie, October 2022, https://www.perkinscoie.com/en/news-insights/security-breach-notification-chart.html.

42 "State Data Breach Notification Laws," Foley & Lardner; see "Cyber Breach Reporting Requirements: An Analysis of Laws Across the United States," American Academy of Actuaries, November 2020, https://www.actuary.org/sites/default/files/2020-11/Cyber_Breach_Reporting.pdf. Encryption is the process of encoding information so that only the sender and intended recipients can access it. Encryption systems often use a public key, available to the public, and a private key, which allows only the intended recipient to decode the message. For a more detailed explanation of encryption, view Lee Bell, "Encryption Explained: How Apps and Sites Keep Your Private Data Safe (and Why That's Important)," *Wired*, June 5, 2017, http://www.wired.co.uk/article/encryption-software-app-private-data-safe.

43 Key Issues Filter – "Encryption Safe Harbor" is Broader Than the General Definition, Breach Notification Law Interactive Map, BakerHostetler, 2022, https://www.bakerlaw.com/BreachNotificationLawMap; see "State Data Breach Notification Laws," Foley & Lardner.

44 See Linn Freedman, "Illinois Data Breach Law Amended and Includes New Twists," Data Privacy & Cybersecurity Insider, June 23, 2016, https://www.dataprivacyandsecurityinsider.com/2016/06/illinois-data-breach-law-amended-and-includes-new-twists/.

45 "Cyber Breach Reporting Requirements: An Analysis of Laws Across the United States," American Academy of Actuaries, November 2020, https://www.actuary.org/sites/default/files/2020-11/Cyber_Breach_Reporting.pdf.

46 Michigan's law caps the civil penalty for failure to provide notice at $750,000 per breach. "Security Breach Notification Chart - Michigan," Perkins Coie, accessed November 2022, https://www.perkinscoie.com/en/news-insights/security-breach-notification-chart-michigan.html.

47 For example, Louisiana's law imposes a $5,000 fine for failure to timely notify the state's Attorney General. Louisiana, by Jurisdiction, OneTrust DataGuidance, accessed June 2023, https://www.dataguidance.com/jurisdiction/louisiana; see "Data Breach Notification Laws by State," IT Governance, July 2018, https://www.itgovernanceusa.com/data-breach-notification-laws.

48 "Cyber Breach Reporting Requirements," American Academy of Actuaries.

49 Actual damages are directly related to the losses incurred by the consumer. "Actual Damages," Cornell Law School, updated June 2022, https://www.law.cornell.edu/wex/actual_damages#:~:text=In%20tort%20law%2C%20actual%20damages,may%20instead%20grant%20nominal%20damages.

50 "State Data Breach Notification Chart," IAPP; see "Cyber Breach Reporting Requirements," American Academy of Actuaries.

51 Statutory damages are established in the statute and are not directly related to losses actually incurred by the consumer. "Statutory Damages," Cornell Law School, updated August 2021, https://www.law.cornell.edu/wex/statutory_damages#:~:text=Statutory%20damages%20are%20a%20type,loss%20caused%20to%20the%20plaintiff.

52 Jonathan Schenker, Michael Buchanan, and Alejandro Cruz, "A Closer Look at the CCPA's Private Right of Action and Statutory Damages," Data Security Law Blog, Patterson Belknap, August 22, 2019, https://www.pbwt.com/data-security-law-blog/a-closer-look-at-the-ccpas-private-right-of-action-and-statutory-damages; see Robert Bateman, "The CCPA/CPRA's Private Right of Action," TermsFeed, updated March 8, 2023, https://www.termsfeed.com/blog/ccpa-private-right-action/.

53 Cal. Civ. Code § 1798.150(a)(1), accessed June 2023, https://leginfo.legislature.ca.gov/faces/codes_displayText.xhtml?division=3.&part=4.&lawCode=CIV&title=1.81.5; *see* James Harvey & Gavin Reinke, "Data Privacy & Security Advisory: The CCPA Could Reset Data Breach Litigation Risks," Alston & Bird, August 19, 2019, https://www.alston.com/en/insights/publications/2019/08/ccpa-could-reset-data-breach.

54 Cal. Civ. Code § 1798.150(a)(1); see Scott Hyman, Genevieve Walser-Jolly, & Elizabeth Farrell, "What is a 'Reasonable Security Procedure and Practice' Under the California Consumer Privacy Act's Safe Harbor," *Quarterly Report* 73, no. 3, (2019), https://www.severson.com/wp-content/uploads/2020/01/CCFLQ-CCPA-Reasonable-Procedures-Article.pdf.

55 Cathy Cosgrove, "CCPA Litigation: Shaping the Contours of the Private Right of Action," IAPP, June 8, 2020, https://iapp.org/news/a/ccpa-litigation-shaping-the-contours-of-the-private-right-of-action/; see Mark Melodia, Ashley Shively, and Mark Francis, "Litigating the CCPA in Court," Holland & Knight, July 22, 2020, https://www.hklaw.com/en/insights/publications/2020/07/litigating-the-ccpa-in-court. Note that the "implementation and maintenance of reasonable security procedures" by a company after a breach does not qualify as a cure. Amelia Gerlicher et al., "2023 Breach Notification Law Update: Changes to Notification and Security Requirements Continue at State and Federal Levels," JDSupra, October 10, 2023, https://www.jdsupra.com/legalnews/2023-breach-notification-law-update-1361087/.

56 As the California's data breach notification law was the first such law in the nation, the definition for "personal information" found in the law is typical of the definitions subsequently enacted by other states (discussed in Section 7.1.2.1.1). California's law defines personal information to be "an individual's first name or first initial and the individual's last name in combination with any one or more of the following data elements, when either the name or the data elements are not encrypted or redacted: Social Security number, driver's license number ..., account number..., medical information, health insurance information, unique biometric data ..., [and] genetic data." Cal. Civil Code § 1798.81.5, accessed November 2022, https://leginfo.legislature.ca.gov/faces/codes_displaySection.xhtml?lawCode=CIV§ionNum=1798.81.5; see Gerlicher et al., "2023 Breach Notification Law Update"; Amy de La Lama, "The Expanded Private Right of Action Under the CPRA," Bryan Cave Leighton Paisner, December 3, 2020, https://www.bclplaw.com/en-US/insights/the-expanded-private-right-of-action-under-the-cpra.html; see Bateman, "The CCPA/CPRA's Private Right of Action"; see also "Does the CCPA Have a Private Right of Action?" TrueVault, accessed October 2023, https://www.truevault.com/learn/ccpa/does-the-ccpa-have-a-private-right-of-action. For a chart of covered data in California, view "CPRA Expanded Private Right of Action," *Data*

Privacy Automation (blog), Securiti, December 16, 2022, https://securiti.ai/blog/cpra-privacy-right-of-action/.

57 These topics are discussed in Chapter 8 [Health Insurance Portability and Accountability Act (HIPAA)] and Chapter 9 [Gramm-Leach-Bliley Act (GLBA)], respectively.

58 The FTC is discussed in Chapter 5 [Federal and State Regulators].

59 Jeremy Feigelson, et al., "The State of State Cybersecurity Laws," *Data Blog*, Debevoise & Plimpton, September 30, 2021, https://www.debevoisedatablog.com/2021/09/30/the-state-of-state-law-cybersecurity-requirements/; see Data Security Laws—Private Sector, National Conference of State Legislatures, updated May 29, 2019, http://www.ncsl.org/research/telecommunications-and-information-technology/data-security-laws.aspx. Note that many states also have passed laws requiring state governments to have security measures in place. See Data Security Laws—State Government, National Conference of State Legislatures, February 14, 2020, http://www.ncsl.org/research/telecommunications-and-information-technology/data-security-laws-state-government.aspx.

60 Cal. Civil Code § 1798.81.5, accessed November 2022, https://leginfo.legislature.ca.gov/faces/codes_displaySection.xhtml?lawCode=CIV§ionNum=1798.81.5; see Assembly Bill 1950, accessed November 2022, http://www.leginfo.ca.gov/pub/03-04/bill/asm/ab_1901-1950/ab_1950_bill_20040929_chaptered.html; see also Scott Hyman, Genevieve Walser-Jolly, and Elizabeth Farrell, "What is a 'Reasonable Security Procedure and Practice' Under the California Consumer Privacy Act's Safe Harbor," Quarterly Report, Volume 73, Number 3, 2019, https://www.severson.com/wp-content/uploads/2020/01/CCFLQ-CCPA-Reasonable-Procedures-Article.pdf.

61 Cal. Civil Code § 1798.81.5.

62 201 CMR 17.00, accessed June 2023, https://www.mass.gov/regulations/201-CMR-1700-standards-for-the-protection-of-personal-information-of-residents-of-the-commonwealth.

63 Feigelson, et al., "The State of State Cybersecurity Laws."

64 Michael Borgia and Daniel Felder, "New Iowa Legislation Creates Cybersecurity Safe Harbor," Davis Wright Tremaine, July 18, 2023, https://www.dwt.com/blogs/privacy--security-law-blog/2023/07/iowa-cybersecurity-breaches-safe-harbor; Feigelson, et al., "The State of State Cybersecurity Laws"; Kayne McGladrey, "Three U.S. Laws are Providing Safe Harbor Against Data Breaches," CyberSecurity Hub, September 8, 2021, https://www.cshub.com/security-strategy/articles/three-us-state-laws-are-providing-safe-harbor-against-breaches.

65 Gerlicher et al., "2023 Breach Notification Law Update"; Dom DiFurio, "4 States Pass Half of All New Cybersecurity Laws Enacted Across the U.S. in 2022," Drata, March 29, 2023, https://drata.com/blog/4-states-passed-nearly-half-of-new-cybersecurity-laws; see "New York State Department of Financial Services Revises Cybersecurity Regulation to Include New Requirements," Gibson Dunn, November 15, 2022, https://www.gibsondunn.com/new-york-state-department-of-financial-services-revises-cybersecurity-regulation-to-include-new-requirements/; Todd Salloum, "Two States Enact Insurance Data Security Laws," *Privacy & Information Security Law Blog*, Hunton Andrews Kurth, May 4, 2022, https://www.huntonprivacyblog.com/2022/05/04/two-states-enact-insurance-data-security-laws/; Sten-Erik Hoidal, "Emerging Trend: States Adopting Cybersecurity Regulations for Financial Services Industry," Fredrikson, July

17, 2017, https://www.fredlaw.com/alert-emerging-trend-states-adopting-cybersecurity-regulations-for-financial-services-industry.

66 The topic is discussed in detail in Chapter 9 (Financial Privacy). See "Disposing of Consumer Report Information? Rule Tells How," Federal Trade Commission, accessed November 2022, https://www.ftc.gov/tips-advice/business-center/guidance/disposing-consumer-report-information-rule-tells-how.

67 Note that these requirements are sometimes incorporated in data breach laws. See Data Disposal Laws, National Conference of State Legislatures, August 27, 2021, https://www.ncsl.org/research/telecommunications-and-information-technology/data-disposal-laws; "U.S. State-Specific Data Disposal Laws," Blancco, 2018, https://www.blancco.com/wp-content/uploads/2021/07/u-s-state-specific-data-disposal-laws.pdf.

68 William Denny, "Legal Responsibility for Safe Disposal of Personal Information," Potter Anderson Corroon, February 21, 2020, https://www.potteranderson.com/newsroom-publications-Legal-Responsibility-for-Safe-Disposal-of-Personal-Data.html.

69 Michael Hill, "The Biggest Data Breach Fines, Penalties, and Settlements So Far," CSO, September 18, 2023, https://www.csoonline.com/article/567531/the-biggest-data-breach-fines-penalties-and-settlements-so-far.html; Ryan Browne, "Fines for Breaches of EU Privacy Law Spike Sevenfold to $1.2 Billion, as Big Tech Bears Brunt," CNBC, January 17, 2022, https://www.cnbc.com/2022/01/18/fines-for-breaches-of-eu-gdpr-privacy-law-spike-sevenfold.html; Jon Porter, "Equifax Agrees to Pay Settlement of Up to $700 Million Over 2017 Data Breach," The Verge, July 22, 2019, https://www.theverge.com/2019/7/22/20703497/equifax-ftc-fine-settlement-2017-data-breach-compensation-fund; *see* Wim Nauwelaerts and Kimberly Peretti, "5 Key Differences in EU and U.S. Breach Notification Regimes," Mondaq, May 11, 2021, https://www.mondaq.com/unitedstates/data-protection/1067056/5-key-differences-in-eu-and-us-breach-notification-regimes; Eric Langland, "Survey of Data Security Requirements in Multistate Breach Settlements," *Privacy Tracker,* IAPP, October 26, 2017, https://iapp.org/news/a/survey-of-data-security-requirements-in-multi-state-breach-settlements/.

CHAPTER 8

Medical Privacy

Special privacy protections for health care date back thousands of years. The modern Hippocratic Oath states, "I will respect the privacy of my patients, for their problems are not disclosed to me that the world may know."[1] There are several reasons why relatively strict privacy laws exist for health care.

First, at the most basic level, medical information is related to the inner workings of one's body or mind. One's individual sense of self may be violated if others have unfettered access to this information. Second, most doctors believe that patients will be more open about their medical conditions if they have assurance that embarrassing medical facts will not be revealed. Third, medical privacy protections can protect employees from the risk of unequal treatment by employers. For instance, a person who uses birth control, has had an abortion, contracted a sexually transmitted disease, been treated for a substance abuse issue, or has undergone psychiatric treatment could potentially be fired if an employer gained access to this information. Health insurers and employers may also have incentives to avoid employing or insuring workers who suffer from expensive medical conditions or who may be at higher risk for such conditions based on their genetic background.

Despite the existence of strict laws protecting medical information within the health care industry, modern insurance and medical practices often use patient medical information quite extensively. For example, information about medical procedures is frequently used to ensure accurate payment for those services. Doctors in one location may wish to access records about a patient's medical treatment in other cities in order to treat the patient appropriately. Researchers also use medical information—sometimes deidentified—in trying to find new patterns as they seek to develop cures for illnesses and promote public health. Records of many patients' outcomes may be used to evaluate health care providers on the overall quality of care provided.

Changing technology plays an important role in how health care is delivered as well as how medical information is collected from individuals. Telemedicine allows a doctor and patient to be in different physical locations when they carry on a medical visit. During the COVID-19 pandemic, telemedicine became the only viable option for many people to interact with their doctor for non-COVID-19-related medical needs. These experiences increased widespread acceptance of telemedicine. After the COVID-19 pandemic, the use of telemedicine is expected to continue growing, both with benefits to patients and the accompanying privacy and security concerns.

This chapter begins with a discussion of the basic privacy and security provisions of the Health Insurance Portability and Accountability Act of 1996 (HIPAA), as updated by the Health Information Technology for Economic and Clinical Health (HITECH) Act of 2009. State health care privacy laws are not discussed here in detail, but it is important to know that HIPAA does not preempt stricter state privacy laws. The California Confidentiality of Medical Information Act (CMIA), for example, expands health information privacy protection duties to providers of software, hardware and online services.[2] Next, the chapter explains the federal protections for records relating to treatment for alcohol and drug abuse that have been in place since the 1970s, currently found in the 2017 version of the Confidentiality of Substance Use Disorder Patient Records Rule. The chapter then discusses the Genetic Information Nondiscrimination (GINA) Act of 2008. The chapter ends with a summary of the privacy protections included in the 21st Century Cures Act.

One potential source of confusion is that an individual's health-related information in the United States is protected differently depending on the setting. For example, HIPAA applies to "covered entities," notably including health care providers and insurers as well as "business associates" that receive data from covered entities. By contrast, health information in the hands of other entities is generally not protected by HIPAA.

Suppose, for instance, that an individual buys a book about a rare form of cancer. That book purchase, along with other book purchases, is covered by the bookstore's privacy policy (if one exists). A California bookstore would also be covered by California's Reader Privacy Act, but would not be covered by HIPAA.[3] Similarly, the records of a website that provides detailed information about this form of cancer may show that the same user has come back repeatedly with questions about the disease. This website is likely outside the scope of HIPAA, yet potentially covered by California's Confidentiality of Medical Information Act.[4]

As another example, consider the legal regulation of wearables, which are electronic devices that individuals can place on their bodies and may collect medical information in real time. When the wearable is provided under the supervision of a medical provider, the health data generally is covered by HIPAA. If the same data comes from a person's smartwatch, however, the data generally goes to a manufacturer or other company outside the scope of

HIPAA. Such a company is generally subject to privacy enforcement by the Federal Trade Commission (FTC) for unfair or deceptive trade practices, as discussed in Chapter 5. Because U.S. privacy law and self-regulatory efforts vary by sector, the privacy professional should examine carefully whether personal information, including health-related information, is covered by HIPAA or some other sector-specific law.[5]

8.1 The Health Insurance Portability and Accountability Act of 1996

Prior to 1996, the United States did not have a comprehensive medical privacy law. HIPAA became law in 1996. By the early 2000s, the HIPAA privacy and security rules had been put in effect. They have been updated periodically since then, most notably by the HITECH Act of 2009.

The initial reason for HIPAA was not to protect privacy and security. Instead, Congress was seeking to meet other goals, including improving the efficiency of health care delivery.[6] To improve efficiency, HIPAA required entities receiving federal health care payments such as Medicare and Medicaid to shift reimbursement requests to electronic formats. At the same time, Congress realized that the shift from paper to electronic reimbursements posed a threat to privacy and security. Accordingly, HIPAA required the U.S. Department of Health and Human Services (HHS) to promulgate regulations to protect the privacy and security of health care information.

Protected health information (PHI) is defined as any individually identifiable health information that is transmitted or maintained in any form or medium; is held by a covered entity or its business associate; identifies the individual or offers a reasonable basis for identification; is created or received by a covered entity or an employer; and relates to a past, present, or future physical or mental condition, provision of health care, or payment for health care to that individual.[7]

Electronic protected health information (ePHI) is any PHI that is transmitted or maintained in electronic media (such as computer hard drives, magnetic tapes, disks, or digital memory cards, all of which are considered electronic storage media). Paper records, paper-to-paper fax transmissions, and voice communications (e.g., telephone) are not considered transmissions via electronic media.[8]

This statutory link to electronic reimbursements helps clarify which health care information is covered under HIPAA. Entities that are directly covered under HIPAA include:[9]

- Health care providers (e.g., doctors' offices, hospitals) that conduct certain transactions in electronic form
- Health plans (e.g., health insurers)
- Health care clearinghouses (e.g., third-party organizations that host, handle, or process medical information)[10]

It is important to understand that HIPAA applies to these covered entities but not to other health care providers and services. For instance, some doctors accept only cash or credit cards and do not bill for insurance.[11] They are not covered by HIPAA. More broadly, individuals reveal medical information in a wide variety of settings, ranging from conversations with friends and colleagues to purchasing books about health care, surfing on health care websites, and even posting medical information online. These sorts of health care information are outside the scope of HIPAA.[12]

Before the HITECH update, business associates were not subject to HIPAA but became subject to privacy and security protections under the written contracts they signed with covered entities. Under HITECH, however, HIPAA privacy and security rules are codified and apply directly to business associates.[13]

Beyond covered entities, HIPAA creates important obligations for business associates, including, for example, cloud storage providers that handle PHI knowingly or unknowingly.[14] Under the Privacy Rule (see Section 8.1.1), a business associate is any person or organization, other than a member of a covered entity's workforce, that performs services and activities for or on behalf of a covered entity, if such services or activities involve the use or disclosure of PHI.[15] Business associates may provide services and activities such as claims processing, data analysis, utilization review and billing as well as legal, actuarial, accounting, consulting, data aggregation, management, administrative, accreditation, and/or financial services.[16]

Before the release of the HHS's final rule, under HITECH, when a covered entity engaged another entity to provide the activities and services described above, the Privacy Rule required that the covered entity enter into a business associate agreement (a contract) with that other entity.[17] This contract would include provisions that passed the privacy and security standard down to the contracting entity. Also, the business associate agreement had to be in writing, although it could be signed electronically as long as such signatures are valid as "written signatures" under the applicable state's contract laws. Modifications to the Security Rule (see Section 8.1.2) in HITECH, however, now require business associates and covered entities to implement reasonable, appropriate safeguards to protect PHI (in addition to signing a business associate agreement).[18] As such, covered entities and business associates should implement security practices that, overall, comply with the Security Rule.[19]

8.1.1 The HIPAA Privacy Rule

In August 2000, the HHS promulgated the regulations on standard electronic formats for health care transactions, known as the Transactions Rule. This was followed in December 2000 by rules concerning the privacy of protected health information, known as the Privacy Rule.[20] The initial HIPAA Privacy Rule was revised somewhat in 2002.[21] In February 2003, the HHS promulgated a final Security Rule. In January 2013, the Privacy and Security rules were modified to implement statutory amendments under HITECH, which is discussed fully following here. The definition of covered entity is the same for all three rules.

8.1.1.1 The Privacy Rule and the Fair Information Privacy Practices

Compared with other U.S. privacy laws, HIPAA provides perhaps the most detailed implementation of the Fair Information Privacy Practices (FIPPs), including requirements concerning privacy notices, authorizations for use and disclosure of PHI, limits on use and disclosure to the minimum necessary, individual access and accounting rights, security safeguards, and accountability through administrative requirements and enforcement. There are also important exceptions to the HIPAA rules. The following are some of the key privacy protections:

- **Privacy notices.** The Privacy Rule generally requires a covered entity to provide a detailed privacy notice at the date of first service delivery. There are some defined exceptions to the notice requirements. For example, a privacy notice does not have to be provided when the health care provider has an "indirect treatment relationship" with the patient or in the case of medical emergencies. The rule is quite specific about elements that must be included in the notice, including detailed statements about individuals' rights with respect to their PHI.
- **Authorizations for uses and disclosures.** Consistent with the statutory goal of improving efficiency in the health care system, HIPAA itself authorizes the use and disclosure of PHI for essential health care purposes: treatment, payment and operations (collectively, TPO), as well as for certain other established compliance purposes. Other uses or disclosures of PHI require the individual's opt-in

authorization. An authorization is an independent document that specifically identifies the information to be used or disclosed, the purposes of the use or disclosure, the person or entity to which a disclosure may be made, and other information. A covered entity may not require an individual to sign an authorization as a condition of receiving treatment or participating in a health plan. Additional, strict rules apply for authorizations to use or disclose psychotherapy notes.[22]

Specific rules define when the opt-in is required for marketing purposes. For instance, face-to-face communications by a covered entity to an individual are not considered marketing.

- **"Minimum necessary" use or disclosure.** Other than for treatment, covered entities must make reasonable efforts to limit the use and disclosure of PHI to the minimum necessary in order to accomplish the intended purpose. As discussed more fully later, covered entities may disclose PHI to a business associate (such as a billing company, third-party administrator, attorney, or consultant) only if the covered entity ensures that the business associate is bound by all the obligations applicable to the covered entity, including the minimum necessary standards.
- **Access and accountings of disclosures.** Under the Privacy Rule, individuals have the right to access and copy their own PHI from a covered entity or a business associate. The right applies to PHI kept in a "designated record set," which is a fairly broad definition including a patient's medical records and billing records or other records used by the covered entity to make decisions about individuals. Only fairly narrow exceptions exist to this right of access. Additionally, individuals have a right to receive an accounting of certain disclosures of their PHI that have been made. A reasonable charge may be assessed to cover the costs of providing access.

  Individuals also have the right to amend PHI possessed by a covered entity. If the covered entity denies the request to amend the PHI, the individual may file a statement that must then be included in any future use or disclosure of the information.
- **Safeguards.** The Privacy Rule requires that covered entities implement administrative, physical, and technical safeguards to protect the confidentiality and integrity of all PHI. The HIPAA Security Rule requires both covered entities and business associates

to implement administrative, physical, and technical safeguards only for ePHI. Like the Privacy Rule, the HIPAA Security Rule aims to prevent unauthorized use or disclosure of PHI. However, the Security Rule also aims to maintain the integrity and availability of ePHI. Accordingly, the Security Rule addresses data backup and disaster recovery, among other related issues.

- **Accountability.** To foster compliance, covered entities are subject to a set of administrative requirements. Covered entities must designate a privacy official who is responsible for the development and implementation of privacy protections. Personnel must be trained, and complaint procedures, along with other procedures, must be in place.

  Accountability is furthered by a range of enforcement agencies. The primary enforcer for the Privacy Rule in the HHS is the Office for Civil Rights (OCR).

8.1.1.2 Limits on and Exceptions to the Privacy Rule

In issuing the Privacy Rule, the HHS stressed the dual goals of protecting PHI while also improving the efficiency of the health care system. As mentioned above, the rule does not require authorizations for the major categories of treatment, payment and health care operations. Other limits on the scope of the rule include deidentified information and medical research.

- **Deidentification.** The Privacy Rule does not apply to information that has been "deidentified"—information that does not actually identify an individual and where there is no reasonable basis to believe that the information can be used to identify an individual.[23] The Privacy Rule provides two methods for deidentifying data: (1) remove all of at least 18 data elements listed in the rule, such as name, phone number, and address or (2) have an expert certify that the risk of reidentifying the individuals is very small.[24]

- **Research.** The Privacy Rule has detailed provisions for how PHI is used for medical research purposes. Research can occur with the consent of the individual, or without consent if an authorized entity such as an institutional review board approves the research as consistent with the Privacy Rule and general rules covering research on human subjects. Research is permitted on deidentified information, and rules are more flexible if only a limited data set is released to researchers.[25]

- **Other exceptions.** The Privacy Rule contains other exceptions under which PHI may be used without consent.[26] These include information used for public health activities; to report victims of abuse, neglect or domestic violence; in judicial and administrative proceedings; for certain law enforcement activities; and for certain specialized governmental functions.[27] A covered entity is required to release PHI to the individual to whom it pertains or to the person's representative, and to the secretary of the HHS to investigate compliance with the privacy rules.
- **Clarification for disclosures of information related to reproductive health care.** After the U.S. Supreme Court overturned Roe v. Wade in 2022, the HHS issued guidance on the disclosure of protected health information related to reproductive health care.[28] According to the HHS, "The Privacy Rule permissions for disclosing PHI without an individual's authorization for purposes not related to health care, such as disclosures to law enforcement officials, are narrowly tailored to protect the individual's privacy and support their access to health services. … The Privacy Rule permits but **does not require** covered entities to disclose PHI about an individual for law enforcement purposes 'pursuant to process and as otherwise required by law,' under certain conditions."[29]

8.1.2 The HIPAA Security Rule

The HIPAA Security Rule was finalized in February 2003 and modified in January 2013.[30] It establishes minimum security requirements for PHI that a covered entity or a business associate receives, creates, maintains, or transmits in electronic form.[31] The Security Rule is designed to require covered entities and business associates to implement "reasonable" security measures in a technology-neutral manner. The goal is for all covered entities and business associates to implement "policies and procedures to prevent, detect, contain, and correct security violations."[32]

The Security Rule is comprised of "standards" and "implementation specifications," which encompass administrative, technical, and physical safeguards. Some of the implementation specifications are required, while others are considered "addressable." This means that the covered entity (or the business associate) must assess whether it is an appropriate safeguard for the entity to adopt. If not, the covered entity (or the business associate) must document why it is not reasonable and, if appropriate, adopt an alternative measure.

The HIPAA Security Rule requires covered entities and business associates to:

- Ensure the confidentiality, integrity, and availability of all ePHI the covered entity or the business associate creates, receives, maintains, or transmits
- Protect against any reasonably anticipated threats or hazards to the security or integrity of the ePHI
- Protect against any reasonably anticipated uses or disclosures of such information that are not permitted or required under the Privacy Rule
- Ensure compliance with the Security Rule by its workforce[33]

As previously noted, the Security Rule strives for a reasonable level of security. Accordingly, the rule permits a covered entity or a business associate to "use any security measures that allow the covered entity or the business associate to reasonably and appropriately implement the standards and implementation specifications."[34] When developing a security program, each covered entity and business associate must consider the following factors:

- The size, complexity and capabilities of the covered entity or business associate
- The covered entity's or the business associate's technical infrastructure, hardware, and software security capabilities
- The costs of security measures
- The probability and criticality of potential risks to electronic protected health information[35]

The HIPAA Security Rule also requires that:

- Each covered entity and each business associate must identify an individual who is responsible for the implementation and oversight of the Security Rule compliance program.[36] This may be the same person who oversees the Privacy Rule compliance program.
- Each covered entity and each business associate must conduct initial and ongoing risk assessments. In particular, the covered entity must "conduct an accurate and thorough assessment of the potential risks and vulnerabilities to the confidentiality, integrity, and availability of electronic protected health information held by the covered entity."[37]

This assessment should identify potential risks and vulnerabilities, each of which must be addressed.

- Each covered entity and each business associate must implement a security awareness and training program for its workforce. Additionally, individual workers must be disciplined if they fail to comply with the policies and procedures.[38]

8.1.3 Telemedicine

During the COVID-19 pandemic, telemedicine became the only viable option for many people to interact with their doctors for care not related to COVID-19.[39] An estimated one in three adults used telemedicine during the pandemic.[40]

An important HIPAA rule change related to privacy and security was one of the drivers for increased use of telemedicine. During the public health emergency, the OCR allowed health care providers to use "nonpublic facing" (meaning one-to-one or one-to-few) videoconferencing technology, even if the technology did not meet all the requirements of the HIPAA Privacy Rule, the HIPAA Security Rule, or the breach notification requirements under HIPAA.[41] Roughly speaking, the rule permitted videoconferencing with secure log-in, but not technologies where unauthorized people could readily join the videoconference.

Nonprivacy legal changes also sped up the adoption of telemedicine during the pandemic. These included:

- **Payment for telemedicine visits.** The Centers for Medicare & Medicaid Services allowed reimbursement for telemedicine visits. Prior to the pandemic, reimbursement was permitted only in very limited circumstances, such as for the patients in rural areas or those seeking medical attention for mental health or substance use issues.[42]
- **Prescribing controlled substances across state lines.** The U.S. Drug Enforcement Agency (DEA) suspended the provisions of the Ryan Haight Online Pharmacy Consumer Protection Act that required an in-person medical exam before prescribing a controlled substance. During the pandemic, qualified prescribers were allowed to prescribe controlled substances to patients regardless of location.[43]
- **Physician licensing across state lines.** Numerous states allowed licensed physicians to obtain temporary licenses in another state to increase access to care via telemedicine.[44] Also, the use of the

Interstate Medical Licensure Compact (IMLC) grew by nearly 50 percent during the pandemic, suggesting that these physicians envision telemedicine continuing after the pandemic.

Post-pandemic, many commentators believe that telemedicine will emerge as an integral part of the U.S. health care system due to (1) increased willingness by patients to use telemedicine, (2) increased willingness by health care providers to use telemedicine, and (3) regulatory changes related to access and payment related to telehealth.[45] Certain specialties, such as mental health treatment,[46] are more likely to experience an increase in telemedicine visits post-pandemic than other specialties, such as those related to surgery.[47] At the time of this writing, it is uncertain which of the privacy and other regulatory changes will stay in effect post-pandemic.[48]

8.1.4 Enforcement

The primary enforcer for both the Privacy Rule and the Security Rule is the OCR, which processes individual complaints and can assess civil monetary penalties of up to approximately $2 million per year per type of violation, as of the writing of this book.[49] The OCR has assessed substantial penalties under HIPAA in recent years.[50] For example, the OCR entered into a settlement agreement in 2018 with Anthem for a record $16 million civil penalty after a cyberattack exposed the ePHI of almost 79 million people.[51] In 2019, the Texas Health and Human Services Commission, a state agency, paid a $1.6 million civil penalty after a software flaw exposed the ePHI of more than 6,000 individuals.[52] In 2020, Premera Blue Cross agreed to pay a civil penalty of $6.85 million dollars after a cyberattack exposed the ePHI of more than 10 million people.[53] The OCR has instituted a program to regularly audit a select number of covered entities and business associates to ensure compliance.[54]

Since 2019, OCR has emphasized enforcement of a patient's right to access records in a timely manner.[55] Many enforcement actions involve a single individual who has been unable to obtain a copy of their protected health information in a timely manner.[56] For example, in 2021, Banner Health agreed to pay a $200,000 civil penalty to settle allegations from two individuals that each waited months to receive copies of requested medical records.[57]

In 2021, Congress enacted the HIPAA Safe Harbor Law, which requires the OCR to consider whether a covered entity has implemented recognized security practices for the prior 12 months. Qualifying security practices go beyond the minimum requirements in the HIPAA Security Rule. Where such practices have been in place, the law provides the OCR discretion to apply leniency in setting fines and corrective action, notably in the event of a data breach.[58]

HIPAA does not include a private right of action for individuals to bring a claim under HIPAA.[59] Individuals who believe that a covered entity or business associate has violated HIPAA's Privacy Rule or Security Rule can file a complaint with the OCR.[60] HIPAA prohibits the covered entity or business associate from discriminating or retaliating against an individual who files a complaint with the OCR.[61]

The U.S. Department of Justice (DOJ) has criminal enforcement authority, with prison sentences of up to 10 years.[62] For the many companies within its jurisdiction, the FTC can bring enforcement actions for unfair and deceptive practices, even for entities covered by HIPAA. State attorneys general can also bring enforcement for unfair and deceptive practices, or pursuant to any applicable state medical privacy law.

8.1.5 Preemption

For the privacy professional, it is important to remember that HIPAA does not preempt state laws that provide more protection than the federal law. In practice, reviewing applicable state laws will be important for ensuring compliance. Topics that should be of particular concern in this review include additional patient rights, added uses or disclosures for PHI, and shortened deadlines for action.[63]

8.1.6 State Laws

The details of state laws that provide more protections than HIPAA are beyond the scope of this book.[64] When reviewing state privacy laws, it is important to understand that certain state laws provide exemptions related to coverage under HIPAA—meaning that complying with HIPAA will be viewed as complying with the state law. When reviewing these exemptions related to HIPAA, privacy practitioners should be alert that certain state laws exempt entities covered by HIPAA while others only exempt data covered by HIPAA.[65]

8.2 The Health Information Technology for Economic and Clinical Health Act

The HITECH Act was enacted as part of the American Recovery and Reinvestment Act of 2009 to promote the adoption and meaningful use of health information technology. HITECH codified and funded the Office of the National Coordinator for Health Information Technology and provided $19 billion in incentives for health care providers to adopt electronic health records and develop a national electronic health information exchange. HITECH also strengthened HIPAA to address the privacy impacts of the expanded use of electronic health records.[66]

8.2.1 Notice of Breach

In the event of unauthorized acquisition, access, use, or disclosure of information, a breach is presumed to have occurred, unless the covered entity or the business associate demonstrates through a risk assessment that there is a low probability that the security or privacy of the information has been compromised.[67] This language provides that covered entities and business associates have the burden of proof that an impermissible use or disclosure did not constitute a breach.[68] If there is a high probability that the security or privacy of the information (financial, reputational, or other) has been compromised, a covered entity must notify individuals within 60 days of discovery.[69] If a business associate discovers a breach, it must notify the covered entity.[70] If the breach affects more than 500 people, the covered entity must notify the HHS immediately, and if the breach affects 500 or more in the same jurisdiction, it must notify the media.[71] All breaches requiring notice must be reported to the HHS at least annually. A breach applies only to "unsecured" information, and a covered entity can avoid liability if it utilizes encryption software to secure information.[72]

In 2021, the HHS announced a settlement agreement with Excellus Health Plan where the health insurer agreed to pay $5.1 million after suffering a 2015 data breach where hackers gained access to the records of more than nine million individuals.[73]

A separate part of HITECH applies to "personal health record" providers.[74] Cloud services for storing an individual's health records are covered by this provision.[75] In 2019, the FTC issued a policy statement clarifying that this rule covers medical apps and wearable devices.[76] The data breach notices required are similar to those for covered entities. These requirements apply even if the provider does *not* seek electronic reimbursement from the U.S. government. The rule is enforced by the FTC.[77]

8.2.2 Increased Penalties

The HHS has issued a final rule pursuant to HITECH that allows for penalties of up to $2 million for the most willful violations and extends criminal liability to individuals who misuse PHI.[78] The enforcement rules provide for penalties even if the covered entity did not know of the violation.[79]

8.2.3 Limited Data

All disclosures by a covered entity should attempt to comply with the definition of a limited data set, and if this is not feasible, data disclosed must be the minimum amount necessary. A "limited data set" refers to protected health information that includes direct identifiers of the individual.[80] Furthermore, patients who directly pay their provider for medical care may restrict their PHI from being disclosed to a health plan unless the disclosure is otherwise required by law.[81]

8.2.4 Electronic Health Records

The $19 billion in funding in HITECH created important incentives for health providers to use electronic health records (EHRs) more extensively. Providers who make "meaningful use" of EHRs can qualify for these funds.[82] In local markets, more practice groups have linked their EHRs with local hospitals. For broader geographic regions, there has been increased sharing of medical information toward the HHS goal of having a National Health Information Network.[83] Sharing of PHI is generally permitted under HIPAA to the extent necessary for treatment, payment, or health care operations. Compliance issues become more important if information shared through EHRs is used for other purposes or with other entities, and such sharing can lawfully be done only with patient consent or under some other provision of HIPAA. Compliance also can become considerably more complex when the laws of different states apply to the same EHR system.

HITECH itself, along with providing funding for greater use of EHRs, made certain changes to HIPAA's legal treatment of EHRs. Covered entities must provide individuals with a copy of their EHR on request and must account for all nonverbal disclosures made within three years on the request.[84] Additionally, covered entities may not sell EHRs without the consent of the patient, and covered entities cannot receive payment for certain marketing plans.[85]

8.3 Confidentiality of Substance Use Disorder Patient Records Rule

Several decades before passage of HIPAA, Congress began its foray into the arena of medical privacy.[86] This federal action was prompted by concern that individuals might not seek medical care for alcohol and substance abuse problems unless the privacy of this information was strictly protected. In

1970, Congress passed the Comprehensive Alcohol Abuse and Alcoholism Prevention, Treatment, and Rehabilitation Act. Two years later, Congress enacted the Drug Abuse Prevention, Treatment and Rehabilitation Act.[87] These confidentiality requirements are implemented in the Confidentiality of Substance Use Disorder Patient Records Rule.[88]

Scope. The scope of the rule covers the disclosure and use of "patient-identifying" information by treatment programs for alcohol and substance abuse.[89] Patient-identifying information is any and all information that could reasonably be used to identify, directly or indirectly, a person who has been diagnosed with a substance abuse issue or has undergone alcohol or substance abuse treatment.[90] In addition, the rule restricts use of any information, whether written or verbal, that could lead to or substantiate criminal charges against a patient concerning their alcohol or drug usage.[91]

Applicability. The law applies to any program that receives federal funding. For purposes of the rule, the term "program" as defined by the rule means any one of the following:

- An individual or entity (other than a general medical facility) who holds itself out as providing, and provides, substance abuse diagnosis, treatment, or referral for treatment
- An identified unit within a general medical facility that holds itself out as providing, and provides, substance abuse diagnosis, treatment, or referral for treatment
- Medical personnel or other staff in a general medical facility whose primary function is provision of the substance abuse diagnosis, treatment, or referral for treatment[92]

Other entities may become subject to the regulation if either a state licensing agency requires them to comply or the clinician uses controlled substances for detoxification, therefore requiring licensing through the DEA.[93]

Disclosure. The program must obtain written patient consent before disclosing information subject to the rule. The consent form may include a general designation that allows disclosure to either individuals or entities so long as those entities have a treating provider relationship with the patient. Upon request, the patient who signs a consent form with a general designation may receive a list of entities to which their information has been disclosed. In addition, the consent form must explicitly describe the type of information that is to be disclosed related to alcohol or drug abuse treatment.[94]

Redisclosure. Redisclosing information obtained from a program is prohibited when that information would "identify, directly or indirectly, an individual as having been diagnosed, treated, or referred for treatment."[95]

Exceptions to consent requirements. Exceptions to the rule that allow disclosures without consent include:

- Medical emergencies[96]
- Scientific research[97]
- Audits and evaluations[98]
- Communications with a qualified service organization (QSO) related to information needed by the organization to provide services to the program[99]
- Crimes on program premises or against program personnel[100]
- Child abuse reporting[101]
- Court order[102]

Security of records. An entity lawfully holding patient-identifying information must have formal policies and procedures in place to protect the security of this information. There are separate requirements for paper and electronic records.[103]

Violations of the Confidentiality of Patient Records for Alcohol and Other Drug Treatment Rule are criminal. The first violation results in a fine of no more than $500. Each subsequent offense is fined not more than $5,000. These violations are reported to the U.S. Attorney's Office.[104]

Entities subject to this rule are likely to also be subject to the HIPAA Privacy Rule.[105] In many areas, these two requirements will have parallel requirements.[106] Privacy practitioners should review both the rule and HIPAA to fully understand when the two do not converge.[107] Also, the rule is similar to HIPAA—it does not preempt state laws that include stricter protections for disclosures than those at the federal level.[108]

8.4 Genetic Information Nondiscrimination Act of 2008

The Genetic Information Nondiscrimination Act (GINA) created new national limits on the use of genetic information in health insurance and employment.[109] In considering GINA, Congress found that genetic testing, before symptoms appeared, would allow individuals to take steps to reduce the likelihood of ultimately developing a disease or disorder. At the same time, such testing could create the risk of misusing that information for health insurance or employment.[110] Concerns about misuse were supported by historical examples of genetic discrimination, such as sterilization programs aimed at those with disorders that were perceived to be genetic, programs aimed at mandating sickle cell testing for African-Americans, and pre-employment genetic screening of federal employees.[111] Generally, GINA prohibits health insurance companies from discriminating on the basis of genetic predispositions in the absence of manifest symptoms or from requesting that applicants receive genetic testing and prohibits employers from using genetic information in making employment decisions.[112]

GINA amended a variety of existing pieces of legislation including, among others, the Employee Retirement Income Security Act (ERISA), the Social Security Act, and the Civil Rights Act. The amendments to ERISA prohibit group health plan providers from adjusting premiums or other contribution schemes on the basis of genetic information, absent a manifestation of a disease or disorder.[113] GINA also amended ERISA to prohibit group health plan providers from requesting or requiring genetic testing in connection with the offering of group health plans, although an exception is carved out for requests for voluntary testing in connection with research.[114] For the research exception to apply, providers must notify the HHS secretary and make clear that compliance is voluntary, that noncompliance will have no effect on enrollment or contributions, and that no genetic information will be used for underwriting purposes.[115]

The amendments to ERISA also allow for governmental enforcement.[116] A statutory penalty is set at $100 for each day of noncompliance (inclusive of the beginning date and date of rectification) with respect to each plan participant or beneficiary, although minimum penalties can rise to $15,000 in certain circumstances.[117] Some liability, however, may be avoided under this section if the grounds for liability could not have been discovered by exercising reasonable diligence.[118]

Similar provisions revise the Public Health Service Act and apply to participants in the individual health insurance market to prohibit adjustments to premiums or other contribution schemes on the basis of genetic information, absent the manifestation of disease or disorder.[119] These revisions prohibit insurers from using a genetic predisposition to find an excludable preexisting condition.[120] Once again, the revisions allow for governmental enforcement against violators. Amendments to the Social Security Act extend similar provisions to the providers of Medicare supplemental insurance policies.[121] GINA also directs the secretary of the HHS to revise HIPAA regulations such that genetic information is considered health information, and the disclosure of such information may not be disclosed by covered entities, pursuant to HIPAA.[122]

Aside from health care insurance, GINA also takes aim at the possibility of employment discrimination based on genetic information in the absence of the manifestation of a disease or disorder.[123] Additionally, the employment-related sections of GINA prohibit discrimination against individuals because they have a family member who has manifested a disease.[124] These sections of GINA revised the Civil Rights Act and apply coextensively with that act.[125] Along with expressly prohibiting discrimination on the basis of genetic information, these portions of GINA prohibit employers from requiring, requesting or purchasing such genetic information about employees or family members unless an express exception applies.[126] Exceptions are provided for instances where:

- Such a request is inadvertent
- The request is part of an employer-offered wellness program that the employee voluntarily participates in with written authorization
- The request is made to comply with the Family and Medical Leave Act (FMLA) of 1993
- An employer purchases commercially and publicly available materials that include the information
- The information is used for legally required genetic monitoring for toxin exposure in the workplace if the employee voluntarily participates with written authorization
- The employer conducts DNA analysis for law enforcement purposes and requests the information for quality-control purposes (i.e., to identify contamination)[127]

These parts of GINA not only apply to employers but also prohibit unions and training programs from excluding or expelling individuals on the basis of such information.[128]

GINA does recognize that employers or unions may have legitimate reasons for possessing such information, such as part of a toxin exposure monitoring program or company-sponsored wellness program.[129] Accordingly, if an employer possesses such information, it must be kept on separate forms in separate medical files, and such files must be treated as confidential employee medical records.[130]

GINA itself does not provide for a private right of action, but—depending on the violation—private rights of action may be available under the federal laws that it revises as well as under similar state laws.[131]

To ensure regulation keeps up with technology, GINA mandates the creation of a commission to review the developments in the science of genetics and make recommendations as to whether to establish a "disparate impact cause of action" under GINA.[132]

8.4.1 Preemption

GINA provides "a floor of minimum protection against genetic discrimination." GINA does not preempt state laws with stricter protections.[133]

8.4.2 State Laws

Although GINA prevents discrimination by employers and health insurers based on genetic information, the federal law does not prevent life insurers, mortgage lenders, schools, or many other entities from treating individuals less favorably based on their genetic information. In 2011, California enacted the California Genetic Information Nondiscrimination Act (CalGINA), which prohibited genetic discrimination in emergency medical services, mortgage lending, housing, education, and other state-funded programs.[134] Several other states have enacted laws to protect individuals from genetic discrimination when seeking life insurance, disability insurance, and long-term care insurance.[135]

8.5 The 21st Century Cures Act of 2016

The 21st Century Cures Act ("Cures Act") has multiple purposes, including to promote medical research and reform mental health treatment.[136] The Cures Act promotes the use and interoperability of electronic health information (EHI), notably by limiting information blocking.[137] It also contains several privacy-specific provisions.

8.5.1 Interaction of information blocking and privacy protection

The Cures Act seeks to balance the use and interoperability of EHI with reasons not to share such data. It emphasizes the usefulness of sharing EHI for purposes including operating health networks, promoting patient access to their EHI, and enabling patients to transfer their EHI more easily to apps or other uses of the patients' choosing. A Cures Act Final Rule has been issued by the Office of the National Coordinator for Health Information Technology (ONC).

The final rule sets forth detailed limits on information blocking, defined as any activity that "is likely to interfere with, prevent, or materially discourage access, exchange, or use of electronic health information."[138] The prohibition on information blocking applies to any (1) health care provider, (2) health IT developers of certified health IT, (3) health information exchanges, or (4) health information networks.[139] ONC can bring enforcement actions for violation of the information-blocking provision of the Cures Act, with a fine up to $1 million.[140]

This general prohibition on information blocking has two categories of exception. First, the final rule recognizes important reasons that can justify the failure to share EHI. These reasons notably include the need to promote the privacy and security of EHI. The final rule defines criteria for when privacy and security can justify information blocking, and organizations subject to the final rule should comply with these criteria in order to both protect privacy and security while also sharing EHI as required by the final rule. Similarly, a decision not to share can be justified where responding to a request would be infeasible and in order to maintain and improve healthy IT performance. Second, the final rule allows an organization to establish procedures for fulfilling requests to access, exchange, or use EHI.[141]

8.5.2 Certification of Health IT Developers

The Cures Act requires the HHS to establish "Conditions and Maintenance of Certifications Requirements for the ONC Health IT Certification Program." There are numerous conditions of certification for health IT developers. Most relevant for purposes of this book are to comply with requirements concerning information blocking and application programming interfaces (APIs). Organizations providing health IT software should consult the detailed applicable requirements.[142]

8.5.3 Promoting Access and Portability for Patient Data

The Cures Act sought to improve patient access to their EHI and make it easier for patients to implement portability for their EHI. To improve this interoperability, covered health IT developers must "publish APIs that allow health information from such technology to be accessed, exchanged, and used without special effort through the use of APIs."[143] As one common example, the API would enable export of the patient's data from a health care provider to a smartphone app.[144] The goal is to provide greater patient control over the data, including by moving data from traditional health care providers to a wider range of destinations, as the patient chooses.

Going forward, there may be ongoing issues about how to achieve this greater data portability while also protecting individual privacy. Traditional health care providers are usually covered entities under HIPAA. They are thus subject to the relatively strict HIPAA privacy and security safeguards, and to enforcement actions by the HHS. By contrast, most apps on a smartphone are outside of HIPAA coverage. Such apps generally are subject to enforcement by the FTC for "unfair and deceptive" trade practices, but a smartphone app's privacy notice often contains fewer privacy protections than HIPAA. Ongoing policy debates are likely about the trade-offs between the benefits of greater patient control over EHI and the risks that can result from weaker privacy and security protections. One way to address the trade-off may be by clear notice to consumers when EHI moves from HIPAA protections to recipients who are not subject to HIPAA.

8.5.4. Other Privacy Provisions in the Cures Act

The Cures Act also contains other privacy-related provisions, including:

- **Certain individual biomedical research information exempted from disclosure under the Freedom of Information Act (FOIA).** To the extent that individual biomedical research information could reveal individual identity, the Cures Act exempts this information from mandatory disclosure under FOIA.[145]
- **Researchers permitted to remotely view PHI.** The Cures Act provides a clarification to existing law that allows medical researchers to remotely review PHI. This remote access must meet minimum safeguards consistent with HIPAA's Privacy and Security rules.[146]
- **Certificates of confidentiality for research.** The Cures Act provides stronger privacy protections for those participating in research, particularly those with alcohol and substance abuse history. The Cures Act requires certificates of confidentiality to be issued by the National Institutes of Health (NIH) for any federally funded research and permits the NIH to issue such certificates at its discretion for research that is not federally funded. These certificates ensure that the research material cannot be used in any legal or administrative proceeding without the consent of the individual involved.[147]

- **Compassionate sharing of mental health or substance abuse information with family or caregivers.** The Cures Act requires the HHS to issue guidance to HIPAA regarding the circumstances under which a health care provider or a covered entity is permitted to discuss with family members or caregivers the treatment of an adult with a mental health disorder or an alcohol or substance abuse disorder.[148]

8.6 Medical Technology

The global revenue for the medical technology (medtech) industry was estimated at $570 billion for 2023.[149] A significant part of medtech includes medical devices such as x-rays, MRIs, and CT scans that are administered only by health care providers. Medtech, however, can also enable individuals to collect health information in real time in the convenience of their own home, test for a variety of medical ailments at home, or access their own electronic health records.[150]

There are different kinds of medtech. Wearables, which are electronic devices placed on a person's body to collect health information, can monitor heart rates or glucose levels in real time. Medical at-home tests provide people with the opportunity to check for genetic markers related to diseases as well as to map their personal DNA. Medical apps assist people in a variety of tasks, such as taking medication at the correct times, calculating the optimal day to become pregnant, and providing access to electronic health records.[151]

When discussing health information in relation to medtech, it is crucial to remember that individuals can be confused when health information is protected in certain situations and not in others.[152] For example, numerous apps exist that allow individuals to store their health records to their phone or other electronic device. These individuals may have a difficult time understanding which apps will provide HIPAA protections to their health data and which will not, as the apps may appear quite similar and may even be downloaded from the same app store.[153]

HIPAA applies to covered entities, including health care providers, as well as business associates that receive data from covered entities. When a covered entity is involved in the use of a wearable, app, or website, the companies providing these products or services are generally either the covered entity or a business associate.[154] In these instances, the individual's data is protected by HIPAA's Privacy Rule and Security Rule, as discussed in Section 8.1.

By contrast, health information in the hands of noncovered entities is generally not protected by HIPAA.[155] In these instances, it is important to understand the types of protection that exist outside of HIPAA for this health information.

8.6.1 Section 5 of the Federal Trade Commission Act of 1914

Section 5 of the FTC Act applies to medtech companies that are covered by HIPAA as well as those that are not. This means the FTC Act is the primary federal statute that applies to the privacy and security practices of companies not covered by HIPAA. Under Section 5 of the FTC Act, medtech companies can face enforcement actions for deceptive trade practices and unfair trade practices, as discussed in Chapter 5.[156] In 2022, the FTC announced that it would focus enforcement on "illegal conduct that exploits Americans' location, health, or other sensitive data," including the practices of medtech companies.[157]

In 2021, Flo Health, a fertility tracking app with approximately 100 million users worldwide, became one of the first medtech companies to agree to a sanction pursuant to Section 5 of the FTC Act. The FTC complaint alleged that the company promised users not to share their health information but disclosed the health information of users to third parties for marketing and analytics purposes.[158]

8.6.2 Federal Food, Drug, and Cosmetic Act

The U.S. Food and Drug Administration (FDA) protects consumers against unlawful medical devices by enforcing the Federal Food, Drug, and Cosmetic Act (FDCA). The act defines a device as an "instrument ... intended for use in the diagnosis of disease or other conditions, or in the ... treatment or prevention of disease."[159] The regulation of medical devices by the FDA can be quite complex, with a system involving levels of risk that in part determine the amount of regulation.[160]

Much of medtech utilized directly by individuals is considered low risk, meaning very little regulation is applicable.[161] In certain instances, this type of medtech can be somewhat more heavily regulated by the FDA. For example, certain medtech that utilizes artificial intelligence (AI) can be considered software as a medical device (SaMD).[162]

Cybersecurity is one area of concern for the FDA.[163] As of the writing of this book, the FDA has issued new guidance to update its cybersecurity guidance that covers "wireless, internet- and network- connected devices, portable media (e.g., USB or CD), and the frequent electronic exchange of medical device-related health information." In the guidance, the FDA focuses on cybersecurity of medtech devices to better protect the overall cybersecurity of health information.[164] In 2023, the FDA also announced that it will "refuse to accept" medical device submissions due to cybersecurity reasons. Device manufacturers must include detailed cybersecurity plans that provide "reasonable assurances" that the devices are cybersecure.[165]

8.6.3 State Laws

Privacy practitioners should be alert to the complex regulatory landscape of state medical privacy laws. Some states have fairly comprehensive medical privacy laws, sometimes with provisions that regulate aspects of medtech.[166] At-home genetic testing is one example where several states have enacted specific privacy laws. By 2020, an estimated 20 percent of people in the United States had taken an at-home genetic test that consumers can buy directly, without the need to involve a doctor.[167] Although these genetic tests would likely be covered by HIPAA if ordered by a doctor, the companies that provide these at-home tests are not generally covered by this federal law. Thus, this sensitive health information —such as a person's likelihood to develop certain diseases—remains largely unregulated at the federal level. Several states, including California, Arizona, and Utah, have enacted laws that require these consumer genetic testing companies—such as 23andMe and Ancestry.com—to provide transparent data collection practices and obtain express consent from individuals to use their data.[168]

8.7 Conclusion

U.S. law about medical and genetic privacy reflects the view that such personal information is particularly sensitive. This chapter has described the comprehensive HIPAA privacy and security rules as updated by the HITECH Act, the Confidentiality of Substance Use Disorder Patient Records Rule, GINA's rules prohibiting discrimination based on genetic personal information, as well as the privacy protections found in the 21st Century Cures Act. That said, there are also compelling reasons to use these categories of personal information. HIPAA notably enables use and disclosure of protected health information for treatment, payment, and health care operations as well as medical research. Similarly, there is great interest in the promise of medical and genetic research. The 21st Century Cures Act aims to balance these often-conflicting goals. Privacy professionals who work with health data need to be aware that not only are strong protections required, but also that such data use is often permitted by the regulations. With the increased use of telemedicine and the explosion of medtech, the skyrocketing amount of data being created will likely intensify the discussion regarding both strong protections and the uses permitted by regulations.

Endnotes

1 Peter Tyson, "The Hippocratic Oath Today," WGBH Educational Foundation, March 27, 2001, https://www.pbs.org/wgbh/nova/body/hippocratic-oath-today.html.

2 For additional information on preemption, view "Does the HIPAA Privacy Rule Preempt State Laws?" Department of Health and human Services, December 28, 2022, https://www.hhs.gov/hipaa/for-professionals/faq/399/does-hipaa-preempt-state-laws/index.html. For more information on health information privacy laws in California in the context of the Health Insurance Portability and Accountability Act and Genetic Information Nondiscrimination Act, *see* Lothar Determann, *California Privacy Law, Fifth Edition* (Portsmouth, NH: IAPP, 2023).

3 See Cal. Civ. Code §§ 1798.90–1798.90.05, accessed June 2023, https://leginfo.legislature.ca.gov/faces/codes_displaySection.xhtml?lawCode=CIV§ionNum=1798.90.5.

4 The website could be covered under HIPAA if it is the website of a covered entity and it collects protected health information as defined under HIPAA. See Cal. Civ. Code §§ 56-59. For a discussion of HIPAA, California's Confidentiality of Medical Information Act and the newly enacted California Consumer Privacy Act, view Sateyender Goel, "California Consumer Privacy Act and the Future of the Health Data Economy," *MedCityNews*, November 7, 2019, https://medcitynews.com/2019/11/california-consumer-privacy-act-and-the-future-of-the-health-data-economy/.

5 For additional information on medical information that is not protected by HIPAA, view Robert Gellman, "Personal Health Records: Why Many PHRs Threaten Privacy," World Privacy Forum, February 20, 2008, https://www.worldprivacyforum.org/wp-content/uploads/2012/04/WPF_PHR_02_20_2008fs.pdf.

6 The protections found in HIPAA are broader than those covered by the earlier laws concerning alcohol and substance abuse treatments records. Section 8.3 discusses the Confidentiality of Substance Use Disorder Patient Records Rule.

7 45 C.F.R. § 160.103, accessed November 2019, https://www.law.cornell.edu/cfr/text/45/160.103.

8 45 C.F.R. § 160.103.

9 "Are You a Covered Entity?" Centers for Medicare & Medicaid Services, updated May 26, 2022, https://www.cms.gov/Regulations-and-Guidance/Administrative-Simplification/HIPAA-ACA/AreYouaCoveredEntity.html.

10 A healthcare clearinghouse means a public or private entity, including a billing service, repricing company, community health management information system or community health information system, and value-added networks and switches that does either of the following functions: (1) processes or facilitates the processing of health information received from another entity in a nonstandard format or containing nonstandard data content into standard data elements or a standard transaction or (2) receives a standard transaction from another entity and processes or facilitates the processing of health information into nonstandard format or nonstandard data content for the receiving entity. 45 C.F.R. § 160.103.

11 "New Rule Protects Patient Privacy, Secures Health Information," Health and Human Services, January 17, 2013, http://www.girardslaw.com/library/HHS_Press_Release_about_New_HIPAA_Rules_2013.pdf.

12 "Medical Privacy: When Is Medical Information Not Covered by HIPAA?" Electronic Frontier Foundation, accessed November 2017, https://www.eff.org/issues/medical-privacy.

13 42 U.S.C. § 17921(2), accessed November 2019, https://www.law.cornell.edu/uscode/text/42/; 45 C.F.R. § 160.103.

14 See Lothar Determann and Oliver Zee, "Cloud Provider Obligations as Business Associates under HIPAA," *Rx Analysis,* The Pharmaceutical and Healthcare Newsletter of Baker & McKenzie's Intellectual Property Practice Group, accessed February 2020, http://f.datasrvr.com/fr1/113/19953/HIPAA_newsletter_CSB28391_October4.pdf.

15 Please note that, in order to be a "business associate" under HIPAA, the person or organization must process protected health information. Entities that do not process protected health information (or whose access to protected health information is truly incidental) are not business associates. Covered entities can themselves be business associates of other covered entities.

16 See HIPAA Privacy Rule and Secondary Uses of Health Information, U.S. Department of Health and Human Services, Office of Civil Rights, July 17-19, 2007, https://www.ncvhs.hhs.gov/wp-content/uploads/2014/08/070717p4.pdf.

17 The HIPAA Privacy Rule only applies to covered entities, not their business associates. The Privacy Rule permits covered entities to disclose protected health information to their business associates if the covered entities obtain satisfactory assurances that the business associate will use the information only for the purposes for which it was engaged by the covered entity, will safeguard the information, and will help the covered entity to comply with some of its duties under the Privacy Rule. "Business Associates," U.S. Department of Health and Human Services, May 24, 2019, https://www.hhs.gov/hipaa/for-professionals/privacy/guidance/business-associates/.

18 The sample business associate contract provided by HHS on its website includes 10 requirements. "Business Associate Contracts," Health Information Privacy, January 25, 2013, www.hhs.gov/hipaa/for-professionals/covered-entities/sample-business-associate-agreement-provisions/index.html. For insight from the U.S. Department of Health and Human Services, view "Summary of the HIPAA Security Rule," October 19, 2022, https://www.hhs.gov/hipaa/for-professionals/security/laws-regulations/.

19 45 C.F.R. § 160.102(b), accessed June 2023, https://www.law.cornell.edu/cfr/text/45/160.102.

20 This HIPAA statute, Transaction Rule, Privacy Rule (with all the amendments), Security Rule, Enforcement Rule, and Breach Notification Rule can be found at https://www.hhs.gov/hipaa/for-professionals/privacy/laws-regulations/combined-regulation-text/index.html, "Combined Regulation Text All Rules, U.S. Health and Human Services, October 19, 2022.

21 For additional information, view "Summary of the HIPAA Privacy Rule," Health and Human Services, October 19, 2022, https://www.hhs.gov/hipaa/for-professionals/privacy/laws-regulations/index.html.

22 For additional information on mental health and substance abuse records, view www.ncbi.nlm.nih.gov/books/NBK19829/ (accessed November 2017). For a discussion of psychotherapy notes, view "Does HIPAA Provide Extra Protections for Mental Health Information Compared with Other Health Information?" U.S. Department of Health and Human Services, September 12, 2017, https://www.hhs.gov/hipaa/for-professionals/

faq/2088/does-hipaa-provide-extra-protections-mental-health-information-compared-other-health.html.

23 45 C.F.R. § 164.502(d), accessed November 2017, https://www.law.cornell.edu/cfr/text/45/164.502.

24 45 C.F.R. § 164.514, accessed November 2017, https://www.law.cornell.edu/cfr/text/45/164.514. For guidance on methods of deidentification, view "Guidance Regarding Methods for De-identification of Protected Health Information in Accordance with the Health Insurance Portability and Accountability Act (HIPAA) Privacy Rule," U.S. Department of Health and Human Services, October 25, 2022, https://www.hhs.gov/hipaa/for-professionals/privacy/special-topics/de-identification/index.html.

25 45 C.F.R. § 164.512(i), accessed November 2017, https://www.law.cornell.edu/cfr/text/45/164.512.

26 45 C.F.R. § 164.512.

27 After the Supreme Court of the United States overturned Roe v. Wade in the 2022 case of Dobbs v. Jackson Women's Health Organization, HHS issued guidance concerning HIPAA's Privacy Rule and disclosures related to reproductive health. The guidance stated that disclosures of PHI without the individual's consent are "narrowly tailored to protect the individual's privacy and support their access to health services." "HIPAA Privacy Rule and Disclosures of Information Related to Reproductive Health Care," U.S. Department of Health and Human Services, June 29, 2022, https://www.hhs.gov/hipaa/for-professionals/privacy/guidance/phi-reproductive-health/index.html#footnote14_348e87m; see Daniel Sulton, "HHS Issues Guidance on Post-Dobbs Protections Under HIPAA Privacy Rule," *The National Law Review*, July 13, 2022, https://www.natlawreview.com/article/hhs-issues-guidance-post-dobbs-protections-under-hipaa-privacy-rule.

28 Roe v. Wade, a 1973 decision of the Supreme Court of the United States, held that the U.S. Constitution recognized a woman's right to terminate her pregnancy by abortion. Roe v. Wade, Supreme Court of the United States, January 22, 1973, https://www.oyez.org/cases/1971/70-18. Roe v. Wade was overturned by the 2022 decision of the Supreme Court of the United States in Dobbs v. Jackson Women's Health Organization, Supreme Court of the United States, June 24, 2022, https://www.oyez.org/cases/2021/19-1392; see Sulton, "HHS Issues Guidance on Post-Dobbs Protections Under HIPAA Privacy Rule."

29 HHS provides the following example: "a covered entity may respond to a law enforcement request made through such legal processes as a court order or court-ordered warrant, or a subpoena or summons, by disclosing only the requested PHI, provided that all of the conditions specified in the Privacy Rule for permissible law enforcement disclosures are met." "HIPAA Privacy Rule and Disclosure of Information Related to Reproductive Health Care," U.S. Department of Health and Human Services.

30 For additional information, view "Summary of the HIPAA Security Rule," U.S. Department of Health and Human Services. In addition, the National Institute of Standards and Technology provides a HIPAA Security Rule kit that can be accessed at https://scap.nist.gov/hipaa/, updated April 20, 2023.

31 HHS considered extending the Security Rule to nonelectronic PHI, so that the provisions mirror the scope of protection offered by the Privacy Rule. See http://nationalacademies.org/hmd/~/media/files/activity%20files/research/hipaaandresearch/hipaabackground.pdf, accessed November 2017. (Note that the financial services counterpart, the Gramm-

Leach-Bliley Act, does not limit applicability of its Safeguards Rule to electronic data. For health insurers subject to HIPAA and the Gramm-Leach-Bliley Act, the security program must encompass paper as well as electronic records.)

32 45 C.F.R. § 164.308, accessed March 2023, https://www.law.cornell.edu/cfr/text/45/164.308; see "Guidance on Risk Analsis," U.S. Department of Health and Human Services, July 22, 2109, https://www.hhs.gov/hipaa/for-professionals/security/guidance/guidance-risk-analysis/index.html.

33 45 C.F.R. § 164.306(a)(1-4), accessed November 2017, https://www.law.cornell.edu/cfr/text/45/164.306.

34 45 C.F.R. § 164.306(b)(1), accessed November 2017, https://www.law.cornell.edu/cfr/text/45/164.306.

35 45 C.F.R. § 164.306(b)(2), accessed November 2017, https://www.law.cornell.edu/cfr/text/45/164.306.

36 45 C.F.R. § 164.308(a)(2), accessed November 2017, https://www.law.cornell.edu/cfr/text/45/164.308.

37 45 C.F.R. § 164.308(a)(1)(ii)(A), accessed November 2017, https://www.law.cornell.edu/cfr/text/45/164.308.

38 45 C.F.R. § 164.308(a)(5)(i), accessed November 2017, https://www.law.cornell.edu/cfr/text/45/164.308.

39 Gary Drenik, "The Future of Telehealth in a Post-Pandemic World," Forbes, June 2, 2022, https://www.forbes.com/sites/garydrenik/2022/06/02/the-future-of-telehealth-in-a-post-pandemic-world/?sh=21bb8ff426e1.

40 See Laura Barrie Smith, Fredric Blavin, "One in Three Adults Used Telehealth during the First Six Months of the Pandemic, but Unmet Needs for Care Persisted," Urban Institute, January 12, 2021, https://www.urban.org/research/publication/one-three-adults-used-telehealth-during-first-six-months-pandemic-unmet-needs-care-persisted.

41 "HIPAA for Telehealth Technology," Telehealth, U.S. Department of Health and Human Services, May 11, 2023, https://telehealth.hhs.gov/providers/telehealth-policy/hipaa-for-telehealth-technology; see Craig Klugman, "Medical Decision Making: Probability and the Art of Shared Decision Making." Family Practice Management, May/June 2021, 9-14, https://www.aafp.org/pubs/fpm/issues/2021/0500/p9.html#fpm20210500p9-b2.

42 "HIPAA for Telehealth Technology," Telehealth, U.S. Department of Health and Human Services; "What Happens to Telemedicine After COVID-19?" Association of American Medical Colleges, October 21, 2021, https://www.aamc.org/news-insights/what-happens-telemedicine-after-covid-19.

43 Libby Baney, Jillian Brady, and Sarah Lloyd-Stevenson, "The Future of Telehealth and the Ryan Haight Act Post-Pandemic," National Association of Boards of Pharmacy, April 22, 2021, https://nabp.pharmacy/news/blog/the-future-of-telehealth-and-the-ryan-haight-act-post-pandemic/; Klugman, "Medical Decision Making."

44 Andis Robeznieks, "Cross-State Licensing Process Now Live in 30 States," American Medical Association, April 26, 2021, https://www.ama-assn.org/practice-management/digital/cross-state-licensing-process-now-live-30-states; see "A Faster Pathway to Physician Licensure," Interstate Medical Licensure Compact, accessed March 2023, https://www.imlcc.org/a-faster-pathway-to-physician-licensure/; Steve North, "These Four Telehealth Changes should Stay, Even After The Pandemic," Family Practice Management, 2021, https://www.aafp.org/pubs/fpm/issues/2021/0500/p9.html#fpm20210500p9-b2.

45 See Oleg Bestsennyy, Greg Gilbert, Alex Harris, and Jennifer Rost, "Telehealth: A Quarter-Trillion-Dollar Post-COVID-19 Reality?" McKinsey & Company, July 9, 2021, "https://www.mckinsey.com/industries/healthcare-systems-and-services/our-insights/telehealth-a-quarter-trillion-dollar-post-covid-19-reality; Brian Bossetta, "Regulatory Attorney Offers Take on Telehealth Privacy Guidance," Medtech Insight, July 12, 2022, https://medtech.pharmaintelligence.informa.com/MT145605/Regulatory-Attorney-Offers-Take-On-Telehealth-Privacy-Guidance?utm_source=hootsuite&utm_medium=&utm_term=&utm_content=&utm_campaign=.

46 Psychotherapy notes receive heightened protections under HIPAA's Privacy Rule. "Does HIPAA Provide Extra Protections for Mental Health Information Compared with Other Health Information?" U.S. Department of Health and Human Services, September 12, 2017, https://www.hhs.gov/hipaa/for-professionals/faq/2088/does-hipaa-provide-extra-protections-mental-health-information-compared-other-health.html.

47 Bestsennyy, Gilbert, Harris, and Rost, "Telehealth: A Quarter-Trillion-Dollar Post-COVID-19 Reality?"

48 "The Future of Telemedicine After COVID-19," OECD, January 20, 2023, https://www.oecd.org/coronavirus/policy-responses/the-future-of-telemedicine-after-covid-19-d46e9a02/; Gary Drenik, "The Future of Telehealth in a Post-Pandemic World," Forbes, June 2, 2022, https://www.forbes.com/sites/garydrenik/2022/06/02/the-future-of-telehealth-in-a-post-pandemic-world/?sh=3dba52c426e1; Jordan Scott, "How Telemedicine Requirements and Policies Will Change Post-Pandemic," HealthTech, July 30, 2021, https://healthtechmagazine.net/article/2021/07/how-telemedicine-requirements-and-policies-will-change-post-pandemic-perfcon; Len Strazewski, "Telehealth's Post-Pandemic Future: Where Do We Go From Here?" AMA, September 7, 2020, https://www.ama-assn.org/practice-management/digital/telehealth-s-post-pandemic-future-where-do-we-go-here; see "HHS Issues Guidance on HIPAA and Audio-Only Telehealth," U.S. Department of Health and Human Services, June 13, 2022, https://www.hhs.gov/about/news/2022/06/13/hhs-issues-guidance-hipaa-audio-telehealth.html.

49 "HIPAA Enforcement," U.S. Department of Health and Human Services, July 15, 2017, https://www.hhs.gov/hipaa/for-professionals/compliance-enforcement/index.html; "Annual Civil Monetary Penalties Inflation Adjustment," Federal Register, October 6, 2023, https://www.federalregister.gov/documents/2023/10/06/2023-22264/annual-civil-monetary-penalties-inflation-adjustment; see "What is the HIPAA Enforcement Rule?" RSI Security, March 23, 2021, https://blog.rsisecurity.com/what-is-the-hipaa-enforcement-rule/.

50 See Sarah Beth Kuyers, Dianne Bourque, and Ellen Janos, "A New Decade of HIPAA—What Can We Expect?" *The National Law Review*, December 23, 2019, https://www.natlawreview.com/article/new-decade-hipaa-what-can-we-expect.

51 "Anthem Pays OCR $16 Million in Record HIPAA Settlement Following Largest U.S. Health Data Breach in History," HHS.org, October 15, 2018, https://www.hhs.gov/about/news/2018/10/15/anthem-pays-ocr-16-million-record-hipaa-settlement-following-largest-health-data-breach-history.html.

52 "OCR Imposes a $1.6 Million Civil Money Penalty Against Texas Health and Human Services Commission for HIPAA Violations," HHS.gov, November 7, 2019, https://www.hhs.gov/about/news/2019/11/07/ocr-imposes-a-1.6-million-dollar-civil-money-penalty-against-tx-hhsc-for-hipaa-violations.html.

53 Steve Alder, "2021-2021 HIPAA Violation Cases and Penalties," *HIPAA Journal*, January 4, 2022, https://www.hipaajournal.com/2020-hipaa-violation-cases-and-penalties/.

54 "HIPAA Privacy, Security, and Breach Notification Audit Program," U.S. Department of Health and Human Services, December 17, 2020, https://www.hhs.gov/hipaa/for-professionals/compliance-enforcement/audit/index.html.

55 "OCR Settles Nineteenth Investigation in HIPAA Right to Access Initiative," U.S. Department of Health and Human Services, January 20, 2023, https://www.hhs.gov/hipaa/for-professionals/compliance-enforcement/agreements/delc/index.html; see Valerie Montague, "Two Years In: Lessons Learned from OCR's Right of Access Initiative Enforcement," Nixon Peabody, October 4, 2021, https://www.nixonpeabody.com/en/ideas/blog/trending/2021/10/04/two-years-in-lessons-learned-from-ocr-right-of-access-initiative-enforcement#:~:text=What%20is%20the%20Initiative%3F,manner%20without%20being%20inappropriately%20charged.

56 For a chart of enforcement actions from 2019 to 2022 in the Right of Access Initiative, see Allen Killworth and Zeina Abu-Hijleh, "HIPAA Enforcement Continues Under Right of Access," *The National Law Review*, April 5, 2022, https://www.natlawreview.com/article/hipaa-enforcement-continues-under-right-access-initiative.

57 Kat Jercich, "Banner Health Agrees to Pay $200K to Settle Potential HIPAA Violations," Healthcare IT News, January 13, 2021, https://www.healthcareitnews.com/news/banner-health-agrees-pay-200k-settle-potential-hipaa-violations; see Jill McKeon, "Top HIPAA Right of Access Cases in 2021, So Far," Health IT Security, August 23, 2021, https://healthitsecurity.com/news/top-hipaa-right-of-access-cases-in-2021-so-far.

58 "HIPAA Safe Harbor Offers Limited But Important Protection," Relias Media, March 1, 2022, https://www.reliasmedia.com/articles/149137-hipaa-safe-harbor-offers-limited-but-important-protection.

59 Steve Alder, "Can a Patient Sue for a HIPAA Violation?" *HIPAA Journal*, January 1, 2023, https://www.hipaajournal.com/sue-for-hipaa-violation/; see "Court Rules No Private Right of Action for HIPAA, But Questions Remain," Relias Media, September 1, 2021, https://www.reliasmedia.com/articles/148467-court-rules-no-private-right-of-action-for-hipaa-but-questions-remain#:~:text=HIPAA%20does%20not%20expressly%20allow,Walder%20Hayden%20in%20Hackensack%2C%20NJ.

60 "How to File a Health Information Privacy or Security Complaint," U.S. Department of Health and Human Services, December 23, 2022, https://www.hhs.gov/hipaa/filing-a-complaint/complaint-process/index.html.

61 "A covered entity or business associate may not threaten, intimidate, coerce, harass, discriminate against, or take any retaliatory action against an individual" who files a complaint, participates in an investigation, or testifies against an entity. 45 CFR § 160.316, accessed July 2022, https://www.law.cornell.edu/cfr/text/45/160.316; see "Whistleblower's Guide to HIPAA," Whistleblower Law Collaborative, August 11, 2020, https://www.whistleblowerllc.com/whistleblower-guide-hipaa/.

62 42 U.S.C. § 1320d-6, accessed November 2017, https://www.law.cornell.edu/uscode/text/42/1320d-6; *see* United States v. Zhou, United States Court of Appeals (9th Cir. 2012) (appeal of misdemeanor conviction for violation of 42 U.S.C. § 1320d-6), accessed November 2017, http://cdn.ca9.uscourts.gov/datastore/opinions/2012/05/10/10-50231.pdf.

63 David Craig, "What You Need to Know about HIPAA and Your State's Privacy Law," *Spruce Blog*, October 10, 2016, https://blog.sprucehealth.com/need-know-hipaa-states-

laws/; see "The Law and Medical Privacy," Electronic Freedom Foundation, accessed October 2017, https://www.eff.org/issues/law-and-medical-privacy. Numerous states have made guides or commentary available about the particulars of their state law requirements. See, e.g., Deven McGraw, Alice Leiter and Christopher Rasmussen, *Rights and Requirements: A Guide to Privacy and Security of Health Information in California,* California Healthcare Foundation, October 2013, https://www.chcf.org/wp-content/uploads/2017/12/PDF-PrivacySecurityGuide.pdf (accessed February 2020); "Patient Privacy," Attorney General of Texas, accessed June 2023, https://www.texasattorneygeneral.gov/consumer-protection/health-care/patient-privacy.

64 Chapter 6 reviews state comprehensive privacy laws while Chapter 7 details state data breach notification laws. For additional resources on states laws that provide more protection than HIPAA, view "State Laws vs HIPAA—What You Need to Know," Abyde, June 8, 2020, https://abyde.com/state-laws-vs-hipaa-what-you-need-to-know/ and "50-State Survey of Health Care Information Privacy Laws, " Seyfarth, 2021, https://www.seyfarth.com/a/web/77459/50-State-Survey-of-Health-Care-Information-Privacy-Laws.pdf.

65 See Mike Tierney, "Data Privacy Laws by State: The U.S. Approach to Privacy Protection," Netwrix, updated March 17, 2023, https://blog.netwrix.com/2019/08/27/data-privacy-laws-by-state-the-u-s-approach-to-privacy-protection/; James Dempsey, "Exceptions in New State Privacy Laws Leave Data Without Security Coverage," IAPP, May 17, 2022, https://iapp.org/news/a/exceptions-in-new-state-privacy-laws-leave-data-without-security-coverage/.

66 42 U.S.C. § 17921, accessed November 2017, https://www.law.cornell.edu/uscode/text/42/17921.

67 45 CFR 164.402, accessed November 2017, https://www.law.cornell.edu/cfr/text/45/164.402.

68 45 CFR 164.402. For additional insight, view "Final Rule: Modified Definition of Breach," HIPAA.com, January 28, 2013, https://www.hipaa.com/final-rule-modified-definition-of-breach/.

69 42 U.S.C. § 17932, accessed November 2017, https://www.law.cornell.edu/uscode/text/42/17932.

70 42 U.S.C. § 17932; 42 U.S.C. § 17932(h), accessed November 2017, https://www.law.cornell.edu/uscode/text/42/17932.

71 42 U.S.C. § 17932(e)(2)-(3), accessed November 2017, https://www.law.cornell.edu/uscode/text/42/17932; 42 U.S.C. § 17932(h), accessed November 2017, https://www.law.cornell.edu/uscode/text/42/17932.

72 42 U.S.C. § 17932(h); see Jessica Davis, "HHS Lacks Effective Communication for HIPAA Breach Reporting Feedback, June 28, 2022, https://www.scmagazine.com/analysis/compliance/hhs-lacks-effective-communication-for-hippa-breach-reporting-feedback.

73 Steve Alder, "Excellus Health Plan Settles HIPAA Violation Case and Pays $5.1 Million Penalty." *HIPAA Journal,* June 18, 2021, https://www.hipaajournal.com/excellus-health-plan-settles-hipaa-violation-case-and-pays-5-1-million-penalty/; see Steve Alder, "May 2022 Healthcare Data Breach Report," HIPAA Journal, June 21, 2022, https://www.hipaajournal.com/may-2022-healthcare-data-breach-report/.

74 Steve Alder, "What is the Relationship Between HITECH, HIPAA, and Electronic Health and Medical Records?" *HIPAA Journal,* January 1, 2023, https://www.

hipaajournal.com/relationship-between-hitech-hipaa-electronic-health-medical-records/.

75 "Complying with the FTC's Health Breach Notification Rule." Federal Trade Commission, January 2022, https://www.ftc.gov/business-guidance/resources/complying-ftcs-health-breach-notification-rule-0; see "Guidance on HIPAA and Cloud Computing." U.S. Department of Health and Human Services, December 23, 2022, https://www.hhs.gov/hipaa/for-professionals/special-topics/health-information-technology/cloud-computing/index.html.

76 "Statement of the Commission on Breaches by Health Apps and Other Connected Devices," Federal Trade Commission, September 15, 2021, https://www.ftc.gov/system/files/documents/public_statements/1596364/statement_of_the_commission_on_breaches_by_health_apps_and_other_connected_devices.pdf.

77 "Health Information Technology ("HITECH") Provisions of the American Recovery and Reinvestment Act of 2009, Title XIII, Subtitle D," Federal Trade Commission, accessed November 2019; https://www.ftc.gov/enforcement/statutes/health-information-technology-hitech-provisions-american-recovery-and; "Complying with the FTC's Health Breach Notification Rule," Federal Trade Commission, January 2022, https://www.ftc.gov/tips-advice/business-center/guidance/complying-ftcs-health-breach-notification-rule; *see* Brad Rostolsky and Steven Boranian, "FTC Issues Final Rule on Notifying Consumers about Breaches of Electronic Health Records," Reed Smith, September 3, 2009, https://www.reedsmith.com/en/perspectives/2009/09/ftc-issues-final-rule-on-notifying-consumers-about.

78 In 2023, the maximum penalty per violation is $2,067,813. "What are the Penalties for HIPAA Violations?" *HIPAA Journal*, accessed October 2023, https://www.hipaajournal.com/what-are-the-penalties-for-hipaa-violations-7096/; see Steve Adler, "HIPAA Omnibus Rule Final Release Issued," *HIPAA Journal*, January 25, 2013, https://www.hipaajournal.com/hipaa-omnibus-rule-final-release-issued/; see also "HITECH Act Enforcement Interim Rule," U.S. Department of Health and Human Services, June 16, 2017, www.hhs.gov/hipaa/for-professionals/special-topics/HITECH-act-enforcement-interim-final-rule/index.html.

79 42 U.S.C. § 17320d-5, accessed November 2017, https://www.law.cornell.edu/uscode/text/42/1320d-5.

80 42 U.S.C. § 17935(a)-(b), accessed November 2017, https://www.law.cornell.edu/uscode/text/42/17935; 45 CFR § 164.522(a)(1)(vi)(A)-(B), accessed April 2017, https://www.law.cornell.edu/cfr/text/45/164.522; see 45 CFR § 164.514(e) (limited data set), accessed November 2017, https://www.law.cornell.edu/cfr/text/45/164.514.

81 45 CFR § 164.522(a)(1)(vi)(A)-(B), accessed November 2017, https://www.law.cornell.edu/cfr/text/45/164.522. For an in-depth discussion, view "Overview of HIPAA/HITECH Act Omnibus Final Rule," Alston & Bird, January 25, 2013, https://www.alston.com/-/media/files/insights/publications/2013/01/ihealth-care-advisoryi--overview-of-hipaahitech-ac/files/click-here-to-view-advisory/fileattachment/13066-hipaahitechomnibusfinalrule.pdf.

82 42 CFR § 412, accessed November 2017, https://www.law.cornell.edu/cfr/text/42/part-412; 42 CFR § 413, accessed November 2017, https://www.law.cornell.edu/cfr/text/42/part-413; 42 CFR § 422, accessed November 2017, https://www.law.cornell.edu/cfr/text/42/part-422; 42 CFR § 495, accessed November 2017, https://www.law.cornell.edu/cfr/text/42/part-495; 45 CFR § 170.32, accessed November 2017, https://www.law.

cornell.edu/cfr/text/45/part-170. For a detailed discussion of Stage 3 of the incentive program, view "Medicare and Medicaid Programs; Electronic Health Record Incentive Program-Stage 3," March 30, 2015, Federal Register, https://www.federalregister.gov/articles/2015/03/30/2015-06685/medicare-and-medicaid-programs-electronic-health-record-incentive-program-stage-3 and "Promoting Interoperability Programs," Centers for Medicare & Medicaid Services, June 12, 2023, https://www.cms.gov/Regulations-and-Guidance/Legislation/EHRIncentivePrograms/index.html?redirect=/ehrincentiveprograms.

83 "Nationwide Health Information Network Exchange," The Office of the National Coordinator for Health Information Technology, accessed November 2019, https://www.healthit.gov/sites/default/files/factsheets/nationwide-health-information-network-exchange.pdf.

84 42 U.S.C. § 17935(c), accessed November 2017, https://www.law.cornell.edu/uscode/text/42/17935.

85 42 U.S.C. § 1936, accessed November 2017, https://www.law.cornell.edu/uscode/text/42/17936.

86 HIPAA is discussed in Section 8.1 of this chapter.

87 "The Confidentiality of Alcohol and Drug Abuse Patient Records Regulation and the HIPAA Privacy Rule: Implications for Alcohol and Substance Abuse Programs," U.S. Department of Health and Human Services, June 2004, https://www.samhsa.gov/sites/default/files/part2-hipaa-comparison2004.pdf. The rule-making authority relating to confidentiality that is granted by these statutes is now codified in 42 U.S.C. § 290dd-2, accessed October 2017, https://www.law.cornell.edu/uscode/text/42/290dd-2.

88 "Confidentiality of Substance Use Disorder Patient Records Rule , 42 C.F.R. Part 2," (formerly Confidentiality of Alcohol and Drug Abuse Patient Records), Federal Register, January 18, 2017, https://www.federalregister.gov/documents/2017/01/18/2017-00719/confidentiality-of-substance-use-disorder-patient-records; *see* "Final Rule: 42 CFR Part 2, Confidentiality of Substance Use Disorder Patient Records," accessed October 2017, American Psychiatric Association, https://www.psychiatry.org/psychiatrists/practice/practice-management/hipaa/42-cfr-part-2.

89 The term used by the rule is *substance use disorder* treatment programs. Section 2.11, Confidentiality of Substance Use Disorder Patient Records Rule, 42 C.F.R. Part 2, January 18, 2017, https://www.federalregister.gov/documents/2017/01/18/2017-00719/confidentiality-of-substance-use-disorder-patient-records.

90 Section 2.11, Confidentiality of Substance Use Disorder Patient Records Rule, 42 C.F.R. Part 2, January 18, 2017, https://www.federalregister.gov/documents/2017/01/18/2017-00719/confidentiality-of-substance-use-disorder-patient-records; "42 CFR Part 2—Final Rule," American Psychiatric Association, https://www.psychiatry.org/File%20Library/Psychiatrists/Practice/Practice-Management/42-CFR-Part-Standards-Comparison.pdf; see "The Confidentiality of Alcohol and Drug Abuse Patient Records Regulation and the HIPAA Privacy Rule," U.S. Department of Health and Human Services.

91 Section 2.12, Confidentiality of Substance Use Disorder Patient Records Rule.

92 Section 2.11, Confidentiality of Substance Use Disorder Patient Records Rule; see "Comparison Chart—1987 rule, 2017 updated final rule, and HIPAA," in "42 CFR Part 2—Final Rule," American Psychiatric Association.

93 Susan Awad, "Confused on Confidentiality? A Primer on 42 CFR Part 2," American Society of Addiction Medicine, August 15, 2013.

94 Section 2.31, Confidentiality of Substance Use Disorder Patient Records Rule; see "Comparison Chart—1987 rule, 2017 updated final rule, and HIPAA Final Rule" in "42 CFR Part 2," American Psychiatric Association.

95 Section 2.32, Confidentiality of Substance Use Disorder Patient Records Rule; see "Comparison Chart—1987 rule, 2017 updated final rule, and HIPAA Final Rule" in "42 CFR Part 2," American Psychiatric Association.

96 Section 2.51, Confidentiality of Substance Use Disorder Patient Records Rule.

97 Section 2.52, Confidentiality of Substance Use Disorder Patient Records Rule. Disclosures for scientific research must meet certain requirements related to protections for human research. See Mark Moran, "Rule Governing Confidentiality of Substance Use Data Updated," Psychiatric News, American Psychiatric Association, February 23, 2017, http://psychnews.psychiatryonline.org/doi/full/10.1176/appi.pn.2017.3a4.

98 Section 2.53, Confidentiality of Substance Use Disorder Patient Records Rule.

99 Section 2.12(c)(4), Confidentiality of Substance Use Disorder Patient Records Rule.

100 Section 2.12(c)(5), Confidentiality of Substance Use Disorder Patient Records Rule.

101 Section 2.12(c)(6), Confidentiality of Substance Use Disorder Patient Records Rule.

102 Section 2.61-2.67, Confidentiality of Substance Use Disorder Patient Records Rule.

103 Section 2.16, Confidentiality of Substance Use Disorder Patient Records Rule.

104 (Name Redacted) Specialist in Health Policy, "Privacy Protections for Individuals with Substance Abuse Disorders: The Part 2 Final Rule in Brief," 4-5, Congressional Research Service, March 17, 2017, https://www.everycrsreport.com/files/20170317_R44790_9f35e7a104d6d5dc1eef64d245f1bf62fcc0f0b0.pdf; *see* Section 2.3-2.4, Confidentiality of Substance Use Disorder Patient Records Rule, 42 C.F.R. Part 2.

105 HIPAA's Privacy Rule is discussed in Section 8.1.1 of this chapter.

106 "The Confidentiality of Alcohol and Drug Abuse Patient Records Regulation and the HIPAA Privacy Rule," Health and Human Services.

107 Comparison charts are available at "Final Rule: 42 CFR Part 2," American Psychiatric Association, and (Name Redacted) Specialist in Health Policy, "Privacy Protections for Individuals with Substance Abuse Disorders: The Part 2 Final Rule in Brief," Congressional Research Service, March 17, 2017, https://www.everycrsreport.com/files/20170317_R44790_9f35e7a104d6d5dc1eef64d245f1bf62fcc0f0b0.pdf.

108 "Confidentiality of Patient Records for Alcohol and Other Drug Treatment," Technical Assistance Publication, Series 13, DHHS Publication No. (SMA) 95-3018, HHS, 1994, http://lib.adai.washington.edu/clearinghouse/downloads/TAP-13-Confidentiality-of-Patient-Records-for-Alcohol-and-Other-Drug-Treatment-103.pdf.

109 Pub. L. 110-233, 122 Stat. 881 (2008), https://www.gpo.gov/fdsys/pkg/PLAW-110publ233/pdf/PLAW-110publ233.pdf; For a summary, view " 'GINA' The Genetic Information Nondiscrimination Act of 2008: Information for Researchers an Health Care Professionals, Department of Health and Human Services," April 6, 2009, https://www.genome.gov/Pages/PolicyEthics/GeneticDiscrimination/GINAInfoDoc.pdf.

110 Pub. L. 110-233, 122 Stat. 881 (2008) at § 2.

111 Pub. L. 110-233, 122 Stat. 881 (2008) at § 2.

112 See generally Pub. L. 110-233, 122 Stat. 881 at §§ 101, 104, 200. For a discussion of a 2019 class-action lawsuit alleging wellness programs violate GINA, view Stephen

Miller, "Workers Sue Yale University over Workplace Wellness Penalties," SHRM, July 24, 2019, https://www.shrm.org/resourcesandtools/hr-topics/benefits/pages/workers-sue-yale-university-over-workplace-wellness-penalties.aspx.

113 Pub. L. 110-233, 122 Stat. 881 (2008) at § 101.

114 Pub. L. 110-233, 122 Stat. 881 (2008) at § 101.

115 Pub. L. 110-233, 122 Stat. 881 (2008) at § 101.

116 Pub. L. 110-233, 122 Stat. 881 (2008) at § 101.

117 Pub. L. 110-233, 122 Stat. 881 (2008) at § 101.

118 Pub. L. 110-233, 122 Stat. 881 (2008) at § 101.

119 Pub. L. 110-233, 122 Stat. 881 (2008) at § 102.

120 Pub. L. 110-233, 122 Stat. 881 (2008) at § 102.

121 Pub. L. 110-233, 122 Stat. 881 (2008) at § 104.

122 As described in 42 U.S.C. § 1171(4)(B) (2006), https://aspe.hhs.gov/report/health-insurance-portability-and-accountability-act-1996#1171; 42 U.S.C. § 1171(4)(B) (2006) at § 105.

123 42 U.S.C. § 1171(4)(B) (2006) § 105 at Title II.

124 42 U.S.C. § 1171(4)(B) (2006) at § 202. Historically, the cases brought by the EEOC for alleged GINA violations relate to employers gaining access to medical histories of the family members of workers. See J. Edward Moreno, "COVID Testing Case Warns Employers on Genetic Bias Law Liability," Bloomberg Law, July 11, 2022, https://news.bloomberglaw.com/daily-labor-report/covid-testing-case-warns-employers-on-genetic-bias-law-liability; Paige Smith, "Genetic Bias Law Has Worked Perfectly, Or Maybe Not At All," Bloomberg Law, January 15, 2020, https://news.bloomberglaw.com/daily-labor-report/genetic-bias-law-has-worked-perfectly-or-maybe-not-at-all.

125 42 U.S.C. § 1171(4)(B) (2006) at §§ 202-205.

126 42 U.S.C. § 1171(4)(B) (2006) at § 202.

127 42 U.S.C. § 1171(4)(B) (2006) at § 202.

128 42 U.S.C. § 1171(4)(B) (2006) at §§ 203-205.

129 42 U.S.C. § 1171(4)(B) (2006) at § 206. For a discussion of GINA and genetic tests paid for by employers, view Ryan Golden, "Report: Apple Pilots Free Genetic Screenings for Employees," HRDive, January 2, 2020, https://www.hrdive.com/news/report-apple-pilots-free-genetic-screenings-for-employees/569620/.

130 42 U.S.C. § 1171(4)(B) (2006) at § 206. Such medical records should be kept in a manner consistent with the practices mandated for employee entrance exams under 42 U.S.C. § 12112(d)(3)(B), accessed November 2017, https://www.law.cornell.edu/uscode/text/42/12112.

131 For example, a private right of action for employment discrimination may be available under Title VII of the Civil Rights Act. "Title VII Of the Civil Rights Act of 1964," U.S. Equal Employment Opportunity Commission, accessed November 2017, https://www.eeoc.gov/laws/statutes/titlevii.cfm. Additionally, 35 states and the District of Columbia have private rights of action for genetic discrimination. "Genome Statue and legislation Database," National Human Genome Research Institute, accessed November 2017, https://www.genome.gov/27552194/.

132 GINA at § 208.

133 "Genetic Discrimination," National Human Genome Research Institute, accessed June 2023, https://www.genome.gov/about-genomics/policy-issues/Genetic-Discrimination.

134 "New California Law Prohibits Genetic Discrimination and Can Result in Significant Damages If Violated," Duane Morris, September 23, 2011, https://www.duanemorris.com/alerts/california_law_prohibits_genetic_discrimination_can_result_significant_damages_if_violated_4222.html; see "Genetic Discrimination," National Human Genome Research Institute.

135 For a link to a searchable data base on relevant state laws, view "Genome Statute ad Legislation Database," National Human Genome Research Institute.

136 Russell Berman, "Congress Nears a Breakthrough on Medical Research Funding," *The Atlantic*, December 1, 2016, https://www.theatlantic.com/politics/archive/2016/12/cures-act-compromise-elizabeth-warren/509228/; The law can be found at Public Law 114-255, December 13, 2016, https://www.congress.gov/114/plaws/publ255/PLAW-114publ255.pdf; For a chart of provisions of the Cures Act that are relevant to data sharing, view Mary Majumder, Christi Guerrini, Juli Bollinger, Robert Cook-Deegan and Amy McGuire, "Sharing Data under the 21st Century Cures Act, Table 1: 21st Century Cures Act provisions relevant to data sharing," *Genetics in Medicine* 19, no 12 (December 2017), https://www.nature.com/articles/gim201759.epdf.

137 Kirk Nahra, "Privacy and Security Impacts of the 21st Century Cures Legislation," *Privacy Tracker*, IAPP, December 19, 2016, https://iapp.org/news/a/privacy-and-security-impacts-of-the-21st-century-cures-legislation/.

138 "21st Century Cures Act: Interoperability, Information Blocking, and the ONC Health IT Certification Program." Federal Register, May 1, 2020, https://www.federalregister.gov/documents/2020/05/01/2020-07419/21st-century-cures-act-interoperability-information-blocking-and-the-onc-health-it-certification; "Information Blocking," HealthIT.gov, accessed June 2023, https://www.healthit.gov/topic/information-blocking.

139 See Peter Swire, "The Portability and Other Required Transfers Impact Assessment (PORT-IA): Assessing Competition, Privacy, Cybersecurity, and Other Considerations," *Georgetown Law Technology Review*, February 2022, https://georgetownlawtechreview.org/the-portability-and-other-required-transfers-impact-assessment-port-ia-assessing-competition-privacy-cybersecurity-and-other-considerations/GLTR-02-2022/.

140 21st Century Cures Act (Public Law 114-255), Section 3022(b)(2)(A), GovInfo, December 13, 2016, https://www.govinfo.gov/app/details/PLAW-114publ255; see Vasilios Kalogredis and Katherine LaDow, "21st Century Cures Act Imposes High Penalties upon Healthcare Providers for Electronic Information Blocking," Lamb McErlane, January 31, 2017, https://www.lambmcerlane.com/articles/21st-century-cures-act-imposes-high-penalties-upon-healthcare-providers-electronic-information-blocking/.

141 "21st Century Cures Act: Interoperability, Information Blocking, and the ONC Health IT Certification Program," Federal Register; see Peter Swire, "The Interoperability and Other Required Transfers Impact Assessment (PORT-IA): Assessing Competition, Privacy, Cybersecurity, and Other Considerations, revised August 25, 2022, https://papers.ssrn.com/sol3/papers.cfm?abstract_id=3689171.

142 "21st Century Cures Act: Interoperability, Information Blocking, and the ONC Health IT Certification Program," Federal Register; see Swire, "The Interoperability and Other Required Transfers Impact Assessment (PORT-IA)."

143 45 C.F.R §170.404, accessed October 2023, https://www.law.cornell.edu/cfr/text/45/170.404.

144 45 C.F.R §170.404 at 25,816.

145 21st Century Cures Act (Public Law 114-255), Sections 2012 and 2013, SciPol, http://scipol.duke.edu/content/21st-century-cures-act-public-law-114-255 (accessed October 2017); see Kathy Hudson and Dr. Francis Collins, "The 21st Century Cures Act—A View from the NIH," The New England Journal of Medicine, (January 12, 2017), www.nejm.org/doi/full/10.1056/NEJMp1615745#t=article.

146 "Twenty-First Century Cures Act Includes HIPAA Provisions," Covington Digital Health, December 23, 2016, https://www.covingtondigitalhealth.com/2016/12/twenty-first-century-cures-act-includes-hipaa-provisions/.

147 21st Century Cures Act (Public Law 114-255); see Richard Eiler, Nesrin Garan Tift, Elizabeth S. Warren, "21st Century Cures Act – HIPAA & Other Privacy Considerations," Bass, Berry & Sims, PLC, *Lexology*, December 16, 2016, https://www.lexology.com/library/detail.aspx?g=dae83798-6229-47a7-9e68-283c0da27d18.

148 William Maruca, "21st Century Cure for a 'Broken' Mental Health System Includes HIPAA Clarification," Fox Rothschild, December 30, 2016, https://hipaahealthlaw.foxrothschild.com/2016/12/articles/articles/21st-century-cure-broken-mental-health-system-includes-hipaa-clarification/; see Maggie Hales, "Compassionate Communication and Mental Health," The HIPAA E-Tool, January 4, 2017, https://thehipaaetool.com/2017-1-4-compassionate-communication-and-mental-health/; Covington Digital Health Team, "Twenty-First Century Cures Act Includes HIPAA Provisions," Covington Digital Health, December 23, 2016, https://www.covingtondigitalhealth.com/2016/12/twenty-first-century-cures-act-includes-hipaa-provisions/.

149 "Medical Technology - Worldwide," Statista, accessed October 2023, https://www.statista.com/outlook/hmo/medical-technology/worldwide.

150 Medtech, TechTerms.com, accessed July 2022, https://techterms.com/definition/medtech#:~:text=Medtech%2C%20short%20for%20%22medical%20technology,several%20new%20medical%20advancements%20possible.

151 Steve Ranger, "Why You Smartwatch and Wearable Devices are the Next Big Privacy Nightmare," ZDNet, January 14, 2019, https://www.zdnet.com/article/smartwatch-data-collection-rush-raises-privacy-backlash-fears/; Robert Kazmi, "Pros and Cons of Genetic Testing: What You Need to Know." Koombea, September 15, 2021, https://www.koombea.com/blog/pros-and-cons-of-genetic-testing/; see "Six Winning Roles for Medtech to Thrive in the Future of Health," Deloitte, 2022, https://www2.deloitte.com/content/dam/Deloitte/us/Documents/life-sciences-health-care/us-lshc-six-winning-roles-for-medtech.pdf. In her 2023 book entitled "The Battle for Your Brain: Defending the Right to Think Freely in the Age of Neurotechnology," Professor Nita Farahany considers "a near-distant future in which it isn't just your heart rate or your oxygen levels or the steps that you're taking that you're tracking, but also your brain activity, where you're wearing wearable brain sensors that are integrated into your headphones and your earbuds." Farahany advocates for an international human right to "cognitive liberty" – "the right to self-determination over our brains

and mental experiences." Alisa Chang, Vincent Acovino, and Justine Kenin, "This Law and Philosophy Professor Warns Neurotechnology is Also a Danger to Privacy," NPR, March 14, 2023, https://www.npr.org/2023/03/14/1163497160/this-law-and-philosophy-professor-warns-neurotechnology-is-also-a-danger-to-priv.

152 See "Using a Health App?" Federal Trade Commission, accessed June 2023, https://www.ftc.gov/sites/default/files/u544718/flo_health_app_infographic_11022020_en_508_0.jpg.

153 See Gaurav Bidasaria, "7 Best Medical Records Apps for Android and iOS in Case of Emergency," Techwiser, May 21, 2020, https://techwiser.com/medical-records-apps/; see also "Health Data Privacy and Third-Party Apps: Reframing the Conversation." Healthcare Innovation, October 13, 2020, https://www.hcinnovationgroup.com/population-health-management/patient-engagement/article/21158201/health-data-privacy-and-thirdparty-apps-reframing-the-conversation; "HHS Guidance Clarifies HIPAA Liability for Use of Third-Party Health Apps." Fierce Healthcare, April 29, 2019, https://www.fiercehealthcare.com/tech/hhs-guidance-clarifies-hipaa-liability-use-third-party-health-apps.

154 The company may itself be a covered entity. "USA: HIPAA and Wearable Technology - Does it Provide Sufficient Protection?" DataGuidance, https://www.dataguidance.com/opinion/usa-hipaa-and-wearable-technology-does-it-provid; see "Facebook is Receiving Sensitive Medical Information from Hospital Websites," The Markup, June 16, 2022, https://themarkup.org/pixel-hunt/2022/06/16/facebook-is-receiving-sensitive-medical-information-from-hospital-websites; see also Evan Peng, "Meta Sued Over Claims Patient Data Secretly Sent to Facebook," Bloomberg, June 17, 2022, https://www.bloomberg.com/news/articles/2022-06-17/meta-sued-over-claims-patient-data-secretly-sent-to-facebook#:~:text=Meta%20Platforms%20Inc.%20was%20sued,for%20some%20health%2Dcare%20providers.

155 Kim Theodos and Scott Sittig, "Health Information Privacy Laws in the Digital Age: HIPAA Doesn't Apply," *Perspectives in Health Information Management* 18, (Winter 2021), https://www.ncbi.nlm.nih.gov/pmc/articles/PMC7883355/.

156 Gicel Tomimbang, "Wearbles: Where Do They Fall Within the Regulatory Landscape?" IAPP, January 22, 2018, https://iapp.org/news/a/wearables-where-do-they-fall-within-the-regulatory-landscape/.

157 Kristinn Cohen, "Location, Health, and Other Sensitive Information: FTC Committed to Fully Enforcing the Law Against Illegal Use and Sharing of Highly Sensitive Data," Federal Trade Commission, July 11, 2022, https://www.ftc.gov/business-guidance/blog/2022/07/location-health-other-sensitive-information-ftc-committed-fully-enforcing-law-against-illegal-use.

158 "Developer of Popular Women's Fertility-Tracking App Settles FTC Allegations that it Misled Consumers about the Disclosure of their Health Data," Federal Trade Commission, January 13, 2021, https://www.ftc.gov/news-events/news/press-releases/2021/01/developer-popular-womens-fertility-tracking-app-settles-ftc-allegations-it-misled-consumers-about. Note that the FTC Commissioners discussed whether an allegation of a violation of the HIPAA Health Breach Notification Rule, which the FTC enforces, should have been added to the case. "Joint Statement of Commissioner Rohit Chopra and Commissioner Rebecca Kelly Slaughter Concurring in Part, Dissention in Part," Federal Trade Commission, January 13, 2021, https://www.ftc.gov/system/files/documents/public_statements/1586018/20210112_final_joint_rcrks_statement_on_flo.pdf; see "Flo gets FTC Slap for Sharing User

Data When Promised Privacy," TechCrunch, January 13, 2021, https://techcrunch.com/2021/01/13/flo-gets-ftc-slap-for-sharing-user-data-when-it-promised-privacy/.

159 "How Did the Federal Food, Drug, and Cosmetic Act Come About?" U.S. Food and Drug Administration, March 28, 2018, https://www.fda.gov/about-fda/fda-basics/how-did-federal-food-drug-and-cosmetic-act-come-about; see Tomimbang, "Wearbles: Where Do They Fall Within the Regulatory Landscape?"

160 For a primer on medtech regulation by the FDA, view Sonia Nath, "Medtech Primer on the FDA Regulatory Landscape," CLS Bulletin, March 11, 2022, https://www.cooley.com/-/media/cooley/pdf/reprints/2022/cls-bulletin-medtech-spotlight---cooley-article.ashx.

161 "General Wellness: Policy for Low Risk Devices," U.S. Food and Drug Administration, September 17, 2019, https://www.fda.gov/regulatory-information/search-fda-guidance-documents/general-wellness-policy-low-risk-devices; "Wearable Medical Devices," Greenlight Guru, accessed June 2023, https://www.greenlight.guru/glossary/wearable-medical-devices. Also, exemptions from FDA review include lifestyle devices unrelated to "diagnosis, cure, mitigation, prevention, and treatment (such as monitoring exercise, reducing stress, and eating habits) as well as software to serve as electronic patient records, "How FDA Regulates Artificial Intelligence Medical Products, August 5, 2021, https://www.pewtrusts.org/en/research-and-analysis/issue-briefs/2021/08/how-fda-regulates-artificial-intelligence-in-medical-products; see amendment in 21st Century Cures Act related to "maintaining or encouraging a healthy lifestyle," "General Wellness: Policy for Low Risk Devices," U.S. Food and Drug Administration.

162 "How FDA Regulates Artificial Intelligence in Medical Products," The Pew Charitable Trusts, August 5, 2021, https://www.pewtrusts.org/en/research-and-analysis/issue-briefs/2021/08/how-fda-regulates-artificial-intelligence-in-medical-products; see "Wearable Medical Devices," Greenlight Guru; Tomimbang, "Wearbles: Where Do They Fall Within the Regulatory Landscape?"; Scott Gottlieb, "Advancing Policies to Promote Safe and Effective Medtech Innovation," U.S. Food and Drug Administration, https://www.fda.gov/news-events/fda-voices/advancing-policies-promote-safe-effective-medtech-innovation; Brian Bossetta, "FDA's Schwartz Says New Draft Cybersecurity Guidance Addresses Emerging Threats." MedTech Insight, April 12, 2022, https://medtech.pharmaintelligence.informa.com/MT145288/FDAs-Schwartz-Says-New-Draft-Cybersecurity-Guidance-Addresses-Emerging-Threats; Kat Jercich, "What Sets FDA Apart?' Medtech Innovation Expert Weighs In," Healthcare IT News, April 11, 2022, https://www.healthcareitnews.com/news/what-sets-fda-apart-medtech-innovation-expert-weighs.

163 "Cybersecurity," U.S. Food and Drug Administration, May 1, 2023, https://www.fda.gov/medical-devices/digital-health-center-excellence/cybersecurity; see "Cybersecurity Guidance," U.S. Food and Drug Administration, May 1, 2023, https://www.fda.gov/medical-devices/digital-health-center-excellence/cybersecurity#guidance.

164 "Cybersecurity in Medical Devices: Quality System Considerations and Content of Premarket Submissions," U.S. Food and Drug Administration, September 27, 2023, https://www.fda.gov/media/119933/download. See "FDA Updates Cybersecurity Guidance for Medical Device Makers," American Hospital Association, September 26, 2023, https://www.aha.org/news/headline/2023-09-26-fda-updates-cybersecurity-guidance-medical-device-makers.

165 "Cybersecurity in Medical Devices: Refuse to Accept Policy for Cyber Devices and Related Systems Under Section 524B of the FD&C Act: Guidance for Industry and Food and Drug Administration Staff," U.S. Food and Drug Administration, March 30, 2023, https://www.federalregister.gov/documents/2023/03/30/2023-06646/cybersecurity-in-medical-devices-refuse-to-accept-policy-for-cyber-devices-and-related-systems-under; see Winston Leung, "New FDA Medical Device Cybersecurity Requirements and How to Simplify Compliance," BlackBerry, June 1, 2023, https://blogs.blackberry.com/en/2023/06/new-fda-medical-device-cybersecurity-requirements; Jessice Davis, "FDA Will Refuse New Medical Devices for Cybersecurity Reasons on Oct. 1," SC Media, March 29, 2023, https://www.scmagazine.com/news/fda-will-refuse-new-medical-devices-for-cybersecurity-reasons-on-oct-1.

166 "State Laws vs. HIPAA: What You Need to Know," Abyde, June 8, 2020, https://abyde.com/state-laws-vs-hipaa-what-you-need-to-know/; "50-State Survey of Health Care Information Privacy Laws," Seyfarth, 2021, https://www.seyfarth.com/a/web/77459/50-State-Survey-of-Health-Care-Information-Privacy-Laws.pdf.

167 "Home Genetic Testing," Consumer Reports, October 2020, https://article.images.consumerreports.org/prod/content/dam/surveys/Consumer%20Reports%20Home%20Genetic%20Testing%20October%202020; see Emily Mullin, "States Are Toughening Up Privacy Laws for At-Home DNA Tests," Wired, October 21, 2021, https://www.wired.com/story/states-are-toughening-up-privacy-laws-for-at-home-dna-tests/.

168 Mullin, "States Are Toughening Up Privacy Laws for At-Home DNA Test,"; see Jill McKeon, "Growing Number of States Enact New Genetic Data Privacy Laws," Health IT Security, October 27, 2021, https://healthitsecurity.com/news/growing-number-of-states-enact-new-genetic-data-privacy-laws.

CHAPTER 9

Financial Privacy

Banking and other financial records have long been treated with high levels of confidentiality. Since medieval days, banks have often kept the identities of their borrower's secret and would not reveal intimate financial details of their customers. One reason for this confidentiality is to encourage borrowers to report honestly to the lender about their other debts and ability to pay. Another priority in the financial sector is to ensure security—thieves and fraudsters can target individuals or transactions if they have access to these details.[1]

This chapter focuses on restrictions on how financial services firms may collect, use and disclose personal information. Financial institutions are also subject to a variety of special rules about when they must disclose personal information. For instance, banks and other financial institutions have a variety of reporting obligations under anti-money-laundering laws. These required disclosures are discussed in Section 9.6.

The chapter begins with the Fair Credit Reporting Act (FCRA), which was enacted in 1970 and substantially updated by the Fair and Accurate Credit Transactions Act of 2003 (FACTA). It next discusses the privacy and security portions of the Gramm-Leach-Bliley Act of 1999 (GLBA), which supplies the general framework for confidentiality of records in the financial services sector. It concludes with the relevant portions of the Dodd-Frank Wall Street Reform and Consumer Protection Act of 2010 (Dodd-Frank Act). That law created a new regulatory agency, the Consumer Financial Protection Bureau (CFPB). The CFPB now has rulemaking authority for the FCRA, as updated by FACTA, as well as for most financial institutions under GLBA, and shares enforcement authority for these with the Federal Trade Commission (FTC) and banking regulators.[2] The chapter also examines existing cryptocurrency regulation in the United States and considers the future regulation of cryptocurrencies.

9.1 The Fair Credit Reporting Act

The United States began regulation of credit reporting during the early days of commercial data processing by computers.[3] The Fair Credit Reporting Act (FCRA) was enacted in 1970 to regulate the consumer reporting industry and provide privacy rights in consumer reports. Specifically, FCRA mandates accurate and relevant data collection, provides consumers with the ability to access and correct their information, and limits the use of consumer reports to defined permissible purposes.[4]

The origins of the FCRA can be traced to the rise of consumer credit in the United States. In the post-World War II era, merchants began to share more in-depth customer data to facilitate lending to households. By the 1960s, consumer credit was critical, but increasingly, individuals were being harmed by inaccurate information that they could neither view nor correct. In response, Congress passed the FCRA, the first federal law to regulate the use of personal information by private businesses.[5]

FCRA amendments in 1996 strengthened consumer access and correction rights and included provisions for nonconsumer-initiated transactions (also known as prescreening). The FCRA was further amended by FACTA, with provisions related to identity theft and other subjects.[6] State financial privacy laws related to credit reporting in general are preempted under FACTA, with the exception of state laws discussed in Section 9.2.[7]

9.1.1 Key Definitions in the FCRA

The FCRA regulates any consumer reporting agency (CRA) that furnishes a consumer report, which is used primarily for assisting in establishing consumers' eligibility for credit.[8] A CRA is any person or entity that compiles or evaluates personal information for the purpose of furnishing consumer reports to third parties for a fee.[9] Three well-known examples of CRAs are Experian, Equifax and TransUnion, which are leading providers of credit information and credit scores. There are thousands of smaller CRAs that compile personal records, such as criminal records or driving histories, for other consumer reporting purposes, such as preemployment screening.[10]

The critical nature of the requirement that the CRA furnish the consumer report to invoke the protections of the FCRA can be illustrated by the lawsuits resulting from the 2017 Equifax breach of nearly 150 million consumers' data. The court's ruling in one of the main class-action lawsuits was that there had *not* been a FCRA violation because Equifax had not "furnished" the stolen data to the hackers.[11]

A consumer report is any written, oral, or other communication of any information by a CRA related to an individual that pertains to the person's credit worthiness, credit standing, credit capacity, character, general reputation, personal characteristics or mode of living which is used "in whole or in part for the purpose of serving as a factor in establishing a consumer's eligibility" for credit, insurance, employment or other business purpose.[12]

The FCRA specifically requires CRAs to:

- Provide consumers with access to the information contained in their consumer reports as well as the opportunity to dispute any inaccurate information
- Take reasonable steps to ensure the maximum possible accuracy of information in the consumer report
- Not report negative information that is outdated: in most cases, this means account data more than seven years old or bankruptcies more than ten years old
- Provide consumer reports only to entities that have permissible purpose under the FCRA
- Maintain records regarding entities that received consumer reports
- Provide consumer assistance as required by FTC rules[13]

The FCRA imposes obligations on organizations that are not CRAs, including **users** (lenders, insurers, employers and others that use consumer reports)[14] and **furnishers** (lenders, retailers and others that furnish credit history or other personal information to the CRAs).[15]

Users must meet several main requirements under the FCRA:

- A user must have a permissible purpose for obtaining a consumer's credit report
- A user must certify to the CRA the permissible purpose for which the user is obtaining the consumer's credit report
- A user must notify the consumer when an adverse action is taken as result of the user obtaining the consumer's credit report[16]

Additionally, users of consumer reports must comply with other requirements, such as record-keeping and securely disposing of the consumer report data.[17] Note that when the user of the consumer report is an employer or prospective employer additional requirements may apply.[18]

Under the FCRA, furnishers' duties related to the information they provide to CRAs include:

- Provide accurate information
- Correct and update information
- Provide notice of dispute
- Respond to information resulting from identity theft[19]

Additionally, companies that extend credit to consumers, even if they do not use consumer reports to make credit decisions, are now required to implement a Red Flags Rule program to detect and deter identity theft (see Section 9.2.2).

9.1.2 CRA Requirements Under the FCRA

Under the FCRA, CRAs have three requirements:

- **CRAs must provide consumers access to the information contained in their consumer reports as well as the opportunity to dispute any inaccurate information.** Upon request by the consumer to the CRA, the CRA shall provide the consumer with access to the information, except for certain detailed exceptions. One of these exceptions permits the CRA to refrain from disclosing "credit scores or any other risk scores or predictors relating to the consumer."[20] The CRA is required to have procedures in place to address a consumer's dispute of information in the consumer's file. Once the CRA receives a dispute from a consumer directly or indirectly (through a reseller), the CRA shall undertake a reasonable investigation to determine if the information is accurate.[21]
- **CRAs must take reasonable steps to ensure the maximum possible accuracy of information in the consumer report.**[22] CRAs are expected to have procedures in place to ensure "maximum possible accuracy" of the information about the individual in the credit report.[23]
- **CRAs must not report negative information that is outdated.** In most cases, this means account data more than seven years old or bankruptcies more than 10 years old. Although the law permits CRAs to report bankruptcies on credit reports for 10 years from the date that the bankruptcy was filed, a notable practice by larger consumer reporting agencies is to remove Chapter 13 bankruptcies after seven years.[24]

9.1.3 User Requirements Under the FCRA

Users, meaning those who use credit reports, are subject to two main types of requirements related to consumer information that is protected by the FCRA. First, the user must meet certain requirements to obtain a credit report from a CRA. Second, the FCRA imposes notice requirements on the user after the user makes a negative decision, known as an adverse action, based at least in part on consumer information covered by the FCRA. This consumer information can be obtained from a CRA, third party, or affiliate.

9.1.3.1 User Obtaining a Consumer Report from a CRA

Users of consumer reports, including employers who use consumer reports in employment decisions as well as lenders, insurers, and others, are required to have a permissible purpose to obtain a credit report. To obtain the credit report, the user must certify to the CRA the specific permissible purpose(s) for which the credit report was obtained as well as the fact that the consumer report will not be used for any other purpose.

- **Users must have a permissible purpose.** Congress has limited the use of consumer reports to protect consumers' privacy. All users must have a permissible purpose under the FCRA to obtain a consumer report. Such purposes include obtaining reports:
    - As instructed by the consumer in writing
    - For the extension of credit as a result of an application from a consumer, or the review or collection of a consumer's account
    - For employment purposes, including hiring and promotion decisions, where the consumer has given written permission
    - For the underwriting of insurance as a result of an application from a consumer
    - When there is a legitimate business need, in connection with a business transaction that is initiated by the consumer
    - To review a consumer's account to determine whether the consumer continues to meet the terms of the account
    - To determine a consumer's eligibility for a license or other benefit granted by a governmental instrumentality required by law to consider an applicant's financial responsibility or status

    - For use by a potential investor or servicer, or current insurer, in a valuation or assessment of the credit or prepayment risks associated with an existing credit obligation
    - For use by state and local officials in connection with the determination of child support payments, or modifications and enforcement thereof
    - In response to a lawfully issued court order or subpoena
    - In addition, creditors and insurers may obtain certain consumer report information for the purpose of making "prescreened" unsolicited offers of credit or insurance[25]
- **Users must provide certifications.** The FCRA prohibits any person from obtaining a consumer report from a CRA unless the person has certified to the CRA the permissible purpose(s) for which the report is being obtained and certifies that the report will not be used for any other purpose.[26]

9.1.3.2 User Notice to Consumers Regarding Adverse Actions

The FCRA imposes requirements on users to notify the consumer when an adverse action is taken. The term "adverse action" is defined very broadly to include all business, credit, and employment actions affecting consumers that can be considered to have a negative impact, such as denying or canceling credit or insurance, or denying employment or promotion.[27] Note that no adverse action occurs in a credit transaction where the creditor makes a counteroffer that is accepted by the consumer.

The FCRA details several adverse actions that can be taken as result of obtaining or reviewing the information contained within a consumer credit report.

- **Adverse actions based on information obtained from a CRA.** If a user takes any type of adverse action (as defined by the FCRA, action that is based, even in part, on information contained in a consumer report), the FCRA requires the user to notify the consumer. The notification may be done in writing, orally, or by electronic means. It must include the following elements:
    - The name, address, and telephone number of the CRA (including a toll-free telephone number, if it is a nationwide CRA) that provided the report

- A statement that the CRA did not make the adverse decision and is not able to explain why the decision was made
- A statement setting forth the consumer's right to obtain a free disclosure of the consumer's file from the CRA if the consumer makes a request within 60 days
- A statement setting forth the consumer's right to dispute directly with the CRA the accuracy or completeness of any information provided by the CRA

- **Adverse actions based on information obtained from third parties that are not consumer reporting agencies.** If a user denies (or increases the charge for) credit for personal, family or household purposes based either wholly or partly upon information from an entity other than a CRA, and the information is the type covered by the FCRA, the law requires that the user clearly and accurately disclose to the consumer their right to be informed of the nature of the information that was relied upon if the consumer makes a written request within 60 days of notification. The user must then provide the disclosure within a reasonable period of time following the consumer's written request.
- **Adverse actions based on information obtained from affiliates.** If a user takes an adverse action involving insurance, employment or a credit transaction initiated by the consumer based on the type of information covered by the FCRA, and this information was obtained from an entity affiliated with the user of the information by common ownership or control, the law requires the user to notify the consumer of the adverse action. The notice must inform the consumer that they may obtain a disclosure of the nature of the information relied upon by making a written request within 60 days of receiving the adverse action notice. If the consumer makes such a request, the user must disclose the nature of the information no later than 30 days after receiving the request. If consumer report information is shared among affiliates and then used for an adverse action, the user must make a similar adverse action disclosure.[28]

9.1.4 Furnisher Requirements under the FCRA

Furnishers, meaning those who furnish credit history or other personal information to the CRAs, have numerous requirements under the FCRA. To ensure that furnishers comply with these requirements, the Furnisher Rule requires furnishers to have policies and procedures in place to ensure the accuracy and integrity of consumer information reported to CRAs—such as ensuring the information reported pertains to the correct person; taking steps to prevent a change in the date of the first delinquent consumer account to a later date so the delinquency remains on the credit report past the time period allowed by the FCRA; and maintaining records for a certain period of time.[29]

- **Furnishers must provide accurate information.** A furnisher is prohibited from reporting information to CRAs about a consumer that the furnisher knows to be inaccurate or that has been disputed by the consumer and established as inaccurate.
- **Furnishers must correct and update information.** A furnisher is required to promptly notify CRAs if the furnisher realizes previously reported information is incorrect or incomplete.
- **Furnishers must provide notice of dispute.** If a consumer disputes the accuracy or completeness of information, the furnisher is required to notify the CRAs of that dispute.
- **Furnisher must respond to information resulting from identity theft.** A furnisher must have procedures in place to respond to a CRA report sent to it related to information resulting from identity theft.[30]

9.1.5 Special Disclosures Under FCRA for Certain Activities

Several activities require special disclosures under the FCRA. One such activity is using creditworthiness to determine a borrower's interest rate, known as risk-based pricing. A second is the use of creditworthiness for employment purposes.

9.1.5.1 Consumer Reports and Risk-Based Pricing

Risk-based pricing is a concept used to describe a practice where lenders offer different interest rates or different loan terms to borrowers based on their creditworthiness. The Risk-Based Pricing Rule requires those offering credit to notify customers if they are receiving less favorable terms because of their credit report.[31]

The FCRA requires disclosure by all persons who use credit scores in making or arranging loans secured by residential real property. These persons must provide credit scores and other information about credit scores to applicants.[32]

Further, in some instances, the person offering credit must provide a risk-based pricing notice to the consumer in accordance with regulations jointly prescribed by the Consumer Finance Protection Bureau (CFPB) and the Federal Reserve Board. These notices are required if a consumer report is used by an individual or organization in connection with an application for credit or a grant, extension, or provision of credit to a consumer on terms less favorable than what is available to a substantial proportion of consumers acquiring loans from or through that person.[33]

9.1.5.2 Consumer Reports and Employment

The FCRA imposes certain additional obligations on organizations that intend to use consumer report information for employment purposes. The user of such information must:

- Make a clear and conspicuous written notification to the consumer before the report is obtained, in a document that consists solely of the disclosure that a consumer report may be obtained by the employer.
- Obtain prior written consumer authorization in order to obtain a consumer report. Authorization to access reports during the term of employment may be obtained at the time of employment.
- Certify to the CRA that the above steps have been followed, that the information being obtained will not be used in violation of any federal or state equal opportunity law or regulation, and that, if any adverse action is to be taken based on the consumer report, a copy of the report and a summary of the consumer's rights will be provided to the consumer.
- Before taking an adverse action, provide a copy of the report to the consumer as well as the summary of the consumer's rights. The user should receive this summary from the CRA. An adverse action notice should be sent after the adverse action is taken.

An adverse action notice also is required in employment situations if credit information (other than transactions and experience data) obtained from an affiliate is used to deny employment.[34]

9.1.6 Special Procedures for Investigations of Suspected Misconduct by Employees

The FCRA provides special procedures for investigations of suspected misconduct by an employee or for compliance with federal, state or local laws and regulations or the rules of a self-regulatory organization, and compliance with written policies of the employer. These investigations are not treated as consumer reports as long as (1) the employer or its agent complies with the procedures set forth in the act, (2) no credit information is used, and (3) a summary describing the nature and scope of the inquiry is provided to the employee if an adverse action is taken based on the investigation.[35]

9.1.7 Investigative Consumer Reports

Investigative consumer reports contain information about a consumer's character, general reputation, personal characteristics, and mode of living. This information is obtained through personal interviews by an entity or person that is a CRA.

Consumers who are the subjects of such reports are given special rights under the FCRA. If a user intends to obtain an investigative consumer report, Section 606 of the FCRA requires that the user of the report disclose its use to the consumer. The disclosure is subject to the following requirements:

- The consumer must be informed that an investigative consumer report may be obtained.
- The disclosure must be in writing and must be mailed or otherwise delivered to the consumer some time before but not later than five days after the date on which the report was first requested.
- The disclosure must include a statement informing the consumer of their right to request additional disclosures of the nature and scope of the investigation, and the summary of consumer rights required by the FCRA. The summary of consumer rights will be provided by the CRA that conducts the investigation.
- The user must certify to the CRA that the required disclosures have been made and that the user will make the necessary disclosure to the consumer.
- Upon written request of a consumer made within a reasonable period of time after the required disclosures, the user must make a complete disclosure of the nature and scope of the investigation.
- The nature and scope disclosure must be made in a written statement that is mailed or otherwise delivered to the consumer no later than five days after the date on which the request was received from the consumer or the report was first requested, whichever is later.[36]

9.1.8 Medical Information Under FCRA

FCRA limits the use of medical information obtained from CRAs, other than payment information that appears in a coded form and does not identify the medical provider.[37] If medical information is to be used for an insurance transaction, the consumer must provide consent to the user of the report, or the information must be coded. If the report is to be used for employment purposes—or in connection with a credit transaction, except as provided in regulations issued by the banking and credit union regulators—the consumer must provide specific written consent and the medical information must be relevant. Any user who receives medical information shall not disclose the information to any other person, except where necessary to carry out the purpose for which the information was disclosed, or as permitted by statute, regulation, or order.[38]

9.1.9 Prescreened Lists

FCRA permits creditors and insurers to obtain limited consumer report information for use in connection with firm unsolicited offers of credit or insurance, under certain circumstances and conditions. This practice is known as prescreening and typically involves obtaining from a CRA a list of consumers who meet certain preestablished criteria. If any user intends to use prescreened lists, that user must: (1) before the offer is made, establish the criteria that will be relied upon to make the offer and grant credit or insurance, and (2) maintain such criteria on file for a three-year period beginning on the date on which the offer is made to each consumer. In addition, any user must include with each written solicitation a clear and conspicuous statement that states:

- Information contained in a consumer's CRA file was used in connection with the transaction.
- The consumer received the offer because they satisfied the criteria for creditworthiness or insurability used to screen for the offer.
- Credit or insurance may not be extended if, after the consumer responds, it is determined that the consumer does not meet the criteria used for screening or any applicable criteria bearing on creditworthiness or insurability, or the consumer does not furnish required collateral.

- The consumer may prohibit the use of information in their file in connection with future prescreened offers of credit or insurance by contacting the notification system established by the CRA that provided the report. The statement must include the address and toll-free telephone number of the appropriate notification system.

Beginning in 2005, the companies that send prescreened solicitations of credit or insurance were required to supply simple and easy-to-understand notices explaining the consumer's right to opt out of receiving such offers.[39] The FTC issued a rule requiring a layered notice with opt-out rights included on the first page. The FTC also issued a new consumer education brochure concerning prescreening.[40]

9.1.10 Enforcement of the FCRA

Enforcement of the FCRA is available through dispute resolution, private litigation, and government actions.[41] The dispute resolution infrastructure permits the consumer to fill a request with the CRA to dispute the accuracy of information and then requires the CRA to investigate the consumer's complaint.[42] If consumers are not satisfied with the dispute resolution process, the individuals have a private right of action, with recent trends including consumers becoming involved in class actions lawsuits.[43] Noncompliance with the FCRA can lead to civil and criminal penalties. In addition to actual damages, violators are subject to statutory damages of a maximum of $1,000 per violation, and a maximum penalty of $4,705 per willful violation.[44] An officer or employee of a CRA who, both knowingly and willingly, provides information concerning an individual from the company's files to someone who is not authorized to receive that information can face criminal penalties and imprisonment.[45]

Government enforcement actions for violations of the FCRA can be brought by the FTC, the CFPB, and state attorneys general.[46] At the federal level, both the FTC and the CFPB share responsibility to enforce the FCRA.[47] Since 1996, state attorneys general have had concurrent enforcement authority with regard to the FCRA.[48] The state attorneys general are required to give notice to the FTC prior to filing suit, and the FTC retains the authority to intervene in the cases brought by the state attorneys general.[49]

An example of FTC enforcement is the 2014 settlement against TeleCheck Services, one of the nation's largest check authorization service companies, for claims that the company failed to follow dispute procedures. The company agreed to pay to a $3.5 million civil penalty.[50] The settlement was part of a broader initiative by the FTC to target the practices of data brokers that sell information to companies making decisions about consumers.[51] In the FTC's first FCRA case involving automated background screening practices, RealPage agreed to pay a $3 million civil penalty in 2018 for claims that the company failed to take reasonable steps to ensure the accuracy of consumer reports.[52]

An example of CFPB enforcement against CRAs is the 2015 case of Clarity Services. The CFPB alleged that the company failed to properly investigate consumers who attempted to dispute information on their credit reports and obtained credit reports without a permissible purpose. As a result, Clarity Services agreed to pay an $8 million civil penalty.[53]

CFPB has also enforced obligations of data furnishers.[54] In 2017, JPMorgan Chase agreed to a settlement where it paid a civil penalty of $4.6 million related to claims that the company failed to have in place reasonable written policies concerning the accuracy of information that it provided to certain CRAs as well as that the company failed to provide consumers with results of investigations where the consumers disputed accuracy of information directly with JPMorgan Chase.[55]

Actions by state attorneys general can be brought by individual states or collectively by multiple states.[56] An example from 2015 involved more than 30 state attorneys general offices that entered into a settlement with Equifax, Experian, and TransUnion, the three main consumer reporting agencies. The settlement related to claims concerning credit report errors, monitoring of data furnishers, and marketing of credit monitoring products to consumers. These companies agreed to pay the participating states $6 million and to adjust their business practices.[57]

9.2 The Fair and Accurate Credit Transactions Act

In 2003, Congress passed FACTA, which made substantial amendments to the FCRA.[58] Under FACTA, stricter state laws are preempted in most areas, although states retain some powers to enact laws addressing identity theft.[59] In addition, FACTA specifically identified certain state laws that would remain in effect. With regard to credit scores, state laws in California and Colorado, as well as state insurance laws regulating the use by insurers of credit-based insurance scores, remain in effect.[60] Pertaining to frequency of free credit reports, the federal law permitted state laws in Colorado, Georgia, Maine, Maryland, Massachusetts, New Jersey, and Vermont to remain in effect.[61]

FACTA enacted a number of consumer protections. It required truncation of credit and debit card numbers, so that receipts do not reveal the full credit or debit card number. It gave consumers new rights to an explanation of their credit scores. It also gave individuals the right to request a free annual credit report from each of the three national consumer credit agencies—Equifax, Experian and TransUnion. Along with other identity theft protections, FACTA required regulators to promulgate a Disposal Rule and a Red Flags Rule.

In 2010, the FTC issued new rules updating the manner of disclosure required by the companies advertising free credit reports.[62] The updates "include prominent disclosures designed to prevent consumers from confusing these 'free' offers with the federally mandated free annual file disclosures." Such a disclosure must be "easily readable," and the rules give examples of fonts that are—and are not—easily readable. As of 2011, the CFPB took over rulemaking authority in this area.[63]

9.2.1 The Disposal Rule

The Disposal Rule requires any individual or entity that uses a consumer report—or information derived from a consumer report—for a business purpose to dispose of that consumer information in a way that prevents unauthorized access and misuse of the data. Consumer reports can be electronic or written. The rule applies to both small and large organizations, including consumer reporting agencies, lenders, employers, insurers, landlords, car dealers, attorneys, debt collectors, and government agencies.

"Disposal" includes any discarding, abandonment, donation, sale, or transfer of information. The standard for disposal requires practices that are "reasonable" to protect against unauthorized access to or use of the consumer data. Factors to consider include the sensitivity of information being disposed of, the costs and benefits of various disposal methods, and available technology.[64] Examples of acceptable, reasonable measures include:

- Burn, pulverize or shred papers containing consumer report information so that the information cannot be read or reconstructed
- Destroy or erase electronic files or media containing consumer report information so that the information cannot be read or reconstructed
- Conduct due diligence and hire a document destruction contractor to dispose of material specifically identified as consumer report information consistent with the rule

Enforcement of the Disposal Rule is by the FTC, the federal banking regulators, and the CFPB. Violators may face civil liability as well as federal and state enforcement actions. Financial institutions that are subject to both the FACTA Disposal Rule and the GLBA Safeguards Rule (discussed in Section 9.3) should incorporate required disposal practices into the information security program that the Safeguards Rule mandates. They should also be aware of any state disposal rules that may impose further requirements.

9.2.2 The Red Flags Rule

The Red Flags Rule was originally promulgated under FACTA, which required agencies that regulate financial entities to develop a set of rules to mandate the detection, prevention, and mitigation of identity theft. The FTC, together with federal banking agencies, authored the Red Flags Rule.[65] As with the rest of the FCRA and FACTA, the CFPB has now gained rulemaking and enforcement authority.

The rule requires certain financial entities to develop and implement written identity theft detection programs that can identify and respond to the "red flags" that signal identity theft. Specifically, the rule applies to financial institutions and creditors. "Financial institution" is defined as all banks, savings and loan associations, and credit unions. It also includes all other entities that hold a transaction account belonging to a consumer. Due to confusion over which entities qualify as covered creditors, however, enforcement of the rule was delayed several times until a clarification was published in 2010.[66]

The Red Flag Program Clarification Act of 2010 was passed in response to concern that the definition of creditor extended to implicate unintended entities, such as attorneys and health providers, simply because they allow customers to pay their bills after the time of service.[67] The clarification narrows the previously broad definition of creditor, as well as the circumstances under which they are covered by the rule. It eliminates entities that extend credit only "for expenses incidental to a service." The rule still applies to entities that, regularly and in the course of business:

- Obtain or use consumer reports in connection with a credit transaction
- Furnish information to consumer reporting agencies in connection with a credit transaction
- Advance funds to or on behalf of someone, except for expenses incidental to a service provided by the creditor to that person[68]

The new law also authorizes regulations that apply the rule to businesses with accounts that should be "subject to a reasonably foreseeable risk of identity theft." The rule does not provide a checklist for specific red flags that must be included in the identity theft detection programs. Rather, the program should generally identify relevant patterns, practices, and specific forms of activity that are red flags of possible identity theft, incorporate these flags into the program, and update the program regularly to reflect changes in risks. Each organization is required to develop its own list of red flags, but examples cited by the FTC include alerts, notifications, or warnings from a consumer reporting agency; suspicious identification documents; suspicious personal identifying data; and unusual use of a covered account.

9.3 Gramm-Leach-Bliley Act

Title V of the Financial Services Modernization Act of 1999 led to the promulgation of both a Privacy Rule and a Safeguards Rule.[69] GLBA was major legislation that reflected and codified the consolidation of the U.S. banking, securities, and insurance industries in the late 1990s. As previously separate types of financial institutions began to merge, substantial concerns arose over how consumer data would be collected, used, and shared among the newly formed holding companies and their subsidiaries within the financial sector.

These privacy provisions were spurred by enforcement actions against major banks for controversial data practices. Prior to GLBA's passage, some leading financial institutions were found to have shared detailed customer information, including account numbers and other highly sensitive data, with telemarketing firms. Subsequently, the firms used the account numbers to charge customers for unsolicited services.

One of the most prominent cases involved U.S. Bancorp and the telemarketing firm MemberWorks.[70] The Minnesota attorney general's office brought suit in 1999, when Congress was considering GLBA. The suit resulted in a $3 million settlement for allegations that the bank had sent detailed customer information to the telemarketing firm, including account numbers and related information that enabled the marketer to directly withdraw funds from the customer account.[71]

The U.S. Bancorp/MemberWorks case focused popular and regulatory attention on the prevalence of data-sharing relationships between banks and third-party marketers. A group of 25 attorneys general brought additional actions against major financial institutions in an attempt to address these practices. Congress responded to these events by including significant privacy and security protections for consumers in GLBA and mandating further rulemaking on privacy and security by the FTC, federal banking regulators, and state insurance regulators. Financial institutions were required to substantially comply with GLBA's requirements in 2001.

The passage of GLBA led to major changes in the structure of the financial services industry and provided for the creation of new financial service holding companies that offer a full range of financial products. It eliminated legal barriers to affiliations among banks, securities firms, insurance companies, and other financial services companies. Under GLBA's privacy provisions, financial institutions are required to:

- Store personal financial information in a secure manner
- Provide notice of their policies regarding the sharing of personal financial information
- Provide consumers with the choice to opt out of sharing some personal financial information

In this discussion of financial data, it is important to note that technology has changed the interaction between customers and banks. Customers no longer need to travel to brick-and-mortar buildings or even interact with the personnel employed by these banks to withdraw money, deposit checks, or apply for loans. In 2000, the Electronic Signatures in Global and National Commerce Act ("E-Sign Act") permitted customers to opt in to online banking.[72] Online banking allows customers to access bank accounts through the internet, and mobile banking permits customers to engage in financial activities with their banks through the use of their cellphones.[73] By 2021, approximately 70 percent of Americans report that they most often access their bank accounts by online or mobile banking.[74]

9.3.1 Scope and Enforcement of GLBA

GLBA applies to financial institutions, which are defined broadly as any U.S. company that is "significantly engaged" in financial activities. Financial institutions include entities such as banks, insurance providers, securities firms, payment settlement services, check-cashing services, credit counselors, and mortgage lenders.

GLBA regulates financial institution management of nonpublic personal information, defined as "personally identifiable financial information (i) provided by a consumer to a financial institution, (ii) resulting from a transaction or service performed for the consumer, or (iii) otherwise obtained by the financial institution." Excluded from the definition are publicly available information and any consumer list that is derived without using personally identifiable financial information.[75]

This encompasses a wide range of information that is not exclusively financial in nature. For example, the name of a financial institution's customer is considered nonpublic personal financial information and is covered under the act because it indicates the existence of a relationship between the institution and the consumer that is financial in nature.

GLBA requires financial institutions to protect consumers' nonpublic personal information under privacy rules that were promulgated originally by the FTC and financial institution (FI) regulators. In 2011, with the passage of the Dodd-Frank Act, the CFPB assumed this rulemaking power, with exceptions for the Securities and Exchange Commission (SEC) and the Commodity Futures Trading Commission (CFTC).

As enacted in 1999, federal financial regulators enforced GLBA for the institutions in their jurisdiction, such as for the Federal Reserve, Office of the Comptroller of the Currency, Federal Deposit Insurance Corporation (FDIC), and SEC.[76] Under GLBA, financial institutions can face civil penalties up to $100,000 per violation. Officers and directors of these financial institutions can face personal liability of up to $10,000 per violation. For intentional violations, owners and directors can face criminal penalties and imprisonment.[77] Banking and related financial institutions that fail to comply with GLBA requirements can also be subject to substantial penalties under the Financial Institutions Reform, Recovery, and Enforcement Act (FIRREA). FIRREA penalties range from up to $5,500 for violations of laws and regulations to a maximum of $27,500 if violations are unsafe, unsound, or reckless; and to as much as $1.1 million for "knowing" violations.[78] For financial institutions not within the jurisdiction of one of the other agencies, the FTC originally had enforcement authority. Under the Dodd-Frank Act, the CFPB also now has enforcement authority for the GLBA Privacy and Safeguards Rules under its general enforcement powers, discussed further in the next two sections.

At the state level, state attorneys general can enforce GLBA. Stricter state laws are not preempted under GLBA.[79] The validity of stricter state laws, however, can be subject to challenge because there is limited preemption under FCRA, so courts would need to determine which federal financial privacy statute governs for a particular state law. Although there is no private right of action under GLBA, failure to comply with certain notice requirements may be considered a deceptive trade practice by state and federal authorities. Some states also have private rights of action for this type of violation.

GLBA's privacy protections generally apply to consumers, or individuals who obtain financial products or services from a financial institution to be used primarily for personal, family, or household purposes. Many of the act's requirements relate to the subset of consumers who are also "customers"—consumers with whom the organization has an ongoing relationship. Financial services companies that do not have such "consumer customers" are not subject to some of GLBA's requirements, such as those related to notice.

Major components of the GLBA Privacy Rule provide that financial institutions must:

- Prepare and provide to customers clear and conspicuous notice of the financial institution's information-sharing policies and practices. These notices must be provided when a customer relationship is established and annually thereafter.
- Clearly provide customers the right to opt out of having their nonpublic personal information shared with nonaffiliated third parties (subject to significant exceptions, including for joint marketing and processing of consumer transactions).
- Refrain from disclosing to any nonaffiliated third-party marketer, other than a consumer reporting agency, an account number or similar form of access code to a consumer's credit card, deposit or transaction account.
- Comply with regulatory standards established by certain government authorities to protect the security and confidentiality of customer records and information, and protect against security threats and unauthorized access to or certain uses of such records or information.

9.3.2 The GLBA Privacy Rule

The GLBA Privacy Rule establishes a standard for privacy notices under which a financial institution must provide initial and annual privacy notices to consumers on specific categories of information and must process opt-outs within 30 days.[80] The privacy notice itself must be a clear, conspicuous and accurate statement of the company's privacy practices and must include:

- What information the financial institution collects about its consumers and customers
- With whom it shares the information
- How it protects or safeguards the information

- An explanation of how a consumer may opt out of having their information shared through a reasonable opt-out process[81]

Provided this notice standard is met, a financial institution may share any information it has with its affiliated companies and joint marketing partners, which are other financial institutions with whom the entity jointly markets a financial product or service.[82] In addition, other than for defined exceptions, a financial institution may also share consumer information with nonaffiliated companies and other third parties, but only after disclosing information-sharing practices to customers and providing them with the opportunity to opt out.

It should be noted that the GLBA prohibits financial institutions from disclosing consumer account numbers to nonaffiliated companies for purposes of telemarketing and direct mail marketing (including through email), even if the consumer has not opted out of sharing the information for marketing purposes. Also, a financial institution must ensure that service providers will not use provided consumer data for anything other than the intended purpose.

There are certain situations in which the consumer has no right to opt out. For example, a consumer cannot opt out if:

- A financial institution shares information with outside companies that provide essential services like data processing or servicing accounts
- The disclosure is legally required
- A financial institution shares customer data with outside service providers that market the financial company's products or services

In 2009, eight federal regulatory agencies issued a model short privacy notice.[83] The model notice implemented the Financial Services Regulatory Relief Act (FSRRA) of 2006, which requires the agencies to propose a succinct and comprehensible model form that allows consumers to easily compare the privacy practices of different financial institutions.[84] Financial institutions that use the model notice satisfy the disclosure requirements for notices, but they are not required to use it.

9.3.3 The GLBA Safeguards Rule

Along with privacy standards and rules, GLBA requires financial institutions to maintain security controls to protect the confidentiality and integrity of personal consumer information, including both electronic and paper records. The regulatory agencies established such standards in the form of a final rule, the Safeguards Rule, which became effective in 2003 and was most recently updated by the FTC in 2021.[85]

The GLBA Safeguards Rule requires financial institutions to develop and implement a comprehensive information security program, which is defined as a program that contains "administrative, technical and physical safeguards" to protect the security, confidentiality, and integrity of customer information.[86] The program must be appropriate for the size, complexity, nature, and scope of the activities of the institution. Thus, like the GLBA Privacy Rule, the Safeguards Rule distinguishes the concepts of security, confidentiality, and integrity but suggests that all three concepts are integral to a complete understanding of security.

The information security program required under the rule must contain certain elements, including a designated employee to coordinate the program, audit systems to determine risk, and certain procedures to take with service providers to ensure that the security of the information is maintained.

Under the GLBA Safeguards Rule, a financial institution must provide the following three levels of security for consumer information:

- **Administrative security**, which includes program definition, management of workforce risks, employee training, and vendor oversight
- **Technical security**, which covers computer systems, networks, and applications in addition to access controls and encryption
- **Physical security**, which includes facilities, environmental safeguards, business continuity, and disaster recovery

Pursuant to the Safeguards Rule, the administrative, technical, and physical safeguards to be implemented must be reasonably designed to (1) ensure the security and confidentiality of customer information, (2) protect against any anticipated threats or hazards to the security or integrity of the information, and (3) protect against unauthorized access to or use of the information that could result in substantial harm or inconvenience to any customer.[87] Maintaining the security of this information essentially means protecting the confidentiality and integrity of information as well as restricting access to it.

The Safeguards Rule does allow for flexibility in implementing a security program. It states that the program must contain safeguards that are "appropriate" to the entity's size and complexity, the nature and scope of the entity's activities, and the sensitivity of any customer information at issue.[88]

The Safeguards Rule requires that certain basic elements be included in a security program. Each institution must:

- Designate an employee to coordinate the safeguards
- Identify and make a written assessment of the risks to customer information in each relevant area of the company's operation and evaluate the effectiveness of the current safeguards for controlling those risks
- Design and implement a safeguard program and regularly monitor and test it
- Select appropriate service providers and enter into agreements with them to implement safeguards
- Evaluate and adjust the program in light of relevant circumstances, including changes in business arrangements or operations, or the results of testing and monitoring of safeguards[89]

With this discussion of security, it is worth pointing out that digital approaches to banking leave customers' financial data susceptible to the vulnerabilities of the technologies at issue: internet-connected computers and cellphones.[90] Methods to address concerns regarding online banking and mobile banking require a combination of measures by the financial institution (such as careful design and updating of the relevant software) and education of the individual consumer, with steps including carefully choosing an operating system; selecting an appropriate internet browser; using firewalls, antivirus programs, and anti-malware programs; and employing strong passwords and encryption.[91] A similar combination of enterprise-side and user-side practices are important to addressing security and privacy concerns for mobile banking.[92] Practitioners should make sure to take into account these online banking and mobile banking concerns when designing programs to comply with the Safeguards Rule.

9.3.4 State Requirements Related to Financial Privacy and Security

Because GLBA does not preempt states from regulating in this area, numerous states have put in place laws or rules specifically focused on financial privacy and security.[93] These states notably include both California and New York.

9.3.4.1 California

The California Financial Information Privacy Act (CFIPA), also known as California SB-1, expands the financial privacy protections afforded under GLBA.[94] CFIPA increases the disclosure requirements of financial institutions and grants consumers increased rights with regard to the sharing of information. Violation of CFIPA in cases of negligent noncompliance can be punished with statutory damages of $2,500 per consumer up to a cap of $500,000 per occurrence. In cases of willful noncompliance, there is no $500,000 damage cap.

Under the legislation, opt-in and opt-out requirements exist for financial institutions as follows: written opt-in consent is required for a financial institution to share personal information with nonaffiliated third parties. Opt-in provisions must be presented on a form titled "Important Privacy Choices for Consumers" and be written in simple English. Additionally, CFIPA grants consumers the ability to opt out of information sharing between their financial institutions and affiliates not in the same line of business. A financial institution does not, however, need to obtain consumer consent in order to share nonmedical information with its wholly owned subsidiaries engaged in the same line of business—insurance, banking or securities—if they are regulated by the same functional regulator.

With the passage of the California Consumer Privacy Act (CCPA) and the California Privacy Rights Act (CPRA), banks and other financial institutions will likely need to review their practices for compliance with the privacy and security requirements of that law.[95] Although the CCPA and the CPRA include a specific provision that intends to avoid conflict with GLBA and CFIPA, experts caution that banks and other financial institutions will need to review their data, dataset by dataset, to determine whether it is covered by GLBA or CFIPA. The concern is that the exemption applies to datasets, and not more generally to the organization that holds that dataset—meaning only the data specifically covered by GLBA or CFIPA will be exempt from the requirements of the CCPA.[96]

9.3.4.2 New York

In 2017, the New York Department of Financial Services (NYDFS) put in place comprehensive and strict cybersecurity regulations for its vast financial industry.[97] Although entities covered by GLBA are already subject to these types of requirements, the New York regulations were the first state-level regulation that went far beyond the requirements of GLBA at the time of implementation.[98]

The New York state financial regulations impose cybersecurity mandates on all covered financial institutions. Covered institutions include state-chartered banks, credit unions, investment companies, licensed lenders, mortgage brokers, life insurance companies, private bankers, commercial banks, and savings and loan associates.[99]

These regulations are in line with the provisions of the National Institute of Standards and Technology (NIST) Cybersecurity Framework.[100] Under the regulations, covered financial institutions are required to implement cybersecurity programs with the following: risk assessments, documentation of security policies, designation of a chief information security officer, limitations on data retention, incident response plan, and audit trails.[101]

For entities already subject to GLBA, it is worth noting several distinctions between the federal law and the New York requirements. The state regulations define nonpublic information more broadly than GLBA's designation of personally identifiable financial information. In addition, the New York regulations have key requirements *not* included in GLBA related to the following topics: personnel, reporting obligations, documentation obligations, and third-party service providers.[102]

It is worth noting that the NYDFS also began regulating virtual currencies in 2015 via its BitLicense regulation. Individuals or businesses that receive, transmit, control, administer, issue, exchange, or maintain custody of virtual currencies must obtain a BitLicense before engaging in these and related activities.[103]

The NYDFS also specifies which virtual currencies licensed individuals and businesses can offer to their customers. As of April 2023, there are 33 virtual currency coins on the NYDFS "Greenlist" which permit any licensed business to use these coins for their approved purpose, i.e., to maintain custody of or to list on their platform.[104] If licensed businesses have an approved coin-listing policy, they may also self-certify that proposed adoption or listing of new coins complies with NYDFS requirements. This allows individuals and businesses to offer new coins to their customers without undergoing a more in-depth review from the NYDFS.[105]

9.4 Dodd-Frank Wall Street Reform and Consumer Protection Act

In response to the financial crisis that became acute in 2008, Congress enacted the Dodd-Frank Act, which was signed into law in June 2010. Along with numerous other reforms, Title X of the act created the CFPB as an independent bureau within the Federal Reserve.

The CFPB oversees the relationship between consumers and providers of financial products and services. It holds broad authority to examine, write regulations, and bring enforcement actions concerning businesses that provide financial products or services, including service providers.[106] The

CFPB has assumed rulemaking authority for specific existing laws related to financial privacy and other consumer issues, such as the FCRA, GLBA, and Fair Debt Collection Practices Act.[107] It has enforcement authority over all nondepository financial institutions, and over all depository institutions with more than $10 billion in assets.[108] For depository institutions with assets of $10 billion or less, CFPB promulgates rules, but enforcement power remains with banking regulators.[109]

One potentially important innovation in the act is a change in the usual language about "unfair and deceptive" acts or practices. As discussed in multiple places in this book, the FTC and state attorneys general have long had the power to enforce against unfair and deceptive acts and practices. The CFPB also can bring enforcement actions for unfairness and deception. In addition, the CFPB has power to enforce against "abusive acts and practices." An abusive act or practice:

- *Materially interferes with the ability of a consumer to understand a term or condition of a consumer financial product or service or*
- *Takes unreasonable advantage of*
    - *A lack of understanding on the part of the consumer of the material risks, costs, or conditions of the product or service;*
    - *The inability of the consumer to protect its interests in selecting or using a consumer financial product or service; or*
    - *The reasonable reliance by the consumer on a covered person to act in the interests of the consumer.*[110]

Because this is relatively new statutory language, the precise meaning of "abusive act or practice" will only become known over time. By its terms, however, enforcement actions for abusive acts or practices may well apply to privacy notices and other aspects of privacy and security protections by financial institutions.

CFPB enforcement authority includes the ability to conduct investigations and issue subpoenas, hold hearings, and commence civil actions against offenders.[111] As of the writing of this book, civil penalties vary from $6,813 per day for federal consumer privacy law violations to $34,065 per day for reckless violations and $1,362,567 for knowing violations.[112] Further, state attorneys general are also authorized to bring civil actions in enforcement of the law or regulations.[113]

9.5 Regulation E of the Electronic Fund Transfer Act (1978)

In 1978, the Electronic Fund Transfer Act (EFTA) was enacted to establish rights of consumers as well as the responsibilities of companies involved in electronic fund transfers. The rule known as Regulation E implements the EFTA. In 2011, the rulemaking authority for EFTA was transferred from the Federal Reserve Board to the CFPB pursuant to the Dodd-Frank Wall Street Reform and Consumer Protection Act.[114]

The term electronic fund transfer (EFT) is defined as any transfer of funds that is initiated through an electronic terminal, telephone, computer, or magnetic tape for the purpose of ordering, instructing, or authorizing a financial institution to debit or credit a consumer's account.[115] Examples include ATM transfers, direct deposits, point-of-sale transfers, and transfers using a debit card.

The definition of a "financial institution" includes:

- Banks, savings associations, credit unions
- Any person that directly or indirectly holds an account belonging to a consumer
- Any person that issues an access device and agrees with a consumer to provide EFT services[116]

In 2021, CFPB issued guidance that Regulation E covered person-to-person payments when they met the definition of EFT, such as those made using companies like Zelle and Venmo. CFPB clarified that unauthorized EFTs are the responsibility of the financial institution, not the consumer.[117] The CFPB issued this clarification in part because of the significant amount of fraud that consumers have fallen victim to using person-to-person payments such as mobile financial apps.[118]

9.6 Required Disclosure Under Anti-Money-Laundering Laws

The privacy and security rules discussed prior typically restrict uses and disclosures of personal information. Financial institutions are also subject to a variety of requirements to retain records and, in some instances, disclose personal financial information to the government. Financial institutions in general have intricate accounting and control systems to document transactions and reduce the risk of fraud. Banks have also long been closely supervised by the government to ensure the safety and soundness of the banks and for other reasons. Financial institutions thus have more detailed record retention rules than most other kinds of companies.

In recent decades, anti-money-laundering laws have become a major additional basis for record retention and mandatory disclosure to the government. U.S. anti-money-laundering laws stem from the Bank Secrecy Act (BSA) of 1970, which targeted organized crime groups and others who used large cash transactions. The laws became stricter as part of the USA PATRIOT Act of 2001, with its focus on antiterrorism efforts. The fundamental goal of anti-money-laundering laws is to "follow the money," per the Financial Crimes Enforcement Network (FinCEN) under the Department of Treasury.[119] The idea of thorough recordkeeping is that it will help detect and deter illegal activity and provide evidence for proving illegality.[120]

Fines for violations of anti-money laundering laws can be significant. In 2022, the Office of the Comptroller of Currency (OCC) and FinCEN issued civil penalties totaling $200 million against a federal savings bank for willfully failing to comply with anti-money-laundering requirements.[121]

9.6.1 The Bank Secrecy Act of 1970

The BSA, also known as the Currency and Foreign Transaction Reporting Act of 1970, authorizes the U.S. treasury secretary to issue regulations that impose extensive recordkeeping and reporting requirements on financial institutions.[122] Specifically, financial institutions must keep records and file reports on certain financial transactions, including currency transactions in excess of $10,000, which may be relevant to criminal, tax, or regulatory proceedings.

The BSA applies broadly to its own definition of financial institutions, which uses different language than GLBA and so may differ in some cases. The BSA applies to banks, securities brokers and dealers, money services businesses, telegraph companies, casinos, card clubs, and other entities subject to supervision by any state or federal bank supervisory authority.[123] The scope of covered institutions has expanded over time to address the problem that criminals have an incentive to exploit whatever institutions are not already covered by the anti-money-laundering laws.

Under the BSA, financial institutions that handle cryptocurrencies are frequently classified as money service businesses. This includes institutions that provide peer-to-peer exchanges, hosted wallet providers, as well as anonymizing service providers like mixers and tumblers. However, some cryptocurrency-related business models may be exempt from the BSA such as decentralized exchanges and mining pools.[124]

The BSA contains regulations relating to currency transactions, transportation of monetary instruments, and the purchase of currency-like instruments. For example, the BSA generally requires currency transactions of $10,000 or more to be reported to the IRS per the regulations, using a Currency Transaction Report, Form 4789. Similarly, the BSA regulations cover purchases of bank checks, drafts, cashier's checks, money orders, traveler's checks, and cryptocurrency transactions of $3,000 or more in currency. The rules require that the entity collect and report information, including the name, address, and Social Security number of the purchaser; the date of purchase; type of instrument; and serial numbers and dollar amounts of the instruments.

The BSA regulates certain wire transfers, including funds transfers and transmittals of funds by financial institutions. Certain funds transfers are exempted from the regulation, however, including funds transfers governed by the EFTA and those made through an automated clearinghouse, ATM, or point-of-sale system.

9.6.1.1 Record Retention Requirements

As part of the overall anti-money-laundering strategy, financial institutions are required to retain categories of records for use in investigations or enforcement actions. Financial institutions are required to maintain records of all extensions of credit in excess of $10,000, but this does not include credit secured by real property. Not all records must be maintained—only those with a "high degree of usefulness."[125] Records that are maintained must include the borrower's name and address, credit amount, purpose of credit, and date of credit. Such records must be maintained for five years.

As to deposit account records, a financial institution must keep the depositor's taxpayer identification number, signature cards, and checks exceeding $100 that are drawn or issued and payable by the bank. With regard to certificates of deposit (CD), the financial institution must obtain the customer name and address, a description of the CD, and the date of the transaction. For wire transfers or direct deposits, a financial institution must maintain all deposit slips or credit tickets for transactions exceeding $100.[126] Additionally, the BSA includes detailed rules regarding information that banks must retain in connection with payment orders.

9.6.1.2 Suspicious Activity Reports

Financial institutions must file a suspicious activity report (SAR) in defined situations. The rationale is that SARs can alert government agencies to potentially suspicious transactions. A SAR must be filed with FinCEN in the following circumstances:

- When a financial institution suspects that an insider is committing (or aiding the commission of) a crime, regardless of dollar amount
- When the entity detects a possible crime involving $5,000 or more and has a substantial basis for identifying a suspect
- When the entity detects a possible crime involving $25,000 or more (even if it has no substantial basis for identifying a suspect)
- When the entity suspects currency transactions aggregating $5,000 or more that involve potential money laundering or a violation of the act[127]

9.6.1.3 BSA Enforcement

As of the writing of this book, penalties for violations of the BSA and its regulations include the following: civil penalties, including fines up to the greater of $25,000 or the amount of the transaction (up to a $100,000 maximum) as well as penalties for negligence ($500 per violation); additional penalties up to $5,000 per day for failure to comply with regulations; penalties of up to $25,000 per day for failure to comply with the information-sharing requirements of the USA PATRIOT Act; and penalties up to $1 million against financial institutions that fail to comply with due diligence requirements. Criminal penalties include up to a $100,000 fine and/or one-year imprisonment and up to a $10,000 fine and/or five-year imprisonment.[128]

While countless enforcement actions have been taken against traditional financial institutions, these potential penalties also extend to financial institutions offering cryptocurrency-related services. In 2020 a $60 million civil penalty was levied against the founder of two cryptocurrency mixers and in 2021 the operator of the longest-running cryptocurrency mixer was arrested for failing to satisfy their obligations under the BSA.[129]

9.6.2 The International Money-Laundering Abatement and Anti-Terrorist Financing Act of 2001

As part of the USA PATRIOT Act, the International Money Laundering Abatement and Anti-Terrorist Financing Act of 2001 expanded the reach of the BSA and made other significant changes to U.S. anti-money-laundering laws.[130] The act gave the U.S. treasury secretary the ability to promulgate broad rules to implement modified Know Your Customer (KYC) requirements and to otherwise deter money laundering.

For covered financial services companies, the major USA PATRIOT Act compliance issues can be grouped into the following categories:

- Information-sharing regulations and participation in the cooperative efforts to deter money laundering, as required by Section 314
- Know Your Customer rules, including the identification of beneficial owners of accounts—procedures required by Section 326
- Development and implementation of formal money-laundering programs as required by Section 352
- Bank Secrecy Act expansions, including new reporting and recordkeeping requirements for different industries (such as broker-dealers) and currency transactions[131]

Going forward, privacy professionals in the financial services sector should be alert to the continuing development of documentation requirements, where the organization may be required to gather and retain personally identifiable information for regulatory purposes.

For example, the Foreign Account Tax Compliance Act of 2010 (FATCA) seeks to target noncompliance with U.S. tax laws for U.S. taxpayers with foreign accounts. To deter tax evasion and require greater withholding of income to these taxpayers, FATCA requires more detailed KYC documentation for both domestic and foreign financial institutions.[132]

More recently, the Anti-Money Laundering Act of 2020 (AML Act) brings the most comprehensive changes to anti-money-laundering regulations since the USA PATRIOT Act. The changes include expanding key definitions to explicitly include virtual currencies in the scope of the BSA, updating whistleblower incentives and protections, and extending subpoena authority for foreign banks with U.S. correspondent accounts.[133]

9.7 Future of Financial Regulation

Cryptocurrencies have gained popularity in part because they are associated with privacy and anonymity. Going forward, the extent of such privacy protections will depend on whether governments adopt a high- or low-regulation approach to cryptocurrencies.[134] If there is a relatively low amount of regulation, then the extent of privacy and anonymity in financial transactions will depend in part of market factors—what degree of privacy exists in the most popular cryptocurrencies. The degree of privacy will also depend in part on technological factors, such as how robust a cryptocurrency is against attack. Even where a cryptocurrency claims to protect privacy, anonymity may not exist in practice, as shown by law enforcement actions that successfully recovered illicit cryptocurrency payments.[135]

Governments may also apply a high level of regulation to cryptocurrencies. Law enforcement agencies fear that anonymous cryptocurrencies will be used to enable ransomware, money laundering, financial sanctions evasion, and other criminal activities. To address such concerns, governments may make it expensive or illegal to convert from a cryptocurrency to the national currency, such as by prohibiting payments in cryptocurrencies to banks and other significant economic actors. Second, governments may issue and support a government-based cryptocurrency.

By 2021, both Japan and China outlawed anonymous cryptocurrencies.[136] China's online currency, known as digital yuan, has few privacy protections.[137] In conclusion, although there has been widespread support for cryptocurrencies due to their potential for privacy protection, it is far from clear that such privacy will actually occur in practice.

9.8 Conclusion

Financial institutions are subject to a wide range of government regulations. The FCRA in 1970 was the first major national data privacy law in the United States, applying notably to consumer reporting agencies, extensions of credit, and purchases of insurance. The overhaul of the financial system in GBLA in 1999 included the GLBA privacy and safeguards requirements, and there have been continuing updates to these legal requirements.

Taken together, these laws mean that financial institutions today must carefully examine their practices with personal information and ensure compliance. As shown by the anti-money-laundering laws, financial institutions at the same time are subject to requirements to retain personal information and disclose it under certain circumstances. The potential complexity of complying with these multiple requirements suggests the usefulness of an overall information management plan for financial institutions, updated over time to meet changing market and regulatory requirements. The future of financial regulation will likely also include strategies for addressing cryptocurrencies.

Endnotes

1 "10 Statistics that Summarize the State of Cybersecurity in Financial Services," Security Boulevard, November 12, 2019, https://securityboulevard.com/2019/11/10-statistics-that-summarize-the-state-of-cybersecurity-in-financial-services/.

2 "Fair Credit Reporting (Regulation V)," Consumer Financial Protection Bureau, accessed November 2017, https://www.consumerfinance.gov/rules-policy/final-rules/fair-credit-reporting-regulation-v/; CFPB Compliance Bulletin 2016-01, Consumer Financial Protection Bureau, February 3, 2016, http://files.consumerfinance.gov/f/201602_cfpb_supervisory-bulletin-furnisher-accuracy-obligations.pdf; 12 C.F.R. 1022, accessed February 2020, National Archives, https://www.ecfr.gov/cgi-bin/text-idx?SID=361693714a362924f3ed1d1b092a548c&mc=true&tpl=/ecfrbrowse/Title12/12cfr1022_main_02.tpl.

3 Mark Furletti, "An Overview and History of Credit Reporting," Federal Reserve Bank of Philadelphia, June 2002, https://www.philadelphiafed.org/-/media/frbp/assets/consumer-finance/discussion-papers/creditreportinghistory_062002.pdf.

4 Chris Jay Hoofnagle, *Federal Trade Commission: Privacy Law and Policy* (New York: Cambridge, 2016), 268–288; see generally Electronic Privacy Information Center, "The Fair Credit Reporting Act (FCRA) and the Privacy of Your Credit Report," accessed November 2017, https://epic.org/privacy/fcra/. For a slightly different drafting of the principles, view *Privacy Online: Fair Information Practices in the Electronic Marketplace: A Federal Trade Commission Report to Congress*, Federal Trade Commission, May 2000, https://www.ftc.gov/reports/privacy-online-fair-information-practices-electronic-marketplace-federal-trade-commission.

5 Hoofnagle, *Federal Trade Commission*; see generally Electronic Privacy Information Center, "The Fair Credit Reporting Act."

6 "Fact Sheet: President Bush Signs the Fair and Accurate Credit Transactions Act of 2003," The White House, December 4, 2003, http://georgewbush-whitehouse.archives.gov/news/releases/2003/12/20031204-3.htm

7 The FCRA provides a narrow list of specific categories where states are preempted from passing laws. These categories include credit monitoring for active-duty military. 15 U.S.C. § 1681t [FCRA § 625], revised September 2018, https://www.ftc.gov/system/files/documents/statutes/fair-credit-reporting-act/545a_fair-credit-reporting-act-0918.pdf; see "Interpretive Rule: The Fair Credit Reporting Act's Limited Preemption of State Laws," Consumer Financial Protection Burueau, June 28, 2022, https://www.consumerfinance.gov/rules-policy/final-rules/the-fair-credit-reporting-acts-limited-preemption-of-state-laws/; see also Kristin Bryan, "Federal Courts Hold that FCRA Preempts State Credit Reporting Restrictions," *The National Law Review* (December 14, 2020), https://www.natlawreview.com/article/federal-court-holds-fcra-preempts-state-credit-reporting-restrictions.

8 15 U.S.C. § 1681a, accessed November 2017, https://www.law.cornell.edu/uscode/text/15/. For additional discussion, view "Credit Reporting Questions," Consumer Affairs, accessed November 2017, https://www.consumeraffairs.com/credit_cards/credit_reporting.html.

9 15 U.S.C. § 1681a, accessed November 2017, https://www.law.cornell.edu/uscode/text/15/1681a.

10 15 U.S.C. § 1681a; 15 U.S.C. § 1681b, accessed November 2017, https://www.law.cornell.edu/uscode/text/15/1681b.

11 "Equifax Dodges FCRA Claims from 2017 Data Breach," *The National Law Review* (January 29, 2019), https://www.natlawreview.com/article/equifax-dodges-fcra-claims-2017-data-breach. For additional information about the 2017 Equifax data breach, view Robert Hackett, "Equifax Underestimated by 2.5 Million the Number of Potential Breach Victims," *Fortune*, October 2, 2017, http://fortune.com/2017/10/02/equifax-credit-breach-total/.

12 15 U.S.C. § 1681a [FCRA § 603], revised September 2018, https://www.ftc.gov/system/files/documents/statutes/fair-credit-reporting-act/545a_fair-credit-reporting-act-0918.pdf.

13 15 U.S.C. § 1681e [FCRA § 607], revised September 2018, https://www.ftc.gov/system/files/documents/statutes/fair-credit-reporting-act/545a_fair-credit-reporting-act-0918.pdf; 15 U.S.C. § 1681g [FCRA § 609], revised September 2018, https://www.ftc.gov/system/files/documents/statutes/fair-credit-reporting-act/545a_fair-credit-reporting-act-0918.pdf.

14 15 U.S.C. § 1681m [FCRA § 615], revised September 2018, https://www.ftc.gov/system/files/documents/statutes/fair-credit-reporting-act/545a_fair-credit-reporting-act-0918.pdf; see "Fair Credit Reporting Act," CFPB Consumer Laws and Regulations, October 2012, https://files.consumerfinance.gov/f/documents/102012_cfpb_fair-credit-reporting-act-fcra_procedures.pdf.

15 15 U.S.C. § 1681s-2, [FCRA § 623], revised September 2018, https://www.ftc.gov/system/files/documents/statutes/fair-credit-reporting-act/545a_fair-credit-reporting-act-0918.pdf; see "Consumer Reports: What Information Furnishers Need to Know," edited February 2023, Federal Trade Commission, https://www.ftc.gov/tips-advice/business-center/guidance/consumer-reports-what-information-furnishers-need-know.

16 15 U.S.C. § 1681m [FCRA § 615]; see "Fair Credit Reporting Act," CFPB Consumer Laws and Regulations.

17 15 U.S.C. § 1681m [FCRA § 615]; see "Fair Credit Reporting Act," CFPB Consumer Laws and Regulations.

18 See Chapter 12 – Workplace Privacy. These requirements apply to the consumer reports of prospective employees and employees both prior to employment and during employment. See Section 604b.

19 15 U.S.C. § 1681s-2, [FCRA § 623]; see "Consumer Reports: What Information Furnishers Need to Know," Federal Trade Commission.

20 15 U.S.C. § 1681g [FCRA § 609], revised September 2018, https://www.ftc.gov/system/files/documents/statutes/fair-credit-reporting-act/545a_fair-credit-reporting-act-0918.pdf.

21 15 U.S.C. § 1681i [FCRA § 611], revised September 2018, https://www.ftc.gov/system/files/documents/statutes/fair-credit-reporting-act/545a_fair-credit-reporting-act-0918.pdf.

22 15 U.S.C. § 1681e [FCRA § 607].

23 15 U.S.C. § 1681e [FCRA § 607]; see Thomas Ahearn, "Fair Credit Reporting Act," Employment Screening Resources, December 21, 2020, https://www.esrcheck.com/2020/12/21/cra-fcra-accuracy-standard/.

24 15 U.S.C. § 1681c [FCRA § 605], revised September 2018, https://www.ftc.gov/system/files/documents/statutes/fair-credit-reporting-act/545a_fair-credit-reporting-act-0918.pdf; "How Do I Get Bankruptcy Removed from My Credit Report?" United States Bankruptcy Court, Central District of California, https://www.cacb.uscourts.gov/faq/

credit-report-how-do-i-get-bankruptcy-removed-my-report; Hilary Back, "What is the Difference Between Chapter 7 and Chapter 13 Bankruptcy?" Experian, April 21, 2021, https://www.experian.com/blogs/ask-experian/bankruptcy-chapter-7-vs-chapter-13/; "How Long Does Bankruptcy Stay on Your Credit Report?" *TransUnion* (blog), May 18, 2021, https://www.transunion.com/blog/credit-advice/how-long-does-bankruptcy-stay-on-credit-report.

25 15 U.S.C. § 1681b [FCRA § 604], revised September 2018, https://www.ftc.gov/system/files/documents/statutes/fair-credit-reporting-act/545a_fair-credit-reporting-act-0918.pdf; see "Fair Credit Reporting Act: Justice Information Sharing," U.S. Department of Justice, accessed July 2022, https://bja.ojp.gov/program/it/privacy-civil-liberties/authorities/statutes/2349; see "CFPB Issues Advisory to Protect Privacy When Companies Compile Personal Data, Consumer Financial Protection Bureau," July 7, 2022, https://www.consumerfinance.gov/about-us/newsroom/cfpb-issues-advisory-to-protect-privacy-when-companies-compile-personal-data/.

26 15 U.S.C. § 1681b [FCRA § 604]; see 15 U.S.C. § 1681e [FCRA § 607].

27 "Using Consumer Reports for Credit Decisions: What to Know about Adverse Action and Risk-Based Pricing Notices," Federal Trade Commission, edited November 2023, https://www.ftc.gov/business-guidance/resources/using-consumer-reports-credit-decisions-what-know-about-adverse-action-risk-based-pricing-notices.

28 15 U.S.C. § 1681m [FCRA § 615]; see Sarah Ammermann, "Adverse Action Notice Requirement Under the ECOA and the FCRA," Consumer Compliance Outlook, accessed March 2022, https://consumercomplianceoutlook.org/2013/second-quarter/adverse-action-notice-requirements-under-ecoa-fcra/.

29 "The Federal Trade Commission, the Consumer Financial Protection Bureau, and the federal banking agencies have each published a Furnisher Rule. The rules are identical in substance." "Consumer Reports: What Information Furnishers Need to Know," Federal Trade Commission, edited February 2023, https://www.ftc.gov/tips-advice/business-center/guidance/consumer-reports-what-information-furnishers-need-know; "Back to Basics, Continued—Frivolous or Irrelevant Disputes; The Furnishers Rule Under the Fair Credit Reporting Act (FCRA)," Dentons, October 30, 2019, https://www.dentons.com/en/insights/newsletters/2019/october/30/consumer-finance-report/back-to-basics-to-be-continued-frivolous-or-irrelevant-disputes.

30 15 U.S.C. § 1681s-2, [FCRA § 623]; see "Consumer Reports: What Information Furnishers Need to Know," Federal Trade Commission.

31 "The Federal Trade Commission, the Consumer Financial Protection Bureau, and the federal banking agencies have each published a Furnisher Rule. The rules are identical in substance." "Consumer Reports: What Information Furnishers Need to Know," Federal Trade Commission.

32 12 CFR Part 1022 (Regulation V), Subpart H, Duties of Users Regarding Risk-Based Pricing, Consumer Financial Protection Bureau, accessed July 2022, https://www.consumerfinance.gov/rules-policy/regulations/1022/73/#a-1-i; Notice to the Home Loan Applicant, Model Form H-3: Model Form for Credit Score Disclosure Exception for Loans Secured by One to Four Units of Residential Real Property, Consumer Financial Protection Bureau, accessed July 2022, https://www.consumerfinance.gov/rules-policy/regulations/1022/h/#ImageH2.

33 12 CFR Part 1022 (Regulation V), Subpart H, Duties of Users Regarding Risk-Based Pricing, Consumer Financial Protection Bureau; see Adam Witmer, "Risk-Based Pricing

vs. Credit Score Disclosure." Compliance Cohort, January 29, 2023, https://www.compliancecohort.com/blog/risk-based-pricing-vs-credit-score-disclosure.

34 15 U.S.C. § 1681d [FCRA § 606], revised September 2018, https://www.ftc.gov/system/files/documents/statutes/fair-credit-reporting-act/545a_fair-credit-reporting-act-0918.pdf; see "Using Consumer Reports: What Employers Need to Know," Federal Trade Commission, October 2016, https://www.ftc.gov/tips-advice/business-center/guidance/using-consumer-reports-what-employers-need-know.

35 "The Fair Credit Reporting Act (FCRA) and the Investigation of Employee Misconduct," FindLaw, November 13, 2017, https://corporate.findlaw.com/business-operations/the-fair-credit-reporting-act-fcra-and-the-investigation-of.html.

36 15 U.S.C. § 1681d [FCRA § 606]; see "Using Consumer Reports: What Employers Need to Know," Federal Trade Commission.

37 According to U.S. Department of Health and Human Services, the provisions of the FCRA concerning limited use of medical information do not conflict with HIPAA's Privacy Rule. "Does the HIPAA Privacy Rule Prevent Reporting to Consumer Credit Reporting Agencies or Otherwise Create Any Conflict with the Fair Credit Reporting Act (FCRA?" U.S. Department of Health and Human Services, December 28, 2022, https://www.hhs.gov/hipaa/for-professionals/faq/267/does-the-privacy-rule-prevent-reporting-to-consumer-credit-agencies/index.html; see "Uses and Disclosures for Treatment, Payment, and Health Care Operations," U.S. Department of Health and Human Services, revised April 3, 2013, https://www.hhs.gov/hipaa/for-professionals/privacy/guidance/disclosures-treatment-payment-health-care-operations/index.html.

38 Elizabeth Young LaBerge, "Considering Medical Information Under FCRA; Housing & Alternative Credit Scores Research," National Association of Federally-Insured Credit Unions, January 31, 2018, https://www.nafcu.org/compliance-blog/considering-medical-information-under-fcra-housing-alternative-credit-scores; Ronald Scott, "Medical Information Protected by the Fair Credit Reporting Act," University of Houston Law Center, March 15, 2004, https://www.law.uh.edu/healthlaw/perspectives/Privacy/040315Medical.html.

39 Consumers can opt out of receiving pre-screened offers either every five years or permanently at the website OptOutPrescreen.com. "Prescreened Credit and Insurance Offers," Federal Trade Commission, May 2021, https://consumer.ftc.gov/articles/prescreened-credit-insurance-offers; see OptOutPrescreen.com, accessed June 2023, https://www.optoutprescreen.com/.

40 "FCRA Compliance: What Every Financial Institution Should Know Before Making 'Firm Offers of Credit,'" Ballard Spahr LLP, January 5, 2017, https://www.ballardspahr.com/alertspublications/articles/2017-01-05-what-every-financial-institution-should-know-before-making-firm-offers-of-credit.

41 Austin Krist, "Large-Scale Enforcement of the Fair Credit Reporting Act and the Role of State Attorney Generals," *Columbia Law Review* 115, no. 8 (2015), http://columbialawreview.org/content/large-scale-enforcement-of-the-fair-credit-reporting-act-and-the-role-of-state-attorneys-general/.

42 15 U.S.C. § 1681i, accessed November 2021, https://www.consumer.ftc.gov/articles/pdf-0091-fair-credit-reporting-act-611.pdf.

43 15 U.S.C. § 1681p, accessed July 2022, https://www.law.cornell.edu/uscode/text/15/1681p. In 2021, the Supreme Court of the United States issued a decision in TransUnion LLC v. Ramirez that consumers must suffer an actual injury to meet the

constitutional requirement of standing. In the class action lawsuit, the lead plaintiff Ramirez had suffered an actual injury when he was denied a car loan due to erroneous information on his credit report; most of the class members did not meet this standard because the erroneous information on their credit reports was not disseminated to third parties. BlankRome, "How SCOTUS Clarified the Spokeo Standard of "Concrete' Harm Necessary to Establish Article III Standing, and What It Means for the Future of Class Actions, JDSupra, July 1, 2021, https://www.jdsupra.com/legalnews/how-scotus-clarified-the-spokeo-9126844/#:~:text=The%20Court%20recognized%20that%20the,driving%20behind%20a%20reckless%20driver.

44 "Adjustments to Civil Penalty Amounts," Federal Register, January 11, 2023, https://www.federalregister.gov/documents/2023/01/11/2023-00382/adjustments-to-civil-penalty-amounts. The precise amount of the penalty is adjusted in relation each year.

45 15 U.S.C. § 1681r [FCRA § 620], revised September 2018, https://www.ftc.gov/system/files/documents/statutes/fair-credit-reporting-act/545a_fair-credit-reporting-act-0918.pdf; see "CFPB Issues Advisory to Protect Privacy When Companies Compile Personal Data," Consumer Financial Protection Bureau, July 7, 2022, https://www.consumerfinance.gov/about-us/newsroom/cfpb-issues-advisory-to-protect-privacy-when-companies-compile-personal-data/.

46 Krist, "Large-Scale Enforcement of the Fair Credit Reporting Act and the Role of State Attorneys General."

47 CFPB Monitor, "How the CFPB and the FTC interact (part 1)," Ballard Spahr, July 7, 2011, https://www.consumerfinancemonitor.com/2011/07/07/how-the-cfpb-and-the-ftc-interact-part-i/. Under the Dodd-Frank Act, rule-making authority shifted from the Federal Trade Commission to the Consumer Financial Protection Bureau, Fair Credit Reporting (Regulation V), Consumer Financial Protection Bureau, updated November 1, 2012, www.consumerfinance.gov/policy-compliance/rulemaking/final-rules/fair-credit-reporting-regulation-v/; see "Fair Credit Reporting Act," Federal Trade Commission, accessed July 2022, https://www.ftc.gov/legal-library/browse/statutes/fair-credit-reporting-act. *See* Section 9.4 of this chapter for a discussion of the Dodd-Frank Act.

48 "The Consumer Credit Reporting Reform Act of 1996," National Credit Union Administration, modified September 25, 2020, https://ncua.gov/regulation-supervision/letters-credit-unions-other-guidance/consumer-credit-reporting-reform-act-1996; *see* Peter P. Swire; "The Consumer Credit Reporting Reform Act and the Future of Electronic Commerce Law," *Electronic Banking Law and Commerce Report* 1, no.6, (November/December 1996), http://peterswire.net/archive/psccrra.htm; Between 1990 and 2010, Congress added explicit grants of state enforcement authority into numerous federal consumer protection laws. Amy Widman and Prentiss Cox, "State Attorney General's Use of Concurrent Public Enforcement Authority in Federal Consumer Protection Laws," University of Minnesota Law School, 2011, http://scholarship.law.umn.edu/cgi/viewcontent.cgi?article=1376&context=faculty_articles.

49 Austin Krist, "Large-Scale Enforcement of the Fair Credit Reporting Act and the Role of State Attorneys General."

50 In 2014, these companies agreed to settle FTC charges that they violated FCRA. The FTC alleged that TeleCheck, as a CRA, did not comply with dispute procedures for consumers whose checks were denied based on information provided by the business. TRS, a company that handles consumer debt taken on by TeleCheck, was alleged to have violated requirements of the FTC's Furnisher Rule, which requires entities furnishing information to CRAs to ensure the accuracy and integrity of the information provided. "Telecheck

to Pay $3.5 Million for Fair Credit Reporting Violations," Federal Trade Commission, January 16, 2014, https://www.ftc.gov/news-events/news/press-releases/2014/01/telecheck-pay-35-million-fair-credit-reporting-act-violations; see Tiffany George, "50 Years of the FCRA," Federal Trade Commission, October 27, 2020, https://www.ftc.gov/business-guidance/blog/2020/10/50-years-fcra.

51 "TeleCheck to pay $3.5 million for Fair Credit Reporting Act violations," Federal Trade Commission.

52 RealPage was a screening background company that provided information to landlords and property managers. From 2012 to 2017, the company is alleged to have created screening reports using an automated system that utilized broad criteria to match applicants to criminal records, with only limited filtering of the results. RealPage's practice led to screening reports that linked some potential renters to criminal records that did not belong to them. "Texas Company Will Pay $3 Million to Settle FTC Charges That It Failed to Meet Accuracy Requirements for its Tenant Screening Reports," Federal Trade Commission, October 16, 2018, https://www.ftc.gov/news-events/news/press-releases/2018/10/texas-company-will-pay-3-million-settle-ftc-charges-it-failed-meet-accuracy-requirements-its-tenant; see George, "50 Years of the FCRA."

53 In the Matter of Clarity Services, Inc., and Timothy Ranney, United States of America Consumer Financial Protection Bureau Administrative Proceeding File No. 2015-CFPB-0030, December 1, 2015, http://files.consumerfinance.gov/f/201512_cfpb_consent-order_clarity-services-inc-timothy-ranney.pdf.

54 See Andrew Smith and Lucille Bartholomew, "Fair Credit Reporting Act and Financial Privacy Update—2017," *The Business Lawyer* 73, no. 73 (Spring 2018), https://www.cov.com/-/media/files/corporate/publications/2018/03/fair_credit_reporting_act_and_financial_privacy_upate_2017.pdf.

55 "CFPB Takes Action Against JPMorgan Chase for Failures Related to Checking Account Screening Information," Consumer Financial Protection Bureau, August 2, 2017, https://www.consumerfinance.gov/about-us/newsroom/cfpb-takes-action-against-jpmorgan-chase-failures-related-checking-account-screening-information/.

56 See Widman and Cox, "State Attorney General's Use of Concurrent Public Enforcement Authority in Federal Consumer Protection Laws."

57 In the Matter of Equifax, Experian, and TransUnion, accessed November 2017, www.ohioattorneygeneral.gov/Files/Briefing-Room/News-Releases/Consumer-Protection/2015-05-20-CRAs-AVC.aspx.

58 16 C.F.R. Part 682, accessed November 2017, https://www.law.cornell.edu/cfr/text/16/part-682; see "The Fair Credit Reporting Act (FCRA) and the Privacy of Your Credit Report," Electronic Privacy Information Center, accessed November 2017, https://epic.org/privacy/fcra/.

59 "CFPB Affirms Ability of States to Police Credit Reporting Markets," Consumer Financial Protection Bureau, June 28, 2022, https://www.consumerfinance.gov/about-us/newsroom/cfpb-affirms-ability-for-states-to-police-credit-reporting-markets/.

60 2003 Changes to the Fair Credit Reporting Act, Consumers Union, accessed February 2020), https://consumerfed.org/pdfs/credit_reporting_summary_of_final_law.pdf;

61 Gail Hillebrand, "After the FACT Act: What States Can Still Do to Prevent Identity Theft," Consumers Reports, January 13, 20224, https://advocacy.consumerreports.org/research/after-the-fact-act-what-states-can-still-do-to-prevent-identity-theft/.

62 16 C.F.R. Part 610.1, accessed November 2017, https://www.law.cornell.edu/cfr/text/16/610.1.

63 12 C.F.R. Part 1022.130, accessed November 2017, https://www.law.cornell.edu/cfr/text/12/1022.130.

64 "Disposing of Consumer Report Information? Rules Tell How," Federal Trade Commission, June 2005, https://www.ftc.gov/tips-advice/business-center/guidance/disposing-consumer-report-information-rule-tells-how.

65 16 C.F.R. 681, accessed November 2017, https://www.law.cornell.edu/cfr/text/16/part-681.

66 "FTC extends enforcement deadline for identity theft Red Flags Rule," Federal Trade Commission, May 28, 2010, https://www.ftc.gov/news-events/press-releases/2010/05/ftc-extends-enforcement-deadline-identity-theft-red-flags-rule.

67 S. 3987 (111th), accessed November 2017, https://www.congress.gov/bill/111th-congress/senate-bill/3987.

68 "Unfurling a new definition of 'creditor' under the Red Flags Rule," Federal Trade Commission, December 7, 2012.

69 Gramm-Leach-Bliley Act, 15 U.S.C. § 6801-6809, accessed November 2017, https://www.law.cornell.edu/uscode/text/15/chapter-94/subchapter-I; see also, "How to Comply with the Privacy of Consumer Financial Information Rule of the Gramm-Leach-Bliley Act," Federal Trade Commission, Jul 2022, https://www.ftc.gov/tips-advice/business-center/guidance/how-comply-privacy-consumer-financial-information-rule-gramm.

70 "Consumer Watch: U.S. Bancorp Pays $3 Million in Privacy Case Settlement," Market Watch, July 1, 1999, www.marketwatch.com/story/consumerwatch-us-bancorp-pays-3-million-in-privacy-case-settlement.

71 The allegations also stated that the marketing firm was using a "negative option," where customers were charged automatically for services unless they later sent a specific request not to be billed.

72 Electronic Signatures in Global and National Commerce Act (E-Sign Act), FDIC Consumer Compliance Examination Manual, January 2014, https://www.fdic.gov/resources/supervision-and-examinations/consumer-compliance-examination-manual/documents/10/x-3-1.pdf; see Sameer Hajarnis, "E-Signatures: Answers to 5 Most Common Questions," *OneSpan Blog*, September 17, 2021, https://www.onespan.com/blog/e-signatures-answers-5-most-common-questions.

73 Eleanor Lumsden, "Securing Mobile Technology & Financial Transactions in the United States," *Berkley Business Law Journal* 9, no. 1 (2012), https://digitalcommons.law.ggu.edu/cgi/viewcontent.cgi?article=1600&context=pubs.

74 "National Survey: Bank Customers Turn to Mobile Apps More Than Any Other Channel to Manage Their Accounts," American Banking Association, October 25, 2021, https://www.aba.com/about-us/press-room/press-releases/bank-customers-turn-to-mobile-apps-more-than-any-other-channel-to-manage-their-accounts.

75 Gramm-Leach-Bliley Act, 15 U.S.C. § 6809, accessed July 2022, https://www.law.cornell.edu/uscode/text/15/6809.

76 Gramm-Leach-Bliley Act, 15 U.S.C. § 6805, accessed July 2022, https://www.law.cornell.edu/uscode/text/15/6805.

77 See Nick Oberheiden, "Gramm Leach Bliley Act: 2 Requirements & 7 Ways to Achieve Compliance, *The National Law Review*, June 3, 2021, https://www.natlawreview.com/article/gramm-leach-bliley-act-2-requirements-7-ways-to-achieve-compliance.

78 Benton Campbell, William Reckler & Brigid Morris, "Understanding FIRREA: Revived Law Expands Government's Enforcement Options," Latham & Watkins LLP, January/February 2014; see Boris Bershteyn, Andrew Good, Ryan Junck, Caroline White, "Biden DOJ Likely To Employ FIRREA as an Enforcement Tool," Skadden, April 5, 2021, https://www.skadden.com/insights/publications/2021/04/biden-doj-likely-to-employ-firrea.

79 In Vermont, the state's Department of Banking, Insurance, Securities, and Health Care Administration adopted opt-in provisions for information sharing. To comply with the regulation, some companies have treated all Vermont residents as having opted out under GLBA. "The Gramm-Leach Bliley Act," Electronic Privacy Information Center, accessed February 2020, https://epic.org/privacy/glba/.

80 "How to Comply with the Privacy of Consumer Financial Information Rule of Gramm-Leach-Bliley Act," Federal Trade Commission, accessed July 2022, https://www.ftc.gov/business-guidance/resources/how-comply-privacy-consumer-financial-information-rule-gramm-leach-bliley-act.

81 Providing a toll-free telephone number or a detachable form with a preprinted address is "reasonable"; requiring someone to write a letter as the only way to opt out is not.

82 The GLBA does not give consumers the right to opt out when the financial institution shares other information with its affiliates. Consumers have this right under the FCRA.

83 "Federal regulators issue final model privacy notice form," Federal Trade Commission, November 17, 2009, https://www.ftc.gov/news-events/press-releases/2009/11/federal-regulators-issue-final-model-privacy-notice-form.

84 Financial Services Regulatory Relief Act of 2006, accessed November 2017, https://www.gpo.gov/fdsys/pkg/BILLS-109s2856enr/pdf/BILLS-109s2856enr.pdf. With regard to the 2021 update to the GLBA Safeguards Rule, "the changes will mean that a broad range of non-banking financial institutions may need to make updates to their data security policies and procedures." "Non-Banking Institutions Will Want to Review Security Measures in the Light of Update to Safeguards Rule, November 4, 2021, https://www.natlawreview.com/article/non-banking-institutions-will-want-to-review-security-measures-light-update-to.

85 16 C.F.R. Part 314, accessed November 2017, https://www.law.cornell.edu/cfr/text/16/part-314; see FTC Safeguards Rule: What Your Business Needs to Know," Federal Trade Commission, May 2022, https://www.ftc.gov/business-guidance/resources/ftc-safeguards-rule-what-your-business-needs-know; Data Security Regulations of Consumer Reporting Agencies, Consumer Data Industry Association, accessed July 2022, https://www.cdiaonline.org/resources/for-reporting-industry-professionals/data-security-regulation-of-consumer-reporting-agencies/.

86 16 C.F.R. Part 314.1(a), accessed November 2017, https://www.law.cornell.edu/cfr/text/16/part-314.

87 16 C.F.R. Part 314.1(a).

88 16 C.F.R. Part 314.3(a), accessed November 2017, https://www.law.cornell.edu/cfr/text/16/part-314.

89 16 C.F.R. Part 314.4, accessed November 2017, https://www.law.cornell.edu/cfr/text/16/part-314; see Glenn Brown, "FTC Amends GLBA Safeguards Rule to Impose Significant

New Privacy Obligations on Financial Institutions," The National Law Review, November 3, 2021, https://www.natlawreview.com/article/ftc-amends-glba-safeguards-rule-to-impose-significant-new-privacy-obligations.

90 "Cybersecurity Resources," FDIC, updated June 26, 2023, https://www.fdic.gov/regulations/resources/cybersecurity/; see Rebecca Lake & Daphne Foreman, "Increase in Digital Banking Raises Consumer Data Protection Concerns: How to Protect Yourself," Forbes, April 5, 2021, https://www.forbes.com/advisor/banking/digital-banking-consumer-data-privacy-concerns/.

91 Steven Abrams, "How to Keep Your Information Safe When Online Banking," *U.S. News & World Report*, October 22, 2018, https://money.usnews.com/banking/articles/how-to-keep-your-information-safe-when-online-banking; Margarette Burnette, "Is Online Banking Safe? How to Boost Your Banking Security," NerdWallet, February 13, 2018, https://www.nerdwallet.com/blog/banking/online-banking-security/.

92 Mobile banking concerns include: the small and portable nature of cell phones make them easy to steal, cell phones can become infected with viruses and infect computers that are connected, and users have a limited ability to delete cookies related to mobile applications. Lumsden, "Securing Mobile Technology & Financial Transactions in the U.S."; For discussion of mobile banking issues, see Anant Bhatia, "Security Concerns Inhibit Mobile Banking Adoption Among Older Consumers," Comscore, June 12, 2015, https://www.comscore.com/Insights/Blog/Security-Concerns-Inhibit-Mobile-Banking-Adoption-Among-Older-Consumers; Tracy Kitten, "6 Top Mobile Banking Risks," May 4, 2012, www.bankinfosecurity.com/6-top-mobile-banking-risks-a-4735; For additional resources, view Zack Whittaker, "Most U.S. Mobile Banking Apps Have Security and Privacy Flaws," TechCrunch, June 11, 2019, https://techcrunch.com/2019/06/11/banking-apps-security-flaws/; Libby Wells and Barbara Whelehan, "Worried about Mobile Banking App Security? Follow these Best Practices," Bankrate, June 30, 2022, https://www.bankrate.com/banking/best-security-practices-for-mobile-banking/.

93 State comprehensive privacy laws are discussed in detail in Chapter 6. GreenbergTrautig provides a detailed analysis of the applicability of state comprehensive laws to financial institutions subject to GLBA. David Zetoony, "Financial Institution Confusion: Are Financial Institutions Fully Exempt from the CCPA, CPRA, VCDPA, and CPA?" GreenbergTrautig, July 1, 2021, https://www.gtlaw-dataprivacydish.com/2021/07/financial-institution-confusion-are-financial-institutions-fully-exempt-from-the-ccpa-cpra-vcdpa-and-cpa/#:~:text=Some%20state%20privacy%20laws%2C%20such,individuals%20who%20have%20obtained%20personal.

94 Cal. Fin. Code § 4050 et seq., accessed November 2017, http://codes.findlaw.com/ca/financial-code/fin-sect-4050.html.

95 The CCPA and the CPRA are discussed in Chapter 6 of this book.

96 "This title shall not apply to personal information collected, processed, sold, or disclosed pursuant to the federal Gramm-Leach-Bliley Act (Public Law 106-102), and implementing regulations, or the California Financial Information Privacy Act (Division 1.4 (commencing with Section 4050) of the Financial Code)." Cal. Civ. Code § 1798.145(e); see Zetoony, "Financial Institution Confusion: Are Financial Institutions Fully Exempt from the CCPA, CPRA, VCDPA, and CPA?"; "The California Privacy Protection Act: Compliance Strategies for Financial Institutions," Debevoise & Plimpton, May 2, 2019, https://www.debevoise.com/insights/publications/2019/04/the-california-consumer-privacy-act.

97 Micheal Buckbee, "NYDFS Cybersecurity Regulation in Plain English," *Varonis* (blog), updated April 18, 2023, https://www.varonis.com/blog/nydfs-cybersecurity-regulation; For details of the regulation, view "Cybersecurity Requirements for Financial Services Companies," New York State, Department of Financial Services, 23 NYCRR 500, accessed June 2023, https://www.dfs.ny.gov/docs/legal/regulations/adoptions/dfsrf500txt.pdf.

98 "FTC's Proposed Amendments to the GLBA Safeguards Rule Seek to Incorporate Requirements from NY DFS Cybersecurity Regulations," Cooley, March 11, 2019, https://cdp.cooley.com/ftcs-proposed-amendments-to-the-glba-safeguards-rule-seek-to-incorporate-requirements-from-ny-dfs-cybersecurity-regulations/?utm_source=Mondaq&utm_medium=syndication&utm_campaign=View-Original; For more details, view "FTC Extends Comment Deadline on Proposed Changes to Safeguards Rule," Federal Trade Commission, May 21, 2019, https://www.ftc.gov/news-events/press-releases/2019/05/ftc-extends-comment-deadline-proposed-changes-safeguards-rule.

99 Juliana De Groot, "What is the NYDFS Cybersecurity Regulation? (And Compliance Tips)," *Data Guardian* (blog), May 6, 2023, https://www.digitalguardian.com/blog/what-nydfs-cybersecurity-regulation-new-cybersecurity-compliance-requirement-financial.

100 Cybersecurity Framework, NIST, accessed November 2019, https://www.nist.gov/cyberframework.

101 Buckbee, "NYDFS Cybersecurity Regulation in Plain English.

102 Michael Krimminger, Cleary Gottlieb Steen & Hamilton, "New York Cybersecurity Regulations for Financial Institutions Enter into Effect," Harvard Law School Forum on Corporate Governance and Financial Regulation, March 25, 2017, https://corpgov.law.harvard.edu/2017/03/25/new-york-cybersecurity-regulations-for-financial-institutions-enter-into-effect/. See Shardul Desai, "The Impact of Cybersecurity Regulations on the Financial Services Industry in 2022," Holland & Knight, January 12, 2022, https://www.hklaw.com/en/insights/publications/2022/01/the-impact-of-cybersecurity-regulations; see also Amelia Gerlicher et al., "2023 Breach Notification Law Update: Changes to Notification and Security Requirements Continue at State and Federal Levels," JDSupra, October 10, 2023, https://www.jdsupra.com/legalnews/2023-breach-notification-law-update-1361087/.

103 Virtual Currency Businesses, New York State, accessed July 2022, https://www.dfs.ny.gov/virtual_currency_businesses; see "The New York BitLicense: What Is It and Who Needs to Have One?" *Capital Fund Law Group* (blog), May 4, 2023, https://www.capitalfundlaw.com/blog/newyorkbitlicense.

104 Virtual Currency Businesses: Main Page," Greenlisted Coins, New York State Department of Financial Services, April 25, 2023, https://www.dfs.ny.gov/virtual_currency_businesses.

105 23 CRR-NY 200.15 Anti-Money Laundering Program, Thomson Reuters Westlaw, New York Codes, Rules and Regulations, June 30, 2021, https://govt.westlaw.com/nycrr/Document/I85908c8f253711e598dbff5462aa3db3; see "Virtual Currency Businesses: Main Page," Department of Financial Services, State of New York, accessed June 2023, https://www.dfs.ny.gov/virtual_currency_businesses.

106 Dodd-Frank Act § 1022, accessed November 2017, https://www.law.cornell.edu/wex/dodd-frank_title_X.

107 Dodd-Frank Act § 1002(12).

108 Dodd-Frank Act § 1002(5); Dodd-Frank Act § 1002 (15); Dodd-Frank Act § 1025.

109 Dodd-Frank Act § 1026.

110 Dodd-Frank Act § 5531.

111 Dodd-Frank Act § 1052(b)-(c).

112 "Civil Penalty Inflation Adjustments," Federal Register, January 3, 2023, https://www.federalregister.gov/documents/2022/01/14/2022-00672/civil-penalty-inflation-adjustments. The precise amount of the penalty is adjusted each year.

113 Dodd-Frank Act § 1041-1042.

114 Electronic Funds Transfer Act, accessed July 2022, https://www.law.cornell.edu/wex/electronic_funds_transfer_act; 12 CFR 1005.3, accessed July 2022, https://www.law.cornell.edu/cfr/text/12/1005.3; "Electronic Funds Transfers FAQs," Consumer Financial Protection Bureau, updated December 13, 2021, https://www.consumerfinance.gov/compliance/compliance-resources/deposit-accounts-resources/electronic-fund-transfers/electronic-fund-transfers-faqs/.

115 Electronic Funds Transfer Act.

116 "Electronic Funds Transfers FAQs," Consumer Financial Protection Bureau.

117 This guidance details when a person-to-person (P2P) payment falls within the definition of an EFT under Regulation E. "Electronic Funds Transfers FAQs," Consumer Financial Protection Bureau.

118 Stacy Cowley & Lananh Nguyen, "When Customers Say Their Money is Stolen on Zelle, Banks Often Refuse to Pay," *The New York Times*, June 20, 2022, https://www.nytimes.com/2022/06/20/business/zelle-money-stolen-banks.html; see Kate Berry, "Zelle is Surprise Lightning Rod in CFPB's Big Tech Inquiry," American Banker, December 20, 2021, https://www.americanbanker.com/news/zelle-is-surprise-lightning-rod-in-cfpbs-big-tech-inquiry; Rob Campbell, "Reg E – Protecting and Preventing Consumers Falling For Social Engineering Scams – What Does it Mean for Banks?" BiometricUpdate.com, September 9, 2021, https://www.biometricupdate.com/202109/reg-e-protecting-and-preventing-consumers-falling-for-social-engineering-scams-what-does-it-mean-for-banks#:~:text=Reg%20E%20provides%20protection%20for,compensation%20for%20any%20losses%20incurred.

119 "What We Do," Financial Crimes Enforcement Network, U.S. Department of the Treasury, accessed November 2017, https://www.fincen.gov/what-we-do.

120 Peter P. Swire, "Financial Privacy and the Theory of High-Tech Government Surveillance," *Washington University Law Quarterly* 77 (1999): 461, http://papers.ssrn.com/sol3/papers.cfm?abstract_id=133340.

121 Sarah Aberg & Gabriel Khoury, "OCC and FinCEN Issue $200 Million in Penalties for BSA-AML Violations," *The National Law Review*, March 28, 2022, https://www.natlawreview.com/article/occ-and-fincen-issue-200-million-penalties-bsa-aml-violations.

122 Financial Recordkeeping and Reporting of Currency and Foreign Transactions Act of 1970, 31 U.S.C. 1051. In addition to the federal Bank Secrecy Act and other regulations that require reporting to the U.S. government, many states also provide for the disclo-

sure of banking records and financial transaction data to state and local law enforcement agencies.

123 With the increased use of cryptocurrency, the regulatory landscape has become complex. In 2019, the U.S. Treasury's Financial Crimes Enforcement Network issued guidance regarding "virtual asset service providers" being treated as "money service businesses"—"which means they must now comply with the long-standing Funds Travel Rule under the Bank Secrecy Act." "CipherTrace Announces Travel Rule Information Sharing Architecture," CipherTrace, August 23, 2019, https://ciphertrace.com/travel-rule-info-sharing-architecture/. To review the complete text of the guidance, view "Application of FinCEN's Regulations to Certain Business Models Involving Convertible Virtual Currencies," FIN-2019-G001, FinCEN Guidance, May 9, 2019, https://www.fincen.gov/sites/default/files/2019-05/FinCEN%20Guidance%20CVC%20FINAL%20508.pdf. Because this is an emerging area of regulation, entities whose business models involve this area may wish to seek the advice of an attorney to ensure compliance with evolving requirements.

124 "Application of FinCEN's Regulations to Certain Business Models Involving Convertible Virtual Currencies," FinCEN Guidance"; see New FinCEN Guidance for Cryptocurrency and Blockchain Businesses, Bloomberg Law, May 2019, https://www.bakerlaw.com/webfiles/IP/2019/Articles/06-06-2019-Jehl-Musiala-Forman-Wasick-FinCENGuidance.pdf.

125 12 U.S.C. § 1829(b), accessed November 2017, https://www.law.cornell.edu/uscode/text/12/1829b.

126 See 31 C.F.R. 1010.410, accessed December 2017, https://www.law.cornell.edu/cfr/text/31/1010.410 (); 31 C.F.R. 1010.430, accessed December 2017, https://www.law.cornell.edu/cfr/text/31/1010.430; 31 C.F.R. 1020.410, accessed December 2017, https://www.law.cornell.edu/cfr/text/31/1020.410.

127 See 12 C.F.R. 21.11, accessed November 2017, https://www.law.cornell.edu/cfr/text/12/21.11; 12 C.F.R. 208.62, accessed November 2017, https://www.law.cornell.edu/cfr/text/12/208.62; 12 C.F.R. 353.3, accessed May 2016, https://www.law.cornell.edu/cfr/text/12/part-353.

128 31 U.S.C. § 5321, accessed November 2017, https://www.law.cornell.edu/uscode/text/31/5321.

129 "First Bitcoin 'Mixer' Penalized by FinCEN for Violating Anti-Money Laundering Laws," Financial Crimes Enforcement Network, U.S. Department of the Treasury, October 19, 2020, https://www.fincen.gov/news/news-releases/first-bitcoin-mixer-penalized-fincen-violating-anti-money-laundering-laws; Nikhilesh De, "U.S. Officials Arrest Alleged Operator of $336M Bitcoin Mixing Service," CoinDesk, April 27, 2021, https://www.coindesk.com/markets/2021/04/27/us-officials-arrest-alleged-operator-of-336m-bitcoin-mixing-service/.

130 International Money Laundering Abatement and Anti-Terrorism Financing Act of 2001, December 4, 2001, https://www.epic.org/privacy/financial/RL31208.pdf; For additional information, see "Unlock Your Guide to AML: U.S. Anti-Money Laundering Requirements: Frequently Asked Questions, Seventh Edition," Protiviti, accessed June 2023, https://www.protiviti.com/sites/default/files/2023-01/Guide-to-US-AML-Requirements-7thEdition-Protiviti.pdf.

131 For an in-depth discussion, view "USA Patriot Act," Financial Crimes Enforcement Network, U.S. Department of the Treasury, accessed November 2017, https://www.fincen.gov/resources/statutes-regulations/usa-patriot-act.

132 "Foreign Account Tax Compliance Act," Internal Revenue Service, accessed November 2017, https://www.irs.gov/businesses/corporations/foreign-account-tax-compliance-act-fatca.

133 "Four Takeaways on BSA/AML Reform Under the Anti-Money Laundering Act of 2020," Thomson Reuters, August 9, 2021, https://legal.thomsonreuters.com/en/insights/articles/4-takeaways-on-bsa-aml-reform#:~:text=The%20AMLA%202020%20also%20establishes,correspondent%20accounts%20in%20the%20U.S.

134 Study Committee, *Cryptography and the Intelligence Community: The Future of Encryption*, (Washington, DC: The National Academies Press, 2022), p. 59, https://nap.nationalacademies.org/catalog/26168/cryptography-and-the-intelligence-community-the-future-of-encryption. Peter Swire, one of the co-authors of this textbook, was a member of the study committee for this book.

135 Julian Dossett, "Are Cryptocurrency Transactions Actually Anonymous?" CNET, June 7, 2022, https://www.cnet.com/personal-finance/crypto/are-cryptocurrency-transactions-actually-anonymous/#:~:text=The%20federal%20focus%20on%20crypto,such%20dealings%20are%20not%20anonymous; "Two Arrested for Alleged Conspiracy to Launder $4.5 Billion in Stolen Cryptocurrency," Office of Public Affairs, U.S. Department of Justice, February 8, 2022, https://www.justice.gov/opa/pr/two-arrested-alleged-conspiracy-launder-45-billion-stolen-cryptocurrency.

136 "Cryptocurrency Regulations Around the World," Comply Advantage, updated June 12, 2023, https://complyadvantage.com/insights/cryptocurrency-regulations-around-world/.

137 "Privacy is likely the biggest concern with the digital yuan. While parties using this currency may not have access to each other's data, the government will have complete visibility across the transaction flow—'controlled anonymity,' as the Chinese government calls it." Shruti Gupta, "China's Digital Yuan is All About Data – and, Perhaps, Control," IndustryWeek, September 1, 2021, https://www.industryweek.com/the-economy/trade/article/21174069/chinas-digital-yuan-is-all-about-dataand-perhaps-control.

CHAPTER 10

Education Privacy

Although education in the United States has been governed largely at the state and local level, education records for institutions that receive federal funding have privacy and security protections under U.S. law. The logic is that grades, disciplinary actions, and other school information about a particular student deserve protection. This chapter discusses the Family Educational Rights and Privacy Act of 1974 (FERPA), the Protection of Pupil Rights Amendment of 1978 (PPRA), as amended, and the interaction between FERPA and the Health Insurance Portability and Accountability Act (HIPAA) Privacy Rule. In addition to these federal laws, practitioners in this area should be careful to follow any state and local laws that apply.

Next, this chapter discusses the issue of education technology ("edtech") companies, where details of students' online activities can be collected when they use edtech products. Advances in technology and online communications have dramatically changed the landscape of education in the United States In past generations, educators utilized textbooks, photocopies, and filmstrips to teach a classroom full of students. Today's classrooms increasingly employ content personalized to each student; social media helps students collaborate across classrooms and online portals allow students to access grades. The prevalence of edtech increased dramatically during the COVID-19 pandemic, when many schools across the United States moved from in-person classroom learning to remote learning for both K-12 schooling and universities.[1] As of the writing of this book, most learning has returned to in-person classroom learning, yet many schools have decided to maintain some level of edtech to supplement traditional in-person classroom learning. This chapter concludes by examining cybersecurity requirements both K-12 schooling and universities.

10.1 The Family Educational Rights and Privacy Act

FERPA is a federal statute that provides students with control over disclosure and access to their education records.[2] FERPA is often referred to as the Buckley Amendment, in reference to Senator James Buckley, who supported its enactment.

10.1.1 Overview of FERPA

The statute generally prevents schools from divulging education record information, such as grades and behavior, to parties other than the student without that student's consent.[3] FERPA includes major aspects of Fair Information Practice Principles (FIPPs), such as notice, consent, access and correction, security, and accountability.

FERPA applies to all educational institutions that receive federal funding—both K-12 schooling and universities.[4] This type of federal funding exists for virtually all public and most private schools, especially at the university level. Specifically, the statute protects the rights of students by providing them with the right to:

- Control the disclosure of their education records to others
- Review and seek amendment of their own education records
- Receive annual notice of their rights under FERPA
- File complaints with the U.S. Department of Education[5]

10.1.2 Key Definitions in FERPA

FERPA includes key definitions such as: student, education record, personally identifiable information (PII), and directory information.

10.1.2.1 Student

Student is defined as "any individual who is or has been in attendance at an educational agency or institution."[6] Attendance is broadly defined to include individuals who are present on campus as well as those who participate via the internet.[7]

The definition of student excludes those individuals who only applied to an educational institution, and even those students who were accepted by the educational institution but did not enroll.[8]

10.1.2.2 Education Record

Education record has a broad meaning. FERPA defines it to include all records that are directly related to the student and maintained by or on behalf of the K-12 school or university. This extends beyond grades and other academic records to include financial aid records, disciplinary records, and others related to the student.[9]

With regard to the more technical aspects of the definition, FERPA defines "record" as "any information recorded in a way, including, but not limited to, handwriting, print, computer media, video or audio tape, film, microfilm, and microfiche."[10] All electronic records and emails are defined as *computer media*.

The term "education record" has several important exceptions.[11] The following records are *not* considered education records under FERPA:

- **Campus police records** created and maintained by campus police for law enforcement purposes[12]
- **Employment records**, when the employee is not a student at the university
- **Applicant records** of those who are not enrolled in the university
- **Alumni records** created by a K-12 school or university after the individual is no longer a student
- **Grades on peer-graded papers**, before they are collected and recorded by a faculty member or other university representative[13]
- **Treatment records** or health records, subject to several requirements[14]

10.1.2.3 Personally Identifiable Information

The Department of Education's definition of PII is similar to other statutory definitions.[15] It includes, but is not limited to:

- The student's name
- The name of the student's parent or other family members
- The student or student's family address
- Personal identifiers such as Social Security number or student number
- Other identifiers, such as date of birth and place of birth
- Other information that, alone or in combination, can be linked to a student and would allow the student to be identified with reasonable certainty
- Information requested by a person whom the school reasonably believes knows the identity of the student to which the education record is linked[16]

Practitioners should be aware that FERPA's definition of PII can overlap with types of information that can be defined as directory information (see Section 10.1.2.4). Examples would include date of birth and place of birth.

The distinctions of how PII and directory information are handled, relevant to disclosures of education records, are discussed in Section 10.1.4.

10.1.2.4 Directory Information

Directory information is broadly defined by FERPA to include information "that would not generally be considered harmful or an invasion of privacy if disclosed."[17] FERPA does not designate specific information types as directory information for every educational institution; rather, it allows individual educational institutions to create their own definitions based on lists of examples provided in the statute and rules laid down by the Department of Education.[18] The examples include name, date and place of birth, address, email address, telephone number, field of study, and honors received.[19]

Before an educational institution can declare information to be directory information and begin using it as such, the institution must provide students with an opportunity to opt out—or block—the release of their directory information. Students cannot use this opt-out to prevent the release of information that falls under a FERPA exception.[20]

The regulations promulgated under FERPA specifically exclude the use of Social Security numbers or student identification numbers as directory information. An educational institution, however, may use student identification numbers as directory information if that number cannot be used to access education records without another factor known only by the authorized user.[21] Therefore, a K-12 school or university cannot use a student identification number as directory information if other information included in directory information combined with the student identification number would enable an unauthorized user to access the student's records.[22]

Practitioners should be aware that the treatment of directory information under FERPA is similar to its treatment under HIPAA. While both statutes require opt-in consent for the use of most personal information, directory information is treated differently requiring the person to opt out if they do not want this category of information to be released.[23]

10.1.3 Holder of the Rights under FERPA

High schools as well as colleges and universities should remain alert to the complex interplay that exists regarding whether the parent or the student holds the rights related to FERPA. The rules regarding the holder of the rights under FERPA are distinct: when the student is enrolled in high school, when the student is enrolled in a college or university, and with regard to the status of the student on their parent's tax return.

10.1.3.1 Student Enrolled in High School

While the student is enrolled in high school, the parent holds the rights under FERPA so long as the student is under the age of 18. When the student turns 18 years old, the rights transfer from the parent to the student. A student may sign a written consent form to grant their parents' permission to view their education records.

10.1.3.2 Student Enrolled in a College or University

For a student who is attending classes at a college or university while also attending high school, the rules regarding high school attendance apply. Once a student is *only* attending a college or university, the student is the holder of the FERPA rights—regardless of age. When the student holds the FERPA rights, the student may sign a written consent form to grant their parents' permission to view their education records.

10.1.3.3 Status of the Student on Their Parents' Tax Return

Even after the rights under FERPA have transferred to the student, a school may disclose to the parents the educational records of the student—without the student's consent—in the circumstance where the student is a dependent for tax purposes.

10.1.4 Disclosure of Education Records

FERPA permits the disclosure of education records in numerous circumstances. One of these instances, when consent is provided by the holder of the FERPA rights, is discussed in detail.

10.1.4.1 Circumstances when Disclosure is Permitted

Disclosure of education records is permitted only if one of the following conditions is met:

- The information is not "personally identifiable"
- The information is "directory information" that the student has not blocked release of
- Consent has been provided by the holder of the rights under FERPA
- The disclosure is made to the holder of the rights under FERPA[24]
- A statutory exception applies, such as for health or safety purposes[25]

PII may still be disclosed if it is determined to be "directory information."[26] Other than the exceptions noted above, nondirectory information, such as grade-point average (GPA), grades, or transcripts are not released without valid consent.[27]

10.1.4.2 Consent Under FERPA

Valid student consent to disclosure must be signed (by hand or electronically), dated, and written. It must also identify:

- The record(s) to be disclosed
- The purpose of disclosure
- To whom the disclosure is being made

Under several statutory exceptions, a school is authorized to disclose PII from an education record without student consent. Educational institutions need meet only one exception for the disclosure to be valid. Schools, however, must use "reasonable methods" to verify the identity of the party to whom they disclose the information. Reasonable methods include PINs, passwords, personal security questions, smart cards and tokens, biometric indicators, and other factors known or possessed only by the user.[28]

Exceptions to the FERPA consent requirements include the following:

- Disclosure to school officials who have determined a "legitimate educational interest" in the records. A legitimate educational interest exists if the record is relevant and necessary to the school official's responsibilities. This group includes school employees and board members as well as third-party vendors (1) the school outsources duties to and (2) are under the direct control of the school regarding use and maintenance of the record.[29] These third parties are not permitted to disclose record information to any other party without consent, and cannot use the record for any purpose other than for which the disclosure was made.[30]
- Disclosure to educational institutions in which a student seeks or intends to enroll, or is currently enrolled, when the disclosure is for a purpose related to the student's enrollment or transfer.
- Disclosure in connection with financial aid that the student has received or for which the student will apply, when the purpose of the disclosure is to determine the student's eligibility for aid, conditions to obtain aid, or amount of financial aid.

- Disclosure to organizations doing research studies for, or on behalf of, educational institutions for the purpose of developing predictive tests, administering student aid programs, or improving school instruction.
- Disclosure to accrediting organizations to fulfill accrediting duties.
- Disclosure to the alleged victim of a forcible or nonforcible sex offense.
- Disclosure of information related to sex offenders and others when the information is provided to the school under federal registration and disclosure requirements.
- Disclosure to a person or entity that is verified as the party that provided or created that record. For example, if a student transfers high schools, the second school can disclose a student's transcript to the original school to verify its authenticity.
- Disclosure to law enforcement or otherwise to comply with a judicial order or subpoena. The school must make reasonable efforts to notify the student prior to the disclosure, unless it is a legal matter that orders nondisclosure.
- Disclosure to appropriate parties in connection with a health or safety emergency, if knowledge of this information is necessary to protect the health or safety of the student or others. The threat of harm must be "articulable and significant," and the school can take the totality of the circumstances into account in making this determination. Information can be disclosed to any individual with the ability to assist in the situation—this includes parents, law enforcement, school officials, spouse or partner, and other educational institutions, among others.[31]

A school is safe from federal scrutiny of its health and safety emergency determination as long as, based on the information available at the time, there is rational basis for the determination. In that case, the Department of Education will not question the determination.

10.1.5 Rights under FERPA

Under the federal law, students have the right to access and review most education records and the right to correction in appropriate circumstances.

10.1.5.1 Right to Access and Review

FERPA provides students with the right to access and review their education records. Once a student has issued a request, the educational institution must provide access to the records within 45 days of that request.[32] It also must respond to reasonable requests from students for explanations of the records. As with other disclosures to third parties, the educational institution must use reasonable measures to verify the identity of the student making the record request.

There are several exceptions to the right of inspection. Students do not have the right to inspect the financial records of their parents, confidential letters of recommendation (if the student has waived the right to inspect those documents), treatment records, attorney-client-privileged information, or records excluded from the definition of education records (such as law enforcement records). Also, when the request pertains to a record containing information about more than one student, the requesting students may access only the parts pertaining to themselves.[33]

10.1.5.2 Right to Correction

Students can request corrections to their education records if they believe the records to be inaccurate, misleading, or in violation of their privacy.[34] This access is intended to allow students to address incorrect records and is not for other purposes. If the request is granted, the records must be corrected within a reasonable time. If the request is denied, the student has a right to request a hearing, which must meet several requirements:

- The student must receive prior and reasonable notice of the time, place, and date.
- The hearing must be held within a reasonable time after the request is made.
- The hearing must be conducted by a party without a direct interest in the outcome.
- The student must be afforded a "full and fair" opportunity to present their case, with or without assistance or representation.
- The decision must be based on the evidence presented at the hearing, delivered in writing, within a reasonable amount of time after the hearing, and must contain a summary and explanation for the decision. If the hearing affirms the student's request, the education record must be amended, and the student must be notified in writing.

If the request is denied, however, the institution must notify the student of their right to place a written statement in the file about the contested record. The statement must then be maintained and disclosed with any release of the contested record.

10.1.6 Enforcement

Parents or eligible students who believe their rights have been violated under FERPA can file formal complaints with the Department of Education.[35] The Family Policy Compliance Officer (FPCO) at the Department of Education investigates complaints. If concerns are found, the FPCO typically provides technical assistance to the educational institution. Violations of FERPA can result in loss of federal funding for the educational institution.[36] FERPA does not provide a private right of action to parents and eligible students.[37]

10.1.7 Preemption

According to the Department of Education, FERPA was intended to establish "a minimum federal standard for record confidentiality and access." FERPA does not preempt state law in this area.[38]

10.1.8 State Laws

In addition to protections at the federal level, student privacy is safeguarded at the state level. Multiple states have provisions in their constitutions or state laws that protect privacy generally, including in the education context.[39] Nearly all states have enacted at least one law specifically focused on student privacy.[40] In addition, the majority of states have enacted laws supplementing FERPA.[41]

In response to recent concerns over the use of student data for targeted advertising, California enacted the first law in the country to prohibit this practice for noneducational purposes—the Student Online Personal Information Protection Act (SOPIPA).[42] California's law became a template for other states around the country that have passed education privacy laws to address edtech company practices.[43] Privacy practitioners should be alert to the changing landscape in this area of privacy regulation.[44]

10.2 FERPA and the Protection of Pupil Rights Amendment

FERPA applies only to information stored in education records, defined as information that (1) directly relates to a student and (2) is maintained by the educational institution or on behalf of the institution. All other general student information that falls outside this definition is not covered by FERPA's consent and disclosure requirements.[45] This has traditionally allowed schools to sell student directory information to commercial entities such as banks or credit card companies unless a parent or student opts out.[46] Congress addressed specific concerns in FERPA by passing the Protection of Pupil Rights Amendment in 1978 and the No Child Left Behind Act in 2001.

10.2.1 Protection of Pupil Rights Amendment of 1978

Congress responded to concerns about the collection and disclosure of student information for commercial purposes by amending FERPA in 1978 with the Protection of Pupil Rights Amendment (PPRA). PPRA requirements apply to all K-12 schools that receive federal funding; the statute, however, does not apply to colleges and universities.

PPRA provides certain rights to parents of minors with regard to the collection of sensitive information from students through surveys. These areas include:

- Political affiliations
- Mental and psychological problems potentially embarrassing to the student and their family
- Sex behavior and attitudes
- Illegal, antisocial, self-incriminating, and demeaning behavior
- Critical appraisals of other individuals with whom respondents have close family relationships
- Legally recognized privileged or analogous relationships, such as those of lawyers, physicians and ministers
- Religious practices, affiliations or beliefs of the student or student's parent
- Income (other than that required by law to determine eligibility for participation in a program or for receiving financial assistance under such program)[47]

10.2.2 No Child Left Behind Act of 2001

The No Child Left Behind Act of 2001 broadened the PPRA to limit the collection and disclosure of student survey information.[48] The amended PPRA now requires schools to:

- Enact policies regarding the collection, disclosure, or use of personal information about students for commercial purposes[49]
- Allow parents to access and inspect surveys and other commercial instruments before they are administered to students[50]
- Provide advance notice to parents about the approximate date when these activities are scheduled[51]
- Provide parents the right to opt out of surveys or other sharing of student information for commercial purposes[52]

10.3 Individuals with Disabilities Education Act

The Individuals with Disabilities Education Act (IDEA) is a federal law that ensures eligible students, who are age 3 to 21, receive a free appropriate public education (FAPE).[53] IDEA requires schools to provide special education services that are tailored to each eligible student through the student's individualized education program (IEP).[54] IDEA provides parents or adult students with the right to inspect educational records, to request explanation of educational records, and to ask that educational records be amended.[55]

The privacy and confidentiality of records for students receiving special education services are protected by IDEA as well as FERPA. IDEA includes specific protections related to the records pertaining to the student's disability as well as to the student's IEP. Schools generally must inform parents or adult students when information related to special education services is no longer needed. Except for certain information that is needed for permanent education records, the school must destroy the information that is no longer needed upon the request of the parents or adult students.[56]

Privacy practitioners should be alert that, in addition to FERPA and IDEA, the records of students with disabilities may be protected by additional federal laws such as the Rehabilitation Act of 1973 and the Americans with Disabilities Act of 1990.[57]

10.4 FERPA and the HIPAA Privacy Rule

Privacy protections for student medical records have been a concern of federal regulators for decades. FERPA became law in the United States in 1974. When HIPAA was enacted in 1996, one important question for the U.S. Department of Health and Human Services (HHS) to address in the Privacy Rule for HIPAA was whether schools would be covered.[58] Although initial drafts of the HIPAA Privacy Rule included schools, the final version of the rule exempted schools where educational records were already subject to the privacy regime of FERPA.[59]

This means that the general rule is that health records are subject to FERPA—and not HIPAA—where a public elementary or secondary school provides a nurse for student health issues.[60] By contrast, FERPA does not apply to private elementary or secondary schools that do not receive federal funding. Health records maintained by one of these private schools are thus subject to the HIPAA Privacy Rule if the school qualifies as a "covered entity" under the federal law.[61]

A university with a health care clinic that treats only students is generally subject to the confidentiality requirements of FERPA relating to the student's health care records.[62] Both FERPA and the HIPAA Privacy Rule typically apply to the college or university health care center that treats both students and nonstudents, such as faculty and staff. In this instance, FERPA applies to the student health records and the HIPAA Privacy Rule applies to the nonstudent health records.[63]

Practitioners in this area should be aware that there may be instances where it is challenging to determine whether FERPA, HIPAA, or both apply. For example, there has been controversy over school-based health care centers that disclose health information to school officials when related to a lawsuit by the student (for instance, in regard to a rape on campus) that pertains to those health records.[64] Another example is the legal requirement for universities to share records within the institution and beyond its borders in an effort to prevent tragedies involving students with mental health issues. These fact settings may be difficult to navigate, particularly if the records include those from the high school and the university as well as records from school and nonschool health care providers and.[65] In these complex legal situations, it may be important to consult an attorney.

10.5 Education Technology

Today's classrooms increasingly employ content personalized to each student: social media helps students collaborate across classrooms and online portals allow students to access grades. The companies that provide computer software, mobile applications (apps), and web-based tools to educators, students, and parents are often referred to as edtech companies.

The impacts from the COVID-19 pandemic significantly increased the use of edtech companies by both schools and universities in the United States. During the pandemic, in-person classroom learning moved to remote learning that was provided through edtech, often for free to those in education settings. Students and parents alike became "instant experts" with edtech that enabled online hosting of teaching material for students, online posting of homework assignments, online communication between teachers and students, and online delivery of grades to students and parents. As of the writing of this book, most learning has returned to in-person classroom learning, yet many schools and universities have decided to maintain some level of edtech to supplement traditional in-person classroom learning. Because edtech focuses on ways to assist educators in providing content electronically, the privacy implications of edtech will continue to increase in importance.[66]

The activities of these edtech companies are subject to the laws discussed in this chapter. Numerous practices of edtech companies raise potential concerns, including surveillance of students across the internet and collection of student data for advertising purposes.[67]

10.5.1 FERPA and Edtech

Edtech was being utilized by schools prior to the COVID-19 pandemic. Google, for example, developed the free Apps for Education—a suite of tools that included Gmail, Google Calendar, Google Docs, and Google Classroom.[68] In 2014, students in California who used Apps for Education sued Google, accusing the company of scanning millions of emails sent to and received by students.[69] The Electronic Privacy Information Center (EPIC), a nongovernmental organization focused on civil liberties and privacy, asserted that Google's practice violated FERPA and advocated for the Department of Education to investigate the company.[70] Soon after the lawsuit was filed, Google agreed to change its business practices to ensure that the information in the emails could not be used for commercial purposes.[71]

During the time period when the lawsuit was pending against Google, the U.S. Department of Education issued guidelines to provide assistance in explaining how FERPA applied in the online arena.[72] This 2014 guidance instructs schools and universities to determine on a case-by-case basis whether the edtech companies that they partner with utilize FERPA-protected data. If so, the schools and universities are required to ensure that FERPA requirements are met.[73]

In 2020, the U.S. Department of Education's Student Privacy Policy Office provided resources related to the requirements for virtual learning. This featured the 2014 guidance along with a framework for evaluating the terms of service of edtech companies.[74]

10.5.2 COPPA and Edtech

In 2022, in response to concerns that students cannot attend class remotely or complete coursework online without being surveilled for commercial purposes, the U.S. Federal Trade Commission (FTC) announced that it would concentrate its scrutiny of potentially illegal practices of edtech companies through its enforcement of the Children's Online Privacy Protection Act (COPPA).[75] The focus by the FTC includes the following areas:

- **Prohibiting use for commercial purposes.** COPPA strictly limits how companies that are covered by the law, including edtech companies, use personal information obtained from children. COPPA prohibits edtech companies from using this information for commercial purposes, such as advertising.
- **Prohibiting unreasonable mandatory collection.** COPPA prohibits edtech companies from requiring children to provide more information than is reasonably necessary for the child to participate in the activity.
- **Prohibiting inappropriate retention.** COPPA prohibits edtech companies from retaining personal information that is obtained from children for longer than reasonably necessary to fulfill the company's purpose for which the data was obtained.
- **Requirements related to security.** COPPA requires edtech companies to have procedures related to the confidentiality, security, and integrity of children's personal data.[76]

10.5.3 Self-Regulation and Edtech

Self-regulation has become a prominent source of privacy rules applied in the educational technology space. The Future of Privacy Forum and the Software and Information Industry Association created a student privacy pledge in 2014, with more than 400 signatories by 2020, including many leading educational technology providers.[77] The updated Student Privacy Pledge 2020 involves specific provisions, including a prohibition on selling student personal information, a ban on using information collected in schools for behavioral targeting of advertisements to students, and a ban on building profiles of students for any purpose other than authorized educational purposes.[78] Violation of the pledge would make a company subject to enforcement as a deceptive trade practice under Section 5 of the FTC Act.[79]

10.6 Cybersecurity Requirements

The education sector holds troves of sensitive data, such as grades, disciplinary actions, and other school information. Modern K-12 schools and universities make use of cloud computing and edtech. This means that a security lapse can pose significant threats to student privacy.[80] To address cybersecurity concerns, K-12 schools and universities have been encouraged to implement the relevant guidelines in the National Institute of Standards and Technology (NIST) Framework.[81]

10.6.1 FERPA and Cybersecurity

Under FERPA, schools are expected to take reasonable security measures to protect student records. It is worth noting that FERPA does not require specific security controls.[82]

Although data breaches are not explicitly addressed in FERPA, such occurrences can lead to violations of FERPA. Data breaches can be investigated by the Department of Education.[83]

10.6.2 Gramm-Leach-Bliley Act and Cybersecurity

With regard to cybersecurity, the Department of Education has provided guidance to universities in possession of financial aid information to remind these institutions that they are covered by the Gramm-Leach-Bliley Act (GLBA) as financial institutions.[84] The GLBA Safeguards Rule, discussed in Chapter 9, requires financial institutions to take defined steps to ensure the security and confidentiality of student financial aid information, including maintaining an information security program, conducting risk assessments, and selecting service providers that can maintain appropriate safeguards.[85]

10.6.3 State Laws and Cybersecurity

Numerous states have enacted laws with various approaches to cybersecurity requirements for education data. For example, California's SOPIPA requires edtech companies to ensure reasonable security measures for student data. New York's Education Law 2-D mandates that school districts put in place cybersecurity policies that adhere to the NIST Cybersecurity Framework.[86]

Also, all 50 states have enacted data breach notification laws.[87] Privacy practitioners should be careful to determine if these laws include data breaches involving K-12 schools as well as universities.[88]

10.7 Conclusion

Because education has traditionally been regulated primarily at the state and local level in the U.S., privacy practitioners should be alert to state and local requirements focused on schools that relate to privacy and cybersecurity. In addition, schools may be covered by more general state protections—such as state constitutional provisions related to privacy, state comprehensive privacy laws,[89] and state data breach notification laws.[90]

U.S. law provides that schools receiving federal funding must abide by the major FIPPs related to education. Such educational institutions therefore must examine their practices to ensure compliance with these relatively detailed rules.

High schools as well as colleges and universities should remain alert to the complex interplay that exists regarding student and parent rights related to FERPA. High schools should be aware of the change in legal status that occurs when a student becomes an adult at the age of 18. At that point, the student is the person in control of rights connected to education records, including grades, rather than the parents. If a student has left high school and is attending only a college or university, the rights under FERPA are held by the student—regardless of the student's age.[91] Even after the rights under FERPA have transferred to the student. However, a school may disclose to the parents the educational records of the student without the student's consent in the circumstance where the student is a dependent for tax purposes.[92]

The impacts from the COVID-19 pandemic have significantly increased the use of edtech companies by both schools and universities in the United States. Privacy professionals should monitor developments in the edtech area because student online activities will continue to generate many new and detailed forms of student personal information. Because the education sector holds troves of sensitive data, such as grades, disciplinary actions, and other school information, privacy practitioners should pay attention to cybersecurity requirements for K-12 schooling as well as universities.[93]

Endnotes

1 In the United States, elementary schools and secondary schools are often referred to as kindergarten through 12th grade schools ("K-12 schools"). Postsecondary schools include colleges and universities.

2 20 U.S.C. § 1232g, accessed November 2017, https://www.law.cornell.edu/uscode/text/20/1232g.

3 20 U.S.C. § 1232g; 34 CFR § 99, accessed November 2017, https://www.law.cornell.edu/cfr/text/34/part-99.

4 20 U.S.C. § 1221, accessed November 2017, https://www.law.cornell.edu/uscode/text/20/1221.

5 20 U.S.C. § 1232g, accessed November 2017, https://www.law.cornell.edu/uscode/text/20/1232g; see Mike Chapple, "Understanding FERPA: How K-12 Schools Can Update Their Data Privacy Approach," *EdTech* (September 20, 2019), https://edtechmagazine.com/k12/article/2019/09/understanding-ferpa-how-k-12-schools-can-update-their-data-privacy-approach-perfcon.

6 34 CFR § 99.3, accessed July 2022, https://www.law.cornell.edu/cfr/text/34/99.3.

7 34 CFR § 99.3.

8 "Under FERPA, a student's admission record only becomes an 'educational record' that requires disclosure if the student matriculates at the university.... This means that students hoping to get a glimpse into why they were rejected by their top school will be unable to gain access to those records." Bradley Boult and Rachel LaBruyere, "The Man Behind the Curtain: College Admissions and FERPA Requests," JDSupra, February 16, 2021, https://www.jdsupra.com/legalnews/the-man-behind-the-curtain-college-3296523/.

9 20 U.S.C. § 1232g.

10 34 C.F.R. § 99.3.

11 Privacy practitioners should be aware that these exceptions in the Family Educational Rights and Privacy Act may be protected under other privacy laws.

12 It should be noted, however, that if the records are shared between campus police and other campus administrators, these are considered education records. "FERPA," Protecting Student Privacy, accessed June 2023, https://studentprivacy.ed.gov/ferpa; "School Resource Officers, School Law Enforcement Units, and The Family Educational Rights and Privacy Act (FERPA), Privacy Technical Assistance Center, February 2019, https://studentprivacy.ed.gov/sites/default/files/resource_document/file/SRO_FAQs_2-5-19_0.pdf.

13 Owasso Independent School District No. 1 v. Falvo, 534 U.S. 426 (2002), https://www.law.cornell.edu/supct/html/00-1073.ZO.html.

14 20 U.S.C. § 1232g, accessed October 2023, https://www.law.cornell.edu/uscode/text/20/1232g. Generally, records that are created or maintained by a professional health practitioner for the purpose of treating a student and not disclosed to anyone except those providing the treatment are considered treatment records. See Joshua Bosin et al., "U.S. Department of Education Issues New FERPA Guidance on Student Health Records," Holland & Knight, April 26, 2023, https://www.hklaw.com/en/insights/publications/2023/04/us-department-of-education-issues-new-ferpa-guidance-on-student.

15 "Personally Identifiable Information for Education Records," Protecting Student Privacy, U.S. Department of Education, accessed July 2022, https://studentprivacy.ed.gov/content/personally-identifiable-information-education-records.

16 34 C.F.R. § 99.3. See generally 20 U.S.C. § 1232g.

17 34 C.F.R. § 99.3(b), accessed November 2017, https://www.law.cornell.edu/cfr/text/34/99.3.

18 20 U.S.C. § 1232g(a)(5)(A)-(B), accessed November 2017, https://www.law.cornell.edu/uscode/text/20/1232g; 34 C.F.R. § 99.3(b)(a), accessed November 2017, https://www.law.cornell.edu/cfr/text/34/99.3.

19 The statute provides the following list: "the student's name, address, telephone listing, date and place of birth, major field of study, participation in officially recognized activities and sports, weight and height of members of athletic teams, dates of attendance, degrees and awards received, and the most recent previous educational agency or institution attended by the student." 20 U.S.C. § 1232g, accessed November 2017, https://www.law.cornell.edu/uscode/text/20/1232g. The rule provides that "directory information includes: the student's name; address; telephone listing; electronic mail address; photograph; date and place of birth; major field of study; grade level; enrollment status (e.g., undergraduate or graduate, full-time or part-time); dates of attendance; participation in officially recognized activities and sports; weight and height of members of athletic teams; degrees, honors, and awards received; and the most recent educational agency or institution attended." 34 C.F.R. § 99.3, accessed November 2017, https://www.law.cornell.edu/cfr/text/34/99.3.

20 34 C.F.R. § 99.7, accessed November 2017, https://www.law.cornell.edu/cfr/text/34/99.7.

21 34 C.F.R. § 99.3(b)(c), accessed November 2017, https://www.law.cornell.edu/cfr/text/34/99.3; For a discussion of Social Security numbers and student ID numbers as electronic personal identifiers, view "Family Educational Rights and Privacy Act (FERPA)," U.S. Department of Education, modified August 25, 2021, https://www2.ed.gov/policy/gen/guid/fpco/ferpa/index.html.

22 For a summary of this issue, view "Privacy Concerns: The Effects of the Latest FERPA Changes," ERIC, accessed November 2017, https://eric.ed.gov/?id=EJ904659.

23 HIPAA defines directory information to include the "patient's name," "location in the facility," "health condition expressed in general terms," and "religious affiliation." "Does the HIPAA Privacy Rule Permit Hospitals and Other Health Care Facilities to Inform Visitors or Callers about a Patient's Location in the Facility and General Condition?" U.S. Department of Health and Human Services, December 28, 2022, https://www.hhs.gov/hipaa/for-professionals/faq/483/does-hipaa-permit-hospitals-to-inform-visitors-about-a-patients-location/index.html.

24 For a discussion of the holder of the rights under the Family Educational Rights and Privacy Act, *see* Section 10.1.3.

25 "Frequently Asked Questions," Protecting Student Privacy, U.S. Department of Education, accessed June 2023, https://studentprivacy.ed.gov/frequently-asked-questions; "Know Your Rights: FERPA Protections for Student Health Records," Protecting Student Privacy, U.S. Department of Education, updated April 2023, https://studentprivacy.ed.gov/resources/know-your-rights-ferpa-protections-student-health-records. Even after the rights under the Family Educational Rights and Privacy Act have transferred to the student, one of the statutory exceptions allows many parents to obtain

the records without the student's consent. In the situation where the student is claimed as a dependent by either parent for tax purposes, both parents are allowed access to the educational records. 34 CFR § 99.31(a)(8), accessed November 2017, https://www.law.cornell.edu/cfr/text/34/99.31.

26 20 U.S.C. § 1232g(a)(5)(A)-(B), accessed November 2017, https://www.law.cornell.edu/uscode/text/20/1232g.

27 The U.S. Department of Education provides guidance to schools on information that can be released: "student's name, address, telephone number, date and place of birth, honors and awards, and dates of attendance." "Family Educational Rights and Privacy (FERPA)," U.S. Department of Education, modified August 25, 2021, https://www2.ed.gov/policy/gen/guid/fpco/ferpa/index.html.

28 34 C.F.R. § 99.31(a)(1)(ii), accessed November 2017, https://www.law.cornell.edu/cfr/text/34/99.31. For a discussion of identification and authentication of identify, view "Family Educational Rights and Privacy Act: Final Rule 34 CFR Part 99."

29 34 C.F.R. § 99.31(a)(1)(i), accessed November 2017, https://www.law.cornell.edu/cfr/text/34/99.31.

30 The "legitimate educational interest" does not have to be academic, just related to any appropriate school function. Also, reasonable security controls must be in place to ensure that parties with a legitimate educational interest are the only ones to access the records. See 34 C.F.R. § 99.31(a)(1)(ii), accessed November 2017, https://www.law.cornell.edu/cfr/text/34/99.31.

31 For an overview from the U.S. Department of Education, view "A Parent Guide to the Family Educational Rights and Privacy Act (FERPA), updated July 2021, https://studentprivacy.ed.gov/resources/parent-guide-family-educational-rights-and-privacy-act-ferpa.

32 34 C.F.R. § 99.10(b), accessed November 2017, https://www.law.cornell.edu/cfr/text/34/99.10.

33 20 U.S.C. § 1232g(a)(1)(A), accessed November 2017, https://www.law.cornell.edu/uscode/text/20/1232g. See also 34 C.F.R. § 99.12(a), accessed November 2017, https://www.law.cornell.edu/cfr/text/34/99.12.

34 20 U.S.C. § 1232g(a)(2), accessed November 2017, https://www.law.cornell.edu/uscode/text/20/1232g.

35 "File a Complaint," Protecting Student Privacy, U.S. Department of Education, accessed October 2019, https://studentprivacy.ed.gov/file-a-complaint.

36 20 U.S.C. § 1232g, accessed October 2019, https://www.law.cornell.edu/uscode/text/20/1232g; see generally "Family Educational Rights and Privacy Act (FERPA)", Electronic Privacy Information Center, accessed October 2019, https://epic.org/privacy/student/ferpa/.

37 "There is no question that the Family Educational Rights and Privacy Act's confidentiality provisions create no rights enforceable under §1983." Gonzaga University v. DOE, 536 U.S. 273 (2002), accessed October 2019https://www.law.cornell.edu/supct/html/01-679.ZS.html; see Daniel Solove, "The Battle for Leadership in Education Privacy Law: Will California Seize the Throne?" *Privacy + Security Blog,* Teach Privacy, April 7, 2014, https://teachprivacy.com/battle-leadership-education-privacy-law-will-california-seize-throne/.

38 "Legislative History of Major FERPA Provisions," Protecting Student Privacy, U.S. Department of Education, updated June 2002, https://studentprivacy.ed.gov/resources/

legislative-history-major-ferpa-provisions; see Solove, "The Battle for Leadership in Education Privacy Law: Will California Seize the Throne?

39 "2023 Consumer Data Privacy Legislation," National Conference of State Legislatures, updated February 15, 2023, https://www.ncsl.org/technology-and-communication/2023-consumer-data-privacy-legislation; "U.S. State Privacy Legislation Tracker," Resource Center, IAPP, updated June 19, 2023, https://iapp.org/resources/article/us-state-privacy-legislation-tracker/; "State Student Data Privacy Laws," Student Privacy Compass, https://studentprivacycompass.org/state-laws/.

40 "State Student Data Privacy Laws," Student Privacy Compass.

41 At least 35 states have enacted laws that supplement FERPA. "State Laws and Legislation," Student Privacy Compass, accessed June 2023, https://studentprivacycompass.org/state-laws-and-legislation/.

42 "SOPIPA: Student Online Personal Information Protection Act," *TermsFeed* (blog), updated February 18, 2023, https://www.termsfeed.com/blog/sopipa/; see "FPF Guide to Protecting Student Data Under SOPIPA: For K-12 School Administrators and Ed Tech Vendors," Future Privacy Forum, November 2016, https://fpf.org/wp-content/uploads/2016/11/SOPIPA-Guide_Nov-4-2016.pdf.

43 "State Laws and Legislation," Student Privacy Compass; "FPF Guide to Protecting Student Data Under SOPIPA" Future Privacy Forum.

44 See Thad Rueter, "What Does the Ed Tech Explosion Mean for Student Privacy," Government Technology, September 2023, https://www.govtech.com/cdg/what-does-the-ed-tech-explosion-mean-for-student-privacy; Kathleen Creel and Tara Dixit, "Privacy and Paternalism: The Ethics of Student Data Collection," The MIT Press Reader, September 15, 2022, https://thereader.mitpress.mit.edu/privacy-and-paternalism-the-ethics-of-student-data-collection/.

45 The Department of Education provides general privacy guidance on the Family Educational Rights and Privacy Act at its Privacy Technical Assistance Center. "Protecting Student Privacy While Using Online Educational Services: Requirements and Best Practices," Privacy Technical Assistance Center, February 2014, https://tech.ed.gov/wp-content/uploads/2014/09/Student-Privacy-and-Online-Educational-Services-February-2014.pdf. The Department of Education includes model terms of service for protecting student privacy while using online educational services. "Protecting Student Privacy While Using Online Educational Services: Model Terms Service," Privacy Technical Assistance Center, revised March 2016, https://studentprivacy.ed.gov/sites/default/files/resource_document/file/TOS_Guidance_Mar2016.pdf.

46 Lynn M. Daggett, "FERPA in the Twenty-First Century: Failure to Effectively Regulate Privacy for All Students," *Catholic University Law Review* 58:59, no. 1 (2008): 100, http://scholarship.law.edu/lawreview/vol58/iss1/4/; see "Frequently Asked Questions," Protecting Student Privacy, U.S. Department of Education.

47 20 U.S.C. § 1232h, https://www.law.cornell.edu/uscode/text/20/1232h. For additional information, *see* "Family Educational Rights and Privacy Act (FERPA)", U.S. Department of Education.

48 No Child Left Behind Act, Pub. L. No. 107-110 § 1061, 115 Stat. 1425, 2083 (2002), accessed November 2017https://www.law.cornell.edu/uscode/text/20/6301. For additional resources on No Child Left Behind, see "No Child Left Behind," U.S. Department of Education, accessed November 2017, www2.ed.gov/nclb/landing.jhtml.

49 20 U.S.C. § 1232h(c), accessed November 2017, https://www.law.cornell.edu/uscode/text/20/1232h.

50 20 U.S.C. § 1232h(c)(1)(F), accessed November 2017, https://www.law.cornell.edu/uscode/text/20/1232h.

51 20 U.S.C. § 1232h(c)(2)(B), accessed November 2017, https://www.law.cornell.edu/uscode/text/20/1232h.

52 20 U.S.C. § 1232h(c)(2)(B), accessed November 2017, https://www.law.cornell.edu/uscode/text/20/1232h.

53 "Statute and Regulations," Individuals with disabilities Education Act, accessed June 2023, https://sites.ed.gov/idea/statuteregulations/; "About IDEA," Individuals with disabilities Education Act, accessed June 2023, https://sites.ed.gov/idea/about-idea/#:~:text=Infants%20and%20toddlers%2C%20birth%20through,services%20under%20IDEA%20Part%20B. Although IDEA is not directly applicable to private schools, the law can apply to students with disabilities who enroll in a private school as a means of providing a free appropriate public education. "Forum Guide to Protecting the Privacy of Student Information, 2.D. FERPA an Special Education Records," National Center for Education Statistics, https://nces.ed.gov/pubs2004/privacy/section_2d.asp#:~:text=IDEA%20protects%20the%20privacy%20of,special%20education%20and%20related%20services.

54 "Learn the Law: IDEA," National Center for Learning Disabilities, accessed June 2023, https://www.ncld.org/get-involved/learn-the-law/idea/.

55 "Confidentiality and Access to Student Records," Center for Parent Information & Resources, accessed June 2023, https://www.parentcenterhub.org/records/.

56 "Forum Guide to Protecting the Privacy of Student Information, 2.D. FERPA an Special Education Records," National Center for Education Statistics.

57 "About IDEA," Individuals with disabilities Education Act, accessed June 2023, https://sites.ed.gov/idea/about-idea/#:~:text=Infants%20and%20toddlers%2C%20birth%20through,services%20under%20IDEA%20Part%20B; Diane Wiscarson and Susana Ramirez, "How do FERPA and HIPAA Privacy Laws Affect Students in Special Education?" *Spectrum Life Magazine*, April 13, 2021, https://www.spectrumlife.org/blog/how-do-ferpa-and-hipaa-privacy-laws-affect-students-in-special-education-642; "Protecting Students with Disabilities: Frequently Asked Questions About Section 504 and The Education of Children with Disabilities," U.S. Department of Education, modified June 1, 2023, https://www2.ed.gov/about/offices/list/ocr/504faq.html.

58 HIPAA is discussed in detail in Chapter 8 of this book.

59 Robert Gellman and Pam Dixon, "Student Privacy 101: Health Privacy in Schools—What Law Applies?" World Privacy Forum, updated January 2017, https://www.worldprivacyforum.org/2015/02/student-privacy-101-health-privacy-in-schools-what-law-applies/; Sandra Barboza, Susan Epps, Randy Byington, and Shane Keene, "HIPAA Goes to School: Clarifying Privacy Laws in the Education Environment," *The International Journal of Law, Healthcare and Ethics* 6, no. 2 (2008), https://dc.etsu.edu/etsu-works/2554/.

60 "Does the HIPAA Privacy Rule Apply to an Elementary or Secondary School?" Health Information Privacy, U.S. Department of Health and Human Services (reviewed July 26, 2013), https://www.hhs.gov/hipaa/for-professionals/faq/513/does-hipaa-apply-to-an-elementary-school/index.html; see Dinsmore and Shohl, LLP, "Understanding the Privacy Rights of HIPAA and FERPA in Schools," *The National Law Review* (January

7, 2011), https://www.natlawreview.com/article/understanding-privacy-rights-hipaa-ferpa-schools. In circumstances where a fee is billed to insurance for medical services provided by the school or by a contractor of the school, the transaction may be deemed a HIPAA transaction. In this situation, the HIPAA Administration Simplification Rules for Transactions and Code Sets may apply to those providing the services. Importantly, the records related to the student's personally identifying information are education records protected by the Family Educational Rights and Privacy Act. If, on the other hand, the school or contractor does not bill the student's insurance for the medical services, HIPAA does not apply; see Sandra Barboza, Susan Epps, Randy Byington, and Shane Keene, "HIPAA Goes to School: Clarifying Privacy Laws in The Education Environment," *The Internet Journal of Law, Healthcare and Ethics* 6, no. 2 (2008), http://ispub.com/IJLHE/6/2/3751.

61 "Are there circumstances in which the HIPAA Privacy Rule might apply to an elementary or secondary school?" Health Information Privacy, U.S. Department of Health and Human Services (reviewed July 26, 2013), https://www.hhs.gov/hipaa/for-professionals/faq/515/are-there-circumstances-in-which-hipaa-might-apply-to-a-school/index.html; *see* Robert Gellman and Pam Dixon, "Student Privacy 101: Health Privacy in Schools – What Law Applies?" updated January 2017, https://www.worldprivacyforum.org/2015/02/student-privacy-101-health-privacy-in-schools-what-law-applies/; The concept of a "covered entity" under HIPAA is discussed in this book in Chapter 8.

62 "FERPA applies to most public and private postsecondary institutions and, thus, to the records on students at the campus health clinics of such institutions. These records will be either education records or treatment records under FERPA, both of which are excluded from coverage under the HIPAA Privacy Rule, even if the school is a HIPAA covered entity." "Joint Guidance on the Application of the Family Educational Rights and Privacy Act (FERPA) and the Health Insurance Portability and Accountability Act of 1996 (HIPAA) To Student Health Records," U.S. Department of Health and Human Services and U.S. Department of Education, November 2008, https://studentprivacy.ed.gov/sites/default/files/resource_document/file/ferpa-hipaa-guidance.pdf; see "Guidance," Protecting Student Privacy, U.S. Department of Education, accessed June 2023, https://studentprivacy.ed.gov/guidance.

63 Milada Goturi and Aaron Lacey, "Is Your Institution of Higher Education Covered by HIPAA?" Thompson Coburn, LLP, February 3, 2016, https://www.thompsoncoburn.com/insights/blogs/regucation/post/2016-02-03/is-your-institution-of-higher-education-covered-by-hipaa-; see "Does FERPA or HIPAA Apply to Records of Students at Health Clinics Run by Postsecondary Institutions?" U.S. Department of Health and Human Services, reviewed July 26, 2013, https://www.hhs.gov/hipaa/for-professionals/faq/518/does-ferpa-or-hipaa-apply-to-records-on-students-at-health-clinics/index.html; "Joint Guidance on the Application of the Family Educational Rights and Privacy Act (FERPA) and the Health Insurance Portability and Accountability Act of 1996 (HIPAA) To Student Health Records," U.S. Department of Health and Human Services and U.S. Department of Education.

64 See Steve Alder, "DoE Considers HIPAA Privacy Standard for FERPA to Close Rape Disclosure Loophole," *HIPAA Journal*, June 18, 2015, https://www.hipaajournal.com/doe-considers-hipaa-privacy-standards-for-ferpa-to-close-rape-disclosure-loophole-7085/.

65 See Gordon Davies, "Connecting the Dots: Lessons from the Virginia Tech Shooting," *Change: The Magazine of Higher Learning* 40, no.1, (August 7, 2010): 8-15, http://naspa.tandfonline.com/doi/pdf/10.3200/CHNG.40.1.8-15.

66 See Rueter, "What Does the Ed Tech Explosion Mean for Student Privacy,"; Daniel Mollenkamp, "As Number of Edtech Providers Grow, Some Say Student Privacy Needs a Reset," EdSurge, May 18, 2023, https://www.edsurge.com/news/2023-05-18-as-number-of-edtech-providers-grow-some-say-student-privacy-needs-a-reset; Taylor Ross, Caitlin Kim and Katherine Rhode, "Protecting Student Data Privacy in the Digital Age," The Regulatory Review, September 18, 2021, https://www.theregreview.org/2021/09/18/saturday-seminar-protecting-student-data-privacy-in-digital-age/; See Caroline Knorr, "Ask Your Kid's School These Essential Student Privacy and Safety Questions," Common Sense Media, August 6, 2018, https://www.commonsensemedia.org/blog/ask-your-kids-school-these-essential-student-privacy-and-safety-questions.

67 See "Governments Harm Children's Rights in Online Learning," Human Rights Watch, May 25, 2022, https://www.hrw.org/news/2022/05/25/governments-harm-childrens-rights-online-learning; "FTC to Crack Down on Companies that Illegally Surveil Children Learning Online," Federal Trade Commission, May 19, 2022, https://www.ftc.gov/news-events/news/press-releases/2022/05/ftc-crack-down-companies-illegally-surveil-children-learning-online; DeVan Hankerson Madrigal, Cody Venzke, Elizabeth Laird, Hugh Grant-Chapman, Dhanaraj Thakur "Report – Online and Observed: Student Privacy Implications of School-Issued Devices and Student Activity Monitoring Software," September 21, 2021, https://cdt.org/insights/report-online-and-observed-student-privacy-implications-of-school-issued-devices-and-student-activity-monitoring-software/.

68 Anya Kamenetz, "Google Hit with a Student Privacy Complaint," *NPR*, December 8, 2015, www.npr.org/sections/ed/2015/12/08/458460509/google-hit-with-a-student-privacy-complaint.

69 In Re: Google Inc. Gmail Litigation, March 18, 2014, http://digitalcommons.law.scu.edu/cgi/viewcontent.cgi?article=1667&context=historical.

70 Ryan Neal, "Google Sued for Data Mining: California Students Claim Violation of Educational Privacy," *International Business Times*, March 18, 2014, www.ibtimes.com/google-sued-data-mining-california-students-claim-violation-educational-privacy-1562198.

71 Michele Molnar, "Google Abandons Scanning of Student Email Accounts," *EdWeek Market Brief*, April 30, 2014, https://marketbrief.edweek.org/marketplace-k-12/google_abandons_scanning_of_student_email_accounts/.

72 Benjamin Herold, "U.S. Department of Education Issues Guidance on Student Data Privacy," *Education Week*, February 25, 2014, https://www.edweek.org/technology/u-s-education-department-issues-guidance-on-student-data-privacy/2014/02; The Department of Education provides general privacy guidance on the Family Educational Rights and Privacy Act at its Privacy Technical Assistance Center, "Protecting Student Privacy While Using Online Educational Services: Requirements and Best Practices," Privacy Technical Assistance Center.

73 The guidance notes that the schools and universities must also comply with other applicable federal, state, and local requirements related to privacy. "Protecting Student Privacy While Using Online Educational Services: Requirements and Best Practices," Privacy Technical Assistance Center.

74 "FERPA and Virtual Learning Related Resources," Student Privacy Policy Office, U.S. Department of Education, March 2020, https://studentprivacy.ed.gov/sites/default/files/resource_document/file/FERPA%20%20Virtual%20Learning%20032020_FINAL.pdf; see "Protecting Student Privacy While Using Online Educational Services: Requirements and Best Practices," Privacy Technical Assistance Center; "Protecting Student Privacy While Using Online Education Services: Model Terms of Service," Protecting Student Privacy, U.S. Department of Education, updated March 2016, https://studentprivacy.ed.gov/resources/protecting-student-privacy-while-using-online-educational-services-model-terms-service.

75 "Policy Statement of the Federal Trade Commission on Education Technology and the Children's Online Privacy Protection Act," Federal Trade Commission, accessed June 2023, https://www.ftc.gov/system/files/ftc_gov/pdf/Policy%20Statement%20of%20the%20Federal%20Trade%20Commission%20on%20Education%20Technology.pdf; see Lisa Oratz et al., "FTC's COPPA Enforcement Action Provides Lessons for Edtech Providers," Perkins Coie, August 21, 2023, https://www.perkinscoie.com/en/news-insights/ftcs-coppa-enforcement-action-provides-lessons-for-edtech-providers.html; Tonya Riley, "FTC Warns It Will Go After Ed Tech Companies Misusing Children's Data," CyberScoop, May 19, 2022, https://www.cyberscoop.com/ed-tech-ftc-coppa/.

76 "FTC to Crack Down on Companies that Illegally Surveil Children Learning Online," Federal Trade Commission; see "FTC to Focus on Edtech Providers in COPPA Enforcement Push, Cooley, May 27, 2022, https://www.cooley.com/news/insight/2022/2022-05-27-ftc-edtech-providers-coppa-enforcement?utm_source=Mondaq&utm_medium=syndication&utm_campaign=LinkedIn-integration.

77 "Student Privacy Pledge Surpasses 400 Signatories," Student Privacy Pledge, March 13, 2020, https://studentprivacypledge.org/news/student-privacy-pledge-surpasses-400-signatories/; "K-12 School Service Provider Pledge to Safeguard Student Privacy 2020," Student Privacy Pledge 2020, accessed July 2022, https://studentprivacypledge.org/privacy-pledge-2-0/.

78 "K-12 School Service Provider Pledge to Safeguard Student Privacy 2020," Student Privacy Pledge 2020.

79 See Alexi Pfeffer-Gillett, "Peeling Back the Student Privacy Pledge," *Duke University Law & Technology Review* 16, no. 1 (2018), https://scholarship.law.duke.edu/cgi/viewcontent.cgi?article=1317&context=dltr.

80 *What You Don't Know Can Hurt You, New Survey Identifies Gaps in K-12 Cybersecurity,* ManagedMethods, 2021-2022, https://get.managedmethods.com/k12-cloud-security-report-2021-22; Shannon Flynn, "Why Students Are at Risk of Data Breaches (and How to Protect Them)," MakeUseOf, June 4, 2022, https://www.makeuseof.com/students-at-risk-of-data-breaches/; "Data Privacy and the Student Data Warehouse," Student Privacy Compass, April 12, 2022, https://studentprivacycompass.org/resource/data-privacy-and-the-student-data-warehouse/.

81 Rebecca Torchia, "5 Reliable K-12 Cybersecurity Resources," EdTech, May 13, 2022, https://edtechmagazine.com/k12/article/2022/05/5-reliable-k-12-cybersecurity-resources; see Cybersecurity Framework, NIST, accessed July 2022, https://www.nist.gov/cyberframework; *NIST Special Publication 800-171 for Higher Education,* Deloitte, 2017, https://www2.deloitte.com/content/dam/insights/us/articles/4321_EDUCAUSE-cybersecurity/4321_EDUCAUSE-Cybersecurity.pdf; April Mardock, "Guide to the NIST Cybersecurity Framework: A K-12 Perspective," May 28, 2019, https://k12cybersecure.com/blog/guide-to-the-nist-cybersecurity-framework-a-k-12-

perspective/; see also "(GEN-16-12) Protecting Student Information," Federal Student Aid, an office of the U.S. Department of Education, July 1, 2016, https://fsapartners.ed.gov/knowledge-center/library/dear-colleague-letters/2016-07-01/gen-16-12-subject-protecting-student-information.

82 Adam Stone, "Understanding FERPA, CIPA, and other K-12 Student Data Privacy Laws," EdTech, April 28, 2022, https://edtechmagazine.com/k12/article/2022/04/understanding-ferpa-cipa-and-other-k-12-student-data-privacy-laws-perfcon; see "Data Security: K-12 and Higher Education," accessed July 2022, Protecting Student Privacy, U.S. Department of Education, https://studentprivacy.ed.gov/Security.

83 "Data Security: K-12 and Higher Education," U.S. Department of Education; "A Parent's Guide for Understanding K-12 School Data Breaches," Privacy Technical Assistance Center, accessed June 2023, https://studentprivacy.ed.gov/sites/default/files/resource_document/file/Parent%20Guide%20to%20Data%20Breach.pdf.

84 GLBA is discussed in detail in Chapter 9.

85 Benjamin Wanger and Pierce Cox, "Update on GLBA Safeguards Rule in Higher Education," BakerHostetler, June 1, 2023, https://www.bakerdatacounsel.com/blogs/update-on-glba-safeguards-rule-in-higher-education/; see Protecting Student Information, GEN-16-12, Federal Student Aid, an office of the U.S. Department of Education, accessed October 2023, https://fsapartners.ed.gov/knowledge-center/library/dear-colleague-letters/2016-07-01/gen-16-12-subject-protecting-student-information; Protecting Student Information, GEN-15-18, Federal Student Aid, an office of the U.S. Department of Education, accessed October 2023, https://fsapartners.ed.gov/knowledge-center/library/dear-colleague-letters/2015-07-29/protecting-student-information.

86 "4 State Student Data Privacy Laws Leading the Way for K-12 Schools," ManagedMethods, January 21, 2021, https://managedmethods.com/blog/state-student-data-privacy-laws/; see "The State of Student Data Privacy Laws: State-by-State Report Card," Parent Coalition for Student Privacy and The Network for Public Education, January 2019, https://iapp.org/media/pdf/resource_center/student_privacy_report_card_1.pdf; Julian Anjorin, "An Overview of Education Law 2-D," Sedara, April 25, 2022, https://www.sedarasecurity.com/education-law-2d/.

87 Chapter 7 includes a discussion of state data breach notification laws.

88 For example, Arkansas amended its data breach notification law in 2021 to include schools. "Recent Amendments to State Breach Notification Laws," Polsinelli, October 19, 2021, https://www.polsinelli.com/publications/recent-amendments-to-state-breach-notification-laws.

89 Chapter 6 focuses on state comprehensive privacy laws.

90 Chapter 7 includes a discussion of state data breach notification laws.

91 "Frequently Asked Questions," Protecting Student Privacy, U.S. Department of Education; "Guidance," Protecting Student Privacy, U.S. Department of Education, accessed June 2023, https://studentprivacy.ed.gov/guidance.

92 34 CFR § 99.31(a)(8), accessed November 2017, https://www.law.cornell.edu/cfr/text/34/99.31.

93 Geoffrey Alphonso, "Empowering Learners and Protecting Privacy: Advancing Data Security in EdTech," Forbes, August 2, 2023, https://www.forbes.com/sites/forbestechcouncil/2023/08/02/empowering-learners-and-protecting-privacy-advancing-data-security-in-edtech/?sh=70f3a3733053.

CHAPTER 11

Telecommunications and Marketing

Telecommunications and marketing involve very important privacy issues. One set of privacy telecommunications issues concerns specific communications channels and methods such as telemarketing, texts, and electronic mail. For these channels, U.S. law has specific rules that regulate how organizations can communicate with individuals for direct marketing and related purposes. Another set of marketing issues concerns the rules that apply to personal information collected by the companies themselves in the course of providing their services. Along with websites, companies in sectors such as telephone, cable, internet service, and social media can potentially learn a great deal about individuals by the phone calls they make, the television shows they watch, and the internet sites they visit. This chapter examines the statutes that govern the commercial use of that type of telephone, cable, and internet activity.[1] The chapter ends by examining the ethics of digital advertising.

11.1 Regulations Governing Telemarketing

U.S. federal and state laws place legal limits on the manner in which organizations can call individuals for marketing and fundraising purposes. Legislators and regulators have issued restrictions in response to complaints by families about deceptive marketing practices as well as unwanted marketing calls.

In examining the legal and theoretical underpinnings of these government actions, it is insightful to compare one traditional privacy tort action known as intrusion on seclusion to telemarking regulations. The tort of intrusion on seclusion imposes liability on "one who intentionally intrudes, physically or otherwise, upon the solitude or seclusion of another or his private affairs or concerns."[2] To succeed in an intrusion tort claim, the plaintiff must show that "the intrusion would be highly offensive to a reasonable person."[3] In contrast with intrusion tort requirements, telemarketing regulations in the United States address milder intrusions, which do not require a showing of "highly offensive" intrusion.

Telemarketing laws in the United States provide considerable detail about what types of intrusions are permitted under federal law. The U.S. Federal Communications Commission (FCC) and the U.S. Federal Trade Commission (FTC) have coordinated closely in their requirements. The FCC issued regulations under the Telephone Consumer Protection Act of 1991 (TCPA) that place restrictions on unsolicited advertising by telephone and facsimile and updated them in 2012 to address robocalls.[4] The FCC has determined that these prohibitions encompass text messages.[5]

The FTC first issued its Telemarketing Sales Rule (TSR) in 1995, implementing the Telemarketing and Consumer Fraud and Abuse Prevention Act. It has since amended the TSR in 2003, 2008, 2010, and 2015.[6] The TSR defines telemarketing as "a plan, program, or campaign which is conducted to induce the purchase of goods or services or a charitable contribution, by use of one or more telephones and which involves more than one interstate telephone call."[7]

The focus of this discussion will be on the FTC rule. This chapter first examines the rules governing how telemarketing calls can be made and then turns to who can receive such calls consistent with the Do Not Call (DNC) list.

11.1.1 Rules Governing How Calls Can Be Made under Telemarketing Laws

The TSR provides detailed rules about many aspects of how telemarketing calls can be made. The majority of telemarketing calls are from legitimate businesses trying to achieve their business goals while satisfying consumers. The telemarketing field, however, has also been plagued with a history of intrusive and fraudulent callers. Such callers sometimes intrude repeatedly on consumers, making frequent calls at inappropriate hours and in other ways that bother consumers. Such callers also sometimes take advantage of their anonymity and physical distance from consumers to try to defraud consumers. This combination of intrusiveness and fraud has led to periodic TSR updates to address new forms of problems for consumers.

The TSR requires covered organizations to:

- Call only between 8 a.m. and 9 p.m.
- Screen and scrub names against the national Do Not Call list
- Display caller ID information
- Identify themselves and what they are selling

- Disclose all material information and terms[8]
- Comply with special rules for prizes and promotions
- Respect requests to call back
- Retain records for at least 24 hours
- Comply with special rules for automated dialers

Under the rules, telemarketing is defined as "a plan, program, or campaign . . . to induce the purchase of goods or services or a charitable contribution" involving more than one interstate telephone call.[9] With some exceptions, all businesses or individuals that engage in telemarketing must comply with the TSR (or the FCC counterpart) as well as applicable state laws.[10] Neither the TSR nor the FCC rules preempt state law. As the FTC notes, compliance is required both of telemarketers—entities that initiate or receive telephone calls to or from consumers—and sellers—the entities that provide or arrange to provide the goods and services being offered.

11.1.1.1 Entity-Specific Suppression Lists

The TSR prohibits any seller (or telemarketer calling on the seller's behalf) from calling any consumer who has asked not to be called again. Sellers and telemarketers are required to maintain internal suppression lists to respect these DNC requests.[11]

11.1.1.2 Required Disclosures

The TSR requires that, at the beginning of the call, before delivering any sales content, telemarketers disclose:

- The identity of the seller
- That the purpose of the call is to sell goods or services
- The nature of those goods or services
- In the case of a prize promotion, that no purchase or payment is necessary to participate or win, and that a purchase or payment does not increase the chances of winning

The FTC has issued guidance on how and when these four basic disclosures must be made. For example, disclosures must be truthful. A company cannot say it is making a "courtesy call" to the consumer if the purpose of the call is telemarketing.

If a call has multiple purposes (such as the sale of different types of products or different overall purposes), disclosures have to be made for all sales purposes. The following examples are from the FTC's "Complying with the Telemarketing Sales Rule" guide:[12]

> *A seller calls a consumer to determine whether he or she is satisfied with a previous purchase and then plans to move into a sales presentation if the consumer is satisfied. Since the seller plans to make a sales presentation in at least some of the calls (the seller plans to end the call if the consumer is not satisfied), the four sales disclosures...must be made promptly during the initial portion of the call and before inquiring about customer satisfaction.*
>
> *However, a seller may make calls to welcome new customers and ask whether they are satisfied with goods or services they recently purchased. If the seller doesn't plan to sell anything to these customers during any of these calls, the four oral sales disclosures are not required. That's the case even if customers ask about the sellers' other goods or services, and the seller responds by describing the goods or services. Because the seller has no plans to sell goods or services during these calls, the disclosures are not required.*

11.1.1.3 Misrepresentations and Material Omissions

The TSR prohibits misrepresentations during the sales call. Telemarketers must provide accurate and complete information about the products and services being offered. They may not omit any material facts about the products or services. There are ten broad categories of information that must always be disclosed:

- Cost and quantity
- Material restrictions, limitations or conditions
- Performance, efficacy or central characteristics
- Refund, repurchase or cancellation policies
- Material aspects of prize promotions
- Material aspect of investment opportunities
- Affiliations, endorsements or sponsorships
- Credit card loss protection
- Negative option features
- Debt relief services

The rule was also amended to require specific disclosures when a telemarketer accepts payment by means other than a credit card or debit card, such as with phone or utility billing. In this case, the seller must obtain "express verifiable authorization." In amending the rule, the commission noted that many new payment methods lacked basic consumer protection provisions that exist in credit card transactions. Because the consumers may not have protections against unauthorized charges, for example, or recourse in the event they are dissatisfied with the goods or services, the TSR now requires telemarketers to meet a higher standard for proving authorization when consumers use new payment methods.

11.1.1.4 Transmission of Caller ID Information

The TSR requires entities that make telemarketing calls to transmit accurate call identification information so that it can be presented to consumers with caller ID services. Each telemarketer may transmit its own name and phone number, or it may substitute the name of the seller on whose behalf the telemarketer is making the call. The telemarketer may also substitute the seller's customer-service telephone number for its number, provided that the seller's number is answered during normal business hours.

Telemarketers are not liable if, for some reason, caller ID information does not reach a consumer, provided that the telemarketer has arranged with its carrier to transmit this information in every call. The FTC guidance states that "telemarketers who can show that they took all available steps to ensure transmission of Caller ID information in every call will not be liable for isolated inadvertent instances when the Caller ID information fails to make it to the consumer's receiver. Nevertheless, a telemarketer's use of calling equipment that is not capable of transmitting Caller ID information is no excuse for failure to transmit the required information."[13]

11.1.1.5 Prohibition on Call Abandonment

The TSR expressly prohibits telemarketers from abandoning an outbound telephone call with either "hang-ups" or "dead air." Under the TSR, an outbound telephone call is abandoned if a person answers it and the telemarketer does not connect the call to a live sales representative within two seconds of the person's completed greeting.

Abandoned calls often result from a telemarketer's use of predictive dialers to call consumers. Predictive dialers promote telemarketers' efficiency by simultaneously calling multiple consumers for every available sales representative. This maximizes the amount of time telemarketing sales representatives spend talking to consumers and minimizes representatives' downtime. But it also means that some calls are abandoned: consumers are either hung up on or kept waiting for long periods until a representative is available.

The use of prerecorded-message telemarketing, where a sales pitch begins with or is made entirely by a prerecorded message, also violates the TSR because the telemarketer is not connecting the call to a live sales representative within two seconds of the called person's completed greeting.[14] For a company to use prerecorded sales messages, it must have the prior express consent (opt-in) of the consumer.[15]

11.1.1.6 Abandonment Safe Harbor

According to the FTC guidance, the abandoned call safe harbor provides that a telemarketer will not face enforcement action for violating the call abandonment prohibition if the telemarketer:

- Uses technology that ensures abandonment of no more than three percent of all calls answered by a live person, measured per day per calling campaign
- Allows the telephone to ring for 15 seconds or four rings before disconnecting an unanswered call
- Plays a recorded message stating the name and telephone number of the seller on whose behalf the call was placed whenever a live sales representative is unavailable within two seconds of a live person answering the call
- Maintains records documenting adherence to the preceding three requirements

To take advantage of the safe harbor, a telemarketer must first ensure that a live representative takes at least 97 percent of the calls answered by consumers. Any calls answered by machine, calls that are not answered at all, and calls to nonworking numbers do not count in this calculation.[16]

Finally, to be within the safe harbor, the telemarketer must keep records that demonstrate its compliance with the other safe harbor provisions. The records must demonstrate both that the per-day, per-campaign abandonment rate has not exceeded three percent and that the ring time and recorded message requirements have been met.

11.1.1.7 Prohibition on Unauthorized Billing

The detailed rules in the TSR have been amended over time to address specific problems that consumers have experienced. For instance, the TSR strictly prohibits telemarketers from billing consumers for any goods or services without the consumer's express, informed consent. If the consumer provides the billing account information to the telemarketer during the call, then express, informed consent can be obtained in any nondeceptive manner.

If, on the other hand, the telemarketer has obtained the consumer's account information from some other source (known as "pre-acquired account information"), the TSR imposes an array of specific requirements on how express, informed consent must be obtained. In particular, the TSR has special requirements for free-to-pay conversion offers (offers that begin with a free trial but then convert to paid service at the end of the trial period). These rules are designed to combat the incidents of unauthorized charges made to consumer accounts where consumers did not understand that the service provider would charge the consumer at the end of the trial period. If pre-acquired account information is used in connection with a free-to-pay conversion offer, the telemarketer must:

- Obtain from the customer at least the last four digits of the account number to be charged
- Obtain the customer's express agreement to be charged for the goods or services using the account number for which the customer has provided at least the last four digits
- Make and maintain an audio recording of the entire telemarketing transaction

If pre-acquired account information is used in connection with any other type of transaction, the telemarketer must still (at minimum) identify the account with enough specificity for the consumer to understand which account will be charged and obtain the consumer's express agreement to be charged using that account number.

11.1.1.8 Updates to the TCPA Rules Concerning Robocalls and Autodialers

In 2012, the FCC revised its TCPA rules governing prerecorded calls (robocalls) and the use of automatic telephone dialing systems (autodialers) to reconcile its rules with the TSR.[17] First, the FCC revised its established business relationship exemption for robocalls. Under the revision, even if a company has an established business relationship with a consumer, it is required to receive prior express written consent for all robocalls to residential lines.[18] Second, the rules include a provision that allows consumers to opt out of future robocalls during a robocall.

In addition, the revisions increase harmonization with the FTC's rules to require "assessment of the call abandonment rate to occur during a single calling campaign over a 30-day period, and if the single calling campaign exceeds a 30-day period, [the FCC requires] that the abandonment rate be calculated each successive 30-day period or portion thereof during which the calling campaign continues." Finally, also consistent with the FTC, robocalls to residential lines made by health care-related entities governed by the Health Insurance Portability and Accountability Act (HIPAA) are exempt from the above requirements.[19]

11.1.1.9 Updates on the FCC Approach to Robotexts

In 2015, the FCC issued an order explicitly stating that text messages sent to wireless devices are subject to the same consumer protections as voice calls under the TCPA. This means that the TCPA prohibits companies from sending text messages via equipment that sends the messages without human intervention, known as "robotexts," absent express consent.[20] The order then altered the definition of prior written consent to require that the consent obtained must include a clear and conspicuous disclosure that telemarking calls or texts can be made with an autodialer or artificial voice. Further, it required that the consent could not be obtained as a requirement of purchase.[21]

In 2017, the FCC provided further guidance on robotexts, including:

- Consent can be revoked by the consumer at any time by any reasonable means
- The mere fact that a consumer's wireless number appears in the contact list of another wireless customer is not sufficient to establish consent
- When a caller has consent for a wireless number and the number has been reassigned, the caller is not liable for the first call but will be liable for subsequent calls if the new consumer makes the caller aware of the change[22]

In 2021, the U.S. Supreme Court limited the TCPA's definition of automatic telephone dialing systems (autodialers) to equipment that has the "capacity to use a random or sequential number generator to either store or produce phone numbers to be called," reversing broad interpretations of autodialers by lower courts that included text messages.[23] The effect of this ruling is to clarify that text message campaigns are permitted under the TCPA—so long as they comply with other requirements of the act.[24]

11.1.1.10 Recordkeeping Requirements

To make enforcement more effective, the TSR requires sellers and telemarketers to keep substantial records that relate to their telemarketing activities. In general, the following records must be maintained for two years from the date that the record is produced:

- Advertising and promotional materials
- Information about prize recipients
- Sales records
- Employee records
- All verifiable authorizations or records of express informed consent or express agreement

These records may be maintained in whatever manner, format, or medium the company uses in the normal course of business. For example, the records may be maintained in electronic or paper formats. Additionally, the TSR requires only one copy of the records to be maintained. Sellers and telemarketers can decide which party should maintain which records as part of the services contract.[25]

In the event of dissolution or termination of the business of a seller or telemarketer, the principal of the business must maintain all records of the business. In the event of a sale, assignment, or other change in ownership of the seller or telemarketer's business, the successor business must maintain the records.

For each type of record previously listed, the TSR includes lists of the information that must be retained. For example, sales records must include (1) the name and last known address of each customer, (2) the goods or services purchased, (3) the date the goods or services were shipped or provided, and (4) the amount the customer paid for the goods or services.

Similarly, for all current and former employees directly involved in telephone sales, records must include (1) the name (and any fictitious name used), (2) the last known home address and telephone number, and (3) the job title(s) of each employee. Additionally, if fictitious names are used by employees, the TSR also requires that each fictitious name be traceable to a specific employee.[26]

11.1.1.11 Enforcement Provisions

The TSR includes significant enforcement provisions and can be enforced by the FTC as well as state attorneys general. The FTC has aggressively enforced the TSR.[27] Violations of the TSR are currently punishable by civil penalties of up to $50,120 per call.[28] The FCC and state attorneys general also actively enforce their counterpart regulations.

The TSR provides for a limited private right of action against telemarketers as an individual must meet the threshold of $50,000 in actual damages to be able to file suit.[29] The ability of plaintiffs to bring a class-action lawsuit under the TCPA has likely been further restricted by the 2021 U.S. Supreme Court case of TransUnion v. Ramirez, where the court found that a plaintiff must show actual harm and not the mere risk of harm to be able to bring a suit.[30]

Additionally, some states have their own versions of TCPA, known as mini-TCPAs, as well as their own telemarketing sales rules that carry additional penalties and may have different requirements.[31] For example, the Louisiana Public Service Commission's DNC General Order has different allowed time frames for making calls, limits established business relationships to six months, and has established its own penalties for violators.[32]

11.1.2 Who Can Be Called: The U.S. National Do Not Call Registry

The U.S. National DNC Registry is perhaps the best known of the FTC's TSR requirements and remains the most popular consumer program ever implemented by the FTC.[33] The program provides a means for U.S. residents to register residential and wireless phone numbers that they do not wish to be called for telemarketing purposes (with specific exceptions, see Section 11.1.2.1).

The DNC Registry provisions took effect in 2003 and require sellers and telemarketers to access the registry prior to making any phone-based solicitations. They are also required to update their call lists every 31 days with new registry information.

The registry is accessed via an automated website at https://telemarketing.donotcall.gov/.[34] Only sellers, telemarketers, and their service providers may access the registry. Each seller must establish a profile by providing identifying information about the organization. The seller then receives a unique Subscription Account Number (SAN) upon payment of the appropriate fee.

Telemarketers accessing the registry on behalf of seller-clients are required to identify the seller-clients and provide the seller-client's unique SAN. Telemarketers access the registry, at no cost, through the use of their seller-client's unique SANs. Their access is limited to the area codes requested and paid for by the seller-client.

The FTC's guidance specifically states that:[35]

> *A telemarketer or other service provider working on behalf of a seller may access the registry directly or through the use of its seller-client's SAN. If access is gained through its seller-client's SAN, the telemarketer or service provider will not have to pay a separate fee for that access. The extent of its access will be limited to the area codes requested and paid for by its seller-client.*
>
> *If a telemarketer or service provider is accessing the registry directly—that is, if a telemarketer or service provider decides to obtain the information on its own behalf—it will have to pay a separate fee and comply with all requirements placed on sellers accessing the registry. Such a telemarketer or service provider will be provided a SAN that can be used only by that company. In other words, that SAN is not transferable.*

This guidance makes it clear that each SAN belongs to a specific seller and SANs are not transferable.

Note that it is a violation of the TSR to place any call to a consumer (absent an exception) unless the registry has been checked. In other words, even a call to a consumer whose phone number is not on the registry is a violation of the TSR if the registry was not checked prior to the call.[36]

The FTC, the FCC, and state attorneys general enforce the DNC Registry, which now contains approximately 250 million participating phone numbers—and is still growing.[37] As of the writing of this book, violations of the rule can lead to civil penalties of up to $50,120 per violation.[38] In addition, violators may be subject to nationwide injunctions that prohibit certain conduct and may be required to pay redress to injured consumers.[39]

11.1.2.1 Exceptions to the DNC Rules

DNC rules apply to for-profit organizations and cover charitable solicitations placed by for-profit telefunders. DNC rules do *not* apply to:

- Nonprofits calling on their own behalf
- Calls to customers with an existing relationship within the last 18 months
- Inbound calls, provided that there is no "upsell" of additional products or services[40]
- Most business-to-business calls

Established Business Relationship Exception. Sellers (and telemarketers calling on their behalf) may call a consumer with whom a seller has an established business relationship (EBR), provided the consumer has not asked to be on the seller's entity-specific DNC list. The TSR recognizes two distinct types of relationships: customers and prospects.

An EBR exists with a customer if the consumer has purchased, rented, or leased the seller's goods or services (or completed a financial transaction with the seller) within 18 months preceding a telemarketing call. The 18-month period runs from the date of the last payment, transaction or shipment between the consumer and the seller.

An EBR exists with a prospect if the consumer has made an application or inquiry regarding the seller's goods and services. This EBR runs for three months from the date of the person's inquiry or application.

Exception Based on Consent. The TSR allows sellers and telemarketers to call consumers who consent to receive such calls. This consent must be in writing, must state the number to which calls may be made, and must include the consumer's signature. A valid electronic signature is acceptable.

Note that the seller's request for consent must be clear and conspicuous. If it is in writing, the request "cannot be hidden; printed in small, pale, or noncontrasting type; hidden on the back or bottom of the document; or buried in unrelated information where a person would not expect to find such a request."[41] If online, the "please call me" button may not be prechecked.

The FTC's guidance also states: "In the FTC's enforcement experience, sweepstakes entry forms often have been used in a deceptive manner to obtain 'authorization' from a consumer to incur a charge or some other detriment. Authorization or permission obtained through subterfuge is ineffective. The FTC scrutinizes any use of such sweepstakes entry forms as a way to get a consumer's permission to place telemarketing calls to her number."[42]

Do Not Call Safe Harbor. The TSR has a DNC Safe Harbor that sellers and telemarketers can use to reduce the risk of liability. Per the guidance:[43]

> *If a seller or telemarketer can establish that as part of its routine business practice, it meets the following requirements, it will not be subject to civil penalties or sanctions for erroneously calling a consumer who has asked not to be called, or for calling a number on the National Registry:*
>
> - *The seller or telemarketer has established and implemented written procedures to honor consumers' requests that they not be called*
> - *The seller or telemarketer has trained its personnel, and any entity assisting in its compliance, in these procedures*

- *The seller, telemarketer, or someone else acting on behalf of the seller . . . has maintained and recorded an entity-specific Do Not Call list*
- *The seller or telemarketer uses, and maintains records documenting, a process to prevent calls to any telephone number on an entity-specific Do Not Call list or the National Do Not Call Registry. This, provided that the latter process involves using a version of the National Registry from the FTC no more than 31 days before the date any call is made*
- *The seller, telemarketer, or someone else acting on behalf of the seller. . . monitors and enforces compliance with the entity's written Do Not Call procedures, [then]*
- *The call is a result of error.*

This DNC Safe Harbor provides an important protection for sellers and telemarketers because violations of the TSR can result in civil penalties, as of the writing of this book, of up to $50,120 per call.[44]

11.1.3 Recent Enforcement Actions Related to Robocalls

In recent years, regulators have increased efforts to deal with the billions of robocalls that U.S. consumers receive every month.[45] In 2019, state attorneys general and telephone companies announced an initiative to fight robocalls. State and federal authorities undertook nearly 100 enforcement actions against illegal robocallers. State authorities focused their efforts on pharmaceutical, credit card, and loan scams. As part of the 2019 initiative to fight robocalls, a dozen of the United States' largest telephone companies pledged to all 50 state attorneys general (plus the District of Columbia) to implement call-blocking technologies and make anti-robocall tools available for free.[46] Also in 2019, the FTC focused enforcement actions on complex operations that often attempted to scam consumers.[47] In 2021, the FCC issued a record fine of $225 million to telemarketers that made approximately one billion robocalls.[48]

11.1.4 State Telemarketing Laws

As neither the TSR nor the FCC rules preempt state laws, the majority of states have enacted telemarketing laws—creating additional legal requirements for telemarketers.[49] For example, more than half the states require that telemarketers obtain a license or register with the state.[50] States can also create their own DNC lists, with differing exceptions, fines, or methods of consumer enrollment from their federal counterpart.[51] Some states require that telemarketers identify themselves at the beginning of the call or that the telemarketer terminate the call without rebuttal if the recipient of the call so desires.[52] Finally, states may require that a written contract be created for certain transactions.[53]

11.2 Fax Marketing

In addition to regulating telemarketing and internet-to-phone short message service (SMS) marketing, the TCPA, which is enforced by the FCC, prohibits unsolicited commercial fax transmissions. Consent can be explicit or inferred from an EBR.[54]

In 2005, Congress amended the TCPA by passing the Junk Fax Prevention Act (JFPA).[55] The JFPA clarified whether consent was required for commercial faxing. The JFPA specifically provides that consent can be inferred from an EBR and permits sending of commercial faxes to recipients based on an EBR as long as the sender offers an opt-out in accordance with the act.[56] Recently, the U.S. Supreme Court decided that faxed invitations that are part of market research surveys and are in exchange for money are not considered "unsolicited" under the TCPA and amended by the JFPA.[57]

Under TCPA, penalties include a private right of action and statutory damages of up to $500 per fax.[58] In 2001, Hooters of Augusta, Georgia, was found to have violated the act and ordered to pay out $12 million in a class action suit.[59] In 2004, the FCC approved a $5.4 million fine against Fax.com for violations of the act.[60]

In 2019, the FCC announced that online cloud-based fax services do not fall under the TCPA and the JFPA. The reasoning is that online fax services that receive faxes (as an email) over the internet do not fall under the definition of telephone facsimile machine and therefore cannot be subject to the junk fax lawsuits.[61]

Some states have enacted their own laws regulating unsolicited commercial fax transmissions. Notably, California attempted to eliminate the TCPA's EBR exception with legislation applicable to unsolicited faxes sent to or from a fax machine located within the state.[62] The law, however, was declared unconstitutional when applied to interstate fax transmissions due to the TCPA's preemption of interstate regulation.[63]

11.3 Controlling the Assault of Non-Solicited Pornography and Marketing Act of 2003

Along with the rules governing commercial telemarketing and faxes, Congress created rules for unsolicited commercial electronic mail in the Controlling the Assault of Non-Solicited Pornography and Marketing (CAN-SPAM) Act of 2003.[64] The act applies to any entity that advertises products or services by electronic mail directed to or originating from the United States. The law covers the transmission of commercial email messages with a primary purpose of advertising or promoting a product or service.

CAN-SPAM was never intended to eliminate all unsolicited commercial email, but rather to provide a mechanism for legitimate companies to send emails to prospects and respect individual rights to opt out of unwanted communications. Spam-filtering software is still widely used to screen out as much of the continuing spam as possible. The act nonetheless has fulfilled an important purpose. It has created the rules of the road for how legitimate organizations send emails, including clear identification of the sender and a simple unsubscribe or opt-out button. The CAN-SPAM Act:

- Prohibits false or misleading headers
- Prohibits deceptive subject lines
- Requires commercial emails to contain a functioning, clearly and conspicuously displayed return email address that allows the recipient to contact the sender
- Requires all commercial emails to include clear and conspicuous notice of the opportunity to opt out along with a cost-free mechanism for exercising the opt-out, such as by return email or by clicking on an opt-out link
- Prohibits sending commercial email (following a grace period of 10 business days) to an individual who has asked not to receive future email
- Requires all commercial email to include (1) clear and conspicuous identification that the message is a commercial message (unless the recipient has provided prior affirmative consent to receive the email) and (2) a valid physical postal address of the sender (which can be a post office box)

- Prohibits aggravated violations relating to commercial emails, such as (1) address-harvesting and dictionary attacks, (2) the automated creation of multiple email accounts, and (3) the retransmission of commercial email through unauthorized accounts
- Requires all commercial email containing sexually oriented material to include a warning label (unless the recipient has provided prior affirmative consent to receive the email)

CAN-SPAM is enforced primarily by the FTC and carries penalties of fines of up to $50,120 per violation.[65] In addition, deceptive commercial email is subject to laws banning false or misleading advertising. The FTC has the authority to issue regulations implementing the CAN-SPAM Act and did so in 2008 to clarify a number of statutory definitions.[66]

CAN-SPAM distinguishes commercial email messages from "transactional or relationship messages," which are messages with a primary purpose to:

- Facilitate or confirm an agreed-upon commercial transaction
- Provide warranty or safety information about a product purchased or used by the recipient
- Provide certain information regarding an ongoing commercial relationship
- Provide information related to employment or a related benefit plan
- Deliver goods or services to which the recipient is entitled under the terms of an agreed-upon transaction

CAN-SPAM contains several requirements generally applicable to the sender of a commercial email message. A sender is anyone who initiates an email message and whose product or service is advertised or promoted by the message. More than one person may be deemed to have initiated a message. The FTC issued a regulation in 2008 clarifying that the entity identified in the "from" line can generally be considered the single sender as long as there is compliance with the other provisions of CAN-SPAM.[67] The 2008 regulation also provides additional detail on (1) a prohibition on having the email recipient pay a fee to opt out, (2) the definition of a valid physical postal address, and (3) the application of the term "person" to apply beyond natural persons.

CAN-SPAM grants enforcement authority to the FTC and other federal regulators, along with state attorneys general and other state officials. Internet service providers that have been adversely affected by a violation may sue violators for injunctive relief and monetary damages. Unlike some state spam laws that are now preempted, the act does not provide for a right of action for other parties. For those authorized to sue, the act provides for injunctive relief and damages up to $250 per violation, with a maximum award of $2 million. The act further provides that a court may increase a damage award up to three times the amount otherwise available in cases of willful or aggravated violations. Certain egregious conduct is punishable by up to five years' imprisonment.

In an example from 2009, a federal judge shut down a company called 3FN based on the FTC's allegations that it had knowingly distributed spam and malware as well as hosted illegal content, such as child pornography.[68]

CAN-SPAM preempts most state laws that restrict email communications, although state spam laws are not superseded by CAN-SPAM to the extent such laws prohibit false or deceptive activity.

11.3.1 Wireless Message Rules Under CAN-SPAM

In addition to the email rules discussed above, the FCC issued rules implementing the CAN-SPAM Act with regard to mobile service commercial messages (MSCMs), including many commercial text messages.

The CAN-SPAM Act defines an MSCM as "a commercial electronic mail message that is transmitted directly to a wireless device that is utilized by a subscriber of a commercial mobile service." The message must have or utilize a unique electronic address that includes "a reference to an internet domain." The FCC also notes in its commentary that the rule is designed to apply only to mail addresses designed by carriers for mobile services messaging. Importantly, the FCC's rules cover messages sent using SMS technology, but do not cover phone-to-phone messages.[69]

The FCC rule defers to the FTC rules and interpretation regarding the definitions of "commercial" and "transactional" (with respect to the mail messages) as well as the mechanisms for determining the primary purpose of messages. Accordingly, the FCC rule must be analyzed in the context of the FTC regulatory framework for the CAN-SPAM Act.

11.3.2 Express Prior Authorization

The CAN-SPAM Act prohibits senders from sending any MSCMs without the subscriber's express prior authorization. Express prior authorization must be obtained for each MSCM, regardless of sender or industry. The FCC requirements are quite detailed, and can be summarized as follows:[70]

- Express prior authorization must be "express," meaning that the consumer has taken an affirmative action to give the authorization. Authorization may not be obtained in the form of a negative option. If the authorization is obtained via a website, the consumer must take an affirmative action, such as checking a box or hitting a button.
- The authorization must also be given prior to the sending of any MSCMs. There is no provision to grandfather existing authorizations that senders may have obtained. Because of the disclosure requirements in these authorizations, the FCC notes that senders who claim they have obtained authorization prior to the effective date of these rules will not be in compliance unless they can demonstrate that these existing authorizations have met each of the requirements in the rule.
- Consumers must not bear any cost with respect to the authorization or revocation processes.
- Each authorization must include certain required disclosures stating that:
    - The subscriber is agreeing to receive MSCMs sent to their wireless device from a particular (identified) sender
    - The subscriber may be charged by their wireless provider in connection with the receipt of such messages
    - The subscriber may revoke the authorization at any time
- These disclosures must be clearly legible and in sufficiently large type (or volume, if given via audio). They must be presented in a manner that is readily apparent to the consumer. These disclosures must be separate from any other authorizations contained in another document. Additionally, if any portion of the authorization/disclosure is translated into another language, then all portions must be translated into that language.
- As noted above, the authorization must be specific to the sender and must clearly identify the entity that is being authorized to send the MSCMs. The FCC rule prohibits any sender from sending MSCMs on behalf of other third parties, including affiliates and marketing partners. Each entity must obtain separate express prior authorizations for the messages it sends.

- Authorization may be obtained in any format, oral or written, including electronic. Although writing is not required, the FCC requires that each sender of MSCMs must document the authorization and be able to demonstrate that a valid authorization (meeting all the other requirements) existed prior to sending the commercial message. The commentary notes that the burden of proof rests with the sender.
- With regard to revocations, senders must enable consumers to revoke authorizations using the same means the consumers used to grant authorizations. (For example, if a consumer authorizes MSCMs electronically, the company must permit the consumer to revoke the authorization electronically.)
- Additionally, the MSCMs themselves must include functioning return email addresses or another internet-based mechanism that is clearly and conspicuously displayed for the purpose of receiving opt-out requests.[71]
- The FCC rule maintains the CAN-SPAM-mandated 10-business-day grace period following a revoked authorization, after which messages cannot be sent.[72]

11.3.3 The Wireless Domain Registry

To help senders of commercial messages determine whether those messages might be MSCMs (rather than regular commercial email), the FCC has created a registry of wireless domain names, available on the FCC website.[73] It is updated on a periodic basis, as new domains are added.

Senders are responsible for obtaining this list and ensuring that the appropriate authorizations exist before sending commercial messages to addresses within the domains. In other words, the requirements listed above will apply to messages sent to any address whose domain name is included on the wireless domain name list.[74]

All commercial mobile radio service providers are required under the domain name list rule to identify all electronic mail domain names that are dedicated for subscribers with wireless devices. The providers are also responsible for updating information on the domain name list to the FCC within 30 days before issuing any new or modified domain names.

11.4 The Telecommunications Act of 1996

The chapter thus far has examined marketing rules for telecommunications channels such as telephones, faxes, emails, and texts. The discussion now turns to rules affecting the telecommunications companies themselves in connection with personal information. The Telecommunications Act of 1996 was a major piece of legislation that reshaped numerous aspects of telecommunications markets.[75] Section 222 of the act governs the privacy of customer information provided to and obtained by telecommunications carriers. Prior to the act, carriers were permitted to sell customer data to third-party marketers without consumer consent. The statute imposed new restrictions on the access, use, and disclosure of customer proprietary network information (CPNI).

11.4.1 CPNI Requirements

CPNI is information collected by telecommunications carriers related to their subscribers. This includes subscription information, services used, and network and billing information as well as phone features and capabilities. It also includes call log data such as time, date, destination, and duration of calls. Certain personal information such as name, telephone number, and address is *not* considered CPNI.

The act imposes requirements on carriers to limit access, use, and disclosure of CPNI. Specifically, carriers can use and disclose CPNI only with customer approval or as required by law.[76] Carriers do not need approval, however, to use, disclose, or provide marketing offerings among service categories to which customers already subscribe. Carriers can also use CPNI for billing and collections, fraud prevention, customer service, and emergency services.

11.4.2 Opt-in and Opt-out Rules for CPNI

The rules concerning opt-in and opt-out for use of CPNI have shifted over time. In 1998, the FCC issued a rule requiring carriers to obtain express consent from customers before using CPNI, even for the carriers' own marketing purposes. This rule was struck down in 1999 in U.S. West, Inc. v. Federal Communications Commission.[77] In that case, the Tenth Circuit found that the opt-in requirement violated the First Amendment speech rights of the carriers. Thus, the standard shifted to an opt-out system for carriers' own use of CPNI. In 2002, the FCC issued final rules requiring carriers to obtain express consent before CPNI could be shared with third parties, but allowed sharing of CPNI with joint venture or independent contractors unless customers opted out within 30 days of being notified. In 2007, the FCC issued new CPNI regulations governing carriers' use and sharing of CPNI.[78] The 2007 CPNI order requires customers to expressly consent, or opt in, before carriers can share their CPNI with joint venture partners and independent contractors for marketing purposes.

The 2007 CPNI order imposes requirements aimed at curbing pretexting, or gaining access to CPNI through fraudulent means. First, carriers must notify law enforcement when CPNI is disclosed in a security breach within seven business days of that breach. Second, customers must provide a password before they can access their CPNI via telephone or online account services. The order also establishes carrier CPNI compliance requirements. Carriers must certify their compliance with these laws annually, explain how their systems ensure compliance and provide an annual summary of consumer complaints related to unauthorized disclosure of CPNI.

11.4.3 Entities Subject to CPNI Requirements

The CPNI requirements apply to telecommunications carriers and voice-over-internet protocol (VoIP) providers that are interconnected with telephone service.[79] As of the writing of this book, the FCC does not regulate streaming video companies, referred to as over-the-top providers (OTT), when the content is provided over the internet or to mobile devices.[80]

As discussed in more detail in the following section, the CPNI requirements historically did not apply to broadband internet service providers (ISPs). In 2016, the FCC issued a detailed regulation that was designed to regulate privacy for customers of broadband ISPs. This regulation was repealed under the Trump administration and new FCC leadership, and ISPs today are subject to the general CPNI requirements of Section 222.

11.5 The Cable Communications Policy Act of 1984

The Cable Communications Policy Act of 1984 regulates the notice a cable television provider must furnish to customers, the ability of cable providers to collect personal information, the ability of cable providers to disseminate personal information, and the retention and destruction of personal information by cable television providers.[81] It also provides a private right of action for violations of the aforementioned provisions and allows for actual or statutory damages, punitive damages, and reasonable attorneys' fees and court costs.[82] The act does not regulate the provision of broadband internet services via cable because the act defines a "cable service" as "one-way transmission to subscribers of . . . video programming or . . . other programming service, and . . . subscriber interaction, if any, which is required for the selection or use of such video programming or other programming service."[83]

At the time of entering into an agreement to provide cable services and on an annual basis thereafter, cable service providers are required to give subscribers a privacy notice that "clearly and conspicuously" informs subscribers of (1) the nature of the personal information collected, (2) how such information will be used, (3) the retention period of such information, and (4) the manner by which a subscriber can access and correct such information.[84] The act further states that a cable TV service provider may only collect personal information that is necessary to render cable services or to detect the unauthorized reception of cable services.[85]

The act limits cable service providers' right to disseminate personal information without the "written or electronic consent" of the subscriber, unless the disclosure is subject to a specified exception.[86] Several exceptions to this provision exist. Specifically, disclosures may be made (1) to the extent necessary to render services or conduct other legitimate business activities, (2) subject to a court order with notice to the subscriber, or (3) if the disclosure is limited to names and addresses and the subscriber is given an option to opt out.[87]

Although the act does not specify a schedule for data retention or destruction, it does mandate that personal information be destroyed when it is no longer needed for the purpose for which it was collected and there are no pending requests for access.[88]

The provision allowing for disclosures of personal information subject to a court order with notice to the subscriber had been read in conflict with the Electronic Communications Privacy Act of 1986 (ECPA), which allows such disclosures without notice to the consumer, as notice may negatively impact an ongoing investigation.[89] In 2011, courts resolved this tension in favor of ECPA due to its later enactment.[90]

11.6 The Video Privacy Protection Act of 1988

The Video Privacy Protection Act of 1988 (VPPA) was passed in response to the disclosure and publication of then-Supreme Court nominee Robert Bork's video rental records.[91] Although the records revealed that Judge Bork watched innocuous films, the disclosure was considered a gross invasion of his privacy.[92]

The act applies to video tape service providers, who are defined as anyone "engaged in the business, in or affecting interstate or foreign commerce, of rental, sale, or delivery of prerecorded video cassette tapes or similar audio visual materials" as well as individuals who receive personal information in the ordinary course of a videotape service provider's business or for marketing purposes.[93] Videotape service providers are prohibited from disclosing customer personal information unless an enumerated exception applies.[94] Exceptions are provided for instances in which the disclosure (1) is made to the consumer themselves; (2) is made subject to the contemporaneous written consent of the consumer; (3) is made to law enforcement pursuant to a warrant, subpoena or other court order; (4) includes only the names and addresses of consumers; (5) includes only names, addresses and subject matter descriptions and the disclosure is used only for the marketing of goods or services to the consumers; (6) is for order fulfillment, request processing, transfer of ownership, or debt collection; or (7) is pursuant to a court order in a civil proceeding and the consumer is granted a right to object.[95]

The act requires that personal information be destroyed "as soon as practicable, but no later than one year from the date the information is no longer necessary for the purpose for which it was collected and there are no pending requests or orders for access to such information."[96]

The act affords a private right of action for violations and allows for actual or statutory damages, punitive damages, and reasonable attorney's fees and court costs.[97] Statutory damages are set at $2,500.[98] There has been active class-action litigation under the VPPA, and several cases, including those against Blockbuster, Netflix and Redbox, suggest that the private right of action extends only to disclosure-related violations and not violations based merely on improper retention.[99] Additionally, the VPPA does not preempt more protective state laws, which may give rise to stricter penalties.[100]

Significant changes to the landscape of video delivery have occurred since the law was enacted in 1988. Netflix, which was founded nearly a decade after the enactment of the VPPA, sought to amend the law in 2011 to address the concept of social media integration for users—a prime example of which was a Facebook feature that would allow Netflix users to share their movie-viewing information with social media friends.[101] To address this concern, Congress adopted the Video Privacy Protection Act Amendments Act of 2012 that allowed for one-time consumer consent that was valid for up to two years, replacing the contemporaneity requirement.[102] Despite this amendment, numerous federal courts have held that the disclosure of an individual's online streaming history along with personal information can be viewed as a potential violation of VPPA.[103] Companies continue to call for a more comprehensive overhaul of the law to address changes in technology, such as social media and streaming video.[104] Privacy professionals should be alert to possible legislative change in this area.

11.7 Digital Advertising

Digital advertising, which is composed of desktop/laptop, mobile, and connected TV advertising, is an integral part of marketing.[105] By 2025, spending on all digital advertising in the United States is expected to exceed $300 billion—with approximately three-fourths of all advertising spending on digital advertising compared with less than one-fourth of all spending on print and television advertising.[106] In 2022, the estimated spending on mobile advertisement was approximately $170 billion—which accounts for about 70 percent of digital advertising spending.[107]

The discussion here focuses on three areas: (1) state laws concerning digital advertising, (2) self-regulatory codes for digital advertising, and (3) digital advertising ethics. Chapter 3 describes the technical side of the digital advertising ecosystem in more detail.

11.7.1 State Laws Concerning Digital Advertising

For decades, states have adopted a variety of laws related to restrictions on digital advertising. The specific topics of these laws vary from protections for consumers who did not want to receive ads to protections for consumers who did not want to be tracked for advertising purposes to protections related to children being targeted for digital adverting. This section examines both state laws that have a specific focus concerning digital advertising and state comprehensive laws that encompass regulation of digital advertising.

11.7.1.1 State Specific Laws Related to Digital Advertising

As there are numerous state laws with restrictions related to digital advertising, this review focuses on two examples of these laws from California, as this state has often been a leader in enacting consumer protection.

In 2003, California passed the California Online Privacy Protection Act (CalOPPA)—the first law in the nation to require operators of commercial websites, including mobile apps, to conspicuously post a privacy notice if they collect personally identifiable information (PII) from those living in California. In 2013, the law was amended to require privacy notice to include information on how the operator responds to Do Not Track signals or similar mechanisms. The law also requires privacy notices to state whether third parties can collect PII about the site's users.[108]

In 2022, California became the first state in the U.S. to enact a law for age-appropriate design requirements—the California Age-Appropriate Design Code Act. The law requires online platforms to consider the "best interest" of child users and to set defaults to protect these users' privacy.[109] The law prohibits behaviors such as using a child's personal information in a manner that is detrimental to the child. Additionally, the law prohibits a company from collecting, sharing, or selling a child's location by default.[110]

11.7.1.2 State Comprehensive Privacy Laws' Impact on Regulation of Digital Advertising

An increasing number of states in the U.S. have adopted laws that comprehensively address the regulation of personal data. Again, using California's approach as it was the first state to adopt such a law, the discussion here focuses on digital advertising aspects of the state laws. In Chapter 6, state comprehensive privacy laws are examined in detail.

For these state laws, an initial consideration is whether a company involved in digital advertising is regulated by these state comprehensive laws. Because the definition of a business may be quite broad in at least some of the state laws, companies that are involved in the collection of data about consumers or that benefit from such collection may need to consult an attorney to determine if they are subject to a particular state comprehensive privacy law. For example, California has passed both the California Consumer Privacy Act (CCPA) and the California Privacy Rights Act (CPRA), which expands and modifies the CCPA. Under the California framework, one of the determining factors for a company being covered under the law is whether it collects personal information on California residents or whether such collection is undertaken on behalf of the company. The California framework also looks at whether the company meets a minimum annual gross revenue, uses the personal information of a minimum number of consumers, or derives at least half of its annual revenue from selling or sharing consumers' personal information.[111]

A next step for determining the impact of these laws on covered companies that engage in digital advertising is to assess the types of practices related to personal data that are regulated. The California framework, for example, protects a broad category of network activity information that is defined to include browsing histories and search histories. In addition, the California framework regulates inferences drawn from personal information used to create profiles. The California framework also restricts cross-device behavioral advertising, defined as targeted advertising based on the consumer's information obtained across websites, services, or applications.[112]

11.7.2 Self-Regulation for Digital Advertising

Realizing the privacy concerns raised by the tracking associated with digital advertising, many companies involved in desktop/laptop advertising and mobile advertising have voluntarily agreed to be bound by self-regulatory principles. Two prominent examples are the Digital Advertising Alliance (DAA) Self-Regulatory Principles for Online Behavioral Advertising and the Network Advertising Initiative (NAI) Code of Conduct.[113]

The DAA is a nonprofit organization that collaborates with businesses, public policy groups, and public officials to establish and enforce "responsible privacy practices across industry for relevant digital advertising, providing consumers with enhanced transparency and control." The self-regulatory principles include guidelines for interest-based advertising in the desktop/laptop environment and the mobile environment as well as cross-device use of data. An important feature of these principles and related self-regulatory initiatives from the DAA is the consumer management of opt-outs.[114]

The NAI is a nonprofit self-regulatory association comprised exclusively of third-party digital advertising companies. The NAI Code of Conduct is a list of self-regulatory principles that all NAI members agree to uphold. The code requires notice and choice with respect to interest-based advertising, limits on the types of data that member companies can use for advertising purposes, and several substantive restrictions on member companies' collection, use, and transfer of data used for online behavioral advertising.[115]

Both sets of principles have enforcement mechanisms. For DAA's Self-Regulatory Principles, the Council of Better Business Bureaus and the Direct Marketing Association provide independent oversight and enforcement.[116] The NAI's Code of Conduct is enforced by its board, and sanctions may include revocation of membership and referral of matters to the FTC.[117] For the wide range of industries engaging in digital advertising, the DAA and NAI requirements can be an important area for careful compliance attention. For companies that have agreed to such codes, a violation is considered an unfair and deceptive practice that can lead to FTC and state attorney general enforcement actions.

It is important to note that companies also choose to constrain their practices in response to public sentiment. One prominent example centers on third-party cookies.[118] In 2020, Apple blocked all third-party cookies from their browser.[119] In 2021, Google also announced it planned to phase out third-party cookies in the near future.[120]

11.7.3 Digital Advertising Ethics

As discussed in more detail in Chapter 4, the issue of ethics can play a significant role in how a company chooses to act in regard to potentially controversial practices related to digital advertising. Because ethics can be thought of as a set of principles that govern a company's behavior, compliance with legal requirements is a starting point in discussions of how a company should act. The next step in ethical decision-making, which often involves the company's chief privacy officer, is how such a company should act when many advertising practices, at least in the United States, are legal but may not be advisable.

Ethical advertising focuses on honesty, accuracy, and fairness in the content of the messaging; the advertising environments that are chosen for the placement of the advertising; and the potential for bias in analysis related to ads.[121] According to Edelman's 2020 Trust Barometer, ethics are more important in creating consumers' trust of a company than competence.[122] Because trust of a company is linked to purchase decisions, each company has a financial incentive to engage in ethical advertising practices.[123]

The Institute for Advertising Ethics (IAE) encourages the use of ethical principles to build a more trusted digital marketplace.[124] Principles include:

- Advertising, public relations, and all marketing communications professionals have an obligation to exercise the highest personal ethics in the creation and dissemination of commercial information to consumers.
- Advertisers should treat consumers fairly based on the nature of the audience to whom the ads are directed, and the nature of the product or service advertised.
- Advertisers should never compromise consumers' personal privacy in marketing communications, and their choices as to whether to participate in providing their information should be transparent and easily made.

As discussed previously, numerous industry groups have enacted codes of conduct that focus on operationalizing practices and behaviors associated with ethical concerns in digital advertising.[125]

Much concern has been raised regarding ethics in targeting of digital advertising: how are consumers targeted, why are they targeted, and what groups should be excluded from targeting. Effective targeting of online ads either at certain groups or particular individuals inherently involves collecting data from these people that will later be used to tailor the placement of advertising. Targeting is central to several specific areas of concern for digital advertising: the use of online behavioral advertising, the manipulation of consumers by dark patterns, and advertising directed at children.

11.7.3.1 Online Behavioral Advertising

There have been persistent criticisms of online behavioral advertising, which the IAPP defines as "advertising that is targeted at individuals based on the observation of their behavior over time."[126] American scholar Shoshana Zuboff, for instance, criticizes such advertising for being part of what she calls "surveillance capitalism."[127]

The tailoring of advertising to the individual person is accomplished by tracking the person across the internet, compiling a profile on the individual, and then using that profile to target advertising. In many instances, consumers are not aware of the tracking that occurs from website to website. In addition, consumers typically have no access to the profiles created about them and no ability to correct inaccuracies in these profiles.[128]

Ethical questions for behavioral advertising focus primarily on whether data should be collected for advertising directed at individuals and how should data be used. Particularly, should companies engage in advertising practices that track users' online activities, often without the consumer's knowledge, and then target ads specifically to that person based on categories such as gender, age, political beliefs, sexual orientation, and medical conditions?

11.7.3.2 Dark Patterns

Dark patterns can be defined as "design practices that trick or manipulate users into making choices they would not otherwise have made and that may cause harm."[129] For digital advertising, dark patterns may include advertising content that appears to be independent or impartial, such as resembling a news story, or manipulative tactics that appeal to a particular demographic.[130]

Ethical questions for dark patterns focus on how data should be used. One issue is how should companies consider targeting ads at certain groups to encourage or discourage certain behaviors? For example, should a company discourage certain groups from voting? Should a certain group be encouraged to engage in higher-risk behaviors (using tobacco-related products or gambling)?

11.7.3.3 Advertising Directed at Children

Ethical concerns exist concerning targeting ads to children who by their very nature are not developmentally mature.[131] In his 2022 State of the Union Address, President Biden stated that the United States should "ban targeted advertising to children."[132]

Ethical questions focus on whether children should not have data collected for advertising and should not be targeted with ads. Age variations within the broad category of children can impact a company's decision. Children ages 6 through 12 are often viewed as distinct from those ages 13 through 18.

11.8 Conclusion

This chapter examined the legal rules that apply to important channels for marketing by telephone, fax, text, and commercial email. It then considered the rules governing how telecommunication companies can use personal information generated in the course of communications activities. Along with the VPPA, special statutes or proposals have long applied to telephone and cable companies, and more recently to broadband internet providers, based on their potential access to individuals' detailed communication and viewing information. Current law places significant limits on how these infrastructure companies can use and disclose personal information that flows through their systems. The chapter ends by discussing topics of digital advertising.

Endnotes

1 Chapter 13 examines rules for government access to the communications, under wiretap and other statutes, that provide lawful access for the government to that data, subject to search warrants and other restrictions.

2 Restatement of the Law, Second, Torts, § 652B, accessed November 2017, https://cyber.law.harvard.edu/privacy/Privacy_R2d_Torts_Sections.htm.

3 Restatement of the Law, Second, Torts, § 652B.

4 47 U.S.C. § 227(b)(1)(A)-(B), accessed June 2016, https://www.law.cornell.edu/uscode/text/47/227; 47 C.F.R. § 64.1200(a)(2)-(3), accessed November 2017, https://www.law.cornell.edu/cfr/text/47/64.1200. For an analysis of significant amendments that took effect in 2013, view Tara Sarosiek, Seamus Duffy, Michael Daly, and Meredith Slawe, "New TCPA Rules Take Effect on October 16, 2013," *TCPA* (blog), http://tcpablog.com/new-tcpa-regulations-take-effect-on-october-16th/#_ednl.

5 In the Matter of Rules and Regulations Implementing the Telephone Consumer Protection Act of 1991, Federal Communications Commission, adopted September 12, 20222, https://www.fcc.gov/document/matter-rules-and-regulations-implementing-telephone-consumer-0.

6 15 U.S.C. § 6101-6108, accessed June 2023, https://www.law.cornell.edu/uscode/text/15/chapter-87; "Complying with Telemarketing Sales Rule," Federal Trade Commission, edited May 2023, https://www.ftc.gov/tips-advice/business-center/guidance/complying-telemarketing-sales-rule.

7 *Federal Register* 68, no 19, January 29, 2003: 4669, Federal Trade Commission, https://www.ftc.gov/sites/default/files/documents/reports/federal-trade-commission-report-congress/dnciareportappenda.pdf.

8 Material terms may include cost, quantity, restrictions, limitations, conditions, no-refund policies, and so forth.

9 Intrastate calls are covered by the Federal Communication Commission's regulations under the Telephone Consumer Protection Act (47 U.S.C. § 227), accessed November 2017, https://www.law.cornell.edu/uscode/text/47/227. These rules are similar to the Telemarketing Sales Rule described herein.

10 Not all telemarketing activities are covered by the Telemarketing Sales Rule. For example, most business-to-business calls are excluded from the rule. Additionally, the Telemarketing Sales Rule applies only to entities subject to Federal Trade Commission jurisdiction, with other entities (such as banks) covered solely by the Telephone Consumer Protection Act referenced in note 1. Finally, some types of calls are partially exempt from the rule. As discussed later in this chapter, calls to existing customers are exempt from the Do Not Call Registry provisions. Inbound calls from customers are also excluded, although upselling during the call will bring it back within the scope of the rule with regard to disclosures, payment provisions, etc.

11 The Telemarketing Sales Rule does provide some latitude for companies that have distinct corporate divisions. In general, such divisions are considered separate sellers under the rule. The Federal Trade Commission specifies two factors that should be used to determine whether Do Not Call requests should be shared among divisions (1) whether there is substantial diversity between the operational structure of the divisions and (2) whether the goods or services sold by the divisions are substantially different from each other. If a consumer tells one division of a company not to call again, a distinct corporate division of the same company may still make calls to that consumer. If the divisions are not distinct, however, the seller may not call the consumer even to offer different goods or services.

12 "Complying with the Telemarketing Sales Rule," under "Requirements for Sellers and Telemarketers: Multiple Purpose Calls," Federal Trade Commission, edited May 2023, https://www.ftc.gov/business-guidance/resources/complying-telemarketing-sales-rule#requirements.

13 "Complying with the Telemarketing Sales Rule," under "Protecting Consumers' Privacy: Transmitting Caller ID Information," Federal Trade Commission, edited May 2023, https://www.ftc.gov/business-guidance/resources/complying-telemarketing-sales-rule#callerID.

14 47 C.F.R. § 64.1200(a)(7), accessed November 2017, https://www.law.cornell.edu/cfr/text/47/64.1200.

15 "Complying with the Telemarketing Sales Rule," Federal Trade Commission, edited May 2023, https://www.ftc.gov/tips-advice/business-center/guidance/complying-telemarketing-sales-rule; Richard Brown, Mark Romance, and Micheal Fitzpatrick, "TCPA: Revisions to FCC Regulations Regarding Prerecorded Voice Message

Calling," Day Pitney, January 12, 2023, https://www.daypitney.com/insights/publications/2023/01/12-tcpa-revisions-fcc-prerecorded-voice-message-calling/.

16 This 3 percent rule applies to each day and each calling campaign. The Federal Trade Commission does not allow a telemarketer to average abandonment rates, even if it is running simultaneous calling campaigns on behalf of different sellers. The Safe Harbor also requires the telemarketer to let the phone ring at least four times (or for 15 seconds). This requirement is designed to ensure that consumers have sufficient time to answer a call. For the small number of calls that are abandoned, the Telemarketing Sales Rule's Safe Harbor requires the telemarketer to play a recorded greeting consisting of the company's name and phone number and a statement that the call was for telemarketing purposes. (The phone number provided in the message must also be one to which the consumer can call to be placed on the company's own Do Not Call list.) This recorded message may not contain a sales pitch. Including a sales message would violate the Federal Communication Commission's rules under the Telephone Consumer Protection Act (47 U.S.C. § 227), accessed November 2017, https://www.law.cornell.edu/uscode/text/47/227, and FCC regulations at 47 C.F.R. § 64.1200, accessed November 2017https://www.law.cornell.edu/cfr/text/47/64.1200.

17 In the Matter of Rules and Regulations Implementing the Telephone Consumer Protection Act of 1991, Federal Communications Commission.

18 47 C.F.R. § 64.1200(a)(3), accessed November 2017, https://www.law.cornell.edu/cfr/text/47/64.1200.

19 For an overview, view "Telephone Consumer Protection Act (TCPA), Robocalls, and Text Messaging," Data Marketing & Analytics, https://thedma.org/resources/compliance-resources/tcpa/ (accessed February 2020).

20 There are certain narrow exceptions (such as emergency notifications). Laura Phillips and Laura Layton, "What's the Purpose of Emergency Purpose Statutory Exemption?" *TCPA* (blog), April 10, 2015, http://tcpablog.com/whats-purpose-emergency-purpose-statutory-exemption/.

21 Tanya Forsheit, Alan Friel, and Melinda McLellan, "FCC's New TCPA Order May Require Companies to Obtain Updated Consents for Marketing Calls and Texts," BakerHostler, July 22, 2015, https://www.dataprivacymonitor.com/enforcement/fccs-new-tcpa-order-may-require-companies-to-obtain-updated-consents-for-marketing-calls-and-texts/.

22 Alan Friel, "FCC Closes Year with Enforcement Advisory on Text Messages," BakerHostler, JD Supra, January 3, 2017, www.jdsupra.com/legalnews/fcc-closes-year-with-enforcement-23350/.

23 Facebook v. Duguid, Oyez, April 1, 2021, https://www.oyez.org/cases/2020/19-511; see Margo Tank, David Whitaker, an Elizabeth Caires, "TCPA: The Supreme Court narrows definition of ATDS, but pitfalls remain." DLA Piper, accessed June 2023, https://www.dlapiper.com/en/us/insights/publications/2021/04/tcpa-the-supreme-court-narrows-definition-of-atds-but-pitfalls-remain/; "The Ripple Effects of the Supreme Court's TCPA Decision: Still Developing for Companies Using Autodialers and Artificial or Prerecorded Voices." *The National Law Review*, June 24, 2021, https://www.natlawreview.com/article/ripple-effects-supreme-court-s-tcpa-decision-still-developing-companies-using-auto.

24 Barry Benjamin and Alexander Borovsky, "Supreme Court Clarifies and Narrows the Definition of an Autodialer Under the TCPA," Kilpatrick Townsend, April 13, 2021, https://kilpatricktownsend.com/en/Blog/classaction/2021/4/Supreme-Court-

Clarifies-and-Narrows-the-Definition-of-an-Autodialer-under-the-TCPA; see Gregg Owen, Supreme Court Ruling Opens the Door to Text Campaigns," Automotive News, September 13, 2021, https://www.autonews.com/sponsored/supreme-court-ruling-opens-door-text-campaigns.

25 As the Federal Trade Commission's guidance states: "Sellers and telemarketers do not have to keep duplicative records if they have a written agreement allocating responsibility for complying with the recordkeeping requirements. Without a written agreement between the parties, or if the written agreement is unclear as to who must maintain the required records, telemarketers must keep employee records, while sellers must keep the advertising and promotional materials, information on prize recipients, sales records, and verifiable authorizations." "Complying with the Telemarketing Sales Rule" under "Who Must Keep Records," Federal Trade Commission, edited May 2023, https://www.ftc.gov/tips-advice/business-center/guidance/complying-telemarketing-sales-rule#whomustkeep.

26 The Telemarketing Sales Rule also includes specific regulations designed to address credit card laundering; telemarketing sales of credit repair programs, loss recovery services, and advance loans; and "telefunding" activities (for-profit companies that call on behalf of charitable organizations).

27 "Record Fines and Restrictive Rules: Agencies Take on the TCPA," McGuireWoods, August 21, 2023, https://www.mcguirewoods.com/client-resources/Alerts/2023/8/record-fines-and-restrictive-rules/.

28 In 2023, the amount of the inflation-adjusted civil penalty rose to $50,120. This amount is subject to annual adjustment. "FTC Publishes Inflation-Adjusted Civil Penalty Amounts for 2023," Federal Trade Commission, January 6, 2023, https://www.ftc.gov/news-events/news/press-releases/2023/01/ftc-publishes-inflation-adjusted-civil-penalty-amounts-2023.

29 15 U.S.C. § 6104 accessed June 2023, https://www.law.cornell.edu/uscode/text/15/6104; see "Private Actions and the Telemarketing Sales Rule," Cove Law, July 13, 2022, https://covelaw.com/private-actions-the-telemarketing-sales-rule/#:~:text=Are%20Private%20Actions%20Permitted%3F,of%20the%20Telemarketing%20Sales%20Rule.

30 TransUnion v. Ramirez, June 25, 2021, https://www.oyez.org/cases/2020/20-297; see Harrison Brown, Jeffery Rosenthal, Deborah Skakel, Ana Tagvoryan, and Scott Wortman, "How SCOTUS Clarified the Spokeo Standard of 'Concrete' Harm Necessary to Establish Article III Standing, and What It Means for the Future of Class Actions," Blank Rome, JD Supra, July 1, 2022, https://www.jdsupra.com/legalnews/how-scotus-clarified-the-spokeo-9126844/#:~:text=The%20Court%20recognized%20that%20the,driving%20behind%20a%20reckless%20driver.

31 See Christine Reilly, "What You Need to Know About Washington's and Oklahoma's New Telemarketing Laws." Manatt, https://www.manatt.com/insights/newsletters/tcpa-connect/what-you-need-to-know-about-washingtons-and-oklah; Brandon White, Travis Sabalewski, Abraham Joshua Colman, "Florida's New Mini-TCPA: What You Need to Know." Holland & Knight, July 14, 2021, https://www.hklaw.com/en/insights/publications/2021/07/floridas-new-mini-tcpa-what-you-need-to-know; "Florida's Mini-TCPA May Be More Broad and More Severe Than Its Federal Telemarketing Counterpart." Blank Rome, July 15, 2021, https://www.blankrome.com/publications/floridas-mini-tcpa-may-be-more-broad-and-more-severe-its-federal-telemarketing.

32 "Do Not Call Program – Frequently Asked Questions for Consumers," Louisiana Public Service Commission, accessed July 2022, https://www.lpsc.louisiana.gov/DNC_ConsumerFAQ.

33 See generally, "Complying with the Telemarketing Sales Rule," Federal Trade Commission, edited May 2023, http://business.ftc.gov/documents/bus27-complying-telemarketing-sales-rule#Glance.

34 "National Do Not Call List – Telemarketer," Federal Trade Commission, accessed June 2023, https://telemarketing.donotcall.gov/.

35 "Q&A for Telemarketers & Sellers About DNC Provisions in TSR," under "Paying For Access," Federal Trade Commission, edited May 2023, https://www.ftc.gov/tips-advice/business-center/guidance/qa-telemarketers-sellers-about-dnc-provisions-tsr#payingforaccess.

36 For additional analysis on Do Not Call regulations, view Kathleen Ann Ruane, "Telemarketing Regulation: National and State Do Not Call Registries," Congressional Research Services, April 1, 2016, https://www.fas.org/sgp/crs/misc/R43684.pdf.

37 In fiscal year 2021, the FTC received more than 5 million complaints concerning violations of DNC. *FTC Issues Biennial Report to Congress on the National Do Not Call Registry,* Federal Trade Commission, January 5, 2022, https://www.ftc.gov/news-events/news/press-releases/2022/01/ftc-issues-biennial-report-congress-national-do-not-call-registry.

38 "Complying with the Telemarketing Sales Rule," Federal Trade Commission; see "FTC Publishes Inflation-Adjusted Civile Penalty Amounts for 2023."

39 For example, the Federal Trade Commission and the Florida Attorney General's Office assessed a $23 million fine to settle allegations that a Florida-based company defrauded seniors by using robocalls to sell medical alert systems. "Settlement with the FTC and Florida Attorney General Stops Operations that Used Robocalls to Fraudulently Pitch Medical Alert Devices to Seniors," Federal Trade Commission, November 13, 2014, https://www.ftc.gov/news-events/press-releases/2014/11/settlement-ftc-florida-attorney-general-stops-operations-used.

40 Upselling is the sale of a product or service in addition to the product or service the customer has purchased. "Complying with the Telemarketing Sales Rule, Federal Trade Commission.

41 "Complying with the Telemarketing Sales Rule," Federal Trade Commission.

42 "Complying with the Telemarketing Sales Rule," Federal Trade Commission.

43 "Complying with the Telemarketing Sales Rule," Federal Trade Commission.

44 "Complying with the Telemarketing Sales Rule," Federal Trade Commission; see "FTC Publishes Inflation-Adjusted Civile Penalty Amounts for 2023."

45 A significant share of these robocalls involve scams. One recent concern has focused on "neighbor spoofing"—a technique where fraudsters call using the same area code and first three digits of the person called to get the victim to pick up and surrender their personal information. "What Is Spoofing?" Caller ID Spoofing, Federal Communications Commission, March 7, 2022, https://www.fcc.gov/consumers/guides/spoofing-and-caller-id; see "Robocalls Response Team: Combating Scam Robocalls & Robotexts," Federal Communications Commission, August 18, 2022, https://www.fcc.gov/spoofed-robocalls; "Robocalls and the Do Not Call Registry," Federal Trace Commission, last accessed July 2022, https://www.ftc.gov/news-events/topics/do-not-call-registry/robocalls; see Margot Saunders & Chris Frascella, "Scam Robocalls: Telecom Providers

Profit," National Consumer Law Center, June 1, 2022, https://www.nclc.org/resources/scam-robocalls-telecom-providers-profit/.

46 These technologies include: SHAKEN (Signature-based Handling of Asserted information using toKENs) and STIR (Secure Telephone Identity Revisited). Brakkton Booker, "Phone Companies Ink Deal with All 50 States to Combat Robocalls," NPR, August 22, 2019, https://www.npr.org/2019/08/22/753524482/phone-companies-ink-deal-with-all-50-states-and-d-c-to-combat-robocalls.

47 Tony Romm, "Crackdown Targets Robocallers That Placed 1 Billion Calls, Federal and State Officials Say," *The Washington Post*, June 25, 2019, https://www.washingtonpost.com/technology/2019/06/25/federal-state-officials-announce-enforcement-efforts-targeting-billion-illegal-robocalls; see FTC, Law Enforcement Partners Announce New Crackdown on Illegal Robocalls," Federal Trade Commission, June 25, 2019, https://www.ftc.gov/news-events/news/press-releases/2019/06/ftc-law-enforcement-partners-announce-new-crackdown-illegal-robocalls.

48 Kif Leswing, "FCC Cracks Down on Robocalls with Record $225 Fine," CNBC, March 18, 2021, https://www.cnbc.com/2021/03/17/spam-callers-get-record-225-million-fine-from-fcc.html.

49 See Christine Reilly, "7th Circuit: TCPA Doesn't Preempt More Restrictive State Robocall Law," CaseText, August 17, 2015, https://casetext.com/analysis/7th-circuit-tcpa-doesnt-preempt-more-restrictive-state-robocall-law.

50 "State Regulations," Allen, Mitchell & Allen PLLC, accessed November 2019, https://telemarketingregulations.com/state-regulations.

51 For examples, view Mississippi's online Do Not Call list registration, "No Call Program," Mississippi Public Service Commission, accessed November 2019, https://www.psc.state.ms.us/nocall/nocall.html; Pennsylvania's Online Do Not Call List registration, "Telephone Information," Pennsylvania Office of Consumer Advocate, accessed June 2023, https://www.oca.pa.gov/telephone/.

52 Kan. Stat. Ann. §§ 50-670 and 50-670a, accessed November 2017, www.kslegislature.org/li_2014/b2013_14/measures/documents/sb308_enrolled.pdf. For a summary of the 2014 changes to the Kansas No-Call Act, see Jeff Hixon, "2014 Update to the Kansas No-Call Act," State Library of Kansas, June 29, 2020, https://kslib.info/Blog.aspx?IID=17.

53 Fla. Stat. § 501.059, accessed November 2017, www.leg.state.fl.us/Statutes/index.cfm?App_mode=Display_Statute&Search_String=&URL=0500-0599/0501/Sections/0501.059.html. For a summary of Florida's law, see "Florida Do Not Call," Florida Department of Agriculture and Consumer Services, accessed June 2023, https://www.fdacs.gov/Consumer-Resources/Florida-Do-Not-Call.

54 "Fax Advertising Policy," Federal Communications Commission, December 8, 2015, https://www.fcc.gov/general/fax-advertising-policy.

55 Junk Fax Prevention Act of 2005, accessed June 2023, https://www.law.cornell.edu/topn/junk_fax_prevention_act_of_2005; see F. Robert Smith, "Fax Advertising: Complying with Federal Junk Fax Laws," Foulston Siefkin, Fall 2009, https://www.foulston.com/uploads/Fax-Advertising-Complying-with-Federal-Junk-Fax-Laws.pdf

56 For purposes of the Junk Fax Prevention Act, "established business relationship" has the same definition as it does in the Federal Trade Commission's Do Not Call rule.

57 The Court described that in the past fax paper and ink were expensive and that is the reason the TCPA was enacted, however it is not costly today. These facsimiles did not seek to sell anything or promote the market research services but were seeking to

obtain responses to their surveys. Christopher R, Murphy, and Travis A. Sabalewski, Holland & Knight Alert, "Second Circuit Rules Faxed Invitation Is Not 'Unsolicited Advertisement' Under TCPA," January 20, 2022, https://www.hklaw.com/en/insights/publications/2022/01/second-circuit-rules-faxed-invitation-is-not-unsolicited-advertisement.

58 Telephone Communications Protection Act, 47 U.S.C. § 227, accessed February 2020, https://www.fcc.gov/sites/default/files/tcpa-rules.pdf. See also "FCC Actions on Robocalls, Telemarketing," Federal Communications Commission, updated July 23, 2018, https://www.fcc.gov/general/telemarketing-and-robocalls.

59 William Glaberson, "Dispute over Faxed Ads Draws Wide Scrutiny After $12 Million Award," *The New York Times*, July 22, 2001, www.nytimes.com/2001/07/22/us/dispute-over-faxed-ads-draws-wide-scrutiny-after-12-million-award.html?pagewanted=all.

60 "FCC Fines Fax.com $5 million for Sending 'Junk Faxes,'" Federal Communications Commission, January 5, 2004, https://www.fcc.gov/document/fcc-fines-faxcom-over-5-million-sending-junk-faxes.

61 "FCC Announces TCPA Junk Fax Prohibitions Do Not Apply to Online Faxes," Hunton Andrews Kurth, December 19, 2019, https://www.huntonprivacyblog.com/2019/12/19/ftc-announces-tcpa-junk-fax-prohibitions-do-not-apply-to-online-faxes/.

62 California Business & Professions Code § 17538.43, accessed November 2019, http://leginfo.legislature.ca.gov/faces/codes_displaySection.xhtml?lawCode=BPC§ionNum=17538.43.

63 Chamber of Commerce of the U.S. v. Lockyer, 2006 WL 462482 (E. D. Cal. 2006). For a summary of the case from the U.S. Chamber of Commerce, view "Chamber of Commerce of the U.S. v. Lockyer, Case Updates," accessed June 2023, https://www.uschamber.com/cases/federal-preemption-and-commerce-clause/chamber-of-commerce-v-lockyer.

64 The CAN-SPAM Act of 2003, 15 U.S.C. 7701, et seq., accessed November 2017, https://www.gpo.gov/fdsys/pkg/PLAW-108publ187/pdf/PLAW-108publ187.pdf.

65 "CAN-SPAM Act: A Compliance Guide for Business," Federal Trade Commission, August 2023, https://www.ftc.gov/business-guidance/resources/can-spam-act-compliance-guide-business.

66 "FTC Approves New Rule Provision Under the CAN-SPAM Act," Federal Trade Commission, May 12, 2008, https://www.ftc.gov/news-events/press-releases/2008/05/ftc-approves-new-rule-provision-under-can-spam-act.

67 16 CFR Part 316, accessed November 2017, https://www.law.cornell.edu/cfr/text/16/part-316.

68 FTC v. Pricewert LLC d/b/a 3FN.net, Triple Fiber Network, APS Communications, and APS Communication, 09 CV-2407 (N.D. Cal. 2009), Federal Trade Commission, updated May 19, 2010, https://www.ftc.gov/enforcement/cases-proceedings/092-3148/pricewert-llc-dba-3fnnet-ftc.

69 In the Matter of Rules and Regulations Implementing the Controlling the Assault of Non-Solicited Pornography and Marketing Act of 2003; Rules and Regulations Implementing the Telephone Consumer Protection Act of 1991, 04-194, Federal Communications Commission, August 12, 2004, https://apps.fcc.gov/edocs_public/attachmatch/FCC-04-194A1.pdf.

70 See "CAN-SPAM: Unwanted Commercial Electronic Email," Federal Communications Commission, updated August 13, 2021, https://www.fcc.gov/general/can-spam.

71 Consumers must not be required to view or hear any further commercial content during the opt-out process (other than institutional identification).

72 See "CAN-SPAM Act: A Compliance Guide for Business," Federal Trade Commission, edited February 2023, https://www.ftc.gov/tips-advice/business-center/guidance/can-spam-act-compliance-guide-business.

73 "Domain Name Downloads," Federal Communications Commission, August 11, 2016, https://www.fcc.gov/consumer-governmental-affairs/about-bureau/consumer-policy-division/can-spam/domain-name-downloads.

74 According to the Federal Communications Commission guidance, messages that are not sent to an address for a wireless device but are only forwarded to a wireless device are not subject to Federal Communications Commission rules on mobile service commercial messages. "Protecting Your Privacy: Phone and Cable," under "Protecting Phone Records," Federal Communications Commission, December 30, 2019, https://www.fcc.gov/consumers/guides/protecting-your-privacy.

75 Telecommunications Act, 47 U.S.C. §222 (1996), accessed November 2017, https://www.law.cornell.edu/uscode/text/47/222.

76 See Electronic Communications Privacy Act discussion in Chapter 13.

77 U.S. West, Inc. v. Federal Communications Commission, 182 F.3d 1224 (10th Cir. 1999), accessed November 2017, http://openjurist.org/182/f3d/1224/us-west-inc-v-federal-communications-commission.

78 *Report and Order and Further Notice of Proposed Rulemaking*, 07-22, Federal Communications Commission, April 2, 2007, https://apps.fcc.gov/edocs_public/attachmatch/FCC-07-22A1.pdf.

79 Public Notice, Annual CPNI Certifications Due March 1, 2012, Federal Communications Commission, February 16, 2012, http://transition.fcc.gov/Daily_Releases/Daily_Business/2012/db0216/DA-12-170A1.pdf. "The FCC requires companies offering telephone or interconnected VoIP services to offer special protections to a category of customer data known as customer proprietary network information (CPNI)." Alexander Brown and David Trapp, "Telecoms & Media 2021," Simmons & Simmons LLP, 2021, https://www.shandpartners.com/wp-content/uploads/2021/09/2021_telecoms_and_Media_Egypt.pdf.

80 According to the FCC, the agency does not regulate "several key communications services." The FCC website particularly notes that the agency does not regulate the following:

- All over-the-top video offerings including: Netflix, YouTube, Amazon Video, and Sling
- All instant messaging and online chat offerings including: WhatsApp, SnapChat, and WeChat
- All social media offerings including: Facebook, Instagram, and Twitter
- All internet cloud offerings including: AWS, IBM Cloud, and Oracle

Michael O'Reilly, "FCC Regulatory Free Zone," FCC, June 1, 2018, https://www.fcc.gov/news-events/blog/2018/06/01/fcc-regulatory-free-arena; see Brown and Trapp, "Telecoms & Media 2021; see also "Broadcasters Push FCC to Reconsider Rules for vMVPDs," NRB, May 26, 2022, https://nrb.org/articles/broadcasters-push-fcc-to-reconsider-rules-for-vmvpds/; John Eggerton, "Big Four Affiliates Push for Regulating VMVPDs." Next TV, April 18, 2022, https://www.nexttv.com/news/big-four-affiliates-push-for-regulating-vmvpds.

81 47 U.S.C. § 551 (2006), accessed November 2017, https://www.law.cornell.edu/uscode/text/47/551.

82 47 U.S.C. § 551(a).

83 47 U.S.C. § 522(6)(A), accessed February 2020, https://www.law.cornell.edu/uscode/text/47/522.

84 47 U.S.C. 551(a).

85 47 U.S.C. 551(b).

86 47 U.S.C. 551(c)(1).

87 47 U.S.C. 551(c)(2).

88 47 U.S.C. 551(e).

89 18 U.S.C. §§ 2703 & 2705, accessed November 2017, https://www.law.cornell.edu/uscode/text/18/2703, https://www.law.cornell.edu/uscode/text/18/2705.

90 See, e.g., In re Application of the United States of America for an Order Pursuant to 18 U.S.C. § 2703(D) Directed to Cablevision Systems Corp., 158 F.Supp.2d 644, Justia, August 10, 2002, http://law.justia.com/cases/federal/district-courts/FSupp2/158/644/2415158/.

91 18 U.S.C. § 2710, accessed November 2017, https://www.law.cornell.edu/uscode/text/18/2710; "The Video Privacy Protection Act: Protecting Viewer Privacy in the 21st Century," 112th Congress (2012) (statement of Rep. Watt), https://www.judiciary.senate.gov/imo/media/doc/CHRG-112shrg87342.pdf.

92 See "Video Privacy Protection Act," Epic.org, accessed November 2017, https://epic.org/privacy/vppa/.

93 18 U.S.C. § 2710(a)(4), accessed November 2017, https://www.law.cornell.edu/uscode/text/18/2710.

94 18 U.S.C. § 2710(b)(1).

95 18 U.S.C. § 2710(b)(2).

96 18 U.S.C. § 2710(e).

97 18 U.S.C. § 2710(c).

98 18 U.S.C. § 2710(c).

99 "Netflix and Blockbuster to amend policies to settle video privacy suits," Lock Lord LLP, *Lexology*, accessed November 2017, www.lexology.com/library/detail.aspx?g=9490362b-5d03-4f20-ae74-3ab4842e0f66; Kevin Sterk and Jiah Chung v. Redbox Automated Retail, LLC, October 23, 2014, http://media.ca7.uscourts.gov/cgi-bin/rssExec.pl?Submit=Display&Path=Y2014/D10-23/C:13-3037:J:Flaum:aut:T:fnOp:N:1440102:S:0.

100 See, e.g., Conn. Gen. Stat. § 53-450, accessed November 2017, http://law.justia.com/codes/connecticut/2012/title-53/chapter-949f/section-53-450; Mich. L. § 445.1712, accessed November 2017, www.legislature.mi.gov/(S(1ldubxv5mkknq0qmykkz0g0r))/mileg.aspx?page=getobject&objectname=mcl-445-1712.

101 "Netflix Backs Amendment to Video Privacy Protection Act," Hunton Andrews Kurth, Lexology, July 25, 2011, www.lexology.com/library/detail.aspx?g=2217f175-7a28-4bb0-aac7-40edeed4a6cd.

102 Julianne Pepitone, "New Video Law Lets You Share Your Netflix Viewing on Facebook," *CNNtech*, January 10, 2013, http://money.cnn.com/2013/01/10/technology/social/netflix-vppa-facebook/. For the text of the amendment, see H.R. 6671 – Video Privacy

Protection Act Amendments Act of 2012, accessed November 2017, https://www.congress.gov/bill/112th-congress/house-bill/6671/text.

103 Nathanial Wood, "Ninth Circuit: Disclosure of Video Viewing History Constitutes Harm Sufficient to Confer Standing in Federal Court," Crowell, December 4, 2017, https://www.crowelldatalaw.com/2017/12/ninth-circuit-disclosure-video-viewing-history-constitutes-harm-sufficient-confer-standing-federal-court/; see "Social Sharing and the U.S. Video Privacy Protection Act: Perilous for Online Video Content Providers," White & Case Technology News Flash, June 25, 2018, https://www.whitecase.com/insight-our-thinking/social-sharing-and-us-video-privacy-protection-act-perilous-online-video; see also Christina Tabacco, "HGTV Online Video Viewers Sue Parent Company for Data Privacy Violations," Law Street, March 15, 2022, https://lawstreetmedia.com/news/tech/hgtv-online-video-viewers-sue-parent-company-for-data-privacy-violations/.

104 See Jonathan Cohn, "Online Viewer Privacy is Regulated by an Act Originally Designed to Protect Video Rentals," *Salon*, August 4, 2019, https://www.salon.com/2019/08/04/online-viewer-privacy-is-regulated-by-an-act-originally-designed-to-protect-video-rentals_partner/; Joshua Jessen and Priyanka Rajagopalan, "Teaching an old law new tricks: The 1988 Video Privacy Protection Act in the modern era," *BloombergBNA* (July 4, 2016), https://www.gibsondunn.com/wp-content/uploads/documents/publications/Jessen-Rajagopalan-Teaching-an-Old-Law-New-Tricks-The-1988-Video-Privacy-Protection-Act-in-the-Modern-Era-BNA-7-4-16.pdf.

105 Ethan Cramer-Flood, "Mobile Advertising is Still King, But More Industries are Looking at Non-Mobile, Thanks to CTV," eMarketer, September 30, 2021, https://www.insiderintelligence.com/content/mobile-advertising-still-king-more-industries-looking-nonmobile-thanks-ctv.

106 "Digital Advertising in 2022: Market & Trend Predictions," eMarketer, April 20, 2022, https://www.insiderintelligence.com/insights/digital-advertising-market-trends-predictions/.

107 Simon Hall, "Mobile Advertising Trends and Technology Adoption by the Numbers," Basis Technologies, August 26, 2022, https://basis.net/blog/mobile-advertising-trends-and-technology-adoption-by-the-numbers.

108 California Online Privacy Protection Act (CalOPPA), Education Foundation, Consumer Federation of California, July 19, 2015, https://consumercal.org/about-cfc/cfc-education-foundation/california-online-privacy-protection-act-caloppa-3/#sthash.tujUzAhM.dpbs; Assembly Bill 370, September 27, 2013, https://leginfo.legislature.ca.gov/faces/billNavClient.xhtml?bill_id=201320140AB370. For a discussion of the interaction of the California Online Privacy Protection Act and the California Consumer Privacy Act, view Kamran Salour, "A Balancing Act: A Brief Overview of California Privacy Laws," BakerHostetler, October 23, 2019, https://www.dataprivacymonitor.com/ccpa/a-balancing-act-a-brief-overview-of-california-privacy-laws/.

109 "California is First State to Adopt Age-Appropriate Design Code," Jones Day, September 2022, https://www.jonesday.com/en/insights/2022/09/california-is-first-state-to-adopt-ageappropriate-design-code-law-alert#:~:text=California%20Is%20First%20State%20to%20Adopt%20Age%2DAppropriate%20Design%20Code%20Law%20Alert,-September%202022%20Alert&text=The%20California%20Age%2DAppropriate%20Design,under%20the%20age%20of%2018; see "Governor Newsom Signs First-in-Nation Bill Protecting Children's Online Data and Privacy,"

Office of Governor Newsom, State of California, September 15, 2022, https://www.gov.ca.gov/2022/09/15/governor-newsom-signs-first-in-nation-bill-protecting-childrens-online-data-and-privacy/#:~:text=AB%202273%20prohibits%20companies%20that,children%20to%20provide%20personal%20information.

110 AB-2273, The California Age-Appropriate Design Code Act, September 16, 2022, https://leginfo.legislature.ca.gov/faces/billTextClient.xhtml?bill_id=202120220AB2273.

111 Jason Gavejian, et al., "California Consumer Privacy Act, California Privacy Rights Act FAQs for Covered Businesses," JacksonLewis, January 19, 2022, https://www.jacksonlewis.com/publication/california-consumer-privacy-act-california-privacy-rights-act-faqs-covered-businesses.

112 Gerald Ferguson, Fernando Bohorquez, Jr., and Yadilsa Diaz, "A Digital Advertising Primer on Preparing for the Post-Cookie World: Part Two," BakerHostetler, January 12, 2022, https://www.bakerdatacounsel.com/data-privacy/a-digital-advertising-primer-on-preparing-for-the-post-cookie-world-part-two/; see Nancy Libin and John Seiver, "California Attorney General Issues Opinion Interpreting 'Inferences' Under CCPA," Davis Wright Tremaine, March 15, 2022, https://www.dwt.com/blogs/privacy--security-law-blog/2022/03/california-ccpa-inferences-disclosures; see also California Attorney General Opinion, No. 20-303, March 10, 2022, https://www.dwt.com/-/media/files/2022/03/20-303.pdf.

113 In 2020, the Mobile Marketing Association plans to release a pledge that is intended to improve its self-regulation. *See* Stuart Thompson and Charlie Warzel, "Twelve Million Phones, One Dataset, Zero Privacy," Opinion, The Privacy Project, *The New York Times*, December 19, 2019, https://www.nytimes.com/interactive/2019/12/19/opinion/location-tracking-cell-phone.html?te=1&nl=the-privacy%20project&emc=edit_priv_20191219.

114 For the specific language of the DAA Self-Regulatory Principles, view "DAA Sefl-Regulatory Principles," Digital Advertising Alliance, accessed November 2019, https://digitaladvertisingalliance.org/principles.

115 For the specific language of the NAI Code of Conduct, view "Guidance for NAI Members: Use of Non-Cookie Technologies for Interest-Based Advertising," Network Advertising Alliance, April 2017, www.networkadvertising.org/sites/default/files/NAI_BeyondCookies_NL.pdf.

116 For detailed information on DAA's enforcement mechanism, view "Enforcement," Digital Advertising Alliance, accessed February 2020, https://digitaladvertisingalliance.org/enforcement.

117 For detailed information on NAI's enforcement mechanism, view "Accountability: The NAI Code and Enforcement Program: An Overview," Network Advertising Initiative, accessed June 2023, https://thenai.org/accountability/.

118 Mark Bergen, "Apple and Google are Killing the (Ad) Cookie. Here's Why," Bloomberg, April 26, 2021, https://www.bloomberg.com/news/articles/2021-04-26/how-apple-google-are-killing-the-advertising-cookie-quicktake?leadSource=uverify%20wall.

119 In essence, if a user would like in-app tracking they would need to opt-in to this approach. Nick Statt, "Apple Updates Safari's Anti-Tracking Tech With Full Third-Party Cookie Blocking," The Verge, March 24, 2020, https://www.theverge.com/2020/3/24/21192830/apple-safari-intelligent-tracking-privacy-full-third-party-cookie-blocking ; see "Apple Block on Third Party Cookies will Change Digital Media

Forever," GlobalData Thematic Research, Verdict, June 23, 2021, https://www.verdict.co.uk/apple-halts-third-party-cookies/.

120 Christine Parizo, "Will Google Kill Third-Party Cookies," TechTarget, March 22, 2022, https://www.techtarget.com/searchcustomerexperience/tip/Will-Google-kill-third-party-cookies.

121 Hitesh Bhasin, "Advertising Ethics – Principles and Tips," Marketing91, June 10, 2023, https://www.marketing91.com/advertising-ethics/; see also Daniel Belanche, "Ethical Limits to the Intrusiveness of Online Advertising Formats: A Critical Review of Better Ad Standards," Journal of Marketing Communications, January 3, 2019, https://www.tandfonline.com/doi/full/10.1080/13527266.2018.1562485?casa_token=ZWJsKqdm-LoAAAAA%3AiAC1ago9diN1e8viof4xGqXXEQlB4nUvIsak_iAT7q-9x_70NBryFmFwWwdrbWfH2dZ7nfqLvPFF.

122 Edelman Trust Barometer 2020, Edelman, https://www.edelman.com/trust/2020-trust-barometer.

123 MJ DePalma, "9 Steps to Build Trust: Ethical Advertising Considerations," *Microsoft Advertising Blog*, January 22, 2021, https://about.ads.microsoft.com/en-us/blog/post/january-2021/9-steps-to-build-trust-ethical-advertising-principles; see Ghulam Nabi, et al., "Ethical Issues in Online Advertising and Its Impact on Consumer Buying Behavior," *Journal of Contemporary Issues in Business Government*, 2020.

124 The Institute for Advertising Ethics (IAE) is an independent body addressing ethical issues in advertising. Principles & Practices, Institute for Advertising Ethics, accessed June 2023, https://www.iaethics.org/principles-and-practices; see DePalma, "9 Steps to Build Trust: Ethical Advertising Considerations.

125 "IAP Code of Conduct," Interactive Advertising Bureau (IAB), accessed June 2023, https://www.iab.com/wp-content/uploads/2015/06/IAB_Code_of_Conduct_10282-21.pdf; "AMA Code of Conduct," American Marketing Association (AMA), accessed June 2023, https://myama.force.com/s/article/AMA-Code-of-Conduct; "Digital Marketers Organization Code of Conduct," Digital Marketers Organization, accessed June 2023, https://digitalmarketers.org/pages/code-of-conduct. Notably, these codes acknowledge that sensitive data, such as information relating to potential medical conditions, necessitate special protection. "Content Taxonomy," Interactive Advertising Bureau (IAB), accessed June 2023, https://www.iab.com/guidelines/content-taxonomy/; "Guidance for NAI members: Health Audience Segments," Network Advertising Initiative (NAI), January 2020, https://thenai.org/wp-content/uploads/2021/07/nai_healthtargeting2020.pdf.

126 "Behavioral Advertising," Resource Center, IAPP, accessed August 2022, https://iapp.org/resources/article/behavioral-advertising-2/; see "Ethical Issues with 3rd Party Behavioral Tracking." AdExchanger, October 31, 2011, https://www.adexchanger.com/the-debate/3rd-party-behavioral-tracking/.

127 Shoshana Zuboff, *The Age of Surveillance Capitalism: The Fight for a Human Future at the New Frontier of Power* (New York: Public Affairs, 2019). For an earlier article on related topics, view Shoshana Zuboff, "Big Other: Surveillance Capitalism and the Prospects of an Information Civilization," *Journal of Information Technology* 30 (2015), https://cryptome.org/2015/07/big-other.pdf.

128 "FTC Staff Report: Self-Regulatory Principles for Online Behavioral Advertising," Federal Trade Commission, February 2009, ftc.gov/sites/default/files/documents/reports/federal-trade-commission-staff-report-self-regulatory-principlesonline-

behavioral-advertising/p085400behavadreport.pdf; see Peter Swire, Justin Hemmings, and Alana Kirkland, "Online Privacy and ISPs: ISP Access to Consumer Data is Limited and Often Less than Access by Others," A Working Paper by the Institute for Information Security & Privacy at Georgia Tech, May 2016, https://peterswire.net/wp-content/uploads/Online-Privacy-and-ISPs-1.pdf; Prepared Statement of Ashkan Soltani, Hearing Before the Committee on Commerce, Science, and Transportation, U.S. Senate, March 16, 2011, https://www.govinfo.gov/content/pkg/CHRG-112shrg73308/html/CHRG-112shrg73308.htm; see also Neil Richards & Woodrow Hartzog, "A Duty of Loyalty for Privacy Law," *Washington University Law Review* 99 (2021) 961, https://papers.ssrn.com/sol3/papers.cfm?abstract_id=3642217.

129 "Staff Report: Bringing Dark Patterns to Light," Federal Trade Commission, September 2022, https://www.ftc.gov/system/files/ftc_gov/pdf/P214800%20Dark%20Patterns%20Report%209.14.2022%20-%20FINAL.pdf; see Harry Brignull, "Dark Patterns: Dirty Tricks Designers Use to Make People Do Stuff," 90 Percent of Everything, July 8, 2010, https://90percentofeverything.com/2010/07/08/dark-patterns-dirty-tricks-designers-use-to-make-people-do-stuff/index.htm.

130 See Irina Ivanova, "How Websites use, 'Dark Patterns' to Manipulate You," CBS News, May 14, 2021, https://www.cbsnews.com/news/manipulative-advertising-technology-dark-patterns/; see also Jan Wiktor and Katarzyna Sanak-Kosmowska, "Manipulation in Online Advertising," (New York: Routledge, 2021), https://www.taylorfrancis.com/chapters/mono/10.4324/9781003134121-4/manipulation-online-advertising-jan-wiktor-katarzyna-sanak-kosmowska?context=ubx&refId=69c84905-42b9-46eb-bd6c-0c4fcce08d5d.

131 Jessica Rich and Darby Hobbs, "Blurred Lines: A Rundown of the FTC Workshop 'Protecting Kids from Stealth Advertising in Digital Media,'" Kelley Drye, October 26, 2022, https://www.adlawaccess.com/2022/10/articles/blurred-lines-a-rundown-on-the-ftc-workshop-protecting-kids-from-stealth-advertising-in-digital-media/; see also Matthew Lapierre and Eunjoo Choi, "Parental Awareness of New Online Advertising Techniques Targeting Children: An Exploratory Study of American Parents," Young Consumers, July 7, 2021, https://www.emerald.com/insight/content/doi/10.1108/YC-12-2020-1271/full; Weng Marc Lim, Sahil Gupta, Arun Aggarwal, Justin Paul and Priyanka Sadhna, "How Do Digital Natives Perceive and React Toward Online Advertising? Implications for SMEs," *Journal of Strategic Marketing*, August 19, 2021, https://www.tandfonline.com/doi/full.

132 "Remarks of President Joe Biden—State of the Union Address as Prepared for Delivery," The White House, March 1, 2022, https://www.whitehouse.gov/briefing-room/speeches-remarks/2022/03/01/remarks-of-president-joe-biden-state-of-the-union-address-as-delivered/; see Steve Dent, "Biden Wants to Ban Advertising Targeted Towards Kids," Engadget, March 2, 2022, https://www.engadget.com/biden-wants-to-ban-advertising-targeted-toward-kids-052140748.html.

CHAPTER 12

Workplace Privacy

This chapter introduces the reader to workplace privacy, with a focus on the sources of law that apply to private-sector employment in the United States. The chapter provides an overview of constitutional law, state contract law, state tort law, and numerous federal laws that impact workplace privacy. The chapter also discusses federal regulatory bodies that protect employee privacy, including the U.S. Department of Labor (DOL), the Equal Employment Opportunity Commission (EEOC), the U.S. Federal Trade Commission (FTC), the Consumer Financial Protection Bureau (CFPB), and the National Labor Relations Board (NLRB). The chapter then provides a framework to examine privacy issues before, during, and after employment.

Technology has transformed the relationship between the employer and the employee, meaning that virtually every phase of the employment relationship includes personal information—from evaluation and hiring, to employee management and monitoring, to termination or departure. Monitoring of employees is one issue that can have significant privacy implications for employees during employment, meaning the approach must be undertaken thoughtfully by employers. For instance, many conversations around the old water cooler, which were hard to monitor, have shifted to texts and emails, which leave a record in the employer's IT system. The cost of video cameras and other sensors has fallen sharply over time. The increasing portion of work conducted with computers and smartphones means that a greater portion of the workday, for many employees, is conducted on systems that are subject to monitoring.

Teleworking is an example where the line between personal and professional environments have blurred. In teleworking, the workday—which is traditionally under the supervision of the employer—and time at home—traditionally considered more private and not usually the business of the boss—no longer have distinct boundaries. The COVID-19 pandemic created a shift of work from offices to homes for many. Privacy and cybersecurity became critical concerns as employers attempted to safeguard customer data being sent to workers and as workers sought to protect the privacy of their home life. Post-pandemic, many experts predict that a larger segment of the job market will continue to seek employment that permits teleworking, either full-time or part-time, which means these privacy and cybersecurity issues will persist.

With the intense amount of personal information in the relationship between the employer and the employee, effective legal compliance and thoughtful management of employee personal information can help reduce the risk of any potential legal claims as well as offer many benefits to both employer and employee.

12.1 Legal Overview

There is no overarching or organized law for employment privacy in the United States. Federal laws apply in specific areas, such as to prohibit discrimination and regulate certain workplace practices, including employment screening and the use of polygraphs and credit reports. State contract and tort law in some instances provide protections for employees, but usually the employee must show fairly egregious practices to succeed. State legislatures have enacted numerous employment privacy laws, providing protections to employees in a bewildering range of specific situations, which often vary state by state. Taken together, there is considerable local variation and complexity on employment privacy issues.

Along with laws protecting privacy, many labor laws in the United States mandate employee data collection and management practices, for instance, to conduct background checks and to ensure and document a safe workplace environment. Companies also have incentives to gather information about employees and monitor the workplace to reduce the risk of being sued for negligent hiring or supervision of employees.[1]

The regulation of employment privacy in the United States stands in contrast with that in nations with comprehensive data protection laws. The European Union, for example, includes employee privacy within its general rules applying to the protection of individuals. Monitoring is permitted only with specific legal justification, and background checks are limited in scope.[2] Generally, employees in the European Union have broad workplace privacy expectations and rights. Companies with employees in the United States and other countries thus must be alert to the possibility that different workplace rules apply in connection with employment privacy.[3] This can be particularly challenging when a multinational corporation's human resources (HR) data systems in one country contain personal information about employees residing in other countries, or even when employees share personal information across borders, such as through email or other communications channels.

12.1.1 Constitutional Law

The U.S. Constitution has significant workplace privacy provisions that apply to the federal and state governments, but they do not affect private-sector employment. Notably, the Fourth Amendment prohibits unreasonable searches and seizures by state actors. Courts have interpreted this amendment to place limits on the ability of government employers to search employees' private spaces, such as lockers and desks.[4]

Some states, including California, have extended their constitutional rights of privacy to private-sector employees.[5] In general for private-sector actors, however, there is no state action, and no constitutional law governs employment privacy.

12.1.2 State Contract, Tort, and Statutory Law

U.S. law looks at the relationship between the employer and employee as fundamentally a matter of contract law. The general rule in the United States is employment at will, which means the employer has broad discretion to fire an employee. That discretion, in turn, has been understood to grant the employer broad latitude in defining other aspects of the employment relationship, such as issues about the employer's knowledge about an employee.

A contract, however, can alter the rules between employer and employee. An individual employee, for instance, might negotiate a contract that says that certain private activities are outside the scope of the employment relationship. More generally, negotiation of a contract can create binding obligations on the employer. If the employer makes promises in a contract to honor employee privacy, then violations of those promises can constitute an enforceable breach of contract.

The most important contracts concerning employee privacy are collective bargaining agreements. Unions have often negotiated provisions that protect employee privacy, including, for instance, limits on drug testing and monitoring of the workplace by the employer.

Turning to tort law, at least three common-law torts can be relevant to employee privacy, although U.S. law generally requires a fairly egregious fact pattern before imposing liability on the employer. First is the tort of intrusion upon seclusion, which states: "One who intentionally intrudes, physically or otherwise, upon the solitude or seclusion of another or his private affairs or concerns, is subject to liability to the other for invasion of his privacy, if the intrusion would be highly offensive to a reasonable person."[6]

A classic example of such intrusion is if the employer puts a camera or peephole in a bathroom or employee changing room—a jury may well find that such surveillance is highly offensive to a reasonable person. Another example could be secret wiretaps or other intrusive surveillance of an employee. Although such an employee tort claim may succeed, this chapter will discuss some of the ways employers can defeat that sort of wiretap claim, such as by an announced policy that the company's computers are owned by the employer and subject to monitoring.

A second tort claim can be "publicity given to private life," which states: "One who gives publicity to a matter concerning the private life of another is subject to liability to the other for invasion of his privacy, if the matter publicized is of a kind that (a) would be highly offensive to a reasonable person and (b) is not of legitimate concern to the public."[7] A plaintiff would need to show a relatively broad dissemination of the facts involved and also that the facts disseminated would be highly offensive to a reasonable person. Courts have been cautious in finding such offensiveness, even for dissemination of a person's salary or other information the employee considers private. Free speech principles under the First Amendment also often provide a defense against such a tort claim.

A third tort claim is for defamation, which focuses on a false or defamatory statement, and is defined as a communication tending "so to harm the reputation of another as to lower him in the estimation of the community or to deter third persons from associating or dealing with him."[8] For employment law, defamation torts can arise if, for instance, a false drug testing report is issued or if a former employer provides a factually incorrect reference to a possible future employer.

Although the common law thus supplies some possible protections for employees, according to *Privacy in Employment Law,* they have a narrow scope: "If privacy is to be protected by law, the task falls largely to the legislatures" rather than to the common-law courts.[9] State legislatures have indeed passed many statutes that affect employee privacy. *Privacy in Employment Law* author Finkin cites some striking examples, such as a California law guaranteeing a woman's right to wear pants at work or the Florida right for employees to shop where they will, free of an employer's dictate. Other state statutes prohibit marital status discrimination, and categories of inquiries regarding prospective employees, such as asking whether a worker has ever filed a claim for worker's compensation benefits.[10] In recent years, a number of states have prohibited employers from requiring employees to disclose the passwords of their social network accounts.[11] Statutes vary enormously state by state, leading to "a patchwork of near bewildering complexity and large lacunae," or gaps.[12]

To summarize on state law and employment privacy, employees tend to have narrow protections under contract, tort, and statutory law. The free market approach of U.S. law applies broadly, except where a discrete problem has arisen and prompted a response by the legal and political system. Against this general backdrop of employer discretion, however, there may be significant state and local laws that apply in a particular setting.

12.1.3 Federal Laws on Employment Privacy

Given this context of relatively limited constitutional or state law protections, a number of federal statutes have been enacted that bear on employment privacy.

12.1.3.1 U.S. Laws Protecting Employee Privacy

The United States has several federal laws prohibiting discrimination. Antidiscrimination laws provide employees with some privacy protection—for example, by limiting questioning with respect to what is being protected, such as age, national origin, or disability.

The United States also has federal laws that regulate employee benefits management. These laws offer certain privacy and security protections for benefits-related information. They also often mandate collection of employee medical information. These laws include the following protections:

- The Health Insurance Portability and Accountability Act of 1996 (HIPAA) contains privacy and security rules that regulate "protected health information" for health insurers, including self-funded health plans[13]
- The Consolidated Omnibus Budget Reconciliation Act (COBRA) requires qualified health plans to provide continuous coverage after termination to certain beneficiaries[14]
- The Employee Retirement Income Security Act (ERISA) ensures that employee benefits programs are created fairly and administered properly[15]
- The Family and Medical Leave Act (FMLA) entitles certain employees to unpaid leave in the event of birth or illness of self or a family member[16]

Other federal laws with employment privacy implications regulate data collection and recordkeeping:

- The Fair Credit Reporting Act (FCRA) regulates the use of consumer reports obtained from consumer reporting agencies (CRAs) in reference-checking and background checks of employees[17]
- The Fair Labor Standards Act (FLSA) establishes the minimum wage and sets standards for fair pay[18]
- The Occupational Safety and Health Act (OSHA) regulates workplace safety[19]
- The Whistleblower Protection Act protects federal employees and applicants for employment who claim to have been subjected to personnel actions because of whistleblowing activities[20]
- The National Labor Relations Act (NLRA) sets standards for collective bargaining, which also apply in social media communications[21]
- The Immigration Reform and Control Act (IRCA) requires employment eligibility verification[22]
- The Securities Exchange Act of 1934 requires disclosures about payment and other information about senior executives of publicly traded companies, as well as registration requirements for market participants such as broker-dealers and transfer agents[23]

Later in this chapter, we will also discuss two statutory regimes that govern specific monitoring practices by employers:

- The Employee Polygraph Protection Act of 1988, which limits employer use of lie detectors[24]
- Electronic surveillance laws, including the Wiretap Act, the Electronic Communications Privacy Act (ECPA) and the Stored Communications Act (SCA)[25]

12.1.3.2 U.S. Regulatory Bodies that Protect Employee Privacy

Employee privacy is protected by several federal agencies, including the U.S. Department of Labor (DOL), the Equal Employment Opportunity Commission (EEOC), the Federal Trade Commission (FTC), the Consumer Financial Protection Bureau (CFPB), and the National Labor Relations Board (NLRB).

The mission of the DOL is "to foster, promote, and develop the welfare of the wage earners, job seekers, and retirees of the United States; improve working conditions; advance opportunities for profitable employment; and assure work-related benefits and rights."[26] To achieve this mission, the department administers a variety of federal laws, FLSA, OSHA and ERISA.

The EEOC works to prevent discrimination in the workplace. The EEOC oversees many laws, including Title VII of the Civil Rights Act, the Age Discrimination in Employment Act of 1967 (ADEA), and Titles I and V of the Americans with Disabilities Act of 1990 (ADA).[27]

Both the FTC and the CFPB regulate unfair and deceptive practices and enforce a variety of laws, including the FCRA, which limits employers' ability to receive an employee's or applicant's credit report, driving records, criminal records, and other consumer reports obtained from a CRA.[28]

The NLRB administers the National Labor Relations Act. The board conducts elections to determine if employees want union representation and investigates and remedies unfair labor practices by employers and unions.[29]

In addition, each state has an agency, often called the Department of Labor, that oversees the state labor laws. These laws include state minimum wage laws and laws limiting work by minors. The same department in most states may administer state unemployment insurance programs and employee rehabilitation programs. Some departments also conduct safety inspections of worker conditions.

12.2 Privacy Issues in the Employment Life Cycle

Workplace privacy issues exist in all stages of the employment life cycle: before, during and after employment. Before employment, employers should consider rules and best practices about background screening, including rules for accessing employee information under the FCRA. During employment, major topics include polygraphs and psychological testing; substance testing; employee monitoring, including phone calls and emails; social media; and bring your own device (BYOD) policies. After employment, the main issues are termination of access to physical and informational assets and proper human resources practices postemployment. It is important to keep in mind that while consumer privacy practices pose a bigger risk for many organizations, HR-related privacy presents a risk for virtually *all* organizations, including organizations in traditional industries that are not focused on data or data privacy.[30]

For privacy professionals whose roles encompass human resources, multiple legal issues can arise in the employment life cycle. In addition to consulting with the legal and information technology (IT) departments, a privacy professional should keep in close contact with the HR experts in the organization. Even before the IT revolution put personnel records on computers, HR professionals had developed good practices for handling confidential information. It is worth noting that one consequence of the long-standing policies in HR is that these departments may be reluctant to adjust policies at the advice of a recently formed privacy team that is seeking to implement more recent developments in privacy.

HR records are often physically segregated from other organization records or handled within IT systems with strict access controls. Because HR records apply to every person in an organization, including the most senior management, HR professionals have a special responsibility to respect the confidentiality of employee information.

Employment laws in the United States often provide employers with more discretion than laws in the European Union and other countries in the handling of personal information. U.S. laws also often vary by state. Organizations thus have to consider which jurisdiction's rules apply to personal information about particular employees.

12.3 Privacy Issues Before Employment

Employers today can have access to a wealth of information about applicants, gathered both directly from the candidates and through searches of public records and private databases. In the United States, the FCRA and antidiscrimination laws create national rules that structure how information is gathered and used preemployment. As in other areas of workplace privacy, states often have additional laws, and egregious practices can create tort suits under the common law. Collective bargaining agreements may also apply. As discussed in other chapters of this book, the privacy professional thus must be aware of both the many beneficial uses of personal information and the legal and other risks that can arise from improper handling of personal information.

12.3.1 Common Reasons for Employee Background Screening

Before employees are hired—or even brought in for an interview—they are often subject to background screening.[31] The type and extent of screening varies depending on the work environment. There are many reasons and motivations for employers to conduct background screening. Some important trends have stimulated an increase in applicant screening.[32] For example:

- The terrorist attacks of September 11, 2001, resulted in heightened attention to security issues and support for more stringent identity verification requirements
- Greater attention to child abuse and abductions has led to laws in almost every state requiring criminal background checks for people who work with children
- Business governance scandals, such as those at Enron and WorldCom, spurred passage of the Sarbanes-Oxley Act (SOX) in 2002, which has increased the incentives for corporate leaders to scrutinize practices in the areas they manage
- The rapid increase of information about candidates from online search and social media sites has made background checks easier[33]

Certain professions are subject to background screening by law. Typically, anyone who works with the elderly, children, or the disabled must now undergo background screening. The federal National Child Protection Act authorizes state officials to access the Federal Bureau of Investigation's (FBI's) National Crime Information Center database for some positions that involve contact with children. Many state and federal government jobs require rigorous background checks to obtain a security clearance.[34] Other groups that are targeted in background checks, depending on the state, include emergency medical service personnel, county coroners, humane society investigators, euthanasia technicians in animal shelters, bus and truck drivers, athletic trainers, in-home repair services, firefighters, gaming (i.e., casino and gambling) industry employees, real estate brokers, and IT workers. The EEOC has cautioned businesses that they should carefully review background screening processes, such as denying employment based on criminal convictions, to ensure that their requirements are job-related and consistent with business necessity.[35]

Employers use background screening to ensure they are hiring the best candidate for the job. Screenings can help determine whether the applicant will fit in the organization's culture and make positive contributions to its growth. Screening can counter false or inflated information provided by job applicants and helps identify candidates who may damage the organization's brand and reputation. In addition, employers seek to mitigate the risk of liability. Careful background screening can help defeat a later claim for negligent hiring, such as if an employee causes harm when there was prior evidence the person was dangerous.[36]

Changing IT has led to changes in screening. An unprecedented amount of candidate data is now available to employers. The sophistication of today's internet search, coupled with the ever-greater amount of information publicly accessible about many people, has enormously expanded the ability of employers to take it upon themselves and screen on the internet. Searches of publicly available information have generally been considered a reasonable practice in the United States. Significant privacy issues can accompany such practices, however, as discussed later in this chapter. For instance, internet searches should not be a basis for making impermissible, discriminatory hiring decisions, and there are laws in numerous states to prohibit more invasive practices, such as requiring candidates to provide their Facebook or other social network passwords so prospective employers can see information that the candidate has taken steps to keep private.[37]

12.3.2 Antidiscrimination Laws as Limits on Background Screening

The United States has several federal laws that prohibit discrimination in employment and have sometimes been used to limit background checks. Notably:

- Title VII of the Civil Rights Act of 1964 bars discrimination in employment due to race, color, religion, sex, and national origin.[38]
- The Equal Pay Act of 1963 bars wage disparity based on sex.[39]
- The Age Discrimination in Employment Act of 1967 bars discrimination against individuals over 40.[40]
- The Pregnancy Discrimination Act of 1978 bars discrimination due to pregnancy, childbirth and related medical conditions.[41]
- The Americans with Disabilities Act of 1990 bars discrimination against qualified individuals with disabilities.[42]
- The Genetic Information Nondiscrimination Act of 2008 bars discrimination based on individuals' genetic information.[43]
- The Bankruptcy Act provision 11 U.S.C. § 525(b) prohibits employment discrimination against persons who have filed for bankruptcy. There is some ambiguity, however, as to whether the statute applies to discrimination prior to the extension of an offer of employment, and courts have read the statute both ways.[44]

The primary purpose of these laws is to prohibit discrimination in hiring and other employment decisions. A secondary effect, however, is that they often affect how interviews and other background screen activities are conducted. For instance, an employer risks possible discrimination claims for interview questions about national origin or race under Title VII, about current or intended pregnancy under the Pregnancy Discrimination Act, about age under the ADEA, or about disability under the ADA. The EEOC has held that Title VII sex discrimination extends to claims based on an individual's sexual orientation or gender identity.[45] Along with these federal laws, many states have their own antidiscrimination laws. Some of these have the same protected classes as the federal laws, and some include additional protected classes. Almost half the states currently prohibit sexual preference discrimination in both public- and private-sector jobs, while other states prohibit such discrimination in public workplaces only.[46] Roughly half the states prohibit discrimination based on marital status.[47]

The complexities of antidiscrimination law are beyond the scope of this book. Extensive case law has grown up under each of these statutes, so that legal research beyond the text of each statute may be needed to assess current good practice. The risk for employers is that their interview questions and other background screening activities may provide evidence of discrimination. On the other hand, information that a candidate is a member of a protected class may be required by statute (such as when age is revealed in the course of verifying eligibility for employment), may be a bona fide occupational qualification, or may become known to the employer for some other nondiscriminatory reason.

In practice, HR professionals often receive detailed training about how to collect information relevant to employment decisions while avoiding practices that increase the risk of an antidiscrimination claim. Many companies have established policies that prohibit discrimination and provide more detailed guidance about what interview and background screening practices are permitted. One strategy to reduce risk is to avoid asking questions that elicit information about membership in a protected class. For instance, avoid asking about membership in organizations that reflect religion or national origin. Another strategy is to be consistent and ask the same questions of all candidates. For instance, the company faces a greater risk of pregnancy or sex discrimination claims if women—but not men—are asked about how long they expect to stay on the job.

12.3.3 The Americans with Disabilities Act and Medical Screenings

The ADA created important restrictions on medical screening of candidates before employment. The law forbids employers with 15 or more employees from discriminating against a "qualified individual with a disability because of the disability of such individual," and specifically covers "medical examinations and inquiries" as grounds for discrimination.[48] Before an offer of employment is made, the ADA permits such examinations and inquiries only where "job-related and consistent with business necessity."[49]

A company may require a medical examination after the offer of employment has been made and may condition the offer of employment on the results of such an examination. Such an examination is permitted only if (1) all entering employees are subjected to such an examination regardless of disability, (2) confidentiality rules are followed for the results of the examination, and (3) the results are used only in accordance with the statutory prohibitions against discrimination on the basis of disability.[50]

The ADA requires an employer to provide reasonable accommodation to qualified individuals who are employees or applicants for employment, unless to do so would cause undue hardship.[51] During the hiring process and before a conditional offer is made, an employer generally may not ask applicants whether they need a reasonable accommodation for the job, except when the employer knows that an applicant has a disability. After a conditional offer of employment is extended, an employer may inquire whether applicants will need reasonable accommodations so long as all entering employees in the same job category are asked this question.[52]

The ADA restrictions on medical examinations and inquiries significantly affect a range of prehiring practices that previously were widespread.[53] Employers can no longer routinely ask questions about prior injuries and illnesses, including prior worker compensation claims. Psychological tests, previously used to predict conditions such as depression or paranoia, may well qualify as medical examinations. The ADA does not cover the use of drugs or alcohol, although it does cover questions about recovered drug addicts and alcoholics. In general, before hiring, employers should use caution about inquiring into the likelihood that a candidate has a covered disability or will seek a reasonable accommodation.

12.3.4 FCRA Restrictions on Background Checks

The FCRA, discussed in more detail in Chapter 9 on financial privacy, regulates how employers perform background checks on job applicants. This law is not limited to background credit checks; it also covers any other type of background check, such as criminal records or driving records, obtained from a CRA. A CRA includes any organization that regularly engages in the assembling or evaluating of consumer information for the purpose of furnishing consumer reports to third parties for a fee.[54]

Under the FCRA, the term "consumer report" includes all written, oral, or other communications bearing on the consumer's creditworthiness, credit standing, credit capacity, character, general reputation, personal characteristics, or mode of living. Examples of inquiries covered by FCRA include a credit report obtained from a credit bureau and a driving history report obtained from an information aggregator. In recent years, the FTC has aggressively enforced FCRA violations against nontraditional CRAs that collect data online and report it to employers.[55] Alleged FCRA violations are frequently litigated by affected individuals as well.

FCRA prohibits obtaining a consumer report unless a "permissible purpose" exists. Permissible purposes, however, include "employment purposes," which in turn include (1) preemployment screening for the purpose of evaluating the candidate for employment and (2) determining if an existing employee qualifies for promotion, reassignment, or retention.

The FCRA also permits employers to obtain an "investigative consumer report" on the applicant if a permissible purpose exists. An investigative consumer report is one in which some of the information is acquired through interviews with neighbors, friends, associates, or acquaintances of the employee, such as reference checks.

To obtain any consumer report under FCRA, an employer must meet the following standards:

- Provide written notice to the applicant that it is obtaining a consumer report for employment purposes and indicate if an investigative consumer report will be obtained
- Obtain written consent from the applicant
- Obtain data only from a qualified consumer reporting agency, an entity that has taken steps to assure the accuracy and currency of the data

- Certify to the CRA agency that the employer has a permissible purpose and has obtained consent from the employee
- Before taking an adverse action, such as denial of employment, provide a pre-adverse-action notice to the applicant with a copy of the consumer report, in order to give the applicant an opportunity to dispute the report
- After taking adverse action, provide an adverse action notice

If employers do not comply with these requirements, they may face civil and criminal penalties, including a private right of action.

In 2003, the Fair and Accurate Credit Transactions Act (FACTA) amended FCRA. The amendments preempted a wide range of state laws on credit reporting, identity theft, and other areas within the FCRA.[56] FACTA, however, specifically left some existing state laws in effect, and the FCRA does *not* preempt states from creating stronger legislation in the area of employment credit history checks. One of these state laws, notably, is the California Investigative Consumer Reporting Agencies Act (ICRAA).[57]

Under the ICRAA, employers must notify applicants and employees of their intention to obtain and use a consumer report. Once disclosure is made, the employer must obtain the applicant or employee's written authorization prior to requesting the report. On the notice and authorization form, employers must enable applicants and employees to check a box to receive a copy of their consumer report any time a background check is conducted. If employers wish to take adverse employment action, they must provide the employee with a copy of the report, regardless of whether the employee waived the right to receive a copy. This exception does not apply to employees suspected of wrongdoing or misconduct.

Ten other states—Colorado, Connecticut, Delaware, Hawaii, Illinois, Maryland, Nevada, Oregon, Vermont, and Washington—currently limit the use of credit information in employment.[58] These states require that credit history information be used only as related to the position applied for. The requisite degree of relation differs among states. While most states require a substantial relationship, Hawaii requires the applicant's credit history to directly relate to an occupational qualification.[59] Additionally, some states allow credit history checks to be performed if the position applied for fits within predefined occupational categories, generally involving financial or managerial responsibility or exposure to confidential information.[60]

12.3.5 Restrictions on Background Checks under Fair Chance to Compete on Jobs Act

The Fair Chance to Compete on Jobs Act (FCA) was enacted in 2019.[61] For many jobs, the FCA restricts federal agencies as well as federal contractors from requesting information related to an applicant's criminal history until a conditional offer of employment has been made to the applicant.[62] Although a discussion of the breadth of state law restrictions on background checks is beyond the scope of this book, practitioners should be aware that FCA is part of a recent type of law known as "Ban the Box Laws." Approximately two-thirds of states and more than 150 municipalities across the U.S. have enacted laws to remove the checkbox on job applications that ask an applicant if they have a criminal history.[63]

12.3.6 Technologies to Screen Potential Employees

In recent years, companies have used a variety of technologies to assist with the hiring process. We will discuss two of these technologies: social media and artificial intelligence (AI).

Social media has increasingly been used to screen prospective hires. Social media sites such as Facebook, LinkedIn, TikTok, and Twitter facilitate easy and immediate sharing, collaboration, and interaction. Businesses now exist that are dedicated entirely to tracking an individual's online presence and screening candidates for predesignated elements selected by the employer. These may include potential drug use, criminal activity, or unsafe behavior. In doing so, employers should be alert to possible legal restrictions.[64] For example, there is the possibility that the FCRA applies to these nontraditional providers of background check information.[65] In addition, although employers are generally legally permitted to use social media in informing their decisions, acting in a discriminatory way in hiring is not. Reviewing applicant's social media pages or posts may provide the basis for discrimination lawsuits if the employer accesses and appears to use information that is legally protected. This includes protected classes such as religion, ethnicity, gender or sexual orientation, political affiliations, and other sensitive information, all of which is commonly available on individuals' social media pages. Employers also face risks when engaging in social engineering—the use of manipulation to gain access to otherwise private information. This includes connecting with potential hires through a false online profile or requesting access to private networks that are not available to the general public. If employers engage in these practices, they may be confronted with invasion of privacy actions for violating the applicant's reasonable expectation of privacy.[66] Employers should thus consider what policies and training should exist to avoid taking actions that could violate legal restrictions, including reviewing information about applicants on social media sites.[67]

Finally, employers should proceed with extreme caution when considering policies that require applicants to divulge access information to private networks as a condition of employment. In 2012, Maryland was the first state to ban employers from asking applicants (or employees) for their social network login information and passwords.[68] As of the writing of this book, approximately half the states have passed similar laws, and Congress has proposed similar legislation.[69]

AI is also being used to screen applicants during the interview stage of the hiring process. When companies conducting job interviews initially adopted video conferencing, the main purpose of this technology was to overcome the distance between the interviewer and the interviewee. Currently, many companies use AI to assess job applicants who appear via video. The AI evaluates the speech patterns, facial expressions, and gestures of the individuals interviewed in an effort to provide insights to those people who are making the hiring decision.[70] Privacy practitioners should be aware of privacy implications of using videotaped interviews as well as the possible biases in the algorithms being introduced into the hiring process.[71]

12.4 Privacy Issues During Employment

A range of workplace privacy issues can arise once an applicant has been hired. The discussion here addresses polygraphs and psychological testing; substance testing; employee monitoring, including of phone calls and emails; and social network monitoring and BYOD policies.[72]

12.4.1 Polygraphs and Psychological Testing

The Employee Polygraph Protection Act of 1988 (EPPA) is a prominent example of federal protection of privacy in the workplace.[73] Under the act and its regulations, issued by the DOL, employers are prohibited from using "lie detectors" on incumbent workers or to screen applicants. A lie detector is defined to include polygraphs, voice stress analyzers, psychological stress evaluators, or any similar device used for the purpose of rendering a diagnostic opinion regarding an individual's honesty.[74] The act prohibits employers from requiring or requesting that a prospective or current employee take a lie detector test. Employers cannot use, accept, refer to, or inquire about lie detector test results. The act also prohibits employers from taking adverse action against an employee who refuses to take a test.[75]

EPPA has exceptions for certain occupations, including for government employees, employees in certain security services, those engaged in the manufacturing of controlled substances, certain defense contractors, and those in certain national security functions. Tests are also allowed in connection with "an ongoing investigation involving economic loss or injury to the employer's business," such as theft, embezzlement, or industrial espionage. Even for such investigations, there must be reasonable suspicion to test an employee, and other protections for the employee apply. An employee cannot be discharged because of the results of a polygraph or for refusing to submit to a polygraph, unless additional supporting evidence also exists.

EPPA requires employers to post the act's essential provisions in a conspicuous location so that employees are aware of its existence. If the act is violated, employers may be subject to a fine from the DOL as well as to private lawsuits. Also, state laws are *not* preempted, and many states have enacted laws further restricting the use of lie detectors in private employment.[76]

EPPA and the ADA together place significant national limits on psychological testing in the workplace. Employers must comply with the rules limiting lie detectors as well as the ADA prohibitions on the use of medical tests, including those designed to test an impairment of mental health. Employers continue to use psychological tests measuring personality traits such as honesty, preferences and habits in hiring and employment, although one expert reports that such tests may be concentrated in specific positions such as management and sales.[77]

12.4.2 Substance Use Testing

Employers test for substance use for varied reasons: (1) to reduce costs resulting from lowered productivity, accidents, and absenteeism caused by drug use; (2) to reduce medical care costs related to drug use; (3) to reduce theft or other illegal activity in the workplace associated with drug trafficking; (4) to bolster corporate image; and (5) to comply with external legal rules that impose or support a drug testing policy.[78]

There is no federal privacy statute that directly governs employer testing of employees for substances such as illegal drugs, alcohol, or tobacco. For public-sector employees, there is considerable case law under the Fourth Amendment about when such testing is reasonable. As previously mentioned, the ADA prohibits discrimination based on disability, although the application of the ADA varies for illegal drugs and alcohol, and for current and past use. The

ADA specifically excludes current illegal drug use from its protections, and a test for drug use is not considered a medical examination.[79] By contrast, the responsible federal agencies have stated that "an alcoholic is a person with a disability and is protected by the ADA if they are qualified to perform the essential functions of the job."[80] Concerning a history of illegal drug use, the U.S. Department of Justice states that "policies that screen out applicants because of a history of addiction or treatment for addiction must be carefully scrutinized to ensure that the policies are job-related and consistent with business necessity."[81]

Federal law mandates drug testing for certain positions within the federal sector, including employees of the U.S. Customs and Border Protection. Federal law also creates regulation for drug testing for employees in the aviation, railroading and trucking industries.[82] The rules preempt state laws that would otherwise limit drug testing.

Drug testing can be used in a variety of settings:

- Preemployment—generally allowed if not designed to identify legal use of drugs or addiction to illegal drugs
- Reasonable suspicion—generally allowed as a condition of continued employment if there is "reasonable suspicion" of drug or alcohol use based on specific facts as well as rational inferences from those facts (e.g., appearance, behavior, speech, odors)
- Routine testing—generally allowed if the employees are notified at the time of hire, unless state or local law prohibits it
- Post-accident testing—generally allowed to test as a condition of continued employment if there is "reasonable suspicion" that the employee involved in the accident was under the influence of drugs or alcohol
- Random testing—sometimes required by law, prohibited in certain jurisdictions, but acceptable when used on existing employees in specific, narrowly defined jobs, such as those in highly regulated industries where the employee has a severely diminished expectation of privacy or where testing is critical to public safety or national security

A majority of states have passed one or more statutes governing the testing of employees for drugs and/or alcohol.[83] States such as Connecticut, Iowa and Minnesota have laws that generally prohibit employee drug tests unless there is reasonable suspicion to test a particular employee, although state law varies on whether employer violation of the statute prevents discharge of an employee who tests positive.[84] There has also been extensive litigation over time under the common law of the various states, on theories including defamation (if the test was inaccurate), negligent testing, invasion of privacy, and violation of contract and collective bargaining agreements.

Generalizing in the face of this state-by-state variation is risky. Cases upholding random drug testing usually involve occupational roles in highly regulated industries or positions that are critical to the protection of life, property, or national security. More invasive tests, such as collection of a blood sample, are more prone to scrutiny than less invasive tests, such as a breathalyzer.

With approximately two-thirds of the states in the United States recently enacting laws legalizing the use of cannabis for medical or recreational purposes, the issue of drug testing employees has become more complicated.[85] Fewer than half of the states that allow individuals to legally use cannabis afford any protections for employees who test positive for the drug. A minority of the state laws that permit legal cannabis use include explicit employee protections.[86] The treatment of employees in sectors regulated by federal law, such as the trucking, aviation, and railroading industries, is complicated. Because cannabis is federally prohibited, employees in these industries must adhere to federal requirements.[87] Privacy practitioners should be prepared to advise management concerning the complexity of crafting drug testing policies that comply with both federal and state laws.[88]

12.4.3 Lifestyle Discrimination

An employee's lifestyle outside of work has generally been regarded as private, unless these actions negatively affect other people or are criminal.[89] In recent years, concerns have been raised about issues such as employees' weight and smoking habits. Employers must use caution when taking negative actions against employees for lifestyle choices.[90]

Weight. The classic example of weight discrimination was in the field of flight attendants, who were told they must remain under a certain weight to be employed. After numerous discrimination lawsuits in the airline industry, the mandate was changed to one requiring a person's weight to be proportional to their height and age.[91] This illustrates how restrictions focused on weight can make a company susceptible to being sued for discrimination.

In the employment context, the EEOC has obtained settlements on behalf of employees who alleged discrimination due to obesity resulting from a physiological disability, yet courts have split in their approach to the topic. This means the details of how the disability will be understood legally are still less than certain at this time.[92]

A current trend concerning weight in the workplace arises in wellness programs that are sponsored by the employer. In 2013, CVS Pharmacy gained national attention when employees were required to provide information on weight as part of a wellness program or face a $600 annual surcharge.[93] Employers should take care to ensure that these attempts to assist their employees do not become avenues for discrimination.

Smoking. Many employers ban smoking tobacco or vaping during work hours or on work property. No federal law protects smokers from discrimination. When designing a policy regarding smoking, employers should be aware that more than half of states have laws that limit smoking bans to the workplace. Under these laws, individuals are protected from discrimination by their employer if they choose to smoke while not at work.[94]

Businesses who have restrictions related to lifestyle issues should clearly explain the business reason for such policies. While concerned for health insurance costs of employees who engage in certain habits, companies should be careful in carrying out the implementation of such policies.[95]

For the privacy professional, it is important to understand this is a developing area of the law. Numerous state laws have been passed to address various lifestyle issues, and more are being considered.[96] Employer policies should be reviewed and updated in light of new developments.

12.4.4 Monitoring in the Workplace

Technological trends have increased the range of ways employers can monitor employees. For example, employees often use company-issued computers, laptops, and smartphones. In the U.S, private-sector employees in general have limited expectations of privacy at the workplace. The physical facilities belong to the employer, and employers in the private sector thus generally have broad legal authority to do monitoring and searches at work.[97] Computers and other electronic equipment are similarly understood to be the property of the employer, with consequent broad employer rights about how the equipment is used.

Organizations should consider establishing formal policies about workplace monitoring and accompanying documents, such as acceptable use policies for IT equipment. These policies may also be required by state law in order for such monitoring to be lawful.[98] Such policies often include when monitoring can or will occur, purposes of data use, to whom data may be disclosed, and the consequences to employees for violations. In special circumstances where additional monitoring is conducted, the employer may be required to describe the approval process and document when it is implemented. Providing employees with notices of these policies helps establish their knowledge and reasonable expectations about workplace activities. Such policies have proven broadly effective in addressing employee claims for improper monitoring.[99]

When developing these policies, companies should be aware that these employer rights are frequently more limited in Europe and other countries, where employees often have a broader set of protections against monitoring under data protection, collective bargaining, and other employment laws. Companies with employees both in the U.S. and abroad thus may need to develop different policies and IT systems that conform to the varying laws.

12.4.4.1 Legal Obligations or Incentives to Monitor Employees

In the U.S., companies often engage in monitoring of employees for a variety of reasons. Certain legal obligations for companies can be fulfilled, at least in part, by monitoring employees. Companies also have a variety of incentives to monitor employees. This means that strong policies both favor and limit monitoring of employees in the workplace.

Because there are numerous reasons and ways to monitor employees, companies should be careful to develop and implement policies related to how data involving employee monitoring is collected, used, transmitted, and stored. Employers should also consider what policies and training should exist to avoid taking actions that could be considered inappropriate, discriminatory, or invasive.[100]

The following are examples related to legal obligations and incentives to monitor:

- **Follow workplace safety and other laws that require or encourage monitoring.** OSHA, for example, requires employers to provide a safe workplace that complies with occupational health and safety standards. These standards require employees to perform tasks in a safe manner to avoid injury. Thus, ensuring compliance with OSHA is one legal reason to monitor employees.[101] For example, monitoring with biometric sensors can help to ensure that workers are performing tasks in a safe manner, such as eye monitors for truck drivers.[102]

- **Improve work quality (e.g., by monitoring service calls with customers).** Call centers and firms that do financial transactions over the phone often record telephone conversations for reasons including agent training, quality assurance, and security/liability. If a dispute arises with a customer after the fact, the recording can often resolve what was said or agreed upon. Such recordings, however, must comply with the rules about phone call recording (see Section 12.4.4.2). As noted in Chapter 11, certain activities that may result in charges placed using preacquired account numbers, such as telemarketing, must be recorded.[103] Note though that for security reasons, call centers often pause the recording functionality when a customer relays full payment card information.

- **Limit liability for employee's actions.** Employers monitor the workplace as a way to defend against a possible tort claim for negligent supervision, especially where the employer is on notice of a specific risk from one employee to other employees or third parties. The claim of negligent supervision is similar to the claim of negligent hiring. In both instances, there is uncertainty about what a jury will find to have been negligent, so employers have an incentive to err on the side of caution to reduce the risk of a successful claim. Also, some business lawyers have counseled companies to monitor email and other employee computer usage to reduce the risk that the employer will be held liable for creating a hostile work environment. An example could be if sexually explicit or racially derogatory material is viewed at work.[104] Note that other experts disagree with this approach.[105]
- **Protect physical security (e.g., by placing video cameras near entrances).** Many U.S. employers use closed-circuit television (CCTV) or other video surveillance in the workplace. Security cameras are often used at the perimeter of a business to deter and detect burglary or other unauthorized intrusion. They are used within a business establishment to deter crimes such as shoplifting and armed robbery and outside to detect drive aways from gas stations or other businesses. They are used within warehouses and other parts of a business to reduce incidents of stealing by employees. Insurance companies may give companies a discount for installing CCTV systems.[106] Employers also may have an interest monitoring the location of company vehicles equipped with GPS to prevent theft. To access certain restricted locations at a company, employees may have to verify their identity using biometrics, such as face scans or hand scans.
- **Protect cybersecurity (e.g., by monitoring activity on computer systems).** Companies today often have in place a variety of systems to monitor electronic communications. Companies routinely run

antispam and antivirus software on emails. The computer security activities of the IT department include a range of intrusion detection and other measures. Depending on the company and job description, there may also be limits on acceptable use of work computers, including bans on accessing websites that are inappropriate for the workplace. Also, to enhance cybersecurity, companies may require face scans or fingerprints for identity verification before accessing computers or other electronic equipment.

- **Protect trade secrets and limit liability for unlicensed transmission of copyrighted material and other confidential company information.** Companies endeavor to protect trade secrets and limit liability concerning leakage of copyrighted and other material. To prevent efforts by employees to obtain such information for nefarious purposes, companies analyze employees' emails, review employees' computer usage, and monitor phone calls. Companies may also track employees' locations to determine if they are meeting with competitors.[107] Improve company reputation. Employers can use social media to their advantage; for example, a strong social media presence helps increase visibility in the marketplace. Social media can be used by employers to stay in touch with customer needs, and its effective use conveys a level of technological sophistication to its followers. It is also a helpful platform for receiving immediate feedback from consumers, clients, and employees at a very low cost. Social media monitoring is used to keep track of current employees to mitigate brand or reputation damage.[108]
- **Try to keep employees on task rather than spending time on personal business.** Although monitoring can be justified to increase productivity by keeping employees on task, there can be serious privacy concerns from excessive video monitoring (such as in changing rooms), monitoring of workplace conversations (such as bugs secretly placed by a supervisor to listen to employees), email and other computer monitoring (such as when emails that an employee believes are personal are reviewed by the employer or screen recording for productivity management).[109]

In this discussion of reasons to monitor employees, it is important to remember that employers often choose not to monitor even where they may have legal ability to do so, for reasons including ethics, cost, and morale.

Monitoring costs include the legal obligations to detect and act on misconduct revealed by the monitoring program.[110]

12.4.4.2 Laws Applying to Types of Monitoring

Federal laws governing wiretaps and access to stored communications are notoriously complex, and electronic monitoring of employees thus should often be done in consultation with a lawyer knowledgeable about the area. Chapter 13 discusses key aspects of these laws. The discussion here focuses on monitoring in the workplace.

Federal and state laws regulate and restrict workplace surveillance activities, including electronic surveillance (such as accessing emails and monitoring internet activities), accessing social media accounts, video surveillance, and monitoring of telephone calls.[111]

Intercepting communications. As discussed in Chapter 13, the Wiretap Act and the Electronic Communications Privacy Act (ECPA) are generally strict in prohibiting the interception of wire communications, such as telephone calls or sound recordings from video cameras; oral communications, such as hidden bugs or microphones; and electronic communications, such as emails. The exact rules for wire, oral, and electronic communications vary, and unless an exception applies, interception of these communications is a criminal offense and provides a private right of action.[112]

Two exceptions to the prohibition on interception often apply in the workplace.[113] Under federal law, interception is permitted:

1. If a person is a party to a call or where one of the parties has given consent[114]
2. The interception is done in the ordinary course of business[115]

An employer who provides communication services, such as a company telephone or email service, has the ability to intercept provided the interception occurs in the normal course of the user's business.[116] An important distinction exists when an employer listens to an employee's purely personal call. In this instance, the employer risks violation of the wiretap laws. As courts have split on how broadly to define the "ordinary course of business," many employers rely on the consent exception for interception of telephone calls.[117] Privacy professionals should be alert to the requirements of relevant state laws on recording phone calls, because some of these laws require one-party consent, while others mandate that all parties to the call consent.[118]

Stored communications. The SCA creates a general prohibition against the unauthorized acquisition, alteration or blocking of electronic communications while in an electronic storage facility that provides electronic communications services.[119] Violations for interceptions can lead to criminal penalties or a civil lawsuit. The law provides for exceptions. Two exceptions that may apply to the employer are for conduct authorized by:

1. "The person or entity providing a wire or electronic communications service" (often the employer)[120]
2. "A user of that service with respect to a communication of or intended for that user"[121]

Generally, employers are permitted to look at workers' electronic communications if the employer's reason for doing so is reasonable and work-related. In the case of City of Ontario v. Quon, the U.S. Supreme Court allowed an employer to review an employee's text messages when the employer was looking at the messages to determine whether the employer's electronic usage policy had been violated. In the case, the employer—the City of Ontario, California—provided the pager used to send the messages at issue. Note that the distinction between private-sector employers and public-sector employers can be particularly important in cases involving ECPA.[122]

In addition, privacy practitioners should be alert to the fact that ECPA generally does *not* preempt stricter state privacy protections. Notably, certain state laws protect email communications.[123]

Social media accounts. As with applicants, employers should proceed with caution when accessing and collecting information from the social media accounts of employees. Employers have not traditionally had access to an employee's personal email account(s), and similar reasoning should be applied to gaining access to the private parts of a person's social network activities.[124] As discussed in Section 12.3.6, approximately half the states in the U.S. currently have laws prohibiting employers from asking employees (or applicants) for access to their social media accounts.[125] In addition, employers must not violate existing antidiscrimination and privacy laws.[126]

Unions and union-organizing activities. Collective bargaining agreements can be an additional limiting factor on an employer's ability to monitor in the workplace. Many such agreements contain provisions designed to limit workplace monitoring or require that a union representative be informed of an employer's monitoring activities. Also, according to the National Labor Relations Board, employees' speech may be protected when social media or other means of electronic communication is used to complain about managers, coworkers or the companies that employ them.[127]

Biometric data. Numerous state laws regulate the collection, use, transmission, storage, and destruction of biometric data. As of the writing of this book, three of these state laws regulate employee data held by employers.[128] The Illinois Biometric Information Privacy Act (BIPA) requires employers to notify employees of their biometric practices and to obtain informed consent from employees for such practices. Employers should be aware that BIPA includes a private right of action, and that numerous employment class action lawsuits have been filed by employees.[129] Texas and Washington also have biometric laws that apply to employers, but do not include a private right of action.[130]

Photo and video surveillance. Federal law generally does not limit the use of either photography or video cameras. For example, cameras and video recordings that do not have sound recordings are outside the scope of the federal wiretap and stored-record statutes. State statutes and common law, however, create limits in some settings. California is like other states in forbidding video recording in areas such as restrooms, locker rooms, and places where employees change clothes.[131] Even in the absence of a statute, employees may be able to bring a common-law tort claim for invasion of privacy, especially where a jury would find the use of the camera to be offensive. In addition, as with other areas of workplace monitoring, collective bargaining agreements may apply.

Postal mail monitoring. U.S. federal law generally prohibits interference with mail delivery. Importantly, mail is considered "delivered" when it reaches a business. As a result, the opening of business letters and packages by a representative of the business does not violate that statute, even if that representative is not the intended recipient. There is, however, some risk involved with monitoring postal mail under state common law. Employers can mitigate this risk by advising employees not to receive personal mail at work, declining to read mail once it is clear it is personal in nature, and maintaining confidentiality for any personal information obtained in the course of monitoring.

12.4.4.3 Policies for Companies Related to Types of Monitoring

Companies should be careful to develop and implement policies related to monitoring in numerous areas, such as: (1) how companies use location-based services, (2) how companies implement data loss prevention (DLP) programs, (3) how the IT department copes with what is called "the consumerization of information technology" or BYOD, and (4) how companies address teleworking. These policies can be particularly complex because each of these areas can blur the line between personal and professional environments, either by bringing the personal environment into the workplace environment or vice versa.

Location-based services (LBS). Mobile phones, GPS devices, and some tablet computers provide geolocation data, which enables tracking of the user's physical location and movements. This creates a category of personal information that typically did not exist before the prevalence of these mobile devices.[132] Employers interested in monitoring the location of company vehicles equipped with GPS may generally do so without legal hindrance, provided that the monitoring occurs for business purposes during work hours, and employees have been informed beforehand.[133]

A company wishing to monitor the location of its employees themselves, however, may face greater legal barriers. Some state laws limit monitoring of employee geolocation data to an extent. Connecticut, for example, prohibits any type of electronic employee monitoring without written notice and provides a civil penalty of $500 for a first offense.[134] California has increased protection for its employees by outlawing the use of "an electronic tracking device to determine the location or movement of a person" as a misdemeanor criminal offense.[135] In addition, the utilization of location-based services to monitor employees runs the risk of incurring invasion of privacy claims in situations where the employee has a reasonable expectation of privacy.

Data loss prevention (DLP). DLP is a strategy used by businesses to ensure that sensitive data is not accessed, misused or lost. DLP software and tools monitor and control endpoint activities, such as employee use of smartphones or laptops.[136] DLP also may include encryption by default or other protections for data in transit.

Another way of understanding DLP is that it combines (1) using information security tools, (2) training employees about acceptable behavior on work devices, and (3) implementing effective standards, policies, and procedures to achieve the desired protection of data.

Privacy concerns have been raised about deployment of DLP. The technology can potentially include surveillance over many or all activities on an endpoint device, such as a phone or laptop that an employee uses. Some endpoint protection programs have included powerful features, such as recording every key stroke, activating the webcam of laptops or smartphones, or tracking the geolocation of the smartphone user without their knowledge.[137] Conducting a privacy impact assessment is good practice, and organizations considering a DLP program should thus consider the likely privacy risks as well as the likely benefits of the program.[138]

Consumerization of information technology (COIT) and bring your own device (BYOD). Individuals today have more IT options than ever before. Computing devices range from traditional desktop computers and laptops to powerful smartphones, tablet computers, and smartwatches. Social networks, web mail, and applications can be accessed across devices. Marked improvement in device capability and widespread internet access allow employees to connect to their online networks from almost any location.

Increasingly, individuals are also using their personal devices for work purposes, blurring the line between personal and professional environments. The COIT trend refers not only to the use of personal computing devices in the workplace but also to online services, such as web mail, cloud storage, and social networking. Traditionally, adoption of high-level IT started with major public- and private-sector organizations, with consumer adoption coming later, after the price became affordable. In recent years, the trend has reversed. Today, IT often emerges in the consumer market and is driven by employees who use their personal devices, accounts, and applications both in and outside of the office for work tasks.[139]

Bring your own device (BYOD) is part of the COIT trend, in which employees use their personal computing devices for work purposes. BYOD offers significant advantages. It allows employees to use the same technology at work that they use at home, which means more flexibility, efficiency and productivity in employee work schedules. Employers benefit from increased accessibility to their employees as well as reduced overhead and workplace device expenses. BYOD, however, presents significant security challenges that stem from the lack of employer control over employee devices. BYOD may expose organizations to security vulnerabilities and threats that they could otherwise protect against with work-issued devices.[140]

Organizations face security risks with BYOD. For example, if an organization's current policy requires specific security controls for company-owned devices but not personal devices, the latter used for work purposes can create risks for the company's data. Data loss prevention or other security controls required for company-owned devices, however, may not be suitable or necessary for personal devices, depending on how they are used. Less security may be adequate, for instance, for personal devices that are not permitted to store sensitive employer data. One consideration is what information triggers breach notification laws—stricter policies may be called for when loss of the device would require breach notices.

BYOD also presents new workplace privacy implications. Private-sector employers often monitor employees' activities on a work network and work-issued devices, but the same monitoring may not be appropriate for personal devices. Employees may feel their privacy is invaded, for instance, if the company monitors their private email and web surfing.

Employers should address both the security and privacy implications in designing BYOD policies. If the employer is engaged in device monitoring or surveillance, it should disclose that information and consider obtaining employee consent. When monitoring and searching the device, exposure of private employee data should be minimized.[141]

When such policies are either not in place or not enforced, employees may be required to provide access to their devices or accounts in response to electronic discovery demands in legal proceedings against the company. For example, an employee who leaves a company for a competitor could be subject to claims such as trade secret theft if the company's data was not completely deleted.[142]

Teleworking. Teleworking exploded during the COVID-19 pandemic and many employees will desire that option post-pandemic. Teleworking allows employees to work from home or other locations out of the office, and the devices used may be provided by the employer or may be owned by the employee. Teleworking employees often discuss company issues via virtual meeting platforms or over the phone.

To protect privacy and cybersecurity, companies may create and enforce policies such as: authorization and authentication of the employee, safety of the employee's home network, patches to address known security vulnerabilities, and employee training concerning phishing and malware.[143] Endpoint security, discussed here as DLP, can be a source of protection for companies, but can be viewed by employees as spyware.

Companies may also need to remind employees that data needs to be protected from family members or others in the home. For instance, work-issued computers should not be used by others in the home, screens should be locked when employees are away from their computers, papers with confidential or customer information should be secured after use, and discarded papers with confidential or customer information should be shredded.[144]

Companies should be aware that employee privacy can be more complicated when the employee is located in their home. Virtual meetings, for example, can have family members visible in the video—including children.

As with BYOD policies, employers should clearly address teleworking issues in company policies and convey to employees the privacy limits and risks when teleworking. If the employer is engaged in monitoring or surveillance, it should disclose that information and determine if employee consent is required. In conducting employee monitoring, exposure of private employee data should be minimized when possible.

12.4.5 Investigation of Employee Misconduct

When alleged employee misconduct occurs, the employer should be aware of issues such as the following:

- Be careful to avoid liability or loss due to failure to take the allegations seriously. Ignoring a problem may allow it to grow or otherwise become more difficult to resolve later.
- Treat the employee with fairness during the investigation to reduce possible employee resentment as well as the risk that later litigation will result in harsher penalties if the employer is seen to have been unfair.
- Follow laws and other corporate policies during the investigation. Particular attention should be given to collective bargaining agreements, which often contain provisions concerning investigations of employee misconduct.
- Document the alleged misconduct and investigation to minimize risks from subsequent claims by the employee.
- Consider the rights of people other than those being investigated, such as fellow employees who could be subject to retaliation or other problems.

Investigations are often conducted in cooperation with an organization's HR office. HR policies often apply to investigations. Progressive and documented discipline for initial or minor infractions can provide a reasoned basis for more serious discipline or termination if necessary. The privacy professional should work with the compliance department to determine the appropriate level of documentation.

Frequently, employers use third parties to investigate employee misconduct. Formerly, this exposed corporations to liability under the FCRA. The FCRA generally requires notice and employee consent when the employer obtains a consumer report. According to an opinion letter issued for the FTC known as the "Vail Letter," if an employer hired an outside organization such as a private investigator or background research firm to conduct these investigations, the outside organization constituted a CRA under the FCRA, and any report furnished to the employer by the outside organization was an "investigative consumer report."[145] Under this opinion, an employer that received these reports was required to comply with the FCRA by providing notice to the suspected employee and obtaining consent, thus destroying the undercover aspect of investigations.[146]

FACTA amended the FCRA to address the problems created by the Vail Letter.[147] Along with other FCRA and FACTA provisions discussed in Chapter 9, FACTA provided that, if certain conditions were met, an employer is no longer required to notify an employee that it is obtaining an investigative consumer report on the employee from an outside organization in the context of an internal investigation. Specifically, FACTA changed the definition of consumer report under FCRA to exclude communications relating to employee investigations from the definition if three requirements are met:

- The communication is made to an employer in connection with the investigation of: (1) suspected misconduct related to employment, or (2) compliance with federal, state, or local laws and/or regulations, the rules of a self-regulatory organization, or any preexisting written employment policies.
- The communication is not made for the purpose of investigating a consumer's creditworthiness, credit standing or credit capacity and does not include information pertaining to those factors.
- The communication is not provided to any person except: (1) the employer or agent of the employer; (2) a federal or state officer, agency, or department, or an officer, agency, or department of a unit of general local government; (3) a self-regulating organization with authority over the activities of the employer or employee; (4) as otherwise required by law; or (5) pursuant to 15 U.S.C. § 1681f, which addresses disclosures to government agencies.[148]

If the employer takes adverse action based on these reports, FACTA requires that the employer disclose a summary of the nature and substance of the communication or report to the employee. This report can be issued after the investigation has been conducted and allows employers to maintain the secrecy of the investigation.[149]

12.5 Privacy Issues After Employment

At the end of the employment relationship, an employer should restrict or terminate the former employee's access to physical and informational assets, follow the correct termination procedures, minimize risks of post-termination claims, help management to transition after the termination, and address any privacy claims that arise.

12.5.1 Access to Physical and Informational Assets

When a person leaves a company or is no longer supposed to have access to specific facilities or information, there should be clear procedures for terminating such access. Basic steps include:

- Secure the return of badges, keys, smartcards, and other methods of physical access
- Disable access for computer accounts
- Ensure the return of laptops, smartphones, storage drives, and other devices that may store company information
- Seek, where possible, to have the employee return or delete any company data that is held by the employee outside of the company's systems
- Remind employees of their obligations not to use company data for other purposes
- Forward clearly marked personal mail, if any, to the former employee but review work-related mail to ensure that proprietary company information is not leaked

Because the departure of employees is a predictable event, IT systems should be designed to minimize the disruption to the company and other employees when a person no longer has authorized access. Access may end not only for a firm employee but also for contractors, interns, and others who have temporary access to company facilities. To take a simple example, the same password should not be used by multiple people because of the need to change the password when one employee leaves.

Privacy professionals may also need to consider appropriate practices for maintaining the HR records of former employees. There can be many reasons for retaining such information, such as to provide references, respond to inquiries about benefits and pensions, address health and safety issues that arise, respond to legal proceedings, and meet legal or regulatory retention requirements for particular types of records. There are also countervailing concerns about the privacy and security of sensitive employment records, and in some jurisdictions (such as in the EU), there may need to be a demonstrable business or legal reason to justify retaining certain personal information.

12.5.2 Human Resources Issues

The HR office is often significantly involved in the period before an employee leaves, especially when employees are not leaving entirely of their own initiative. The HR office often will have detailed and sensitive information about an employee's performance in the period before termination. This sort of information is gathered, for instance, to document the basis for the company's decisions in case the former employee brings a wrongful termination or other claim against the employer. The HR office should have in place consistent policies to deal with the retention of employee records after an employee leaves the company, addressing records such as background checks, employee contracts, performance appraisals, and medical information.[150]

A similar level of care is appropriate for post-termination contacts with the employee. External communications to the former employee should be crafted with care, especially if the termination resulted from misconduct. Communications with remaining employees, customers, and others should meet company goals while refraining from disparaging the former employee.

When an employer is asked to provide references for the former employee, HR, working with legal counsel, should have basic guidelines but collaborate on an appropriate response in more complex circumstances. Companies balance reasons to provide references with the risk of a suit for defamation. The law can vary significantly state by state.[151] The common law imposes no duty on a former employer to supply a reference for a former employee, but some modern state statutes do require references for specific occupations, such as airplane pilot and public school teacher. The common law provides what is known as a "qualified privilege" for employers to report their experience with and impressions of the employee, to help in defense against defamation suits. In recent years, publicity about winning defamation suits has made some employers reluctant to provide references. On the other hand, state legislatures have responded by passing laws that are designed to encourage accurate reports about former employees. A company also often has good reasons to provide references, including to retain goodwill with former employees, whose statements will affect the company's reputation and with whom the company may do business in the future.

12.6 Conclusion

This chapter introduced major themes relating to privacy in the workplace. In the United States, constitutional protections apply specifically to government employees. Contract and tort remedies can provide protections to employees, but they apply in a relatively narrow set of circumstances. States have enacted a considerable number of statutory protections, but the protections exist against a general backdrop of a free-market approach to employment and workplace privacy.

Technology has transformed the relationship between the employer and the employee, and allows the line between personal and professional environments to blur. Monitoring of employees is one issue that can have significant privacy implications for employees during employment, meaning the approach must be undertaken thoughtfully by employers. Investigation of alleged employee misconduct often involves employers reviewing detailed electronic data collected from the employee, meaning the employer must carefully follow legal requirements as well as its own policies. With the uptick in teleworking, employers must ensure the privacy and cybersecurity of company data, while employees have heightened concerns regarding privacy within their home.

Personal information is involved in virtually every phase of the employment relationship—from evaluation and hiring, to employee management and monitoring, to termination or departure. As organizations grow, expand to new geographies, and involve larger numbers of outside partners and vendors, the employment privacy challenges become more acute. Global employers must navigate through a complex patchwork of applicable U.S., EU, and international workplace privacy laws.

Effective legal compliance and thoughtful management of employee personal information can help reduce the risk of any potential legal claims as well as offer many benefits to both employer and employee. These benefits include minimizing the risk of information mishandling, disclosure, or theft; increasing employee morale; and improving the working relationship between employer and employee.

Endnotes

1 See Bridget Miller, "Pros and Cons of Employee Monitoring," *HR Daily Advisor* (September 25, 2019), https://hrdailyadvisor.blr.com/2019/09/25/pros-and-cons-of-employee-monitoring/.

2 See Sara Jodka, "The GDPR Covers Employee/HR Data and It's Tricky, Tricky (Tricky) Tricky: What HR Needs to Know," DickinsonWright, April 2018, https://www.dickinson-wright.com/news-alerts/the-gdpr-covers-employee-hr-data-and-tricky.

3 See Lothar Determann and Lars Brauer, "Employee Monitoring Technologies and Data Privacy—No One-Size-Fits-All Globally," *Privacy Advisor*, IAPP, May 1, 2009, https://iapp.org/news/a/2009-05-employee-monitoring-technologies-differ-globally/; Lothar Determann and Robert Sprague, Intrusive Monitoring: Employee Privacy Expectations Are Reasonable in Europe, Destroyed in the United States, *Berkeley Technology Law Journal*, 26: 979 (2011), https://papers.ssrn.com/sol3/papers.cfm?abstract_id=2298902.

4 O'Connor v. Ortega, 480 U.S. 709 (1987), https://supreme.justia.com/cases/federal/us/480/709/case.html; "Public Employee Privacy Rights: When is an Employee's Workplace His Castle?" Kronick, September 17, 2017, https://kmtg.com/news/publications-and-articles/public-employee-privacy-rights-when-is-an-employees-workplace-his-castle/.

5 California Constitution, Art. 1, § 1, accessed November 2017, https://leginfo.legislature.ca.gov/faces/codes_displayText.xhtml?lawCode=CONS&division=&title=&part=&chapter=&article=I; see Workplace Privacy, FindLaw, June 20, 2016, https://corporate.findlaw.com/law-library/right-to-privacy-in-the-workplace-in-the-information-age.html.

6 Restatement (Second) of Torts, § 652B, https://cyber.law.harvard.edu/privacy/Privacy_R2d_Torts_Sections.htm.

7 Restatement (Second) of Torts, § 652D, sed November 2017, https://cyber.law.harvard.edu/privacy/Privacy_R2d_Torts_Sections.htm.

8 Restatement (Second) of Torts, §§ 558–559, sed November 2017, https://yalelawtechdotorg.files.wordpress.com/2013/10/info-privacy-handout.pdf.

9 Matthew W. Finkin, *Privacy in Employment Law*, 3d edition (Arlington, VA: BNA Books, 2009), xlv.

10 "State Statutes Prohibiting Marital Status Discrimination in Employment," accessed November 2023, https://www.unmarriedamerica.org/ms-employment-laws.htm. See, e.g., Cal. Gov't Code 12940, accessed June 2016, http://leginfo.legislature.ca.gov/faces/codes_displaySection.xhtml?lawCode=GOV§ionNum=12940; N.Y. Exec. Law § 296 (2015), accessed February 2020, https://law.justia.com/codes/new-york/2015/exc/article-15/296; Del. Code Ann. Tit. 19, § 711, accessed November 2017, http://delcode.delaware.gov/title19/c007/sc02/; See, e.g., Illinois Right to Privacy in the Workplace Act, 820 I.L.C.S. § 55, accessed November 2017, https://www.ilga.gov/legislation/ilcs/ilcs3.asp?ActID=2398&.

11 "State Social Media Privacy Laws," National Conference of State Legislatures, updated August 8, 2022, https://www.ncsl.org/technology-and-communication/privacy-of-employee-and-student-social-media-accounts. Additionally, employers should avoid requiring prospective employees to divulge access information to private networks as a condition of employment.

12 Finkin, *Privacy in Employment Law*.

13 Health Insurance Portability and Accountability Act, 42 U.S.C. §§ 300gg-300gg-2, accessed February 2020, https://www.law.cornell.edu/uscode/text/42/chapter-6A/subchapter-XXV/part-A/subpart-I.

14 Consolidated Omnibus Budget Reconciliation Act of 1986, 42 U.S.C. §§ 300bb-1-300bb-8, accessed July 2023, https://www.law.cornell.edu/uscode/text/42/chapter-6A/subchapter-XX.

15 Employee Retirement Income Security Act of 1974, 29 U.S.C. §§ 1001-1461, accessed November 2017, https://www.law.cornell.edu/uscode/text/29/1001.

16 Family Medical Leave Act of 1993, 29 U.S.C. §§ 2601-2654, accessed November 2017, https://www.law.cornell.edu/uscode/text/29/chapter-28.

17 Fair Credit Reporting Act, 15 U.S.C. §§1681-1681v, accessed February 2020, https://www.law.cornell.edu/uscode/text/15/chapter-41/subchapter-III.

18 Fair Labor Standards Act of 1938, 29 U.S.C. §§ 201-219, accessed November 2017, https://www.law.cornell.edu/uscode/text/29/chapter-8.

19 Occupational Safety and Health Act of 1970, 29 U.S.C. §§ 651-678, accessed November 2017, https://www.law.cornell.edu/uscode/text/29/chapter-15.

20 Whistleblower Protection Act of 1989, Public Law No. 101-112, 5 U.S.C. §§ 1201 et seq., accessed July 2023, https://www.govinfo.gov/content/pkg/COMPS-11779/pdf/COMPS-11779.pdf; Whistleblower Protection Enhancement Act of 2012, accessed November 2017, https://www.congress.gov/112/bills/s743/BILLS-112s743enr.pdf.

21 National Labor Relations Act, 29 U.S.C. §§ 151-159, accessed February 2020, https://www.law.cornell.edu/uscode/text/29/chapter-7/subchapter-II.

22 Immigration Reform and Control Act of 1986, 8 U.S.C. §§ 1324a-b, accessed November 2017, https://www.law.cornell.edu/uscode/text/8/1324a.

23 Securities and Exchange Act of 1934, 15 U.S.C. § 78A, accessed November 2017, https://www.law.cornell.edu/uscode/text/15/78a.

24 Employee Polygraph Protection Act of 1988, 29 U.S.C. §§ 2001-2009, accessed November 2017, https://www.law.cornell.edu/uscode/text/29/2001.

25 Wiretap Act, 18 U.S.C. §§ 2510-2522, accessed November 2017, https://it.ojp.gov/PrivacyLiberty/authorities/statutes/1284; Electronic Communications Privacy Act, 18 U.S.C. §§ 2510-2511, accessed November 2017, https://it.ojp.gov/privacyliberty/authorities/statutes/1285; Stored Communications Act, 18 U.S.C. §§ 2701-2712, accessed February 2020, https://www.law.cornell.edu/uscode/text/18/part-I/chapter-121.

26 "About Us: Our Mission," U.S. Department of Labor, accessed November 2019, https://www.dol.gov/general/aboutdol.

27 "Overview," U.S. Equal Employment Opportunity Commission, accessed July 2023, https://www.eeoc.gov/overview.

28 See Fair Credit Reporting Act, 15 U.S.C. §§ 1681 et seq., accessed November 2017, https://www.law.cornell.edu/uscode/text/15/1681 and "Using Consumer Reports: What Employers Need to Know," Federal Trade Commission, October 2016, https://www.ftc.gov/tips-advice/business-center/guidance/using-consumer-reports-what-employers-need-know; see also Thomas Ahearn, "Seven-Year Measuring Period for Criminal Charges Under FCRA Runs from Date of Entry Not Disposition," May 20, 2019, https://www.esrcheck.com/2019/05/20/seven-year-criminal-charges-fcra/.

29 "What We Do," National Labor Relations Board, accessed July 2023, https://www.nlrb.gov/about-nlrb/what-we-do.

30 For an in-depth look at these topics, view Matthew Finkin, "Chapter 7: Privacy and Autonomy," *Employee Rights & Employment Policy Journal* 21(2), (December 1, 2016): 589-621, https://papers.ssrn.com/sol3/papers.cfm?abstract_id=2879088.

31 State laws vary on the permissible timing of when a background check can be undertaken. *See* Andy Yoder, "State Laws and Background Checks: What You Need to Know," *Justifacts,* updated July 29, 2019, https://www.justifacts.com/state-laws-and-background-checks-what-you-need-to-know/.

32 For a detailed discussion of the topic, see Julie Totten, "Balancing Workplace Technology and Privacy in the 21st Century," Orrick, 24-35, March 22, 2017.

33 "Employment Background Checks: A Jobseeker's Guide," PrivacyRights.org, revised January 17, 2019, https://www.dioceseofjoliet.org/siteimages/peace/documents/Jail_and_Prison_Ministry/Jobseekers_Guide_to_Employment_Background_Checks.pdf.

34 "Employment Background Checks," PrivacyRights.org.

35 "Enforcement Guidance on the Consideration of Arrest and Conviction Records in Employment Decisions Under Title VII of the Civil Rights Act," U.S. Equal Employment Opportunity Commission, April 25 2012, https://www.eeoc.gov/laws/guidance/enforcement-guidance-consideration-arrest-and-conviction-records-employment-decisions; "EEOC Updates Guidelines on Criminal Records to Prevent Employment Discrimination during Background Checks," *ESR News Blog,* January 2, 2013, https://www.esrcheck.com/2013/01/02/eeoc-updates-guidance-on-criminal-records-to-prevent-employment-discrimination-during-background-checks/.

36 "Background Checks: What Employers Need to Know," Joint publication of the U.S. Equal Employment Opportunity Commission and the Federal Trade Commission, accessed July 2023, https://www.eeoc.gov/laws/guidance/background-checks-what-employers-need-know.

37 "Nebraska's New Workplace Privacy Act Restricts Employer Access to Employee Internet Accounts," Baird Holm LLP, April 22, 2016, https://www.bairdholm.com/blog/nebraskas-new-workplace-privacy-act-restricts-employer-access-to-employee-internet-accounts/.

38 Civil Rights Act of 1964, Title VII, 42 U.S.C. §§ 2000e-2000e-17, accessed February 2020, https://www.law.cornell.edu/uscode/text/42/chapter-21/subchapter-VI.

39 Equal Pay Act of 1963, accessed July 2023, https://www.eeoc.gov/statutes/equal-pay-act-1963.

40 Age Discrimination in Employment Act of 1967, 29 U.S.C. § 621, accessed November 2017, https://www.law.cornell.edu/uscode/text/29/chapter-14.

41 Pregnancy Discrimination Act, Title VII, 42 U.S.C. §§ 2000e-2000e-17, accessed November 2017https://www.law.cornell.edu/uscode/text/42/chapter-21/subchapter-VI.

42 Americans with Disabilities Act, 42 U.S.C. §§ 12101-12213, accessed February 2020, https://www.law.cornell.edu/uscode/text/42/chapter-126.

43 Genetic Information Nondiscrimination Act of 2008, 42 U.S.C. § 2000ff, accessed November 2017, https://www.law.cornell.edu/uscode/text/42/chapter-21F.

44 Scott Riddle, "Can I Lose My Job if I File for Bankruptcy?" Georgia Bankruptcy Law Network, accessed February 2020, https://www.gabankruptcylawyersnetwork.com/2013/11/can-i-lose-my-job-if-i-file-for-bankruptcy/. For an in-depth discussion,

view Samantha Orovitz, "The Bankruptcy Shadow: Section 525(b) and the Job Applicant's Sisyphean Struggle for a Fresh Start," *Emory Bankruptcy Developments Journal* 29, no. 2 (2013), http://law.emory.edu/ebdj/content/volume-29/issue-2/comments/bankruptcy-shadow.html.

45 "Protections Against Employment Discrimination Based on Sexual Orientation or Gender Identity," U.S. Equal Employment Opportunity Commission, accessed October 2023, https://www.eeoc.gov/laws/guidance/protections-against-employment-discrimination-based-sexual-orientation-or-gender.

46 See Susan Miller, "'Shocking Numbers:' Half of LGBTQ Adults Live in States Where No Laws Ban Job Discrimination," USA Today, October 8, 2019, https://www.usatoday.com/story/news/nation/2019/10/08/lgbt-employment-discrimination-half-of-states-offer-no-protections/3837244002/.

47 "State Statutes Prohibiting Marital Status Discrimination in Employment," accessed July 2023, https://www.unmarriedamerica.org/ms-employment-laws.htm.

48 Americans with Disabilities Act of 1990, 42 U.S.C. § 12112(a), accessed November 2017, https://www.law.cornell.edu/uscode/text/42/12112.

49 42 U.S.C. § 12112(b)(4).

50 42 U.S.C. § 12112(b)(3).

51 "Enforcement Guidance on Reasonable Accommodation and Undue Hardship Under the ADA," U.S. Equal Employment Opportunity Commission, accessed July 2023, https://www.eeoc.gov/laws/guidance/enforcement-guidance-reasonable-accommodation-and-undue-hardship-under-ada.

52 A recent trend related to the ADA is whether the law protects potential future disabilities. In several court cases, an employment action was taken against an individual by a company that perceived the person could develop an impairment that could impair their ability to perform essential job functions. Despite the fact that the companies succeeded in the recent cases, it is worth noting that the EEOC may view these potential future disabilities as protected conditions under the ADA. Privacy professionals should be aware that this topic is a complex and unsettled area of the law. Harris Mufson, Laura Fant, and Jacob Hirsch, "Emerging Trend: ADA Does Not Cover Potential Future Disabilities," *The National Law Review* (November 13, 2019), https://www.natlawreview.com/article/emerging-trend-ada-does-not-cover-potential-future-disabilities.

53 Paul F. Gerhart, "Employee Privacy Rights in the United States," *Comparative Labor Law Journal* 17 (1995): 195.

54 Fair Credit Reporting Act, 15 U.S.C. § 1681a, accessed July 2023, https://www.ftc.gov/legal-library/browse/statutes/fair-credit-reporting-act.

55 Leslie Fair, "Where HireRight Solutions Went Wrong," Federal Trade Commission, August 8, 2012, https://www.ftc.gov/business-guidance/blog/2012/08/where-hireright-solutions-went-wrong. For an in-depth discussion, view Alan Kaplinsky and John Culhane, Jr., "FTC continues aggressive FCRA enforcement against data brokers," Ballard Spahr LLP, January 23, 2014, https://casetext.com/analysis/ftc-continues-aggressive-fcra-enforcement-against-data-brokers-by-the-consumer-financial-services-group.

56 Fair Credit Reporting Act, 15 U.S.C. § 1681t, accessed November 2017, https://www.ftc.gov/enforcement/rules/rulemaking-regulatory-reform-proceedings/fair-credit-reporting-act.

57 Investigative Consumer Reporting Agencies Act, 1.6A Cal. Civ. Code §§ 1786-1786.60, accessed November 2017, https://leginfo.legislature.ca.gov/faces/codes_displayText.xhtml?lawCode=CIV&division=3.&title=1.6A.&part=4.&chapter=&article=1.

58 Lisa Guerin, "Can an Employer Check My Credit Score?" NOLO, accessed October 2023, https://www.nolo.com/legal-encyclopedia/can-prospective-employers-check-your-credit-report.html; see Anna Grozdanov, "What are Employment Credit Checks, and Are They Legal?" Lexington Law, January 5, 2022, https://www.lexingtonlaw.com/blog/credit-101/employment-credit-checks.html.

59 See, e.g., Conn. Gen. Stat. § 31-51tt, accessed November 2017, https://www.cga.ct.gov/current/pub/titles.htm; Md. Code, Lab. & Empl. § 3-711, accessed February 2020, https://law.justia.com/codes/maryland/2013/article-gle/section-3-711/; Wash. Rev. Code § 19.182.020, accessed November 2017, http://apps.leg.wa.gov/rcw/default.aspx?cite=19.182.020; Haw. Rev. Stat. § 378-2.7, accessed November 2017, http://law.justia.com/codes/hawaii/2010/division1/title21/chapter378/378-2-7.

60 See, e.g., Cal. Lab. Code § 1024.5, accessed February 2020, http://leginfo.legislature.ca.gov/faces/codes_displaySection.xhtml?lawCode=LAB§ionNum=1024.5; 820 Ill. Comp. Stat. § 70/10, accessed November 2017, https://www.ilga.gov/legislation/ilcs/ilcs3.asp?ActID=3277&ChapterID=68.

61 Susan Corcoran, Richard Greenberg, Francis Wilson, "Federal Contractor Obligations Under Fair Chance Act," *The National Law Review*, January 9, 2022, https://www.natlawreview.com/article/federal-contractor-obligations-under-fair-chance-act; see Dennis Damp, "Fair Chance Act: OPM Takes Steps to Improve Your Chances to Compete for a Federal Job," Clearance Jobs, September 13, 2023, https://news.clearancejobs.com/2023/09/13/fair-chance-act-opm-takes-steps-to-improve-your-chances-to-compete-for-a-federal-job/; see also "Incarceration to Employment: A Comprehensive Strategy to Expand Employment Opportunities for Formerly Incarcerated Persons," The White House, April 2022, https://www.whitehouse.gov/wp-content/uploads/2022/04/Incarceration-to-Employment-Strategy.pdf.

62 "Fair Chance Act: Restricting Timing of Criminal History Inquiries Begins to Take Effect," Husch Blackwell, January 26, 2022, https://www.huschblackwell.com/newsandinsights/fair-chance-act-restricting-timing-of-criminal-history-inquiries-begins-to-take-effect; "FAQ: Fair Chance to Compete for Jobs Act of 2019," National Employment Law Project, December 17, 2019, https://www.nelp.org/publication/faq-fair-chance-to-compete-for-jobs-act-of-2019/.

63 "Ban the Box," National Conference of State Legislatures, updated June 29, 2021, https://www.ncsl.org/research/civil-and-criminal-justice/ban-the-box.aspx; "List of States and Municipalities with Ban-the-Box Laws," AccuSource, accessed July 2023, https://accusource-online.com/list-of-states-and-municipalities-with-ban-the-box-laws/#:~:text=34%20states%20and%20over%20150,with%20Ban%20the%20Box%20legislation; "Ban the Box: U.S. Cities, Counties, and State Adopt Fair Hiring Policies," National Employment Law Project, October 1, 2021, https://www.nelp.org/publication/ban-the-box-fair-chance-hiring-state-and-local-guide/.

64 Nicole Pozzi, "Shoulder Surfing: A Fourth Amendment Violation," Cardozo Arts & Entertainment Law Journal, April 24, 2015, https://cardozoaelj.com/2015/04/24/shoulder-surfing-a-fourth-amendment-violation/.

65 See "Social Media and the FCRA: What You Need to Know," *Background Investigations Blog*, Alliance Worldwide Investigative Group, February 2, 2018, https://

alliancerisgroup.com/social-media-and-the-fcra-what-you-need-to-know/. For additional resources, view Lesley Fair, "The Fair Credit Reporting Act & Social Media: What Businesses Should Know," Federal Trade Commission, June 23, 2011, https://www.ftc.gov/business-guidance/blog/2011/06/fair-credit-reporting-act-social-media-what-businesses-should-know.

66 In 2006, Hewlett Packard's chairman Patricia Dunn authorized the use of false pretenses to investigate press leaks originating from the board of directors, a practice termed "pretexting." The investigative tactics were widely condemned, triggering congressional hearings and both federal and state felony charges against Dunn and others. For a detailed overview of the case, *see* Miriam Hechler Baer, "Corporate Policing and Corporate Governance: What Can We Learn from Hewlett-Packard's Pretexting Scandal?" *University of Cincinnati Law Review* 77: 523 (2008).

67 See Joseph Lazzarottie and Jason Gavejian, "Third Circuit Rules in Favor of Employer Who Monitored Former Employees' Social Media Accounts," *The National Law Review*, March 25, 2019, https://www.natlawreview.com/article/third-circuit-rules-favor-employer-who-monitored-former-employees-social-media. For a detailed discussion, view Totten, "Balancing Workplace Technology and Privacy in the 21st Century," 42-43.

68 Melissa Coretez Goemann, "Maryland Passes Nation's First Social Media Privacy Protection Bill," American Civil Liberties Union, May 4, 2012, https://www.aclu.org/blog/maryland-passes-nations-first-social-media-privacy-protection-bill.

69 "Social Media Privacy Laws in Employment: 50-State Survey," Justia, September 2022, https://www.justia.com/employment/employment-laws-50-state-surveys/social-media-privacy-laws-in-the-workplace-50-state-survey/; "Privacy of Employee and Student Social Media Accounts," National Conference of State Legislatures, August 8, 2022, https://www.ncsl.org/technology-and-communication/privacy-of-employee-and-student-social-media-accounts.

70 Zahira Jaser, Dimitra Petrakaki, Rachel Starr & Ernesto Oyarbide-Magana, "Where Automated Job Interviews Fall Short," Harvard Business Review, January 27, 2022, https://hbr.org/2022/01/where-automated-job-interviews-fall-short; Tyrone Richardson, "AI's Eyes on Job Interviews Prompts Law on Disclosure, Data Use," *Bloomberg Law*, June 12, 2019, https://news.bloomberglaw.com/privacy-and-data-security/ais-eyes-on-job-interviews-prompts-law-on-disclosure-data-use.

71 Tam Harbert, "Regulations Ahead of AI: Business Leaders are Discussing the Responsible Use of Artificial Intelligence. Soon They May Need to Walk the Walk." SHRM, April 2, 2022, https://www.shrm.org/hr-today/news/all-things-work/pages/regulations-ahead-on-artificial-intelligence.aspx; Adam Forman and Nathaniel Glassner, "Hiring by Algorithm: Legal Issues Presented by the Use of Artificial Intelligence in Sourcing and Selection," *The National Law Review*, March 17, 2021, https://www.natlawreview.com/article/hiring-algorithm-legal-issues-presented-use-artificial-intelligence-sourcing-and; see Simone Francis and Zachary Zagger, "New York City Adopts Final Rules on Automated Decision-Making Tools, AI in Hiring," The National Law Review, April 8, 2023, https://www.natlawreview.com/article/new-york-city-adopts-final-rules-automated-decision-making-tools-ai-hiring; Rebecca Heilweil, "Illinois Says You Should Know if AI is Grading Your Online Job Interviews," Vox, January 1, 2020, https://www.vox.com/recode/2020/1/1/21043000/artificial-intelligence-job-applications-illinios-video-interivew-act; Nicol Turner Lee and Samantha Lai, "Why New York City is Cracking Down on AI in Hiring," Brookings, December 20, 2021, https://

www.brookings.edu/blog/techtank/2021/12/20/why-new-york-city-is-cracking-down-on-ai-in-hiring/.

72 For a general overview of these topics, view "Workplace Privacy Laws: 10 Things All Employers Should Know," Rocket Lawyer, accessed July 2023, https://www.rocketlawyer.com/business-and-contracts/employers-and-hr/company-policies/legal-guide/workplace-privacy-laws-10-things-all-employers-need-to-know; Kenny Brown, "What are Employee Privacy Rights," Chron, August 25, 2020, https://smallbusiness.chron.com/employee-privacy-rights-1239.html.

73 Employee Polygraph Protection Act, 29 U.S.C. §§ 2001-2009, accessed February 2020, https://www.law.cornell.edu/uscode/text/29/chapter-2

74 Employee Polygraph Protection Act, 29 U.S.C. § 2001(3).

75 Finkin, *Privacy in Employment Law,* 159–173.

76 Finkin, *Privacy in Employment Law,* 175.

77 Finkin, *Privacy in Employment Law,* 184.

78 Finkin, *Privacy in Employment Law,* 67.

79 "Americans with Disabilities Act Questions and Answers," ADA National Network, 2013, https://adata.org/guide/americans-disabilities-act-questions-and-answers.

80 "Americans with Disabilities Act Questions and Answers," ADA National Network.

81 "Questions and Answers: The Americans with Disabilities Act and Hiring Police Officers," U.S. Department of Justice, updated February 25, 2020, https://archive.ada.gov/copsq7a.htm. For additional discussion on the concept of business necessity, view "Consideration of Arrest and Conviction Records," Equal Employment Opportunity.

82 49 U.S.C. § 1834 (App.) (aviation), accessed November 2017, https://www.law.cornell.edu/uscode/text/49/subtitle-VII; 45 U.S.C. § 431 (App.) (railroading), accessed November 2017, https://www.law.cornell.edu/uscode/text/45/431; and 49 U.S.C. § 277 (App.) (trucking), accessed November 2017, https://www.law.cornell.edu/uscode/text/49.

83 "State by State Legal Status Guide: Workplace Drug and Alcohol Testing Laws," Alere Toxicology, August 2016, https://www.edrugtest.com/Messages_from_Admin/Statebystatelaw_Guide_89046.pdf.

84 Finkin, *Privacy in Employment Law,* 138–140.

85 As of the writing of this book, 38 states and the District of Columbia allow the medical use of cannabis. "State Medical Cannabis Laws," National Conference of State Legislatures, June 22 2023, https://www.ncsl.org/health/state-medical-cannabis-laws; see Lisa Nagele-Piazza, "What is a 'Safety-Sensitive' Job Under State Marijuana Laws," SHRM, October 5, 2021, https://www.shrm.org/resourcesandtools/legal-and-compliance/employment-law/pages/what-is-a-safety-sensitive-job-under-state-marijuana-laws.aspx.

86 See Candice Norwood, "Can Medical Marijuana Get You Fired? Depends on the State," Governing, May 6, 2019, https://www.governing.com/topics/mgmt/gov-medical-marijuana-legalization-workplace-policies.html.

87 Cole Lauterbach, "New Illinois Pot Law Says Users Must Be Impaired before Employers Can Punish," *The Telegraph,* November 26, 2019, https://www.thetelegraph.com/news/article/Changes-coming-in-Illinois-for-job-related-drug-14864358.php. At the writing of this book, numerous efforts are underway at the federal level to reform the federal prohibition on marijuana. See Tom Angell, "Vote to Federally Legalize

Marijuana Planned in Congress," *Forbes*, November 16, 2019, https://www.forbes.com/sites/tomangell/2019/11/16/vote-to-federally-legalize-marijuana-planned-in-congress/#6b81ab61201b; Angelica LaVito, "US Lawmakers Look to Legalize Pot in 'Historic' Marijuana Reform Hearing," *CNBC*, July 10, 2019, https://www.cnbc.com/2019/07/10/us-lawmakers-look-to-legalize-pot-in-historic-marijuana-reform-hearing.html.

88 See Nathaniel Glassner, Anastasia Regne, Eric Emanuelson Jr., "Marijauna Legalization Rundown: Recent Judicial Decisions," September 14, 2021, https://www.workforcebulletin.com/2021/09/14/marijuana-legalization-rundown-recent-judicial-decisions/; Thomas Ahearn, "Court Dismisses Lawsuit of Employee Fired for Positive Marijuana Drug Test, August 9, 2021, https://www.esrcheck.com/2021/08/09/court-dismisses-lawsuit-positive-marijuana-drug-test/.

89 See "Lifestyle Discrimination in the Workplace: Your Right to Privacy under Attack," American Civil Liberties Union, March 12, 2002, https://www.aclu.org/other/lifestyle-discrimination-workplace-your-right-privacy-under-attack.

90 In certain instances, applicants may be able to raise legal claims against potential employers for discrimination based on lifestyle choices of the applicant. See Thom Cope, "Lifestyle Discrimination: Is It Legal?" Mesh Clark Rothschild, accessed October 2017, https://www.mcrazlaw.com/lifestyle-discrimination-is-it-legal/.

91 See Carol Kleiman, "Flight Attendants Win Fight Over Weight Rules," *Chicago Tribune*, March 13, 1991, http://articles.chicagotribune.com/1991-03-13/news/9101230213_1_professional-flight-attendants-weight-rules-american-airlines.

92 Melissa Legault, "Does Obesity Qualify as a Disability Under the ADA? – It Depends on Who You Ask (US)," *The National Law Review*, April 11, 2019, https://www.natlawreview.com/article/does-obesity-qualify-disability-under-ada-it-depends-who-you-ask-us; see Jim Griffin, "Is Obesity a Disability Under the ADA?" Management Association, April 19, 2016, https://www.hrsource.org/maimis/Members/Articles/2016/04/April_19/Is_Obesity_a_Disability_Under_the_ADA_.aspx.

93 Amy Langfield, "CVS to Workers: Tell Us How Much You Weigh or It'll Cost You $600 a Year," *CNBC*, March 20, 2013, https://www.cnbc.com/id/100573805.

94 See Thom Cope, "Lifestyle Discrimination"; Ellie Williams, "Can Employers Discriminate Against Smokers?" Chron, accessed November 2019, http://work.chron.com/can-employers-discriminate-against-smokers-18507.html.

95 It is worth noting that the Affordable Care Act prohibits premium increases because someone is obese. See Chelan David, "Understanding the legal ramifications of lifestyle discrimination," Smart Business, December 2, 2015, www.sbnonline.com/article/understanding-the-legal-ramifications-of-lifestyle-discrimination/.

96 See Donna Ballman, "States with Pro-Employee Laws: No Firing for Legal Off-Duty Activity," *LexisNexis Newsroom Labor and Employment Law*, December 18, 2014.

97 See Frank J. Cavico, "Invasion of Privacy in the Private Employment Sector: Tortious and Ethical Aspects," *Houston Law Review* 30 (1993): 1304–1306.

98 For example, see Conn. Gen. Stat. § 31-48d, revised January 1, 2023, https://www.cga.ct.gov/current/pub/titles.htm; 19 Del. C. § 705, accessed November 2017, http://delcode.delaware.gov/title19/c007/sc01/index.shtml.

99 David Bender, Bender on Privacy and Data Protection § 10.02 (Dayton, OH: LexisNexis, 2011).

100 "Workplace Privacy," Society for Human Resource Management, accessed April 3, 2023, https://www.shrm.org/resourcesandtools/tools-and-samples/toolkits/pages/workplaceprivacy.aspx; Michael Acarian, "Monitoring Employees: GPS and Other Workplace Privacy Concerns," SHRM, January 27, 2015, https://www.shrm.org/ResourcesAndTools/hr-topics/risk-management/Pages/Monitoring-Employees-GPS.aspx; see "How Much Employee Monitoring is Too Much?," American Bar Association, January 2018, https://www.americanbar.org/news/abanews/publications/youraba/2018/january-2018/how-much-employee-monitoring-is-too-much-/. For a detailed discussion, view Totten, "Balancing Workplace Technology and Privacy in the 21st Century," 42-43.

101 "Occupational Injury and Illness Recording and Reporting Requirements," Occupational Safety and Health Administration, U.S. Department of Labor, 29 C.F.R Parts 1904 and 1952, January 19, 2001, https://www.osha.gov/pls/oshaweb/owadisp.show_document?p_table=FEDERAL_REGISTER&p_id=16312.

102 See Julie Weed, "Wearable Tech That Tells Drowsy Truckers It's Time to Pull Over," *The New York Times*, February 6, 2020, https://www.nytimes.com/2020/02/06/business/drowsy-driving-truckers.html; see also Muhammad Qasim Khan and Sukhan Lee, "Gaze and Eye Tracking: Techniques and Applications in ADAS," National Center for Biotechnology Information, National Library of Medicine, NIH, December 2019, https://www.ncbi.nlm.nih.gov/pmc/articles/PMC6960643/.

103 See generally 16 C.F.R. § 310.5(a), accessed November 2017, https://www.law.cornell.edu/cfr/text/16/310.5.

104 "You & the Law: Quick, Easy-to-Use Advice on Employment Law 2" National Institute of Business Management (2002).

105 An authority on employment law, Professor Matthew Finkin, has disagreed, saying: "The bald fact is that employers have no more a duty to monitor their employees' email, to assure that untoward messages are not being communicated, than they have a duty to place hidden microphones or cameras at the water coolers to detect sexually offensive remarks or leering glances." Matthew Finkin, "Information Technology and Workers' Privacy: The United States Law," *Comparative Labor Law and Policy Journal* 23 (2002): 471. Courts that have addressed the issue have stressed that the speech involved must be so pervasive as to alter working conditions, so the risk of such claims may well be lower than business lawyers believed when internet usage was first becoming common. E.g., Custis v. DiMaio, 46 F. Supp. 2d 206 (E.D.N.Y. 1999), accessed November 2017, http://law.justia.com/cases/federal/district-courts/FSupp2/46/206/2488236/.

106 Bennett Conlin, "5 Ways Your Business Can Benefit From Security Cameras," *business.com*, updated April 14, 2023, https://www.business.com/articles/5-ways-your-company-can-benefit-from-security-cameras/.

107 Fisher Phillips, "Protecting Trade Secrets Through Employee Surveillance: Risky Business?" Fisher Phillips, accessed July 2023, https://www.fisherphillips.com/news-insights/non-compete-and-trade-secrets-blog/protecting-trade-secrets-through-employee-surveillance-risky-business.html; "Safeguarding Trade Secrets in the Information Age: Sample Communications Policy," FindLaw, March 26, 2008, https://corporate.findlaw.com/intellectual-property/safeguarding-trade-secrets-in-the-information-age-sample.html; see Shena Crowe and Teresa Thompson, "Strategies for Protecting Your Trade Secrets and Data from the Insider Threat—a Law Enforcement and Litigation View," Minnesota CLE, May 2018, https://www.minncle.org/eaccess/1020751801/405_806_Thompson.pdf.

108 Patricia Abril, Avner Levin and Alissa Riego, "Blurred Boundaries: Social Media Privacy and the Twenty-First-Century Employee," *American Business Law Journal* 49 (January 2012), https://www.researchgate.net/publication/228311105_Blurred_Boundaries_Social_Media_Privacy_and_the_Twenty-First-Century Employee.

109 See Jodi Kantor and Arya Sundaram, "The Rise of the Worker Productivity Score" *The New York Times*, August 14, 2022, https://www.nytimes.com/interactive/2022/08/14/business/worker-productivity-track ing.html. Time management has become a concerning trend where employers are tracking their employees. Today, more companies in various industries are using monitoring technologies to track their employee's productivity. Workplace tracking is done through various means including, screen recording and cameras snapping shots of employees faces to verify if in fact the employee is working.

110 See "What are the Privacy Rights of Employees?" *The Science Times*, November 11, 2019, https://www.sciencetimes.com/articles/24248/20191111/what-are-the-privacy-rights-of-employees.htm.

111 For additional information, view "Workplace Privacy and Employee Monitoring," PrivacyRights.org, revised March 25, 2019, https://www.privacyrights.org/workplace-privacy-and-employee-monitoring. An overview of the issues involved can be found in Julie Totten's "Balancing Workplace Technology and Privacy in the 21st Century," 14-24.

112 See Totten, "Balancing Workplace Technology and Privacy in the 21st Century," 9-11.

113 See Brenda Sharton and Karen Neuman, "The Legal Risks of Monitoring Employees Online," *Harvard Business Review*, December 14, 2017, https://hbr.org/2017/12/the-legal-risks-of-monitoring-employees-online.

114 18 U.S.C. § 2511(2)(D), accessed November 2017, https://www.law.cornell.edu/uscode/text/18/2511.

115 18 U.S.C. § 2511(2)(a)(i), accessed November 2017, https://www.law.cornell.edu/uscode/text/18/2511.

116 Martha W. Barnett and Scott D. Makar, "In the Ordinary Court of Business: The Legal Limits of Workplace Wiretapping," *Communications and Entertainment Law Journal* 10 (1988): 715.

117 Finkin, *Privacy in Employment Law*, 365-369.

118 "Summary of Consent Requirements for Taping Telephone Conversations," aapsonline.org, accessed October 2017, https://www.aapsonline.org/judicial/telephone.htm.

119 See Sharton and Neuman, "The Legal Risks of Monitoring Employees Online."

120 18 U.S.C. § 2701(c)(1), accessed November 2017, https://www.law.cornell.edu/uscode/text/18/2701.

121 18 U.S.C. § 2701(c)(2), accessed November 2017, https://www.law.cornell.edu/uscode/text/18/2701.

122 Although City of Ontario v. Quon illustrates the point, the case itself is more complex because the employer was a government entity. In such an instance, the Fourth Amendment is implicated when monitoring occurs—which means the government would typically need to seek a warrant to conduct the search. In the case, Quon raised claims pursuant to both the Fourth Amendment and the Stored Communications Act. See W. Scott Blackmer, "Quon: US Supreme Court Rules against Privacy on Employer-

Issued Devices," *Info Law Group* (blog), June 17, 2010, https://www.infolawgroup.com/blog/2010/06/articles/privacy-law/quon-us-supreme-court-rules-against-privacy-on-employer-issued-devices; "Workplace Privacy and Employee Monitoring," Privacy Rights Clearinghouse, revised March 25, 2019, https://www.privacyrights.org/consumer-guides/workplace-privacy-and-employee-monitoring.

123 "On a state level, only Connecticut and Delaware require that employers notify employees about monitoring of email and internet beforehand." Helen Poliquin, "What Are the US Employee Monitoring Laws? The 101 FAQ [Up to Date]" *The BeeBole Blog*, October 11, 2018, https://beebole.com/blog/employee-monitoring/.

124 Seyfarth Shaw, "Questions Remain About Social Media Privacy Rights during Workplace Investigation," *Employment Law Outlook*, Seyfarth, October 1, 2015, www.laborandemploymentlawcounsel.com/2015/10/social-media-privacy-rights-during-workplace-investigations/; see Joseph Lazzarottie and Jason Gavejian, "Third Circuit Rules in Favor of Employer Who Monitored Former Employees' Social Media Accounts," *The National Law Review*, March 25, 2019, https://www.natlawreview.com/article/third-circuit-rules-favor-employer-who-monitored-former-employees-social-media.

125 "Privacy of Employee and Student Social Media Accounts," National Conference of State Legislatures, updated August 8, 2022, https://www.ncsl.org/technology-and-communication/privacy-of-employee-and-student-social-media-accounts; Sachi Clements, "State Laws on Social Media Password Requests by Employers," Nolo, accessed July 2023, https://www.nolo.com/legal-encyclopedia/state-laws-on-social-media-password-requests-by-employers.html#:~:text=Employers%20may%20require%20employees%20to,used%20solely%20for%20such%20purposes.

126 Several recent decisions by the National Labor Relations Board have found that employees' speech is protected when they use social media to complain about managers, coworkers or the companies that employ them. Steven Greehhouse, "Even if It Enrages Your Boss, Social Net Speech Is Protected," *The New York Times*, January 21, 2013, www.nytimes.com/2013/01/22/technology/employers-social-media-policies-come-under-regulatory-scrutiny.html?_r=1&pagewanted=all&pagewanted=print. For additional details from the National Labor Relations Board, view "The NLRB and Social Media," National Labor Relations Board, accessed November 2019, https://www.nlrb.gov/rights-we-protect/rights/nlrb-and-social-media.

127 Thomas Payne, "Employee Social Media Complaints: Employers Beware," Barnes & Thornburg LLP, February 2, 2022, https://btlaw.com/en/insights/blogs/labor-relations/2022/employee-social-media-complaints-employers-beware; Steven Greenhouse, "Even if It Enrages Your Boss, Social Net Speech Is Protected," *The New York Times*, January 21, 2013, www.nytimes.com/2013/01/22/technology/employers-social-media-policies-come-under-regulatory-scrutiny.html?_r=1&pagewanted=all&pagewanted=print. For additional details view "The NLRB and Social Media," National Labor Relations Board; see generally Brian Heater, "US Labor Secretary Marty Walsh on Automation and Unionization." TechCrunch, July 21, 2022, https://techcrunch.com/2022/07/21/us-labor-secretary-marty-walsh-on-automation-and-unionization/?utm_medium=TCnewsletter&tpcc=TCstartupsnewsletter&utm_campaign=TCstartupsweekly.

128 Smith, John. "U.S. Biometric Laws & Pending Legislation Tracker," JD Supra, May 13, 2021, https://www.jdsupra.com/legalnews/u-s-biometric-laws-pending-legislation-5729436/#:~:text=LAW%20%C2%A7%20201%2Da.,as%20provided%20by%20

other%20laws; see F. Mario Trujillo and Jon Frankel, "Texas Starts Enforcing its Biometric Law" *ZwillGen Blog*, updated June 13, 2023, https://www.zwillgen.com/privacy/texas-cubi-law-and-biometric-privacy/#:~:text=In%20Texas%2C%20CUBI%20regulates%20%E2%80%9Cbiometric,and%20consent%20is%20first%20given.

129 Anjali Das, "Beware of BIPA and Other Biometric Laws – BIPA Class Actions Can Result in Astronomical Damages," Reuters, July 3, 2023, https://www.reuters.com/legal/legalindustry/beware-bipa-other-biometric-laws-bipa-class-actions-can-result-astronomical-2023-07-03/; Susan Lorenc, Dremian Moore, James Schreve, Ryan Gehbauer, "BIPA Litigation Update: Cothron's Impact and Employer BIPA Defense Affirmed," Thompson Coburn, May 24, 2023, https://www.thompsoncoburn.com/insights/blogs/cybersecurity-bits-and-bytes/post/2023-05-24/bipa-litigation-update-cothron-s-impact-and-employer-bipa-defense-affirmed; Adam Forman and Nathaniel Glassner, "Employers Take Heed: Follow Illinois Biometric Privacy Rules or Risk a Losing Battle," JD Supra, February 17, 2022, https://www.jdsupra.com/legalnews/employers-take-heed-follow-illinois-4684209/#:~:text=The%20Illinois%20Biometric%20Information%20Privacy,in%20this%20case%20employees)%20with; "Recent Surge in Class Actions Involving Biometric Data: What Employers Need to Know and Do Now," Epstein Becker Green, January 3, 2018, https://www.ebglaw.com/insights/recent-surge-in-class-actions-involving-biometric-data-what-employers-need-to-know-and-do-now/. Note that Michigan has made it illegal for employers to require employees to be microchipped, which is typically used either for productivity measurements or to replace timecards. Loukia Papadopoulos, "Michigan Passes Bill to Make it Illegal to Forcefully Microchip Employees," Interesting Engineering (July 1, 2021), June 28, 2020, https://interestingengineering.com/innovation/michigan-passes-bill-to-make-it-illegal-to-forcefully-microchip-employees.

130 Ana Tagvoryan, Brooke Lley, and David Oberly, "Learn the Rules on Employers' Use of Biometric Data," SHRM, April 1, 2019, https://www.shrm.org/resourcesandtools/legal-and-compliance/employment-law/pages/regulation-employer-use-biometric-data.aspx; see "Tracking U.S. State Consumer Data Privacy Legislation," HuschBlackwell, September 12, 2023, https://www.huschblackwell.com/2023-state-biometric-privacy-law-tracker; see also Peter Strelitz, "CUBI: Everything You Need to Know About Texas' Biometric Law and Beyond," Segal McCambridge, January 28, 2021, https://www.segalmccambridge.com/blog/cubi-everything-you-need-to-know-about-texas-biometric-law-and-beyond/; Covington and Burling, "Washington State Becomes Third State with Biometric Law," *The National Law Review*, June 1, 2017, https://www.natlawreview.com/article/washington-state-becomes-third-state-biometric-law.

131 Cal. Lab. Code § 435, accessed February 2020, https://leginfo.legislature.ca.gov/faces/codes_displaySection.xhtml?lawCode=LAB§ionNum=435. Michigan's statute is broader, forbidding installation of a device for observing or photographing a "private place" as defined by the statute. Mich. Comp. Laws § 750.539d, accessed November 2017, www.legislature.mi.gov/(S(ivmaxvahnreeqq1ysth2seun))/mileg.aspx?page=getObject&objectName=mcl-750-539d.

132 Elizabeth Austermuehle, "Monitoring Your Employees through GPS: What Is Legal and What Are Best Practices?" *Greensfelder* (blog), February 18, 2016, www.greensfelder.com/business-risk-management-blog/monitoring-your-employees-through-gps-what-is-legal-and-what-are-best-practices.

133 David Munkittrick, "GPS in the Workplace," *Proskauer Privacy Blog*, April 30, 2012, http://privacylaw.proskauer.com/2012/04/articles/workplace-privacy/gps-in-the-workplace/.

134 Conn. Gen. Stat. § 31-48d, accessed November 2017, http://law.justia.com/codes/connecticut/2014/title-31/chapter-560/section-31-94.

135 Cal. Pen. Code § 637.7, accessed November 2017, http://codes.findlaw.com/ca/penal-code/pen-sect-637-7.html.

136 Juliana De Groot, "What is Data Loss Prevention (DLP)? A Definition of Data Loss Prevention," *Data Insider*, Digital Guardian, April 28, 2023, https://digitalguardian.com/blog/what-data-loss-prevention-dlp-definition-data-loss-prevention.

137 Vadim Zdor, "DLP vs. Privacy Laws," *InfoWatch*, September 14, 2011, https://infowatch.com/blog/2328.

138 See Sharton and Neuman, "The Legal Risks of Monitoring Employees Online."

139 Chris Brook, "The Ultimate Guide to BYOD Security: Definition & More," *Data Insider*, Digital Guardian, November 7, 2022, https://digitalguardian.com/blog/ultimate-guide-byod-security-overcoming-challenges-creating-effective-policies-and-mitigating.

140 "Bring Your Own Device … at Your Own Risk," PrivacyRights.org, revised October 1, 2014, https://privacyrights.org/consumer-guides/bring-your-own-device-byod-your-own-risk.

141 See Totten, "Balancing Workplace Technology and Privacy in the 21st Century," 46-50.

142 The topics related to civil litigation and governments investigations are further discussed in Chapter 13.

143 "Data Privacy Concerns: Tips for Teleworking During Coronavirus," Shipman & Goodwin LLP, April 8, 2020, https://www.shipmangoodwin.com/insights/data-privacy-concerns-tips-for-teleworking-during-coronavirus.html; "Cybersecurity Considerations for Telework," Venable LLP, April 1, 2020, https://www.venable.com/insights/publications/2020/04/cybersecurity-considerations-for-telework; see generally "Telework," Cybersecurity and Infrastructure Security Agency, accessed July 2023, https://www.cisa.gov/topics/risk-management/coronavirus/telework-guidance-and-resources.

144 "Data Privacy Concerns: Tips for Teleworking During Coronavirus," Shipman & Goodwin LLP.

145 Advisory Opinion to Vail (04-05-99), Federal Trade Commission, April 5, 1999, https://www.ftc.gov/policy/advisory-opinions/advisory-opinion-vail-04-05-99.

146 Rod Fliegel, "The FACT and How It Affects FCRA and Employment Investigations (the Vail Letter)," Littler, January 15, 2004, https://www.littler.com/publication-press/publication/fact-and-how-it-affects-fcra-and-employment-investigations-vail-letter.

147 Fliegel, "The FACT and How It Affects FCRA and Employment Investigations."

148 Fliegel, "The FACT and How It Affects FCRA and Employment Investigations."

149 Fliegel, "The FACT and How It Affects FCRA and Employment Investigations."

150 Elizabeth Gonzalez, "How Long to Keep Employee Files: Everything Small Business Owners Need to Know," The Ascent, May 18, 2022, https://www.fool.com/the-ascent/small-business/human-resources/articles/how-long-to-keep-employee-files/.

151 Finkin, *Privacy in Employment Law*, 267–295.

CHAPTER 13

Privacy Issues in Civil Litigation and Government Investigations

This chapter examines privacy issues that arise when a company is responding to civil litigation and government investigations. Before trial, a company may receive civil "discovery" requests (requests for information by each party in a lawsuit). In the course of a law enforcement or national security investigation, an organization may face requests or orders to produce information. At a civil or criminal trial, the tradition of public records and open courtrooms in the United States means that additional personal information may be revealed.

Historically, outside counsel and in-house lawyers often played the predominant role in determining what personal information would be disclosed in the course of investigations or litigation. Disclosures in litigation were often undertaken manually, after lawyers, paralegals, or other individuals read through document files to determine what had to be produced.

Today, disclosures in investigations and litigation are more likely to be made through cooperative efforts of lawyers with a company's privacy and information technology (IT) professionals. Companies that hold large amounts of personal information often have information management plans that set policies for how and when disclosures will occur. Those plans are created through collaborative efforts that include experts on relevant privacy requirements and implementation through automated IT systems. To avoid data breaches, authorization may be required by specific, responsible people in the organization. To ensure implementation of company policies, audit trails are often in place concerning disclosures of sensitive information to third parties, including for investigation and litigation purposes. With this convergence of professionals for privacy, law, and IT, organizations often need a more systematic approach to responding to investigations and litigation.

This chapter begins with an outline of how disclosures may be required, permitted, or forbidden by law. Organizations sometimes are required by law either to disclose or not to disclose personal information. In other situations, the organization faces a choice about whether and how to make such disclosures. The chapter next turns to civil litigation. Since the 2007 revisions to the Federal Rules of Civil Procedure, the U.S. tradition of public records in litigation has been paired with requirements that lawyers redact certain sensitive personal information before it goes into court files. Since 2006, federal civil litigation has operated under the "e-discovery" rules, which require automated and large-scale production of emails and other corporate documents during the discovery process prior to trial. These large volumes of disclosure raise important privacy issues, illustrating the need for privacy professionals to work closely with lawyers and IT professionals.

The chapter then turns to privacy issues in law enforcement investigations. Protecting privacy is a major theme of the Fourth Amendment to the U.S. Constitution, which prohibits the government from making unreasonable searches and seizures. The Fourth Amendment sets limits on both physical searches and searches for personal information through wiretaps and access to company records. Fourth Amendment principles have also informed several statutes, including wiretap laws, the Electronic Communications Privacy Act (ECPA), the Right to Financial Privacy Act (RFPA) (applying to financial institutions), and the Privacy Protection Act (PPA) (applying to reporters and media companies). Privacy professionals need to be aware of these statutes, as a company can face legal consequences, depending on the context, for turning over either too much or too little information. This section of the chapter ends with a discussion of evidence stored in other countries, and how the Clarifying Lawful Overseas Use of Data Act (CLOUD Act) and the updated Budapest Convention address this issue.

The chapter concludes with an examination of privacy issues and national security investigations in the era of Edward Snowden's intelligence leaks in 2013. Under the Foreign Intelligence Surveillance Act (FISA) of 1978, communications providers can face especially complex rules about when and in what way they are permitted or required to provide information to the government. For both the law enforcement and national security discussions in this chapter, the goal is not to provide enough detail to answer the questions of specialized practitioners. Rather, the goal is to set forth the basic principles and specific provisions that apply to a wide range of organizations as well as provide insight into the reforms that were put in place after the Snowden leaks.

13.1 Disclosures Required, Permitted, or Forbidden by Law

For investigations and litigation, the law can be complex about when information must be disclosed, when the organization has a choice about whether to disclose, and when the organization is prohibited from disclosing.

Sometimes the same statute requires production of information in some circumstances, such as when a judge issues a court order, but prohibits production of the same information in other circumstances, such as when no court order exists.

13.1.1 Disclosures Required by Law

Certain U.S. laws require disclosure of personal information held by an organization. Chapter 9 discussed the Bank Secrecy Act (BSA) and related reporting requirements designed to reduce money laundering. Other examples of required disclosure are:

- The U.S. Food and Drug Administration (FDA) requires health professionals and drug manufacturers to report serious adverse events, product problems, or medication errors suspected to be associated with the use of an FDA-regulated drug, biologic, device, or dietary supplement under the Food, Drug and Cosmetic Act (FDCA).[1]
- The U.S. Department of Labor's (DOL's) Occupational Health and Safety Administration (OSHA) requires compilation and reporting of information about certain workplace injuries and illnesses.[2]
- Many states require reporting of certain types of injuries and medical conditions, such as abuse, gunshot wounds, immunization records, or specific contagious diseases. The Health Insurance Portability and Accountability Act (HIPAA) permits disclosure of protected health information where disclosure is "required by law."[3]

Outside of these regulatory systems, records sometimes must be disclosed during an investigation or in the course of litigation. The discussion in this chapter of e-discovery will describe how parties to civil litigation in the United States are routinely required to produce emails, documents, and other company records containing substantial personal information. In litigation, discovery—which essentially means information disclosed to another party in a lawsuit before trial—is governed by the rules of civil and criminal procedure, as overseen by state and federal judges.

Companies with information relevant to a government investigation or civil litigation may receive a subpoena, which is an instruction to produce a witness or records. For instance, Federal Rule of Civil Procedure 45 says that a subpoena must:

- State the court from which it is issued
- State the title of the action and its civil-action number

- Command each person to whom it is directed to do the following at a specific time and place: attend and testify; produce designated documents, electronically stored information, or tangible things in that person's possession, custody or control; or permit the inspection of premises
- Set out the text of the rules describing a person's right to challenge or modify the subpoena

The party seeking information must "serve" the subpoena (deliver it to the subject in a legally sufficient way), which puts that person on notice of the obligation to respond and of the recipient's right to seek to quash or modify the subpoena. The rule states that the issuing court "may hold in contempt a person who, having been served, fails without adequate excuse to obey the subpoena."[4] Contempt of court can result in fines or imprisonment.

Differing legal standards may, of course, apply to civil (private) litigation and to government investigations, and standards also vary depending on the types of records sought. For instance and explored later in this section, law enforcement can get history of dialed phone numbers and similar information under a pen register order. A judge issues that type of order under the relatively easy-to-meet standard that the information "is relevant to an ongoing investigation."[5] The stored content of records may be accessed under court orders defined by 18 U.S.C. § 2703(d), which require the government to provide a judge with "specific and articulable facts showing that there are reasonable grounds" to believe communications are relevant to a criminal investigation.[6]

One step stricter is the traditional search warrant issued by a judge or magistrate under the Fourth Amendment to the U.S. Constitution, which requires showing that there is probable cause that a crime has been, is, or will be committed. Even stricter is the standard for a telephone wiretap, which has the requirements of a probable cause warrant as well as other requirements, such as when alternative means of getting the evidence have been exhausted.[7] This range of standards is intended to provide more protection for more sensitive information—a list of phone numbers called is easier to get than permission to listen to an entire telephone conversation.

13.1.2 Disclosures Permitted by Law

For some categories of information, an organization is permitted, but not required, to disclose personal information. HIPAA itself, for instance, requires very few disclosures. The HIPAA Privacy Rule requires covered entities to disclose protected health information (PHI) only to the individual to whom it pertains and to the U.S. Department of Health and Human Services (HHS) in the course of an enforcement action.[8] It permits (but does not require) companies to disclose PHI when required to do so by another applicable law, such as the state laws that require reporting of medical information. HIPAA also permits covered entities to disclose PHI for reasons including public health, law enforcement, and national security.

After the U.S. Supreme Court overturned Roe v. Wade in 2022, the HHS Office of Civil Rights issued guidance concerning permitted disclosures and reproductive health care.[9] According to the guidance, the HIPAA Privacy Rule clarified that a covered entity would not be permitted to make a disclosure of PHI to law enforcement as "required by law" where the state law does not expressly require the reporting, such as when a state law prohibits abortion but does not require the hospital to report individuals to law enforcement. The 2022 HHS Office of Civil Rights guidance also clarified that the HIPAA Privacy Rule would permit a covered entity to disclose PHI in response to a law enforcement request made through legal process such as a court order or court-ordered warrant.[10]

Another example is the "computer trespasser" exception (sometimes called the "hacker trespasser" exception) created by Section 217 of the USA PATRIOT Act.[11] In general, a law enforcement officer needs to have a court order or some other lawful basis to intercept wire or electronic communications. As discussed later in the chapter, the owner or operator of a computer system can face penalties under ECPA for providing access to law enforcement without following legally mandated procedures. Section 217 of the USA PATRIOT Act permits, but does not require, the owner or operator of a computer system to provide such access in defined circumstances. For computer trespassers, law enforcement can now perform interceptions if:[12]

- The owner or operator of the protected computer authorizes the interception of the computer trespasser's communications on the protected computer
- The person acting under color of law (in an official capacity) is lawfully engaged in an investigation
- The person acting under color of law has reasonable grounds to believe the contents of the computer trespasser's communications will be relevant to the investigation
- Such interception does not acquire communications other than those transmitted[13]

13.1.3 Disclosures Forbidden by Law

Many of the privacy laws discussed in this book forbid disclosures of categories of personal information to categories of recipients. These laws often use either an opt-in or an opt-out requirement to help accomplish their restrictions.[14] For instance, HIPAA and the Children's Online Privacy Protection Rule (COPPA) forbid disclosures of covered information to third parties unless there is opt-in consent or a different exception applies. The Gramm-Leach-Bliley Act (GLBA) forbids disclosures to third parties if the individual has opted out. Many websites of companies not covered by GLBA similarly provide an opt-out, and disclosures in violation of such promises can trigger Section 5 enforcement under the Federal Trade Commission (FTC) Act.

In the context of investigations and litigation, evidentiary privileges can also prohibit disclosure. These privileges are generally defined under state law.[15] One example is the attorney-client privilege, which means that an attorney cannot be compelled to testify or produce records about a client concerning matters within the scope of the representation. As with other privacy rules, there can be exceptions to the attorney-client privilege, such as client consent or to prevent imminent physical harm to another person. Other common evidentiary privileges include doctor-patient, priest-penitent, and spousal privilege. Where these apply, a doctor, member of the clergy, or spouse cannot be compelled to testify about the other party, absent consent or some other exception. Nationally, a person accused of a crime in state or federal court can assert the privilege against self-incrimination under the Fifth Amendment to the U.S. Constitution.

13.2 Privacy and Civil Litigation

A large amount of personal information may be disclosed to parties in the course of civil litigation. Courts can issue protective orders to prohibit disclosure of personal information revealed in litigation, and attorneys increasingly are required to redact Social Security numbers and other sensitive information when filing documents with the courts. The systematic management of personal information has also become more prominent since the 2006 adoption of the e-discovery rules, which often require civil litigants to turn over large volumes of a company's electronic records in litigation.

13.2.1 Public Access to Court Records, Protective Orders, and Required Redaction

The United States has a strong tradition of public access to government records, including under the federal Freedom of Information Act (FOIA) and state open records laws. States and localities often provide access to a wide range of public records, including birth and death records, professional and business licenses, real estate ownership and appraisal records, voter registration records, and many more. The activities of courts historically have also been public records. Criminal and civil trials in the United States are almost always open for the public to attend. Historically, people could also go to the local courthouse and read the materials submitted to the court, including documents and other exhibits introduced at trial. With the growth of the internet, court systems began to consider putting their records online for beneficial reasons such as providing transparency in government and reducing the cost of storing and accessing records.

Placing court records on the internet, however, also raised privacy issues. Paper records stored in local courthouses provided practical obscurity for most of the information because of the expense and difficulty of searching the records. Online, searchable public records greatly reduced this obscurity. In 2000, the federal bankruptcy courts proposed placing their records online, including Social Security numbers, bank account numbers, and the amount in each account. Internet publication of these details raised the risk that these accounts would be the target of identity fraud. The federal government issued a report on the privacy issues, and the bankruptcy court rules were amended to protect Social Security numbers and privacy.[16] The Administrative Office of U.S. Courts and the Center for Legal and Court Technology have held multiple conferences in Williamsburg, Virginia, with extensive documentation of how state and federal courts address the issues of privacy and public access to court records.[17] Certain categories of records often receive greater protection, including juvenile, financial, and medical records.

One response to public access to court records has been for litigants to seek protective orders for personal information. With a protective order, a judge determines what information should not be made public and what conditions apply to those who may access the protected information. Rule 26(c) of the Federal Rules of Civil Procedure states that a party may seek a protective order providing that confidential information may not be revealed or must be revealed in a particular way—such as "attorney's eyes only"—during litigation. The moving party must demonstrate good cause, and a court will apply a three-part test in deciding whether to grant the request. First, the resisting party must show the information to be confidential. Second, the requesting party must show that the information is relevant and necessary to the case. Third, the court must weigh the harm of disclosure against the need for the information.[18]

The HIPAA Privacy Rule, similarly, discusses the standards for a "qualified protective order" (QPO), which applies in state courts that are not covered by the Federal Rules of Civil Procedure. A QPO prohibits the parties from using or disclosing PHI for any purpose other than the litigation or proceeding for which such information was requested. It also requires the return to the covered entity or destruction of the PHI (including copies) at the end of the litigation.[19] If a QPO is in place, a covered entity complies with privacy requirements for disclosure in litigation or administrative proceedings.

More generally, court rules today require redaction of certain personal information by the litigants themselves. **Redaction** is the practice of identifying and removing or blocking information from documents being produced pursuant to a discovery request or as evidence in a court proceeding. One important example is the 2007 adoption of Rule 5.2 of the Federal Rules of Civil Procedure, "Privacy Protection for Filings Made with the Court." The rule applies to both paper and electronic filings and to both parties and nonparties filing documents. Specifically, attorneys are required to redact documents so that no more than the following information is included in court filings:

- The last four digits of the Social Security number and taxpayer identification number
- The year of the individual's birth
- If the individual is a minor, only the minor's initials
- The last four digits of the financial account number[20]

Certain exemptions may apply, and parties may request that filings be made under seal without redaction when appropriate. In cases where additional protection may be necessary, parties can seek protective orders. If granted, the protective order may require additional redaction or may restrict electronic access to the court filings.[21] Enforcement and penalties apply for other violations of court rules.[22]

Rule 49.1 of the Federal Criminal Rules of Procedure and Rule 9037 of the Federal Rules of Bankruptcy Procedure contain similar redaction requirements.[23] In criminal proceedings, city and state of the home address are a fifth category requiring redaction so that the precise home address is not revealed.[24]

Federal district courts often have supplementary redaction or privacy requirements that apply in their court proceedings. Similarly, state and local courts have increasingly adopted redaction requirements. Attorneys and privacy professionals thus should be mindful of the privacy procedure rules that may apply depending on where the litigation takes place.

13.2.2 Electronic Discovery

Prior to trial, the parties usually engage in discovery. In discovery, the information typically is exchanged with the other party or parties and their attorneys. In doing so, there may be confidentiality protections such as protective orders and redaction requirements. Information exchanged in discovery also raises at least the possibility that it will be disclosed more broadly, such as in a trial or public court filing, or because those who receive the information in discovery may disclose it to others.

Since the 2006 revisions to the Federal Rules of Civil Procedure, electronically stored information (ESI) has become an increasingly large focus of pretrial discovery in U.S. litigation.[25] The discovery of ESI, generally known as e-discovery, has become an important subdiscipline in law and technology. E-discovery implicates both domestic privacy concerns and issues arising in transborder data flows.

Managing e-discovery and privacy begins with a well-managed data retention program. In designing a retention policy, it should be remembered that ESI takes not only obvious forms such as email or word processing documents, but can also manifest itself as databases, web pages, server logs, instant messaging transcripts, voicemail systems, virtual meetings, social networking records, thumb drives, or even micro SD cards found in smartphones.[26] An important source of standards and best practices for managing electronic discovery compliance through data retention policies is the Sedona Conference.[27] Regarding email retention, the Sedona Conference offers four key guidelines:

- Email retention policies should be administered by interdisciplinary teams composed of participants across a diverse array of business units
- Such teams should continually develop their understanding of the policies and practices in place and identify the gaps between policy and practice

- Interdisciplinary teams should reach consensus as to policies while looking to industry standards
- Technical solutions should meet and parallel the functional requirements of the organization

Database design should also be considered when addressing a company's retention policies. When done in good faith, data that is "transitory in nature, not routinely created or maintained by [d]efendants for their business purposes, and requiring of additional steps to retrieve and store" may be considered outside the duty of preservation.[28] Retention policies should also consider employee hard drives. While it may be an accepted practice to wipe and reimage personal computers after an employee is terminated so that the computer can be provided to a new employee, "in order to take advantage of the good faith exception [to discovery obligations], a party needs to act affirmatively to prevent the system from destroying or altering information, even if such destruction would occur in the regular course of business."[29] One solution to this problem is to collect forensic images of such devices prior to reassignment.

Initial problems with invasion of privacy concerns related to such retention can be countered by clearly articulating a usage policy for employees. For example, by discouraging employees from using their company email accounts for personal communications, a company can reduce the future risk of handing over sensitive or embarrassing information when complying with a discovery request. Similarly, placing limits on the permitted uses of company computers may aid in preventing later forensic discovery of hard drives from revealing private information about employees. Conversely, employees should be discouraged from conducting company business on personal devices to prevent the subsequent risk of an invasion of privacy if an employer needs to examine such devices.[30]

While these best practices are widely accepted, it should be noted that where discovery obligations are in direct conflict with business practices, the discovery obligations will likely prevail. When a court finds conflict between a corporate retention policy and a discovery request, the court will likely apply a three-factor test: (1) a retention policy should be reasonable considering the facts of the situation, (2) courts may consider similar complaints against the organization, and (3) courts may evaluate whether the organization instituted the policy in bad faith.[31] Finally, in regard to retention policies, it must be remembered that even a reasonable policy may need to be suspended in the face of a litigation hold, which exists when the company is on notice of discovery because litigation is already underway.[32]

U.S. sectoral laws such as HIPAA and GLBA create some tension between broad pretrial discovery powers and privacy protections. Generally, however, these laws exist in harmony with discovery obligations. For example, the HIPAA Privacy Regulation specifically addresses when protected health information may be disclosed during discovery. First, a covered entity may disclose PHI if the subject of those records authorizes their release.[33] Second, absent a release, a covered entity may release PHI subject to a court order.[34] Third, a covered entity may disclose PHI subject to a discovery request if satisfactory assurances are provided. An assurance is satisfactory under HIPAA if the parties seeking the request for information have agreed to a qualified protective order and have submitted it to the court, or if the party seeking the information has requested a qualified protective order from the court.[35] A qualified protective order requires both that the parties are prohibited from using or disclosing the PHI for any purpose other than the litigation and that the PHI will be returned or destroyed at the end of the litigation.[36]

Similarly, under GLBA, a financial institution may disclose otherwise protected information "to comply with federal, state, or local laws, rules, and other applicable legal requirements; to comply with a properly authorized civil, criminal, or regulatory investigation or subpoena or summons by federal, state, or local authorities; or to respond to judicial process or government regulatory authorities having jurisdiction over the financial institution for examination, compliance, or other purposes as authorized by law."[37] Federal courts have been willing to read this clause to encompass civil discovery requests, although protective orders should still be obtained by those disclosing the information.[38]

The issue of transborder data flows creates a more complicated situation. When engaged in pretrial discovery in U.S. courts, parties can be caught between conflicting demands. On the one hand, they must comply with U.S. discovery rules that expressly recognize the importance of broad preservation, collection, and production. The rules therefore generally require the disclosure of all information relevant to the claims or defenses in a case that are in a party's possession, custody or control—and this extends to information globally. On the other hand, parties may also face compliance obligations under foreign laws that place an emphasis of the protection of personal data and recognize privacy as a fundamental right.

For instance, the EU General Data Protection Regulation (GDPR) makes e-discovery with European nations subject to even more restrictions.[39] Consequently, a conflict can arise between a U.S. requirement to produce documents and another country's laws, which may prohibit transfer of personal information out of that country and/or prohibit disclosure to third parties without the data subject's consent.[40]

U.S. courts have taken different approaches to resolving this conflict.[41] Some courts have sought to resolve this tension by requiring production by those parties that sought to take advantage of U.S. jurisdiction, such as the plaintiff who filed the lawsuit.[42] Other courts, however, have extended data production requirements even to parties that did not seek the benefit of U.S. courts, with the U.S. Supreme Court even stating "it is well settled that [foreign] statutes do not deprive an American court of the power to order a party subject to its jurisdiction to produce evidence even though the act of production may violate that statute."[43] Another approach has been to focus on the nature or type of the documents at issue, such as by requiring the foreign parties to prepare a privacy log describing the documents without disclosing the contents of the documents, so that the court could differentiate among documents.[44] Balancing broad discovery demands in the U.S. with foreign privacy restrictions remains a challenging issue for many organizations, with no simple resolution thus far of the legal conflicts.

The production of transborder data may also be avoided by invoking the Hague Convention on the Taking of Evidence.[45] Under the treaty, the party seeking to displace the Federal Rules of Civil Procedure bears the burden of demonstrating that it is more appropriate to use the Hague Convention and must establish that the foreign law prohibits the discovery sought. Such prohibitions may be established by expert testimony. Aerospatiale v. S.D. of Iowa outlines the factors that an American court may use to reconcile the conflict.[46] These factors include:[47]

- The importance of the documents or data to the litigation at hand
- The specificity of the request
- Whether the information originated in the United States
- The availability of alternative means of securing the information
- The extent to which the important interests of the United States and the foreign state would be undermined by an adverse ruling

The fifth factor is often referred to as being the most important. For example, when victims of a terrorist attack sued a British bank for aiding and abetting a terrorist organization, British bank secrecy laws did not preempt the discovery request, because the information was central to the case, and the disclosure would advance both American and British interests in combating terrorism.[48] Courts have also been willing to look to additional factors, such as the good faith of the party resisting compliance, in applying such a test. Obtaining evidence through the Hague Convention is far more expensive and time-consuming than typical discovery requests under the Federal Rules; it is often a means of last resort for U.S. litigators with no other recourse for obtaining the necessary evidence.[49]

Once data has been culled for e-discovery, preservation and transport present final considerations. Data may be "preserved in place" by maintaining it in its native repository, or it may be preserved in a separate form.[50] For transfer, data should be encrypted, and the key transferred by a secure second method of transport. If shipped as physical media (such as a hard drive or optical media), it should be transported in a manner that preserves an audit trail. Alternatively, data may be transferred by using a secure connection, such as secure file transfer protocol (SFTP). Organizations producing thousands of pages of documents in discovery will often need a plan to address sensitive personal information, including a process for identifying and redacting or withholding such information where possible, maintaining confidentiality under a protective order where it must be disclosed, and seeking to "claw back" or otherwise remediate inadvertent disclosures of such information.

13.3 Law Enforcement and the Role of Privacy Professionals

Along with civil litigation, a company can face requests to provide personal information in connection with criminal investigations and litigation. The discussion here begins with an introduction to Fourth Amendment limits on law enforcement searches. Fourth Amendment cases have articulated some of the most fundamental concepts used by privacy lawyers and other privacy experts in the United States, including the "reasonable expectation of privacy" test developed in the context of government wiretaps.[51] The discussion then moves to other statutes that can apply to criminal investigations, including HIPAA, ECPA, the SCA, the RFPA and the PPA. This section concludes with a discussion of evidence stored in other countries, and explains how the recently enacted CLOUD Act addresses this issue.

This chapter does not attempt to provide the many details that prosecutors and criminal defense lawyers need to know about the handling of personal information in criminal litigation. Nor does it go into the complex details of ECPA and the SCA, as those laws apply to communications providers such as telephone companies and email services. Instead, the focus is on general principles and issues that can arise in a wide range of companies.

13.3.1 Fourth Amendment Limits on Law Enforcement Searches

The Fourth Amendment to the Constitution provides: "The right of the people to be secure in their persons, houses, papers, and effects, against unreasonable searches and seizures, shall not be violated, and no warrants shall issue, but upon probable cause, supported by oath or affirmation, and particularly describing the place to be searched."[52]

The Fourth Amendment's limits on government power stem in part from objections to "general warrants" used by the British king's customs inspectors before the American Revolution. Officers of the Crown could get one general warrant and search all the houses in a neighborhood or town when looking for contraband goods. At the most basic level, the Fourth Amendment authorizes reasonable government searches while setting limits on their scope and how they are issued. The U.S. Supreme Court has stated: "The overriding function of the Fourth Amendment is to protect personal privacy and dignity against unwarranted intrusion by the State."[53]

The Fourth Amendment provides a ban against "unreasonable searches and seizures" by the government. For search warrants, the government must show "probable cause" that a crime has been, is or is likely to be committed. Search warrants must be supported by specific testimony, often provided by a police officer. A neutral magistrate (judge) approves the search warrant. They cannot be general warrants, but instead must describe the place to be searched with particularity.

Evidence gathered by the government in violation of the Fourth Amendment is generally subject to what is called the "exclusionary rule"—meaning that the evidence can be excluded from the criminal trial. The exclusionary rule creates a powerful incentive for criminal defendants to seek to show that the government has violated the Fourth Amendment. Consequently, state and federal courts have issued an enormous number of judicial decisions interpreting the Fourth Amendment, and the case law is notably complex.

Company privacy professionals are not likely to encounter the type of search warrant that provides the police physical entry to a house, automobile, or other private space. The legal rules are likely to be more important when the government seeks to conduct surveillance in connection with a company's facilities. For instance, the government might conduct wiretaps using the facilities of a telephone company or email service. In addition, and increasingly over time, the government may seek to gain access to company databases containing personal information about customers, employees and others.

Telephone wiretap law has been important to the last century of Fourth Amendment jurisprudence. In the 1928 case of Olmstead v. United States, a majority of the Supreme Court held that no warrant was required for wiretaps conducted on telephone company wires outside of the suspect's building.[54] The majority emphasized that the purpose of the Fourth Amendment was to protect the home and other private spaces. In one of the most famous statements about privacy, Justice Louis Brandeis argued in dissent that new technologies meant that the Fourth Amendment must have a "capacity of adaptation to a changing world." He said: "The makers of our Constitution . . . conferred, as against the government, the right to be let alone—the most comprehensive of rights and the right most valued by civilized men. To protect that right, every unjustifiable intrusion by the government upon the privacy of the individual, whatever the means employed, must be deemed a violation of the Fourth Amendment."[55]

The Supreme Court essentially overruled Olmstead in the 1967 case of Katz v. United States.[56] The majority stated: "What a person knowingly exposes to the public, even in his own home or office, is not a subject of Fourth Amendment protection. But what he seeks to preserve as private, even in an area accessible to the public, may be constitutionally protected." The court found that a warrant was needed for a police bug in a restaurant, placed to hear the calls behind the closed doors of a phone booth.

Katz is best remembered today for the widely cited "reasonable expectation of privacy" test. In a concurring opinion, Justice John Marshall Harlan stated: "There is a twofold requirement, first that a person have exhibited an actual (subjective) expectation of privacy and, second, that the expectation be one that society is prepared to recognize as 'reasonable.'"[57]

In practice, important exceptions exist to the requirement of a warrant where a reasonable expectation of privacy exists. The "in public" and "third-party" exceptions are especially important to privacy professionals. The case of Katz itself said that what a person knowingly exposes to the public is not protected by the Fourth Amendment. Police thus have broad discretion to follow a suspect down the street or take advantage of other information that is in plain view. The Supreme Court has also held that information a person puts into the hand of someone else—a third party—is not protected by the Fourth Amendment. For instance, the court has held that the Fourth Amendment does not require a warrant for the police to get a person's checking account records or the list of phone numbers a person has called.[58] The court has stated that the individual consented to letting the bank or phone company have that information, so the companies can lawfully turn the information over to the government without a search warrant. The third-party doctrine has been especially important in connection with company privacy practices—companies are generally permitted under the Constitution to turn over customer and employee records to the government (although statutory and other legal limits may apply).

In the 2012 case of United States v. Jones, the Supreme Court signaled important changes to the in public and third-party exceptions. The court held unanimously that a warrant was needed when the police placed a Global Positioning System (GPS) device on a car and tracked its location for over a month. The majority decision emphasized that the police had trespassed onto the car when they physically attached the GPS device. Four of the nine justices, however, would have held that a search occurred even without the physical attachment, and even for movements that took place entirely in public. A fifth justice seemed to indicate sympathy for this constitutional limit on surveillance of "in public" activities, and also stated that the time had come to reexamine the third-party doctrine.[59]

The 2014 case of Riley v. California was an important decision where the Supreme Court unanimously held that the contents of a cellphone cannot be searched unless law enforcement officers first obtain a search warrant.[60] The justices ruled that the data on a cellphone was quantitatively (the amount of data) and qualitatively (the kind of data) different than the contents that would normally be found in a physical container, which was the analogy the government had proposed to the court. As to the quantity of data, the court noted the immense storage capacity of cellphones as well as the ability to link to remote storage. With regard to the quality of data, the court opined that internet searches can reveal a person's interests, and location information can pinpoint an individual's movement over time.[61]

In the 2018 case of Carpenter v. United States, the Supreme Court reduced the scope of the third-party doctrine.[62] Prior to the determination of this case, a person did not legally have a reasonable expectation of privacy in records held by a third party—including bank records and telephone pen registers—so a warrant was not required for records held by third parties.[63] This is the concept known as the third-party doctrine. In 2018, the court acknowledged that cellphone usage was integral to modern life and noted that cell site location information could reveal intimate details about the habits of individuals' lives. In Carpenter, the court determined that law enforcement officers must secure a warrant to access at least certain records held by third parties—namely, cell site location information.[64]

These three recent cases by the Supreme Court requiring search warrants—Jones, Riley, and Carpenter—suggest that the Supreme Court is seeking to update Fourth Amendment doctrine to adapt to changing technology and may place further limits on the third-party doctrine as it relates to digital data.[65] Applying legal rules such as the third-party doctrine is further complicated when the accused did not themselves provide their data to the relevant company, such as: (1) DNA databases that are examined to identify relatives of the person who submitted the DNA sample and (2) videos from electronic doorbells that are utilized to investigate individuals other than the person who installed the doorbell.[66] As of the writing of this book, neither of these issues have been directly addressed by the U.S. Supreme Court, but privacy professionals should be on the lookout for possible updates concerning the application of the Fourth Amendment.

In 2022, the U.S. Supreme Court overturned Roe v. Wade—the 1973 case that stated the U.S. Constitution recognized a woman's right to terminate her pregnancy by abortion. After this recent U.S. Supreme Court decision, the legality of an abortion was decided by each state in the United States.[67] In states that outlaw abortion, state and local law enforcement may send legal process, such as a warrant, for data related to an illegal abortion to a company headquartered in a state that does not outlaw abortion. In response to this situation that impacted many technology companies headquartered in California, California enacted its own law that prohibits a company from responding to other states' abortion-related warrants.[68] This creates a conflict of law, similar to those seen in the international cross-border context (discussed in Section 13.3.8). Privacy practitioners should be alert that this type of conflict of law between U.S. states could result in a case before the U.S. Supreme Court.[69]

The overturning of Roe v. Wade also heightened concerns about geofence warrants. Geofencing is a technology that allows companies to target digital advertising to people within a virtually fenced area—such as within a certain proximity of an abortion clinic. The collection of data for this advertising purpose means that data can then be acquired by law enforcement using a geofence warrant. These geofence warrants have been challenged in lower courts—sometimes successfully and other times not successfully—under the bar against general warrants.[70] As of the writing of this book, the U.S. Supreme Court has not ruled on the legality of such warrants.[71]

13.3.2 Statutes That Go Beyond Fourth Amendment Requirements

Several federal statutes affect law enforcement access to personal information. Some of the statutes placed additional requirements on law enforcement after the Supreme Court held that the Constitution did not require search warrants in the relevant circumstances. For instance, the Right to Financial Privacy Act of 1978 was passed after the Supreme Court held that the Fourth Amendment did not apply to checking accounts, and the Electronic Communications Privacy Act of 1986 was passed after the court held that it did not apply to telephone numbers called.[72] In these instances, Congress has required some legal process for law enforcement to access the records, but the requirements are not as strict as a probable cause warrant approved by a neutral magistrate. These two statutes are examples of disclosure to law enforcement that is prohibited unless the statutory requirements are met.

Some law enforcement provisions permit—but do not require—companies to release personal information to law enforcement. HIPAA illustrates the sometimes complex trade-offs between protecting confidentiality and providing information for law enforcement purposes. The general rule in HIPAA is that PHI may be disclosed to third parties, including law enforcement, only with opt-in consent from the patient. Unauthorized disclosures can lead to enforcement by HHS. Section 512(f), however, goes into considerable detail about precisely when disclosure to law enforcement is permitted.[73] Disclosure is permitted pursuant to a court order or grand jury subpoena, or through an administrative request, if three criteria are met:

- The information sought is relevant and material to a legitimate law enforcement inquiry
- The request is specific and limited in scope to the extent reasonably practicable in light of the purpose for which the information is sought
- Deidentified information could not reasonably be used

Disclosure is also permitted in other specific instances, such as about a crime on the premises, about decedents in connection with a suspected crime, in emergencies, and about victims of a crime even in the absence of patient consent if a multifactor test is met. Limited information may in some instances also be released for identification and location purposes.

As discussed at the beginning of the chapter, other statutes require the release of personal information to law enforcement. Companies thus can face multiple, potentially conflicting laws about when and how to disclose to law enforcement. HIPAA addresses this problem by saying that disclosure is permitted when it is "required by law," even if a disclosure does not otherwise fit within the law enforcement or other exception.[74]

13.3.3 The Wiretap Act, Electronic Communications Privacy Act, and Stored Communications Act

From strictest to most permissive, federal law has different rules for (1) telephone monitoring and other tracking of oral communications, (2) privacy of electronic communications, and (3) video surveillance, for which there is little applicable law. Federal law is also generally stricter for real-time interception of a communication, as contrasted with retrieval of a stored record. In each area, states may have statutes that apply stricter rules.[75] Furthermore, monitoring that is offensive to a reasonable person can give rise to claims under state invasion of privacy or other common-law claims.[76]

13.3.3.1 Intercepting Communications

Federal law is generally strict in prohibiting wiretaps of telephone calls. The Wiretap Act today derives from Title III of a 1968 anticrime law, and its rules are thus often called Title III requirements.[77] The law applies to wire communications, which includes a phone call or other aural communication made through a network. The law also applies to oral communications, such as hidden bugs or microphones, and defined as "any oral communication uttered by a person exhibiting an expectation that such communication is not subject to interception under circumstances justifying such expectation."[78]

The Electronic Communications Privacy Act (ECPA) extended the ban on interception to electronic communications, which essentially are communications, including emails, that are not wire or oral communications.[79] The exact rules for wire, oral and electronic communications vary.[80] Unless an exception applies, however, interception of these communications is a criminal offense and provides a private right of action.

The prohibition on interception has a number of exceptions, each of which may have its own nuances requiring an expert to analyze. Under federal law, interception is permitted if a person is the party to the call or if one of the parties has given consent.[81] A number of states, however, have the stricter rule that all of the parties to the call must consent.[82] This all-party consent requirement is why customers often hear a message giving notice that a call is being recorded for quality assurance or other purposes. With the increase in businesses using video conferencing, privacy practitioners should be alert that video conferencing may fall within the protections of state laws that require all-party consent.[83]

A second exception relevant to many companies is concerning interception done in the ordinary course of business.[84] This exception can apply where the device used for the interception is "furnished to the subscriber or user by a provider of wire or electronic communication service in the ordinary course of its business."[85] This language, for instance, supports the ability to intercept for an employer who provides the communication service, such as the company telephone or email service. To qualify for the exception, the interception itself must also be in the normal course of the user's business.[86] Normal course of business here would apply to routine monitoring in a call center or scanning of company emails for viruses or other malware. By contrast, the employer listening to an employee's purely personal call would risk running afoul of the wiretap laws. Courts have split on how broadly to define "ordinary course of business," which is a reason that many employers rely instead on the consent exception for interception of telephone calls.[87] Note that the federal law is *not* preemptive, so if an organization is monitoring or recording calls, it runs the risk of violating the stricter law in the "all-party consent" states mentioned above—it should not rely on any of these exceptions outside the specific state.[88]

13.3.3.2 Stored Communications

The Stored Communications Act (SCA) was enacted as part of ECPA in 1986.[89] It creates a general prohibition against the unauthorized acquisition, alteration, or blocking of electronic communications while in electronic storage in a facility through which an electronic communications service is provided.[90] As for interceptions, violations can lead to criminal penalties or a civil lawsuit, so an expert in the SCA should generally be consulted before turning over such records in a law enforcement investigation. For monitoring within a company, the exceptions are simpler than for interceptions. The SCA has an exception for conduct authorized "by the person or entity providing a wire or electronic communications service," which will often be the company.[91] It also has an exception for conduct authorized "by a user of that service with respect to a communication of or intended for that use."[92] In general, legal limits on interceptions are stricter than limits for access to stored records.

It should also be noted that ECPA does *not* preempt stricter state privacy protections, and that state laws may protect email communications. For example, Delaware law prohibits employers from "monitor[ing] or otherwise intercept[ing] any telephone conversation or transmission, electronic mail or transmission, or internet access or usage" without prior written notice and daily electronic notice.[93] Similarly, Connecticut law requires that "each employer who engages in any type of electronic monitoring shall give prior written notice to all employees who may be affected, informing them of the types of monitoring which may occur. Each employer shall post, in a conspicuous place which is readily available for viewing by its employees, a notice concerning the types of electronic monitoring which the employer may engage in."[94]

13.3.3.3 Preservation Orders

The SCA states that a provider of wire or electronic communication services or a remote computing service, upon the request of a governmental entity, shall take all necessary steps to preserve records and other evidence in its possession pending the issuance of a court order or other process.[95] In such instances, the company must have a technical ability to preserve those records. This is similar to litigation holds when a company must preserve records during civil litigation.[96]

13.3.3.4 Pen Register and Trap-and-Trace Orders

Traditionally, a pen register recorded the telephone numbers of outgoing calls, and a trap-and-trace device recorded the telephone numbers that called in to a particular number. ECPA provided for pen register and trap-and-trace orders from a judge under the relatively lenient legal standard of "relevant to an ongoing investigation."[97] The USA PATRIOT Act expanded the definitions beyond telephone numbers to include "dialing, routing, addressing, or signaling information" transmitted to or from a device or process. The USA FREEDOM Act set new rules for national security investigations, prohibiting the use of pen register and trap-and-trace orders for bulk collection and restricting their use to circumstances where there were specific selectors such as an email address or telephone number.[98]

13.3.4 The Communications Assistance to Law Enforcement Act

The U.S. Communications Assistance to Law Enforcement Act of 1994 (CALEA), sometimes referred to as the Digital Telephony Bill, lays out the duties of defined actors in the telecommunications industry to cooperate in the interception of communications for law enforcement and other needs relating to the security and safety of the public.[99] It notably requires "telecommunications carriers" to design their products and services to ensure that they can carry out a lawful order to provide government access to communications. The Federal Communications Commission (FCC) has implemented CALEA through various rulemaking processes.[100]

CALEA applies to telecommunications carriers, but not to other information services. As enacted, therefore, the law was interpreted not to apply to internet services. In 2004, however, the U.S. Department of Justice (DOJ), the Federal Bureau of Investigation (FBI) and the Drug Enforcement Administration (DEA) petitioned to expand the interpretation of the scope of the legislation. In 2005, the FCC issued an order that providers of broadband internet access and voice-over-internet protocol (VoIP) services were telecommunications services when they interconnect with traditional telephone services, and so they now operate under CALEA requirements.[101]

13.3.5 Cybersecurity Information Sharing Act

The Cybersecurity Information Sharing Act (CISA) became law in 2015. The statute permits the federal government to share unclassified technical data with companies about how networks have been attacked and how successful defenses against such attacks have been carried out.[102] Correspondingly, CISA encourages companies to voluntarily share information with the federal government, state and local governments, and other companies and private entities. Under the law, the company's release of information about "cyberthreat indicators" and "defensive measures" receives certain protections.[103] These include limitations on liability, non-waiver of privileges, and exemption from FOIA disclosure. Participation by companies is voluntary. In addition, CISA authorizes companies to monitor and implement certain defensive measures on their information systems in an effort to counter cyberthreats.[104]

The specific provisions of CISA include:

- **Authorization for a company to share or receive "cyberthreat indicators" or "defensive measures."** Pursuant to CISA, a company is authorized to share with the federal government, state and local governments, and other companies and private entities "cyberthreat indicators"[105] and "defensive measures" for a "cybersecurity purpose"[106] or receive such information from these entities.[107]

- **Requirement for company to remove personal information before sharing.** For sharing to qualify for protections under CISA, the company's actions must be done in accordance with certain requirements.[108] For example, a company intending to share a "cyberthreat indicator" must first remove—or implement a "technical capacity" configured to remove—any information that is not directly related to a threat and that the company is aware at the time relates to a specific individual.[109]
- **Sharing information with federal government does not waive privileges.** Sharing information with the federal government does not waive privileges, such as attorney-client privilege. Importantly, there is no similar provision for sharing with state and local governments or other companies.[110]
- **Shared information exempt from federal and state FOIA laws.** Information shared pursuant to CISA is exempt from disclosure under FOIA as well as under any state or local provisions "requiring disclosure of information or records."[111]
- **Prohibition on government using shared information to regulate or take enforcement actions against lawful activities.** Information shared under CISA "shall not be used by any Federal, State, tribal, or local government to regulate, including an enforcement action, the lawful activities of any non-Federal entity or any activities taken by a non-Federal entity pursuant to mandatory standards, including activities related to monitoring, operating defensive measures, or sharing cyberthreat indicators." The information may be used, however, to develop or implement new cybersecurity regulations.[112]
- **Authorization for company's monitoring and operating defensive measures.** According to the act, a company is authorized to "monitor" and "operate defensive measures" on its own information system—or, with written authorization, another party's system—for cybersecurity purposes.[113]
- **Protection from liability for monitoring activities.** Under CISA, the company is protected from liability for its monitoring activities. Note, however, that there is no corresponding liability protection for operating defensive measures.[114]

During the discussions prior to the passage of CISA, numerous privacy concerns were raised.[115] In part to address these concerns, the act requires the federal government to publish guidelines concerning the use and dissemination of shared information.[116]

13.3.6 Right to Financial Privacy Act

The special requirements of the Right to Financial Privacy Act (RFPA) of 1978 apply to disclosures by a variety of financial institutions, including banks, credit card companies, and consumer finance companies.[117] RFPA states that "no Government authority may have access to or obtain copies of, the information contained in the financial records of any customer from a financial institution unless the financial records are reasonably described" and meet at least one of these conditions:

- The customer authorizes access
- There is an appropriate administrative subpoena or summons
- There is a qualified search warrant
- There is an appropriate judicial subpoena
- There is an appropriate formal written request from an authorized government authority[118]

By its terms, RFPA applies only to requests from federal agencies, although over a dozen states have similar requirements.[119] It applies to the financial records of individuals and partnerships of fewer than five people. With limited exceptions, customers must receive notice in advance of the government request for the records, and they have the right to challenge disclosure of such records. As with other privacy statutes, a number of important exceptions exist. Financial institutions that produce records under the RFPA are eligible for reimbursements for reasonably necessary costs. Penalties for violation can include actual damages to the customer, punitive damages, and attorney's fees.

13.3.7 Media Records and the Privacy Protection Act

The Privacy Protection Act of 1980 provides an extra layer of protection for members of the media and media organizations from government searches or seizures in the course of a criminal investigation.[120] PPA was passed in the wake of the 1978 Supreme Court case of Zurcher v. Stanford Daily.[121] In that case, police used a search warrant to look through a newspaper's unpublished photographs of a demonstration. Lower courts found the search unlawful, saying that the government should have used less invasive methods than a full search of the newspaper's premises. The Supreme Court, however, found that valid search warrants "may be used to search any property" where there is probable cause to believe that evidence of a crime will be found.

Under PPA, government officials engaging in criminal investigations are not permitted to search or seize media work products or documentary materials "reasonably believed to have a purpose to disseminate to the public a newspaper, book, broadcast or other similar form of public communication." In practice, rather than physically searching a newsroom, "the PPA effectively forces law enforcement to use subpoenas or voluntary cooperation to obtain evidence from those engaged in First Amendment activities."[122]

PPA applies to government officers or employees at all levels of government. It applies only to criminal investigations, not to civil litigation. Several states provide additional protections.[123] Violation can lead to penalties of a minimum of $1,000, actual damages, and attorney's fees.

One important exception is if there is probable cause to believe that a reporter has committed or is in the process of committing a crime. This PPA exception does not apply if the member of the media's only crime is possession, receipt, or communication of the work product itself. Other exceptions exist, such as to prevent death or serious injury or where there is reason to believe documents will be destroyed or concealed if the materials were requested through a subpoena.[124]

PPA was drafted to respond to physical police searches of traditional newspaper facilities. Going forward, courts may face claims that PPA is significantly broader, because disseminating "a public communication" may apply to blogs, other web publishing, and perhaps even social media.[125]

13.3.8 Evidence Stored in a Different Country

With the growth of cloud storage of records, including by web email and social network providers, evidence for a criminal case is more frequently held in a different country—a phenomenon that has been called "the globalization of criminal evidence."[126] Prosecutors and companies thus face an increasing number of cases that raise the issue of whether the domestic rules for accessing evidence apply to communications and other records held abroad. This section discusses: (1) the U.S. Clarifying Lawful Overseas Use of Data Act (CLOUD Act) and (2) the Second Additional Protocol to the Budapest Convention.

13.3.8.1 The U.S. CLOUD Act

The CLOUD Act, passed in 2018, marks a major change in how cross-border access to evidence may develop. Part 1 of the act addresses how the DOJ can access content of communications held by companies located in the United States. Part 2 of the act creates a new mechanism for other countries to access the content of communications held by U.S. service providers.[127]

The first part of the CLOUD Act mooted the pending Supreme Court case of United States v. Microsoft.[128] The case gained national attention in 2016 when the federal appellate court in New York ruled that the SCA did not require the company to provide electronic evidence that was stored outside of the United States, meaning the warrant was not valid for the contents of an email account that Microsoft stored overseas.[129] In 2017, the DOJ appealed the case to the Supreme Court. In oral arguments before the Supreme Court in 2018, Microsoft argued that the U.S. warrant had no legal force because the emails being sought were stored outside the United States, in Ireland. The DOJ argued that Microsoft could access the data from within the United States, and thus the place where the data happened to be stored did not matter.[130] The first part of the CLOUD Act resolved this legal issue, providing that the kind of compelled disclosure orders at issue in the Microsoft Ireland case applies "regardless of whether such communication, record, or other information is located within or outside of the United States."[131]

The second part of the CLOUD Act creates a new mechanism for other countries to access the content of communications held by U.S. service providers. This statutory mechanism is intended to address this major concern faced by foreign law enforcement.[132]

As background, ECPA prohibits U.S. service providers from disclosing content of communications to law enforcement except through a warrant or an appropriate request through a mechanism such as a mutual legal assistance treaty (MLAT).[133] When foreign law enforcement submit a request to the Unites States via the MLAT process, the request needs to show "probable cause" (the U.S. legal standard)—despite the fact that the crime occurred outside the United States. This MLAT process has been an increasing source of frustration for many governments, particularly since so much cloud-based data is held by U.S.-based providers. The MLAT process takes an estimated 10 months (global average) for law enforcement to receive electronic evidence.[134]

If the United States and a foreign government sign an agreement pursuant to the second part of the CLOUD Act, foreign law enforcement would be able to go *directly* to service providers for communications content. The foreign government, specifically, can target communications of *non*-U.S. citizens and residents, without the need to use the MLAT process or to get approval from a U.S. judge that probable cause exists.[135]

The CLOUD Act authorizes these executive agreements only for countries meeting human rights and rule of law requirements. Notably, an executive agreement must include designated safeguards both at the level of each individual request and at an institutional level.[136]

As of the writing of this book, the U.S./UK Executive Agreement and U.S./Australia Executive Agreement have been negotiated.[137] The U.S. has also announced negotiations with Canada and the European Union concerning possible CLOUD Act executive agreements.[138]

13.3.8.2 The Second Additional Protocol to the Budapest Convention

In 2004, the first international treaty to focus explicitly on cybercrime—the Council of Europe Convention on Cybercrime ("the Budapest Convention") —entered into force.[139] The treaty mandated participating countries outlaw certain cybercrimes, enact evidence-gathering rules, and cooperate with investigations across national borders. As of the writing of this book, more than 60 countries around the world have ratified this treaty—including the United States.[140]

The Second Additional Protocol to the Budapest Convention was negotiated as a way to assist countries in dealing with the globalization of criminal evidence that had occurred in the nearly two decades since the Budapest Convention first went into effect.[141] Although the details of the Second Additional Protocol are beyond the scope of this book, the topics addressed include:

- Expedited production of subscriber information and traffic data by allowing an order from the requesting country to, in essence, be treated as an order in the country where the request is being sent
- Direct disclosure of subscriber information and domain name registration information by allowing law enforcement to make requests directly to a service provider in another country
- Emergency requests by law enforcement for stored subscriber information, stored traffic data, and stored content in another country

The Second Additional Protocol also requires protections for personal data. These protections can be accomplished in several ways: a domestic law ensuring data protection, a binding agreement between the requesting party and the receiving country concerning law enforcement requests,[142] and even a nonbinding agreement between the two countries.[143]

The Second Additional Protocol opened for signatures of the parties to the original treaty in 2022. The United States is one of the countries that has signed this protocol.[144]

13.4. National Security and the Role of Privacy Professionals

Compared with the law enforcement issues discussed in the previous section, somewhat different rules and issues arise when the government seeks personal information for national security purposes. This section briefly explains the key differences. It then provides an overview of FISA as amended by the USA PATRIOT Act in 2001 and more recently by the 2015 USA FREEDOM Act.[145] As with the discussion above of ECPA, the discussion here does not delve into as many details of the law as would be needed by attorneys who work for the government or communications providers. Instead, the focus is on issues that can arise in a wide range of companies. Notably, any company can be faced with a request for records under Section 215 of the USA PATRIOT Act, and a significant range of companies can receive a national security letter (NSL).

13.4.1 Introduction to Debates About National Security Surveillance

National security wiretaps and other national security searches create a fundamental constitutional question. Under Article II of the Constitution, defining executive powers, the president is commander-in-chief of the armed forces, and the Supreme Court has stated the president has "plenary" powers in foreign affairs.[146] On the other hand, Article III of the Constitution grants judicial power to the Supreme Court and lower courts. In 1967, in Katz v. United States, the Supreme Court underscored the importance of judges under the Fourth Amendment—wiretaps require a warrant signed by a neutral magistrate.[147]

The ongoing and difficult question is where the president's inherent authority leaves off and where judicial and legal limits on that authority apply. The decision in Katz stated that its warrant rules applied for ordinary wiretaps used for domestic law enforcement rather than national security. A few years later, the court expressed skepticism about a general exception for national security cases, in part out of concerns that the term "national security" was too vague and could extend too far. In the Keith case, the court specifically left undecided the extent of the president's power to conduct wiretaps without warrants "with respect to the activities of foreign powers, within or without this country."[148]

In passing FISA in 1978, both supporters and critics of broad surveillance powers achieved important goals. Supporters of surveillance gained a statutory system that expressly authorized foreign intelligence wiretaps, lending the weight of congressional approval to surveillance that did not meet all the requirements of ordinary Fourth Amendment searches. Critics of surveillance institutionalized a series of checks and balances on the previously unfettered discretion of the president and the attorney general to conduct surveillance in the name of national security.

The attacks of September 11, 2001, led to important changes to FISA, as part of the USA PATRIOT Act passed in the aftermath. Supporters of the changes emphasized the new types of national security threat posed by Al Qaeda and international terrorism. The original FISA statute was passed during the Cold War, when a major target of national security efforts was to track the activities of Soviet Union agents and its allies. For instance, foreign intelligence wiretaps could be used in connection with communications of the Soviet Embassy or people who worked there. By contrast, the war on terrorism after 2001 involved threats from hard-to-detect individuals who had few or no links to foreign governments. Supporters of broader surveillance argued that foreign intelligence wiretaps should be used more often and with more flexible legal limits. The USA PATRIOT Act provided more of that flexibility.

Over time, however, national security surveillance received a major new round of criticism. *The New York Times* and other newspapers published detailed stories that showed large numbers of national security wiretaps and access to stored communications records without judicial authorization.[149] Among other lawsuits, the largest telephone companies were sued for tens of billions of dollars under the SCA for their role in providing records to the government.[150] Other reports revealed that the number of NSLs for communications and other records was orders of magnitude higher than previously stated by the government.[151]

In the wake of these disclosures, Congress considered FISA once again, notably in the FISA Amendment Act of 2008.[152] This statute gave legal authorization to some of the new surveillance practices, especially where one party to the communication is reasonably believed to be outside of the United States. It granted immunity to the telephone companies so they would not be liable for the records they had provided to the government in the wake of 9/11. The new rules also required more reporting from the government to Congress, and put limits on some of the secrecy about NSLs and other government requests for records in the national security realm.

Additional public debate and reform proposals emerged after the revelations made by Edward Snowden, which began in June 2013. Snowden released tens of thousands of classified documents to media outlets, detailing government programs collecting massive amounts of information on both citizens and noncitizens. The revelations were met with mixed emotions, with some commentators calling him a patriot or whistleblower for his actions and others calling him a traitor. Whatever the judgment may be about the actions, the Snowden revelations reinvigorated the discussion surrounding national security and information privacy.

Beginning soon after June 2013, President Obama worked with two independent review efforts, staffed by people briefed at the TS/SCI level (Top Secret/Sensitive Compartmented Information), the highest level of security clearance. The President's Review Group on Intelligence and Communications Technology ("Review Group"), including an author of this book, Peter Swire, made 46 recommendations in its late 2013 report.[153] When President Obama made his major speech on surveillance reform in January 2014, the Review Group was told that 70 percent of its recommendations were being adopted in letter or spirit. Others have been adopted since. The Privacy and Civil Liberties Oversight Board (PCLOB), an independent agency in the executive branch, released detailed reports on the Section 215 and Section 702 surveillance programs, making numerous recommendations.[154] Overall, PCLOB made 22 recommendations in its Sections 215 and 702 reports, and virtually all have been accepted and implemented.

The Snowden revelations led to significant reforms in U.S. surveillance law and practices. These reforms included passage of the USA FREEDOM Act in 2015, which, among multiple provisions, ended bulk collection under the Section 215 program, and the Judicial Redress Act of 2016, which extends U.S. Privacy Act protections to certain non-U.S. persons. There have also been numerous administrative changes.[155]

For privacy professionals, history since the Snowden revelations illustrates the competing values that come into play when the government makes a national security request for personal information. Company employees, including privacy professionals, generally have a strong desire to help where possible with national security requests. On the other hand, as shown by negative reactions to some surveillance activities post-Snowden, providing information too broadly can lead to legal, public relations, and civil liberties objections.

Responding to national security requests is more complicated because U.S. privacy laws have varying scope and differing definitions for national security exceptions. For instance, HIPAA permits disclosure of PHI "to authorized federal officials for the conduct of lawful intelligence, counter-intelligence, and other national security" under the National Security Act.[156] GLBA has a privacy exception that is more vaguely worded, "for an investigation on a matter related to public safety."[157] By contrast, COPPA and its implementing regulation make no mention of a national security exception.[158] Privacy professionals, IT professionals who provide access to records, and attorneys thus may need to do research in particular settings to determine what sorts of national security disclosures are permitted, for what sorts of records, and to which agencies.

Debates about encryption provide another illustration of the tension between national security and law enforcement on the one hand, and civil liberties concerns and limits on lawful sharing of personal information on the other.[159] In the 2016 case of Apple v. FBI that garnered international attention, the FBI sought the assistance of Apple to gain access to the encrypted phone of one of the assailants in a high-profile shooting in San Bernardino.[160] The FBI obtained a court order requiring Apple to assist the government by creating a custom operating system that would disable key security features on the iPhone.[161] Apple filed a motion with the court asking it to reconsider its decision, expressing the company's concern that complying with the order would result in building a back door into the encryption for all iPhones of that particular model phone.[162] On one side of this case, law enforcement sought information in a mass shooting, and they secured a warrant before proceeding. On the other side, a preeminent technology company warned that its compliance with the order could weaken the technology that protects privacy around the world.[163] The specific court case involving Apple ended when the FBI announced that it had gained access to the encrypted phone without the assistance of the company, but the debate about the government accessing encrypted data led to hearings and proposed legislation in Congress.[164] This debate has been framed by national security and law enforcement agencies as the "going dark" problem—the idea that encryption blinds the ability of officials to see evidence—while civil liberties experts have countered that the current environment is the "Golden Age of Surveillance," due to the explosive growth of personal data that is amassed in databases.[165]

13.4.2 Overview of the Foreign Intelligence Surveillance Act

FISA establishes standards and procedures for electronic surveillance that collects "foreign intelligence" within the United States. FISA orders can be issued when foreign intelligence gathering is "a significant purpose" of the investigation.[166] For law enforcement cases, court orders issue based on probable cause of a crime; FISA orders instead issue on probable cause that the party to be monitored is a "foreign power" or an "agent of a foreign power." FISA orders issue from a special court of federal district court judges, the Foreign Intelligence Surveillance Court (FISC). Historically, only attorneys for the U.S. government appeared before the FISC. The USA FREEDOM Act created a group of independent experts in the area of privacy and civil liberties, known as an *amicus curiae*, to brief the FISC on novel or significant matters of law.[167]

In addition to wiretap orders, FISA authorizes pen register and trap-and-trace orders (for phone numbers, email addresses, and other addressing and routing information) and orders for video surveillance.

Due to the secrecy of government surveillance of agents of foreign powers, entities that receive a FISA order to produce records generally cannot disclose the fact of the order to the targets of investigation. There is generally no disclosure after the fact to the target of a FISA wiretap as there is for law enforcement wiretaps. Nonetheless, there have been significant increases in transparency over time about FISA surveillance. Companies are now allowed to publish statistics about the number of FISA orders and NSLs they receive.[168] Under the USA FREEDOM Act, the government issues yearly transparency reports with more detail than previously, and the U.S. government has declassified a substantial number of orders from the FISC.[169] Over time, FISA orders have grown so that they outnumber traditional law enforcement wiretap orders.[170] The legal details of FISA can be important for communication providers, such as telephone companies and email services, but such issues arise much less often for most other companies.[171]

13.4.3 Section 215 Orders

Section 215 of the USA PATRIOT Act of 2001 received a great deal of public attention after documents released by Edward Snowden stated that the National Security Agency (NSA) had created a database containing a substantial fraction of call detail information for domestic U.S. telephone calls. The USA FREEDOM Act of 2015 ended bulk collection conducted under Section 215, requiring requests by government officials to be based upon specific selectors, such as a telephone number.[172] Section 215 expired when Congress failed to reauthorize it in 2020.[173]

13.4.4 Section 702

Section 702 refers to a provision in the Foreign Intelligence Surveillance Act Amendments Act of 2008 (FISAA), which revised FISA.[174] Section 702 applies to collection of electronic communications that take place within the United States and only authorizes access to the communications of targeted individuals for listed foreign intelligence purposes. One legal question answered by Section 702 was how to govern foreign-to-foreign communications for interception of content that has been stored within the United States. This inquiry is important because communications between two non-U.S. persons is now often stored within the United States due to the growing use of U.S.-based providers for web mail, social networks, and other services.

The basic structure of Section 702 is that the FISC must annually approve certifications by the director of national intelligence and the attorney general setting the terms for Section 702 surveillance.[175] To target the communications of any person, the government must have a foreign intelligence purpose to conduct the collection and a reasonable belief that the person is a non-U.S. citizen located outside of the United States.[176] Section 702 can provide access to the full contents of communications, not just metadata such as to/from information. The court annually reviews and must approve targeting criteria documenting how targeting of a particular person will lead to the acquisition of foreign intelligence information.[177]

Two surveillance programs are authorized under Section 702: PRISM and Upstream. The PRISM program became famous when it was publicly named in one of the first stories based on the Snowden documents.[178] The operation of PRISM resembles data requests made in other settings to service providers. In PRISM collection, acting under a Section 702 court order, the government sends a judicially approved and judicially supervised directive requiring collection of certain "selectors," such as an email address. The directive goes to a U.S.-based service provider. The company's lawyers have the opportunity to challenge the government request. If there is no appeal to the court, the provider is compelled to give the communications sent to or from that selector to the government.[179]

In addition to PRISM, Section 702 supports intelligence collection commonly referred to as the Upstream program. Upstream targets internet-based communications as they pass through physical internet infrastructure located within the Unites States.[180] Upstream is designed to only acquire internet communications that contain a tasked selector. To do so, Upstream filters internet transactions that pass through the internet backbone to eliminate potential domestic transactions; these are then further screened to capture only transactions containing a tasked selector. Emails and other transactions filtered with a tasked selector are stored for access by the NSA, while information that is filtered out is never accessed by the NSA or anyone else.

In 2018, Congress adopted several amendments to Section 702, including requirements for querying procedures consistent with the Fourth Amendment, restrictions on the use of information pertaining to U.S. persons in criminal proceedings, and congressional oversight of "about" collection.[181] Privacy practitioners should be alert for possible changes to Section 702 as Congress regularly reconsiders the details of this provision of FISA.[182]

13.4.5 National Security Letters

An NSL is a category of subpoena that, prior to the PATRIOT Act in 2001, was used narrowly, only for certain financial and communication records of an agent of a foreign power, and only with approval of FBI headquarters.[183] The PATRIOT Act expanded use of NSLs. The number of NSLs rose to tens of thousands per year, with most involving the records of U.S. citizens. Separate and sometimes differing statutory provisions now govern access, without a court order, to communication providers, financial institutions, consumer credit agencies, and travel agencies.[184] As the use of NSLs grew after 2001, a series of reports by the inspector general of the DOJ criticized the lack of effective procedures for implementing rules governing NSLs and related investigatory tools.[185]

As amended in 2006, NSLs can be issued by authorized officials, often the special agent in charge of an FBI field office. The precise language in the statutes varies, but NSLs generally can seek records relevant to protect against international terrorism or clandestine intelligence activities. NSLs can be issued without any judicial involvement. Under the 2006 amendments, however, recipients can petition to a federal court to modify or set aside an NSL if compliance would be unreasonable or oppressive.[186]

The USA PATRIOT Act included strict rules against disclosing that an organization had received an NSL. After court decisions questioned this ban on disclosure on First and Fourth Amendment grounds, the 2006 amendments said that recipients are bound to confidentiality only if there is a finding by the requesting agency of interference with a criminal or counterterrorism investigation or for other listed purposes.[187] Recipients were allowed to disclose the request to those necessary to comply with the request and to an attorney for legal assistance. Recipients could also petition a court to modify or end the secrecy requirement. Breach of the confidentiality requirements, however, was treated as a serious offense, punishable by up to five years of imprisonment and fines of up to $250,000 for an individual.[188]

Reforms in the area of NSLs have focused on the indefinite secrecy previously imposed on companies that received these. In 2014, President Obama announced the indefinite secrecy would change. As of 2015, the FBI now presumptively terminates NSL secrecy for an individual order when an investigation closes, or no more than three years after the opening of a full investigation.[189]

13.5 Conclusion

Many privacy issues can arise in the course of investigations and litigation. Companies can face complex legal rules about when they are required to or forbidden from disclosing personal information, and when they have a choice about whether to do so. Companies grapple with new and challenging issues related to data as technology evolves.[190] As the volume of records involved in investigations and litigation has mounted, the earlier case-by-case approach led by lawyers has evolved into a greater role for organization policies and procedures under more comprehensive information management plans. Lawyers, privacy professionals, and IT experts increasingly must work together to meet the organization's goals while still complying with privacy and disclosure requirements.

Endnotes

1 U.S.C. Title 21, Chapter 9, accessed November 2017, https://www.law.cornell.edu/uscode/text/21/chapter-9.

2 See U.S. Department of Labor, Occupational Health and Safety, accessed November 2017, https://www.osha.gov/pls/oshaweb/owadisp.show_document?p_table=FEDERAL_REGISTER&p_id=16312.

3 Covered entities, such as hospitals, are permitted to disclose protected health information (PHI) without the individual's consent when there is a mandate contained in law that compels the entity to make that disclosure of PHI and the mandate is enforceable in a court of law. 45 C.F.R. § 164.512(a)(1), accessed November 2017 https://www.law.cornell.edu/cfr/text/45/164.512.

4 Fed. R. Civ. Pro. 45(g), accessed November 2017, https://www.law.cornell.edu/rules/frcp/rule_45.

5 18 U.S.C. § 3123(a), accessed November 2017, https://www.law.cornell.edu/uscode/text/18/3123.

6 18 U.S.C. § 2703(d), accessed November 2017, https://www.law.cornell.edu/uscode/text/18/2703.

7 18 U.S.C. §§ 2510-2522, accessed November 2017, https://www.law.cornell.edu/uscode/text/18/2510.

8 45 C.F.R. § 164.524, accessed November 2017, https://www.law.cornell.edu/cfr/text/45/164.524; 45 C.F.R. § 164.528, accessed November 2017, https://www.law.cornell.edu/cfr/text/45/164.528; 45 C.F.R. § 164.502(a)(2), accessed November 2017, https://www.law.cornell.edu/cfr/text/45/164.502.

9 Roe v. Wade, a 1973 decision of the Supreme Court of the United States, held that the U.S. Constitution recognized a woman's right to terminate her pregnancy by abortion. Roe v. Wade, Supreme Court of the United States, January 22, 1973, https://www.oyez.org/cases/1971/70-18. Roe v. Wade was overturned by the 2022 decision of the Supreme Court of the United States in Dobbs v. Jackson Women's Health Organization, Supreme Court of the United States, June 24, 2022, https://www.oyez.org/cases/2021/19-1392; see Daniel Sutton, "HHS Issues Guidance on Post-Dobbs Protections Under HIPAA Privacy Rule," July 13, 2022, https://ogletree.com/insights/hhs-issues-guidance-on-post-dobbs-protections-under-hipaa-privacy-rule/.

10 "HIPAA Privacy Rule and Disclosures of Information Relating to Reproductive Health," Office for Civil Rights, U.S. Department of Health and Human Services, June 29, 2022, https://www.hhs.gov/hipaa/for-professionals/privacy/guidance/phi-reproductive-health/index.html.

11 18 U.S.C. §§ 2510-2511, accessed November 2017, https://www.law.cornell.edu/uscode/text/18/2510.

12 The USA PATRIOT Act defines a "computer trespasser" as "a person who accesses a protected computer without authorization." 18 U.S.C. § 2510(21), accessed November 2017, https://www.law.cornell.edu/uscode/text/18/2510.

13 Section 217 of the USA PATRIOT Act, accessed November 2017, https://www.law.cornell.edu/uscode/text/18/2511.

14 Opt-in provisions require a potential customer to choose to be involved in the organization's services before the organization can act. Opt-out provisions apply to existing customers who receive services from the organization, and who can individually exercise the ability to end receiving such services. Jeanne Hopkins, "The Ultimate Glossary: 44 Email Marketing Terms Marketers Must Know," *HubSpot* (blog), updated June 10, 2021, https://blog.hubspot.com/blog/tabid/6307/bid/7595/the-ultimate-glossary-44-email-marketing-terms-marketers-must-know.aspx.

15 The scope of evidentiary privileges in the federal courts is defined by the courts and generally is similar to state law. For civil cases, the evidentiary privileges are governed by Federal Rules of Evidence 501, accessed November 2017, https://www.law.cornell.edu/rules/fre/rule_501.

16 "The Clinton-Gore Plan to Enhance Consumers Financial Privacy: Protecting Core Values in the Information Age," The White House, May 1, 2000, https://clintonwhitehouse3.archives.gov/WH/New/html/20000501_4.html. For a more detailed discussion, view "Financial Privacy" at PeterSwire.net, accessed November 2017, http://peterswire.net/archive/psfinancialpage.htm; Rule 9037. Privacy Protection for Filings Made with the Court, Federal Rules of Bankruptcy Procedure, accessed November 2019, https://www.law.cornell.edu/rules/frbp/rule_9037. The 2019 amendments to the bankruptcy rules provide a procedure for redacting documents previously filed. Cooley LLP, "Blog: Amendments to the Federal Rules of Bankruptcy

Procedure Take Effect December 1, 2019," JDSupra, November 5, 2019, https://www.jdsupra.com/legalnews/blog-amendments-to-the-federal-rules-of-35425/.

17 See Conferences, Center for Legal & Court Technology, accessed November 2019, https://law.wm.edu/academics/intellectuallife/researchcenters/clct/.

18 See Madanes v. Madanes, 186 F.R.D. 279, 288 (S.D.N.Y. 1997), accessed November 2019, http://law.justia.com/cases/federal/district-courts/FSupp/981/241/2282097/.

19 45 C.F.R. § 164.512(e), accessed November 2019, https://www.law.cornell.edu/cfr/text/45/164.512.

20 Fed. R. Civ. Pro. 5.2, accessed November 2019, https://www.law.cornell.edu/rules/frcp/rule_5.2.

21 Fed. R. Crim. Pro. 49.1(e), accessed November 2017, https://www.law.cornell.edu/rules/frcrmp/rule_49.1.

22 11 U.S.C. § 105(a), accessed November 2017, https://www.law.cornell.edu/uscode/text/11/105.

23 Rule 49.1 of the Federal Rules of Criminal Procedure, accessed November 2019, https://www.law.cornell.edu/rules/frcrmp/rule_49.1; Rule 9037. Privacy Protection for Filings Made with the Court, Federal Rules of Bankruptcy Procedure.

24 Fed. R. Crim. Pro. 49.1(a)(5), accessed November 2017, https://www.law.cornell.edu/rules/frcrmp/rule_49.1.

25 See generally "Federal Rule Changes Affecting E-Discovery Are Almost Here - Are You Ready This Time?," accessed July 2023, https://www.ediscoverylaw.com/wp-content/uploads/2015/10/Rules-Amendment-Alert-100115.pdf.

26 Mark Diamond, "How to Implement a Record Retention Schedule for Electronic and Other Records," Association of Corporate Counsel, February 22, 2017, https://www.acc.com/resource-library/how-implement-record-retention-schedule-electronic-and-other-records; see Reda Chouffani, "Is it Legal to Record Virtual Meeting and Video Conferences?" TechTarget, June 3, 2021, https://www.techtarget.com/searchcontentmanagement/tip/Is-it-legal-to-record-virtual-meetings-and-video-conferences.

27 The Sedona Principles, Third Edition: Best Practices, The Sedona Conference, October 2017, https://thesedonaconference.org/publication/The_Sedona_Principles.

28 In a footnote, the court notes, "Although Federal Rule of Civil Procedure 37(e) is not cited by the parties, and does not apply under the circumstances of this case, by analogy the Rule is useful in understanding what steps parties should take to preserve electronic evidence. Rule 37(e) states: 'Absent exceptional circumstances, a court may not impose sanctions under these rules on a party for failing to provide electronically stored information lost as a result of the routine, good faith operation of an electronic information system.'" Arista Records LLC v. Usenet.com, Inc., 608 F. Supp. 2d 409, 413 (S.D.N.Y. 2009), https://www.courtlistener.com/opinion/1465022/arista-records-llc-v-usenet-com-inc/. In 2015, Federal Rule of Civil Procedure 37(e) (Rule 37) was rewritten to add a reasonable component to preservation, examining "whether the data should have been preserved" when litigation was likely and "whether the data loss resulted from a failure to take reasonable steps to preserve" the data. See Gretchen Moore, "A Rule 37 Refresher – As Applied to a Ransomware Attack," *The National Law Review*, July 14, 2022, https://www.natlawreview.com/article/rule-37-refresher-applied-to-ransomware-

attack?utm_source=Robly.com&utm_medium=email&utm_campaign=2022-07-18NLRCybersecurity+Legal+News&utm_content=44be3ffd0371d62f091c28115253b27f.

29 Doe v. Norwalk Cmmunity College, 248 F.R.D. 372, 378 (D. Conn. 2007), accessed July 2023, https://casetext.com/case/doe-v-norwalk-community-college.

30 Cf. Wal-Mart Stores v. Lee, 348 Ark. 707 (Ark. 2002), accessed November 2017, https://www.courtlistener.com/opinion/1383972/wal-mart-stores-inc-v-lee/.

31 Lewy v. Remington Arms Co., 836 F.2d 1104, 1111 (8th Cir. Mo. 1988), accessed November 2017, http://cyber.law.harvard.edu/digitaldiscovery/library/spoliation/lewy.html.

32 Zubulake v. UBS Warburg LLC, 220 F.R.D. 212, 218 (S.D.N.Y. 2003). ("Once a party reasonably anticipates litigation, it must suspend its routine document retention/destruction policy and put in place a 'litigation hold' to ensure the preservation of relevant documents."), accessed November 2017, https://cdn2.hubspot.net/hub/179343/file-357162524-pdf/docs/zubulake_v__ubs_warburg_llc.pdf.

33 45 C.F.R. § 164.502(a)(1)(iv), accessed November 2017, https://www.law.cornell.edu/cfr/text/45/164.502.

34 45 C.F.R. § 164.512(e)(1)(I), accessed November 2017, https://www.law.cornell.edu/cfr/text/45/164.512.

35 45 C.F.R. § 164.512(e)(iv)(A & B), accessed November 2017, https://www.law.cornell.edu/cfr/text/45/164.512.

36 45 C.F.R. § 164.512(e)(v), accessed November 2017, https://www.law.cornell.edu/cfr/text/45/164.512.

37 15 U.S.C. § 6802(e)(8), accessed November 2017, https://www.law.cornell.edu/uscode/text/15/6802.

38 Marks v. Global Mortgage Group, Inc., 218 F.R.D. 492 (S.D. W. Va. 2003), https://casetext.com/case/marks-v-global-mortgage-group-inc.

39 For a detailed discussion of the U.S. perspective and the EU perspective on these discovery requests, view Gary Weingarden and Matthias Artzt, "Stuck in the Middle with You: When U.S. Discovery Orders Hit GDPR," IAPP, January 26, 2021, https://iapp.org/news/a/stuck-in-the-middle-with-you-when-u-s-discovery-orders-hit-the-gdpr. For an overview of the impacts of the General Data Protection Regulation to e-discovery, view David Kessler, Jamie Nowak, and Sumera Khan, "The Potential Impact of Article 48 of the General Data Protection Regulation on Cross Border Discovery from the United States," *The Sedona Conference Journal* 17, no. 2 (2016), https://www.nortonrosefulbright.com/-/media/files/nrf/nrfweb/imported/20170126--the-potential-impact-of-article-48-of-the-general-data-protection-regulation-on-cross-bord.pdf.

40 See Fred H. Cate and Margaret P. Eisenhauer, "Between a Rock and a Hard Place: The Conflict between European Data Protection Laws and U.S. Civil Litigation Document Production Requirements," *BNA Privacy and Security Law Report* 229 (2007); Peter Swire, "When Does GDPR Act as a Blocking Statute: The Relevance of a Lawful Basis for Transfer," Cross-Border Data Forum, November 4, 2019, at https://www.crossborderdataforum.org/when-does-gdpr-act-as-a-blocking-statute-the-relevance-of-a-lawful-basis-for-transfer.

41 Doug Austin, "Cross-Border Discovery and the Battle Between Relevancy and Data Protection Concerns," JD Supra, July 14, 2022, https://www.jdsupra.com/legalnews/cross-border-discovery-and-the-battle-1747022/. For example, the Pennsylvania court in

Giorgi Global Holdings v. Smulski found that, when the defendant is a U.S. citizen sued in the U.S., that party bears the burden of showing that GDPR bars production of relevant documents. Doug Austin, "Court Finds that GDPR Doesn't Protect Polish Resident from Responding to Discovery Requests: eDiscovery Case Law," eDiscovery Today, June 25, 2020, https://ediscoverytoday.com/2020/06/25/court-finds-that-gdpr-doesnt-protect-polish-resident-from-responding-to-discovery-requests-ediscovery-case-law/. In *Cadence Design System v. Syntronic,* the California court found no conflict between U.S. discovery requirements and China's Personal Information Protection Law (PIPL) because "the Court's order to produce computers for inspection in the United States creates a legal obligation sufficient to invoke the exception" in the Chinese law. Doug Austin, "PIPL Doesn't Prohibit Production of Computers, Court Rules: eDiscovery Case Law," eDiscovery Today, July 14, 2022, https://ediscoverytoday.com/2022/07/14/pipl-doesnt-prohibit-production-of-computers-court-rules-ediscovery-case-law/.

42 Spain v. American Bureau of Shipping, 2006 WL 3208579 (S.D.N.Y. 2006). For an analysis of the case, view Catrien Noorda and Stefan Hanloser, *E-discovery and Data Privacy: A Practical Guide,* (Kluwer Law International, 2010).

43 Columbia Pictures, Inc. v. Bunnell, 245 F.R.D. 443, 453 (C.D. Cal. 2007) (quoting Societe Nationale Industrielle Aerospatiale v. United States Dist. Court for S. Dist. IA, 482 U.S. 522 (1987)), https://casetext.com/case/columbia-pictures.

44 In Re Xarelto (Rivaroxaban) Products Liability Litigation, MDL No. 2592, 2016 WL 2855221 (E.D. La) May 16, 2016. For a discussion of the case, see Stephan Cornell, "E-Discovery in Cross-Border Litigation: The 'Blocking Statute Defense,'" Fox Rothschild, May 25, 2016, http://www.foxrothschild.com/publications/e-discovery-in-cross-border-litigation-the-blocking-statute-defense/.

45 20: Convention of 18 March 1970 on the Taking of Evidence Abroad in Civil or Commercial Matters, Hague Conference on Private International Law, https://www.hcch.net/en/instruments/conventions/full-text/?cid=82.

46 Societe Nationale Industrielle Aerospatiale v. United States Dist. Court for S. Dist. IA, 482 *U.S. 522 (1987),* https://supreme.justia.com/cases/federal/us/482/522/case.html.

47 Societe Nationale Industrielle Aerospatiale v. United States Dist. Court for S. Dist. IA, 482 U.S. at 568.

48 Weiss v. Nat'l Westminster Bank, PLC, 242 F.R.D. 33 (E.D.N.Y. 2007), https://casetext.com/case/weiss-v-national-westminster-bank.

49 Aimée Canty, "Getting Discovery Across Borders: Four Tips (and Some Obstacles) for Litigation Across International Lines," ABA, March 23, 2020, https://www.americanbar.org/groups/litigation/committees/pretrial-practice-discovery/practice/2020/getting-discovery-across-borders/.

50 Albert Barsocchini, "Preserve in Place v. Collect to Preserve," Law.com, August 24, 2009, https://www.law.com/almID/4dcafb2a160ba0ad57001895/.

51 Katz v. United States, 389 U.S. 347 (1967), https://supreme.justia.com/cases/federal/us/389/347/case.html.

52 Fourth Amendment to the U.S. Constitution, National Archives, accessed November 2019, https://www.archives.gov/founding-docs/constitution.

53 Schmerber v. California, 384 U.S. 757 (1966), https://supreme.justia.com/cases/federal/us/384/757/case.html.

54 Olmstead v. United States, 277 U.S. 438 (1928), https://supreme.justia.com/cases/federal/us/277/438/case.html.

55 Olmstead v. United States, 277 U.S. 438 (1928), Brandeis dissent.

56 Katz v. United States, 389 U.S. 347.

57 Katz v. United States, 389 U.S. 347, Harlan concurrence.

58 United States v. Miller, 425 U.S. 435 (1976) (checking account records), https://supreme.justia.com/cases/federal/us/425/435/; Smith v. Maryland, 442 U.S. 735 (1979) (phone-calling records), https://supreme.justia.com/cases/federal/us/442/735/case.html.

59 United States v. Jones, 132 S. Ct. 945 (2012), https://supreme.justia.com/cases/federal/us/565/400/.

60 Riley v. California, 134 S. Ct. 2473 (2014), https://supreme.justia.com/cases/federal/us/573/373.

61 Marc Rotenberg and Alan Butler, "Symposium: In Riley v. California, a Unanimous Supreme Court Sets Out Fourth Amendment for Digital Age," *SCOTUSblog*, June 26, 2014, www.scotusblog.com/2014/06/symposium-in-riley-v-california-a-unanimous-supreme-court-sets-out-fourth-amendment-for-digital-age/.

62 Carpenter v. United States, 585 U.S. (2018), https://supreme.justia.com/cases/federal/us/585/16-402/.

63 "Pen registers" are records of dialed phone numbers. In Carpenter, the records at issue had been acquired under the Electronic Computer Privacy Act's requirement for "specific and articulable facts." The court determined this was not sufficient protection for the cell-location data. The third-party doctrine, which states there is no reasonable expectation of privacy in information shared with a third-party business, arises from U.S. Supreme Court cases including United States v. Miller and Smith v. Maryland. In United States v. Miller, the Court held that a defendant had no reasonable expectation of privacy in the bank records associated with revenue he earned through making bootleg liquor with an unregistered still and on which he did not pay taxes. United States v. Miller, 425 U.S. 435 (1976), 436. The Court pointed to Katz's language stating that "[w]hat a person knowingly exposes to the public . . . is not a subject of Fourth Amendment protection." Carpenter v. United States, 442 (citing Katz v. United States). The court in United States v. Miller noted that "the Fourth Amendment does not prohibit the obtaining of information revealed to a third party and conveyed by him to Government authorities, even if the information is revealed on the assumption that it will be used only for a limited purpose and the confidence placed in the third party will not be betrayed." United States v. Miller, 443. The same principle was applied in Smith v. Maryland where the court held that a pen register was covered under the third-party doctrine. Smith v. Maryland, 442 U.S. 735 (1935), 743-744. The court reasoned that "when he used his phone, petitioner voluntarily conveyed numerical information to the telephone company and 'exposed' that information to its equipment in the ordinary course of business. In so doing, the petitioner assumed the risk that the company would reveal to police the numbers he dialed." Smith v Maryland 744. For further discussions concerning the third-party doctrine, view Peter Swire, Justin Hemmings, and Suzanne Vergnolle, "A Mutual Legal Assistance Case Study: The United States and France," *Wisconsin International Law Review* 34, no. 323 (2017), https://papers.ssrn.com/sol3/papers.cfm?abstract_id=2921289 and Orin Kerr, "The Case for the Third-Party Doctrine," *107 Mich. L. Rev.* 561 (2009), https://repository.law.umich.edu/mlr/vol107/iss4/1/.

64 Carpenter v. United States, 585 U.S. (2018). For an analysis of the Carpenter v. United States ruling, view Kimberly Kiefer Peretti and James Harvey, "U.S. Supreme Court Builds on Individuals' Privacy Rights," Alston & Bird, July 26, 2018, https://www.alston.com/en/insights/ publications/2018/07/us-supreme-court-builds-on-individuals-privacy.

65 See Florencio Travieso and Em Lyon, "The Legal Implications of Digital Privacy," Government Technology, January 15, 2019, https://www.govtech.com/public-safety/The-Legal-Implications-of-Digital-Privacy.html; *see* also Marley Degner, "Riley and the Third-Party Doctrine," Pillsbury, April 9, 2015, https://www.pillsburylaw.com/siteFiles/Publications/AR_Riley_and_the_thirdparty_doctrine_Degner_4915.pdf.

66 "The thorny questions of third-party sharing don't neatly apply to the criminal suspects in genetic-genealogy cases, because they haven't themselves uploaded their DNA." Rafil Kroll-Zaidi, "Your DNA Test Could Send a Relative to Jail," *The New York Times*, January 3, 2022, https://www.nytimes.com/2021/12/27/magazine/dna-test-crime-identification-genome.html.

67 Roe v. Wade, a 1973 decision of the Supreme Court of the United States, held that the U.S. Constitution recognized a woman's right to terminate her pregnancy by abortion. Roe v. Wade, Supreme Court of the United States, January 22, 1973, https://www.oyez.org/cases/1971/70-18. Roe v. Wade was overturned by the 2022 decision of the Supreme Court of the United States in Dobbs v. Jackson Women's Health Organization, Supreme Court of the United States, June 24, 2022, https://www.oyez.org/cases/2021/19-1392.

68 "New Protections for People Who Need Abortion Care and Birth Control," Office of Governor Gavin Newsom, September 27, 2022, https://www.gov.ca.gov/2022/09/27/new-protections-for-people-who-need-abortion-care-and-birth-control/; see Brian Fung and Clare Duffy, "California Bars Tech Companies from Complying with Other States' Abortion-Related Warrants," CNN Business, September 29, 2022, https://www.cnn.com/2022/09/29/tech/california-tech-abortion-warrant-ban/index.html.

69 Aaron Cooper, "Two Americas: Cross-Border Data Requests Post-Dobbs," *Lawfare* (blog), September 22, 2022, https://www.lawfareblog.com/two-americas-cross-border-data-requests-post-dobbs; Dana Brusca, Bart Huff, Marc Zwillinger, "California Poised to Enact Law Prohibiting Electronic Service Providers from Complying with Out-of-State Legal Process Relating to Abortion Inquiries," *ZwillGenBlog*, September 2, 2022, https://www.zwillgen.com/law-enforcement/california-prohibiting-electronic-communication-services-providers-complying-out-of-state-legal-process-abortion-inquiries/.

70 As discussed earlier in this section, a general warrant specifies the offense but allows the government official to determine the persons to be arrested and the places to be searched. Steagald v. United States, 451 U.S. 20 (1981), https://www.oyez.org/cases/1980/79-6777.

71 Isha Marathe, "Post-'Dobbs,' Privacy Attorneys Prepare for Increased Data Surveillance," Law.com, June 27, 2022, https://www.law.com/legaltechnews/2022/06/27/post-dobbs-privacy-attorneys-prepare-for-increased-data-surveillance/; see Orin Kerr, "The Fourth Amendment and Geofence Warrants: A Critical Look at United States v. Chatrie," *Lawfare* (blog), March 12, 2022, https://www.lawfareblog.com/fourth-amendment-and-geofence-warrants-critical-look-united-states-v-chatrie; Nathaniel Sobel, "Do Geofence Warrants Violate the Fourth Amendment," *Lawfare* (blog), February 24, 2020, https://www.lawfareblog.com/do-geofence-warrants-violate-fourth-amendment; see also "Geofence Warrants and the Fourth Amendment," *Harvard Law Review* 134, no. 7, May 10, 2021, https://harvardlawreview.org/2021/05/geofence-warrants-and-the-fourth-amendment/.

72 12 U.S.C. § 3401 et seq., accessed November 2017, https://www.law.cornell.edu/uscode/text/12/chapter-35; 18 U.S.C. § 2510 et seq., accessed July 2023, https://www.law.cornell.edu/uscode/text/18/2510.

73 45 C.F.R. § 164.512(f), accessed November 2017, https://www.law.cornell.edu/cfr/text/45/164.512.

74 45 C.F.R. § 164.512(a), accessed November 2017, https://www.law.cornell.edu/cfr/text/45/164.512.

75 See Erin Pauley, "Conflicts Among Federal and State Wiretap Statutes Present Practical Challenges for Businesses," *The National Law Review*, September 26, 2018, https://www.natlawreview.com/article/conflicts-among-federal-and-state-wiretap-statutes-present-practical-challenges.

76 In 2019, users of a popular home video device sued its makers after hackers were able to access video feeds and taunt individuals inside the owners' houses. The legal claims in the case include invasion of privacy, negligence, and violation of unfair competition. Christina Carrega, "Amazon, Ring Face $5 Million Proposed Class Action Lawsuit that Alleges Camera 'Vulnerable' to Cyber-Attacks," *ABC News*, December 27, 2019, https://abcnews.go.com/US/amazon-ring-face-million-proposed-class-action-lawsuit/story?id=67948687.

77 Omnibus Crime Control and Safe Streets Act of 1968, Pub. L. No. 90-351, accessed November 2017, https://transition.fcc.gov/Bureaus/OSEC/library/legislative_histories/1615.pdf.

78 18 U.S.C. § 2510, accessed November 2017, https://www.law.cornell.edu/uscode/text/18/2510.

79 18 U.S.C. § 2510.

80 ECPA permits law enforcement to compel a provider to disclose information using a subpoena, a 'd order,' or a search warrant – depending on the type of data sought. "Searching and Seizing Computers and Obtaining Electronic Evidence in Criminal Investigations," U.S. Department of Justice, July 2002, https://cyber.harvard.edu/practicallawyering/Week9DOJECPAExcerpt.pdf. Law enforcement can compel a provider to produce basic subscriber information, such as name, address, and payment method for services, using a subpoena. 18 U.S.C. § 2703(c), https://www.law.cornell.edu/uscode/text/18/2703. The legal threshold is relatively low that law enforcement must meet to obtain a subpoena for evidence relevant to a criminal investigation. To compel a provider to produce all other non-content customer records, law enforcement must obtain a 'd order' – so named because it refers to section d of the statute. 18 U.S.C. § 2703(d), https://www.law.cornell.edu/uscode/text/18/2703. For a 'd order' to be issued, a judge must determine that law enforcement has met the standard of "specific and articulable facts" to believe that the data sought is relevant to the criminal investigation – a higher standard than required for a subpoena. In practice, law enforcement must obtain a search warrant to access the content of email communications. To obtain a search warrant, a judge must determine that the standard of "probable cause" has been met by law enforcement – a constitutional standard and a higher standard than is required for a 'd order.' 18 U.S.C. § 2703(a) (for content held for 180 days or less), https://www.law.cornell.edu/uscode/text/18/2703; see United States v. Warshak, 631 F.3d 266 (6th Circuit 2010) (interpreting ECPA to say that requests for content of communications, such as emails, require a judge-issued warrant based on probable cause), https://www.opn.ca6.uscourts.gov/opinions.pdf/10a0377p-06.pdf; see also Robert Peters, et al.,

"Not an Ocean Away, Only a Moment Away: A Prosecutor's Primer to Obtaining Remotely Stored Data," *Mitchell Hamline Law Review* 47, no. 3 (2021), (stating that the "Warshak court ruled that the Fourth Amendment required law enforcement to procure a search warrant authorizing the examination of the emails' content"), https://open.mitchellhamline.edu/cgi/viewcontent.cgi?article=1257&context=mhlr; DeBrae Kennedy-Mayo, Peter Swire, Sreenidhi Srinivasan, and Madhulika Srikivasan, "India-U.S. Data Sharing for Law Enforcement: Blueprint for Reforms," Observer Research Foundation, January 17, 2019, (stating that because of the "U.S. Supreme Court's history of applying strict Fourth Amendment protections to changing technologies, observers have expressed their belief that there is a strong likelihood the Warshak approach would be adopted if the US Supreme Court were to review this topic"), https://www.orfonline.org/wp-content/uploads/2019/01/MLAT-Book-_v8_web-1.pdf.

81 18 U.S.C. § 2511(2)(D), accessed November 2017, https://www.law.cornell.edu/uscode/text/18/2511.

82 Charles Kennedy and Peter Swire, "State Wiretaps and Electronic Surveillance After September 11," *Hastings Law Journal* 54: 971 (2003) (Appendix A listing state wiretap laws), https://www.peterswire.net/archive/appendix_A_state_wiretap_laws.pdf. For a current list of state laws, view "Reporters Recording Guide," Reporter's Committee for Freedom of the Press, accessed July 2023, https://www.rcfp.org/reporters-recording-guide.

83 Justin Tomevi and Katelyn Rohrbaugh, "Legal Risks of Recording Video Conference Calls," Barley Snyder, June 2, 2020, https://www.barley.com/legal-risks-of-recording-video-conference-calls/; see Chouffani, "Is it Legal to Record Virtual Meeting and Video Conferences?"

84 8 U.S.C. § 2511(2)(a)(i), accessed November 2017, https://www.law.cornell.edu/uscode/text/18/2511.

85 8 U.S.C. § 2510(5), accessed November 2017, https://www.law.cornell.edu/uscode/text/18/2510.

86 Martha W. Barnett and Scott D. Makar, " 'In the Ordinary Court of Business': The Legal Limits of Workplace Wiretapping," *Communications and Entertainment Law Journal* 10 (1988): 715.

87 Matthew W. Finkin, *Privacy in Employment Law,* Third Edition (Arlington, VA: BNA Books, 2009), 365–369.

88 For instance, for a call from a state with one-party telephone recording notification to California, the latter's two-party notification law outweighs the one-party notification law—that is, both or all parties must consent to the telephone call recording. Kearney v. Salomon Smith Barney Inc., 39 Cal. 4th 95 (2006), http://caselaw.findlaw.com/ca-supreme-court/1099204.html.

89 18 U.S.C. §§ 2701-2712, accessed November 2017, https://www.law.cornell.edu/uscode/text/18/part-I/chapter-121.

90 "At inception, Section 2703(b) of the SCA, on its face, permitted the government to obtain certain content from 'remote computing services' (which would include many cloud providers) without a warrant or showing of probable cause, provided the content has been in storage for more than 180 days. In U.S. v. Warshak, the Sixth Circuit addressed whether this was constitutional, concluding that 18 U.S.C. §2703(b) violated the Fourth Amendment to the extent it permitted the government to obtain emails from a remote computing service without showing probable cause. ... Though the ruling applies

only in the Sixth Circuit, the Department of Justice has agreed, as a matter of policy, to follow *Warshak* generally and to seek warrants to obtain email content." Kate Lucente and Andrew Serwin, "The Government in Your Cloud," DLA Piper, July 24, 2019.

91 18 U.S.C. § 2701(c)(1), accessed November 2017, https://www.law.cornell.edu/uscode/text/18/2701.

92 18 U.S.C. § 2701(c)(2), accessed November 2017, https://www.law.cornell.edu/uscode/text/18/2701.

93 19 Del. C. § 705, accessed November 2017, http://codes.findlaw.com/de/title-19-labor/de-code-sect-19-705.html.

94 Conn. Gen. Laws. Chap. 557, § 31-48d, accessed November 2017, https://www.cga.ct.gov/current/pub/chap_557.htm.

95 18 U.S.C. § 2703(f), accessed November 2017, https://www.law.cornell.edu/uscode/text/18/2703.

96 "A litigation hold, also known as a 'preservation order' or 'hold order' is a temporary suspension of the company's document retention destruction policies for the documents that may be relevant to a lawsuit or that are reasonably anticipated to be relevant." "Litigation Hold Law and Legal Definition," USLegal, accessed November 2019, https://definitions.uslegal.com/l/litigation-hold/.

97 18 U.S.C. § 3123, accessed November 2017, https://www.law.cornell.edu/uscode/text/18/3123.

98 H.R. 2048 USA FREEDOM Act of 2015, https://www.congress.gov/bill/114th-congress/house-bill/2048/text. For additional information, view Peter Swire, "US Surveillance Law, Safe Harbor, and Reforms Since 2013," December 17, 2015, https://fpf.org/wp-content/uploads/2015/12/White-Paper-Swire-US-EU-Surveillance.pdf.

99 Communications Assistance to Law Enforcement Act of 1994, 47 U.S.C. §§ 1001-1021 (1994), https://www.law.cornell.edu/uscode/text/47/chapter-9.

100 See "Communications Assistance for Law Enforcement," Federal Communications Commission, updated July 6, 2023, https://www.fcc.gov/public-safety-and-homeland-security/policy-and-licensing-division/general/communications-assistance.

101 American Council on Education v. FCC, 451 F.3d 226 (D.C. Cir. 2006), http://openjurist.org/451/f3d/226/american-council-on-education-v-federal-communications-commission.

102 The act authorizes classified information to be shared with entities that have the appropriate security clearances. Cybersecurity Information Sharing Act of 2015, Section 103(a), https://epic.org/privacy/cybersecurity/Cybersecruity-Act-of-2015.pdf; see Boris Segalis, Andrew Hoffman, and Kathryn Linsky, "Federal Cybersecurity Information Sharing Act Signed into Law," *Data Protection Report*, Norton Rose Fulbright (January 3, 2016), https://www.dataprotectionreport.com/2016/01/federal-cybersecurity-information-sharing-act-signed-into-law/.

103 The configuration of a firewall mechanism would be an example of a "defensive measure." Hanley Chew and Tyler Newby, "The Cybersecurity Information Sharing Act of 2015"; see Rick Link, "What You Need to Know about the Cybersecurity Information Sharing Act of 2015" *ISACA Now Blog*, ISACA, January 2016; Examples of "cyberthreat indicators" include malware found on a company's network and IP addresses associated with botnet command and control servers. Hanley Chew and Tyler Newby, "The Cybersecurity Information Sharing Act of 2015: An Overview," *Fenwick Privacy*

Bulletin, Fall 2016, Fenwick & West LLP, October 24, 2016, https://www.fenwick.com/Publications/Pages/Fenwick-Privacy-Bulletin-Fall-2016.aspx.

104 Brad Karp, Paul, Weiss, Rifkind, Wharton & Garrison LLP, "Federal Guidance on the Cybersecurity Information Sharing Act of 2015," Harvard Law School Forum on Corporate Governance, March 3, 2016, https://corpgov.law.harvard.edu/2016/03/03/federal-guidance-on-the-cybersecurity-information-sharing-act-of-2015/; *see* Segalis, Hoffman, and Linsky, "Federal Cybersecurity Information Sharing Act Signed into Law."

105 CISA defines "cyber threat indicator" as "[I]nformation that is necessary to describe or identify:
(A) malicious reconnaissance, including anomalous patterns of communications that appear to be transmitted for the purpose of gathering technical information related to a cybersecurity threat or security vulnerability;
(B) a method of defeating a security control or exploitation of a security vulnerability;
(C) a security vulnerability, including anomalous activity that appears to indicate the existence of a security vulnerability;
(D) a method of causing a user with legitimate access to an information system or information that is stored on, processed by or transiting an information system to unwittingly enable the defeat of a security control or exploitation of a security vulnerability;
(E) malicious cyber command or control;
(F) the actual or potential harm caused by an incident, including a description of the information exfiltrated as a result of a particular cybersecurity threat;
(G) any other attribute of a cybersecurity threat, if disclosure of such attribute is not otherwise prohibited by law;
(H) any combination thereof;"
Cybersecurity Act of 2015, Section 102(6), https://epic.org/privacy/cybersecurity/Cybersecruity-Act-of-2015.pdf.

106 CISA defines a "cybersecurity purpose" as "the purpose of protecting an information system or information that is stored on, processed by or transiting an information system from a cybersecurity threat or security vulnerability." Cybersecurity Information Sharing Act of 2015, Section 102(4).

107 Cybersecurity Information Sharing Act of 2015, Section 104(c)(1).

108 Cybersecurity Information Sharing Act of 2015, Section 106(b)(1).

109 Cybersecurity Information Sharing Act of 2015, Section 104(d)(2)(A), (B).

110 Cybersecurity Information Sharing Act of 2015, Section 105(d)(1).

111 Cybersecurity Information Sharing Act of 2015, Section 105(d)(3).

112 Cybersecurity Information Sharing Act of 2015, Section 105(d)(5)(D)(i), (ii).

113 Cybersecurity Information Sharing Act of 2015, Section 104(a)(1)(A)–(C), (b)(1)(A)–(C).

114 Cybersecurity Information Sharing Act of 2015, Section 106(a); see generally Karp, Weiss, Rifkind, Wharton & Garrison LLP "Federal Guidelines on the Cybersecurity Information Sharing Act of 2015."

115 See Boris Segalis, Andrew Hoffman and Kathryn Linsky, "Federal Cybersecurity Information Sharing Act Signed into Law"; Graeme Caldwell, "Why You Should be Concerned about the Cybersecurity Information Sharing Act," *TechCrunch*, February 7, 2016, https://techcrunch.com/2016/02/07/why-you-should-be-concerned-about-cisa/.

116 "Privacy and Civil Liberties Final Guidelines: Cybersecurity Information Sharing Act of 2015," U.S. Department of Homeland Security and U.S. Department of Justice (June 15, 2018), https://www.cisa.gov/sites/default/files/publications/Privacy%20and%20Civil%20Liberties%20Guidelines%20under%20the%20Cybersecurity%20Information%20Sharing%20Act%20of%202015_0.pdf.

117 12 U.S.C. §§ 3401-3422, accessed November 2017, https://www.law.cornell.edu/uscode/text/12/chapter-35.

118 12 U.S.C. § 3402, accessed November 2017, https://www.law.cornell.edu/uscode/text/12/3402.

119 The Right to Financial Privacy Act, Epic.org, accessed November 2017, https://epic.org/privacy/rfpa/.

120 42 U.S.C. §§2000aa to 2000aa-7, x accessed November 2017, https://www.law.cornell.edu/uscode/text/42/chapter-21A.

121 Zurcher v. Stanford Daily, 436 U.S. 547 (1978), https://supreme.justia.com/cases/federal/us/436/547/case.html.

122 Chapter Three: Existing Federal Privacy Laws, Center for Democracy & Technology, November 30, 2008, https://cdt.org/insight/existing-federal-privacy-laws/.

123 Nine states are listed on the summary of the act provided by the Electronic Privacy Information Act. The Privacy Protection Act of 1980, EPIC.org, accessed November 2019, https://epic.org/privacy/ppa/.

124 42 U.S.C. § 2000aa(b)(3), accessed November 2017, https://www.law.cornell.edu/uscode/text/42/2000aa.

125 For an in-depth discussion of evolving technology, view Elizabeth Uzelac, "Reviving the Privacy Protection Act of 1980," *Northwestern University Law Review* 107, no. 3 (2013), http://scholarlycommons.law.northwestern.edu/cgi/viewcontent.cgi?article=1057&context=nulr.

126 Peter Swire, "Why Cross-Border Government Requests for Data Will Keep Becoming More Important," *Lawfare* (blog), May 23, 2017, https://www.lawfareblog.com/why-cross-border-government-requests-data-will-keep-becoming-more-important.

127 Peter Swire and Jennifer Daskal, "Frequently Asked Questions about the U.S. CLOUD Act," Cross-Border Data Forum, April 16, 2019, https://www.crossborderdataforum.org/frequently-asked-questions-about-the-u-s-cloud-act/.

128 Peter Swire and Jennifer Daskal, "What the CLOUD Act Means for Privacy Pros," *Privacy Tracker*, IAPP, March 26, 2018, https://iapp.org/news/a/what-the-cloud-act-means-for-privacy-pros/.

129 Microsoft v. United States, 829 F.3d 197, 220 (2d Cir. 2016). This interpretation, that a warrant could not compel production of electronic evidence held by a U.S. company outside the United States, surprised some commentators. Jennifer Granick, "The Microsoft Ireland Case and the Future of Digital Privacy," *Just Security*, July 18, 2016, https://www.justsecurity.org/32076/microsoft-ireland-case-future-digital-privacy/. Until the Microsoft Ireland case (so called because the evidence at issue was housed by Microsoft in Ireland), leading email and social network services have been based in the United States, so the U.S. government could gain evidence in law enforcement investigations by ordering production through the U.S. corporate headquarters. By contrast, other governments have had to meet the requirements of U.S. law, such as the Electronic Communications Privacy Act, to gain access to email, social network,

or other electronic evidence held by these companies. Other countries aside from the United States have thus needed to use the mutual legal assistance process, and so had to meet probable cause or other U.S.-defined standards for gaining the evidence. See Greg Stohr, "Microsoft Email-Access Fight With U.S. Gets Top Court Review," *Bloomberg Politics*, October 16, 2017, https://www.bloomberg.com/news/articles/2017-10-16/microsoft-email-access-fight-with-u-s-gets-supreme-court-review; Andrew Woods, "A Primer on Microsoft Ireland, the Supreme Court's Extraterritorial Warrant Case," *Lawfare* (blog), October 16, 2017, https://www.lawfareblog.com/primer-microsoft-ireland-supreme-courts-extraterritorial-warrant-case.

130 See Jennifer Daskal, "Microsoft Ireland Argument Analysis: Data, Territoriality, and the Best Way Forward," *Harvard Law Review* (blog), February 28, 2018, https://blog.harvardlawreview.org/microsoft-ireland-argument-analysis-data-territoriality-and-the-best-way-forward/.

131 H.R.4943 CLOUD Act, accessed November 2019, https://www.congress.gov/bill/115th-congress/house-bill/4943. For a discussion of the concept of "possession, custody, or control" in the CLOUD Act, view the article by Justin Hemmings, Sreenidhi Srinivasan, and Peter Swire, "Defining the Scope of 'Possession, Custody, or Control' for Privacy Issues and the Cloud Act," *Journal of National Security Law and Policy* 631 (January 2020), https://papers.ssrn.com/sol3/papers.cfm?abstract_id=3469808.

132 Swire and Daskal, "Frequently Asked Questions about the U.S. CLOUD Act."

133 A Mutual Legal Assistance Treaty is a formal agreement between countries to seek and exchange evidence located in their jurisdictions upon requests from another country that is party to the treaty. "Promoting Public Safety, Privacy, and the Rule of Law Around the World: The Purpose and Impact of the CLOUD Act," U.S. Department of Justice, April 2019, https://www.justice.gov/opa/press-release/file/1153446/download.

134 This statistic is an average for all requests from all countries, and no statistics related to specific countries were included. Richard a. Clarke, et. Al., *Liberty and Security in a Changing World: Report and Recommendations of the President's Review Group on Intelligence and Communications Technologies*, December 12, 2013, 227, https://obamawhitehouse.archives.gov/sites/default/files/docs/2013-12-12_rg_final_report.pdf.

135 Swire and Daskal, "Frequently Asked Questions about the U.S. CLOUD Act."

136 Peter Swire and Justin Hemmings, "Recommendations for the Potential U.S.-U.K. Executive Agreement under the CLOUD Act," *Lawfare* (blog), September 13, 2018, https://www.lawfareblog.com/recommendations-potential-us-uk-executive-agreement-under-cloud-act; *see* Jennifer Daskal and Peter Swire, "Why the CLOUD Act is Good for Privacy and Human Rights," *Lawfare* (blog), March 14, 2018, https://www.lawfareblog.com/why-cloud-act-good-privacy-and-human-rights.

137 Georgia Wood and James Lewis, "The CLOUD Act and Transatlantic Trust," Center for Strategic & International Studies, March 29, 2023, https://www.csis.org/analysis/cloud-act-and-transatlantic-trust; "CLOUD Act Agreement Between the Governments of the U.S. and Australia," U.S. Department of Justice, updated August 11, 2023, https://www.justice.gov/criminal-oia/cloud-act-agreement-between-governments-us-and-australia; "United States and Australia Enter CLOUD Act Agreement to Facilitate Investigations of Serious Crime," U.S. Department of Justice, December 15, 2021, https://www.justice.gov/opa/pr/united-states-and-australia-enter-cloud-act-agreement-facilitate-investigations-serious-crime; "Landmark U.S.-UK Data Access

Agreement Enters into Force," U.S. Department of Justice, October 3, 2022, https://www.justice.gov/opa/pr/landmark-us-uk-data-access-agreement-enters-force; see Paul Greaves and Peter Swire, "New Developments for the U.K. and Australian Executive Agreements with the U.S. Under the CLOUD Act," Cross-Border Data Forum, July 19, 2020, https://www.crossborderdataforum.org/new-developments-for-the-u-k-and-australian-executive-agreements-with-the-u-s-under-the-cloud-act-2/; Jennifer Daskal and Peter Swire, "The U.K.-U.S. CLOUD Act Agreement is Finally Here, Containing New Safeguards," Lawfare (blog), October 8, 2019, https://www.lawfareblog.com/uk-us-cloud-act-agreement-finally-here-containing-new-safeguards

138 "CLOUD Act Resources," U.S. Department of Justice, updated October 24, 2023, https://www.justice.gov/criminal-oia/cloud-act-resources; see Thomas Claburn, "U.S., Canada to Figure Out Rules on Cops and Feds Accessing People's Data Across Borders," The Register, March 23, 2022, https://www.theregister.com/2022/03/23/us_canada_cloud_act/; "EU-U.S. Announcement on the Resumption of Negotiations on an EU-U.S. Agreement to Facilitate Access to Electronic Evidence in Criminal Investigations," European Commission, March 2, 2023, https://commission.europa.eu/news/eu-us-announcement-resumption-negotiations-eu-us-agreement-facilitate-access-electronic-evidence-2023-03-02_en; Peter Swire, "EU and U.S. Negotiations on Cross-Border Data, Within and Outside of the CLOUD Act Framework," Cross-Border Data Forum, April 13, 2019, https://www.crossborderdataforum.org/eu-and-u-s-negotiations-on-cross-border-data-within-and-outside-of-the-cloud-act-framework/

139 In 2001, the treaty opened for signatures in Budapest, Hungary. This led to the treaty being referred to as the Budapest Convention. "20 Years of the Convention on Cybercrime: Join the Celebration," Council of Europe, September 28, 2021, https://www.coe.int/en/web/cybercrime/-/20-years-of-the-convention-on-cybercrime-join-the-celebration-.

140 Jennifer Daskal and DeBrae Kennedy-Mayo, "Budapest Convention: What is it and How is it Being Updated?" Cross-Border Data Forum, July 2, 2020, https://www.crossborderdataforum.org/budapest-convention-what-is-it-and-how-is-it-being-updated/; see DeBrae Kennedy-Mayo, "In Search of a Balance Between Police Power and Privacy in the Cybercrime Treaty," Richmond Journal of Law & Technology, 2002, https://scholarship.richmond.edu/jolt/vol9/iss1/5/.

141 A protocol supplements the original treaty. A country that has ratified the original treaty is only bound to the protocol if the country officially approves the protocol. For the Budapest Convention, the First Additional Protocol focused on racism and xenophobia. Note that the U.S. did not ratify the First Additional Protocol. See Additional Protocol to the Convention on Cybercrime concerning the criminalization of acts of a racist and xenophobic nature committed through computer systems, Council of Europe, 2003, https://rm.coe.int/168008160f; Additional Protocol to the Convention on Cybercrime concerning the criminalization of acts of a racist and xenophobic nature committed through computer systems, Council of Europe, Status as of 11/7/2023, https://www.coe.int/en/web/conventions/full-list?module=signatures-by-treaty&treatynum=189.

142 The EU-U.S. Umbrella Agreement and Executive Agreements under the CLOUD Act fall into this category. DeBrae Kennedy-Mayo and Peter Swire, "Update to Budapest Convention Expected to be Finalized This November," Cross-Border Data Forum, October 11, 2021, https://www.crossborderdataforum.org/update-to-budapest-convention-expected-to-be-finalized-this-november/?cn-reloaded=1.

143 Kennedy-Mayo and Swire, "Update to Budapest Convention Expected to be Finalized This November."

144 Second Additional Protocol to the Cybercrime Convention on Enhanced Co-operation and Disclosure of Electronic Evidence, Council of Europe, accessed July 2022, https://www.coe.int/en/web/cybercrime/second-additional-protocol.

145 The Foreign Intelligence Surveillance Act of 1978, Pub. L. No. 95-511, 92 Stat. 1783 (1978), https://www.govinfo.gov/content/pkg/STATUTE-92/pdf/STATUTE-92-Pg1783.pdf; "USA Freedom Act: What's in, what's out," *The Washington Post*, June 2, 2015, https://www.washingtonpost.com/graphics/politics/usa-freedom-act/.

146 United States v. Curtiss-Wright Export Corp., 299 U.S. 304 (1936), https://supreme.justia.com/cases/federal/us/299/304/case.html.

147 Katz v. United States, 389 U.S. 347.

148 United States v. United States District Court (known as the Keith case), 407 U.S. 297 (1972), https://supreme.justia.com/cases/federal/us/407/297/case.html.

149 James Risen and Eric Lichtblau, "Bush Lets U.S. Spy on Callers Without Courts," *The New York Times*, December 16, 2005, www.nytimes.com/2005/12/16/politics/bush-lets-us-spy-on-callers-without-courts.html?_r=0.

150 Peter Swire and Judd Legum, "Telcos Could Be Liable for Tens of Billions of Dollars for Illegally Turning Over Phone Records," *ThinkProgress*, May 11, 2006, http://thinkprogress.org/politics/2006/05/11/5300/telcos-liable/.

151 "Testimony of Peter Swire before the U.S. Senate Judiciary Committee, "Responding to the Inspector General's Findings of Improper Use of National Security Letters by the FBI," April 11, 2007, https://www.judiciary.senate.gov/imo/media/doc/swire_testimony_04_11_07.pdf.

152 Foreign Intelligence Surveillance Act Amendments Act of 2008, Pub. L. 110-261, 2008.

153 One of the Review Group Report's most widely publicized findings was that the use of Section 215 telephony metadata was not essential to preventing attacks and could readily have been obtained in a timely manner using conventional Section 215 orders. The full report is available at *Liberty and Security in a Changing World: Report and Recommendations of the President's Review Group on Intelligence and Communications Technology*, December 12, 2013, https://obamawhitehouse.archives.gov/sites/default/files/docs/2013-12-12_rg_final_report.pdf.

154 *Report on the Telephone Records Program Conducted under Section 215 of the USA PATRIOT Act and on the Operations of the Foreign Intelligence Surveillance Court*, Privacy and Civil Liberties Oversight Board, January 23, 2014, https://irp.fas.org/offdocs/pclob-215.pdf; *Report on the Surveillance Program Operated Pursuant to Section 702 of the Foreign Intelligence Surveillance Act*, Privacy and Civil Liberties Oversight Board, July 2, 2014, https://irp.fas.org/offdocs/pclob-702.pdf.

155 A full list of reforms is presented in Peter Swire, "US Surveillance Law, Safe Harbor, and Reforms Since 2013," December 17, 2015, https://fpf.org/wp-content/uploads/2015/12/White-Paper-Swire-US-EU-Surveillance.pdf.

156 45 C.F.R. § 164.512(k)(2), accessed November 2017, https://www.law.cornell.edu/cfr/text/45/164.512.

157 15 U.S.C. § 6803(e), accessed November 2017, https://www.law.cornell.edu/uscode/text/15/6803.

158 15 U.S.C. § 6501, accessed November 2017, https://www.law.cornell.edu/uscode/text/15/6501.

159 Leslie Harris, "House Passage of Cybersecurity Bill CISPA Wasn't a Complete Loss," *The Daily Beast,* April 30, 2012, www.thedailybeast.com/articles/2012/04/30/house-passage-of-cybersecurity-bill-cispa-wasn-t-a-complete-loss.html.

160 Elizabeth Weise, "Apple v. FBI Timeline: 43 Days that Rocked Tech," *USA Today,* March 15, 2016, https://www.usatoday.com/story/tech/news/2016/03/15/apple-v-fbi-timeline/81827400/.

161 For specifics of the request by the FBI and the order issued by the court, see "Apple v. FBI," EPIC.org, accessed November 2019, https://epic.org/amicus/crypto/apple/.

162 Arjun Kharpal, "Apple vs FBI: All You Need to Know," *CNBC,* March 29, 2016, https://www.cnbc.com/2016/03/29/apple-vs-fbi-all-you-need-to-know.html.

163 Jedidiah Bracy, "Why the Apple Crypto Case Goes beyond One Company's Privacy Battle," IAPP, February 18, 2016, https://iapp.org/news/a/why-the-apple-crypto-case-goes-beyond-one-companys-privacy-battle/.

164 "Apple, FBI go to Capitol Hill to talk encryption," IAPP, March 2, 2016, https://iapp.org/news/a/apple-fbi-go-to-capitol-hill-to-talk-encryption/.

165 See Sean Gallagher, "Barr Says the US Needs Encryption Backdoors to Prevent 'Going Dark.' Um, What?" *Ars Technica,* August 4, 2019, https://arstechnica.com/tech-policy/2019/08/post-snowden-tech-became-more-secure-but-is-govt-really-at-risk-of-going-dark/; see also Fergus Hunter, "Facebook Refuses to Compromise on Privacy, Firing Back at Australia, US, and UK," *The Sydney Morning Herald,* December 11, 2019, https://www.smh.com.au/politics/federal/facebook-refuses-to-compromise-on-privacy-firing-back-at-australia-us-and-uk-20191210-p53ik7.html. For an analysis of encryption encountered in U.S. wiretaps, view Darlene Storm, "2015 Wiretap Report: No wiretap denied, encryption rarely encountered," *ComputerWorld,* July 5, 2016, https://www.computerworld.com/article/3091824/2015-wiretap-report-no-wiretap-denied-encryption-rarely-encountered.html.

166 FISA is codified at 50 U.S.C. §§ 1801-1811, accessed November 2017, https://www.law.cornell.edu/uscode/text/50/chapter-36/subchapter-I.

167 This is one of the reforms instituted in the USA FREEDOM Act. USA FREEDOM Act, Section 401, accessed November 2017, https://iapp.org/media/pdf/resource_center/Freedom_Act_Amendments_FINAL.pdf.

168 USA Freedom Act, Section 604, accessed November 2019, https://www.congress.gov/114/bills/hr2048/BILLS-114hr2048enr.pdf. Examples of these reports are located on the websites of Facebook and Google. Meta Transparency Center, accessed July 2023, https://govtrequests.facebook.com/government-data-requests; *Google Transparency Report,* accessed July 2023, https://transparencyreport.google.com/user-data/overview?user_requests_report_period=authority:US. Although transparency reports are standard practice with major tech companies, the practice is less common with businesses that sell products for "smart homes." Zack Whittaker, "Many Smart Home Device Makers Still Won't Say if They Give Your Data to the Government," *TechCrunch,* December 11, 2019, https://techcrunch.com/2019/12/11/smart-home-tech-user-data-government/; Cory Doctorow, "'Smart Home' Companies Refuse to Say Whether Law Enforcement is Using Your Gadgets to Spy on You," Boing Boing, October 20, 2018, https://boingboing.net/2018/10/20/the-walls-have-ears.html.

169 *2015 FISA Report*, U.S. Department of Justice, April 28, 2016, https://www.justice.gov/nsd/nsd-foia-library/2015fisa/download.

170 Wiretap reports, United States Courts, accessed July 2023, https://www.uscourts.gov/statistics-reports/analysis-reports/wiretap-reports.

171 For detailed analysis of USA FREEDOM Act amendments to FISA, view https://iapp.org/media/pdf/resource_center/Freedom_Act_Amendments_FINAL.pdf, accessed November 2017.

172 Jodie Liu, "So What Does the USA Freedom Act Do Anyway?" *Lawfare* (blog), June 3, 2015, https://www.lawfareblog.com/so-what-does-usa-freedom-act-do-anyway.

173 Sharon Bradford Franklin, "Rethinking Surveillance on the 20th Anniversary of the Patriot Act," Just Security, October 26, 2021, https://www.justsecurity.org/78753/rethinking-surveillance-on-the-20th-anniversary-of-the-patriot-act/; see India McKinney, "Victory: Government Finally Releases Secretive Court Rulings Sought By EFF," Electronic Frontier Foundation, August 22, 2022. https://www.eff.org/deeplinks/2022/08/victory-government-finally-releases-secretive-court-rulings-sought-eff.

174 Amendments Act of 2008, Pub. L. 110-261 (2008), https://www.govtrack.us/congress/bills/110/hr6304/text.

175 See National Security Agency Director of Civil Liberties and Privacy Office Report, *NSA's Implementation Of Foreign Intelligence Surveillance Act Section 702*, National Security Agency, April 16, 2014, https://www.nsa.gov/about/civil-liberties/reports/assets/files/nsa_report_on_section_702_program.pdf.

176 President's Review Group on Intelligence and Communications Technologies, *Liberty and Security in a Changing World: Report and Recommendations of The President's Review Group on Intelligence and Communications Technologies*, Appendix A at 263, December 12, 2013, https://obamawhitehouse.archives.gov/sites/default/files/docs/2013-12-12_rg_final_report.pdf.

177 Peter Swire, "Chapter 3: Systemic Safeguards in the US System of Foreign Intelligence Surveillance Law," Professor Peter Swire Testimony in Irish High Court Case, Alston & Bird, accessed November 2017, https://www.alston.com/-/media/files/insights/publications/peter-swire-testimony-documents/chapter-3--systemic-safeguards-in-the-us-sytem-of.pdf?la=en.

178 The initial story about PRISM was incorrect in important respects, but those inaccuracies have been widely repeated. The actual PRISM program is not even a bulk collection program, much less the basis for "mass and indiscriminate surveillance" when data is transferred from the EU to the United States. *See* Peter Swire, "US Surveillance Law."

179 Privacy and Civil Liberties Oversight Board, *Report on the Surveillance Program Operated Pursuant to Section 702 of the Foreign Intelligence Surveillance Act*, 7, July 2, 2014, https://www.pclob.gov/library/702-Report.pdf.

180 "Upstream collection is different from PRISM collection because the acquisition occurs not with the compelled assistance of United States [Internet service providers], but instead with the compelled assistance (through a Section 702 directive) of the providers that control the telecommunications backbone over which communications transit." Privacy and Civil Liberties Oversight Board, *Report on the Surveillance Program Operated Pursuant to Section 702 of the Foreign Intelligence Surveillance Act.*

181 Emma Kohse, "Summary: The FISA Amendments Reauthorization Act of 2017," *Lawfare* (blog), (January 18, 2018), https://www.lawfareblog.com/summary-fisa-amendments-reauthorization-act-2017. For a discussion of these recent reforms, view Peter Swire and Richard Clarke, "Reform Section 702 to Maintain Fourth Amendment Principles," *Lawfare* (blog), October 19, 2017, https://www.lawfareblog.com/reform-section-702-maintain-fourth-amendment-principles; Susan Hennessey and Benjamin Wittes, "Don't Reform Section 702 Just for the Sake of Reform," *Lawfare* (blog), October 16, 2017, https://www.lawfareblog.com/dont-reform-section-702-just-sake-reform.

182 Sharon Bradford Franklin, "Rethinking Surveillance on the 20th Anniversary of the Patriot Act," Just Security, October 26, 2021, https://www.justsecurity.org/78753/rethinking-surveillance-on-the-20th-anniversary-of-the-patriot-act/; see George Croner, "New Statistics Confirm the Continuing Decline in the Use of National Surveillance Authorities," Lawfare, May 24, 2022, https://www.lawfareblog.com/new-statistics-confirm-continuing-decline-use-national-surveillance-authorities.

183 Peter Swire, "Responding to the Inspector General's Findings." For additional detail, view Peter Swire, "The System of Foreign Intelligence Surveillance Law," *George Washington Law Review* 72:1306 (2004), http://ssrn.com/abstract=586616.

184 Charles Doyle, "National Security Letters in Foreign Intelligence Investigations: Legal Background," Congressional Research Service, July 30, 2015, www.fas.org/sgp/crs/intel/RL33320.pdf.

185 *A Review of the Federal Bureau of Investigation's Use of Exigent Letters and Other Informal Requests for Telephone Records*, Office of the Inspector General, U.S. Department of Justice, January 2010, https://www.oversight.gov/sites/default/files/oig-reports/s1001r.pdf.

186 18 U.S.C. § 3511, accessed November 2017, https://www.law.cornell.edu/uscode/text/18/3511.

187 Doe v. Ashcroft, 334 F.Supp. 2d 471 (S.D.N.Y. 2004), www.clearinghouse.net/detail.php?id=12966; Doe v. Gonzales, 386 F.Supp.2d 66 (D.Conn. 2005), https://www.courtlistener.com/opinion/2372515/doe-v-gonzales/.

188 18 U.S.C. § 1510, accessed November 2017, https://www.law.cornell.edu/uscode/text/18/part-I/chapter-73.

189 Exceptions are permitted only if a senior official determines that national security requires otherwise in the particular case and explains the basis in writing. "IC on the Record," Office of the Director of National Intelligence. For additional information, view Peter Swire, *"US Surveillance Law, Safe Harbor, and Reforms Since 2013."*

190 As of the writing of this book, continual use of location tracking, searching of DNA databases, and utilization of facial recognition are notable practices raising privacy concerns as the data that is collected, stored, and analyzed has the potential to be used in both civil and criminal lawsuits. See Lee Hale et al., "When it Comes to the Dangers of AI, Surveillance Poses More Risk than Anything," NPR, March 2, 2023, https://www.npr.org/2023/03/02/1160714485/when-it-comes-to-the-dangers-of-ai-surveillance-poses-more-risk-than-anything; Heather Federman, "Privacy and Data Protection in the Wake of Dobbs," Security, September 29, 2022, https://www.securitymagazine.com/articles/98414-privacy-and-data-protection-in-the-wake-of-dobbs; Paige St. John, "The Untold Story of How the Golden State Killer was Found: A Covert Operation and Private DNA," *The Los Angeles Times*, December 8, 2020, https://www.latimes.com/california/story/2020-12-08/man-in-the-window; Khari Johnson, "Meta's VR Headset Harvests Personal Data Right Off Your Face," *Wired*, October 13, 2022, https://www.wired.com/story/metas-vr-headset-quest-pro-personal-data-face/.

CHAPTER 14

The GDPR and International Privacy Issues

As discussed in Chapter 1, governments around the world vary in their approach to privacy law, policy, and regulation. As of the writing of this book, more than 160 nations globally have enacted significant privacy laws that apply to companies doing business within their borders (including e-commerce) and with their citizens.[1] Notable countries that have recently enacted or are currently enacting significant privacy protections include China,[2] India,[3] and Brazil.[4] The evolving privacy rules outside of the United States often impact business practices that relate to privacy.

As also discussed in Chapter 1, the first wave of modern privacy laws—beginning in the 1970s—was based on fair information practices (FIPs), which originated with the U.S. government. Today, the worldwide template for privacy laws related to the protection of data is the 2018 update to the comprehensive EU privacy requirements—the General Data Protection Regulation (GDPR).[5] The EU requirements apply broadly to companies with assets and employees in the European Union, to companies that sell to individuals in the European Union, and to data stored in the European Union.

Fines for violations of the GDPR can be as much as four percent of worldwide revenues. This means that, for a company with worldwide revenues of $1 billion, the maximum fine is $40 million, while the maximum fine can be $4 billion for a company with worldwide revenues of $100 billion. These sanctions are significant enough to garner the attention of even the top management in businesses.

Since a series of decisions by the Court of Justice of the European Union (CJEU), referred to as "Schrems I" and "Schrems II" (discussed in detail in Section 14.7.3), the EU legal system has closely scrutinized the surveillance practices of those countries where EU data is transferred—highlighting particular complexity in the data flowing from the European Union to the United States.

14.1 Overview of the General Data Protection Regulation

Key provisions introduced in the GDPR include (1) requirements for processing data, (2) individual rights, (3) notification of security breaches, (4) designation of data protection officers (DPOs), (5) sanctions of up to four percent of worldwide revenues, and (6) rules for international transfers.[6] Under the broad definition in the European Union under the GDPR, companies doing business in the European Union have the legal obligation to comply with these comprehensive privacy requirements, subject to potentially very large fines.[7]

14.2 Key Terms

The key terms in the GDPR include personal data, sensitive personal data, data subject, controller, processor, consent, data protection authority (DPA), and DPO. These terms have specific meanings under EU law that may appear to U.S. practitioners to be terms of art.

14.2.1 Personal Data

"Personal data" is broadly defined in the GDPR as any data "related to an identified or identifiable natural person." This means a person who can be identified directly or indirectly. If data can be grouped together to lead to an identification, the pieces constitute personal data. Data that has been deidentified, encrypted, or pseudonymized remains personal data if it can be used to reidentify the person. Data is *only* considered "anonymized" if the process used is irreversible.[8] Examples of personal data include:

- First and last name
- Home address
- Email address including a first and last name
- Identification card number
- Location data
- IP address (often *not* personally identifiable information (PII) in the United States)
- Cookie ID (often *not* PII in the United States)
- Advertising identifier on phone

- Data held by doctor or hospital, even separated from the patient's name

Examples *not* considered personal data include registration number for a company, email addresses such as support@business.com, and anonymized data.[9]

14.2.2 Sensitive Personal Data

Sensitive personal data is a special category of personal data that receives additional protections under the GDPR. Sensitive personal data includes:

- Race or ethnic origin
- Political opinions
- Religious or philosophical beliefs
- Trade union membership
- Genetic data
- Biometric data
- Health data
- Sex life or sexual orientation

Unless a specific exception applies under the GDPR, sensitive personal data requires the business to obtain "explicit consent" from the person to process the data for a specified purpose.[10]

14.2.3 Data Subject

With regard to the GDPR, the concept of data subject is critical to understanding the regulation. Essentially, a data subject is the person whose data is being processed.[11] According to one of the official comments to the GDPR, known as a recital, a data subject is any natural person whose data is being collected, stored or processed.[12] To understand which data subjects have rights under GDPR, it is important to consider the meaning of data subject in conjunction with the definition of personal data and the territorial scope of the law. When EU-based establishments are processing the personal data of data subjects located outside of the European Union, GDPR rights apply. Similarly, when establishments based outside of the European Union are monitoring the behavior of or targeting goods or services to data subjects in the European Union, GDPR rights apply.

14.2.4 Controller

The term "controller" refers to an individual or entity that "determines the purposes and the means of the processing of personal data."[13] In simple terms, the controller is the company that directs the processing of data to further its business objectives.

Under the GDPR, the obligations of controllers include the following:

- Implement data protection by default and by design
- Provide instructions to processors
- Ensure data security
- Report data breaches
- Cooperate with DPAs
- Appoint a DPO for the business
- Identify legal basis for processing
- Maintain data processing records
- Conduct data protection impact assessments (DPIAs)[14]

14.2.5 Processor

The term "processor" in the GDPR means an individual or entity that "processes personal data on behalf of the controller."[15] The GDPR requires the processor to be governed by instructions provided by the controller in a contract. Generally speaking, the controller should bear more of the legal responsibility under the GDPR than the processor. Requirements flow downstream to a subprocessor (like a subcontractor).

Under the GDPR, the obligations of processors include the following:

- Compliance with instructions of the controller
- Confidentiality
- Record of processing activities
- Data security
- Data breach reporting
- Cooperation with DPAs[16]

14.2.6 Consent

Consent is a concept that is foundational to the GDPR. For U.S. practitioners, the definition of consent in the GDPR may be much more detailed and elaborate than expected. The term "consent" is defined as follows: freely given, specific, informed, and an unambiguous indication of the data subject's wishes.[17]

For consent to be valid under the GDPR, the business must provide the data subject with the following for the consent to be deemed informed:

- Controller's identity
- Purpose of processing for which consent is sought
- Types of data that will be collected
- Information about the right to withdraw consent
- Information about automated processing
- Risks of transfers outside the European Union

Under the GDPR, a data subject may express their consent by statement or by clear affirmative action. Note that businesses are responsible for being able to demonstrate that consent was obtained, and for ensuring that the data subject was provided sufficient information to make the consent informed.[18]

14.2.7 Data Protection Authorities

DPAs are responsible for enforcing data protection laws at a national level, and providing guidance on the interpretation of those laws. DPAs are independent public authorities that investigate and enforce data protection laws.[19] There is one DPA in each EU member state (a country in the European Union) except for Germany, which has a federal DPA with jurisdiction over the public sector and 16 Lander (or state-level) DPAs with jurisdiction over the commercial sector.[20]

14.2.8 Data Protection Officer

The DPO is the primary point of contact on data protection issues within a business that is based in the European Union. The DPO facilitates and reviews the company's GDPR compliance. With regard to qualifications, the DPO must have expertise in data protection law relevant to the data processing of the company. Critically, the DPO must *not* have any conflicts of interest—

meaning the DPO must *not* have duties related to processing personal data that conflict with duties related to monitoring.[21]

Which entities must appoint a DPO? The answer is not based on the entity being a controller or a processor. Several key factors in determining the need for a DPO:

- Are the data subjects from the European Union?
- Is the data in/from the European Union?
- Is there large-scale monitoring of data subjects?
- Is there large-scale processing of sensitive personal information?
- Where is the company based?

Importantly, the term "data protection officer (DPO)" is used to refer to the representative for companies based in the European Union. For companies that do *not* have a physical presence inside the European Union, the company must appoint an "EU representative"—notably, someone who is subject to enforcement proceedings pursuant to the GDPR. For non-EU companies with subsidiaries in the European Union, the picture is somewhat complex.[22]

14.3 General Principles

The GDPR contains seven key principles that are the foundation of the regulation underpinning the rights it affords as well as its requirements and rules. These key principles form the framework for a company's GDPR compliance program, and all processing of personal data must abide by these principles. The seven key principles are as follows:

- Lawfulness, fairness and transparency
- Purpose limitation
- Data minimization
- Accuracy
- Storage limitation
- Integrity and confidentiality
- Accountability[23]

14.3.1 Lawfulness, Fairness, and Transparency

Processing of personal data must be lawful and fair. This means that companies should have a legal basis for processing personal data and that data subjects should be made aware of the rules and safeguards as well as the risks associated with their data.[24] In addition, processing of personal data must be made transparent to data subjects so that they understand to what extent personal data concerning them is or will be processed. The principle of transparency, which is intrinsically linked to fairness, requires that any communication (such as privacy notices) be concise, easily accessible, and written using clear and plain language that it is easy to understand (in particular, when providing information to children).[25]

14.3.2 Purpose Limitation

Personal data must be collected for specified, explicit, and legitimate purposes.[26] The specific purposes for which personal data are processed should comply with all applicable laws (e.g., privacy, contract, employment) at all times during the data life cycle and should be clearly expressed to data subjects.[27] Thus, companies need to determine what personal data they need to collect and why before collecting personal data.

The purpose limitation principle also requires that personal data not be further processed—any processing activity following collection such as storage—in a manner that is incompatible with the original purpose for which it was collected. Whether further processing is incompatible will need to be assessed on a case-by-case basis considering the following key factors:[28]

- The relationship between the purposes of collection and the purposes of further processing
- The nature of the personal data and the safeguards adopted to ensure fair processing
- The reasonable expectations of the data subjects and the impact of further processing on the data subjects

The GDPR makes it clear that further processing for archiving purposes in the public interest, scientific, or historical research purposes or statistical purposes is *not* considered to be incompatible with the original purposes.[29]

14.3.3 Data Minimization

Processing of personal data must be adequate, relevant, and limited to what is necessary considering the purposes of processing.[30] When determining the purpose of a processing activity, a company should carefully consider what personal data is necessary to achieve that purpose and subsequently collect and process only the necessary personal data. For instance, compliance with the data minimization principle requires the deletion or anonymization of personal data that is no longer necessary and that any data retention period be limited to a strict minimum.[31]

14.3.4 Accuracy

Personal data must be accurate and, where necessary, kept up to date.[32] The accuracy principle requires that every reasonable step is taken to ensure that personal data that is inaccurate is erased or rectified without delay.

14.3.5 Storage Limitation

Personal data must be kept for no longer than is necessary for the purposes of processing, which is interlinked with the data minimization principle.[33] The data retention period should reflect the purposes of processing, legal obligations, and industry best practices. The GDPR does allow the storage of personal data for longer periods if processed solely for archiving purposes in the public interest, scientific or historical research purposes, or statistical purposes. To ensure that personal data is kept only as long as necessary, companies should establish time limits to review or erase the personal data stored.[34]

14.3.6 Integrity and Confidentiality

Through appropriate technical or organizational measures, personal data must be processed in a way that ensures a level of security appropriate to the risk of processing the personal data.[35] A company should take into account the state of the art; the costs of implementation; and the nature, scope, context, and purposes of processing, as well as the risk of varying likelihood and severity for the rights and freedoms of individuals.[36]

14.3.7 Accountability

Under the accountability principle, a controller is responsible for and must be able to demonstrate compliance with the six principles in Sections 14.3.1–14.3.6.[37] The accountability principle aims to move privacy from theory to practice by requiring that the processes underlying privacy policies and procedures are implemented appropriately and effectively.[38] Accountability measures include documenting personal data breaches (including those not requiring notification), maintaining a record of processing activities, and conducting DPIAs.[39]

14.4 Data Subject Rights

A cornerstone of the GDPR is providing individuals with control over their personal data.[40] To allow individuals to exercise such control, the GDPR provides the following rights: the right to be informed of transparent communication and information, right of access, right to rectification, right to erasure, right to restrict processing, right to data portability, right to object, and right *not* to be subject to automated decision-making.[41]

Controllers are responsible for facilitating the exercise of these rights and must respond to rights requests within one month of receipt of the request (or, where necessary, within three months) in writing or, if requested, orally.[42] The identity of the requestor should be verified using reasonable measures such as asking for a form of photo identification. Generally, controllers cannot charge a fee to requestors; however, controllers may charge a fee to cover administrative costs for requests that are manifestly unfounded or excessive or for requests for additional copies of information previously provided.[43] In certain instances, a controller may refuse to act on a request either because an exemption exists, or it is manifestly unfounded or excessive.[44]

14.4.1 Right to Be Informed of Transparent Communication and Information

Providing individuals with control over their personal data is only possible when they understand what a company is doing with their personal data. To help ensure that data subjects are properly informed, and as a part of the principle of transparency, the GDPR requires that controllers provide certain information on their processing and handling of personal data to data subjects when they collect personal data. This is commonly referred to as a privacy notice.[45] Where personal data is not collected directly from data subjects, the data subjects must be informed of details they would not be aware of, such as the source of personal data concerned.[46]

Controllers should take into account the nature, circumstances, scope, and context of their processing activities when balancing the requirements under the GDPR to provide comprehensive information in a concise form. Examples of different forms of privacy notices include a layered approach (short overview of key information linking to additional layers of detailed information), just-in-time notices (information relevant to the personal data about to be collected), and privacy dashboards (information and privacy preference management in one centralized area).[47]

14.4.2 Right of Access

The GDPR provides data subjects with the right to obtain the following from controllers: confirmation as to whether a controller is processing the data subject's personal data, a copy of the personal data, and other information that should already be provided in a privacy notice.[48] When data subjects exercise their right of access, the request is often called a "subject access request." A subject access request allows data subjects to understand the what, why, and how regarding a controller's personal data-processing activities, which in turn allows them to verify the lawfulness of processing.[49] Given the scope of information a controller may have to provide to data subjects under this right, the right of access is often the gateway to data subjects exercising other rights under the GDPR.

14.4.3 Right to Rectification

While the accuracy principle requires that personal data must be accurate, the right to rectification supplements this principle by allowing data subjects to require controllers to confirm the accuracy of their personal data. The GDPR provides data subjects with the right to have inaccurate personal data corrected and, taking into account the purposes of processing, to have incomplete personal data completed.[50] Personal data may be completed via a supplementary statement.

14.4.4 Right to Erasure ("Right to Be Forgotten")

Under the GDPR, data subjects have the right to have personal data erased in certain circumstances. This right is known as the right to erasure or the "right to be forgotten."

The right applies where:

- "The personal data are no longer necessary … [for] the purposes for which they were collected or otherwise processed"
- "The data subject withdraws consent on which the processing is based … and where there is *no* other legal ground for the processing"
- "The data subject objects to processing [based on legitimate interests] and there are *no* overriding legitimate grounds for the processing"
- "The personal data have been unlawfully processed"
- "The personal data have to be erased for compliance with a legal obligation"

- "The personal data have been collected ... [to offer] information society services [to children]"[51]

Under a valid erasure request, a controller must delete the relevant personal data, including from backup systems, unless an exemption applies, such as processing necessary to comply with a legal obligation or for the establishment, exercise, or defense of legal claims. Further, where a controller has made the personal data publicly available online, the controller must use reasonable measures to inform other controllers processing the personal data to erase any links to or copies of the personal data.[52]

14.4.5 Right to Restriction of Processing

As an alternative to the right to erasure, data subjects have the right to restriction of processing, which allows them to limit the way their personal data is processed. The GDPR defines "restriction of processing" as "the marking of stored personal data with the aim of limiting their processing in the future."[53] Methods of restriction include temporarily moving data to another system, making personal data unavailable to users, or removing data from a website.[54] The right applies where:

- "The accuracy of the personal data is contested," and the controller is verifying the accuracy
- "The processing is unlawful," and the data subject prefers to have the use of their personal data restricted rather than having it erased
- "The controller no longer needs the personal data," but the data subject requires it for the establishment, exercise or defense of legal claims
- "The data subject has objected to processing" pursuant to the GDPR, and the controller is verifying whether its legitimate grounds override those of the data subject[55]

The GDPR requires controllers to communicate any rectification or erasure of personal data and any restriction of processing to each recipient to whom they have disclosed the personal data, unless this is impossible or involves disproportionate effort. The information required to make such communications should be documented in the record of processing activities.[56]

14.4.6 Right to Data Portability

The GDPR further strengthens data subjects' control and access to their personal data with the right to data portability. This right allows data subjects to port data to themselves *or* to another controller.[57] Data subjects may request that the data is provided in a structured, commonly used, and machine-readable format such as a CSV or Excel file. The right *only* applies (1) to personal data provided by the data subject (actively and knowingly provided by the data subject or observed data provided by the data subject through the use of the service or device, such as search history or location data), (2) where the processing is based on consent or the performance of a contract, *and* (3) when the processing is carried out by automated means.[58] The right to data portability cannot adversely affect the rights and freedoms of others, including trade secrets or intellectual property rights.[59]

14.4.7 Right to Object

The right to object allows data subjects to require controllers to stop processing their personal data. When a data subject objects to the processing of their personal data for direct marketing purposes, a controller must cease all such processing, including any related profiling activities.[60] Data subjects may also object to the processing of personal data based on one of the following legal bases: (1) a task carried out in the public interest, (2) the exercise of official authority, or (3) legitimate interests; however, these objections do not trigger an absolute right. In these circumstances, data subjects must provide reasons as to why they are objecting to the processing, and controllers may refuse to act on the request if (1) they have compelling legitimate grounds overriding those of the data subject or (2) the processing is necessary for the establishment, exercise, or defense of legal claims.[61]

14.4.8 Right Not to Be Subject to Automated Decision-Making

Similar to the right to be informed, the right not to be subject to automated decision-making applies without any action by data subjects. This right is in the form of a general prohibition on fully automated decision-making, including profiling, that has a legal or similarly significant effect (e.g., cancellation of a contract, entitlement to or denial of a social benefit, or denial of citizenship).[62] A controller cannot carry out such processing unless the decision is (1) necessary for the performance of a contract between the data subject and controller, (2) authorized by law (e.g., monitoring and preventing fraud), or (3) based on the data subject's explicit consent.[63]

14.5 Breach Notification and Response

The GDPR defines a "data breach" as "a breach of security leading to the accidental or unlawful destruction, loss, alteration, unauthorized disclosure of, or access to, personal data transmitted, stored or otherwise processed."[64] Recall that personal data is defined as "any information relating to an identified or identifiable natural person." This means the concept of data breach is broader under the GDPR than under most U.S. laws.[65]

In 2022, the annual aggregate number of data breach notifications reported pursuant to the requirements of the GDPR was approximately 110,000. During that time period, the Netherlands had the most breaches notifications per capita, followed closely by Denmark. Since the GDPR went into effect in 2018, the DPAs in Germany and the Netherlands have received the most notices of data breaches.[66]

The GDPR authorizes fines for data breaches up to four percent of a company's worldwide revenues. This topic will be further discussed in Section 14.6 on enforcement.

14.5.1 Notice Required from Controllers

The GDPR requires controllers to report data breaches to the relevant DPA within 72 hours of becoming aware of a breach, where feasible. Controllers are "aware" of a breach when they have a reasonable degree of certainty that a security incident has compromised personal data.[67] If for any reason the controller *cannot* make this deadline, they are required to provide the reasons for the delay with the notification.[68] Controllers are not required to report a breach if it is unlikely to result in a risk to individuals' rights and freedoms, but controllers must still document the details of the breach (e.g., nature of the breach, personal data affected, likely consequences of the breach, remedial measures taken, and decision whether to report to the DPA).

14.5.2 Notice Required from Processors

Processors are required to notify controllers "without undue delay" after discovering a breach. Controllers should strongly consider including specific instructions for how to handle this notice requirement in the contract between controller and processor.

14.5.3 Notice to Data Subjects

If a data breach occurs that is likely to result in a *high* risk to individuals' rights and freedoms, the controller must notify affected data subjects without undue delay. At a minimum, the notification must be in "clear and plain language" and must include:[69]

- The name and contact of the DPO (or appropriate person)
- The likely consequences of the data breach
- Any measures taken by the controller to mitigate the breach

Note that the controller is exempt from notifying data subjects when (1) the risk of harm is low because the affected data is protected (such as encrypted data), (2) the controller has taken steps to protect the data subject from harm (such as suspended accounts), and (3) the notice would impose disproportionate effects on the controller (and would still require public notice of the breach).[70]

14.6 Enforcement

At least some commentators believe that the major difference between the 1995 Data Protection Directive and the GDPR relates to fines. EU data protection law in the 1990s was often aspirational. Today, with significant fines part of the picture, EU data protection law is a compliance regime.

With fines as large as four percent of worldwide revenues, it is important for companies to understand the complaint process, liability for compensation, and levels of fines.

14.6.1 Complaint Process

An administrative complaint can be initiated by a data subject or by a DPA. A data subject can file an administrative complaint with a DPA. A data subject can file complaints with the courts in EU member states where the alleged issue occurred; where they reside, or where they work. A DPA can initiate a complaint or can address a complaint filed by a data subject.[71] Once a DPA has a complaint, there must be an assessment to determine whether more than one DPA has a similar complaint. A lead DPA must be determined. After assessing the complaint, the DPA must decide whether to impose an administrative fine.[72]

When the DPA handles a complaint initiated by a data subject, the data subject has the right to bring the complaint to a national court if (1) the data subject is not satisfied with the decision of the DPA, or (2) the DPA does not inform the data subject—within three months—of the outcome of the complaint or of the progress on the complaint.

In addition, the data subject has the right to seek a judicial remedy against the controller or processor. The judicial proceeding against the controller or processor should take place in the EU member state (1) where the controller or processor is established or (2) where the data subject has "habitual residence."[73]

14.6.2 Liability for Compensation

Under the GDPR, both the controller and the processor can be liable to data subjects for harm caused by unlawful processing of personal data. Controllers are liable for any damages caused by unlawful processing. Processors are liable for processing in violation of the GDPR obligations on processors and for processing in violation of instructions given by the controller.

If a controller and a processor are involved in the same processing where damage occurred, each is liable for the entire damage. Once the data subjects involved have been fully compensated, the controller or processor is entitled to compensation from the other relevant parties corresponding to their part in the responsibility for the damage.

In a situation where there are joint controllers, each controller is liable for the entire damage. Once the data subjects involved have been fully compensated, then the controllers involved can bring proceedings to recover portions of the damages from each other.[74]

The GDPR provides that both controllers and processors are exempt from liability when they are "not in any way responsible for the event giving rise to the damage."[75]

14.6.3 Levels of Fines

Since the GDPR came into effect in 2018, European regulators have handed out several notable fines.[76] In 2022, Instagram was fined €405 million concerning improper handling of children's data.[77] Also, in 2022, Facebook was fined €265 million related to a complaint of data scraping.[78] In 2021, Amazon was fined €746 million related to lack of consent for cookies.[79]

For companies, it is important to understand that the GDPR has two levels of fines. Higher-level fines can be up to four percent of global annual revenues. Lower-level fines can be up to two percent of global annual revenues.[80]

Higher-level fines focus on infringements related to basic principles of processing (including conditions of consent, lawfulness of processing, and processing of special categories of personal data), rights of data subjects, and transfers of personal data to a recipient outside the European Union. In this higher-level category, the maximum fines are the greater of €20 million or four percent of global annual revenue.

Lower-level fines include infringements related to integrating data protection by default or by design, records of processing, cooperation with DPAs, security of processing data, notification to DPAs of a data breach, communication of a data breach to data subjects, and designation of a DPO. For the lower-level category, the maximum fines can be the greater of €10 million or two percent of global annual revenues.[81]

In addition to these fines, member states are permitted to impose criminal sanctions for violation of the GDPR. As of the writing of this book, at least ten countries have adopted criminal sanctions.[82]

14.7 Overview of EU Requirements for International Data Transfers

The GDPR governs cross-border transfers of personal data.[83] Under the GDPR, transfers of personal data from the European Union and Norway, Liechtenstein, and Iceland—which is known as the European Economic Area or EEA—to non-EEA countries or international organizations are prohibited unless one of the following transfer mechanisms can be relied upon: an adequacy decision, an appropriate safeguard (e.g., standard contractual clauses, binding corporate rules), or a derogation (e.g., explicit consent).[84]

This section analyzes these numerous EU requirements for international data transfers. In the first subsection, we examine transfers to adequate countries. The second subsection details permissible methods to transfer data to other "third countries"—countries without an adequacy decision that are outside the EEA. Both appropriate safeguards and derogations are discussed.

This section concludes with a discussion of transfers between the European Union and United States. As of the writing of this book, two agreements—U.S.-EU Safe Harbor and EU-U.S. Privacy Shield—have been put in place and subsequently struck down by the CJEU. In July 2023, the EU-U.S. Data Privacy Framework was finalized. Many expect that this third agreement will be challenged as insufficient in the EU legal system.

14.7.1 Transfers to Adequate Countries

Personal data is permitted to flow freely from the European Union to countries that have adopted legal protections that EU law deems "adequate"—meaning that each country's protections have been assessed to be "essentially equivalent" to those found in the GDPR.[85] As of the writing of this book, countries and territories deemed adequate for purposes of the GDPR are Andorra, Argentina, Canada,[86] Faroe Islands, Guernsey, Isle of Man, Israel, Japan, Jersey, New Zealand, South Korea, Switzerland, the United Kingdom, the United Sates,[87] and Uruguay.[88] The grant of an adequacy decision is subject to periodic review.[89]

It is worth noting that an initial threshold for an adequacy decision appears to involve an assessment of whether the country's government upholds democratic principles and has an established rule of law.[90]

14.7.2 Transfers to Other "Third Countries"

The GDPR prohibits data transfers to other "third countries"—countries without an adequacy decision that are outside the EEA—unless the transfer is subject to an appropriate safeguard or a derogation applies. Part of the EU assessment is the extent to which the recipient country has rule-of-law protections within a democracy.[91]

14.7.2.1 Appropriate Safeguards

According to the GDPR, the term "appropriate safeguards" include the following:

- A legally binding and enforceable instrument between public authorities or bodies
- Binding corporate rules
- Standard data protection clauses adopted by the European Commission
- Standard data protection clauses adopted by a DPA and approved by the European Commission
- An approved code of conduct, together with binding and enforceable commitments of the non-EEA controller or processor
- An approved certification mechanism together with binding and enforceable commitments of the non-EEA controller or processor
- Contractual clauses authorized by the DPA of the controller or processor transferring the data outside of the EEA
- Administrative arrangements between public authorities authorized by the DPA in the country from which the transfer is being made[92]

Among these safeguards, it is important for privacy practitioners to understand the following two transfer mechanisms utilized by many companies. These mechanisms provide for lawful transfers of personal data from the European Union to the United States.

- **Standard contractual clauses (SCCs).** For SCCs, a company contractually promises to comply with EU law and to submit to the supervision of a DPA.[93] In practice, SCCs are the most common legal basis for transferring personal data.[94]
- **Binding corporate rules (BCRs).** BCRs provide that a multinational company can transfer data between countries, including among affiliated entities, *after certification* of its practices by a DPA.[95]

14.7.2.2 Derogations

If a transfer is not covered by an adequacy decision or appropriate safeguard, the GDPR provides derogations or conditions under which a transfer may occur. ("Derogation" is a term often used in the European Union where the term "exception" would be used in the United States.) The derogations allow for a transfer if the data subject has provided explicit consent to the transfer or if the transfer is necessary for one of the following:

- The performance of a contract between the data subject and controller (including pre-contractual measures) and the transfer is occasional
- The performance or conclusion of a contract concluded in the interest of the data subject between the controller and a third party and the transfer is occasional
- Important reasons of public interest
- The establishment, exercise or defense of legal claims and the transfer is occasional
- The protection of the vital interests of an individual incapable of giving consent[96]

A transfer is also allowed if made from a public register.[97] Finally, as a last-resort derogation, a transfer may take place if none of the other derogations apply if it is necessary for the purposes of compelling legitimate interests and if it meets all of the specified requirements under the GDPR, including notifying the DPA of the transfer.[98] The EDPB and other EU regulators have interpreted the scope of these derogations relatively narrowly, citing case law permitting derogations only so far as is "strictly necessary."[99]

14.7.3 Transfers from the European Union to the United States

Throughout the writing of this book, the legal authorization to transfer data between the European Union and the United States has transformed from a stable process to one that is in flux. Privacy practitioners should be keenly aware that this critical area of cooperation between the European Union and the United States could change rapidly and dramatically, depending on the outcome of European court cases or negotiations between the European Union and the United States.

14.7.3.1 Schrems I Case

Until 2015, many U.S. companies that did business in the European Union participated in the U.S.-EU Safe Harbor program to provide a lawful basis for EU data to be transferred to the United States under the EU Data Protection Directive in place at that time, which was the pre-cursor to the GDPR.

In 2015, the CJEU struck down the Safe Harbor program in the case of Schrems v. Data Protection Commission (Schrems I case).[100] This decision was made in significant part based on concerns about U.S. government surveillance, as made public by the 2013 Snowden disclosures.[101]

14.7.3.2 Schrems II Case

In 2016, the EU-U.S. Privacy Shield—the successor agreement to the U.S.-EU Safe Harbor—was put in place. The agreement set forth (1) commitments by U.S. companies, (2) detailed explanations of U.S. laws, and (3) commitments by U.S. authorities. U.S. companies that imported personal data from the European Union under the Privacy Shield accepted obligations on how that data could be used, and those commitments were legally binding and enforceable.

In 2020, the CJEU struck down the Privacy Shield in the case of Data Protection Commissioner v. Facebook Ireland and Schrems (Schrems II case). [102] In Schrems II, the Court again raised concerns about the perceived lack of legal protections from U.S. government surveillance for EU data being transferred to Facebook, which is headquartered in the United States.[103]

It is important to note that, although the Schrems II case involved a U.S.-based company, the language of the Schrems II case states that the decision applies generally to all "third countries"—with potentially significant implications for countries outside of the European Union, such as China,[104] that provide *fewer* protections against government surveillance than the United States.[105]

14.7.3.3 EU-U.S. Data Privacy Framework

In July 2023, the European Union and the United States finalized the requirements of the EU-U.S. Data Privacy Framework. From the U.S. side, this meant that the United States put in place safeguards to address the concerns raised by the European Court of Justice in the Schrems II case. With the issuance of President Joe Biden's Executive Order 14086,[106] the United States agreed: (1) to ensure that surveillance activities would comply with the "necessity and proportionality" standard; and (2) to establish an independent data protection review court to provide European citizens the ability to complain when they believe their personal data has been collected inappropriately by U.S. intelligence agencies.[107] As part of implementing the requirements of this Executive Order, the United States designated the European Union and its member states as "qualifying states," meaning the U.S. determined that surveillance programs in Europe adequately protect the rights of U.S. citizens.[108] After the United States put these measures in place, the European Commission issued its adequacy decision for the United States.[109] As of the writing of this book, many expect that the EU-U.S. Data Privacy Framework will be challenged as insufficient in the EU legal system.[110]

14.8 Recent Developments in Global Data Flows

The impact of GDPR has been significant, both in countries adopting their own GDPR-like data protection statutes as well as in companies adopting practices for cross-border data flows based on interpretations of the requirements of EU law. There have also been numerous developments in global data flows that are not derived from GDPR. In part acknowledging that most countries in the world are not likely to qualify for an adequacy decision under the EU's GDPR, the Asian-Pacific Economic Cooperation (APEC) undertook an approach to allow trade while providing privacy protections.[111] Realizing the need for common principles for government access to personal data held by private companies, the Organisation for Economic Co-operation and Development (OECD) has engaged in a multi-year process to develop these principles.[112]

14.8.1 Global Cross-Border Privacy Rules Forum Based on Existing APEC Framework

As of the writing of this book, APEC has published a declaration concerning an international approach to allow trade between participating countries while providing assurances regarding how data will be handled. Canada, Japan, the

Republic of Korea, the Philippines, Singapore, Chinese Taipei, and the United States announced in 2022 the establishment of an international certification system based on the existing APEC Cross-Border Privacy Rules and Privacy Recognition for Processors (PRP) Systems.[113] The new approach, known as the Global Cross-Border Privacy Rules Forum (Global CGPR Forum), will technically be independent of the existing APEC framework, allowing non-APEC members to participate.[114]

14.8.2 OECD Common Principles for Government Access to Personal Data Held by Private Companies

In 2022, the OECD adopted a declaration on common principles for government access, both for law enforcement and national security purposes, to personal data held by private companies. The principles focus on the following topics: legal basis for government access; pursuit of legitimate aims and in conformity with the rule of law; requirements for approval; appropriate handling of personal data; transparency; oversight; and appropriate remedies. Numerous governments are involved in these negotiations including Australia, Canada, the European Union, New Zealand, the United Kingdom, and the United States.[115]

14.9 Conclusion

For companies doing business outside the United States, an increasingly important aspect of information management is ensuring compliance with the laws in non-U.S. countries. Even companies operating within the United States may be covered if their websites are accessed from the European Union or other jurisdictions with strict privacy rules. For companies affected by non-U.S. laws, compliance efforts often focus on rules governing international data flows and data breaches. Since 2018, the requirements of the EU's GDPR have become increasingly important—both because most businesses with an internet presence are doing business in Europe, and because many countries around the world are implementing privacy laws to protect data that are patterned after the GDPR. Thus, familiarity with the GDPR is important for most privacy professionals in the United States.

Endnotes

1 Graham Greenleaf, "*Global Data Privacy Laws 2023: 162 National Laws and 20 Bills,*" 181 *Privacy Laws & Business International Report* 1, (February 10, 2023): 2-4, https://papers.ssrn.com/sol3/papers.cfm?abstract_id=4426146. For a searchable database, see "Data Protection Laws of the World," DLA Piper, accessed October 2023, https://www.dlapiperdataprotection.com/#handbook/world-map-section/c1_RU; Francesca Casalini, Javier Lopez Gonzalez and Taku Nemoto, "Mapping Commonalities in Regulatory Approaches to Cross-Border Data Transfers," Organisation for Economic Co-operation and Development (OECD) Trade Policy Paper, May 2021, https://www.oecd-ilibrary.org/trade/mapping-commonalities-in-regulatory-approaches-to-cross-border-data-transfers_ca9f974e-en;jsessionid=9M_Msj7seEBO28Cf3Rb0ybdofqqitbLo9mu1C9zU.ip-10-240-5-97.

2 "China Topic Page," Resource Center, IAPP, last accessed November 2022, https://iapp.org/resources/topics/china-3/; see Derek Ho and Mandy Zhu, "China Cross-Border Data Transfer Mechanism and Its Implications," IAPP, August 23, 2022, https://iapp.org/news/a/china-cross-border-data-transfer-mechanism-and-its-implications/; see also Graham Webster, "Topic Guide: Personal Information Protection Law," DigiChina, October 31, 2021, https://digichina.stanford.edu/work/knowledge-base-personal-information-protection-law/; "Translation: Data Security Law of the People's Republic of China," DigiChina, June 29, 2021, https://digichina.stanford.edu/work/translation-data-security-law-of-the-peoples-republic-of-china/. As of the writing of this book, China has handed out the largest fine for violations of privacy and cybersecurity laws. In 2022, the Cybersecurity Administration of China fined Didi Global, the Chinese ride-sharing company, approximately $1.2 billion. Michael Hill, "The 12 Biggest Data Breach Fines, Penalties, and Settlements So Far," CSO Online, September 12, 2022, https://www.csoonline.com/article/3410278/the-biggest-data-breach-fines-penalties-and-settlements-so-far.html; Evelyn Cheng, "China Fines Didi More than $1 Billion for Breaking Data Security Laws," CNBC, July 21, 2022, https://www.cnbc.com/2022/07/21/china-fines-didi-more-than-1-billion-for-breaking-data-security-laws.html.

3 "India Topic Page," Resource Center, IAPP, last accessed November 2022, https://iapp.org/resources/topics/india-2/. At the time of the writing of this book, India is considering the Digital Personal Data Protection Act of 2022. "India Proposes Digital Personal Data Protection Act of 2022," IAPP, November 18, 2022, https://iapp.org/news/a/india-proposes-digital-personal-data-protection-act-2022/; Jagmeet Singh and Manish Singh, "India Proposes Permitting Cross-Border Data Transfers with Certain Countries in New Privacy Bill," *TechCrunch*, November 18, 2022, https://techcrunch.com/2022/11/18/india-digital-data-protection-bill-2022-draft/; see Justin Sherman, "India's Sudden Reversal on Privacy Will Affect the Global Internet," Slate, September 5, 2022, https://slate.com/technology/2022/09/india-data-protection-bill-fourth-way.html; see also Sindhuja Balaji, "India Finally Has a Data Privacy Framework—What Does It Mean for Its Billion-Dollar Tech Industry?" *Forbes*, August 3, 2018, https://www.forbes.com/sites/sindhujabalaji/2018/08/03/india-finally-has-a-data-privacy-framework-what-does-it-mean-for-its-billion-dollar-tech-industry/#4f886e870fe8.

4 Brazilian General Data Protection Law (LGPD), Resource Center, IAPP, updated October 2020, https://iapp.org/resources/article/brazilian-data-protection-law-lgpd-english-translation/; see Renato Leite Monteiro, "The New Brazilian General Data Protection Law—a Detailed Analysis," *Privacy Tracker*, IAPP, August 15, 2018, https://iapp.org/news/a/the-new-brazilian-general-data-protection-law-a-detailed-analysis/.

5 Prior to the GDPR, Europe's data protection regime focused on the 1995 Data Protective Directive. The goals for this regime were often aspirational. Today, with significant fines in the GDPR, EU data protection law is a compliance regime.

6 Regulation (EU) 2016/679 of the European Parliament and of the Council of 27 April 2016 on the protection of natural persons with regard to the processing of personal data and on the free movement of such data, and repealing Directive 95/46/EC (General Data Protection Regulation)', EUR-Lex, https://eur-lex.europa.eu/eli/reg/2016/679/oj. For a discussion of the regime in the EU, see "Data Protection," European Commission, accessed November 2019, https://ec.europa.eu/info/law/law-topic/data-protection_en; see Jan Dhont, Delphine Charlot and Jon Filipek, "The EU General Data Protection Regulation – Europe Adopts Single Set of Privacy Rules," *Privacy & Data Security Blog,* Alston & Bird, December 16, 2015, https://www.alstonprivacy.com/the-eu-general-data-protection-regulation-europe-adopts-single-set-of-privacy-rules/.

7 "The GDPR introduces two principles with regard to territorial applicability: establishment and extra-territorial effect." In other words, the GDPR applies to companies that are established in the EU as well as to companies that are not established in the EU, if those companies handle EU data in certain prescribed ways. Matthias Artzt, "Territorial Scope of the GDPR from a U.S. Perspective," IAPP, June 26, 2018, https://iapp.org/news/a/territorial-scope-of-the-gdpr-from-a-us-perspective/.

8 General Data Protection Regulation, Article 4, accessed November 2022, https://gdpr.eu/article-4-definitions/; *see* "What Is Personal Data?" European Commission, accessed November 2019, https://ec.europa.eu/info/law/law-topic/data-protection/reform/what-personal-data_en. For an overview of key terms in the General Data Protection Regu, view Detlev Gabel and Tim Hickman, "Chapter 5: Key Definitions – Unlocking the EU General Data Protection Regulation," White & Case, April 5, 2019, https://www.whitecase.com/publications/article/chapter-5-key-definitions-unlocking-eu-general-data-protection-regulation.

9 "What Is Personal Data?" European Commission; *see* Jenna Kersten, "What is GDPR Personal Data and Who Is a GDPR Data Subject?" *KirkpatrickPrice* (blog), June 7, 2018, https://kirkpatrickprice.com/blog/what-is-gdpr-personal-data-and-who-is-a-gdpr-data-subject/; see also Luke Irwin, "The GDPR: What Exactly is Personal Data," IT Governance, March 22, 2022, https://www.itgovernance.eu/blog/en/the-gdpr-what-exactly-is-personal-data (noting the importance of context in determining what is deemed personal information).

10 General Data Protection Regulation, Article 9, accessed November 2022, https://gdpr.eu/article-9-processing-special-categories-of-personal-data-prohibited/; see "What Personal Data is Considered Sensitive?" European Commission, accessed November 2022, https://ec.europa.eu/info/law/law-topic/data-protection/reform/rules-business-and-organisations/legal-grounds-processing-data/sensitive-data/what-personal-data-considered-sensitive_en; see also Natasha Lomas, "Sensitive Data Ruling by Europe's Top Court Could Force Broad Privacy Reboot," *TechCrunch,* August 2, 2022, https://techcrunch-com.cdn.ampproject.org/c/s/techcrunch.com/2022/08/02/cjeu-sensitive-data-case/amp/.

11 "Data Subject" Resource Center, IAPP, accessed November 2022, https://iapp.org/resources/article/data-subject/.

12 General Data Protection Regulation, Recital 26, accessed November 2019, https://gdpr.eu/recital-26-not-applicable-to-anonymous-data/; see Leonard Wills, "A Very Brief Introduction to GDPR Recitals," American Bar Association, May 1, 2019, https://www.

americanbar.org/groups/litigation/committees/minority-trial-lawyer/practice/2019/a-very-brief-introduction-to-the-gdpr-recitals/.

13 General Data Protection Regulation, Article 4; *see* Detlev Gabel and Tim Hickman, "Chapter 10: Obligations of Controllers – Unlocking the EU General Data Protection Regulation," White & Case, April 5, 2019, https://www.whitecase.com/publications/article/chapter-10-obligations-controllers-unlocking-eu-general-data-protection.

14 General Data Protection Regulation, Article 4; *see* Gabel and Hickman, "Chapter 10: Obligations of Controllers – Unlocking the EU General Data Protection Regulation."

15 General Data Protection Regulation, Article 4; General Data Protection Regulation, Article 28, accessed November 2022, https://gdpr.eu/article-28-processor/; see Kumar Venkatesh and Teodora Pimpireva, "The Processor: Always a Bridesmaid, Never a Bride," *Privacy Tracker*, IAPP, October 30, 2018, https://iapp.org/news/a/the-processor-awakens-episode-gdpr/. For a detailed discussion of processors obligations, view Detlev Gabel and Tim Hickman, "Chapter 11: Obligations of Processors – Unlocking the EU General Data Protection Regulation," White & Case, April 5, 2019, https://www.whitecase.com/publications/article/chapter-11-obligations-processors-unlocking-eu-general-data-protection.

16 General Data Protection Regulation, Article 4; General Data Protection Regulation, Article 28; see Venkatesh and Pimpireva, "The Processor: Always a Bridesmaid, Never a Bride." For a detailed discussion of processors obligations, see Gabel and Hickman, "Chapter 11: Obligations of Processors – Unlocking the EU General Data Protection Regulation."

17 General Data Protection Regulation, Article 4; *see* Detlev Gabel and Tim Hickman, "Chapter 5: Key Definitions – Unlocking the EU General Data Protection Regulation," White & Case, April 5, 2019, https://www.whitecase.com/insight-our-thinking/chapter-5-key-definitions-unlocking-eu-general-data-protection-regulation; see also Andrew Clearwater and Brian Philbrook, "Practical Tips for Consent under the GDPR," *Privacy Tracker*, IAPP, January 23, 2018, https://iapp.org/news/a/practical-tips-for-consent-under-the-gdpr/; Mark Young and Joseph Jones, "EU Regulators Provide Guidance on Notice and Consent under GDPR," *The National Law Review*, December 14, 2017, https://www.natlawreview.com/article/eu-regulators-provide-guidance-notice-and-consent-under-gdpr.

18 General Data Protection Regulation, Article 4; see Gabel and Hickman, "Chapter 5: Key Definitions – Unlocking the EU General Data Protection Regulation"; *see also* Clearwater and Philbrook, "Practical Tips for Consent Under the GDPR"; Young and Jones, "EU Regulators Provide Guidance on Notice and Consent Under GDPR."

19 Detlev Gabel and Tim Hickman, "Chapter 14: Data Protection Authorities – Unlocking the EU General Data Protection Regulation," White & Case, April 5, 2019, https://www.whitecase.com/publications/article/chapter-14-data-protection-authorities-unlocking-eu-general-data-protection.

20 "What are Data Protection Authorities (DPAs)?" European Commission, accessed November 2022, https://ec.europa.eu/info/law/law-topic/data-protection/reform/what-are-data-protection-authorities-dpas_en.

21 General Data Protection Regulation, Article 37, accessed November 2019, https://gdpr.eu/article-37-designation-of-the-data-protection-officer/; see Detlev Gabel and Tim Hickman, "Chapter 12: Impact Assessments, DPOs and Codes of Conduct – Unlocking the EU General Data Protection Regulation," White & Case, April 5, 2019, https://

www.whitecase.com/publications/article/chapter-12-impact-assessments-dpos-and-codes-conduct-unlocking-eu-general-data; Nate Lord, "What Is a Data Protection Officer (DPO)? Learn about the New Role Required for GDPR Compliance in 2019," *Digital Guardian*, December 28, 2022, https://digitalguardian.com/blog/what-data-protection-officer-dpo-learn-about-new-role-required-gdpr-compliance.

22 Gabel and Hickman, "Chapter 10: Obligations of Controllers – Unlocking the EU General Data Protection Regulation"; Focal Point Insights, "Understanding the DPO and EU Representative Roles under the GDPR," Focal Point, April 26, 2018, https://blog.focal-point.com/understanding-the-dpo-and-eu-representative-roles-under-the-gdpr; Lothar Determann, "Representatives under Art. 27 of the GDPR: All of Your Questions Answered," IAPP, June 12, 2018, https://iapp.org/news/a/representatives-under-art-27-of-the-gdpr-all-your-questions-answered/.

23 General Data Protection Regulation, Article 5, accessed November 2019, https://gdpr.eu/article-5-how-to-process-personal-data/); "What Data Can We Process and Under Which Conditions?" European Commission, accessed November 2019, https://ec.europa.eu/info/law/law-topic/data-protection/reform/rules-business-and-organisations/principles-gdpr/what-data-can-we-process-and-under-which-conditions_en.

24 General Data Protection Regulation, Article 5(1)(a), accessed November 2022, https://gdpr.eu/article-5-how-to-process-personal-data/; see General Data Protection Regulation, Article 6, accessed November 2022, https://gdpr.eu/article-6-how-to-process-personal-data-legally/; General Data Protection Regulation, Article 9, accessed November 2019, https://gdpr.eu/article-9-processing-special-categories-of-personal-data-prohibited/; General Data Protection Regulation Recital 39, accessed November 2019, https://gdpr.eu/recital-39-principles-of-data-processing/.

25 General Data Protection Regulation, Article 12, accessed November 2019, https://gdpr.eu/article-12-how-controllers-should-provide-personal-data-to-the-subject/; "Guidelines on transparency under regulation 2016/679 (wp260rev.01)," Article 29 Working Party, last revised and adopted April 11, 2018, https://ec.europa.eu/newsroom/article29/item-detail.cfm?item_id=622227; "What Information Must Be Given to Individuals Whose Data is Collected?" European Commission, accessed November 2019, https://ec.europa.eu/info/law/law-topic/data-protection/reform/rules-business-and-organisations/principles-gdpr/what-information-must-be-given-individuals-whose-data-collected_en.

26 General Data Protection Regulation, Article 5(1)(b), accessed November 2019, https://gdpr.eu/article-5-how-to-process-personal-data/.

27 "Can Data Be Processed by Anyone?" European Commission, accessed November 2019, https://ec.europa.eu/info/law/law-topic/data-protection/reform/rules-business-and-organisations/principles-gdpr/purpose-data-processing/can-data-be-processed-any-purpose_en.

28 "Opinion 03/2013 on Purpose Limitation (wp203)," Article 29 Working Party, April 2, 2013, https://ec.europa.eu/justice/article-29/documentation/opinion-recommendation/files/2013/wp203_en.pdf.

29 General Data Protection Regulation, Article 5(1)(b).

30 General Data Protection Regulation, Article 5(1)(c), accessed November 2019, https://gdpr.eu/article-5-how-to-process-personal-data/; Guidelines 2/2019 on the processing of personal data under Article 6(1)(b) General Data Protection Regulation in the context of the provision of online services to data subjects (Version 2.0) October 8, 2019, https://edpb.europa.eu/our-work-tools/our-documents/smernice/guidelines-

22019-processing-personal-data-under-article-61b_en; "How Much Data Can Be Collected?" European Commission, accessed November 2019, https://ec.europa.eu/info/law/law-topic/data-protection/reform/rules-business-and-organisations/principles-gdpr/how-much-data-can-be-collected_en.

31 General Data Protection Regulation, Recital 39, accessed November 2019, https://gdpr.eu/recital-39-principles-of-data-processing/.

32 General Data Protection Regulation, Article 5(1)(d), accessed November 2019, https://gdpr.eu/article-5-how-to-process-personal-data/; "For How Long Can Data Be Kept and Is It Necessary to Update it?" European Commission, accessed November 2019, https://ec.europa.eu/info/law/law-topic/data-protection/reform/rules-business-and-organisations/principles-gdpr/how-long-can-data-be-kept-and-it-necessary-update-it_en.

33 General Data Protection Regulation, Article 5(1)(e), accessed November 2019, https://gdpr.eu/article-5-how-to-process-personal-data/; "For How Long Can Data Be Kept and Is It Necessary to Update It?" European Commission.

34 General Data Protection Regulation, Recital 39.

35 General Data Protection Regulation, Article 5(1)(f), accessed November 2019, https://gdpr.eu/article-5-how-to-process-personal-data/.

36 General Data Protection Regulation, Article 32, accessed November 2019, https://gdpr.eu/article-32-security-of-processing/.

37 General Data Protection Regulation, Article 5(2), accessed November 2019, https://gdpr.eu/article-5-how-to-process-personal-data/; "Opinion 3/2010 on the principle of accountability (wp173)," Article 29 Working Party, July 13, 2010, https://ec.europa.eu/justice/article-29/documentation/opinion-recommendation/files/2010/wp173_en.pdf.

38 Opinion 3/2010 on the principle of accountability (wp173), Article 29 Working Party.

39 General Data Protection Regulation, Articles 30, 33 and 35, accessed November 2019, https://gdpr.eu/article-30-records-of-processing-activities/; https://gdpr.eu/article-33-notification-of-a-personal-data-breach/; https://gdpr.eu/article-35-impact-assessment/.

40 General Data Protection Regulation, Recital 7, accessed November 2019, https://gdpr.eu/recital-7-the-framework-is-based-on-control-and-certainty/.

41 General Data Protection Regulation, Articles 12–23, accessed November 2019, https://gdpr.eu/article-12-how-controllers-should-provide-personal-data-to-the-subject/; General Data Protection Regulation, Recitals 58–73, accessed February 2020, https://gdpr.eu/recital-58-the-principle-of-transparency/; see General Data Protection Regulation, Chapter 3: Rights of the Data Subject, accessed November 2019, https://gdpr-info.eu/chapter-3/.

42 General Data Protection Regulation, Article 12(3), accessed November 2019, https://gdpr.eu/article-12-how-controllers-should-provide-personal-data-to-the-subject/; "How Should Requests from Individuals Exercising Their Data Protection Rights Be Dealt With?" European Commission, accessed November 2019, https://ec.europa.eu/info/law/law-topic/data-protection/reform/rules-business-and-organisations/dealing-citizens/how-should-requests-individuals-exercising-their-data-protection-rights-be-dealt_en.

43 General Data Protection Regulation, Article 12(5), accessed November 2019, https://gdpr.eu/article-12-how-controllers-should-provide-personal-data-to-the-subject/.

44 General Data Protection Regulation, Article 12(5).

45 General Data Protection Regulation, Articles 13 and 14, accessed November 2019, https://gdpr.eu/article-13-personal-data-collected/; https://gdpr.eu/article-14-personal-data-not-obtained-from-data-subject/; "Guidelines on transparency under regulation 2016/679 (wp260rev.01)," Article 29 Working Party.

46 General Data Protection Regulation, Article 14; "Guidelines on transparency under regulation 2016/679 (wp260rev.01)," Article 29 Working Party.

47 "Guidelines on transparency under regulation 2016/679 (wp260rev.01)," Article 29 Working Party.

48 General Data Protection Regulation, Article 15, accessed November 2019, https://gdpr.eu/article-15-right-of-access/; "What Personal Data and Information Can an Individual Access on Request?" European Commission, accessed November 2019, https://ec.europa.eu/info/law/law-topic/data-protection/reform/rules-business-and-organisations/dealing-citizens/what-personal-data-and-information-can-individual-access-request_en.

49 General Data Protection Regulation, Recital 63, accessed November 2019, https://gdpr.eu/recital-63-right-of-access/.

50 General Data Protection Regulation, Article 16, accessed November 2019, https://gdpr.eu/article-16-right-to-rectification/.

51 General Data Protection Regulation, Article 17, accessed November 2019, https://gdpr.eu/article-17-right-to-be-forgotten/; "Do We Always Have to Delete Personal Data if a Person Asks?" European Commission, accessed November 2019, https://ec.europa.eu/info/law/law-topic/data-protection/reform/rules-business-and-organisations/dealing-citizens/do-we-always-have-delete-personal-data-if-person-asks_en; see "Everything You Need to Know about the Right to Be Forgotten," GDPR.EU, accessed November 2019, https://gdpr.eu/right-to-be-forgotten/.

52 General Data Protection Regulation, Article 17; Recital 66, accessed November 2022, https://gdpr.eu/recital-66-right-to-be-forgotten/; see Stephen Gardner and Andrea Vittorio, "Blockchain's Forever Memory Confounds EU 'Right to be Forgotten,'" Bloomberg Law, August 3, 2022, https://news.bloomberglaw.com/privacy-and-data-security/businesses-adopting-blockchain-question-eus-strict-privacy-law.

53 General Data Protection Regulation, Article 4(3), accessed November 2019, https://gdpr.eu/article-4-definitions/.

54 General Data Protection Regulation, Recital 67, accessed November 2019, https://gdpr.eu/recital-67-restriction-of-processing/.

55 General Data Protection Regulation, Article 18, accessed November 2019, https://gdpr.eu/article-18-right-to-restriction-of-processing/.

56 General Data Protection Regulation, Article 19, accessed November 2019, https://gdpr.eu/article-19-notification-obligation/.

57 General Data Protection Regulation, Article 20, accessed November 2019, https://gdpr.eu/article-20-right-to-data-portability/; "Guidelines on the right to data portability under Regulation 2016/679 (wp242 rev.01)," Article 29 Working Party; "Can Individuals Ask to Have Their Data Transferred to Another Organisation?" European Commission, accessed November 2019, https://ec.europa.eu/info/law/law-topic/data-protection/reform/rules-business-and-organisations/dealing-citizens/can-individuals-ask-have-their-data-transferred-another-organisation_en.

58 General Data Protection Regulation, Article 20, Guidelines on the right to data portability under Regulation 2016/679 (wp242 rev.01), European Data Protection

Board; "Can Individuals Ask to Have Their Data Transferred to Another Organisation?" European Commission.

59 General Data Protection Regulation, Article 20, Guidelines on the right to data portability under Regulation 2016/679 (wp242 rev.01); "Can Individuals Ask to Have Their Data Transferred to Another Organisation?" European Commission. For an examination of how the right to data portability potentially comes into conflict with other goals, including competition and cybersecurity, see Peter Swire, "The Portability and Other Required Transfers Impact Assessment (PORT-IA): Assessing Competition, Privacy, Cybersecurity, and Other Considerations," 6 Georgetown Law Tech Review 57 (2022), https://georgetownlawtechreview.org/the-portability-and-other-required-transfers-impact-assessment-port-ia-assessing-competition-privacy-cybersecurity-and-other-considerations/GLTR-02-2022/.

60 General Data Protection Regulation, Article 21, accessed November 2019, https://gdpr.eu/article-21-right-to-object/; General Data Protection Regulation, Recital 70, accessed November 2019, https://gdpr.eu/recital-70-right-to-object-to-direct-marketing/; "Guidelines on automated individual decision-making and profiling for the purposes of regulation 2016/679 (wp251rev.01)" Article 29 Working Party; "What Happens if Someone Objects to My Company Processing Their Personal Data?" European Commission, accessed November 2019, https://ec.europa.eu/info/law/law-topic/data-protection/reform/rules-business-and-organisations/dealing-citizens/what-happens-if-someone-objects-my-company-processing-their-personal-data_en.

61 General Data Protection Regulation, Article 21; General Data Protection Regulation, Recital 70; "Guidelines on automated individual decision-making and profiling for the purposes of Regulation 2016/679 (wp251rev.01)," Article 29 Working Party.

62 See "Artificial Intelligence and Automated Individual Decision Making, Including Profiling, under Art. 22 GDPR," FieldFisher, June 30, 2023, https://www.fieldfisher.com/en/insights/artificial-intelligence-and-automated-individual-decision-making; "GDPR & Artificial Intelligence: The Rise of the Machines and Article 22," Scott Technology Attorneys, November 10, 2021, https://scottandscottllp.com/gdpr-artificial-intelligence-the-rise-of-the-machines-and-article-22/; see also Sebastiao Barros Vale and Gabriela Zanfir-Fortuna, "FPF Report: Automated Decision-Making Under the GDPR – A Comprehensive Case Law Analysis," Future of Privacy Forum, May 17, 2022, https://fpf.org/blog/fpf-report-automated-decision-making-under-the-gdpr-a-comprehensive-case-law-analysis/.

63 General Data Protection Regulation, Article 22, accessed November 2019, https://gdpr.eu/article-22-automated-individual-decision-making/; "Guidelines on automated individual decision-making and profiling for the purposes of Regulation 2016/679 (wp251rev.01)," Article 29 Working Party; "Are There Restrictions on the Use of Automated Decision-Making?" European Commission, accessed November 2019, https://ec.europa.eu/info/law/law-topic/data-protection/reform/rules-business-and-organisations/dealing-citizens/are-there-restrictions-use-automated-decision-making_en; see Avi Gesser, et al., "New Automated Decision-Making Laws: Four Tips for Compliance," Debevoise & Plimpton, June 25, 2022, https://www.debevoisedatablog.com/2022/06/25/new-automated-decision-making-laws-four-tips-for-compliance/.

64 General Data Protection Regulation, Article 4; *see* Gabel and Hickman, "Chapter 5: Key Definitions – Unlocking the EU General Data Protection Regulation."

65 General Data Protection Regulation, Article 34, accessed November 2022, https://gdpr.eu/article-34-communication-of-a-personal-data-breach/; *see* Detlev Gabel and Tim

Hickman, "Chapter 2: Complying with the GDPR – Unlocking the EU General Data Protection Regulation," White & Case, April 5, 2019, https://www.whitecase.com/publications/article/chapter-2-complying-gdpr-unlocking-eu-general-data-protection-regulation; Gabel and Hickman, "Chapter 10: Obligations of Controllers – Unlocking the EU General Data Protection Regulation; Lee Matheson, "Top 10 Operational Responses to the GDPR: Part 8: Data Breach and the GDPR," IAPP, March 12, 2018, https://iapp.org/news/a/top-10-operational-responses-to-the-gdpr-part-8-data-breach-and-the-gdpr/; "GDPR Processor Obligations," TaylorWessing, accessed July 2023, https://www.taylorwessing.com/-/media/taylor-wessing/files/germany/2020/08/tw_2020_gdpr_new_processor_obligations_en.pdf.

66 Ross McKean, Ewa Kurowska-Tober and Heidi Waem, "DLA Piper GDPR Fines and Data Breach Survey: January 2023," DLA Piper, January 25, 2023, https://www.dlapiper.com/en-gb/insights/publications/2023/01/dla-piper-gdpr-fines-and-data-breach-survey-january-2023.

67 "Guidelines on Personal data breach notification under Regulation 2016/679 (wp250rev.01)," Article 29 Working Party, last revised and adopted February 6, 2018, https://ec.europa.eu/newsroom/article29/item-detail.cfm?item_id=612052.

68 Gabel and Hickman, "Chapter 2: Complying with the GDPR; Gabel and Hickman, "Chapter 10: Obligations of Controllers."

69 General Data Protection Regulation, Article 34; Gabel and Hickman, "Chapter 2: Complying with the GDPR"; Gabel and Hickman, "Chapter 10: Obligations of Controllers"; Lee Matheson, "Top 10 Operational Responses to the GDPR: Part 8; "GDPR Processor Obligations," TaylorWessing.

70 General Data Protection Regulation, Article 34; see Gabel and Hickman, "Chapter 2: Complying with the GDPR"; Gabel and Hickman, "Chapter 10: Obligations of Controllers"; Lee Matheson, "Top 10 Operational Responses to the GDPR: Part 8"; "GDPR Processor Obligations," TaylorWessing.

71 "What are Data Protection Authorities (DPAs)?" European Commission.

72 General Data Protection Regulation, Articles 77, 78, and 79, accessed November 2019, https://gdpr.eu/article-77-data-subjects-right-to-lodge-a-complaint/; https://gdpr.eu/article-78-judicial-remedy-against-a-supervisory-authority/; https://gdpr.eu/article-79-judicial-remedy-against-a-controller-or-processor/; see University of Groningen, "Rights Concerning Complaints and Judicial Remedies," Future Learn, accessed November 2019, https://www.futurelearn.com/courses/general-data-protection-regulation/0/steps/32422; see also Maria P. "Protecting Your Online Business from GDPR Privacy Complaints," Privacy Policies, updated July 1, 2022, https://www.privacypolicies.com/blog/gdpr-privacy-complaints/.

73 Gabel and Hickman, "Chapter 14: Data Protection Authorities – Unlocking the EU General Data Protection Regulation."

74 Detlev Gabel & Tim Hickman, "Chapter 16: Remedies and Sanctions – Unlocking the EU General Data Protection Regulation," White & Case, April 5, 2019, https://www.whitecase.com/publications/article/chapter-16-remedies-and-sanctions-unlocking-eu-general-data-protection; see Remedies and Liabilities, Bird & Bird, accessed November 2019, https://www.twobirds.com/~/media/pdfs/gdpr-pdfs/71--guide-to-the-gdpr--remedies-and-liabilities.pdf?la=en&hash=502A5A5A0B5A5FF77E97E1F4DE206F0D7AAD7F3C.

75 General Data Protection Regulation, Article 82, accessed November 2019, https://gdpr.eu/article-82-data-subjects-right-to-compensation-and-liability/; see Gabel and Hickman, "Chapter 16: Remedies and Sanctions"; see Remedies and Liabilities, Bird & Bird.

76 "GDPR Enforcement Tracker," CMS, accessed October 2023, http://www.enforcementtracker.com/; see "30 Biggest GDPR Fines So Far (2020, 2021, 2022)," Tessian, May 5, 2022, https://www.tessian.com/blog/biggest-gdpr-fines-2020/. For a cumulative summary of fines imposed, view "Statistics: Fines Imposed Over Time," CMS, accessed October 2023, https://www.enforcementtracker.com/?insights.

77 "Irish DPC Finalizes 405 Million Euro Fine Against Instagram," IAPP, September 15, 2022, https://iapp.org/news/a/irish-dpc-finalizes-405m-euro-fine-against-instagram.

78 "Data Protection Commission Announces Decision in Facebook 'Data Scraping' Inquiry," Press Release, Irish Data Protection Commissioner, November 28, 2022, https://www.dataprotection.ie/en/news-media/press-releases/data-protection-commission-announces-decision-in-facebook-data-scraping-inquiry.

79 Sam Shead, "Amazon Hit with $887 Million Fine by European Privacy Watchdog," CNBC, July 30, 2021, https://www.cnbc.com/2021/07/30/amazon-hit-with-fine-by-eu-privacy-watchdog-.html.

80 General Data Protection Regulation, Article 83, accessed November 2019, https://gdpr.eu/article-83-conditions-for-imposing-administrative-fines/; see Gabel and Hickman, "Chapter 16: Remedies and Sanctions."

81 "What Are the GDPR Fines?" GDPR.EU, accessed July 2023, https://gdpr.eu/fines/.

82 General Data Protection Regulation, Article 84, accessed November 2019, https://gdpr.eu/article-84-member-state-penalties/; see Gabel and Hickman, "Chapter 16: Remedies and Sanctions".

83 Although the term "transfer" is a key concept in the GDPR, the term is not defined within the text of the document. General Data Protection Regulation, Chapter 5, Articles 44-50, accessed November 2022, https://gdpr.eu/tag/chapter-5/; General Data Protection Regulation, Recitals 101-116, accessed November 2022, https://gdpr.eu/Recital-101-General-principles-for-international-data-transfers/. In 2021, the European Data Protection Board (EDPB) issued guidance concerning its interpretation of "transfer." "Guidelines 05/2021 on the Interplay Between the Application of Article 3 and the Provisions on International Transfers as Per Chapter V of the GDPR," European Data Protection Board, November 18, 2021, https://edpb.europa.eu/system/files/2021-11/edpb_guidelinesinterplaychapterv_article3_adopted_en.pdf; see Gretchen Scott, et al., "EDPB Defines a 'Transfer' Under the GDPR," Goodwin Privacy Blog, December 2, 2021, https://www.goodwinprivacyblog.com/2021/12/02/edpb-defines-a-transfer-under-the-gdpr/.

84 General Data Protection Regulation, Chapter 5, Article 44 – 50; see Anna Myers, "Top 10 Operational Impacts of the GDPR: Part 4 – Cross-Border Data Transfers," *Privacy Advisor*, IAPP, January 19, 2016, https://iapp.org/news/a/top-10-operational-impacts-of-the-gdpr-part-4-cross-border-data-transfers/.

85 General Data Protection Regulation, Article 45, accessed November 2022, https://gdpr.eu/article-45-adequacy-decision-personal-data-transfer/; Schrems v. Data Protection Commissioner (C-362/14) EU:C:2015:650, October 6, 2015, https://eur-lex.europa.eu/legal-content/EN/TXT/?uri=CELEX%3A62014CJ0362; see "Essentially Equivalent: A Comparison of the Legal Orders for Privacy and Data Protection in the European Union and the United States," Sidley Austin, January 25, 2016, https://www.sidley.com/~/

media/publications/essentially-equivalent---final.pdf; see also Laura Drechsler and Irene Kamara, "Essential Equivalence as a Benchmark for International Data Transfers After Schrems II," Research Handbook for EU Data Protection, July 7, 2021, https://papers.ssrn.com/sol3/papers.cfm?abstract_id=3881875.

86 Canada's adequacy decision relates to "commercial organizations." "Adequacy Decisions: How the EU Determines if a Non-EU Country has an Adequate Level of Data Protection," European Commission, accessed October 2023, https://ec.europa.eu/info/law/law-topic/data-protection/international-dimension-data-protection/adequacy-decisions_en; See Abigail Dubiniecki and Constantine Karbaliotis, "'Schrems II': Impact on Data Flows with Canada," IAPP, August 14, 2020, https://iapp.org/news/a/schrems-ii-impact-on-data-flows-with-canada/.

87 The adequacy decision of the U.S. relates to "commercial organisations participating in the EU-U.S. Data Privacy Framework." "Adequacy Decisions: How the EU Determines if a Non-EU Country has an Adequate Level of Data Protection," European Commission, accessed October 2023, https://ec.europa.eu/info/law/law-topic/data-protection/international-dimension-data-protection/adequacy-decisions_en; see Lisa Thomas, "EU Adopts Adequacy Decision for EU-U.S. Data Privacy Framework," The National Law Review, July 10, 2023, https://www.natlawreview.com/article/eu-adopts-adequacy-decision-eu-us-data-privacy-framework.

88 "Adequacy Decisions: How the EU Determines if a Non-EU Country has an Adequate Level of Data Protection," European Commission, accessed October 2023, https://ec.europa.eu/info/law/law-topic/data-protection/international-dimension-data-protection/adequacy-decisions_en.

89 General Data Protection Regulation, Article 45. After the Schrems II decision (discussed in Section 14.7.3), Brookings reported, "[W]hat does the Commission really know as to how the national security agencies in Israel, Japan, or Argentina collect, use or share EU personal data. … [T]his suggests that all adequacy decisions by the Commission must be treated as potentially suspect and open to being declared invalid by the CJEU." Joshua Meltzer, "The Court of Justice of the European Union in Schrems II: The Impact of GDPR on Data Flows and National Security," Brookings, August 5, 2020, https://www.brookings.edu/research/the-court-of-justice-of-the-european-union-in-schrems-ii-the-impact-of-gdpr-on-data-flows-and-national-security/.

90 For example, a recent European report stated, "The country report on the People's Republic of China (PRC) gives context to the Chinese legal system. It is held that the PRC is not a democratic, liberal state, nor does it have a rule of law. Therefore, it cannot be considered as having the ability to provide people with the protection of personal data equivalent to the EU." Milieu Consulting, "Government Access to Data in Third Countries," European Data Protection Board, November 2021, https://edpb.europa.eu/system/files/2022-01/legalstudy_on_government_access_0.pdf. In line with this conclusion about the Chinese system, the Freedom on the Net Report 2022 finds, "Conditions for internet users in China remained profoundly oppressive and confirmed the country's status as the world's worst abuser of internet freedom for the eighth consecutive year. … China's authoritarian regime has become increasingly repressive in recent years. The ruling Chinese Communist Party (CCP) is tightening control over the state bureaucracy, the media, online speech, religious groups, universities, businesses, and civil society associations, and it has undermined its own already modest rule-of-law reforms." "Freedom on the Net 2022: China," Freedom House, accessed November 2022, https://freedomhouse.org/country/china/freedom-net/2022.

91 According to the 2021 report on third countries prepared for the EDPB, "Each country section [for China, India, and Russia] presents a first subsection aimed to answer the research question concerning the general situation of the countries as regards human rights, and specifically the right to privacy and data protection. It provides an overview concerning rule of law, respect for human rights and fundamental freedoms in the observed countries. ... Subsequently, the country reports include a subsection illustrating the purposes, conditions, and oversight mechanisms of government access to personal data in each of the three countries." Milieu Consulting, "Government Access to Data in Third Countries."

92 General Data Protection Regulation, Article 46, accessed November 2022, https://gdpr.eu/article-46-appropriate-safeguards-personal-data-transfers/.

93 "Standard Contractual Clauses (SCC)", European Commission, accessed November 2019, https://ec.europa.eu/info/law/law-topic/data-protection/international-dimension-data-protection/standard-contractual-clauses-scc_en.

94 "SCCs are among the most widely used mechanisms for transferring personal data out of the EU. Firms from a broad range of sectors and countries rely on SCCs – not just consumer facing companies from the United States. ... [M]ost companies (90 percent) used SCCs for business-to-business sales and service ..." Nigel Cory, Ellysse Dick, & Daniel Castro, "The Role and Value of Standard Contractual Clauses in the EU-U.S. Digital Trade," Information Technology & Innovation Foundation, December 17, 2020, https://itif.org/publications/2020/12/17/role-and-value-standard-contractual-clauses-eu-us-digital-trade/; see "Data Transfers and Effectiveness of Supplementary Measures," Digital Europe, May 17, 2021, https://www.digitaleurope.org/resources/data-transfers-and-effectiveness-of-supplementary-measures/.

95 General Data Protection Regulation, Article 47, accessed November 2019, https://gdpr.eu/article-47-binding-corporate-rules/; "Binding Corporate Rules (BCR)," European Commission, accessed November 2019, https://ec.europa.eu/info/law/law-topic/data-protection/international-dimension-data-protection/binding-corporate-rules-bcr_en.

96 General Data Protection Regulation, Article 49, accessed November 2019, https://gdpr.eu/article-49-when-can-personal-data-be-transfered/; "Guidelines 2/2018 on derogations of Article 49 under Regulation 2016/679, European Data Protection Board," May 25, 2018, https://edpb.europa.eu/our-work-tools/our-documents/smjernice/guidelines-22018-derogations-article-49-under-regulation_en.

97 Tess Blair, "Data Transfer in the GDPR: The Public Register Derogation," Morgan Lewis, July 1, 2019, https://www.morganlewis.com/pubs/2019/07/data-transfer-in-the-gdpr-the-public-register-derogation.

98 Tess Blair, "Transfer of Data in the GDPR: The Definition of Legitimate Interest," Morgan Lewis, October 2, 2018, https://www.morganlewis.com/pubs/2018/10/the-edata-guide-to-gdpr-transfer-of-data-in-the-gdpr-the-definition-of-legitimate-interest.

99 "[D]erogations and limitations in relation to the protection of personal data must apply only in so far as is strictly necessary." Guidelines 2/2019 on the Processing of Personal Data Under Article 6(1)(b) GDPR in the Context of the Provision of Online Services to Data Subjects, European Data Protection Board, October 8, 2019, https://edpb.europa.eu/sites/default/files/files/file1/edpb_guidelines-art_6-1-b-adopted_after_public_consultation_en.pdf.

100 Schrems v. Data Protection Commissioner (C-362/14) EU:C:2015:650.

101 "Schrems I," Resource Center, IAPP, accessed November 2022, https://iapp.org/resources/article/schrems-i/.

102 In Schrems II, the European Court of Justice criticized the U.S. legal system as lacking individual redress and proportionality with regard to government surveillance practices. CJEU 16 July 2020, C-311/18, Schrems II, https://curia.europa.eu/juris/document/document.jsf?text=&docid=228677&pageIndex=0&doclang=EN&mode=lst&dir=&occ=first&part=1&cid=9924207; see Theodore Christakis, "After Schrems II: Uncertainties on the Legal Basis for Data Transfers and Constitutional Implications for Europe," *European Law Blog*, July 21, 2020, https://europeanlawblog.eu/2020/07/21/after-schrems-ii-uncertainties-on-the-legal-basis-for-data-transfers-and-constitutional-implications-for-europe/.

103 "Schrems II (aka Schrems 2.0)," Resource Center, IAPP, accessed November 2022, https://iapp.org/resources/article/schrems-ii-aka-schrems-2-0/; see "The Definitive Guide to Schrems II," *OneTrust DataGuidance* (blog), November 22, 2022, https://www.dataguidance.com/resource/definitive-guide-schrems-ii.

104 Peter Swire, "The U.S., China, and Case 311/18 on Standard Contractual Clauses," *European Law Blog*, July 15, 2019, https://europeanlawblog.eu/2019/07/15/the-us-china-and-case-311-18-on-standard-contractual-clauses/.

105 Milieu Consulting, "Government Access to Data in Third Countries," (stating the report examines transfers of personal data to third countries after the Schrems II case with a focus on the "legislation and practice in China, India, and Russia"); see Peter Swire, "Foreign Intelligence and Other Issues in the Initial Opinion in Schrems II," *Lawfare (blog)*, December 23, 2019, https://www.lawfareblog.com/foreign-intelligence-and-other-issues-initial-opinion-schrems-ii; Peter Swire, "The U.S., China, and Case 311/18 on Standard Contractual Clauses," *European Law Blog*, July 15, 2019, https://europeanlawblog.eu/2019/07/15/the-us-china-and-case-311-18-on-standard-contractual-clauses/.

106 "Enhancing Safeguards for United States Signals Intelligence Activities," President Joe Biden's Executive Order 14086 of October 7, 2022, Federal Register, https://www.federalregister.gov/documents/2022/10/14/2022-22531/enhancing-safeguards-for-united-states-signals-intelligence-activities.

107 Emily Benson and Elizabeth Duncan, "Temporarily Shieled? Executive Action and the Transatlantic Data Privacy Framework," Center for Strategic & International Studies, October 7, 2022, https://www.csis.org/analysis/temporarily-shielded-executive-action-and-transatlantic-data-privacy-framework; see Theodore Christakis, Kenneth Propp, and Peter Swire, "The Redress Mechanism in the Privacy Shield Successor: On the Independence and Effective Powers of the DPRC," *Privacy Advisor*, IAPP, October 11, 2022, https://iapp.org/news/a/the-redress-mechanism-in-the-privacy-shield-successor-on-the-independence-and-effective-powers-of-the-dprc/.

108 Peter Swire, "A Guide to the Attorney General's Finding of 'Reciprocal' Privacy Protections in the EU," *Privacy Advisor*, IAPP, July 18, 2023, https://iapp.org/news/a/a-guide-to-the-attorney-generals-finding-of-reciprocal-privacy-protections-in-eu/; see "Designation Pursuant to Section 3(f) of Executive Order 14068, Office of the Attorney General, June 30, 2023, https://www.justice.gov/d9/2023-07/Attorney%20General%20Designation%20Pursuant%20to%20Section%203%28f%29%20of%20Executive%20Order%2014086%20of%20the%20EU%20EEA.pdf; see also "Memorandum in Support of Designation of the European Union and Iceland, Liechtenstein, and Norway

as Qualifying States Under Executive Order 14086," U.S. Department of Justice, National Security Division, October 7, 2022, https://www.justice.gov/d9/2023-07/Supporting%20Memorandum%20for%20the%20Attorney%20General%27s%20designation%20of%20EU-EEA.pdf.

109 Thomas, "EU Adopts Adequacy Decision for EU-U.S. Data Privacy Framework"; see "Commercial Sector: Adequacy Decision on the EU-U.S. Data Privacy Framework," European Commission, July 10, 2023, https://commission.europa.eu/law/law-topic/data-protection/international-dimension-data-protection/eu-us-data-transfers_en.

110 Foo Yun Chee, "EU Seals New U.S. Data Transfer Pact, But Challenge Likely," Reuters, July 10, 2023, https://www.reuters.com/technology/eu-announces-new-us-data-transfer-pact-challenge-ahead-2023-07-10/; Ross McKean, Ewa Kurowska-Tober, and Heidi Waem, "DLA Piper GDPR Fines and Data Breach Survey: January 2023," DLA Piper, January 25, 2023, https://www.dlapiper.com/en-gb/insights/publications/2023/01/dla-piper-gdpr-fines-and-data-breach-survey-january-2023; see "European Commission Gives EU-U.S. Data Transfers Third Round at CJEU," NOYB, July 10, 2023, https://noyb.eu/en/european-commission-gives-eu-us-data-transfers-third-round-cjeu.

111 The APEC Privacy Framework is discussed in Chapter 1.

112 The OECD Guidelines are discussed in Chapter 1.

113 Mark Scott and Vincent Manancourt, "Washington Goes on the Global Privacy Offensive," Politico, May 6, 2022, https://www.politico.eu/article/washington-data-privacy-global-rules-restrictions/; APEC Cross-Border Privacy Rules Go Global," The National Law Review, April 21, 2022, https://www.natlawreview.com/article/apec-cross-border-privacy-rules-go-global.

114 "Global Cross-Border Privacy Rules Declaration," U.S. Department of Commerce, accessed July 2022, https://www.commerce.gov/global-cross-border-privacy-rules-declaration; see "What is the Cross-Border Privacy Rules System?" Asia-Pacific Economic Cooperation, updated June 2023, https://www.apec.org/about-us/about-apec/fact-sheets/what-is-the-cross-border-privacy-rules-system; see also "Global Cross-Border Privacy Rules – Guidance and Resources," Resource Center, IAPP, July 2023, https://iapp.org/resources/article/global-cbpr-resources/; Mark Young and Sam Jungyun Choi, "Global CBPR Forum: A New International Data Transfer Mechanism," Covington, May 2, 2023, https://www.insideprivacy.com/cross-border-transfers/global-cbpr-forum-a-new-international-data-transfer-mechanism/.

115 "Declaration on Government Access to Personal Data Held by the Private Sector," Organisation for Economic Co-operation and Development (OECD), December 13, 2022, https://legalinstruments.oecd.org/en/instruments/OECD-LEGAL-0487; see Natasha Lomas, "OECD Adopts Declaration on Trusted Government Access to Private Sector Data," TechCrunch, December 14, 2022, https://techcrunch.com/2022/12/14/oecd-declaration-trusted-government-access/; see also Theodore Christakis, Kenneth Propp, and Peter Swire, "Towards OECD Principles for Government Access to Data," *Lawfare* (blog), December 20, 2021, https://www.lawfareblog.com/towards-oecd-principles-government-access-data.

About the Authors

Peter Swire, CIPP/US

Peter Swire is the J.Z. Liang Chair in the Georgia Institute of Technology School of Cybersecurity and Privacy, and a Professor of Law and Ethics in the Scheller College of Business at the Georgia Institute of Technology. Swire is senior counsel with the cybersecurity and privacy practice of Alston & Bird, LLP, and is research director of the Cross-Border Data Forum.

In 2018, Swire was named an Andrew Carnegie Fellow for his research on cross-border data flows. In 2015, the International Association of Privacy Professionals awarded Swire its Privacy Leadership Award. In 2013, he served as one of five members of President Obama's Review Group on Intelligence and Communications Technology. From 2009 to 2010, he was special assistant to the president for economic policy in the National Economic Council. He is a senior fellow with the Future of Privacy Forum and has served on the National Academy of Sciences Forum on Cyber Resilience.

Under President Clinton, Swire was the chief counselor for privacy in the U.S. Office of Management and Budget. He was the first person to have U.S. government-wide responsibility for privacy policy. In that role, his activities included being White House coordinator for the HIPAA Privacy Rule and helping negotiate the U.S.-EU Safe Harbor agreement for transborder data flows.

Swire is the author of eight books and numerous scholarly papers. He has testified often before Congress and has been quoted regularly in the press.

Swire graduated from Princeton University, summa cum laude, and from Yale Law School, where he was an editor of the *Yale Law Journal*. He also studied at L'Institut d'études européennes in Brussels, Belgium.

DeBrae Kennedy-Mayo, CIPP/US

DeBrae Kennedy-Mayo is a faculty member in Law and Ethics in the Scheller College of Business at the Georgia Institute of Technology. Kennedy-Mayo works directly with Peter Swire, serving as part of a small team at Georgia Tech who research, write, and teach on legal and policy issues concerning privacy and cybersecurity. Kennedy-Mayo also speaks internationally on these topics.

With Swire, Kennedy-Mayo is the co-author of the 2018 edition and the 2020 edition of this book as well as numerous articles and publications. Kennedy-Mayo is also a Senior Fellow with the Cross-Border Data Forum.

Kennedy-Mayo has been an attorney for approximately 20 years. She has spent most of her career working in government, acting as both an assistant attorney general for the state of Georgia and as an assistant district attorney in several Georgia counties. Prior to becoming an attorney, Kennedy-Mayo worked for President Jimmy Carter at The Carter Center as part of The America Project. Kennedy-Mayo has also pursued several entrepreneurial ventures.

Kennedy-Mayo graduated with honors from Winthrop University, where she was awarded the Wylie Mathematics Scholarship. Kennedy-Mayo graduated with honors from Emory University School of Law, where she was named an Atlanta Law School Foundation Fellow.

Index

B

C

D

F

H

I

J

K

L

M

N

O

Q

R

S

T

U

V

W

Z